FDR

FDR

*Transforming the Presidency
and Renewing America*

Iwan Morgan

BLOOMSBURY ACADEMIC
LONDON · NEW YORK · OXFORD · NEW DELHI · SYDNEY

BLOOMSBURY ACADEMIC
Bloomsbury Publishing Plc
50 Bedford Square, London, WC1B 3DP, UK
1385 Broadway, New York, NY 10018, USA
29 Earlsfort Terrace, Dublin 2, Ireland

BLOOMSBURY, BLOOMSBURY ACADEMIC and the Diana logo are trademarks
of Bloomsbury Publishing Plc

First published in Great Britain 2022

Cover design by Catherine Wood
Cover image: Portrait of Franklin D Roosevelt by Vincenzo Laviosa, 1932.
(© GraphicaArtis/Getty Images)

A catalogue record for this book is available from the British Library.

A catalog record for this book is available from the Library of Congress.

ISBN: HB: 978-0-7556-3716-4
ePDF: 978-0-7556-3719-5
eBook: 978-0-7556-3717-1

Typeset by Deanta Global Publishing Services, Chennai, India
Printed and bound in Great Britain

To find out more about our authors and books visit www.bloomsbury.com and
sign up for our newsletters.

To Juno and Ronan
May they grow up in a better, safer world.

Contents

Illustrations

All images courtesy of the Franklin D. Roosevelt Museum and Library (with ID number), unless stated otherwise.

1   FDR delivering his inaugural address, 4 March 1933 (63-124)

2   FDR giving the first of his 998 news conferences, a key element in his public-communications strategy, 8 March 1933 (courtesy Getty Images – 514679386)

3   FDR visiting Civilian Conservation Corps Camp Big Meadow, Virginia, 12 August 1933, with Secretary of Agriculture Henry Wallace and Assistant Secretary of Agriculture Rexford Tugwell (on his left), Secretary of the Interior Harold Ickes (second right) and aide Louis Howe (third right) (54499)

4   FDR signing the Gold Reserve Act of 1934, the culmination of the early New Deal's currency programme, with Treasury Secretary Henry Morgenthau standing to his right (courtesy Federal Reserve), https://commons.wikimedia .org/wiki/File:Franklin_Delano_Roosevelt_signs_Gold_Bill_1934.jpg

5   FDR delivering his seventh Fireside Chat on 28 April 1935 to explain the New Deal's goals for work relief and social insurance (4849311)

6   A billboard announcing a Works Progress Administration work-relief project in Baton Rouge, Louisiana, with FDR's name prominently displayed (52-235)

7   FDR signing the Social Security Act, 14 August 1935, with Senator Robert Wagner (D-New York) and Secretary of Labor Frances Perkins immediately behind him (courtesy Library of Congress), https://commons.wikimedia.org/ wiki/File:Signing_Of_The_Social_Security_Act.jpg

8   Eleanor Roosevelt visiting a Works Progress Administration Negro Nursery School, Des Moines, Iowa, 8 June 1936 (64-141)

9   1936 campaign publicity, Women's Division, Democratic National Committee (53-227 (725))

10 New Deal liberalism at high tide: FDR, Governor Herbert Lehman (D-New York) and Senator Robert Wagner greet the crowd at the president's final address in his successful re-election campaign at Madison Square Gardens, New York, 31 October 1936, https://commons.wikimedia.org/wiki/File:Campaign_rally_at _Madison_Square_Garden._FDR,_Gov._Lehman,_Sen._Wagner._October_31, _1936_(8100592017).jpg

Preface

This book examines how Franklin D. Roosevelt transformed the American presidency to deal with the two great crises faced by the United States in the first half of the twentieth century – the Great Depression and the Second World War. In doing so, he was instrumental in bringing modern America into being. FDR is already the subject of numerous biographies, but relatively less is written on how he changed the office of president. This volume appears when the presidency is in crisis as a result of Donald Trump's polarizing tenure and its aftermath. Accordingly, it is opportune to remind readers what great presidential leadership looks like through examination of Roosevelt's establishment of his office as the driving force of American politics and government.

FDR has loomed large in my thinking, teaching and research as a historian of the United States. I have cheerfully accepted designation as a 'presidential historian', not a fashionable identification in a discipline where the scholarly pendulum was swinging away from 'great man' history. To my mind, understanding the presidency is one of the necessary elements to understand the United States and understanding the Roosevelt presidency is essential to understand the possibilities and shortcomings of the modern office he created. This does not make me an uncritical admirer of either the presidency in general or the FDR model in particular. I am, however, much more persuaded of their benefits than their drawbacks.

I began my academic career in the early 1970s when the perilous consequences of the strong presidency bequeathed by FDR were becoming evident in the imperial presidency forged by his successors. I wrote this book when the anti-democratic impulses of the presidency were once more on display. My approach is shaped by an assertion made at the time of Watergate, which has stayed in my mind ever since. In the foreword to his seminal study *The Imperial Presidency*, historian Arthur Schlesinger, Jr, observed in 1973, 'We need a strong Presidency – but a strong Presidency *within the Constitution.*' By and large, FDR governed in accordance with that dictum, albeit with some transgressions that confirm the need for a purposeful president to be subject to effective democratic control.

The volume begins with an assessment of FDR's significance as presidential leader and ends with a review of his legacy for his successors. The chapters in between follow a thematic rather than chronological organization. If this mode of structuring the analysis downplays the huge array of issues facing FDR at any one time, it allows better understanding of how he changed the presidency, enlarged its responsibilities and expanded its authority across so many fields of leadership. Of course, these diverse fields, far from being separate domains, are all interconnected in the complex tapestry of Roosevelt's presidency. Accordingly, attention is drawn, where appropriate, to their connectivity in the patterns of his leadership.

The opening chapter considers Roosevelt's pre-presidential life to assess how this equipped him with the personality, skills and values to become an effective president. The others are divided into three discrete sections of four chapters each: the first examines Roosevelt's use of the presidency in support of liberal socio-economic activism during his first two terms in office; the next, the hinge that connects the other sections, considers his development of the presidency as an institution of government; the final section assesses his expansion of presidential power through his leadership in the international arena as chief diplomat, commander-in-chief and national-security exponent.

Within this framework, Chapter 2 assesses FDR's establishment of the presidency as chief legislator during the Hundred Days of 1933, Chapter 3 examines his use of the presidency to develop a new welfare state in the mid-1930s, Chapter 4 considers how he made the role of economic manager a fundamental part of the presidential job description and Chapter 5 explains how his limited initiatives on racial issues made African-American rights a legitimate issue of presidential concern that his successors would build upon.

Chapter 6 assesses Roosevelt's administrative style and his modernization of the governing capacity of his office through eventual establishment of the Executive Office of the President, Chapter 7 examines his clashes with the Supreme Court over the legitimacy of the New Deal and the ultimate triumph of his 'living Constitution' ideals, Chapter 8 analyses FDR's role as Democratic Party leader in effecting a political realignment that supported the development of a liberal national state and Chapter 9 evaluates his reinvention of the public presidency in support of his leadership of popular opinion.

Chapter 10 explains why FDR played second-fiddle to Congress in the neutrality debates of the 1930s and how he established presidential ascendancy in foreign policy when war raged in Europe in 1939–41, Chapters 11 and 12 assess how Roosevelt enhanced presidential power as the most assertive commander-in-chief in any foreign war in American history – the former considers how he structured his command operations and insisted on primacy in determining military strategy, while the latter focuses on his role in making America the 'arsenal of democracy' and in holding together the US–Soviet–British Grand Alliance, and, finally, Chapter 13 examines his invention of the national-security presidency that linked America's safety and well-being at home to development of a world order based on peace, democracy and freedom.

The analysis is based on a combination of primary and secondary research. My hopes of an extended research visit to the Franklin D. Roosevelt Library in Hyde Park, New York, fell victim to the Covid pandemic that hit the whole world in 2020–1. I was fortunate, however, to benefit from its digitized collections that gave me access to many rich documentary sources. I also drew on the work of other scholars working in the field. My citations record my obligations to these authors, who are too numerous to name here but that does not lessen my gratitude to them.

There have been occasions when I thought to delay completion of the project until travel restrictions eased, but the uncertainty about when there would be a return to something approximating normality was a forceful deterrent. In weighing up my options, I reasoned that it was better to finish the book without completing all possible research than risk not finishing it at all. From what I have learned about FDR, I think that he would have approved that decision. I earnestly hope that readers are of the same mind.

Acknowledgements

I have received a great deal of assistance in researching and writing this book. I should begin by thanking my original editor at I.B. Tauris, Joanna Godfrey, for suggesting I write a book on FDR after completing my earlier biography of Ronald Reagan. Equally, I record my gratitude to my current editors, Tomasz Hoskins and Nayiri Kendir, for helping me see the project through to conclusion.

I could not have written the book without the benefit of excellent digitized collections, most notably the FRANKLIN repository at the Franklin D. Roosevelt Library, the *Foreign Relations of the United States* series and the American Presidency Project. I am equally indebted to the many scholars whose work on FDR not only made him more understandable to me but also constituted an essential foundation for my own writing.

I also thank successive cohorts of students, undergraduate and postgraduate, at City of London Polytechnic/London Guildhall University, University of London School of Advanced Study and University College London, who have helped me learn about the US presidency in general and FDR in particular through teaching them for nearly half a century. I am particularly grateful for discussions with MA students on my *US Presidents and the Presidency* module at the University of London's Institute for the Study of the Americas and UCL's Institute of the Americas.

I thank friends and colleagues Gareth Davies, Tony McCulloch, Andrew Rudalevige and Mark White for illuminating discussions about presidential leadership. I additionally express gratitude to David Reynolds for his guidance on FDR's wartime strategy. A big thanks, furthermore, to Professor Maxine Molyneux and Professor Jonathan Bell for establishing as directors of the UCL Institute of the Americas a departmental culture that enabled teaching and research to flourish and for their support of my own work.

Finally, and most importantly, my family has kept me going in this venture. As always, my wife, Theresa, has borne the brunt of my obsession with US presidents and has managed to keep me aware that there are other things in life. Without her love and support, I could not have undertaken this writing project, let alone complete it – or indeed any other in my career. My daughter Eleanor has been an unfailing source of good cheer, encouragement and interest in the evolving manuscript – as well as a supplier of books about American presidents and IT-problem fixer. My son Humphrey has been somewhat more distant from the undertaking, based as he is in Japan, but has been a regular discussant about contemporary American politics and parallels with the past. During the time the book was written, the birth of my first two grandchildren, Juno and Ronan, has been the greatest of joys, hence its dedication to them.

Prologue

FDR and the American presidency

Franklin Delano Roosevelt was sworn in as America's thirty-second president shortly after midday on Saturday, 4 March 1933. The day in Washington had dawned bleak, cold and grey, matching the nation's mood. Aside from Abraham Lincoln amid the secession crisis in 1861, no president had taken office in more difficult circumstances. With the Great Depression well into its fourth year, fear, insecurity and uncertainty about the present had extinguished the forward-looking optimism of the American national character. The richest nation on earth in the 1920s, the United States was now in the grip of the worst economic downturn in its history. From the top of prosperity in mid-1929 to the deepest point of depression in early 1933, economic output fell by 30 per cent, new construction by 78 per cent, business investment by an incredible 98 per cent, aggregate farm income by two-thirds and personal income by 44 per cent. When FDR became president, at least 25 per cent of the nation's workforce – some thirteen million people – were unemployed, an official figure widely considered low, more than a third of those who had jobs were working part-time and a goodly portion of those fully employed were on reduced wages. With many families unable to maintain mortgage payments, home foreclosures averaged more than a thousand a day and farm foreclosures were triple that level.[1]

Meanwhile, depositor runs that had resulted in suspension of over 2,200 banks in 1930–1 started anew in the final days of Herbert Hoover's administration. With the financial system close to meltdown, many state governments ordered a 'bank holiday' that temporarily or indefinitely closed all banks within their jurisdiction. Their number rose to thirty-four when the governors of New York and Illinois, home to the main centres of finance, issued such pronouncements in the pre-dawn hours of Inauguration Day. With the whole economy now in jeopardy, the dispirited Hoover told an aide, 'We are at the end of our string.'[2]

The largest Inauguration Day crowd in history, lining eight deep on the procession route and numbering over 100,000 in the Capitol Plaza, looked for reassurance from the new president. First Lady Eleanor Roosevelt told reporters afterwards, 'It was very, very solemn, and a little terrifying. The crowds were so tremendous, and you felt that they would do anything – if only someone would tell them what to do.'[3] Her husband worried that authoritarian voices would be the ones doing the telling if popular hopes invested in his leadership fell flat. Some four weeks earlier, Adolf Hitler had become Chancellor of Germany on the promise that his Nazi regime would renew the country's greatness. FDR had no illusions that America's democratic traditions would prevent its embrace of dictatorship if economic conditions worsened. Told by a friend that he would go down in history as America's greatest or worst president depending on whether he restored prosperity, FDR responded, 'If I fail, I shall be the last one.'[4]

Far from failing, FDR would be re-elected three times to become America's longest-serving president with a tenure of twelve years and thirty-nine days. Two monumental crises dominated his time in office. His leadership during America's greatest economic depression and its greatest foreign war transformed the presidency from a rather small, personalized institution into the driving force of national government. In effect, he was both the leader-in-chief responsible for giving direction to domestic, foreign and defence policy and the interpreter-in-chief whose rhetoric provided meaning, vision and reassurance for the American people in hard times and in dangerous times.

FDR may not have invented the modern presidency – that distinction goes to his kinsman Theodore Roosevelt – but he was the first fully to understand its capacity for national leadership.[5] Wary of creating an elected king, the Constitution of 1787 had given the president limited independence from the other branches of national government and somewhat imprecise powers. In Article I, the founders signalled their preference for congressional authority by delegating most of the federal government's powers to the legislative branch. Until the early twentieth century, the president was predominantly a chief clerk mainly responsible for the administration of laws enacted by Congress. Personal ambition or national crisis sometimes produced a chief-executive president capable of vigorous leadership. The pantheon of strong presidents prior to the 1930s only featured George Washington (1789–97), Thomas Jefferson (1801–9), Andrew Jackson (1829–37), James Polk (1845–9), Abraham Lincoln (1861–5), Theodore Roosevelt (1901–9) and Woodrow Wilson (1913–21). FDR's assertive leadership resolved the chief clerk-chief executive conundrum forever more. All his successors aspired to be a strong president and were measured against the model that he had established.[6]

In essence, the Roosveltian transformation of the presidency entailed change from a republican president to a presidential republic. The institution became the centre of political, governmental and policy leadership to a greater degree than ever before. As John F. Kennedy remarked in 1963, '[T]he Presidency is the center of the play of pressure, interest, and idea in the Nation; and the presidential office is the vortex into which all the elements of national decision are irresistibly drawn.'[7] Thanks to FDR's adept use of his authority in meeting the tests of depression and war, the presidency acquired the heroic image of saviour whom the public expected to rescue the nation whenever its prosperity, well-being or security was under threat. His successors, historian Jon Roper observed, 'had to operate in a climate of cultural expectations moulded around the hope for similar inspirational leadership'.[8]

The architect of America's welfare state and warfare state, Roosevelt ranks among its greatest presidents, but his record occasions some ambivalence. US scholarly polls that rate presidential performance usually place FDR in the top three alongside Abraham Lincoln and George Washington. Though occasionally in top spot, Lincoln's habitual status, Roosevelt is more often second or third. Perhaps indicative of his greater reputation abroad, the first UK scholars' presidential poll (conducted by the author in 2011) placed him first, also his position in the follow-up British survey in 2017.[9]

Americans seemingly prefer Lincoln's moral strength amid the Civil War and Washington's republican gravitas in establishing the presidency over FDR's willingness to use ambiguity, deceit and indirection if it suited his purpose. An admiring historian, Arthur Schlesinger, Jr, acknowledged that he could be wilful, ruthless and mendacious in the cold skill with which he played the political game. Far from being uniformly heroic, his Depression-era leadership was a mix of boldness and caution, perfectly captured by James MacGregor Burns, author of the first great Roosevelt biography, in its Machiavelli-inspired subtitle, *The Lion and the Fox*.[10] Much the same could be said of his leadership during the Second World War. As Roosevelt himself readily admitted in private, 'You know I am a juggler, and I never let my right hand know what my left hand does. . . . I may be entirely inconsistent, and furthermore I am perfectly willing to mislead and tell untruths if it will help win the war.'[11] Another grey area in Roosevelt's record is his wartime role in planting the seeds of the 'imperial presidency' that routinely flouted the constitutional limits on its power during the Cold War and the War on Terror in the name of the nation's security. Despite sincere intent to relinquish emergency powers once the war was won, his cutting of constitutional corners to secure victory established dangerous precedents.[12]

Conservative aversion to FDR's socio-economic activism also affected his historical reputation. Disdain for his legacy has smouldered in the hearts of succeeding generations of Republican right-wingers. They could never forgive him for creating the liberal state that proved so hard to demolish when power passed to them in the late twentieth century. An exception was Ronald Reagan, a one-time Democrat who voted for Roosevelt in all four of his presidential elections and remained a great admirer after converting to Republicanism. According to him, FDR's Democratic successors had turned what he intended as emergency programmes into a permanent welfare state. Others on the right were less generous in blaming Roosevelt for establishing a big-government political economy that throttled private enterprise through overspending, overtaxing and overregulation until Reagan's presidency restored the market as the engine of growth. Conservatives have long subscribed, too, to the belief that an ailing Roosevelt surrendered the nations of Eastern Europe to the Soviet Union at the Yalta conference of 1945. Sixty years later, President George W. Bush trumpeted this conviction in declaring: 'The agreement at Yalta followed in the unjust tradition of Munich and the Molotov-Ribbentrop Pact. Once again, when powerful governments negotiated, the freedom of small nations was somehow expendable.'[13]

The ultimate indicator of national ambivalence about FDR is the Twenty-second Amendment's constitutional imposition of two-term limits on his post-Harry Truman successors. Approved in 1947 by a Republican-controlled Congress with help from Southern Democrats, this was the posthumous revenge of bipartisan conservatives against FDR. Yet it had sufficient support in the country to be ratified with relative ease by the requisite thirty-six states (only two – Massachusetts and Oklahoma – rejected it) within four years. While most Americans evidently approved FDR's breaking of George Washington's two-term convention by electing him to third and fourth terms in the emergency circumstances of 1940 and 1944, many also favoured constitutional restraints to ensure that this did not set a precedent.

FDR's presidential leadership certainly manifested flaws, but its positives were vastly more significant. As historian Jeremi Suri observed, 'Roosevelt's personal commitment to decency, democracy and cooperation disciplined the powers he harnessed for the benefit of millions of citizens.'[14] Seeing America's well-being as inextricably bound with the well-being of international society, he employed the presidency to build a more humane socio-economic order at home and establish a rules-based world order capable of sustaining peace after the Second World War. Whatever his Machiavellian qualities, Roosevelt exuded an authenticity that enabled him to gain the trust of most of his fellow citizens. A patrician who looked and sounded different from them, he still managed to communicate his identification with their needs and they in turn identified with him. FDR established a new intimacy between the people and their president that would endure until the political polarization of the early twenty-first century.

It is important not to be swept up in the 'great man' theory that exceptional leaders make history irrespective of broader structural and societal factors at work. Nevertheless, America and the world would have been very different had Franklin Roosevelt not become president, which very nearly happened. On the evening of 15 February 1933, he escaped an attempted assassination by Italian–American anarchist Giuseppe Zangara at Bay Front Park, Miami, where he had stopped off from a pre-inauguration yachting vacation to make some brief remarks from the back of a Buick convertible to the large crowd gathered there. Sitting in the car just 25 feet from where the would-be assassin fired off five pistol shots, the president-elect was extremely lucky to escape injury. Some bystanders were wounded, mortally so in the case of Mayor Anton Cermak of Chicago, who was chatting with FDR to mend fences for not having supported his nomination at the Democratic National Convention. With his car about to speed off to safety, Roosevelt calmly ordered the driver to stop so that Cermak could be placed next to him and taken to the nearest hospital. His unruffled demeanour under fire inspired popular confidence that he was capable of commensurate bravery in meeting the worsening economic crisis head-on as president. 'To a man', *Time* magazine asserted, 'his country rose to applaud his cool courage in the face of death. He is a martyr president at the start of his term.'[15]

Had the president-elect been killed, his running mate, John Nance Garner, a Texan conservative with isolationist preferences, would have taken the oath of office. In that event there would have been no New Deal and no presidential prodding of the nation to resist international aggression. This alternative scenario underlines the immense significance of Roosevelt's accession to the presidency. He was living proof of Thomas Carlyle's assertion, '[I]n all epochs of the world's history, we shall find the Great Man to have been the indispensable saviour of his epoch; the lightning, without which the fuel never would have burnt.'[16]

Roosevelt launched his presidency with one of the greatest inaugural addresses. Aide Raymond Moley had worked for several months on a draft that highlighted the sick state of the economy and the resultant national despair but conveyed little of the dynamic energy the new president would bring to office. FDR's courage in the face of attempted assassination inspired a revised version that projected him as the saviour the nation needed. The president-elect worked with Moley to produce the near-final draft at his Hyde Park home on the night of 27 February. Their collaboration honed a speech that promised vigorous presidential leadership to get the country out of crisis, expressed through plain words like 'firmness', 'courage' and 'attack'.

Roosevelt's delivery of his inaugural address in tones radiating strength, determination and authority maximized its impact on the audience, including an estimated fifty million radio listeners. At 1,880 words, it was a case of less being more – his three Republican predecessors had delivered longer orations (3,672 words in Herbert Hoover's case) to say nothing worthy of remembrance.[17] All the great inaugural addresses – and there have not been many – have a line that defines a president's image forever more. In FDR's case, his opening remarks projected confidence that the United States would surmount the awful times through the famous exhortation (inserted on the advice of aide Louis Howe): 'This great Nation will endure as it has endured, will revive and will prosper. So, first of all, let me assert my firm belief that the only thing we have to fear is fear itself – nameless, unreasoning, unjustified terror which paralyzes needed efforts to convert retreat into advance.'

FDR was clear where the blame for the nation's predicament lay and from whence salvation would come. From his patrician lips emanated the populist critique:

Plenty is at our doorstep, but a generous use of it languishes in the very sight of the supply. Primarily this is because rulers of the exchange of mankind's goods have failed through their own stubbornness and their own incompetence, have admitted their failure, and have abdicated. . . . The money changers have fled from their high seats in the temple of our civilization. We may now restore that temple to the ancient truths.

The use of 'we' in this instance meant the government he led and the American people's support for it. Henceforth leadership to restore the economy would come from Washington DC rather than the titans of business and finance, who had promised everlasting prosperity in the booming 1920s.

Making it plain that putting people back to work was the national government's immediate priority, Roosevelt trenchantly asserted, 'This Nation asks for action, and action now'. He briefly enumerated measures that could be taken to kick-start the process of recovery, before proclaiming: 'We must act and act quickly'. Having outlined 'the lines of attack', he announced, 'I shall presently urge upon a new Congress, in special session, detailed measures for their fulfillment'. With this promise, FDR made it clear that the presidency would be the essential force driving recovery efforts. While expressing hope that 'the normal balance of Executive and legislative authority may be wholly adequate to meet the unprecedented task before us', he had no qualms about making a 'temporary departure' if conditions required. As the address drew to a close, Roosevelt unambiguously affirmed his resolve:

We do not distrust the future of essential democracy. The people of the United States have not failed. In their need they have registered a mandate that they want direct, vigorous action. They have asked for discipline and direction under leadership. They have made me the present instrument of their wishes. In the spirit of the gift, I take it.[18]

Just over twelve years later, Franklin D. Roosevelt died aged sixty-three of a cerebral haemorrhage on 12 April 1945 at the Warm Springs White House in Georgia. He had gone there for a restorative break after the rigours of the Yalta conference and the huge journeys there and back. The exhausting demands of war leadership shortened his life. Despite ill health, he ran for re-election in 1944 to fulfil his responsibilities as commander-in-chief to secure final victory in the war and as diplomat-in-chief to negotiate with Joseph Stalin and Winston Churchill a sustainable peace based on Great Power cooperation. A peerless foreign-war president, Roosevelt had given his life to these intersecting causes. He is rightly listed among the Harvard dead of the Second World War in his alma mater's Memorial Church. As his executive secretary poignantly recorded in his diary, 'In the quiet beauty of the Georgia spring, like a thief in the night, came the day of the Lord. The immortal spirit no longer supported the failing flesh, and at 3.35 p.m. the President gave up the ghost.'[19]

FDR's transformation of the presidency was fundamental to America's renewal from its nadir in the early 1930s. He left the United States much more prosperous, much more powerful and much more confident than when he took office. America was close to achieving a status for which a new term had to be devised – 'superpower'. It was near to victory over Adolf Hitler's Germany after which it would turn its full force against Japan. Its booming economy had demonstrated in wartime renewed capacity to deliver strong growth and high employment. Many of its citizens could look forward to greater socio-economic security in peacetime, thanks to the New Deal's legacy. Finally, in contrast to its retreat from collective-security obligations after the Great War, it stood ready to play the major role in shaping the postwar world. At the time he died, Roosevelt was revising a Jefferson Day speech that he would deliver next day by radio. The two paragraphs he added to the prepared draft constituted his last personal message to America. In words reminiscent of his first as president amid economic crisis twelve years earlier, Roosevelt called on his country to be bold in building a sustainable peace: 'The only limit to our realization of tomorrow will be our doubts of today. Let us move forward with strong and active faith.'[20]

FDR's pre-presidency

The making of a leader

Franklin Delano Roosevelt was born on 30 January 1882 at Springwood, near Hyde Park, New York, into an old, moneyed and well-connected family. His privileged background helped him rise to the presidency, but other factors were just as important. He developed a driving ambition more typical of self-made men in pursuit of political rather than financial advancement. A quick study, he learned the art of politics and the craft of government during tenures in state and federal offices. An attack of polio that left him without the use of his legs at age thirty-nine seemingly threatened his inexorable rise, but the determination not to be limited by disability only intensified his presidential aspirations. These diverse elements in FDR's character and experience made him the president he became.

Roosevelt's parents belonged to the social elite that was America's closest equivalent to an aristocracy, its pedigree defined by ancestral settlement in colonial times, long-established wealth and commitment to public service. By the 1880s business tycoons were leading America's march to modern economic might, making themselves ostentatiously super-rich in the process. Despite being surpassed in wealth, the thoroughbred heritage of families like the Roosevelts kept them atop the social order. These self-designated 'best people' considered themselves necessary counterweights to the materialism of the new-money class in undertaking public service and charitable activities that cemented societal solidarity in times of great change.[1]

The American origins of FDR's father, James, went back seven generations to a Calvinist Dutch family – whose name meant 'rose field' – come to New Amsterdam in the 1640s. FDR's mother, Sara, traced her Delano lineage back to Calvinist Huguenot and English Puritan Pilgrims who settled the Plymouth Colony in the early 1620s. 'May you always bear in mind', James counselled his teenage son, 'that in the past – on both sides of your ancestry – they have a good record and have borne a good name.'[2] Franklin inherited his parents' deep pride that their forbears had helped to build America since its earliest days. He took the oath of presidential office with his hand on the family Bible, open at 1 Corinthians 13. Published in 1686 in Dutch, it remains the oldest Bible ever used in an inauguration, the only one not in English – and the only one used for four consecutive swearings-in.

The middle stretch of the Hudson Valley was home to a succession of patrician estates that followed each other down the east bank of the broad, slow-moving river.

James Roosevelt's 1,000-acre Springwood domain lay close to the centre of this cluster. The family residence was a comfortable and spacious seventeen-room mansion whose lived-in feel made it quite different from the garishly grand houses favoured by the nouveau riche. Given a pony when four, little Franklin accompanied his father on regular morning rides round his manor, sharing the sense of being masters of all they surveyed. For FDR, the house, the estate and the Hudson became, in biographer Geoffrey Ward's words, 'the great constants in his life', to where he would always return to recharge himself physically and emotionally as his political career progressed.[3] Arguably, no other president has possessed such a strong sense of identity with any single place.

Though the Roosevelts and Delanos were old-wealth families, they were not averse to making new money. James made profitable investments in coal, railroads and shipping in the mid-nineteenth century, but his speculative ventures incurred losses during the economically volatile 1870s and 1890s. Even so, he left a sizeable financial estate worth $713,000 – equivalent to about $20 million in 2020 values – on his death in 1900, with a third each after taxes and expenses going to Sara, older son James (from his first marriage) and the eighteen-year-old Franklin (held in trust until he was twenty-one).[4] Sara, the much younger second wife that he married in 1880, was independently wealthy, thanks to a $1.2 million inheritance in 1898 from her father, Warren Delano, who made a fortune trading tea and opium in China. The adult FDR claimed a special understanding of that country from his grandfather's stories while remaining blissfully ignorant of the nefarious source of his wealth.

Alongside moneymaking, estate management and travel, James made time for his patrician obligations as a pillar of Hyde Park's Episcopalian church, overseer of its public school, township supervisor and mainstay of community charities. On his death, the nineteen-year-old Franklin assumed all his father's social responsibilities, but his sense of noblesse oblige towards common folk would find far grander expression as New York governor and US president. His governmental activism provoked many of the so-called best people to designate him a traitor to his class. Dubbed 'democracy's aristocrat' by James MacGregor Burns, Roosevelt understood that some redistribution of wealth and power was necessary to make America a better country.[5]

Nothing in Franklin's youth suggested that he would become a rebel blue blood. He grew up in a family that gave him supreme security, unbounded self-confidence and an understanding of his obligations. His doting parents let him have anything he wanted while expecting him to be responsible, unselfish and well behaved in return. They inculcated in him the lesson that life was about duty, work and achievement rather than self-indulgent pleasure. Delighted to have another son at age fifty-three, James schooled him in the role of estate squire that he was expected one day to undertake. When FDR became president, Sara was asked if she had always thought this was his destiny. 'Never, oh never', she answered. 'The highest ideal I could hold up before our boy – to grow up to be like his father, straight and honorable, just and kind, an upstanding American.'[6]

Despite paternal anticipation that Franklin's role in life was to be the Ringwood squire, his upbringing instilled grander ambition. A child made the centre of his parents' universe might either be left unprepared for life's challenges or, as in FDR's case, grow up confident, resilient and focused on advancement. As historian Joseph Persico put it, 'The rarity of hearing the word 'no' leads him to expect that anything is possible and to expect success as his due. Young Franklin saw the world in this light.'[7] This also bred the self-centred assumption that he could count on the support of family, friends and subordinates to get ahead without necessarily reciprocating in kind. It was a feature of FDR's political career that he surrounded himself with people who saw their role in life as being to serve him. When they were no longer useful or wholly committed in their dedication, he had no compunction in seeking new devotees.[8]

Though Sara was only twenty-seven when she gave birth, an excruciating 24-hour labour that threatened her baby's life prompted medical advice against another pregnancy. Franklin consequently became the centre of her life – and remained so for the rest of her days. As a child he engaged in small-scale rebellions against the highly structured life she supervised while developing a keen sense of how far he could push the limits. Needing emotional privacy when away at school and college in his teens, he revealed in letters to her only what he knew she wanted to hear about his activities. This established a lifelong pattern of concealing his thoughts while seeming to reveal them. Despite exuding warmth, charm and good cheer in adulthood, FDR possessed what speechwriter Robert Sherwood called a 'thickly forested interior' that hid his inner self from view.[9] As president, he often kept allies and adversaries guessing about his true intentions in order to maintain freedom of manoeuvre to advance them.

His parents wanted young Franklin to experience the outside world in the manner befitting their privileged class. The Roosevelts usually spent the winter social season in their Manhattan town house. In early 1887 they had an extended stay in Washington DC during which James took Franklin to visit with his friend, President Grover Cleveland, at the White House. In high summer, the Roosevelts retreated to their large vacation cottage on Campobello Island, where father, son and guests sailed the family sloop off the Maine coast. In combination with boating on the Hudson, these outings made Franklin a skilled sailor with a love of all seafaring matters. His passion for studying navigation maps gave him a prodigious knowledge of the world's seaways that would serve him well as Assistant Secretary of the Navy in the First World War and commander-in-chief in the Second World War.[10]

The young FDR also became familiar with the transatlantic world through eight visits made to Europe by age fifteen. The well-connected Roosevelts gained entrée to elite society in England, France and Germany. In preparation for this, Sara arranged a succession of governesses and tutors to home-school Franklin with a particular brief to make him proficient in French and German. On the first of their annual visits to the German spa town of Bad Nauheim, where James took the waters after suffering a heart attack in 1890, Sara enrolled her son for a six-week term at a local *Stadtschulle*, his solitary experience of public education. Such was his linguistic proficiency and ingrained self-confidence that he found the experience enjoyable rather than daunting. 'I go to the public school with a lot of little mickies', he wrote two cousins, 'and we have German reading, German dictation, the history of Siegfried, and arithmetic. I like it very much.'[11] FDR's language skills would prove useful during his presidency – he was able to translate Adolf Hitler's radio broadcasts during the Munich crisis of 1938 for the benefit of aides, and he could converse in French during wartime meetings with Charles de Gaulle, who refused to speak English. By then, he had become the world's best-known stamp collector, a passion that began at age nine when Sara gave him her own childhood collection to stimulate his interest in geography and foreign travel.

At age fourteen, Franklin was enrolled at Groton, the exclusive boarding school founded in 1884 some 35 miles north of Boston by Episcopalian minister Endicott Peabody. Pitched into spartan conditions, the hitherto pampered boy followed a rigorous daily schedule, slept in a tiny cubicle and received a weekly allowance of just 25 cents, but adjusted quickly. Classmates remembered him as self-confident to the point of cockiness, showing occasional defiance of authority to prove himself one of the boys without ever going too far and being highly competitive in everything he did.

Groton gave Roosevelt a first-rate classical education, provided his first experience of public speaking through school debates and exposed him to social humanitarianism through its charitable activities. Modelling his school on Thomas Arnold's Rugby, Peabody wanted to instil manly Christian virtues in his charges to prepare them for future positions of leadership. His emphasis on privileged-class duty to serve others reinforced the message from Franklin's parents. His exhortations never to rest on one's laurels also made a deep impression on the teenage boy. What Peabody's Sunday sermons did not do was instil in Roosevelt a deep religiosity. As an adult, he certainly believed in the existence of heaven and hell and sought God's help through prayer but wore his beliefs lightly. When Eleanor Roosevelt asked his views on their children's religious learning, he replied, 'I never really thought about it. I think it is just as well not to think about things like that too much.'[12]

In 1900, Roosevelt entered Harvard as a sophomore after a strong performance in the entrance examinations excused him freshman requirements. A history major, he sailed through the next three years producing passable but undistinguished scholarship with little effort. One exception, written after inheriting his father's community responsibilities, was a term paper exploring the history of the Roosevelts in colonial times. Though light on evidence, it concluded that some old families had not proved enduringly important because of their lack of 'progressiveness'. The 'very democratic spirit' of the Roosevelts, in contrast, had guaranteed them lasting significance. 'They have never felt', he avowed, 'that [because] they were born in a good position they could put their hands in their pocket and succeed. They have felt, rather, that being born in a good position, there was no excuse for them if they did not do their duty by the community.'[13]

Extra-curricular activities were Franklin's route to becoming a big man on campus. Too slight in frame for the sports-field, he devoted his energies to various clubs and societies, undertook charitable work and fraternized with fellow students of like background at dinners and social occasions wherein he discovered the joys of nicotine and good scotch. His ultimate goal was membership of Porcellian, Harvard's most exclusive social club, for which he was passed over – something resented for the rest of his life. As compensation, Roosevelt threw himself into working on the campus newspaper, *The Harvard Crimson*, rising to become president in the 1903–4 school year. Though his editorial tenure was unremarkable, it ensured his reputation as a college notable.

While still at Harvard, Franklin shocked his mother at Thanksgiving 1903 with news of his engagement. He had hidden from her his courtship of distant cousin Eleanor Roosevelt, a childhood playmate and now a nineteen-year-old young woman with whom he had fallen in love after a chance meeting brought them together again. Wanting a better match, Sara got the pair to defer their wedding in the hope of them drifting apart, but it finally went ahead on 17 March 1905. For Franklin, marriage was a way to escape his mother's close attention, to have a large family as compensation for being an only child and to build a future with a woman whose social concerns and activism he deeply respected. Above all, it was a love match – in the words of Eleanor's principal biographer, 'their affinity was chemical, intellectual, total'.[14]

In their first eleven years of marriage the Roosevelts produced six children – in order of age, Anna, James, Franklin (who died aged seven months in 1909), Elliott, Franklin Delano, Jr, and John. They had a yearly income of $12,000 from inheritances plus the $500 salary Franklin made as a law clerk with a Wall Street firm, a job secured through family connections after passing the state bar exam. Though sufficient for the bottom end of an upper-class lifestyle, including household-staff costs, this did not pay for suitable housing, vacations and school fees. For big-ticket outlays, the Roosevelts depended on Sara's subventions that gave her considerable control over their lives. Increasingly resentful of her mother-in-law's domination, Eleanor tearfully pleaded at the outset of her third pregnancy for her husband to do something about the situation, but he was uncomprehending of her unhappiness. In this matter, Franklin showed a capacity for ignoring contentious issues on which he did not wish to pronounce, a trait characteristic of his presidency. Eleanor also had to endure his self-indulgent routine of daytime work and evening socializing that left little time to help her raise their family.

Behind the façade of life as a lightweight, Roosevelt intended a change of course that would take him to new heights. At a bull session to discuss career objectives, the 25-year-old Franklin unveiled his presidential ambitions to fellow clerks. Years later, one of them recalled the plan he outlined: 'First, a seat in the State Assembly, then an appointment as Assistant Secretary of the Navy . . ., and finally the governorship of New York. Anyone who is Governor of New York has a good chance to be President with any luck.'[15] Such was Roosevelt's air of authority that no one sniggered at his intent to follow the route that his kinsman, the current president, had taken to the White House.

To the end of his life, Franklin considered Theodore Roosevelt 'the greatest man I ever knew'.[16] Being distantly related as fifth cousins earned him social kudos at Groton and Harvard. He took to wearing pince-nez, Theodore's trademark, when diagnosed as short-sighted. More significantly, TR's ascent to the presidency changed FDR's youthful outlook that politics was a dirty business unfit for a gentleman. Now one of the 'best people' was fulfilling the obligation to serve by holding the top job in American government – and doing so with energy and style. Hopes of emulating his kinsman likely focused his fierce ambition and competitiveness on a career in the same arena. Marriage to Eleanor, one of TR's clan of Oyster Bay (Long Island) Roosevelts, brought him into her uncle's circle. The engaged couple attended his inauguration on 4 March 1905, lunched at the White House after the ceremony and danced at the inaugural ball. A fortnight later, Uncle Ted gave away his orphaned niece at her wedding. 'Well, Franklin', he joked, 'there's nothing like keeping the name in the family.'[17]

Unlike the Oyster Bay branch, the Hyde Park Roosevelts were Democrats, albeit of the conservative variety. James Roosevelt was a small-government, sound-money, pro-business Democrat in the manner of Grover Cleveland. Though Franklin inherited his father's political outlook, his views changed with the times. Industrialization, urbanization and immigration, which were rapidly transforming early-twentieth-century America, brought social and economic dislocations in their wake. In response, the new Progressive movement energized one of the most productive periods of reform in American history. It demanded curbs on big business, amelioration of urban and labour conditions, corruption-free politics and administrative improvements in pursuit of greater efficiency in government. Entering politics when Progressive currents were reaching full flow, Roosevelt enthusiastically supported the new orthodoxy that activist government was essential to resolve the problems of a new America.

An invitation from local Democrats in 1910 to contest the state senate seat encompassing his own Dutchess County and two others marked Franklin's entrée into politics. The odds seemed hopeless since the predominantly rural constituency was a Republican stronghold. However, Roosevelt had two powerful advantages: his famous name drew much press attention and the Republicans were seriously divided, nationally and locally, between Old Guard conservatives and Progressives championed by the now out-of-office Theodore Roosevelt. Hiring a shiny red automobile to travel the district and lavishly self-funding his campaign, Franklin had the time of his life on the stump. Running on an anti-bossism platform of efficiency and economy in government, he won the seat with 52 per cent of the vote, part of a Democratic sweep in state and nation.[18]

On taking office in Albany, the novice politico joined upstate Democrats seeking to block Tammany Hall boss Charles Murphy from nominating a henchman as US senator. Roosevelt's name brought the insurgents press coverage, his spacious rented house became their campaign headquarters, and he served as their spokesman because his wealth shielded him from Tammany reprisals. After weeks of deadlock, Murphy offered the now dwindling opposition a face-saving deal to withdraw his nominee in return for acceptance of another Tammany-approved candidate. Despite this inglorious outcome, the episode had given the young freshman more publicity than many state legislators gained in a lifetime. In addition to front-page coverage in *The New York Times*, he found himself being referred to as 'the Galahad of the insurgency' in friendly newspapers.[19]

Having won his spurs as a good-government champion, Roosevelt needed to engage with socio-economic reforms directly relevant to ordinary people's lives if he was to ride onto the national stage. He lent support to many such causes without playing a significant part in their promotion. The Progressive issue that truly claimed his heart was conservation, a devotion inherited from his father. Nevertheless, there were signs that Roosevelt was developing the social-contract philosophy of government that would guide him as president. In one address, he argued that the quest for personal gain should give way to the primacy of the communal and national interest embodied in a more powerful government. Though little more than a simplified version of Theodore

Roosevelt's New Nationalism address of 1910, it foreshadowed the New Deal's effort to redefine freedom in societal terms. What would drive politics henceforth, Roosevelt avowed, was 'the struggle for liberty of the community rather than liberty of the individual', thereby giving liberty 'a higher and nobler meaning'.[20]

Unlike the mature FDR, the younger one did not inspire admiration from his co-partisans. The regular Democrats of New York City's Tammany Hall organization, which he disdained as inherently corrupt, thought him self-satisfied and snobbish, while reformers found him haughty, charmless and insufferable. According to Frances Perkins, a social worker and labour lobbyist who became the first woman to hold a Cabinet seat as Secretary of Labor in FDR's administration, '[H]e had a youthful lack of humility, a streak of self-righteousness, and a deafness to the hopes, fears, and aspirations which are the common lot.' When polio made him more empathetic, FDR admitted to her, 'I was an awfully mean cuss when I first went into politics.'[21]

An exception to the litany of disdain was the unqualified devotion that Roosevelt inspired in one journalist during the battle with Boss Murphy. 'Almost from [our] very first meeting', Louis Howe later remarked, 'I made up my mind that . . . nothing but an accident could keep him from becoming president.'[22] Addicted to politics, the asthmatic reporter's gnomic ugliness and dishevelled manner ruled out a career in that arena, so he projected his ambitions onto Roosevelt. Blessed with shrewd instincts, he became his idol's most important adviser for the next quarter century. Hauteur and inexperience did not prevent Roosevelt from appreciating that the offbeat Howe could help his star to rise. This was the first manifestation of his capacity for attracting devoted subordinates and understanding how best to employ their talents.[23]

Sensing that national politics offered better hope for Progressive causes and his own advancement, Roosevelt was an early supporter of Governor Woodrow Wilson (D-New Jersey) in his bid for the Democratic presidential nomination of 1912. He deeply admired Wilson's dedication to the public interest against the dual threats of bossism and big business. Despite Tammany's opposition, his man won the day at the Democratic National Convention in Baltimore. Soon afterwards Democratic prospects received a boost when Theodore Roosevelt bolted the Republican Party to run as the presidential candidate of the newly formed Progressive Party in protest at what he considered the foul means by which President William Taft had secured the Republican nomination over him. Despite gaining just 41.8 per cent of the popular vote on Election Day (still the lowest winning share since Abraham Lincoln in 1861), Wilson romped home with over 80 per cent of the Electoral College vote courtesy of the Taft–Roosevelt split. The outcome was a clear victory for progressivism, if not the Progressive Party, as TR took 27.4 per cent of the popular vote compared to Taft's 23.2 per cent share.

Roosevelt's reward for backing Wilson was appointment as Assistant Secretary of the Navy. He was the youngest person ever to hold TR's old post, where he enjoyed considerable latitude because his pacifist-inclined superior, Southern newspaperman Josephus Daniels, was more interested in domestic issues. Despite his political and administrative inexperience, Roosevelt was supremely confident of making the most of his position. 'I will have to work like a new turbine to master this job – but it will be done even if it takes all summer', he wrote his mother.[24] Critical for FDR's political development, the Navy post taught him not only to think big in government but also how to get things done and overcome the obstruction of mid-level bureaucrats. Regular testimony before congressional committees acquainted him with how they functioned and how to impress them. With the help of Louis Howe, ensconced as his personal assistant, he learned that feeding the press information about Washington goings-on earned him favourable newspaper coverage in return. Overcoming his disdain for patronage politics, FDR discovered much about the national Democratic Party through social interactions with state committeemen visiting Washington to secure defence jobs for the folks back home. Another first was having to engage with labour leaders, whose support was vital for industrial peace in the Navy yards. According to Frances Perkins, a new Roosevelt emerged in this period, one who had 'learned to be a politician'.[25]

Nevertheless, the old one was still on show in the contempt manifested for Josephus Daniels, whom Roosevelt considered a hayseed. Taking it upon himself to put the Navy on alert when war broke out in Europe in August 1914, he wrote Eleanor, 'I am *running* the real work, although Josephus is here. He is bewildered by it all, very sweet but very sad!'[26] Daniels would have been justified in getting his disrespectful subordinate fired but desisted from belief that he was destined for greatness. Roosevelt's brash conviction of his own superiority was also evident in his ill-judged quest to become New York's Democratic candidate for US senator in 1914, a campaign that ended in crushing primary defeat at the hands of his Tammany-backed opponent. This experience persuaded him to seek a modus vivendi with the organization that was the essential source of urban Democratic votes in the Empire State.

More than compensating for this failure, the outbreak of war in Europe raised the profile of FDR's Washington job. Long a devotee of the big-navy ideas of Alfred Thayer Mahan, the greatest American strategist of the nineteenth century, he had called in vain for naval expansion to promote US interests abroad since taking up post. 'Our national defense must extend all over the western hemisphere', he declared in 1914, 'must go out a thousand miles into the sea . . . and over the seas wherever our commerce may be.'[27] The European war intensified his conviction that the United States had to become a great sea power. Sensing that America would be dragged into the conflict, he began leaking about the inadequate state of the Navy to the administration's Republican critics, including TR. In self-justification, he wrote Eleanor, 'The country needs the truth about the Army and Navy instead of the soft mush about everlasting peace which so many statesmen are handing out to a gullible public.'[28]

In early 1917, Germany's announcement of unrestricted submarine warfare against all shipping entering the war zone it proclaimed around Britain made US belligerency inevitable. Wilson appeared before a joint session of Congress on 2 April to request a declaration of war. For Roosevelt, this outcome was an object lesson in the futility of wishful hoping for peace with aggressors, one that shaped his own thinking as president some twenty years later. Wilson's war message was also important for his political education. Understanding that Americans wanted to fight for idealistic purposes, the president pronounced the nation's participation in the conflict essential to 'make the world safe for democracy'.[29] This influenced FDR's own announcement in

1941 of the Atlantic Charter as a war aim even before America became a belligerent in the Second World War.

To advance his political career, FDR sought to enlist in the armed forces once America declared war but Wilson considered him too valuable in his Navy post. His responsibilities now included managing a greatly expanded departmental bureaucracy, approving a plethora of naval contracts, overseeing warship construction and ensuring that labour problems did not disrupt production. Having to cut through red tape to get things done was valuable experience for expediting Lend-Lease assistance to Britain and Russia a quarter century later. Still hankering for action, FDR persuaded Daniels to let him make an inspection tour of naval forces in France in July–August 1918. This gave him the chance to visit the front near Chateau-Thierry, getting closer to the fighting than was wise for a senior civilian official.[30] However indirect this experience of war, it afforded Roosevelt first-hand understanding of conditions on the western front and a degree of self-respect that he had not been entirely desk-bound for the duration.

FDR's personal life was soon pitched into career-threatening crisis when Eleanor discovered his affair with her one-time social secretary, Lucy Mercer. The Roosevelts had been growing apart for some years before he embarked on the extramarital liaison sometime in 1916. Handsome, dashing and outgoing – to say nothing of being self-centred – Franklin lived social life to the full. For him, parties, golf and hob-nobbing with cronies were a necessary diversion from the cares of office. Eleanor, by contrast, disliked what she considered frivolous social occasions where she felt shy and awkward. Her own father's alcoholism made her fearful that social drinking was just a step away from excess. As she later admitted, 'I was so serious and a certain kind of orthodox goodness was my ideal and ambition. . . . What a tragedy it was if in any way my husband offended against these ideals of mine – and, amusingly enough, I never told him what I expected!'[31] Eleanor's withdrawal from the marriage bed after the birth of her last child, John, in March 1916 made a relationship breakdown inevitable. She later confided to daughter Anna that sex with Franklin was something she had endured rather than enjoyed. What she really craved was emotional intimacy, but her husband's ingrained habit of never fully revealing his thoughts and feelings denied her that. Having performed her wifely duty in producing six children, she would maintain a separate bedroom for the rest of their lives together.[32]

Enlisting Sara's support, Eleanor confronted FDR with Lucy Mercer's love letters which she had found when unpacking his luggage on his return from France seriously ill with double pneumonia. She presented him with an ultimatum either to stop seeing Lucy or to divorce her, the kiss-of-death for his political ambitions. Sara also threatened to cut him off without a penny from the family inheritance if he left his wife and children. Unwilling to sacrifice family and career, FDR promised never to see Lucy again, but she remained the love of his life. Losing her may well have strengthened his determination to become president as the only justification for relinquishing the emotional happiness she brought him. Following Lucy's marriage to wealthy socialite Winthrop Rutherfurd, the pair began meeting in secret at irregular intervals from the mid-1920s onwards. Whether FDR was sexually active after contracting polio is unclear but he enjoyed close friendships with women who gave him their unqualified admiration, an emotional need Eleanor could not meet. Among them was Margaret 'Daisy' Suckley, a close companion and confidante during the presidential years, whose diary is a valuable portrait of his thoughts and moods in wartime.[33]

Unloved by her mother, who died when she was eight, Eleanor had transferred her affection to her father, who died an alcoholic two years later. Being put in the care of an unsympathetic grandmother and a cruel governess compounded her feelings of abandonment. Her husband's infidelity renewed her sense of being deserted, killing the love she had felt for him. In many ways, however, it was what finally made her self-reliant. 'The bottom dropped out of my own particular world and I faced myself, my surroundings, my world honestly for the first time', she later told biographer Joseph Lash.[34] She renewed the social activism in which she had found fulfilment before marriage and motherhood and began forging her own political agenda.

Though no longer in a conventional marriage, ER entered into a highly effective political partnership with FDR, often prodding him to take more liberal positions than he intended. 'Men and women who live together through long years get to know one another's failings', she later wrote:

> but they also come to know what is worthy of respect and admiration in those they live with and in themselves. . . . He might have been happier with a wife who was completely uncritical. That I was never able to be, and he had to find it in other people. Nevertheless I think I acted sometimes as a spur, even though the spurring was not always wanted or welcome.

In a bitter-sweet postscript that captured FDR's capacity to get what he wanted from those close to him, she added, 'I was one of those who served his purposes.'[35] In fact Eleanor did far more because she played an essential part in Franklin's rise to presidency. Without her, he might not have made it to that pinnacle and he certainly would not have had anyone he trusted so entirely to act as his political eyes, ears and legs as he adjusted to disability.

While the Roosevelts weathered their marital crisis, the Wilson administration was engulfed in political crisis over the Great War peace settlement. The Treaty of Versailles that the president negotiated in two rounds of talks with his European allies pitched national politics into turmoil. Wilson had gone to Paris seeking a settlement that embodied his vision of an international order based on liberal principles of democracy, free trade, self-determination for the new nations of Central and Eastern Europe and an end to traditional imperialism. Dreading a resurgent Germany, Britain and France insisted on a punitive settlement that imposed reparation payments, territorial cessions and colonial losses on their defeated foe. For Wilson, accordingly, the only hope of lasting peace lay in American participation in a postwar League of Nations that would guarantee collective security against aggressor states. FDR had witnessed some of the conference spectacle while in Paris with Eleanor during an assignment to oversee reduction of the US naval presence in France. In February 1919 the Roosevelts voyaged home on the same warship carrying Wilson back to America with the draft covenant of the League of Nations. 'The United States must go in', the president told them over lunch one day, 'or it will break the heart of the world, for she is the only nation that all feel is disinterested and all trust.'[36]

Wilson's liberal internationalism flew in the face of Theodore Roosevelt's insistence that military strength, national self-interest and balance-of-power politics governed international relations. Following TR's sudden death in January 1919, Senator Henry Cabot Lodge (R-Massachusetts) assumed leadership of the fight against the Treaty of Versailles. He made acceptance of it conditional on amendments to the League covenant, in particular that Congress should authorize any American commitment to defend member-nations. Forced by illness to curtail a nationwide tour to promote his internationalist vision, the president returned to the White House where in October 1919 he suffered a devastating stroke that incapacitated him for the remainder of his tenure. With neither Wilson nor Lodge willing to back down, Senate ratification of the treaty was now doomed.

Although FDR supported the president to the full in public, in private he favoured compromise. He was beginning to grapple with the issue that would shape his foreign policy as president – how to reconcile Woodrow Wilson's idealism with Theodore Roosevelt's realism. He became a national spokesman for Wilsonianism out of conviction that America's membership of the League of Nations was essential to preserve its new status as a Great Power. By staying outside, he warned in June 1919, the United States might revert to 'an old Chinese wall policy of isolation', but if inside, it would have 'an important, perhaps even a controlling voice' in international affairs. In this and other addresses, however, he continued to insist on America having strong armed forces to operate in a dangerous world, even if this necessitated universal military training.[37]

As the 1920 elections approached, Roosevelt's rising star gained him second spot on the Democratic ticket headed by Governor James Cox of Ohio. Campaigning far more vigorously than customary for a vice-presidential candidate, he visited thirty-two states (only the 'solid' South missed seeing him) to deliver addresses with two main themes – the need to continue progressive reform at home and to join the League of Nations as the surest means of marshalling America's moral and military power in support of world peace. Despite his prodigious efforts, a national yearning for normalcy carried the Republicans to a landslide victory. Warren Harding was elected president with a popular-vote margin of 60 to 34 per cent, the largest since the Civil War, but Roosevelt's political fortunes survived this debacle unscathed. He had proved an effective national campaigner, had made useful party contacts and had learned much about reading the electorate's mood, all of which marked him out as a future Democratic leader.

Returning to private life in New York, Roosevelt practised law and took a well-paid position with a bond-surety business while awaiting his moment to resume the quest for high office. The severe attack of polio that he suffered while vacationing at Campobello in August 1921 put his ambitions on hold and made physical recovery his immediate priority. As its alternative name of infantile paralysis suggested, poliomyelitis was a disease that killed or crippled children but only one per cent of adult victims suffered lasting damage. With a two-week incubation period, the virus probably entered FDR's body in late July when his duties as president of the Boy Scout Foundation of New York took him up the Hudson to visit a summer encampment at Bear Mountain.

Feeling spent and unwell after a hectic day of non-stop exertion, Roosevelt went to bed early on 10 August and collapsed after getting up to shave the next morning.

It was the last time he ever walked. The paralysis caused a frightening loss of bladder, bowel and sexual organ functions. Two weeks elapsed before a specialist called from New York diagnosed the disease. Although Roosevelt's upper body organs eventually returned to normal, the principal muscles of leg movement would remain severely paralysed. Refusing to accept his condition as permanent, he spent most of the next seven years seeking to regain use of his legs. When one therapy failed, he would try another, a willingness to experiment that later found parallels in his approach as president to combatting the Great Depression.

In March 1922, Roosevelt accepted the necessity of wearing 14-pound steel braces, belted at the waist, locked at the knees and fully encasing both limbs, just to help him stand. After much practice, he developed the strength, stamina and balance to use crutches for traversing short distances. A wheelchair became another requirement for mobility. FDR rejected conventional models to design his own for construction by the Hyde Park blacksmith. He opted for an easy-access armless kitchen chair mounted on rollers, accepting the trade-off that this required someone to push him in preference to having the self-propelling benefits of large side-wheels that advertised the sitter's immobility. Despite failing to rebuild his withered limbs, intensive exercise gave him a muscular torso with arms to match, thereby creating an outward image of vitality.[38]

Polio enhanced FDR's political ambitions in order to prove himself as capable as his able-bodied self. He would repeatedly avow, 'I'm not going to be conquered by a childish disease.' According to Elliott Roosevelt, the disability enhanced his father's long-standing personal characteristics: 'His stability became more stable, his optimism more optimistic, and notwithstanding his inability to walk, even his independent nature was intensified.' Roosevelt's ally Felix Frankfurter similarly commented of his best-known trait, 'With most people, optimism is an evasion or an anodyne; with F.D.R. it is an energy, a driving force for overcoming the obstructions and difficulties of life. It is that energy in him, I think, which explains his triumph over [polio].'[39]

Aware that contemporary attitudes to 'cripples' as pitiable and incapable prohibited popular acceptance of one becoming president, Roosevelt hid his paralysis with help from family and friends. Thanks to their elaborate deceptions, in which the press collaborated, most Americans thought him relatively undamaged by polio. After years of intense effort, he strengthened this misperception through appearing to walk short distances in public, mainly to deliver podium addresses. In reality he was using his exercise-strengthened hip muscles to swing his braced legs while grasping the right arm of a companion, necessarily a sturdy one, with his left hand and steadying his right hand by leaning on a cane. Only FDR's close circle was aware of his utter dependence on round-the-clock assistance from a team of valets to get him in and out of bed, dress and undress him, take him to the bathroom and carry him up and down steps.

Eleanor Roosevelt strongly encouraged her husband's continued hopes for high office because she thought 'his very life depended . . . on his ability to remain active, interested and ambitious in public life'. In alliance with Louis Howe, she opposed her mother-in-law's efforts to have him live quietly in Springwood, an act of resistance that finally freed her from Sara's control. FDR's disability also brought Eleanor out of his imposing shadow – it 'made me stand on my own two feet' she remarked – even as it brought them closer in other ways.[40] The political partnership they developed during his early polio years laid the foundations for her role as a valued associate in the White House years. During FDR's absence from the political arena, Eleanor became his surrogate as campaigner and fundraiser for New York Democrats. A sought-after speaker, always introduced as 'Mrs Franklin D. Roosevelt', she was initially nervous on the podium but soon became an accomplished performer with Louis Howe's help. A supporter of progressive causes, she was a leading light in numerous women's organization, all of them useful channels for promoting the Roosevelt name and for educating her husband about women's concerns. Finally, she herself developed what Frances Perkins called 'a remarkable reportorial quality' to keep him abreast of what she saw and heard on her political travels.[41]

As well as making him more appreciative of Eleanor's talents, polio shaped FDR's outlook in other ways important for his presidency. Only someone having experienced his ordeal could reassure Americans at the depth of the Great Depression that all they had to fear was fear itself. His habitual cheeriness became more pronounced in public as a consequence of having to conceal the severity of his disability. The optimism he radiated was an asset for his presidential relationship with the American people but made some critics question his fitness as a candidate for office amid the hard times of 1932. One commentator remarked that FDR was 'all light and no darkness; all faith and no skepticism; all bright hope and no black despair. One expects shadow and depth in a great man.'[42]

In reality, Roosevelt had sometimes manifested 'black despair' in private during the early polio years. One witness was Marguerite 'Missy' LeHand, an indispensable personal assistant since joining the 1920 vice-presidential campaign. Every late winter from 1923 to 1926, she accompanied FDR on long cruises around Florida with a group of friends. In her recall, a depressed Roosevelt sometimes stayed in bed till noon until he managed a gay face for his companions' benefit. More than any other individual, Missy helped him cope psychologically with his paralysis, even when president. In addition to being his de facto chief of staff from 1933 to 1941, she met his need for companionship in the White House, helped him relax and strove to maintain his good cheer.[43]

Those who knew him believed that polio had purged Roosevelt of his arrogance and insensitivity. Louis Howe sensed a more empathetic and reflective FDR emerging from the bedridden early months: '[H]e was flat on his back with nothing to do but think. . . . He thought of others who were ill and afflicted or in want. He dwelt on many things that had not bothered him much before.' In Frances Perkins's estimate, FDR became 'completely warmhearted, with a humility of spirit and with a deeper philosophy. Having been to the depths of trouble, he understood the problems of people in trouble.' Of similar mind, Eleanor Roosevelt remarked that he would have been 'a president of a different kind without polio', one less able to convey compassion for people needing help, something elemental to his success in office.[44] Roosevelt's polio-disabled biographer Hugh Gallagher offers a powerful rebuttal to anyone doubting the impact of the disease on him: 'I have never met anyone for whom the paralysis was not . . . the most vital-shaping event of his life.'[45]

A desire to help others afflicted with the disease prompted FDR's purchase in 1926 of a spa resort in Warm Springs, Georgia, some 90 miles south of Atlanta, with the idea of turning it into a rehabilitation centre. A visit two years earlier convinced him of the potential restorative power of its 88-degree spring-sourced pool for his limbs. Roosevelt covered the purchase price of $195,000 through a mortgage that obligated two-thirds of the money inherited from his father. In early 1927 he established the non-profit Georgia Warm Springs Foundation, to which he assigned the property with the task of managing it, paying off the mortgage and refunding his personal investment. Roosevelt remained deeply involved in raising charitable donations to fund modernization of the facilities, pay staff costs and finance treatment of low-income patients. With help from skilled therapists, polio sufferers who spent time at Warm Springs learned how to cope with their handicap, making them better able to function in society.[46]

A successful philanthropic venture, Warm Springs demonstrated that Roosevelt was still capable of achieving large goals that he set for himself. His visits to the spa were also important in bringing him into contact with the South for the first time. Hitherto unaware of the region's rural poverty, with which he would grapple as president, he was shocked to encounter it while taking drives through the Georgia countryside in his modified Ford, driven entirely through hand controls. Annual sojourns at Warm Springs also turned him into something of a part-time Southerner, an identity useful for his presidential ambitions.

Although polio had temporarily sidelined FDR's hopes for national office, it had done so when 1920s prosperity underwrote Republican ascendancy. The Democrats became hopelessly split along rural versus urban lines over the sociocultural issues of immigration, religion and ethnicity. More than anything else, Prohibition delineated intra-party divisions between the mostly old-stock 'dries' of the South and West and the predominantly ethnic 'wets' of the Northern industrial cities. The 1924 Democratic National Convention that met in New York laid bare the party's fault lines by taking 103 ballots to nominate a compromise candidate, corporate attorney John Davis. This no-hoper went down to crushing defeat at the hands of Calvin Coolidge. The Democratic ticket retained the Solid South, but its popular-vote share slumped to 28.8 per cent – the party's worst-ever performance – owing to competition from the temporarily revitalized Progressive Party.[47]

Roosevelt himself emerged once more with enhanced status from the ashes of Democratic defeat. In his first public engagement since illness, his nominating speech for the presidential candidacy of Governor Alfred E. Smith (D-New York) was the high spot of the national convention. Moving on crutches, he traversed the 15 feet from the back of the platform to the rostrum, one specially tested to ensure he could lean on it while speaking. FDR practised for hours each day for several weeks to be able to do this. 'Nobody knows how that man worked. . . . Oh, he struggled', commented a friend who witnessed his efforts. His 34-minute address succeeded in praising Smith without offending the other candidates. Widely lauded for his physical courage in delivering it, the speech helped to establish FDR as the epitome of reason and unity in a badly divided party. His confident patrician voice also played well with a much larger audience than the one in the hall as the 1924 national conventions were the first to be covered by radio.[48]

Hoping that Democrats would be amenable to change after electoral catastrophe, Roosevelt looked to position himself as a key figure in their revival. In December

1924 he sent some 3,000 party notables a letter canvassing thoughts on what needed to be done and laying out 'certain fundamental truths' that he considered the necessary starting point for debate. As well as calling for organizational and financial improvements, he urged the Democrats to become 'the party of progress and liberal thought' in opposition to a Republican party that had forsaken Theodore Roosevelt's legacy to become the voice of pro-business conservatism. Roosevelt urged his party to unite around a progressive programme of socio-economic reform instead of giving vent to regional, ethnic and religious antagonisms that found toxic expression in cultural politics. The replies ranged far and wide in their diagnosis of Democratic ailments, giving FDR an unrivalled repository of knowledge about party issues. Seizing the mantle of harmonizer, he sounded out Democratic chieftains in March 1925 about holding a national conference to discuss the way forward. Fears that this would only provide a forum to reaffirm existing animosities proved too strong. Nevertheless, the initiative was significant in establishing Roosevelt as the foremost advocate of Democratic unity. If the party was not yet ready to come together, it would eventually need a leader who could reconcile its supporters in the urban North with those of the South and West.[49]

Roosevelt's unity manoeuvres aroused suspicion in Al Smith's camp that he was angling for the 1928 presidential nomination. In reality, his plan was to run for governor of New York in 1932 and the White House four years later against a non-incumbent Republican. Accordingly, FDR willingly nominated Smith for president at the Democratic National Convention in Houston, where his first-ballot victory made him the first Roman Catholic to run for the office. Needing to carry New York to win the White House, the Democratic standard-bearer asked Roosevelt to run for governor to strengthen the ticket, a request to which FDR reluctantly acceded for fear that he would incur blame if Smith lost their home state. The Republican press greeted his candidacy by rubbishing his physical capacity for office. In a typical broadside, the *New York Evening Post* called it 'pathetic and pitiless . . . [The governorship] is killing hard work . . . for a man struggling out of one of the most relentless of modern diseases'.[50]

To counter this assault, FDR embarked on what was probably the most intensive speaking campaign hitherto mounted by a New York gubernatorial candidate. His stamina and courage enabled him to surmount the daily physical challenges with gusto. Samuel Rosenman, a Smith aide delegated to serve FDR as speechwriter, was soon hard-pressed to maintain the hectic schedule of major addresses. He marvelled at Roosevelt's capacity to edit mundane speech drafts into engaging talks with progressive themes that captivated audiences. Throughout the campaign, FDR focused his animus on Republican leaders rather than Republican voters, many of whom he hoped to attract to his column. It was a practice that he continued in all his national campaigns. 'There are thousands of people who call themselves Republicans', he once told Rosenman, 'who think as you and I do about government. They are enrolled as Republicans because their families have been Republicans for generations – that's the only reason.'[51]

Al Smith succumbed to landslide national defeat at the hands of Herbert Hoover, losing New York in the process by 103,000 votes. In contrast, FDR eked out a narrow victory by some 25,500 votes, less than 1 per cent of the total cast, thanks to his greater support upstate. Despite victory bringing him out of Smith's giant shadow, he had to fight off efforts to recast it. Expecting Roosevelt to make regular visits to Warm Springs, the former incumbent kept a suite of hotel rooms in Albany in anticipation of running the governorship behind the scenes. FDR's refusal to appoint Smith's principal lieutenants to their old posts in the state administration was in effect a declaration of independence. As he explained to Frances Perkins, whom he appointed as state industrial commissioner over his predecessor's objections that a woman could not run the Department of Labor, 'I've *got* to be Governor of the state of New York and I've got to be it *myself*.'[52] To underline this, he put his own people into key positions in the state house. Spurned in his repeated offers to confer on policymaking, Smith found himself an outsider in his former domain. Quitting Albany for good, he made himself rich as head of the company that built and managed the Empire State Building in New York City. His simmering resentment at being overtaken on the greasy pole of politics by someone he considered a lesser man would later find expression in open antagonism to FDR when president.

Despite their falling-out, Smith and Roosevelt are bound together in history as co-founders of the modern Democratic Party and its liberal mission. A third-generation American whose grandparents emigrated from Germany, Italy and Ireland, raised a Catholic on New York's Lower East Side and the product of Tammany politics, Smith made an unlikely collaborator for the patrician FDR. Nevertheless, his record of social reform to benefit the urban working classes as four-term governor of New York foreshadowed parts of the New Deal agenda at national level. Furthermore, his losing race for president in 1928 was immensely significant in mobilizing a new urban-ethnic base for the national Democratic Party that FDR would build upon in the 1930s. Though Roosevelt's star ultimately eclipsed Smith's, he never lost sight of their ties, even when his erstwhile ally condemned the New Deal for excessive centralization. 'I just can't understand it', he told Frances Perkins, 'All the things we have done in the federal government are like the things Al Smith did as governor of New York. They're the things he would have done as president.'[53]

Despite falling short of Smith's record as a gubernatorial reformer, Roosevelt's Albany tenure proved an important preparation for his presidency. Regular press conferences kept him in the eye of urban newspaper readers, establishment of a news bureau to distribute information about state affairs brought him to the attention of outlying rural areas lacking a daily newspaper and widely publicized inspection tours of state facilities undertaken each summer – often on a houseboat – brought him to places where previous chief executives had not ventured. In a foretaste of his 'Fireside Chats' as president, FDR also used radio to mobilize support for his leadership. Meanwhile, he worked with Democratic state committee chieftain James Farley to strengthen party organization, particularly in rural counties. His popularity bolstered by these operations, FDR stormed to landslide re-election by 725,000 votes in 1930, the largest majority in New York history hitherto and double Smith's best showing, which established him as front runner for the Democratic presidential nomination in 1932.[54]

A Republican-controlled assembly constrained Roosevelt's capacity to enact ambitious legislation in his first term in office, exemplified by the significant scaling down of his old-age pension initiative to ensure its enactment in 1930. Even so, there was little in his early agenda to suggest that he was a budding New Dealer. When Herbert Hoover urged governors to accelerate public works, FDR insisted that New York would only do so within the limits of 'estimated receipts from revenues without increasing taxation'.[55] In March 1930, he established a committee to coordinate public and private efforts to help the jobless, an initiative copied by thirty-one other states, but this could not stem the rising tide of unemployment. Meanwhile Roosevelt ignored clear warnings from a gubernatorial fact-finding committee about banking malpractice. When New York City's Bank of the United States collapsed through criminal fraud in December 1930, with the loss of 450,000 deposits valued at $2 million, an impenitent governor told the Republican legislature, 'The responsibility for strengthening the banking law rests with you. . . . Any further delay is inexcusable.'[56]

As economic conditions worsened, Roosevelt adopted a more activist stance that foreshadowed his approach as president. In January 1931 he convened a conference in Albany with the governors of six other states to discuss means of combatting unemployment with a team of eminent economists assembled by Frances Perkins. Despite failing to produce an effective programme for concerted action, this initiative manifested Roosevelt's willingness to consult academic specialists that became a feature of his presidency. By late summer, an exponential rise in joblessness threatened to overwhelm New York's public-welfare system and private charities, which ranked among the best organized and funded in the nation. In response, Roosevelt delivered a message to a special session of the legislature calling for a large-scale relief programme. 'The duty of the State towards the citizen', he proclaimed, 'is the duty of the servant to the master. . . . One of these duties . . . is that of caring for those of its citizens who find themselves unable to obtain even the necessities for mere existence without the aid of others.'[57]

To fulfil this obligation, Roosevelt advocated the creation of the Temporary Emergency Relief Administration (TERA) to oversee the distribution of $20 million in unemployment aid, as both 'home relief' (the dole) and 'work relief' (cash wage for employment on public projects). This was to be funded by doubling the state income tax paid by the well off. Faced with his threat to veto an insufficient measure and his relentless campaign of radio broadcasts, Republican leaders gave him what he wanted. The first state relief agency in the nation, TERA put to work some 30 per cent of the able-bodied unemployed, mainly on small-scale public works, in its first eight months of operation but lacked the resources to help the majority of New Yorkers who had lost their job.[58]

In promoting TERA's enactment, Roosevelt articulated a public philosophy that would later find embodiment in the New Deal. He now insisted that Americans had a right to expect their government to protect them against socio-economic problems over which they had no control as individuals. At the outset of his governorship, he asserted that his administration had an obligation to safeguard citizens from disease, physical injury and old-age want. Amid deepening economic crisis, he added unemployment and economic insecurity to this list. He further believed that the beneficiaries of the economic system had a duty to assist the needy on grounds of enlightened self-interest. 'In the final analysis', he had declared in accepting the Democratic gubernatorial nomination in 1928, 'the progress of our civilization will be retarded if any large body of citizens falls behind.' Such thinking indicated that Roosevelt had moved beyond the agenda of early-twentieth-century progressivism to embrace modern liberalism's identification of economic security as a fundamental right. This evolution signified lack of emotional attachment to America's individualistic traditions. A twentieth-century man in outlook, FDR regarded government-sponsored change as necessary for the nation's advancement.[59]

Roosevelt was the ablest and best qualified of the prospective candidates for the 1932 Democratic presidential nomination, something not universally recognized. In a typical criticism, columnist Walter Lippmann dismissed him as 'a highly impressionable person, without a firm grasp of public affairs . . . a pleasant man who, without any important qualifications for the office, would very much like to be President'.[60] This preposterous misjudgement underestimated the ability, skill and courage displayed in his pre-presidential life and ignored what he had achieved in the Navy Department and the New York governorship. Even so, FDR himself was not entirely free from self-doubt about his capacity to be an effective president. On the night of his election, while son James removed his leg braces and put him to bed, Roosevelt admitted, 'I'm afraid I may not have the strength to do this job.'[61] This was a very human acknowledgement that he would need the will, bravery and endurance to face each day greater challenges than any president excepting Lincoln while knowing that the lower half of his body would always fail him. By now FDR accepted that he would never walk again, but his leadership would lift his stricken country to its feet.

Chief legislator

FDR and the Hundred Days

Franklin D. Roosevelt's name is forever associated with the New Deal programme that embedded the liberal state at the heart of modern America's development. He presided over the most productive period of governmental activism in US history, beginning with the unprecedented enactment of fifteen major laws in his first hundred days in office from March to June 1933.[1] No predecessor had hitherto pursued a legislative programme remotely comparable in scale over the entire course of his tenure, let alone at its outset. By the end of the Hundred Days, Roosevelt's success in recommending, promoting and enacting his early New Deal measures had established him as the chief legislator of American government.

Roosevelt introduced the term 'New Deal' into America's political lexicon in his address accepting the 1932 presidential nomination at the Democratic National Convention in Chicago. In its peroration, he vowed, 'I pledge you, I pledge myself, to a new deal for the American people.' Breaking with tradition. FDR had flown to Chicago to accept the nomination in person, rather than waiting for a party committee to come to the gubernatorial mansion in Albany with news of his selection, thereby symbolizing that he would not be bound by outworn customs in the 'unprecedented and unusual times'.[2] He had no idea that he was christening a political era in promising a 'new deal'. When drafting the address, speechwriter Samuel Rosenman attached little importance to the phrase, which he may have derived from a series of articles that economist Stuart Chase had begun to publish in *The New Republic* on convention eve. Next day's newspaper reports paid it little heed but Rollin Kirby's editorial cartoon in the *New York World-Telegram* presciently depicted a farmer staring up in hope at a plane passing overhead with the words 'New Deal' displayed on its wings. The term quickly came to epitomize what Roosevelt stood for. As Rosenman reflected, 'Within a short time it became a commonplace – the watchword of a fighting political faith.'[3]

Thinking the New Deal fundamentally an election slogan, some scholars claim that FDR improvised its initiatives after taking office. Others find its basic programmatic formulation in his 1932 campaign statements devised with help from the 'Brain Trust' of Columbia University professors, Raymond Moley, Rexford Tugwell and Adolf Berle, who continued advising him in the interregnum between election and inauguration.[4] The argument that the New Deal followed a grand design is more persuasive. As historian David Kennedy remarked, it put in place 'a set of institutional arrangements that constituted a more coherent pattern than is dreamed of in many philosophies . . . [and] can be summarized in a single word – security'.[5] Of course, New Deal goals are often summarized alliteratively in three words, rather than one – 'relief', 'recovery' and 'reform'. For Roosevelt, all three were significant, but 'reform' was the essence of his programmatic legacy. The New Deal envisaged the national state as the instrument of economic security for business, bankers, farmers, workers, homeowners and vulnerable individuals. Its principal aim was not to destroy capitalism, as some critics charged, but to create a stable marketplace that distributed its benefits more evenly.

Roosevelt's most systematic articulation of this agenda in the 1932 campaign was his address to San Francisco's Commonwealth Club. Drafted by Adolf Berle, its central theme was the need to modernize the tenets of the old faith of American individualism in recognition that the twentieth-century economy was in mature stage of development which did not offer comparable opportunities for personal advancement as its nineteenth-century predecessor. 'A glance at the situation today', Roosevelt asserted, 'only too clearly indicates that equality of opportunity as we have known it no longer exists.' The challenge facing America was no longer development of new resources, expansion of production or headlong pursuit of wealth. It was 'the soberer, less dramatic business of administering resources and [industrial] plants already in hand, of seeking to reestablish foreign markets for our surplus production, of meeting the problem of underconsumption, of adjusting production to consumption, of distributing wealth and products more equitably, of adapting existing organizations to the service of the people. The day of enlightened administration has come.' The new task of government in relation to business was 'to assist the development of an economic declaration of rights, an economic constitutional order'. Under the new terms of the old social contract, every man had a right to life that encompassed 'a comfortable living'. To this end, Roosevelt proclaimed, 'Our Government formal and informal, political and economic, owes to everyone an avenue to possess himself of a portion of [America's] plenty sufficient for his needs, through his own work.'[6]

Though Roosevelt could envision the New Deal's ultimate destination at this early stage, he lacked a precise chart to get it there. There would be improvisations, missteps and course adjustments on the way. FDR also recognized that he could only go as fast as political circumstance and popular support allowed. Moreover, the New Deal could appear to be going in different directions at the same time in its dizzying creation of new agencies. Arguably the best summation of the leadership challenge facing the new president came from across the Atlantic. 'Roosevelt', Winston Churchill wrote in 1934, 'is an explorer who has embarked on a voyage as uncertain as that of Columbus, and upon a quest which might conceivably be as important as the discovery of the New World.'[7]

Roosevelt was on this journey because his diagnosis of the Great Depression's cause was diametrically different from Herbert Hoover's. Though not the do-nothing president of Democratic caricature, the Republican incumbent had largely relied on indirect initiatives to encourage recovery at home. This reflected not only his abhorrence of statist solutions as the harbingers of socialism but also his conviction that the roots of economic catastrophe lay outside the United States. As he saw matters, the Wall Street Crash of 1929 had only precipitated a 'normal recession', from which America was steadily recovering until hit by the shock waves of financial crisis in Europe in mid-1931. In Hoover's reckoning, the Great Depression was the coming home to roost of the Great War's destabilizing legacy of unsustainable reparation payments imposed on Germany by the Versailles peace treaty and the huge war debts owed the United States by Britain, France, Belgium and Italy, which depended on German reparations to keep up repayments. Focused on restoring European financial stability, he saw no purpose in stimulus spending and other interventions directed at domestic recovery. 'We cannot legislate ourselves out of world economic depression', he declared in 1931.[8]

FDR placed no credence in what Rexford Tugwell dismissed as 'Hoover's thesis – or alibi – that the depression had come "on us from abroad" as a result of dislocations from the war'. In his interpretation, the slump originated from internal economic and institutional shortcomings, notably the maldistribution of wealth that led to over-saving by the rich and under-consumption by the rest of the nation, the overproduction of the farm economy, the structural weakness of the banking system and the reckless greed of an unregulated Wall Street. As Raymond Moley remarked, the Roosevelt camp was adamant that 'the heart of the recovery program was and must be domestic'.[9]

The stark differences between Hoover and FDR found expression on the campaign trail. Voters could hardly have been unaware that the incumbent would eschew socio-economic activism if re-elected and the challenger intended a raft of federal initiatives in support of relief, recovery and reform. As Election Day neared, Hoover increasingly warned that a Roosevelt victory would impose an alien philosophy of government on the country. In his last major address, he asserted that the 'so-called new deals would destroy the very foundations of the American system of life'.[10]

Roosevelt went on to win a larger share of popular votes (57.4 per cent) and Electoral College votes (89 per cent) than any Democratic presidential candidate hitherto. His coat-tails helped congressional Democrats gain their largest-ever majorities in the House of Representatives (313 to 117 seats) and Senate (59 to 36 seats). Buoyed by this landslide, FDR outlined an ambitious agenda for his presidency in a short article for the mass-circulation magazine *Liberty*, which many newspapers summarized for their readers. Roosevelt claimed 'a mandate truly national in scope . . . to meet the depression boldly and give the American people a new deal in their political and economic life'. He then outlined legislative goals that included unemployment relief, farm relief, public-power development, public works and stock-market regulation. 'The Constitution', he asserted, 'clearly contemplated that the Presidency might, without overstepping its proper functions, provide a degree of leadership for the varied points of view represented in the Congress.'[11]

On his inauguration as president, FDR published a book based on his speeches and written articles on the causes of the Great Depression and their resolution. This best-selling volume was entitled *Looking Forward*, an intentional parallel with Edward Bellamy's famous utopian novel *Looking Backward, 2000-1887*, which imagined the huge improvements in technology, social welfare and quality of life in twenty-first-century America compared to the unequal state of affairs in the late nineteenth century. In its introduction, FDR optimistically asserted, 'America is new. It is in the process of change and development. It has the great potentialities of youth.' Exhorting his countrymen to meet the challenges of the depression, he promised them an administration that would implement the changes necessary to benefit the nation as a whole.[12]

Even in defeat, Hoover sought to divert FDR from developing the New Deal. As established by Amendment XII of the Constitution in the horse-and-buggy days of 1804, four months elapsed between the election and inauguration of the new president. Concern that the country might face a leadership vacuum amid economic crisis had induced Congress in February 1932 to approve Amendment XX moving the inauguration forward to 20 January, but this was not ratified in time to abbreviate the Hoover-Roosevelt interregnum. When another wave of bank panics threatened financial collapse in early 1933, Hoover asked FDR to join him in restoring public confidence. On 18 February he despatched a Secret Service agent with a handwritten message to the president-elect, in which he brazenly claimed that his measures had put the economy back on track by Election Day only for recovery to be derailed by uncertainties as to Roosevelt's intentions. 'I am convinced', Hoover asserted, 'that a very early statement by you upon two or three policies of your Administration would serve greatly to restore confidence and cause a resumption of the march of recovery.' He urged FDR to forswear inflation of the currency, deficit budgets and public projects that would overburden government borrowing. What the outgoing president wanted, he told Senator David Reed (R-Pennsylvania), was to get his Democratic successor to agree 'the abandonment of 90% of the so-called New Deal'.[13] Unsurprisingly, FDR would have nothing to do with a treaty of surrender to a defeated foe.

On becoming president, Roosevelt wasted no time in getting to grips with the banking crisis that Hoover had tried to exploit to sidetrack the New Deal. On his first night in office, he directed new Treasury Secretary William Woodin to have an emergency bank bill ready for congressional consideration within five days. On 5 March, he issued an executive order calling Congress back into special session on 9 March and secured Cabinet support for another proclamation halting transactions in gold and declaring a four-day national bank holiday.[14] The bank holiday announcement had three significant effects: it bought time to frame legislation and put pressure on Congress to assent expeditiously to the measure, it turned the current maze of state-mandated bank closures into a uniform approach that established federal responsibility for meeting the crisis and it enabled FDR to invoke patriotic unity in support of his actions.

The Roosevelt administration drew on the expertise of Hoover officials who had been dealing with the financial crisis for weeks without being able to persuade the outgoing president to take bold action. These included Treasury Secretary Ogden Mills, Treasury Undersecretary Arthur Ballantine and Federal Reserve general counsel Walter Wyatt, the author of the bank holiday proclamation signed by FDR. William Woodin, a Republican for Roosevelt in 1932, served as the administration's point man, with support from Raymond Moley, on the informal task force that devised the emergency banking legislation, but they were secondary actors.[15]

Presented with the draft bill on 8 March, Roosevelt met with congressional leaders of both parties that evening to secure their support for it. What became the Emergency Banking Act (EBA) of 1933 gave him almost total jurisdiction over bank credit, foreign exchange and gold purchases. This arguably represented the largest grant of authority to any president hitherto in America's peacetime history. Further enhancing executive power, the measure licensed the Treasury to reorganize insolvent banks deemed capable of eventually reopening their doors and authorized the Hoover-created Reconstruction Finance Corporation (RFC) to make capital-boosting stock purchases in these institutions.

When Congress reconvened on 9 March, it received a blunt 427-word presidential message urging the bill's rapid enactment as vital to restore confidence in the banking system. Despite having just one printed copy in its possession, the House of Representatives approved the measure sight unseen in a voice vote after less than forty minutes of debate. 'The house is burning down', asserted Minority Leader Bertrand Snell (R-New York), 'and the President of the United States says this is the way to put out the fire.'[16] The bill went immediately to the Senate where it encountered opposition from Western progressives for its lack of deposit insurance, but still sped to unamended approval by 73 votes to 7. The EBA received the president's signature at 8.36 in the evening, less than eight hours after its introduction in Congress. The next day, FDR issued an executive order that set procedures to reopen banks found to be sound, differentiated between banks in the Federal Reserve System and those under state regulation, and codified restrictions on gold and silver.[17]

The bank holiday was extended for Treasury and Federal Reserve officials to undertake a feverish examination of which banks could be safely reopened in the week beginning 13 March. It remained unclear whether people would leave their savings in those designated as sound and, just as important, return money they had previously withdrawn. Roosevelt understood that only his personal appeal could provide reassurance about the security of bank deposits. This was the purpose of his radio address to the nation on Sunday evening, 12 March 1933. In what was probably the single most important public communication of his New Deal presidency, FDR was wholly successful in persuading Americans that their money was safe in the reopened banks. 'Confidence and courage are the essentials in carrying out our plan', he told his huge audience. 'You people must have faith; you must not be stampeded by rumours or guesses. . . . We have provided the machinery to restore our financial system; it is up to you to support and make it work.'[18]

Within three days, some 12,000 banks, 70 per cent of the nation's total, had resumed operations. Long lines formed outside the first to open, but now people were there to return money into their accounts. By the end of March, $1.2 billion in currency was back in the banking system. By mid-April, another 1,300 banks had received approval to reopen, and in time a further 3,100 were reorganized with help from RFC stock purchase. Some 1,100 (6 per cent of the total) had to be liquidated as incapable of meeting federal standards, but the EBA drafters had feared that a third of all banks might suffer this fate. Explaining popular belief in the solvency of the reopened banks, Agnes Meyer, wife of Federal Reserve chair Eugene Meyer, wrote in her diary on 14 March, 'The people trust this admin. as they distrusted the other. This is the secret of the whole situation.'[19]

The work of Hoover men rather than New Dealers, the EBA was clearly an improvisation to meet an emergency but FDR still put his own stamp on it. Had Hoover closed the banks, the restrictions on gold purchases would have been a temporary expedient until the situation stabilized. Roosevelt, by contrast, intended them as the first step in taking the United States off the gold standard, a prerequisite for an inflationary strategy for recovery (reviewed in Chapter 4). That said, the EBA was predominantly conservative in character because speedy resolution of the banking emergency dictated reliance on policies at hand.

In Raymond Moley's words, the measure aimed to rally the confidence 'first, of the conservative business and banking leaders of the country, and then through them, of the public generally'. As a consequence, he famously remarked, 'Capitalism was saved in eight days'.[20] Western progressives later claimed that the emergency represented a lost opportunity to take the banks into public ownership. Senator Bronson Cutting (R-New Mexico) insisted that 'the nationalization of banks could have been accomplished without a word of protest'.[21] The need for expeditious reopening of banks meant that nationalization never came into consideration during EBA's formulation. Even if it had, the federal government simply lacked the administrative machinery to operationalize such a radical course of action in 1933.

Despite its conservatism, the EBA was critically significant in generating momentum for the legislative whirlwind of the Hundred Days. Never before had any law had such immediately measurable effect in overcoming such a grave crisis. Roosevelt's presidency was up and running with a spectacular success to its name and the promise of more to come. Having badly misjudged FDR's capabilities in 1932, columnist Walter Lippmann offered fulsome praise for what he had done in his first ten days in office:

> The great achievement . . . has been the revival of the people's confidence in themselves and in their institutions. They believe they have a leader whom they can follow. They believe they have a government which can act. They believe again that with human intelligence, a resolute will, and a national discipline the measures that have to be taken can be devised and executed.[22]

Roosevelt quickly scored two further successes that consolidated his status as legislative leader. To reassure business and banking, the EBA drafters urged him to re-balance government finances that the Great Depression had plunged into the red under Hoover. According to Raymond Moley, Roosevelt was receptive to their exhortations because 'Dutch thrift' was ingrained in his character, manifested by his 'noticeably economic' record as New York governor.[23] Bureau of the Budget director Lewis Douglas, a leading light of the new administration, produced a spending retrenchment bill that the president sent to Congress on 10 March. This gave him broad executive powers to cut veterans' benefits, the single largest component of federal spending, and to reduce federal salaries by up to 15 per cent. All told it would achieve savings of $0.5 billion, equivalent to some 10 per cent of annual budget outlays. In a trenchant message urging enactment of what became the Economy Act of 1933, FDR warned Congress that the large budget deficits accrued under his predecessor had contributed to economic stagnation, rising unemployment and the banking collapse.[24] So great was his prestige that the House of Representatives enacted the bill the day after its introduction. The veterans' lobby succeeded in holding it up in the Senate – but only for three days.

To speed things along, FDR sent a three-sentence message to the legislature urging immediate legalization of 3.2 per cent alcohol-strength beer and wine. With the country tiring of the Prohibition experiment, a constitutional amendment repealing it, approved by the lame-duck Congress in February, was moving towards state ratification, attained in December 1933. Roosevelt's beer bill struck a chord with Americans too thirsty to wait till then for a legal drink. The House approved it within twenty-four hours and sent it to the Senate. As FDR knew, the upper chamber's rules required it first to complete consideration of the Economy bill before taking up another measure. Duly swallowing the budgetary castor oil, the Senate chased it down with the beer bill the following day.

Less than two weeks into office, FDR had bested the veterans and the dries, two of the most influential lobbies in Washington. He had originally anticipated that Congress would adjourn once the banking crisis was resolved and return in regular session in December to enact bills that his administration would have prepared in the interim. The legislature's early willingness to do his bidding encouraged him to keep it in Washington to consider measures as they became ready. '[W]e seem to be off to a good start', Roosevelt wrote a banker friend, 'and I hope to get through some important legislation while the feeling of the country is so friendly.'[25]

If the first three legislative initiatives of his presidency had hardly taken America in a new direction, succeeding measures launched the New Deal as a reform programme. Henceforth it would become more difficult to maintain consensus, even among his advisers. FDR outlined his vision for federal intervention in the agricultural and industrial sectors in his next Fireside Chat on 7 May. After reading an early draft, Raymond Moley remarked that his proposals constituted 'an enormous step away' from America's laissez-faire traditions. 'If that philosophy hadn't proved to be bankrupt', the president replied, 'Herbert Hoover would be sitting here right now. I never felt surer of anything in my life than I do of the soundness of this passage.'[26]

FDR dealt first with the desperate plight of agriculture, which occupied some 21 per cent of the nation's labour force. In difficulties throughout the 1920s because of overproduction and increased foreign competition, farmers received some 60 per cent less for their commodities in 1932 than in 1929, itself hardly a boom year. This made it impossible for many to keep up with mortgage payments and state-tax obligations, leading to an epidemic of foreclosures on the Great Plains and in the Midwest Corn Belt. Displaying their anger more readily than the urban unemployed, some farmers went on strike in refusing to take their products to market, some used intimidation to force through penny bids at foreclosure sales and some formed armed groups to deter judges and sheriffs from ordering and enforcing dispossessions. In January 1933, American Farm Bureau Federation leader Edward O'Neal warned a Senate subcommittee, 'Unless something is done for the American farmer we will have revolution in the countryside within less than twelve months.'[27]

The recipient of a massive farm vote in 1932, FDR understood the political imperative of tackling the rural crisis. Beyond such calculations, he had argued throughout the 1920s that national prosperity was unsustainable if not shared by the agricultural sector. By 1933, he was one of many in Washington who believed that farmers' lack of purchasing power was prolonging the Great Depression. In time, agricultural planners would realize that the holistic solution to declining commodity prices lay in restoring urban demand. Had he known this in 1933, FDR would still have prioritized agricultural recovery. While agriculture accounted for just 8 per cent of national economic output, far less than industry, finance and services, farm interests had the support of conservative Southern Democrats who formed the core of party and committee leadership in Congress. Accordingly, putting farmers first gave the president cover for the unprecedented expansion of the central state that the New Deal would engender.

FDR met with Secretary of Agriculture Henry Wallace and Assistant Secretary Rexford Tugwell at the White House on 8 March to discuss the farm situation. All three were supporters of the Voluntary Domestic Allotment Plan, developed in 1929 by Milburn Wilson, professor of agricultural economics at Montana State College, who wanted to incentivize cutbacks in agricultural production through government payments to farmers willing to reduce their acreage. Tugwell had persuaded Roosevelt to give broad endorsement to Wilson's proposal in his major election address on farm issues at Topeka, Kansas. To his mind, the allotment plan offered the perfect middle ground between the anarchy of agrarian overproduction and the tyranny of direct controls. It would also assist the establishment of national land planning, something he considered essential for a modern farm economy subject to technological change and international competition. 'We can make . . . [the farmer] contribute towards a long-run program in this way', Tugwell told a group of congressional progressives. 'We can plan for him and with him.'[28]

The integration of agriculture into the national economy by bringing supply into line with demand and assigning the federal government regulatory power over production was controversial. Some farm organizations preferred solutions more attuned to the agrarian ideal of independent farmers maximizing the bounty of the land. To expedite intervention before spring ploughing produced another bumper harvest to depress prices further, FDR accepted Wallace's proposal to draft legislation that incorporated multiple approaches but allowed the Secretary of Agriculture to implement the most appropriate option. A brilliant plant scientist who helped revolutionize corn farming, Wallace was an expert on commodity prices and the editor-publisher of *Wallace's Farmer*, the weekly journal that his grandfather had made into the voice of Midwestern agriculture. To his mind, farmers were at the mercy of market demand because they could not regulate production like manufacturers. 'In agriculture', he declared, 'supply sets the price. In industry, price sets the supply.'[29] Accordingly, government needed to do for the farmer what the farmer could not do for himself through enforced reduction of surpluses.

Summoned to a conference in Washington on 10–11 March, farm leaders agreed to an outline Agricultural Adjustment bill that aimed to raise farm income to parity, namely the cost–price ratio for commodities in the golden age of agriculture from 1909 to 1914. This omnibus measure contained: a domestic allotment scheme, funded on FDR's insistence through a new tax on food processors rather than from deficit finance; subsidies for farm exports; and a market-agreement provision requiring processors to pay farmers a minimum price for specified products. As agricultural journalist Russell Lord observed, the bill was 'fantastically elastic' in its inclusion of 'almost anything anybody could think up'.[30] Once the conference adjourned, Department of Agriculture officials spent some frantic days drafting the complex legislation for despatch to Congress on 16 March. Wallace and Tugwell composed an accompanying presidential statement to which FDR added a passage of his own. 'I tell you frankly', it warned, 'that it is a new and untrod path, but I tell you with equal frankness that an unprecedented condition calls for the trial of new means to rescue agriculture.'[31]

Belatedly recognizing that the bill offered no protection for farmers facing the threat of foreclosure, Roosevelt signed an executive order on 27 March consolidating the federal government's existing rural credit agencies into the Farm Credit Administration under the leadership of Henry Morgenthau, his Hudson valley neighbour and friend. Morgenthau's chief adviser, Cornell economist William Myers, devised a mortgage-relief proposal for inclusion in the farm bill. Under its terms, $2 billion in land-bank bonds would fund emergency loans, with maximum interest of 4.5 per cent and five-year grace before repayments commenced, to head off foreclosures and refinance existing mortgages. The volume of mortgage that the new agency advanced in 1933 was over four times the total for the entire land-bank system in 1932. Congress validated its powers in the Emergency Farm Mortgage Act, enacted as part of the omnibus farm bill, and supplemented them in the Farm Credit Act of 1933, signed by FDR on 16 June. Among the most successful initiatives of the Hundred Days, the Farm Credit Administration held some two-fifths of all farm-mortgage debt by 1940.[32]

In the House of Representatives, where rules curtailed debate, Democratic leaders shepherded the administration's farm measure to approval with relative ease. In the Senate, farm-state members inserted a cost-of-production fixed-price amendment that effectively guaranteed funding for ever-increasing farm surpluses. At FDR's bidding, House members of the conference committee charged with reconciling the different bills succeeded in eliminating this in the final legislation. Wallace remained on guard against its resurrection by farm interests who 'refuse to admit that surpluses, by wrecking prices, can destroy farmers without contributing one iota to feeding and clothing the needy'.[33]

FDR was more sympathetic to another proposal that emerged from congressional deliberations over the farm bill. Concerned that bank failures, bankruptcies and hoarding had reduced the volume of dollars in circulation by 50 per cent since 1929, many rural legislators regarded monetary inflation as essential for agricultural recovery. Senator Elmer Thomas (D-Oklahoma) fused together various reflation measures into a bill that authorized the president partially to re-monitize silver, devalue the dollar and issue greenbacks unsupported by gold. Seeing it as the most acceptable of the various inflationary panaceas, Roosevelt decided to accept the measure if modified to allow him greater discretion over monetary expansion. To appease sound-money advocates in his own circle, Roosevelt delegated Treasury aide James Warburg to redraft the bill. In final form, it gave the president unprecedented authority to control monetary policy through the securities operations of the US Treasury and the Federal Reserve, but placed a $3 billion cap on printing greenbacks and limited dollar devaluation to 50 per cent maximum. Disdainful of inflationary solutions, Warburg congratulated himself in his diary for 'bringing an insane proposal back to the realms of sanity'.[34]

Congress finally sent farm legislation containing the Agricultural Adjustment Act, the Emergency Farm Mortgage Act and the Thomas Amendment for presidential approval on 12 May. In a political trade, FDR had persuaded Senator Ellison 'Cotton Ed' Smith (D-South Carolina), an outspoken advocate of volume in cotton production, to release the bill from his Senate Agriculture Committee in return for the appointment of his ally, George Peek, to head the Agricultural Adjustment Administration, the new agency that would administer the farm programme. Putting a long-time opponent of production restraint in charge of the body responsible for enforcing it stored up problems for later but facilitated the measure's enactment.

Meanwhile, FDR had taken his first steps to help the unemployed in establishing the Civilian Conservation Corps (CCC), the New Deal initiative with best claim to be his brainchild. As New York governor, he had launched a programme that put some 10,000 unemployed men to work on forestry schemes. On the morning of 9 March, before his presidency was a week old, Roosevelt summoned the secretaries of Agriculture, Interior and War to the White House to hear his idea for putting some 500,000 unemployed men in rural camps to plant trees, protect forests and control floods. Interior officials were delegated to come back with a draft bill by 9.30 pm that same evening. This became the basis for the proposal sent to Congress on 21 March with an accompanying presidential message that the CCC would conserve forest resources, curb flooding and deliver 'moral and spiritual value' by rescuing a 'vast army' of the unemployed from enforced idleness through provision of work in 'healthful surroundings'.[35] The authorizing legislation sailed through Congress to be signed into law by FDR on 31 March.

CCC was a rare example of successful interdepartmental collaboration under the New Deal: Interior and the Forest Service organized the work projects, the Army managed the camps and Labor oversaw the recruitment process. FDR delighted in visiting the camps to talk with enlistees over lunch, often with some Cabinet members in tow. While CCC went down in history as embodying a 'New Deal for Youth', this was not what he had envisaged. Frank Persons, a Department of Labor official with expert knowledge of youth unemployment, was responsible for stipulating that recruits should be males aged between eighteen and twenty-five (later seventeen to twenty-eight). The CCC enrolled nearly 275,000 young men in 1,300 camps in its first three months and over three million in its nine-year existence. Enlistees were mainly drawn from families on local relief, who received $25 of their $30 monthly wage. The average recruit signed on aged eighteen, stayed nine months and gained 12–30 pounds in weight, thanks to three square meals a day. CCC's public-investment record included construction of 125,000 miles of road, 46,854 bridges and over 300,000 anti-erosion dams; planting of 3 billion trees; laying of 89,000 miles of telephone wire; and over 8 million hours of firefighting. It offered a life-changing experience that instilled self-confidence in many participants. One recalled sixty years later, 'There was pride in the work. We built something, and I knew I helped . . . it was something you could take pride in, and there wasn't a lot of pride available in those days.'[36]

Shortly after CCC's establishment, the New Deal took its first steps to enhance unemployment relief. The Emergency Relief and Construction Act of 1932 had established the first large-scale federal welfare programme in history in response to the imminent collapse of state-local relief. It financed 60 per cent of all unemployment relief through direct loans to the states, but its $300 million appropriation was exhausted by the time Roosevelt became president. FDR's early preoccupation with the banking crisis and farm issues slowed his response to the groundswell of support in Congress for grants-in-aid to the states to fund unemployment relief. It required the intervention of Harry Hopkins, director of New York's Temporary Emergency Relief Administration (TERA), to appraise him that a new federal agency was needed to oversee this disbursement. Roosevelt asked three congressional supporters of federal relief, Senator Edward Costigan (D-Colorado), Senator Robert La Follette Jr (R-Wisconsin) and Senator Robert Wagner (D-New York), to draw up the required legislation. Following on from his distinguished record as a social reformer in New York state government in alliance with Al Smith, a fellow alumnus of Tammany politics, this was Wagner's first of many contributions to FDR's agenda that would make him the most significant New Dealer in the Senate. The trio's bill established the Federal Emergency Relief Administration (FERA) with $500 million funding, half going to individual states on the basis of one federal dollar for every three they spent on relief and half to be disbursed at the agency director's discretion. Following speedy enactment, it went to FDR for signing on 12 May.[37]

Never a member of FDR's inner circle in Albany, Hopkins became a key New Dealer through being appointed FERA director. A product of small-town Iowa, he was imbued with the social gospel of applying Christian ethics to alleviate poverty while a student at Grinnell College. Moving to New York City after graduation in 1912, he rose rapidly through the ranks of its social-work establishment. His experiences among the immigrant communities on the Lower East Side convinced him that joblessness, not moral defect, was the root of poverty. Impatient with red tape, he put a premium on expediting federal assistance for relief. On his first day as FERA director, he commandeered a desk in a hallway at the Reconstruction Finance Corporation, got hold of unprocessed state relief-loan applications and disbursed $5 million in grants within two hours. With no time or money to create a large federal bureaucracy, Hopkins relied on state organizations to administer FERA funds but used his control of purse strings to insist that governors professionalize their relief operations as a condition for aid. Though the cash dole was FERA's main instrument of assistance, Hopkins drew on his TERA experience to prod states into operating work relief, a more expensive form of aid but better suited to giving the unemployed self-respect.[38]

The jobless were not the only group requiring assistance in urban America, where many families struggled to maintain payments on homes bought in the prosperous 1920s. The standard mortgage was a short-term loan, usually of three to five years, covering only interest. It was expected that rising property equity would make for automatic refinancing but average housing values fell by one-third from 1926 to 1932. Middle-class families unable to get adequate re-mortgage terms faced bank foreclosure on their homes. FDR called on Congress to provide security against enforced liquidation as 'a proper concern of Government'.[39] In response, it created the Home Owners Loan Corporation (HOLC) to purchase and refinance mortgages in default. Lenders received full compensation at original home values in the form of government bonds paying 4 per cent interest. Capitalized by the US Treasury, HOLC had authority to issue $2 billion in bonds, later raised to $4.75 billion, enabling it to purchase approximately one-fifth of all urban mortgage-debt by the time its enabling legislation expired in June 1936. It succeeded in reducing non-farm foreclosure rates by half from 1933 to 1937, refinanced loans at low interest with long-term notes (typically 5 per cent over fifteen years) and kept the dream of free-and-clear homeownership alive for more than a million middle-class families. HOLC also put money in federal coffers, reporting profits of $11 million on finally closing its accounts in 1948.[40]

A child of the country, Roosevelt had greater interest in solving rural problems than urban ones, showing himself capable of thinking on a vastly ambitious scale to uplift the impoverished Tennessee Valley that extended through seven Southern states. Overworked soil, erosion, springtime flash floods and lack of electricity made for primitive agriculture that barely yielded a living for its typical farm family. The valley's greatest asset was the hydroelectric-generating potential of a turbulent river system, a political battleground between public-power champions and private utilities. A series of rapids at Muscle Shoals, Alabama, caused the Tennessee river to drop by almost the height of Niagara Falls over a 37-mile stretch. During the Great War, the federal government had commenced constructing the Wilson Dam to provide flood control and cheap power for its new nitrate plants at Muscle Shoals, a project completed in 1924. Senator George Norris (R-Nebraska) twice secured congressional approval for public ownership of the Muscle Shoals development. Neither measure survived veto, respectively by Calvin Coolidge and Herbert Hoover, both of whom objected to federal sale of electricity in competition with private business. Signalling his different mindset, FDR invited Norris to join him on an inspection tour of Muscle Shoals in January 1933. During their trip, the president-elect outlined a bold vision for the entire valley's redevelopment. 'Is he really with you?' reporters later asked the venerable senator, who replied, 'He is more than with me because he plans to go even further than I did.'[41]

Like Norris, Roosevelt regarded public power as both a source of cheap electricity and a pricing yardstick to deter profit-gouging by private utilities. As New York governor, he had contemplated harnessing the Saint Lawrence's hydroelectric potential to provide cheap electricity akin to neighbouring Ontario's public-power system. Enlarging his vision on the national stage, FDR conceived an integrated programme for Tennessee Valley modernization. As outlined to reporters before his inauguration, this entailed generation of up to three million horsepower of electricity at Muscle Shoals, an even greater volume at other dams to be built (sixteen in total between 1933 and 1944), the construction of flood control reservoirs, the dredging of a navigable ship canal (eventually stretching 650 miles from Knoxville on the Tennessee to Paducah on the Ohio), reforestation of bare hillsides, anti-erosion measures, improvements in farming techniques, upgrade of health and education services, establishment of model communities for the resettlement of valley residents and the urban unemployed from outside the region, and the introduction of small-scale diversified industry. 'We have been going at these projects piecemeal ever since the days of TR', he asserted. 'I believe it is now time to tie up all these various developments into one great comprehensive plan.'[42]

Securing legislation to operationalize this vision was one of Roosevelt's greatest achievements in the Hundred Days. On 10 April he asked Congress to create the

Tennessee Valley Authority (TVA) as a public corporation charged with implementing regional renewal that 'touches and gives life to all forms of human concern'.[43] Though worried that FDR had underestimated the so-called power trust's capacity to safeguard private utilities, Norris piloted to approval a Senate bill that perfectly embodied presidential wishes. As he had feared, the utility conglomerates succeeded in getting the House to approve a measure that served their interests. Entering the fray with gusto, FDR used all his influence to ensure that the reconciliation conference committee adopted the Norris bill in its entirety. Following speedy approval by both chambers, this went for presidential signature on 18 May.

While Roosevelt was taking on the power trust, he sought to discipline big finance for its part in precipitating the 1929 crash. Even Herbert Hoover had suspected speculators of conspiring to sell other peoples' stock short to make a profit on their own holdings. Encouraged by him, the Republican-led Senate Banking and Currency Committee held investigations that got nowhere until Ferdinand Pecora became its chief counsel in January 1933. A 51-year old, Sicilian-born immigrant son of a cobbler, Pecora had worked his way through law school to become assistant New York district attorney before moving into private practice. Subpoenaing a mountain of documents from investment banks, his team of lawyers discovered that about half of the $450 billion securities issued in the free-and-easy 1920s were worthless. Pecora took his first big scalp during cross-examination of Charles Mitchell, president of the National City Bank (forebear of Citigroup), the man known on Wall Street as 'Sunshine Charley' because of his unabashed optimism about the securities he was selling – particularly the worthless ones. Mitchell had pioneered the integration of commercial banking with investment banking and brokerage but in eight days of testimony he was forced to admit the unloading of poor stocks onto unsuspecting small investors by his bank's security house and his own evasion of income tax. Pecora's investigatory net widened to compel J. P. Morgan and other investment bankers to testify on their questionable practices. The additional misdemeanours he uncovered included tax avoidance by creating paper losses on stock sales, issuance of stock to rescue bad loans made by the parent commercial bank and protection of favoured clients by selling them stock below market values.[44]

The Pecora investigations elevated Wall Street regulation into a New Deal priority. The Truth in Securities bill that Roosevelt sent to Congress on 29 March was the work of Huston Thompson, a Wilsonian Democrat and former chair of the Federal Trade Commission. The accompanying presidential message lauded it for replacing the principle of caveat emptor in securities transactions to put 'the burden of telling the whole truth on the seller'.[45] Expert criticism of its inadequacies during hearings conducted by the House Interstate Commerce Committee convinced Chairman Sam Rayburn (D-Texas) that an entirely new measure was needed. Asked to help by FDR aide Raymond Moley, Harvard law professor Felix Frankfurter recruited three of his former students to draft workable legislation. New York corporate lawyer Benjamin Cohen, Reconstruction Finance Corporation aide Tommy Corcoran and James Landis of the Harvard Law School holed up in Washington's Carlton Hotel, one block from the White House, to do their work.

In the first of many New Deal bill-drafting initiatives by Frankfurter protégés, the trio produced a measure requiring full and fair disclosure. The administration bill had granted immense but imprecise powers over stock registration to the Federal Trade Commission, an agency liberals deemed too cosy with business. The Cohen-Corcoran-Landis alternative established clear standards to ensure that registration became a matter of mechanistic routine and imposed responsibility for truthful disclosure not only on a corporation's directors but also its accountants, lawyers and appraisers. For his part, Rayburn shielded the politically inexperienced trio from the hostility of Wall Street attorneys sent to pick apart their handiwork during committee hearings. Once put before the full House, the bill received overwhelming approval, but the Senate had meanwhile adopted the Thompson-drafted proposal. Roosevelt's switch of support to Rayburn's measure, whose superiority he readily acknowledged, ensured its adoption by the conference committee. When a banker warned that the legislation would deter investment, FDR responded, 'Don't worry. . . . It will not hurt any honest seller of securities and some of them are seeing things at night!'[46]

In his signing statement, Roosevelt acknowledged that the hastily drafted legislation corrected 'some of the evils which have been so glaringly revealed in the private exploitation of the public's money' but was only a first step 'in a program to restore some old-fashioned standards of rectitude' without which 'economic well-being cannot be achieved'.[47] It placed enormous responsibilities on the Federal Trade Commission which lacked the organizational machinery to discharge them robustly. It entirely avoided regulation of security exchanges, a key area of malpractice. Loopholes in its technical requirements also meant that dubious start-up ventures of the kind exposed by the Pecora hearings could easily qualify for registration. '[O]bserve how slightly the Act would have touched those exhibits in our Hall of Horrors', warned Yale law professor and future New Dealer William O. Douglas.[48] Nevertheless, the measure established the fundamental principle that stock-issuing corporations owed full disclosure to investors, raised the ethical and professional standards of the accounting profession, and established securities regulation as a legitimate obligation of the federal government. Keen to obtain legislation while the Pecora investigations had the financial community on the ropes, Roosevelt had not demanded more than he thought it would accept without a battle. 'It is conservative rather than extreme', former Brain Truster Adolf Berle commented. 'The protection it gives is minimum rather than maximum.'[49]

More immediately effective in regulating Wall Street and longer in gestation was another banking reform, which reflected outrage over Pecora's findings that the line between commercial and investment banking had grown dangerously thin in the 1920s. The savings of millions of commercial bank depositors had leaked into the stock-and-bond accounts of their Wall Street security affiliates, resulting in a liquidity crisis of unprecedented proportions when the stock market hit the skids. To address this problem, Senator Carter Glass (D-Virginia) and Representative Henry Steagall (D-Alabama) won congressional approval for the Banking Act of 1933 (better known as Glass-Steagall). This required the separation of commercial banking from investment banking, allowed commercial banks one year to divest their security affiliates, created the Federal Deposit Insurance Corporation (FDIC) to guarantee individual bank accounts up to $2,500 and strengthened the Federal Reserve's control over the supply of money and credit, notably through establishment of the Federal Open Market

Committee to coordinate buying and selling of government securities. FDR considered vetoing Glass-Steagall out of concern that the high cost of deposit insurance would unfairly penalize strong banks just to protect weak ones. Despite relenting when the likelihood of being overridden became apparent, he signalled his reservations in not offering a celebratory statement when signing the law on 16 June.

Deposit insurance went into effect on 1 January 1934, initially for a six-month period that was quickly extended to eighteen months. FDIC was made permanent and its guarantee doubled to $5,000 by the Banking Act of 1935. Its mere existence reassured depositors that their money was safe in banks, thereby consigning runs to history, with the consequence that deposit-insurance premiums remained low. Whereas some 4,000 banks had failed in 1933, only 61 did so in 1934, all but nine of which lacked deposit insurance. Between 1934 and 1960, depositors lost $706,000 in failed banks on aggregate annual average, compared with $146 million yearly from 1921 to 1933. Drawing a veil over his initial reservations, Roosevelt jubilantly asserted in 1938 that FDIC 'amply justifies the confidence which we placed in deposit insurance as an effective means of protecting the ordinary bank depositor'. Two conservative economists later adjudged its establishment 'the single most important structural change' in the economy since the Civil War because of its success in preventing bank panics.[50]

On the day he signed Glass-Steagall, a New Deal success story, FDR put his name to a bill establishing its least effective agency, the National Recovery Administration (NRA), created by the most hastily improvised, ill thought-out and unwieldy legislation of the Hundred Days. Its genesis lay in Roosevelt's desperate need to head off congressional enactment of the 'thirty-hour bill', sponsored by Senator Hugo Black (D-Alabama). Hitherto, the New Deal had not featured legislation to galvanize expansion of industrial employment owing to contradictions between the myriad panaceas on offer. While FDR awaited crystallization of thinking, Senate Democrats stepped into the breach in promoting a spread-the-work measure that prohibited from interstate commerce goods made in enterprises where employees laboured longer than a thirty-hour week.

Rubbishing claims that the Black bill would create some six million additional jobs in one bold stroke, critics feared that it would smother not stimulate the economy. Some jobs, they warned, would be difficult to perform in thirty-hour weeks, some industries would find it impossible to recruit suitably qualified additional labour and employers would slash wages for everyone working fewer hours. Wary of antagonizing Black's supporters, Roosevelt delegated Frances Perkins to suggest necessary amendments in testimony before the House Committee on Labor on 17 April. With Eleanor Roosevelt looking on from the galleries to signify that she spoke for the president, the Secretary of Labor cannily voiced support for the measure in principle while undermining it by insisting on significant changes, most notably minimum-wage protection.[51]

In the meantime, a number of groups worked on a comprehensive programme for industrial recovery. Raymond Moley recruited General Hugh Johnson, briefly a member of Roosevelt's Brain Trust, to devise a proposal for government-business cooperation based on the War Industries Board that had organized industrial mobilization during the Great War. Within a few days he produced a draft bill providing for nationwide regimentation of industry as if for war. It suspended anti-trust laws, authorized presidential sanction of business agreements pertaining to competition and labour practices and allowed federal licensing of industrial codes to ensure compliance. A group headed by Senator Robert Wagner produced a recovery plan featuring public works, direct loans to industry and federal authorization of trade association agreements. Another group helped by Rexford Tugwell recommended using trade associations as instruments of national economic planning. The principal drafters got to make their case to FDR on 10 May. After hearing them out, the president suggested they lock themselves in a room – budget director Lewis Douglas's office was the chosen venue – and not come out till they agreed on a measure. Their labours produced a compromise proposal that welded together their disparate ideas, minus industrial loans whose repayment would be difficult to enforce.[52]

On 17 May the president sent what became the National Industrial Recovery Act (NIRA) to Congress accompanied by a message calling for speedy approval of the necessary machinery for 'a great cooperative movement throughout all industry in order to obtain wide reemployment, to shorten the working week, to pay a decent wage for the shorter week and to prevent unfair competition and disastrous overproduction.'[53] Despite speedy House enactment, Western progressives inserted anti-trust provisions in the Senate version to prevent the industrial codes from becoming charters for business monopolies. Corporate insistence that price-fixing was essential for recovery induced the conference committee to reject this amendment. The reconciled bill narrowly got through the Senate by 46 votes to 39 on 13 June.

As finally enacted, Title I of NIRA established the National Recovery Administration with a two-year lifespan to oversee a massive process of federal-sanctioned cartelization. It gave the president ultimate power to approve codes drawn up by trade groups for an entire industry provided they were not monopolistic, to amend these if necessary and to impose a code in an industry that failed to agree on one. NIRA exempted the industrial codes from anti-trust laws but said little about what they should contain, other than for labour standards. Section 7 of Title I stipulated their obligation to provide for maximum hours, minimum wages and desirable work conditions. The codes also had to guarantee workers' right to organize and bargain collectively through representatives of their own choosing. The legislation therefore embodied two conflicting theories of economic recovery: one held that business confidence could be restored and new investment generated by curbing destructive competition and insuring profits; the other deemed that expansion of purchasing power required raising wages, holding down prices and spreading work. Lacking the machinery to reconcile its contrary mission goals, the NRA became a battleground for rival interests and ended up, in the words of journalist Ernest Lindley, an 'administrative, economic and political mess'.[54]

Title II of NIRA created the Public Works Administration (PWA) with an appropriation of $3.3 billion to fund federal-supported construction projects. The champions of pump-priming within the Roosevelt administration, Frances Perkins and Rexford Tugwell, had wanted an allocation of $5 billion, but FDR was leery of such vast expenditure, a stand encouraged by the penny-pinching Lewis Douglas. Left to his own devices, Roosevelt might have stuck with the $900 million of projects identified by Herbert Hoover as worthy of federal support. The popularity of public works in Congress induced him to settle for a sum midway between what Hoover and Perkins wanted.[55] Worried that this huge outlay would impair government credit, the president insisted that NIRA contain a levy on capital stock and excess profits to cover interest payments on money borrowed to fund the programme.

Hugh Johnson's service on the War Industries Board and his role in formulating the enabling legislation made him the obvious choice to head the NRA, but there could be no illusions about him being a team player. A man of indefatigable energy and egotism, the general started lining up people for NRA and PWA posts before being appointed to take charge and without consulting the president. Seeking to harness his ability, FDR made Johnson responsible to a committee of Cabinet members heading the departments with which the NRA would need to work. He also removed public works from the general's jurisdiction on the supposed grounds that asking any one man to administer Titles I and II would be 'an inhuman burden'. Johnson's flabbergasted reaction when told this after a Cabinet meeting on 16 June aroused concern that he might air his grievance to the press. 'Stick with Hugh', FDR whispered to Perkins. 'Keep him sweet. Don't let him explode.' For the next few hours Johnson found himself being driven round Washington until he regained sufficient composure to accept the truncated post.[56]

The separation of NRA and PWA responsibilities weakened their coordination in support of recovery. Johnson had anticipated using public works to induce acceptance of the industrial codes he expected to negotiate with business. Whether this was possible was another matter because of the time-consuming challenges of assembling a new bureaucracy, selecting appropriate projects and ensuring graft-free operations. Put in charge of PWA, Secretary of the Interior Harold Ickes interpreted his mandate as being to approve expenditures on large-scale construction projects after careful review that these were in the public interest.[57] Under his leadership, the agency would develop a national infrastructure that laid the foundations for the remarkable expansion of the American economy in the 1940s and 1950s. In the short term, PWA was less successful in boosting employment because it prioritized meticulous project development ahead of fast-tracking people into work. By January 1934, it had committed its $3.3 billion allocation, but actual outlays lagged far behind.[58]

With the adjournment of Congress on 16 June, the Hundred Days of 1933 came to an end. The legislation signed by FDR had decisively resolved the bank crisis, devised new bureaucratic structures to reorganize key sectors of the nation's economy, developed mortgage financing by government to rescue hard-pressed farm owners and homeowners, launched the greatest public-works programme and the boldest regional-planning experiment hitherto in American history, and built significantly on the narrow foundations of unemployment relief promulgated under Herbert Hoover. All this added up to a record of high-speed policy innovation unmatched by any predecessor or successor – indeed all those who came to office after FDR would find themselves measured in their first hundred days against his impossible standard.

Reflecting on Roosevelt's impact on the national psyche in 1933, Hugh Johnson commented that America 'could have got a dictator a lot easier than Germany got Hitler' but for his restoration of popular confidence in the national government.

Rexford Tugwell, who agreed with Johnson on little else, similarly remarked that the United States was confronted on FDR's inauguration 'with a choice between an orderly revolution – a peaceful and rapid departure from past concepts – and a violent and disorderly overthrow of the whole capitalist structure'. According to another perceptive commentator, Roosevelt's leadership had restored 'three magnificent things' that America had appeared in danger of losing in early 1933: hope, action and self-respect.[59]

Newspapermen made up for underestimating FDR in 1932 by praising him to the skies in 1933. Veteran *Baltimore Sun* correspondent Fred Essary typically remarked, 'Roosevelt the Candidate and Roosevelt the President are two different men. . . . The oath of office seems suddenly to have transfigured him from a man of mere charm to one of dynamic aggressiveness.'[60] Such effusiveness overlooked the reality that the New Deal's launch in the Hundred Days was a collaborative venture, not an exclusively presidential one. Only the measures establishing the CCC and the TVA were FDR's own inventions. The EBA was the work of holdovers from the Hoover administration, others in the administration with support from affected constituencies took the lead in shaping the farm bill and the industrial recovery bill, and Congress played an important role in shaping key measures – even seizing the initiative from FDR in the case of the Thomas Amendment, the securities legislation and the Glass-Steagall Act. Roosevelt's indispensable role was to instil a sense of urgency that government had to act, to give direction to the New Deal and to use his immense influence to expedite congressional approval of legislation enacted in its name.

Regardless of his limited authorship of the early New Deal, Roosevelt established a new presidential role as chief legislator in the Hundred Days. Excepting Glass-Steagall, he was involved in some way or other in launching all the major bills that eventually became law. Virtually every one of these initiatives was sent to Congress with a trenchant presidential statement of its necessity. Whenever it looked as if the legislature might not produce the kind of measure he wanted, FDR used his influence to ensure that it did his bidding, as was the case with the various components of the omnibus farm bill and the 'share-the-work' bill.

FDR traded on his authority as party leader and his electoral mandate to keep his Democratic troops in line behind the early New Deal. For now, his expansion of federal activism had support from Southerners desperate to restore the farm economy and keen to regulate Wall Street and the big banks, long villains in rural America's eyes. Significantly, the New Deal's initial lack of provision for African Americans posed no challenge to racial hierarchies. The loyalty of conservative Democrats withered when it changed direction in the mid-1930s to identify with the needs of urban America, a shift with significant implications for the distribution of power in the national party.

Popular opinion attributed the unprecedented outpouring of the Hundred Days legislation exclusively to FDR rather than Congress, thanks to his highly effective public communications. The uplifting oratory of the inaugural address, the reassuring tones of the Fireside Chats, the messages to Congress and the regular signing statements all conditioned this outlook. FDR also benefited immensely from favourable coverage in the newspapers, courtesy in no small part to his bi-weekly press conferences. Equally important, he was almost deified on newsreel screens as America's saviour, especially in documentaries that were as popular with movie audiences as the main features of the theatre programme. Typical of the latter, *The Fighting President*, an hour-long cinematic political biography of FDR, culminated with a heroic montage of his achievements in his first month in office.[61] Accordingly, it was hardly surprising that in trying to make sense of the bewildering transformation of government that had taken place in barely three months, ordinary citizens personified Roosevelt as its architect and embodiment.

The intimate relationship that Roosevelt established with the American people in 1933 endured throughout his tenure. Another significant development for his presidency was its acquisition of responsibility for economic management, a role implicit in the currency and gold powers granted initially by the Emergency Banking Act and later the Thomas Amendment. Most importantly, the legislative blitzkrieg of 1933 enhanced the power and authority of his office by placing it at the heart of the activist national state.

If the Hundred Days was crucial to the transformation of the presidency, it also stored up problematic consequences. The plethora of federal agencies established to administer the new programmes created challenges of administrative coordination for FDR. Their resolution eventually required the establishment in 1939 of new executive mechanisms within the White House that enhanced presidential capacity to secure bureaucratic compliance with his objectives. The early New Deal's unprecedented expansion of federal authority also raised questions about its constitutional legitimacy that would embroil FDR in confrontation with the judicial branch of government in the mid-1930s. The Supreme Court's ultimate acceptance of Washington's socio-economic activism added up to a constitutional revolution of immense significance for presidential leadership of public policy.

The New Deal was far from a finished product when the congressional session of 1933 came to an end. In all but one of the next five years – election-affected 1936 was the exception – there were major additions to its legislative output. These initiatives sought to either remedy existing programmes or develop new measures to address overlooked or unresolved problems. As the emergency circumstances of 1933 receded, FDR would encounter much greater difficulty in enacting administration bills without having them weakened through amendment by congressional conservatives, particularly in the case of socio-economic initiatives aimed at disadvantaged groups. Nevertheless, Congress would still look to the president to frame its legislative agenda. This was the overriding legacy of the Hundred Days.

New Dealer

FDR and socio-economic reform

According to New Dealer Rexford Tugwell, Franklin D. Roosevelt's fundamental goals on assuming the presidency were to bring about 'a better life for all Americans, and a better America to live it in'.[1] In 1933–4, he focused on the recovery and reform of the financial, business and agricultural sectors. Thereafter his agenda became more directly concerned with the socio-economic needs of ordinary Americans. The early New Deal offered security for those in danger of losing assets they already possessed: bankers and bank depositors, industrialists, investors, homeowners and mortgage creditors, and farm owners. Roosevelt's later initiatives offered a different form of security through provision of work relief, social insurance, workplace rights and assistance for renters. This change in the character, tone and class identification of the New Deal shaped historical memory of him as a great reformer.

In his public discourses of 1934–5, Roosevelt redefined freedom as socio-economic security underwritten by national government. No speech better summed up this philosophy than his special message to Congress in June 1934. 'Among our objectives', he avowed, 'I place the security of the men, women and children of the Nation first.' Spelling out his meaning, he identified 'three great objectives – the security of the home, the security of livelihood, and the security of social insurance' as 'a minimum of the promise that we can offer to the American people'. These constituted 'a right which belongs to every individual and every family willing to work'.[2] Paying tribute to the New Deal's advancement of these goals, Columbia University philosopher Irwin Edman wrote in his popular history of democratic thought, published in 1941, that economic security had 'at last been recognized as a political condition of personal freedom'.[3]

For conservatives like Herbert Hoover, the New Deal's expansion of federal authority undermined rather than underwrote personal liberty.[4] Addressing this concern in a Fireside Chat in September 1934, Roosevelt insisted that only a benevolent national government could ensure the security of its people in a modern industrial economy, where wealth was concentrated and individuals were vulnerable to the vicissitudes of life. 'I am not for a return to that definition of liberty', he declared, 'under which for many years a free people were being regimented into the service of a privileged few. I prefer and I am sure you prefer that broader definition of liberty under which we are moving forward to greater freedom, to greater security for the average man than he has ever known before in the history of America.'[5]

The early New Deal's failure to achieve economic recovery made it imperative to redefine freedom. The National Recovery Administration (NRA) was incapable of fulfilling its mission to revitalize and reform the industrial sector through development of industry-wide codes of fair competition to regulate production levels, prices, hours of work and wages. The task of devising charters capable of reconciling the interests of big and small business, regional diversity and the divisions between capital and labour was beyond it. Furthermore, the NRA made no effort to change discriminatory employment practices affecting African Americans and women. Making matters worse, it operated under inept leadership. General Hugh Johnson's boundless energy, tub-thumping oratory and talent for cajolery suggested that he could speedily establish a new government partnership with business. Underneath his tough exterior, however, lurked personal insecurities that found expression in bluster, bullying and binge-drinking.

Johnson enlisted FDR's support for a public-relations campaign reminiscent of the Great War's Liberty Bond drives to promote the NRA codes. In a Fireside Chat on 24 July 1933, the president urged every business in the country to display 'a badge of honour' to signify their cooperation with the agency.[6] This was the Blue Eagle, wings spread, clutching lightning bolts in one talon and an industrial cog in the other, above the NRA slogan in red, 'We do our part'. Agency officials barnstormed the country to spread the word that buying from enterprises exhibiting this emblem was the patriotic way to propel the nation towards employment recovery. Keeping FDR's name to the fore, Johnson mounted huge public events to boost the Blue Eagle. On 13 September, officially designated 'the President's NRA Day', a great parade of some 250,000 people representing New York City's many occupations marched up Fifth Avenue, watched by a crowd of a million-and-a-half people. Festivities of this kind, replayed on a smaller scale throughout the nation, served to identify the New Deal's entire recovery strategy with the NRA, arousing popular expectations of better times that were doomed to disappointment.[7]

FDR and Johnson were misguided in their mutual conviction that invoking patriotic unity would secure corporate support for fair competition. The first code negotiated with a big industry showed that private interest was uppermost for business. Cotton textile producers were desperate to end the cut-throat competition, overproduction and price discounting that afflicted the myriad small mills stretching from New England to the Appalachian South. Their trade association agreed a code that stipulated a forty-hour week for labour, a minimum weekly wage of $12 and abolition of child labour, but allowed industry control of production and prices in return for these concessions. It also exempted 'learners' from the wages-and-hours guarantees, thereby enabling owners to fire existing employees and re-hire them in the new category. Intending to sign the code for a four-month trial period, FDR let Johnson persuade him that this would deter cooperation from other industries. Accordingly cotton textiles set a precedent for trading off presidential prerogative to require acceptable terms for the sake of code agreement by large industries.[8]

All the big industries had agreed a code by mid-September, but there were some individual holdouts. Johnson organized the automobile industry without Henry

Ford, who refused to put 'that Roosevelt buzzard' on his cars, a recusancy that did not prevent his company increasing its market share of auto sales in 1933. Far more commonly, corporate leaders were willing partners because the NRA allocated primary responsibility for code-drafting to the trade associations that were under their control. Johnson was confident that the force of public opinion whipped into patriotic fervour by the Blue Eagle campaign would keep business from exploiting its privileged position over labour and consumers. Accordingly, the quantity rather than the quality of codes was his measure of NRA success. During a Cabinet meeting in late July, Roosevelt light-heartedly remarked that Johnson had recently rushed into his office to have him sign three codes on the spot and then sped out to seek others. 'He hasn't been seen since', FDR joked. Though the story got lots of laughs, it signified that the president had lost control over code-making.[9]

Reporter George Leighton's investigation of corporate practice under the NRA produced a bleak conclusion: 'Any supposition that business intends to "govern itself" in the spirit of the New Deal is preposterous. The profit motive is still solidly in the saddle.'[10] Trade associations crafted industry-wide codes that met general NRA requirements while containing terms favouring big business. These often imposed production specifications that smaller enterprises found hard to meet, divided up marketing territories to discourage new competitors, condoned price-fixing, established minimum-wage levels that rapidly became the maximum and set maximum hours with loopholes allowing them to be sidestepped. Many businesses circumvented code-ordained collective-bargaining rights for workers through establishing company unions that were the lapdogs of management. In 1934, class antagonisms spilled over into violent strikes in Minneapolis, San Francisco and Toledo, which resulted in recognition of independent unions. Elsewhere, labour suffered bloody defeats in industries where workers were vulnerable to intimidation. The United Textile Workers called out its 400,000 widely scattered members in what was then the largest strike in American history to compel mill operators to honour the wages-and-hours terms of the Cotton Textile Code, but it collapsed in the face of violent suppression in the South.[11]

FDR went down in history as a champion of labour despite being an inconsistent supporter during the industrial strife of 1933–4. Though happy to better the lot of workers through NRA initiatives, he was not enthusiastic about empowering their unions, demonstrated by his stand on the vexed issue of exclusive representation. On 1 March 1934, the National Labor Board, the NRA's largely ineffectual mediation body, ruled that the union receiving most votes in a government-supervised representation election had won the exclusive right to represent all workers. Roosevelt's personal intervention in another recognition dispute between the United Auto Workers and the automobile companies effectively rejected this principle. On 25 March, he announced a settlement that provided for proportional, rather than exclusive, representation, thereby legitimizing company unions.[12] Led by Senator Robert Wagner (D-New York), labour's allies in Congress prepared to enact new legislation that strengthened union rights. To head them off, Roosevelt issued an executive order on 29 June establishing the National Labor Relations Board (NLRB) in place of the National Labor Board. Given greater authority than its predecessor, it settled the representation issue through the Houde case ruling that any organization designated as bargaining agent by the majority of employees 'had the right . . . to be treated by the employer as the exclusive bargaining agency of all the employees in the unit'.[13]

When it became clear that the country was not flying back to prosperity on the Blue Eagle's wings, popular disillusion with the NRA was inevitable. Despite FDR finally sacking the increasingly inebriated Johnson in September 1934, there was no saving the agency. Roosevelt hoped that it could be reorganized as a prelude to congressional reauthorization for another two years. 'The fundamental purposes and principles of the Act are sound', he declared. 'To abandon them . . . would spell the return of industrial and labor chaos.'[14] The new director, Chicago attorney Donald Richberg, gambled that obtaining Supreme Court validation of the agency's authority to regulate business would facilitate its legislative renewal. The test case he chose for this purpose was *Schechter v U.S.* pertaining to NRA regulation of the kosher poultry industry. Appearing before the high bench to argue the case in person, Richberg contended that an extraordinary economic crisis warranted extraordinary government powers. A unanimous judgement on 27 May 1935 ruled against the constitutionality of the agency's code-writing operations. The 'sick chicken case', as the press dubbed it, brought the Blue Eagle to earth. After conferring with the president at the White House, Richberg emerged to announce that the NRA was being wound up because its industrial codes were unenforceable as a matter of law.[15]

The early New Deal's other agency of economic recovery, the Agricultural Adjustment Administration (AAA), encountered problems of a different kind. George Peek, appointed its director to ease Senate approval of the omnibus farm bill in 1933, disagreed with the agrarian planning ideals of its principal authors, Secretary of Agriculture Henry Wallace and Assistant Secretary Rexford Tugwell. His preferred solution for the farm crisis was the subsidized export of unrestricted agricultural surpluses. 'I did not have the slightest idea', he later remarked disingenuously, 'that in its administration [AAA] would become principally an instrument to regiment the farmer through acreage control.'[16] Wallace signalled his opposite commitment in getting the AAA, established late in the 1933 farm calendar, to order the ploughing-up of crops already planted and the slaughter of millions of pregnant sows and piglets already born as a production-control exigency. The destruction, undertaken when many families lacked adequate food, was a public-relations disaster that saddled AAA with a reputation for heartlessness. An unrepentant Wallace commented, 'They were emergency acts made necessary by the almost insane lack of world statesmanship during the period 1920 to 1932. . . . I would tolerate it only as a cleaning up of wreckage of the old days.'[17]

Bureaucratic in-fighting turned AAA into a house divided against itself. On one side stood Peek and his band of administrators, many of them long-standing US Department of Agriculture (USDA) officials transferred to the new agency. They were at heart agricultural industrialists dedicated to the interests of landlords and food processors and driven by one overriding concern. 'The job's simple', Peek asserted. 'It's just to put up farm prices.'[18] Aligned against them was a group of young New Dealers, many of them Ivy League-trained lawyers with no experience of farming. Their goal was not just to restore commodity prices but to provide a decent standard of living for farm labourers, tenants and sharecroppers, regardless of race. The reformers were based in the AAA legal division, headed by General Counsel Jerome Frank, an ally of Rexford Tugwell. From Peek's perspective, they wanted to turn AAA 'from a device to aid the farmers into a device to introduce the collectivist system of agriculture into this country'.[19]

The reformers emerged victorious in the opening battle but lost the war. In late 1933, Peek clashed with Tugwell over his plan to dump heavily subsidized American butter on the European market, which contradicted efforts to limit farm production. Drawn into the dispute, FDR accepted Tugwell's suggestion that Peek should have a face-saving transfer to the post of 'special assistant to the president' with a brief to pursue foreign agricultural trade agreements in coordination with the Department of State, headed by ardent free trader Cordell Hull. For the president this was a means of burying Peek away in a post of little power, from which he would resign in disillusion in December 1935.[20]

Despite Peek's removal, AAA was still divided over whether its mission was economic or social. Voluntary participation in its production-control programme came with the inducement of cash payments for farm owners who reduced their output. The USDA's Bureau of Agricultural Economics annually calculated the acreage to be removed from cultivation for each major crop and set livestock targets in order to boost commodity prices by bringing supply into line with demand. It also determined how much the federal government would pay for diminution of agricultural production. The AAA then faced the daunting task of issuing millions of individual contracts to participating farmers setting out their acreage and commodity reduction obligations and their financial compensation for meeting these. The only way it could do so was by enlisting the help of existing organizations, both governmental and non-governmental, that were already deeply involved in the farm economy. Accordingly, the AAA recruited the USDA's Extension Service county agents and the county directors of the American Farm Bureau Federation to head up new production-control units established in every rural county in the nation. This made the agency largely indistinguishable from the existing farm bureaucracy and the biggest farm group, thereby ensuring its primary identification with the economic interests of farm owners in the upper and middle echelons of agriculture.[21]

The AAA's strategy of controlling farm production through generous financial inducement helped in boosting farm income by 50 per cent and reducing farm indebtedness by $1 billion during FDR's first term. When campaigning for re-election, Roosevelt exulted that his administration had delivered 'security for those who have spent their lives in farming; opportunity for real careers for young men and women on the farms; a share for farmers in the good things of life abundant enough to justify and preserve our instinctive faith in the land'.[22]

These fine words belied the reality that the AAA made no provision for some 4.5 million farm labourers, sharecroppers and tenants, constituting about a third of the agrarian workforce. In theory landowners were to share their federal benefits with them but few did. In the cotton South, many sharecroppers and tenants found themselves evicted by owners seeking to meet AAA acreage-reduction obligations. In Arkansas, they fought back by joining the inter-racial Southern Tenant Farmers Union (STFU) only to be beaten into submission by the whips and guns of the 'riding bosses' and police lackeys of the local cotton lords. After being roughed up when speaking for the union in the ill-named town of Birdsong, habitual Socialist Party presidential candidate Norman Thomas went to the White House to appeal for Roosevelt's intervention. Reliant on Southern Democrats' support in Congress, FDR refused to put the entire New Deal at risk for the sake of the STFU. 'Now come, Norman', he remonstrated, 'I'm a damn sight better politician than you are. I know the South, and there is arising a new generation of leaders and we've got to be patient.'[23]

AAA reformers rushed in where the president feared to tread. Alger Hiss, a 28-year old Harvard graduate who had never seen Dixie's cotton fields, drafted a ruling 'that no signer of a [AAA] contract, no owner of land could get rid of his tenants'. On 1 February 1935, Jerome Frank promulgated this as an administrative directive for cotton contracts, only to be overruled by new AAA director Chester Davis. Unwilling to risk confrontation with Dixie Democrats, he sacked Frank and four of his Legal Division officials with the approval of Henry Wallace. The purge marked the end of AAA attempts to address the structural and racial inequalities inherent in the South's cotton economy.[24]

Shedding social-mission aspirations may have saved AAA from the wrath of congressional conservatives, but the agency fell afoul of the Supreme Court's broad assault on the New Deal. In early 1936 the *US v. Butler* judgement struck down production controls and the processing tax that funded them as unconstitutional expansions of federal regulatory authority. To circumvent this, the Soil Conservation and Domestic Allotment Act of 1936 provided payments from congressional appropriations for famers who reduced their acreage of soil-depleting crops, notably cotton and wheat, and increased their soil-conserving crops, especially new commodities like soybeans. This was an inadequate substitute for the original scheme because its monetary incentives for farmer participation were less generous than those funded from the processing tax. Its shortcomings for production control became evident when the drought-free summer of 1937, the first in the West since 1929, produced record harvests.

Following the Supreme Court's change of heart on New Deal constitutionality, Roosevelt's farm programme entered a third phase with the enactment of the Agricultural Adjustment Act of 1938. This made a start in establishing an ever-normal granary (federal purchase of surplus commodities to safeguard against future crop failures), made soil conservation a permanent programme, authorized crop loans and offered wheat farmers insurance against drought. Its complex quota and marketing provisions caused initial confusion among farmers, particularly those in the Midwest and West, whose resentments cost the Democrats dear in the midterm elections. The bumper yields of wheat and cotton, the result of another good summer in 1939, compelled the administration to fall back on export subsidies to dump surpluses abroad in complete violation of original New Deal intent. Only the loss of foreign markets caused by war in Europe, which forced farmers to accept production control as an essential prop for commodity prices in 1940, saved the farm programme.[25]

Despite twists and turns, the New Deal succeeded in stabilizing the agrarian economy by the end of FDR's second term, saving it from ever again suffering devastating depressions. The general economic status of the farm population also underwent significant improvement during Roosevelt's tenure. All this was achieved at cost of a reduction in the number of farm units by 15 per cent between 1930 and 1950. Tenant numbers underwent precipitous decline from 2.7 million to 1.4 million over this period as landlords removed acreage from cultivation to qualify for AAA payments. Many farmers also used their government money to purchase modern machinery that lessened the need for labouring help. As the farm population declined, the size of farm units mushroomed by 35 per cent over the course of FDR's presidency. Bigger farms laid the foundations for the expansion of agribusiness that would turn much of farming into a corporate enterprise in the postwar era. Some rationalization of agriculture had been necessary because there were too many people working the land, but the process was brutal for the losers. Summing up Roosevelt's reform record in the sector, historian Theodore Saloutos observed, 'With all its limitations and frustrations, the New Deal, by making operational the ideas and plans that had long been in the minds of agricultural researchers and thinkers, constituted the greatest innovative epoch in the history of American agriculture.'[26]

Despite his initial focus on business and agricultural recovery, Roosevelt was aware that the unemployed needed help to get through the winter of 1933–4, one of the harshest on record. In early November he sanctioned a bold proposal from Harry Hopkins to create a new agency, the Civil Works Administration (CWA), charged with speedy placement of four million people on federal work-relief projects at an initial cost of $400 million drawn from Public Works Administration (PWA) funds. Though he would later fret over their competing jurisdictions, Harold Ickes readily assented to the transfer of money from his agency to the new one headed by Hopkins. 'There was a general feeling', he acknowledged, 'that we really are in a very critical condition, and that something drastic and immediate should be done to bolster the situation.'[27]

Once Roosevelt established CWA through executive order on 9 November 1933, Hopkins built its bureaucracy from scratch. He transferred staff from the Federal Emergency Relief Administration (FERA), used the existing state relief organizations as its local arm and enlisted the Veterans' Administration, which had a national system of disbursement in place, as CWA paymaster. To develop work projects, he solicited ideas from other federal departments and the states and pinched a good few that the slower-moving PWA had under consideration. Thanks to Hopkins's organizational genius, CWA got 2.4 million people into work in its first month and boosted its rolls beyond four million within another month. Magnificent achievement as this was, another eight million of the unemployed remained beyond its reach.

Placing great importance on the self-worth and dignity of the jobless, CWA hired half its workers from relief rolls and half from the needy unemployed without subjecting anyone to a means test. It paid a wage, at the prevailing minimum rate (40 cents an hour in the South, 60 cents in the North), as opposed to giving handouts. Hopkins loved hearing about the wife of a CWA worker saying, 'We aren't on relief any more. My husband is working for the Government.' In its five-month life, CWA issued close on $834 million in pay cheques, with the help of a supplemental appropriation from Congress. In return, its employees upgraded some 500,000 miles of secondary roads, refurbished 40,000 schools, laid 12 million feet of sewer pipes (and installed

150,000 privies for rural families) and constructed 3,700 playgrounds and athletic fields. 'Long after the workers of the CWA are dead and gone and these hard times are forgotten', Hopkins proudly remarked, 'their efforts will be remembered by permanent useful works in every county of every state.'[28]

Much as FDR admired what Hopkins had achieved, he worried about its financial and social consequences. If the CWA continued into the summer, he told the National Emergency Council on 23 January 1934, it would 'become a habit with the country.... We must not take the position that we are going to have permanent depression.'[29] Shortly afterwards, he decreed that CWA be wound up by 31 March, an order that Hopkins carried out with his usual despatch, albeit reluctantly. FERA, which prioritized dole assistance, resumed full responsibility for the New Deal's much-reduced relief operations. Nevertheless, CWA's success in putting the unemployed to work stood in stark contrast to NRA's failure to get businesses to boost employment. Accordingly, its organizing principle would have an all-important afterlife within a year of its last rites being read.

Meanwhile, Roosevelt added another two dozen measures to the New Deal roster in 1934. '[E]ven though the orthodox protest and the heathen roar', he wrote Colonel Edward House, a confidante since their days in the Wilson administration, 'I think we can keep the tide on the flood for a good long time to come.'[30] The most significant recovery initiative was the National Housing Act, drafted by a presidential task force headed by banker Marriner Eccles. With almost a third of the jobless formerly employed in construction, the measure aimed to resuscitate the homebuilding industry, dubbed by FDR 'the wheel within the wheel to move the whole economic engine'. It established the Federal Housing Administration (FHA) to encourage greater lending for home construction and refurbishment through provision of government insurance for private mortgages as a safeguard against default. From 1935 to 1939 the agency insured 400,000 new housing units, about a quarter of the total number financed through the mortgage market, but this was hardly pump-priming on the scale required. Obliged not to operate at a loss by congressional amendment to its enabling legislation, the FHA developed a banker-like aversion to risk and social purpose. It hardly ever insured rental housing, the predominant low-income accommodation, because this was subject to profit constraints like rent control. It red-lined urban districts settled or likely to be settled by African Americans, whose presence was considered certain to undermine property values. The FHA's insurance programme made home mortgages less onerous in financial terms, while its real-estate assessment regulations did much to establish minimum standards for housing construction. Nevertheless, its preference for supporting detached, owner-occupied homes set on an ample lot meant that the New Deal put in place a structure of financial security that ultimately enabled private money to build suburbia and neglect the inner city.[31]

The most significant reform initiative in 1934 was the Securities and Exchange Act that established federal oversight of stock exchanges to prevent 'unnecessary, unwise, and destructive speculation'.[32] Congressman Sam Rayburn (D-Texas), chair of the House Interstate Commerce Committee, and Senator Duncan Fletcher (D-Florida), chair of the Senate Banking Committee, introduced into their respective chambers an administration bill that New Deal aides Benjamin Cohen and Tommy Corcoran had been working on for months. Going much further than the Securities Act of 1933, this established a new principle that the financial affairs of stock-issuing corporations were matters of public interest that should be conducted in the open. Horrified at the prospect of outside scrutiny, Wall Street girded for war, but FDR was not for turning. He wrote Rayburn and Fletcher that Americans 'in overwhelming majority' wanted effective stock-exchange regulation and their bill met the 'minimum requirements' for so doing. Accordingly, he concluded, 'I do not see how any of us could afford to have it weakened in any shape, manner or form.'[33]

The legislation created the Security and Exchange Commission (SEC), endowed it with discretionary authority to regulate some twenty stock exchanges, required the detailed financial reports of listed companies to be filed with SEC, restricted the capacity of floor traders and insiders to manipulate the market and empowered the Federal Reserve to regulate margin requirements for stock trading on credit. Pleased with the outcome, FDR wrote to Adolf Berle, one of the intellectual influences on the bill, '[T]he fundamental trouble with this whole Stock Exchange crowd is their complete lack of elementary education. I do not mean lack of college diplomas, etc, but just inability to understand the country or the public or their obligation to their fellow man.'[34]

Telling aides that 'it takes a thief to catch a thief', FDR chose Joseph P. Kennedy, notorious for insider trading and market manipulation on Wall Street in the free-and-easy 1920s, to lead SEC.[35] Speaking for outraged progressives, journalist John T. Flynn remarked that he had expected the president to appoint someone acceptable to Wall Street 'in obedience to his well-known policy of carrying water on both shoulders', but not in his 'wildest dreams' had he anticipated the selection of a speculator. When this object of scorn resigned from SEC in September 1935, the same reporter admitted that he had 'disappointed the expectations of his critics'.[36] Kennedy cracked down on fraudulent selling of securities in stock exchanges through negotiation rather than litigation and self-enforcement rather than coercion. His legacy was a commission philosophy that balanced the need for profits and probity. Building on this, Kennedy's successors, James Landis and William Douglas, erected a legal framework that even Wall Street applauded for implanting order and trust in the financial markets for the next half-century.

While the New Deal continued to seek recovery and regulatory reform in the second half of the depression decade, Roosevelt's annual message to Congress in January 1935 signified new priorities. Declaring that 'social justice . . . has become a definite goal', he itemized specific initiatives to make this a reality. Roosevelt cloaked his innovative intent in the garb of orthodoxy: 'We seek [change] through tested liberal traditions, through processes which retain all of the deep essentials of that republican form of representative government first given to a troubled world by the United States.'[37]

For some commentators, the shift in course was a response to grassroots discontent fomented by Senator Huey Long (D-Louisiana) and radio priest Father Charles Coughlin, both of whom charged that the New Deal was too cosy with business and banks. Elliott Roosevelt, for example, adjudged that it was 'designed to cut the ground from under the case of the demagogues'.[38] At this juncture popular support was growing for Long's 'Share the Wealth' programme that purported to confiscate annual income over $1 million and inheritances over $5 million for redistribution among ordinary Americans in the form of a 'household estate' of $5,000. This was sheer fantasy – even if all such wealth were in liquid form, its reallocation through the most punitive tax levies imaginable would have given every household just $400 and harmed more than helped the economy.

Far from turning left to outmanoeuvre his demagogic critics, Roosevelt was acting from conviction that the New Deal needed to do more to help people in need. He exploited the Long-Coughlin clamour to warn conservatives that irresponsible radicals would run wild if his new measures were defeated. Accordingly, he met with Edmond Coblentz, William Randolph Hearst's chief editor, to get a message to the media mogul, a vituperative critic: 'I am fighting Communism, Huey Longism, Coughlinism' to save capitalism from 'crackpot ideas'. In like vein, he wrote Newton Baker, formerly a Wilsonian Progressive but now a conservative corporate attorney, 'One of my principal tasks is to prevent bankers and businessmen from committing suicide!'[39]

With the Great Depression entering its sixth year, pessimism that many of the jobless would never again find work in private industry was taking hold among New Dealers. In a Fireside Chat in June 1934 Roosevelt had warned Americans that the federal government would have to spend vast sums on relief for years to come. 'We may as well recognize that fact', he asserted. Of like mind, Harry Hopkins commented, 'Intelligent people have long since left behind them the notion that . . . the unemployed will disappear as dramatically as they made their appearance after 1929. . . . For them a security program is the only answer.'[40] The Democratic gains in the 1934 midterm congressional elections in defiance of the historic trend that the president's party lost seats in off-year contests provided the opportunity to expand the New Deal – and, equally, the obligation to seize the moment. 'All of us', Roosevelt told Vice President John Garner, 'have an increased responsibility for the very fact that the country has such great confidence that we can better conditions everywhere.'[41]

With the CWA's success in mind, the president wrote Colonel House, 'What I am seeking is the abolition of relief altogether. I cannot say so out loud yet but I hope to be able to substitute work for relief.'[42] Roosevelt wanted the federal government to quit 'the business of relief' because he feared that the dole 'induces a spiritual and moral disintegration fundamentally destructive to the national fibre'. In contrast, he approved its substitution with work-relief which inculcated 'self-respect . . . self-reliance and courage and determination'.[43] A key influence on presidential thinking, Harry Hopkins told FERA aides shortly after the midterms, 'Boys – this is our hour. We've got to get everything we want – a works program, social security, wages and hours, everything – now or never. Get your minds to work on developing a complete ticket to provide complete security for the folks of this country up and down and across the board.'[44]

Hopkins holed up with his men in the St Regis Hotel in New York to labour for several days developing a plan for a massive programme of work relief, which he presented to FDR at Warm Springs. This provided the broad rationale for Roosevelt's request to the new Congress for an Emergency Relief Appropriation of $4.8 billion. The 'Big Bill', as he liked to call it in private, asked for the largest peacetime appropriation hitherto in American history to address what its architects regarded as the long-term, perhaps permanent, incapacity of the private economy to provide employment for all who wanted it. Enacted on 8 April, the measure earmarked some funding for the Civilian Conservation Corps and the PWA but allowed the president discretion to allocate the rest on new agencies that he would create through executive orders. One initiative, the Rural Electrification Administration, helped to improve living standards in rural America over the next decade-and-a-half through bringing cheap power to farm homes, nearly 90 per cent of which lacked electricity in 1935. The most immediately significant outcome of the Big Bill, however, was the establishment of the Works Progress Administration (WPA) that federalized the funding, administration and operation of all work relief.

WPA employed able-bodied relief recipients to work on permanently useful, self-liquidating, labour-intensive projects. The 1.5 million recipients of FERA aid too sick, old or handicapped to work were placed back in the care of local institutions, most of which lacked the resources to provide adequate assistance. Meanwhile, at least five million of the unemployed not on relief rolls were left outside the scope of federal largesse. Within the limits of its remit, WPA employed 8.5 million people at an aggregate cost of some $11 billion over its eight-year existence, with a peak enrolment of 3.3 million in late 1938.[45] Since half of labour-market participants aged between sixteen and twenty-four were jobless, FDR also created the National Youth Administration as a WPA subsidiary. To encourage the needy young to stay in school or college, it paid them stipends to undertake on-campus tasks, assistance that reached 400,000 students by 1937.

WPA's establishment as an independent agency under Harry Hopkins engendered jurisdictional rivalry with Harold Ickes, who had wanted it for his PWA empire.[46] To curb their feuding, Roosevelt decreed that projects costing under $25,000 should generally go to the WPA and above to the PWA, but the canny Hopkins stayed several steps ahead of his rival. In one case, WPA got the go-ahead to build a sewer system for Atlanta, Georgia, by dividing the job into dozens of individual contracts. Nevertheless, the warring officials were essential complementary cogs in the New Deal's public-works strategy. Hopkins strove to spend money as quickly as possible for the benefit of the here-and-now, whereas the penny-pinching Ickes favoured projects benefiting posterity. It was highly unlikely that either could have done the other's job or been an effective czar of a single agency combining public works and work relief.

Roosevelt thought of making the 'Big Bill' even bigger by including old-age pensions, unemployment insurance and national healthcare within an integrated strategy for sustainable socio-economic security. Instead he split these elements into separate legislation to facilitate enactment and pre-empt comprehensive constitutional challenge. The resultant Social Security Act (SSA) of 1935 had the most significant legacy of any New Deal measure. According to Frances Perkins, Roosevelt 'always regarded [it] as the cornerstone of his administration'.[47] Nevertheless, its evolution from blueprint to legislation was a tortuous process involving the interplay of idealism, political pressure, constitutional calculation and financial constraints.

Perkins had accepted Cabinet appointment as Secretary of Labor with the aim of promoting social insurance into law. The Triangle Shirtwaist Company fire of March 1911, which killed 146 mostly female employees in a Manhattan factory that violated even minimal notions of health and safety, made her a lifelong believer in governmental responsibility to protect workers. A prim New Englander with no small talk, Perkins was a resolute battler on behalf of the underprivileged during a long career in state and national government. It scandalized her that the United States alone among advanced nations lacked a national system of unemployment compensation and old-age pensions. She single-handedly pressed for social insurance at early Cabinet meetings when FDR's priority was the economic emergency. Wearing a trademark felt tricorn hat atop oval-faced features and small of frame, she was initially underestimated by male colleagues, who did not take well the discovery that their first impressions were wrong. 'I continue to be astonished at Miss Perkins' lack of sense of proportion', Harold Ickes complained of her capacity to fight for the president's ear.[48]

As Roosevelt's own vision of economic security took shape, he found himself increasingly attracted to the goal of comprehensive social insurance. According to Rexford Tugwell, this became his great panacea for ensuring 'permanent well-being for the people of the United States'. On 29 June 1934, he announced the formation of a Committee on Economic Security (CES), chaired by Perkins and composed of Treasury Secretary Henry Morgenthau, Henry Wallace, Attorney General Homer Cummings and Harry Hopkins, with the brief to formulate a social insurance programme through consultation with experts. University of Wisconsin economist Edwin Witte, appointed staff director, played a key role in shaping the group's deliberations. In the first flush of enthusiasm, FDR told Perkins, 'There is no reason why everybody in the United States should not be covered . . . from the cradle to the grave they ought to be in a social insurance system.' Sensing that the huge financial costs militated against a universal approach, she was more realistic in urging that CES base its recommendations on 'a practical knowledge of the needs of our country, the prejudices of our people, and our legislative habits'.[49]

Casting a shadow over CES deliberations was what General Counsel Thomas Eliot called 'the omnipresent question of constitutionality', namely the concern that the Supreme Court would strike down an entirely federalized social insurance.[50] The imperative of creating a mixed system effectively ruled out inclusion of healthcare insurance, which many states viewed with suspicion as socialized medicine, particularly Southern ones where racial prejudices reinforced such animus. It also presented a potential obstacle to the funding of unemployment insurance from taxed employer contributions because some states might hold out for competitive advantage in attracting industries from participating states. A worried Eliot remarked, 'Some way must be found to induce *all* the states to enact these laws. But what way? How?' The answer came from an unexpected source. A long-time supporter of unemployment insurance, Supreme Court justice Louis Brandeis used back channels to counsel that writing a tax-offset device into unemployment insurance would induce states to devise their own programmes on pain of having a portion of their tax revenues appropriated to fund a federal programme. Its inclusion in the authorizing legislation ensured that all forty-eight states established unemployment-insurance programmes conforming to minimal national standards, while varying widely in the benefits paid.[51]

Devising adequate old-age assistance proved even more problematic because of FDR's insistence that 'the funds necessary to provide this insurance should be raised by contribution rather than an increase in general taxation'. If pensions were free, he anticipated constant grassroots clamour to raise them. In Eliot's assessment, funding pensions through payroll levies on employers and employees increased the risk of judicial repudiation on grounds that 'the Constitution gave Congress no authority to go into the insurance business'. There were even greater doubts about the fairness of old-age assistance partially financed through a regressive tax on workers. The United States would find itself alone among modern industrial nations in operating social insurance without financial input from national government. Under its system, workers would effectively end up paying for employer contributions because these costs would be passed on to them through higher consumer prices. Furthermore, the initial collections of these taxes, scheduled for 1937, would suck purchasing power from employees' pockets to the detriment of a recovering economy. Warned of all this by Perkins, Roosevelt jauntily replied, 'We can't help that. We have to get it started or it will never start.'[52]

Whatever the constitutional and economic perils, Roosevelt was prepared to risk them because of his absolute opposition to funding social insurance from general taxes. 'No dole', he would repeatedly tell Perkins. 'No money out of the Treasury.' When challenged on this by public administration expert Luther Gulick in 1941, FDR explained the trade-off he had felt obliged to undertake:

> I guess you're right on the economics, but those taxes were never a problem of economics. They are politics all the way through. We put the payroll contributions in there so as to give the contributors a legal, moral and political right to collect their pensions and unemployment benefits. With those taxes in there, no damn politician can ever scrap my social security program.[53]

To facilitate congressional enactment, Perkins and her planners created a scale of payments based on previous earnings, a practice in line with private insurance principles. There was still the conundrum of what benefits were due older workers who would have paid relatively little into the system on retirement. If strict actuarial rules were followed, an employee making five years of contributions from an average monthly wage of $50 would receive a monthly annuity of just 24 cents; even ten years of paying in would net only 78 cents. The CES solution was to grant workers over forty-five in 1935 far more generous pension payments than their contributions warranted – at cost of creating an accrued liability in the Social Security trust fund to be met from general taxes sometime between 1965 and 1980. 'Ah', Roosevelt remarked on hearing it, 'but this is the same old dole under another name. . . . We can't do that.' Almost immediately, he swung 180 degrees to acknowledge need for 'a solid plan which will give some assurance to old people of systematic assistance on retirement'. Otherwise, he worried, Congress could be tempted to consider a more extravagant pension scheme in response to grassroots pressure.[54]

To assuage presidential concern, the CES devised a hybrid financing scheme based on an initial payroll tax of 1 per cent of earnings split fifty-fifty between workers and employers and rising gradually to a combined 5 per cent in 1956. This would pay in part for more generous payments to early retirees than their contributions warranted, with the rest coming from a one-off federal appropriation in the mid-1960s, after which the programme would become self-funding. Henry Morgenthau's unexpected intervention prompted further changes. Despite signing off on the final CES report, he began a personal campaign against any federal subsidization of contributory insurance as a fraud on the taxpayer. The Treasury Secretary persuaded FDR that the payroll tax should start at 2 per cent, shared equally by employers and employees, to build up a reserve of nearly $50 billion by 1980, thereby relieving the federal government of its future obligation. According to Perkins, Morgenthau had pestered Roosevelt until he finally said 'Oh, all right, Henry, all right' to get some peace.[55] This explanation ignores FDR's own reservations about the accumulated deficit being funded from general taxation. Morgenthau's solution likely received his assent because it allowed him to have his pension cake and to eat it free from guilt about subsidization.

Despite its limitations, the Social Security plan that went to Congress offered beneficiaries an unprecedented measure of 'security against the hazards and vicissitudes of life'. The term 'social security' had not yet entered the political lexicon, so FDR fashioned understanding of it as offering the freedom of economic security to different groups in society – workers, the temporarily unemployed, retirees, indigent aged, dependent children and the impoverished sick.[56] The administration measure did not try to outbid the pension promises contained in the Townsend Plan, the brainchild of elderly California doctor Francis Townsend, which envisaged getting workers to retire at sixty on a monthly federal pension of $200, financed by a sales tax. It spawned the first mass-lobby for old-age security in the nation's history in the form of Townsend Clubs that claimed membership of five million and adherents in excess of twenty million in 1935. Experts like Edwin Witte dismissed this beguiling vision for costing annually more than double the aggregate of federal, state and local tax receipts to support the 9 per cent of Americans aged sixty or more. Exploiting congressional concerns about Townsend Plan costs, FDR described his own proposal as a cautious assessment of what was possible without straining the capacity of business and workers to underwrite social insurance. Now was not the time, he warned, to endanger the 'precious' goal of social security 'by attempting to apply it on too ambitious a scale'.[57]

Witte assumed primary responsibility for explaining the administration bill in two days of testimony before the House Ways and Means Committee, with Perkins lending her heavyweight support when he finished. All seemed to go well until Morgenthau's testimony put another spoke in their wheel in his committee appearance on 5 February. Professing to support universal old-age assistance in principle, he expressed scepticism that the Internal Revenue Service was administratively capable of collecting such broad-based employee contributions as currently envisaged. Accordingly, he recommended excluding from coverage agricultural labourers, household servants and establishments with fewer than ten employees. These strictures hit at the very occupations employing well over nine million of the nation's most insecure workers, notably African-American and Latino farm workers, female domestics and the ethnic young working in small urban enterprises.[58]

Morgenthau's intervention offered a rationale for conservatives on the Ways and Means Committee and the Senate Finance Committee to demand amendments that whittled down the costs of social security by eliminating coverage for these vulnerable employment categories. Needing Southern Democrats to support the bill, Roosevelt did not lift a finger to prevent its retrenchment. As originally framed, the legislation could very well have driven them to make common cause with conservative Republicans in opposing it. An editorial in a leading Mississippi newspaper offered unambiguous expression of regional hostility to coverage for farm labour. 'The average Mississippian', it declared, 'can't imagine chipping in to pay pensions for able-bodied Negroes to sit around in idleness on front galleries, supporting all their kinfolk on pensions, while cotton and corn crops are crying out for workers to get them out of the grass.'[59]

Once redrafted, the bill sped through the House of Representatives by 372 votes to 33 in April and the Senate by 77 votes to 6 in June. As finally approved in reconciled form, the Social Security Act of 1935 provided for unemployment insurance, old-age pensions and categorical assistance (funded through a combination of general taxes and matching state grants) for specified groups – fatherless families with dependent children, the blind, the physically handicapped and the indigent elderly. Signing the law on 14 August, Roosevelt acknowledged that it 'represents a cornerstone in a structure which is being built but is by no means complete'.[60] Undoubtedly the single most important piece of social legislation in US history, the SSA laid the foundations for a peculiarly American welfare state that established a two-tier system based on social security, which rewarded recipients for working, and public assistance, which provided limited aid for those unable to work. By insisting on contributory social insurance, albeit out of political calculation rather than moral principle, Roosevelt had created a social-welfare programme that primarily benefited Americans holding steady jobs throughout their working lives rather than those trapped in poverty.

The SSA was the most significant of five major bills and a host of lesser but still important ones enacted during what went down in Washington folklore as the 'second Hundred Days', stretching from early June to late August 1935. Few observers would have predicted this outcome at the end of May. At that point, the 'Big Bill' constituted FDR's solitary legislative success of note. Despite the midterm mandate for reform, Roosevelt found himself on the defensive in the face of an anti-lynch law filibuster and the uncertain constitutional fate of the New Deal. Harold Ickes confided to his diary that the president somehow had to 'reaffirm the position of vigorous leadership' displayed in 1933.[61]

The Supreme Court's *Schechter* decision provided the charge of political electricity that galvanized FDR into action. In early June he told congressional leaders that four major bills required enactment before the legislature adjourned: the social security bill, a labour bill, a banking reform and a public-utility holding company reform. On 19 June, he added a wealth tax to his 'must' list. Administration emissaries became regular callers in Democratic congressional offices to press the Roosevelt agenda. Any waverer received a presidential telephone call that mixed coaxing and command to bring him onside. In the sweltering heat of the Washington summer, endured without benefit of air conditioning, legislators ended up doing the president's bidding before heading home in exhaustion. Congressional leaders at one point considered issuing a unilateral declaration of adjournment to escape the draining humidity but desisted from knowledge that Roosevelt would call them back into special session.

The immediate outcome of renewed presidential assertiveness was the National Labor Relations Act. When the Supreme Court's invalidation of NRA struck down existing labour protections, Roosevelt put the measure developed by Senator Robert Wagner on his 'must' list. With the president only a secondary influence in securing what American Federation of Labor president William Green called 'the Magna Carta of Labor', the legislation rightly became known by its real author's name. The Wagner Act established a new National Labor Relations Board with unprecedented authority to call plant elections, certify the unions that workers chose to represent them on the basis of majority rule and proscribe anti-union activities by employers. Unlike its various forerunners, the NLRB's three-member board was entirely composed of public appointees rather than representatives drawn from business, labour and consumers. Its principal mission was to safeguard labour rights as defined in law rather than engage in disinterested mediation to end strikes. A large legal staff ensured the effectiveness of NLRB's enforcement machinery. According to one of its leading attorneys, Thomas Emerson, the Wagner Act's establishment of a government structure to protect labour 'was a major triumph of the New Deal. . . . It provided a counterforce to industry. The concept was entirely in the right direction.'[62]

This strongly pro-labour legislation could only have gotten through Congress in the unusual circumstances of 1935. Conservatives did little to block its enactment in the expectation that the Supreme Court would rule it unconstitutional. Southern Democrats contented themselves with amending the bill to exclude agricultural labour and domestic servants from its coverage. Business leaders, in contrast, had no intention of complying with legislation that they considered unconstitutional. General Motors boss Alfred Sloan sounded the call to arms: 'Industry, if it has any appreciation of its obligations to future generations, will fight this proposal to the very last.'[63] Accordingly, the Wagner Act marked a new phase in labour's struggle for recognition rather than its final victory.

Meanwhile, FDR's long-time enmity to the 'power trust' put him at the forefront of the campaign to secure the Public Utilities Holding Company Act (PUCHA). Defined as entities that controlled other companies through share-ownership, holding companies were common throughout the business world, but public-power supporters regarded their widespread presence in the utility industry as wholly pernicious. Operating within complex, highly leveraged structures that shielded them from regulation, eight such enterprises controlled three-quarters of the nation's private electricity supply in 1932. Seeing no hope of regulating them to safeguard consumers against excessive charges, FDR was set on their elimination.

Charged with drafting the requisite legislation, Ben Cohen and Tommy Corcoran met FDR's abolitionist intent with a 'death penalty' provision allowing the Securities and Exchange Commission to compel dissolution of any holding company that extended beyond a discrete geographical region and failed to demonstrate economic necessity for its existence. The utility industry mounted a lavishly funded counter-campaign when the bill came before Congress in February 1935. As well as employing an army of lobbyists, it organized mass-mailings of constituent protests, most of which were fabricated. Wary of defeat, Roosevelt initially left his congressional allies to battle the utility assault unaided before finally rallying to the cause. Fearful that the president was throwing in the towel, Senator Burton K. Wheeler (D-Montana) sought an early morning meeting at the White House in early June to ascertain his intentions.

Still abed and puffing away at his first cigarette of the day, Roosevelt nonchalantly scrawled a note of support for the 'death penalty' on some scrap paper. When the Senate debated removing it from the bill, Wheeler's reading of the president's words was instrumental in securing its survival by a single vote. The House of Representatives proved a tougher nut to crack because the mass-mailings had made many Democrats nervous. The lower chamber twice voted by large majorities for a bill shorn of the death penalty.

With the conference committee unable to reconcile the House and Senate versions, PUCHA looked set to die until a complicated compromise saved the day. The bill finally signed by FDR on 26 August authorized federal regulation of interstate transmission of electricity and gas, wiped out holding companies more than twice removed from operating companies and allowed holding companies to exist only one level above consumer operations if their economic necessity could be justified to SEC. Although legal challenges to the legislation slowed its implementation, utility holding companies had divested assets worth $12 billion and reduced the number of affiliates under their control from some 2,000 to 300 by 1948.[64]

Another of Roosevelt's 'must' bills struck at the rich in mainly symbolic fashion. Having earlier decried any need for new taxes to raise revenue, he surprised Congress with a message calling for a wealth tax. This was the solitary initiative of his 1935 agenda undertaken in response to the Long-Coughlin grassroots agitation. 'Our revenue laws', he declared, 'have operated in many ways to the unfair advantage of the few, and they have done little to prevent an unjust concentration of wealth and economic power.' This prefaced requests for 'very high taxes' on large incomes, stiffer inheritance taxes, a graduated corporate income tax and taxes on intercorporate dividends offered by holding companies.[65] Roosevelt wrapped the Treasury-produced tax package in the cloak of fiscal necessity to reduce the budget deficit, but it would raise a mere $250 million in additional revenues, less than 10 per cent of the 1934 federal tax take. Quite clearly, the proposal had more to do with politics for the president. As one congressman remarked, 'This is a hell raiser not a revenue raiser.' Roosevelt also found gratification in getting back at his wealthy enemies. Gleefully giving Harold Ickes a personal reading of the tax message, he remarked at one point, 'That is for Hearst.'[66]

Having lain down his marker, Roosevelt acquiesced without protest to congressional amendments. The final legislation promulgated higher brackets for annual incomes in excess of $1 million, culminating in a top band of 79 per cent for those above $5 million, a levy that hit only one man in the country – oil baron John D. Rockefeller. It levied a modest estate tax instead of the tough inheritance tax that FDR initially requested, raised gift taxes and imposed a token corporate tax. As a means of wealth redistribution, the measure was a damp squib – it took nothing of note from the richest 1 per cent and entirely spared those of smaller but still substantial fortune. In political terms, it fitted well with the strategy of lambasting economic elites that FDR adopted for his successful re-election campaign in 1936 but was counterproductive in another regard. Taking a leaf out of Theodore Roosevelt's largely rhetorical assaults on big-business trusts, FDR intended the wealth tax to assert the primacy of the national interest over private selfishness and to warn the corporate community of what might be in store if it persisted in attacking his programmes. Instead of cowing the forces of entrenched wealth, the measure only hardened their opposition to the New Deal's socio-economic turn.

The final item in Roosevelt's must list, the Banking Act, was the crowning achievement of his agenda to bring currency and credit under federal control. The Banking Act of 1933 had granted statutory recognition to the Federal Open Market Committee (FOMC), a hitherto informal body established during the Great War to buy and sell Treasury bonds, operations that greatly influenced the money supply, credit volume and interest rates. It initially operated under the control of the Federal Reserve's New York regional bank, which was largely responsive to private banking interests based in the nation's financial capital. Drafted by newly appointed Federal Reserve Board chair Marriner Eccles, the original version of the 1935 legislation aimed to centralize control of the Federal Reserve System in Washington DC. It encountered powerful opposition from both private banking interests and Senator Carter Glass (D-Virginia), who wanted to preserve the Federal Reserve largely as he had helped to create it in 1913 when chair of the House Banking and Currency Committee. Their alliance stymied the bill for months before FDR stamped it as 'must' legislation.[67] When Glass settled for substantially rewriting details of the bill, his amendments did not undermine the Roosevelt-Eccles goal of transforming the Fed into a modern central bank. The legislation empowered the president to appoint (subject to Senate confirmation) the seven members of the newly named Federal Reserve Board of Governors and designate one to chair it (hitherto the Treasury Secretary's role), endowed it with direct and exclusive authority over FOMC, gave it control over the appointment of chief officers to Federal Reserve regional banks and increased its powers to determine interest rates and reserve requirements within the entire banking system.[68]

The intensive pace of the second Hundred Days left Roosevelt physically and emotionally exhausted. Weariness may have underlain his response to a plea from Roy Howard, chairman of the Scripps-Howard newspaper chain, urging 'recess from further experimentation' in order the restore business confidence. The administration's 'basic program', FDR replied, 'has now reached substantial completion and the "breathing spell" of which you speak is here – very decidedly so'.[69] He likely intended the pause to last until re-election provided a mandate for further reform to benefit needy Americans.

Vowing to continue his administration's efforts to help the vulnerable, Roosevelt declared in his second inaugural address, 'I see one third of a nation ill-housed, ill-clad, ill-nourished. . . . The test of our progress is not whether we add more to the abundance of those who have much; it is whether we provide enough for those who have too little.' Nevertheless, he recognized that the times were now less advantageous to that cause because an improving economy dulled commitment to social justice.[70] This was a prescient assessment of how New Deal expansion would fare in his second term.

Roosevelt made some effort to help rural and urban renters largely overlooked by his previous initiatives. In March 1935, he had used a portion of 'Big Bill' appropriations to create the Resettlement Administration under Rexford Tugwell to alleviate rural poverty. Tugwell hoped to resettle 500,000 impoverished farmers from sub-marginal land onto good soil and give them modern equipment, but lack of funds limited the tally to 4,441. The Farm Tenancy Act of 1937, a congressional initiative given FDR's blessing, replaced the Resettlement Administration with the Farm Security Administration (FSA). The first agency to do anything substantial for the rural underclass, this extended rehabilitation loans to farmers, granted low-interest, long-term loans to enable tenants to buy farms and established a chain of sanitary, well-run camps to accommodate migrant labour – many of them dispossessed farm families – as they travelled the countryside looking for work. FSA was also scrupulous in seeking to ensure that African Americans benefited from its programmes. The agency's redistributive ambitions ensured that it never received the wherewithal from Southern-dominated congressional committees to fulfil its social-justice mission. Its impoverished constituents lacked power, while its opponents – notably agribusinesses that wanted cheap labour and Southern landlords who benefited from regional peonage – had ample political influence.[71]

The later New Deal also fell short in its efforts to help urban renters. In late 1934 FDR told the National Emergency Council that he wanted to help what he estimated to be forty million people without decent housing, but desisted from promoting Robert Wagner's public-housing legislation for nigh on three years. Showing that his heart was not in the cause, Roosevelt flippantly told a delegation of housing reformers that his solution for clearing the slums of New York's Lower East Side was simple: 'You don't need money and laws; just burn it down.' The Wagner bill gained Senate approval for the second year running in August 1937 but looked likely to fail again in the House. Roosevelt's relatively tepid endorsement emphasizing the measure's benefits to the construction industry finally got it over the line. The Wagner-Steagall Act of 1937 created the United States Housing Authority as a public corporation within the Department of the Interior and made $500 million available in sixty-year loans at 3 per cent interest for local housing authorities to construct public housing. By 1941, it had sponsored 130,000 new units in over 300 projects nationwide, a modest beginning in the quest to improve low-income housing. Reformers estimated that it would require $2.5 billion just to demolish New York's tenements to make space for modern dwellings.[72]

Roosevelt's most significant second-term initiative to enhance the economic security of low-income Americans was the Fair Labor Standards Act (FLSA) of 1938. Another Cohen-Corcoran collaboration, the original measure introduced in Congress in May 1937 guaranteed workers engaged in interstate commerce a 'living wage' for a workweek with set maximum hours, enforceable by a new body with extensive powers, the Labor Standards Board. A much-amended and weaker measure, with oversight responsibility placed in the Department of Labor rather than a powerful new body, finally made it onto the statute books fourteen months later. To maintain their region's low-wage structure as an inducement for business relocation from elsewhere in the country, Southern Democrats insisted on minimum-pay guarantees of just 25 cents an hour, instead of the originally intended 40 cents. Despite its retrenchment, the FLSA immediately improved wages for approximately 300,000 employees, reduced hours for 1 million workers and prohibited child labour. However, its benefits did not extend to workers not engaged in interstate commerce, most evidently agricultural labour and domestic servants, occupations in which African Americans and women respectively predominated.[73]

The FLSA was the New Deal's last attempt to improve conditions for the bottom one-third of the nation, but FDR had one big shot left in his economic-security locker. In January 1939, he proposed significant improvements in the Social Security programme, now so popular that Congress willingly did his bidding. The changes added over a million people to the system (farm workers and domestics remained outside), made more generous calculation for benefits, allowed pension benefits for wives aged over sixty-five of insured husbands and made provision for the widows and children of insured workers who died before reaching retirement age. These changes, one analyst observed, 'transformed Social Security from a retirement program for workers into a *family-based* economic security program'.[74] They also established a tradition of steady improvement of the social insurance system.

An almost simultaneous presidential recommendation for matching federal grants to the states to expand their public-health programmes was not enough to enact Robert Wagner's enabling bill. As this setback demonstrated, FDR found it much more difficult to advance socio-economic reform in his second term in the face of growing bipartisan conservative opposition in Congress. From 1933 through 1939 he had unquestionably done more than any other president hitherto to bring the freedom of economic security to many millions of Americans, but much was left undone. New Deal initiatives aimed at the disadvantaged represented no more than a beginning, albeit an important one that laid the foundations on which later presidents and legislators could build in the quarter century after the Second World War.

Roosevelt's growing difficulties from the mid-1930s onwards in enacting New Deal measures that helped Americans in the lower half of the income distribution provided a more accurate gauge of his transformation of the presidency's role as chief legislator than the heady successes of the Hundred Days of 1933. No longer driven by a sense of crisis, Congress reasserted its responsibilities, in the words of historian Ira Katznelson, 'as a forum where detailed answers could be created to the main substantive challenges of a historically dense and difficult era'.[75] Given that executive and legislative authority remained fundamentally separate in a system of institutionally shared powers of government, Congress's determination to exercise its constitutional right to debate and decide on law-making was hardly surprising. That said, FDR continued to act as chief legislator through his ability to set the terms for congressional deliberations. In this regard the presidency's capacity for unitary agenda-setting and ascendancy in public communication were powerful advantages over the legislature's pluralistic and particularistic tendencies.

When putting the recovery programme almost entirely in the president's hands in the crisis circumstances of 1933, Congress had still asserted its prerogative to shape the legislative outputs that emanated from Roosevelt's recommendations. In several cases it had improved and expanded upon what the president advocated. This happened infrequently in later years. The National Labor Relations Act of 1935 was the most significant example. More typically Congress restricted and retrenched New Deal proposals seeking to uplift disadvantaged groups. This was the fate of, among other measures, the National Housing Act of 1934, the Social Security Act of 1935 and the Fair Labour Standards Act of 1938.

Conservative Southern Democrats, who exercised disproportionate influence in the standing committees that reported out socio-economic bills, spearheaded efforts to constrain New Deal liberalism. The guardians of their region's racial order, they succeeded in excluding African Americans from new federal programmes that promised to improve their lot. Convinced that their traditional ascendancy in the national party was unshakeable, Dixie conservatives had been confident in 1933 of being able to shape the New Deal to suit the white South's interests. The new urban and class-based Democratic Party that emerged under FDR put them on the defensive. No longer confident of controlling the course of the New Deal, they looked to clip its liberal wings with the support of conservative co-partisans from other regions. Initially, they sought amendments that weakened Roosevelt's legislative proposals without killing them. Following Republican revival in the 1938 midterms, however, conservative Democrats grew bolder in establishing an informal coalition with the opposition party in Congress that succeeded in stalling the New Deal as a whole.

During his first term, Roosevelt's use of the presidential podium to mould popular support enhanced his ability to persuade Congress to do his bidding. FDR's rhetoric struck a chord with the public in envisioning a fairer and more balanced society brought about by an activist government. In this regard, historian Robert McElvaine suggested, he was in tune with the widespread desire, shared by working-class and middle-class Americans alike, for a 'moral economics' amid the distress of the depression.[76] In his second term, Roosevelt's policy missteps temporarily blunted his success as a public communicator. The attempted reorganization of the Supreme Court in 1937 and the onset of the sharp recession of 1937–8 dented his popularity, encouraging the development of bipartisan conservative opposition in Congress.

By late 1938, the New Deal had effectively run its course as a legislative reform programme. As the economy came out of recession, FDR recognized that the most immediate way of improving the lives of millions of Americans was to get them into decently paid work. It was necessary, he avowed in his 1939 message to Congress, 'to reinvigorate the processes of recovery in order to preserve our reforms, and to give every man and woman who wants to work a real job at a living wage'.[77] What gave these words significance was Roosevelt's conviction that he now had a feasible strategy to achieve this end.

4

Economic manager

FDR's political economy

Franklin D. Roosevelt added the role of economic manager to the president's job description. None of his predecessors had assumed systematic responsibility for managing employment, prices and currency values. When the economy slumped, nineteenth-century presidents assumed that it would self-correct without federal intervention, an outlook that persisted during the sharp postwar recession of 1920–1, the last before the Great Depression. Herbert Hoover's acceptance of public spending increases, tax cuts and budget deficits in 1930–1 offered a nod towards modern ideas of economic management before he retreated into orthodoxy. These temporary initiatives did not qualify him as the founder of the modern presidency's most important responsibility besides that of safeguarding the nation from external threat. The credit for that momentous expansion of presidential purpose was uniquely FDR's.

Roosevelt proved a confident, creative and mostly shrewd economic manager. According to Robert Jackson, a member of his inner circle, '[T]he mental processes of the President . . . did not impress me as being grounded in economic theory or practice . . . he had never devoted himself to much study of the economic processes of the country.'[1] This assessment is plain wrong. FDR knew enough about economics to be disdainful of traditional doctrines. 'I have no sympathy', he told Americans, 'for the professional economists who insist that things must run their course and that human agencies can have no influence on economic ills. One reason is that I happen to know that professional economists have changed their definition of economic laws every five or ten years for a very long time.'[2]

Receptive to new ideas in his quest for recovery, Roosevelt consulted scholarly proponents of reflation, notably Irving Fisher of Yale, James Harvey Rogers of Harvard and George Warren of Cornell, and like-minded financial experts, such as Alexander Sachs of Lehman Brothers. He was also familiar with the ideas of popular pro-growth economists like Stuart Chase, William Trufant Foster and Waddill Catchings. In their best-selling tome *The Road to Plenty*, published in 1928, Foster and Catchings advanced the bold claim that consumption regulated production, not vice versa as in the classical orthodoxy of Say's Law, and insisted that government spending was the surest guarantee of adequate consumer income. FDR had scrawled on the flyleaf of his personal copy, 'Too good to be true – you can't have something for nothing.'[3] Nevertheless, he was a regular reader of Foster's Depression-era articles advocating a compensatory public-works programme. Meanwhile, the economist whose name became a byword for new thinking in the 1930s, John Maynard Keynes, did everything possible to bring his ideas to Roosevelt's attention. It was evident, however, that FDR had an eclectic approach to economics that eschewed devotion to any single doctrine. As historian Elliot Rosen observed, 'Whatever ideas Roosevelt accepted from others, it was he who untangled the threads and he alone who made the great decisions of the day.'[4]

Roosevelt's record as economic manager in the Great Depression is conventionally considered a failure because US involvement in the Second World War was what finally restored prosperity. Nevertheless, it can be argued that the fundamental idea underlying the New Deal, the need for state-sponsored economic security, saved American capitalism amid its greatest crisis and laid the foundations for long-term economic growth. Many on the right, by contrast, claim that Roosevelt's expansion of government in pursuit of reform prolonged the slump. Jim Powell of the Cato Institute asserted in 2003,

> FDR didn't make the recovery of private, productive employment his top priority. . . . His goal was 'reform' not recovery. Accordingly, the New Deal taxed money away from the private sector, and government officials, not private individuals, made the spending decisions, New Deal laws determined what kind of people businesses must hire, how much they must be paid, what prices businesses must charge, and it interfered with their ability to raise capital.[5]

In reality, the New Deal balance sheet of recovery and reform was much healthier than conservatives admit. Though there is no formal definition of economic depression, two broadly used criteria are either a 10 per cent decline in gross domestic product (GDP) or a slump lasting more than three years with an unemployment rate rising above 10 per cent.[6] On the latter measure, the Great Depression began in August 1929 and ended in late 1941. By contrast, the annual GDP index, which computes the market value of the goods and services produced over the course of a year, puts America coming out of economic downturn in March 1933. Measured thus, the slump was actually shorter at forty-three months duration than that of 1873–9, which lasted sixty-five months, but the 30 per cent fall in GDP over its course was unparalleled. In the Great Recession of 2007–9, for example, the American economy experienced a 4.2 per cent decline in GDP.

Given the severity of the early 1930s slump, it was hardly surprising that some key economic indicators took so long to regain their pre-Depression levels. Nevertheless, real GDP (adjusted for inflation) grew at an average annual rate of 8 per cent in FDR's first term, the greatest expansion of output and industrial production in any four-year period in America's peacetime history. In the manufacturing sector, employment numbers and corporate profits were close to their 1929 levels by 1937, but productivity gains meant that less labour was needed than in the past to boost output. Unemployment remained high because industry could not absorb newcomers entering the labour market each year nor workers displaced from agriculture. The downturn that started in mid-1937 produced a sharp fall in real GDP over twelve months, but economic output expanded annually at better than 8 per cent in 1939–40. According to economist Christina Romer, later to chair Barack Obama's Council of Economic Advisers, 'These rates of growth are spectacular, even for an economy pulling out of a severe depression.'[7] Despite this, the annual unemployment rate only twice fell below 15 per cent (14.3 per cent in 1937 and 14.6 per cent in 1940) in Roosevelt's first two terms.

Concern that America's economy had reached a mature stage of development, as voiced in FDR's Commonwealth Club Address in the 1932 campaign, fashioned the New Deal's initial strategies for industrial and agricultural recovery. The drive to restore balance, stability and security, key concepts in the administration's economic thinking, signified expectation that recovery would restore the previous level of prosperity but do little to generate expansion beyond that. Only in Roosevelt's second term did the New Deal focus on economic growth and development as explicit goals to achieve recovery from the recession of 1937–8.[8]

FDR instituted a veritable revolution in monetary policy in support of the early New Deal's recovery strategy, one that would also facilitate the later shift towards economic expansion. A belated follower of Keynesian fiscal prescriptions, he was an early devotee to the British economist's gospel that a managed currency was the necessary first step to full recovery in America and elsewhere. That said, his principal inspiration on this score was George Warren rather than Keynes. As Rexford Tugwell reflected, FDR 'behaved in what later came to be called the Keynesian manner' because he operated in 'an intellectual climate' of unorthodoxy in which many economic thinkers were seeking solutions to the Great Depression.[9]

From its outset, Roosevelt's recovery programme was fixed on an inflationary strategy pursued through price-fixing and dollar devaluation, methods that had little in common beyond their diagnosis that higher prices were essential for economic uplift. Price-fixing entailed a structural approach to price behaviour in agriculture and industry through measures that limited output in the former and facilitated cartelization in the latter. Dollar devaluation, by contrast, sought to raise the general price level. In marked contrast to their respective proponents, Roosevelt saw both as valid ways of counteracting the deflationary spiral. Devaluationist Irving Fisher commented, 'FDR thinks of them as similar – merely two ways of raising prices! But one changes the monetary unit to restore it to normal while the other spells scarce food and clothing when many are starving or half-naked.' Conversely, structuralist Rexford Tugwell disdained devaluation because it ignored the problem of overproduction.[10]

Price-fixing in agriculture was only partially successful in the 1930s because the collapse in farm commodity prices had been so great in 1929–32 (63 per cent compared to 15 per cent for industrial prices). Net farm income more than doubled from $2 billion in 1932 to $4.6 billion in 1939 but remained well below the 1929 level of $6.1 billion. How far this improvement was attributable to Agricultural Adjustment Administration (AAA) production control was unclear. Adverse climate conditions like dust storms, drought and floods helped reduce farm output in FDR's first term. Greater rainfall, mechanization and improvements in agricultural techniques produced bumper harvests in his second term. In response, the Agricultural Adjustment Act of 1938 established a stronger framework for production controls, price supports and surplus-crop storage. In the industrial sector, meanwhile, the National Recovery Administration was instrumental in breaking the vicious deflationary cycle of the early 1930s. Once its industrial codes sanctioned business cartelization as a means of price-fixing, consumer prices began a steady rise, but the blessings of this inflation accrued predominantly to corporate profits.

Devaluation initiatives proved more successful, long-lasting and broadly beneficial than price-fixing. In his fourth Fireside Chat in October 1933, FDR explained that he wanted to raise prices, secure prosperity and then seek stability – in that order, all of which depended on reducing the gold value of the dollar. 'The definite policy of the Government', he avowed, 'has been to restore commodity price levels. . . . When we have restored the price level, we shall seek to establish and maintain a dollar which will not change its purchasing and debt-paying power during the succeeding generation.' To do so, the United States 'must take firmly in its own hands the control of the gold value of our dollar', thereby safeguarding it against any adverse effects of economic and political developments abroad. 'This is a policy and not an expedient', Roosevelt asserted. 'We are thus continuing to move toward a managed currency.'[11]

Excepting emergency suspensions in wartime, America had adhered to a gold standard since the Coinage Act of 1834 set the value of the dollar at $20.67 to an ounce of pure gold as a way of controlling speculative bubbles resulting from bankers' over-issuance of cheap credit, which undermined trust in paper money. Every domestic economic exchange henceforth had a value in gold, redeemable on demand by holders of paper money. This permitted US adherence to an international gold standard that facilitated trade between nations tying their currencies to the yellow metal. As the nineteenth century progressed, gold became bankers' money because its relative scarcity safeguarded the value of credit. Holding mortgages and other forms of debt, farmers in the American West pressed for inflation to ease their repayments and get higher prices for their commodities. Democrat William Jennings Bryan ran on a platform of unlimited coinage of silver to expand the money supply in the 1896 presidential election, but Republican William McKinley's victory consolidated the power of gold. The subsequent Gold Standard Act of 1900 required all forms of money issued or coined by the United States to be maintained at parity value with the $20.67 an ounce price of gold. In 1913, the Democrats under Woodrow Wilson tried once more to make currency and credit more readily available through creation of the Federal Reserve System with the power to print paper currency. However, the enabling legislation bowed to financial-sector demands for stability by requiring the new central bank to keep gold in its vaults equal to 40 cents worth of every dollar it issued, an obligation that limited the elasticity of the new money.[12]

Two decades later, gold's defenders insisted that it alone guaranteed the soundness of America's money amid the Great Depression, while critics saw a yellow monster gnawing the vitals of the economy. For devaluationists, the spiral of decline resulted from the cruel combination of deflation and debt: the prices people received for their commodities and work went down as the economy slumped, but repayments on mortgages and other credit remained steady because of the dollar's gold-denominated value. Their solution was to raise the price level to the debt level through abandoning the gold standard. One way of slaying the behemoth was to resurrect the white knight of silver monetization, advocated by Western Democrats, but FDR feared that this could produce runaway inflation. Changing the dollar's value in terms of gold offered a more controllable means of raising the price level.

This idea gained credence during the interregnum among Roosevelt's farm advisers, received exposition from George Warren in his correspondence with the president-elect (an access gained courtesy of his former Cornell student, Henry Morgenthau) and was brought to FDR's attention by informal adviser Felix Frankfurter, an avid reader of John Maynard Keynes's newspaper columns that were reproduced in the *New York Herald Tribune*. In March 1933, Keynes himself sent the new president a copy of his pamphlet, *The Means to Prosperity*, an expanded version of four articles he had written for *The Times* urging monetary and fiscal expansion to stimulate recovery.[13]

The bank panic of early 1933 was critical in shaping FDR's determination to abandon the gold standard. In his inaugural address, he declared it essential to provide for 'an adequate but sound currency', words that implied this intent. Next day, George Warren risked a 250-mile flight in a small plane from Ithaca, home of Cornell University in upstate New York, to Washington to urge this course of action on the new president in person, only to find himself behind the curve. Thanks to Henry Morgenthau, he got an audience with Roosevelt just in time to hear of the impending declaration to close the banks and prohibit the export or hoarding of gold and silver. In his diary, Warren recorded the president remarking with considerable glee, 'We are now off the gold standard.'[14]

If FDR's 20 April announcement of the export embargo on gold bullion, coin and certificates marked the formal abandonment of the gold standard, the proclamation of 6 March and the Emergency Banking Act (EBA) enacted three days later had already made this a reality. Under the EBA, Americans could no longer turn their dollars into gold and could be required to return gold already in their possession to the government in exchange for other money. Fearful of hoarding penalties, thousands of people turned up the day after its enactment at Federal Reserve banks in New York, Chicago and elsewhere to hand in their personal caches. The value of privately held gold, $77 million in 1929, had mushroomed to $284 million in the bank panic of early 1933, but dropped to $80 million by 31 March. To mop up that residue, Roosevelt issued an executive order requiring its return to the government by 1 May. In a final flourish, he secured congressional abrogation of the gold clause in public and private contracts on 5 June.[15]

Roosevelt's approach to the World Economic Conference, meeting in London in mid-1933 to discuss international solutions to the global economic crisis, was entirely consistent with this strategy. When news leaked that the British were holding private talks with other delegations to secure international currency stabilization at values disadvantageous to the American dollar, he messaged Secretary of State Cordell Hull, chairman of the US delegation, on 20 June to resist the manoeuvres of the 'banker-influenced cabinets' of Europe. The continuing intrigues prompted FDR to send his 'bombshell message' of 2 July, read out by Hull to a shocked conference the following day. It would, he declared, be 'a catastrophe amounting to a world tragedy' to fixate on exchange stability before recovery was in place. Rejecting the 'old fetishes of so-called international bankers', FDR called for planned national currencies with 'a continuing purchasing power which does not greatly vary in terms of the commodities and need of modern civilization'.[16] Covering the conference as a reporter, Keynes felt vindicated in his earlier assessment that Roosevelt alone among world leaders had a realistic approach to restoring prosperity. Lauding the president's intervention as 'magnificently right' in its understanding that economic growth had to precede currency stability, the economist urged all governments to follow his lead to 'put men back to work by all the means at our disposal until prices have risen to a level appropriate to the existing debts and other obligations fixed in terms of money'.[17]

Roosevelt's commitment to a managed currency was accompanied by a shake-up of his economic advisers. Raymond Moley, FDR's closest pre-presidential aide, quit the administration in disillusion with his monetary policy. Meanwhile, George Warren and James Harvey Rogers took advisory positions in the Commerce Department and Jacob Viner of the University of Chicago joined the Treasury in similar capacity. Eugene Black, an advocate of monetary expansion, took over as Federal Reserve chair following the resignation of Eugene Meyer, an investment banker appointed by Herbert Hoover. When Black died from a heart attack in December 1934, his successor was Utah banker Marriner Eccles, who had a Westerner's appreciation for cheap credit and an understanding that deficit spending was necessary to boost consumption (based on his reading of Foster and Catchings rather than Keynes). Assuming that Wall Street's support safeguarded him from dismissal, George Harrison, the New York Federal Reserve president, threatened to stop Open Market Committee purchase of government bonds unless FDR changed monetary course. Roosevelt brought him to heel by letting it be known that, if necessary, he would 'show those fellows what real inflation looked like' through use of his Thomas Amendment authority to produce currency.[18]

At this juncture Roosevelt was desperate for inflation because the spike in farm prices that followed AAA's establishment had subsided. 'The West', he wrote his mother, 'is seething with unrest and must have higher values to pay off their debts.' The clamour was equally strong in the hitherto quiescent cotton belt. Even a sound-money man like Senate Finance Committee chair Pat Harrison (D-Mississippi) warned, 'Commodity prices have got to go up. I favor some sort of rational inflation. We've got to do more than we are doing.'[19] Federal loans of 10 cents for every pound that cotton growers kept off the market and massive wheat purchases to feed relief workers provided short-term palliatives, but Roosevelt required a durable solution.

To meet this need, George Warren advanced a 'commodity dollar' theory that the price of gold controlled the general price level. In his schema, the surest way to generate inflation was to raise the dollar-cost of purchasing gold, a thesis that received exposition in a weighty academic tome replete with charts purporting to demonstrate past movements in gold and commodity prices operating in tandem. With no time to read this, FDR got the economist to explain his theory in person at Hyde Park in mid-August. This tutorial was reinforced with written advice that the most effective way of raising prices was to reduce the gold value of the dollar by ordering the Treasury to make regular purchases of gold at steadily increasing prices. Whether FDR wholly bought into Warren's recommendations is a matter of doubt, but they offered him a programme of action when he desperately needed one. Obtaining an audience with the president on 21 September in the hope of reasserting sound-money orthodoxy, banker and informal adviser James Warburg found him firm in the conviction that if wheat and cotton prices did not rise, 'I shall have marching farmers'. Angered by Warburg's insensitivity to rural distress, Roosevelt never called for his counsel again.[20]

To put Warren's ideas into practice, Roosevelt had to circumvent Treasury and Justice Department doubts about his authority to order buying and selling of gold at prices higher than the legally prescribed $20.67 an ounce. Dean Acheson, effectively running the Treasury as Undersecretary in the absence of the seriously ill William Woodin, also expressed ethical concern that dollar devaluation violated government obligation to protect the value of bonds issued for public sale to fund the growing budget deficit. Bureaucratic succour was forthcoming when Farm Credit Administration (FCA) lawyers advised that the Reconstruction Finance Corporation (RFC) could be empowered to handle the buying of gold in the domestic market. Accordingly, Roosevelt commanded Acheson to support the new policy at a White House showdown on 19 October. 'The President has ordered me to do it', a furious Acheson reported to the RFC board. 'I will carry out his orders.'[21] Nonetheless, he continued to obstruct presidential purpose through sanctioning exports of gold at the gold-standard dollar price. Determined to assert his authority, Roosevelt gathered all his economic advisers at the White House on the evening of 29 October to read the riot act. 'We are all in the same boat', he declared. 'If anyone does not like the boat, he can get out of it.' Gold purchases were an essential administration policy to avert 'an agrarian revolution in this country'.[22]

In consultation with FCA chief Henry Morgenthau and RFC director Jesse Jones, Roosevelt took personal responsibility for determining the price level for buying gold, a power never before exercised by an American president – or since. Relishing the opportunity to kindle the fires of recovery, Roosevelt told Morgenthau, 'I have had the shackles on my hands for months now, and I feel for the first time as though I had thrown them off.'[23] FDR met with his two accomplices every morning in his bedroom to determine the gold purchase price while breakfasting on coffee and soft-boiled eggs. Their only guiding principle was to push the level ever higher at divergent daily margins to confuse speculators. The buying spree commenced on 25 October at a price of $31.36, high enough to persuade the markets of Roosevelt's resolve but low enough to discredit rumours that he would go above $36. The next day it was set 18 cents higher and the day after 22 cents higher again. While FDR revelled in the game, Morgenthau grew increasingly uncomfortable with what was being done. When deliberating a price increase between 18 and 22 cents on 4 November, the president settled on 21 cents. Seeking to cheer up his collaborator, FDR joked, 'It's a lucky number because it's three times seven.' Recounting the episode in his diary, Morgenthau remarked, 'If anybody ever knew how we really set the gold price through a combination of lucky numbers, etc., I think that they really would be frightened.'[24]

It quickly became clear that markets were hedging their bets by arbitraging the differing price of gold in America and abroad, thereby diluting the domestic effect of Roosevelt's ploy. To eliminate the price differential, he determined that the United States should buy gold on the international market, a move necessitating foreign exchange operations that George Harrison agreed to have the New York Fed undertake. Around this time, Acheson gave the president an undated, handwritten letter of resignation to use whenever required. Doubting his loyalty, Roosevelt seized the opportunity to appoint Morgenthau in his stead on 16 November – and placed the new man in charge of the Treasury after Woodin resigned on 31 December.

'Those who knew Morgenthau well', James Warburg disparagingly remarked, 'interpreted this to mean that the President would now be his own Secretary of the Treasury'. More realistically, Morgenthau himself commented, 'The President wanted a Treasury Department which would play its proper role in his campaign on prices; he wanted a Secretary who would be loyal and try to get things done; so he threw me in to plug the hole'. Devoted to FDR, he told an aide that 'the most important thing in his life was his relationship with the President'.[25] Loyal without being obsequious, Morgenthau resisted FDR at times – though never in public. When requested in early 1935 to destabilize the dollar to influence Supreme Court deliberations over the constitutionality of the gold clause abrogation of 1933, he replied, 'Mr President, don't ask me to do this'.[26] News of his appointment to replace Acheson left no doubt about FDR's commitment to dollar devaluation. Accordingly, the price of gold on the London markets shot up to overtake the administration's declared price for gold.

With farm prices rising slowly by comparison, it became evident that FDR's gold purchase strategy had not achieved its immediate objective. Nevertheless, it did enough to douse rural militancy, ease repayment of farm debts and lay the foundations for stabilization of the dollar's gold price. Having undertaken only two price manipulations in December, Roosevelt terminated the experiment in mid-January 1934. He now asked Congress for authority to revalue the dollar at no more than 60 per cent of its former weight in gold, sanction Treasury ownership of all monetary gold in the United States and establish a Treasury currency stabilization fund drawn from government profits on the revalued gold in its possession. The resultant legislation, the Gold Reserve Act, one of the most important New Deal initiatives, receives only brief coverage in standard histories. Signing it on 30 January, the day he turned fifty-two, FDR showed greater awareness of its significance in calling it 'the nicest birthday present I ever had'.[27] The next day the president met with his economic advisers to decide the dollar's new value. The figure of $35 an ounce, a devaluation of 59.06 per cent, came close to matching everyone's preference. Roosevelt issued a proclamation fixing this as the dollar's value in relation to an ounce of gold while reserving the right to amend it in accordance with national interest.[28] As things turned out, America's currency would hold steady at this level until 1971.

The United States once more had a dollar with a fixed value in gold but almost everything about it was different from the currency Roosevelt inherited. The new dollar was worth significantly less than the old one, could not be transferred from paper form into gold by ordinary citizens, had a gold value that was only used to settle international accounts and was pegged to this only as long as the president adjudged that economic circumstances required. The Gold Reserve Act completed the monetary changes that started with FDR's initiatives in the first week of his presidency. Under the old gold standard, the United States had subordinated the value of the dollar to the value of gold, but their respective positions were now reversed. Roosevelt and his advisers were at greater liberty to pursue economic policies deemed necessary for the public good because their control over the dollar's exchange value enabled them to protect domestic credit structures. Flights of gold to banks outside the United States and foreign currency revaluations could no longer send shock waves through the American economy. The Gold Reserve Act, furthermore, made the Treasury a co-producer of credit and currency, alongside the independent Federal Reserve, based on its control over America's upwardly valued and monetized gold reserves. This established monetary management as an instrument of national policy, thereby giving FDR the opportunity to pursue a moderately expansionary fiscal policy in the mid-1930s without danger of crowding out private business from access to loan capital for investment.[29]

In political terms, the drive for a managed currency produced an open break between the president and what he called 'the Mellon-Mills influence in banking and certain controlling industries'.[30] This was a reference to the conservative Treasury Secretaries of the recent Republican administrations, Andrew Mellon (1921–32) and Ogden Mills (1932–3). Desperate for gold-standard restoration to safeguard credit values, many banking and corporate leaders regarded the president's monetary strategy as ultimate proof that he could not be trusted with the economy's financial health and the regulation of their enterprises. For his part, Roosevelt was furious that 'a very definite drive was made by New York bankers and political forces led by Ogden Mills' in November 1933 to secure the British government's agreement to return to the gold standard if the United States did so first. Suspicious that his critics were selling American interests downriver to serve their own needs, he delegated George Harrison to make unofficial approaches to ascertain Britain's willingness to return to gold, queries that produced negative responses from the Bank of England and the UK Treasury.

For FDR, the intrigues were proof that he was locked in a battle to save the New Deal from the forces of deflation. 'The real truth of the matter is', he wrote Colonel Edward House, 'that a financial element in the larger centers has owned the Government ever since the days of Andrew Jackson, and I am not wholly excepting the Administration of W.W. [Woodrow Wilson] The country is going through a repetition of Jackson's fight with the Bank of the United States – only on a far bigger and broader basis.' This sentiment foreshadowed Roosevelt's re-election campaign as a modern-day Jackson doing battle with selfish economic elites in the name of the people. The sense of being Old Hickory's legatee grew stronger as his first term progressed. After visiting the Hermitage, the great man's Tennessee home, in late 1934, FDR remarked, 'The more I learn about Andy Jackson, the more I love him.'[31]

John Maynard Keynes staunchly supported Roosevelt's monetary strategy as 'a middle course between old-fashioned orthodoxy and the extreme inflationists'. The president, he declared, had done nothing 'which need be disturbing to business confidence' in establishing a stable dollar that would only be revalued if economic circumstances necessitated. It was his hope that other countries would follow America's lead, thereby laying the foundations for a modern international monetary system that provided sufficient liquidity, stability and flexibility to underwrite global prosperity.[32] For now, however, Keynes was more concerned to see the United States achieve economic recovery as an example to other democracies still mired in depression.

Meeting Keynes at a very liquid dinner at King's College, Cambridge, on 6 December 1933, Harvard law professor Felix Frankfurter (currently spending the academic year at All Souls College, Oxford) urged him to give Roosevelt the benefit of his advice. The economist's 'Open Letter to the President' appeared in *The New York Times* on 31 December after FDR received a private copy. It began with the paean: 'You have made yourself the Trustee for those in every country who seek to mend the evils of our condition by reasoned experiment within the framework of the existing social system. If you fail, rational change will be gravely prejudiced throughout the world, leaving orthodoxy and revolution to fight it out.'[33] This was the prelude to a trenchant but constructive critique of Roosevelt's record.

Rubbishing the theory that the price of gold controlled commodity prices, Keynes commented, '[T]he recent gyrations of the dollar have looked more to me like a gold standard on the booze than the ideal managed currency of my dreams.' He recommended stabilizing the dollar at a gold price that suited America's interests but reserving the right to make future adjustments, a policy that FDR would pursue of his own accord in the Gold Reserve Act. Most significantly, Keynes advised Roosevelt against making inflation his first priority: 'The stimulation of output by increasing aggregate purchasing power is the right way to put prices up; and not the other way round.' The means of doing so was to expand federal outlays through deficit spending. For Keynes, 'Nothing else counts in comparison with this.' Ending on a positive note, he declared, 'The United States is ready to roll towards prosperity, if a good hard shove can be given in the next six months.'[34]

Columnist Walter Lippmann wrote to Keynes that the open letter had a positive effect on FDR. It certainly got him an invitation to tea at the White House on 28 May 1934 while visiting the United States to receive an honorary doctorate from Columbia University. The conventional wisdom, based on comments recorded in Secretary of Labor Frances Perkins's memoir, holds that there was no meeting of minds at this encounter. 'I saw your friend Keynes', FDR told her afterwards. 'He left a whole rigmarole of figures. He must be a mathematician rather than a political economist.' Seeing Perkins on his round of Washington meetings, Keynes admitted that he had 'supposed the president was more literate, economically speaking'. The principals themselves offered more positive assessments of their exchange in letters to Frankfurter – 'I had a grand talk with Keynes and liked him immensely', FDR remarked, while Keynes called their 'tête-à-tête . . . fascinating and illuminating'.[35]

Two weeks before meeting with Keynes, Roosevelt had spoken of the sufficiency of public expenditure levels and the possibility of balancing the budget before long.[36] After their encounter, he placed more emphasis on raising the level of deficit spending. Journalist Arthur Krock had no doubts that the president had absorbed some of the economist's ideas. Of like mind, New Dealer Rexford Tugwell wrote in his diary, 'I was inclined to feel that Keynes had more success than the rest of us in rounding out for the President the policy as a whole and fitting the parts together. . . . After Keynes's visit, I fancied we heard a good deal less about economy and a balanced budget.'[37] Already unravelling before he communed with Keynes, Roosevelt's relationship with conservative budget director Lewis Douglas declined rapidly thereafter. In late April they had clashed over whether the budget should be balanced in 1936 to boost business confidence. 'That is too far in the future', Roosevelt insisted. 'Why worry about the future?'[38] Douglas finally resigned on 31 August to conduct an open campaign alongside James Warburg against the economic evils of unbalanced budgets and managed currencies. Meanwhile, George Warren's counsel for further dollar devaluation while economizing on spending, the very opposite of what Keynes wanted, extinguished his influence as a presidential economic adviser.[39]

Before returning home, Keynes published another open letter to FDR. A panegyric to deficit spending, it asserted that aggregate monthly outlays of $300 million during the Civil Works Administration's lifetime had been immensely helpful to the economy but expressed concern that their decline to $200 million following the agency's termination would harm recovery. 'If it were to rise to $400 million monthly', Keynes proclaimed, 'I should be quite confident that a strong business revival would set in by the autumn. So little divides a retreat from an advance.' This did Roosevelt no favours because he came under immediate conservative attack for wanting to spend at such eye-watering rates. According to Lewis Douglas's notes of their meeting on 11 June, the day after the Keynes letter appeared, the president became angry when asked if he planned monthly spending of $400 million. Banging his fist on the desk, Roosevelt declared:

> I am getting God damned sick and tired of having imputed to me things I have never said. . . . You have been reading Arthur Krock and Maynard Keynes. . . . I never said I was going to spend at that rate. . . . I am just as Scotch as you and I have some Dutch in me also, and I want to save just as much as you want to save.[40]

Regardless of this outburst, Keynesian-style fiscal thinking clearly influenced the New Deal from 1934 onwards. Though the British economist's magnum opus was two years away from publication, his ideas had already received thorough public exposition.[41] In his credo, consumption was more important than production in generating economic growth, recession resulted from under-consumption and government spending was the best agency for recovery. During a slump, he wanted public spending to compensate for the private economy's decline. If this idea was not new, Keynes broke fresh ground in advancing the multiplier theory to justify it: government should borrow to fund programmes that gave money in some form or another to the unemployed; they would quickly spend it on life's necessities; and those whom they paid for these would re-spend their portions. In his estimate, the multiplier effect of deficit finance would yield a boost to consumption at least double the value of the original government outlay, leading to reduced unemployment, increased production and greater capital investment in industry. Keynes recognized that increased investment was vital for improved productivity, on which sustained economic growth was ultimately dependent. In his view, it was the expectation of profit that generated new investment, and the key to this was a high consumption-full employment economy that could be achieved through adept fiscal policy.

Harry Hopkins nailed his colours to the Keynesian mast in justifying generous funding for the Works Progress Administration (WPA). 'Recovery through government expenditures', he asserted, 'requires that Government money automatically goes to the lowest economic strata. It is there that occurs automatically the greatest number of respendings.'[42] However, the New Deal deficits needed to be far bigger for the loan-finance prescription to work. Only in Fiscal Years (FY) 1934 and 1936 did the budget imbalance exceed 5 per cent GDP (respectively 5.8 per cent and 5.4 per cent, compared with the average of 9 per cent GDP in the Great Recession deficits of FY2009–11). Only in three New Deal budgets (FY1934, FY1936 and FY1939) did total federal spending exceed 10 per cent GDP (the high being 10.6 per cent in FY1934). Meanwhile, the growth in tax receipts from 3.4 per cent GDP in FY1933 to 7.5 per cent GDP in FY1938, the result of an improving economy, constrained the benefits of higher spending.[43]

In his first term, FDR accepted the need for deficit spending but justified it more in social than economic terms. In one of their exchanges, he remonstrated with Lewis Douglas that conservatives 'do not speak of the necessity for relieving suffering – they lack a sense of human needs'. In May 1935, he told Congress,

> Every authorization of expenditure . . . has been predicated not on the mere spending of money to hasten recovery, but on the sounder principle of preventing the loss of homes and farms, of saving industry from bankruptcy, of safeguarding bank deposits, and most important of all – giving relief and jobs through public work to individuals and families faced with starvation.[44]

A full-blooded economic defence of deficits would have been risky because the so-called balanced-budget rule still exercised a strong hold. Over the previous 150 years, two of every three federal budgets had been in balance, with deficits occurring mainly during wars and recessions as temporary aberrations to the norm of fiscal rectitude.[45]

According to Keynes, deficit spending of any ilk, useful or not, encouraged the propensity to consume. In his famous example of pyramid-building, he reasoned that '"wasteful" loan expenditures may nevertheless enrich the community on balance'.[46] Roosevelt, by contrast, was reluctant to sanction outlays for what he deemed non-emergency purposes. This explained his long-standing resistance to enhancing veterans' benefits, a recurring issue in his first term. In May 1935, the American Legion and its congressional allies secured enactment of legislation requiring immediate payment in government-issued greenbacks of the bonus for the First World War servicemen, ten years earlier than scheduled. FDR went in person to Congress to deliver a veto message, which the Senate upheld. In January 1936, with forthcoming elections in mind, both chambers approved by large margins a similar measure but funded by Treasury bonds. On this occasion, Roosevelt's veto went down to defeat. In boosting federal outlays by more than a fifth, the veterans' bonus provided a stimulus for the whole economy.[47]

Roosevelt's stand against the bonus reflected his conviction that reducing the deficit was the necessary prelude to balancing the budget, to his mind the ultimate proof that the New Deal had succeeded in conquering the economic crisis. 'Restoration of the national income, which shows continuing gains for the third successive year', he told Congress in 1936, 'supports the normal and logical policies under which agriculture and industry are returning to full activity. Under these policies we approach a balance of the national budget'. FDR reassured campaign audiences later in the year that the economy had turned the corner, thereby putting a balanced budget within reach. At

Forbes Field, Pittsburgh, the venue in the 1932 campaign of his trenchant charge that Herbert Hoover's deficits were dangerously excessive, he defended the effectiveness of his own in relieving unemployment and destitution. '[W]e had to balance the budget of the American people before we could balance the budget of the national Government', he asserted. Thanks to New Deal outlays, 'The national income has gone up faster than we dared then to hope. Deficits have been less than we expected. Treasury receipts are increasing.' On the basis of this success, he expressed confidence that federal tax revenues 'will, within a year or two, be sufficient to care for all ordinary and relief expenses of the Government – in other words, to balance the budget'.[48] Determination to make good on that prediction induced FDR to commit the greatest economic error of his presidency.

Roosevelt misinterpreted improving indicators as proof that recovery was at hand. In the first half of 1937, personal income, wholesale prices, industrial production, corporate profits, employment and, most significantly, national income were all well up on their 1932 levels, generating widespread optimism that real prosperity was around the corner. As some Americans celebrated Independence Day by splashing out on holiday activities, *Business Week* expressed confidence that the economy's buoyancy brought 'hope, faith and clarity' to business.[49] Stubbornly high unemployment, the stagnation of private investment and the sluggishness of some major industries like automobiles should have given cause for concern. Fiscal changes also presaged the danger of boom becoming bust: in 1936 the economy received a one-off $1.7 billion stimulus from the early payment of the veterans' bonus; in 1937 the inaugural collection of social insurance taxes sucked $1 billion in purchasing power from workers' pay packets.

Two of Roosevelt's lieutenants, Treasury Secretary Henry Morgenthau and Federal Reserve chair Marriner Eccles, battled for his ear as to whether recovery was imminent. Only the second Jew to hold a Cabinet position in American history, Morgenthau made an unlikely protagonist in bureaucratic politics: he was not an intellectual heavyweight (he dropped out of Cornell before graduating), lacked formal training in economics and had little business experience (he was a gentleman farmer before entering government). Willing to tolerate deficits for depression relief, he feared their inflationary consequences if continued amid recovery. As Roosevelt's second term began, Morgenthau thought it time 'to strip off the bandages, throw away the crutches and see if American enterprise could stand on its own two feet'.[50] Marriner Eccles became the highest-ranking Mormon in US government hitherto when appointed Federal Reserve chair. A former Republican with a successful career in business, banking and investment, he was an early convert to the belief 'that the only way we could get out of the depression was through government action in placing purchasing power in the hands of people who were in need of it'. Though his brief was monetary policy, he was a consistent advocate of greater deficit spending. Premature efforts to balance the budget, he warned FDR in December 1936, would 'lead to a new wave of deflation and reverse the process of recovery thus far set in motion'.[51]

A balanced budget was a cause close to Roosevelt's heart, but his head also inclined him to pursue one. Convinced that recovery was nigh, he began to worry that rising inflation, once seen as the economy's salvation, was on the verge of becoming a threat.

In political terms, too, FDR calculated that restoration of fiscal responsibility would facilitate congressional enactment of further New Deal reforms in his second term. At a meeting with his warring advisers in early April 1937, he made a forthright declaration of his preferences. 'God, if he'd only say publicly what he told him [Eccles], it would be marvelous', Morgenthau exulted to Treasury aides.[52] Roosevelt soon did so in a message to Congress calling for the removal or deferral of all non-essential expenditures in order to 'eliminate this deficit in the coming fiscal year'. Unable to contain his delight, Morgenthau recorded in his diary, 'The President gave me . . . everything that I asked for. . . . He must have come to the conclusion that if he wants his administration to go forward with his reform program he must have a sound financial foundation.'[53]

When the spending cuts came into operation in the second half of 1937, they exacerbated a recession that had commenced in midyear. Corporate leaders blamed the downturn on industry's loss of confidence from the president's prolonged business-bashing, but monetary changes were far more significant. The gold sterilization policy that the Treasury Department instituted in late 1936 did most damage. Once the Roosevelt administration had stabilized the banks and the dollar, the outflow of gold from the United States reversed course. Amid increasing turbulence in Europe, a net inflow averaging some $1.7 billion a year from 1935 to 1938 made its way to America's safe haven. The Treasury initially bought this gold in exchange for gold certificates that became the basis for an expanding supply of money and credit helpful to economic recovery. To house the government's precious hoard, the Public Works Administration began constructing a new two-storey concrete depository at Fort Knox, Kentucky, in 1935. By late 1936, concern was mounting that the tide of gold imports could distort the money supply. The Treasury began buying specie out of its general funds, instead of through money-creating certificates, and sterilized it in an inactive account. The Federal Reserve's decision to counteract inflationary pressures through raising reserve requirements for member banks exacerbated the contractionary effect of gold sterilization on the money supply. To maintain their reserve positions, banks began curtailing lending and selling investments, thereby undermining business confidence.[54]

The economy faltered in the late spring before tanking in the autumn of 1937. Over the recession's thirteen-month course, real GDP slumped by 11 per cent, industrial production fell by 32 per cent and unemployment rose from 14.3 per cent to 19 per cent of the labour force, making it the third-worst downturn in American history. Panic selling of stocks in October 1937, an episode all too reminiscent of Wall Street's collapse eight years earlier, prefaced a three-fifths decline in prices by midyear 1938. After a winter that bore uncomfortable resemblance to that of 1932–3, absent the bank failures, the human cost was manifest in the quadrupling of relief rolls in many industrial cities.

FDR's determination to see through his balanced-budget goal slowed his response to the crisis. In October 1937, he told Senator John Bankhead (D-Alabama), 'I propose to be very definite this fall in saying that if Congress exceeds my spending estimates, which will provide a balanced budget, . . . [members] can stay in session or come back once a week in special session throughout the year until they give me additional taxes to make up the loss.' A week later, amid the Wall Street panic, he informed Congressman

John McCormack (D-Massachusetts), 'I personally cannot get very excited about the national seriousness of the drop in stocks. . . . This present decline has hit only a comparatively small number of people who insist on continuing to speculate with margin accounts.'[55] Fed up with corporate carping that the New Deal was to blame for the recession, Roosevelt told the Cabinet that business was engaged in an 'unconscious conspiracy' in the form of a capital strike to compel reversal of the administration's social and regulatory initiatives.[56]

FDR's public expressions of confidence in the essential soundness of the economy made him sound like Hoover in the early 1930s. His insistence that the downturn was a recession rather than a depression provided critics with alliterative ammunition to dub it the 'Roosevelt Recession'. John Maynard Keynes worried that the downturn could endanger democracy abroad if not quickly reversed. In February 1938, he wrote the president a private letter urging the need to take immediate steps to stimulate consumption. The key to recovery, Keynes declared, was the revival of demand through an increase in government spending on public works. Since there was great need for home construction, he advised FDR to put 'most of your eggs in this basket'. Irritated rather than inspired by counsel that also warned his attacks on business were counterproductive, Roosevelt put his name to a non-committal response drafted by the Treasury.[57]

Throughout the winter of 1937–8, Roosevelt offered neither clarity nor cogency about the direction of economic policy. Assuming the role of fiscal conscience, Morgenthau urged him to press forward with balancing the budget as the necessary precondition for restoring business confidence. At times, FDR appeared to heed this counsel, on other occasions he rubbished it. After Morgenthau received a particularly sarcastic dressing down at one Cabinet meeting, Harold Ickes noted with satisfaction that he 'looked and acted like a spanked child'.[58] The opposing camp found it no less frustrating to deal with Roosevelt. Eccles began to wonder whether he 'really knew what the New Deal was'. In early 1938, Ickes remarked in his diary, 'It looks to me as if all the courage has oozed out of the president. He has let things drift. There is no fight and no leadership'.[59]

With no sign of recovery by March, Eccles sent Roosevelt his strongest exhortation to reflate the economy with a dose of compensatory expenditure. 'The greatest threat to democracy today', he warned, 'lies in the growing conviction that it cannot work. . . . I urge that you provide the democratic leadership that will make the system work. Only in that way can the growing threat of Fascism be overcome.' He decried the 'recent policy of comparative inaction' for undermining the morale of FDR's supporters at home and giving 'a new lease of life to the reactionaries'.[60] If this message gave Roosevelt food for thought, he was not ready to order from the Keynesian menu until the dangers of inertia were apparent. A run of opinion polls recorded growing popular dissatisfaction with him over the recession, Nazi Germany's execution of the *Anschluss* with Austria on 12 March lent weight to warnings that the spread of fascism fed on America's economic failure and the stock market collapsed once more on 25 March.

A still undecided FDR departed for a break in Warm Springs, where a delegation of spenders caught up with him on 1 April. Seriously ill with stomach cancer that had necessitated major surgery and grieving for his wife, who had succumbed to breast cancer, Harry Hopkins was hitherto absent from the intra-administration economic debates. Following extended recuperation, he travelled to Georgia with a group of like-minded New Dealers in tow to reinforce his advocacy of compensatory spending. Leon Henderson (WPA's chief economic adviser), Aubrey Williams (National Youth Administration director) and Beardsley Ruml (a director of the New York Federal Reserve) came armed with a memorandum written by Lauchlin Currie, special adviser to Eccles.

Currie had written the original version at his boss's invitation in November 1937 to tutor the Federal Reserve Board in a Keynesian understanding of the downturn. In the months that followed, it became a spending manifesto, with repeatedly updated versions being sent out for comment to a network of supporters spread throughout the New Deal bureaucracy. FDR himself was finally ready to heed its central argument that 'a very substantial increase in the Government's contribution to national buying power' was the best antidote to the recession. It still required Ruml's reassurances that the federal government had always been in the business of stimulating purchasing power through its infrastructure investments, protective tariffs and land grants to railroads to satisfy the president that he could justify the Keynesian turn as a continuation of American political tradition. Roosevelt returned to Washington the next day to put together a compensatory spending programme in consultation with key New Deal officials.[61]

The spenders' bête noire was also down in Georgia working on a balanced-budget strategy for recovery while vacationing at the Sea Island luxury resort. On his return to Washington on 10 April, Morgenthau went straight to the White House to make his pitch, only to find FDR's mind already made up. 'We have been travelling fast this last week', the president remarked, 'and you will have to hurry to catch up.' When Morgenthau queried the costs, he responded airily, 'Oh, we have all that.' The angry Treasury Secretary reported to his own staff the next day on the spenders' victory, 'They have stampeded him like cattle.' Returning to the White House for a conference with congressional leaders about the new programme, Morgenthau caused consternation in warning that it would put the FY1939 budget in the red by at least $3.5 billion, an intervention that earned him a presidential rebuke in private for breaking ranks. Two days later, he astounded FDR by threatening to resign: 'You are asking the general, in charge of finances, to carry out a program when he had nothing to do with the planning.' Morgenthau soon relented in recognition that his dispute with the president was over means not ends, but his chief economic adviser, Jacob Viner, did quit.[62]

Roosevelt's recommendations 'to stimulate further recovery' went to Congress on 14 April. They featured increased appropriations for the WPA and other relief agencies, new funding for public works and credit easing through Treasury 'desterilization' of the gold supply and Federal Reserve reduction of reserve requirements (neither of which required congressional authorization). The request totalled some $2 billion in increased spending, $950 million in new federal loans (mainly for Public Works Administration projects) and $2.1 billion in credit relaxation, making for an aggregate stimulus of $5 billion. Commending the programme as vital to boost purchasing power, FDR declared, 'At this immediate time we suffer from a failure of consumer demand.'[63]

That same evening the president delivered a Fireside Chat, drafted in part by Leon Henderson, to explain the compensatory programme to the American people. The address put across three basic messages about its rationale. First, renewed prosperity was essential for the nation's security from the threat posed by foreign dictatorships: 'Your Government, seeking to protect democracy, must prove that Government is stronger than the forces of business depression.' Second, the recovery initiatives 'followed tradition as well as necessity' in accordance with American government's historic mission to promote economic growth. Finally, and most significantly, instead of being a necessary evil to alleviate suffering, deficit spending was a positive good that would underwrite the economy's well-being for the benefit of all: '[W]e suffer primarily from a failure of consumer demand because of lack of buying power. It is up to us to create an economic upturn.' The federal government would deploy its fiscal resources 'to put idle money and idle men to work, to increase our public wealth and to build up the health and strength of our people – and to help our system of private enterprise to function'.[64]

The adoption of compensatory spending contributed to a substantial upward turn in the economy, but some liberals at the time and later dismissed its significance. According to *The New Republic*, the programme was 'not large enough to do more than prevent the existing situation from growing worse'. Biographer James MacGregor Burns likewise considered FDR's Keynesian turn of 1938 too little, too late. In his assessment the president's eclecticism had 'cut him off from the one economist and the one economic idea' offering a likely route to recovery. 'A Keynesian solution', he asserted, 'involved an almost absolute commitment, and Roosevelt was not one to commit himself absolutely to any political or economic method'.[65] These criticisms did not do justice to initiatives that were instrumental in raising FY1939 outlays by a third over FY1938 levels, boosting the deficit from 0.1 per cent GDP to 3.1 per cent GDP and significantly easing credit.

Eccles was no longer fighting a solitary battle for compensatory outlays within the administration. A host of younger economists sympathetic to Keynesian ideas had by now found federal employment. Newly appointed as Commerce Secretary, Harry Hopkins aspired to make it his department's mission to disseminate their thinking that a sustained fiscal and credit stimulus was needed to produce a high level of employment. Signalling awareness of their views, FDR appointed the Federal Reserve's Keynesian guru, Lauchlin Currie, one of his special assistants within the White House Office, created by the Executive Reorganization Act of 1939. Currie's performance in this post underlined the importance of the president having direct access to economic counsel. This was instrumental in the later establishment of the Council of Economic Advisers within the Executive Office of the President in 1946.[66]

To Keynesian chagrin, the coalition of conservative Democrats and Republicans that ruled the roost in the post-midterm Congress was resistant to compensatory spending. To stimulate economic growth, FDR proposed in spring 1939 that the Reconstruction Finance Corporation be authorized to borrow about $3.8 billion which it could spend or lend on self-liquidating public-works projects outside the normal budget in the coming years, with a target of $800 million set for FY1940. The plan came under immediate conservative attack for its regularization of federal intervention in the economy in the long term rather than just in emergency conditions. Despite gaining Senate approval, it went down to defeat in the House of Representatives. Nor was there support in the country at large for additional federal spending. In late 1938 a Gallup poll found that 61 per cent of respondents thought outlays too high, 10 per cent too low and 29 per cent about right. Accordingly, FDR did not risk investing his prestige in a Fireside Chat on behalf of the spend-lend bill.[67]

Keynesians still managed to find a back door to propound their ideas via the Temporary National Economic Committee (TNEC), a congressional body ostensibly established to investigate business monopoly as a cause of recession. With FDR's support, Executive Secretary Leon Henderson used the committee hearings as a channel for compensatory thinking. Justifying this, Roosevelt informed the TNEC chair, Senator Joseph O'Mahoney (D-Wyoming), that it was necessary to ascertain 'why a large part of our vast reservoir of money and savings have remained idle in stagnant pools' and 'why the dollars which the American people save each year are not yet finding their way back into productive enterprise in sufficient volume to keep our economy turning at the rate required to bring about full employment'.[68] The star Keynesian witness, Alvin Hansen of Harvard, advanced his 'stagnation thesis' that the economy was now in a mature stage of development lacking the dynamic elements that had powered American prosperity in the past, notably rapid population growth, territorial expansion and fresh investment opportunities in innovative technology and manufacturing. In his assessment, the recession of 1937–8 was proof that private capital was incapable of making good any withdrawal of fiscal or monetary stimuli, so deficit budgets would have to be a permanent feature of American government to underwrite national wealth and jobs.[69]

Roosevelt and his Keynesian allies had to wait for defence orders to boost the economy to the point that unemployment fell below 10 per cent for the first time in his presidency in 1941. A president whose economic record featured an average annual rate of unemployment of 18.6 per cent over two terms of office would be considered an abject failure in other times. However, the slump of 1929–33 was so deep that average GDP annual growth in excess of 6 per cent in the New Deal years (even with negative growth in 1933 and 1938) was insufficient to soak up the pool of jobless. The boom generated by military spending in the Second World War ultimately dispelled stagnationist theory about America's economic limits while also demonstrating that large federal outlays were now indispensable to the expansion of national prosperity. As Keynes himself recognized, 'It is, it seems, impossible for a capitalistic democracy to organize expenditure on the scale necessary to prove my case – except under war conditions.'[70]

One of Franklin D. Roosevelt's most significant legacies was his transformation of the presidency's role as economic manager. He had recast monetary policy through his evisceration of the old gold standard and the establishment of a managed currency better suited to the national interest. The dollar that emerged from the currency initiatives of 1933–4 was to all intents and purposes the Roosevelt dollar. Similarly momentous developments on the fiscal side of economic management took longer to come about. Congressional conservatism initially limited Roosevelt's scope for boosting national income through enhanced federal expenditure until the crisis of war tilted the political balance in his favour. Having to fight what could be termed a gross-national-product war that largely turned on which side could outproduce the other ensured that the pursuit of economic growth became the new orthodoxy for peacetime. As a consequence, all FDR's successors regarded the management of prosperity in pursuit of a high employment-low inflation-strong growth economy as a fundamental responsibility.

Second emancipator

FDR and African Americans

Many African Americans looked on Franklin D. Roosevelt as a second emancipator who did more for their race than any president since Abraham Lincoln. Accustomed to government neglect of their needs, they received unprecedented socio-economic assistance from the New Deal. 'You must be a God Sent man', a Black Mississippian wrote FDR in 1934. 'You have made a great change since you have ben president. . . . You ben Bread for the hungry and clothes for the naked.'[1] Though Roosevelt's civil-rights initiatives were hesitant and half-hearted by comparison, they still represented the most significant federal contribution to the Black struggle for equality since Reconstruction. Accordingly, his presidency marked a veritable revolution in African-American expectations of a better tomorrow in which they shared fully in America's promise of economic, social and political freedom. As Mary McLeod Bethune, the child of former slaves and now the foremost Black New Dealer, declared in 1938, 'We are on our way.'[2]

Already economically marginalized, African Americans were reduced to their lowest ebb since slavery by the Great Depression. In 1930 half of them lived in the rural South, where fully four-fifths eked out a precarious existence as tenant farmers, sharecroppers and wage-labourers. With the collapse in cotton prices, many quit the countryside to seek work in Dixie's cities, where they found whites taking what were once considered Black jobs like cleaners, janitors and road-sweepers. Those who went North fared no better – Black male unemployment in New York, Philadelphia, Chicago and Detroit in early 1933 averaged above 40 per cent and for women it was even higher at 55 per cent.[3]

Nothing about Roosevelt's pre-presidential career encouraged African Americans to see him as their saviour. Roy Wilkins of the National Association for the Advancement of Colored People (NAACP) thought him an aloof patrician 'with no natural feel for the sensibilities of black people, no compelling inner commitment to their cause'.[4] A Northern Democrat with presidential ambitions, Roosevelt had courted his party's dominant Southern wing for more than a quarter century. The first rule of national politics in his book was deference to Dixie on matters of race. As Assistant Secretary of the Navy under Woodrow Wilson, FDR had overseen the Jim-Crowing of his department in line with the segregation of federal offices in Washington DC by a Southern-dominated administration. After buying Warm Springs as a spa for polio sufferers, he happily announced himself an adopted Georgian, an identity in which he found no difficulty in conforming with Southern racial mores on visits there. Focused on restoring the 'Solid South' lost by Al Smith in 1928, he made no effort to win Black votes in his 1932 campaign and returned unanswered the NAACP questionnaire soliciting his views on racial issues.[5]

As the party of Lincoln, Republicans had long received support from African Americans but had grown indifferent to their interests. Having carried five of the eleven former Confederate states in 1928, Herbert Hoover was willing to drive Blacks out of the party as the price of advancing it in the South.[6] Despite this, antipathy to FDR ensured that the historic ties binding African Americans to the Republican Party endured in the 1932 election. One of the few Black leaders to urge a new affiliation, *Pittsburgh Courier* editor Robert Vann declared in a speech at Cleveland on 11 September, 'I see millions of Negroes turning the picture of Abraham Lincoln to the wall. This year I see Negroes voting a Democratic ticket.'[7] For most of the African-American press, by contrast, a second term for Hoover, however bad, was preferable to having FDR in the White House. Voicing this sentiment, an article in *The Crisis*, the NAACP organ, warned that a vote for Roosevelt was a vote for segregation.[8]

Black voters needed little prompting to follow the old ways. Barely 5 per cent of African Americans based in the South could cast ballots because of suffrage restrictions, but they remained overwhelmingly Republican in defiance of Dixie's lily-white Democrats. Despite horrendous Black unemployment, Hoover captured two-thirds of the African-American vote outside the South, a larger share than he won in 1928. Few of those who went against tradition did so with any enthusiasm. In Seattle, Revels Cayton, a labour activist and the grandson of Hiram Revels, the Mississippi Republican who had become the first Black US senator in 1870–1, found his father sitting dejectedly at home on Election Day because he had just voted Democrat for the first time. 'Well Roosevelt's going to feed ya', the younger man reassured the older one, who replied, 'Yes, that's true, but the Republican party *freed* me.'[9]

Owing African Americans nothing for his election, FDR had no cause to prioritize their problems and every reason to be circumspect about offending Southern Democrats whose support in Congress he needed.[10] He was of one mind with long-time adviser Louis Howe about the imperative of favouring 'our Southern brethren' over 'our anxious Negro brethren'. Determined to focus on economic rather than racial problems, FDR was clear on one thing: 'First things come first, and I can't alienate certain votes I need for measures that are more important at the moment by pushing any measures that would entail a fight.'[11] Other than Secretary of the Interior Harold Ickes, none of the Cabinet or agency heads thought differently. When some New Dealers in time grew bolder on race, Roosevelt had no hesitation in putting them right about reality as he saw it. 'Politics is the art of the possible', he lectured National Youth Administration (NYA) director Aubrey Williams. 'I do not believe in attempting something for the purpose of one's image. I believe you should never undertake anything unless you have evidence that you have at least a 50-50 chance of winning.'[12]

Early relief and recovery ventures were far from even-handed towards African Americans and in some instances were fundamentally harmful to them. The Agricultural Adjustment Administration's prioritization of landlord interests accelerated decline in Black tenant and sharecropper numbers in the South. The National Recovery Administration (NRA) became an object of Black scorn. 'Before the Blue Eagle', one African American told a reporter, 'we was just one-half living, but now we is only one-third living.'[13] The cotton-industry code exempted low-paying jobs in which Blacks predominated from NRA minimum-wage standards. Over one hundred codes permitted geographical variations that enabled Southern industries to pay their employees lower wages. Taking their cue from this, many regional employers ignored the wage codes altogether in the case of Black workers. Unwilling to risk confrontation with Southern Democrats, FDR washed his hands of responsibility for improving African-American labour conditions in the South. 'It is not the purpose of this Administration', he declared, 'to impair Southern industry by refusing to recognize traditional differentials.'[14] Few Blacks regretted the demise of an agency whose initials stood for 'Negro Run Around' or 'Negroes Ruined Again' in their mind.

The Civilian Conservation Corps (CCC), established to put unemployed and unmarried young men to work on natural-resource conservation projects, fell short of the anti-discriminatory ideals of its enabling legislation.[15] Young Blacks saw it as a great chance to acquire skills and earn money. Future federal judge Leon Higginbotham recalled that for his peers in Trenton, New Jersey, '[I]t was as important as going to Princeton University – they had status.'[16] With selection devolved to state and local CCC offices, those in the South were slow to enrol African Americans. The national headquarters had to threaten withholding funds to secure Black recruitment in Alabama, Florida, Georgia and, most notably, Mississippi. CCC director Robert Fechner, a conservative Southerner, remained hostile to large-scale African-American participation in its work. With the president's concurrence, he insisted that CCC camps should be rigidly segregated, other than in New England and parts of the West where Black numbers were too small to make up full companies of recruits. Under pressure from civil-rights organizations and with an election approaching, FDR agreed in 1936 to relax the rule requiring Black camps to be supervised and officered only by whites. By then, African Americans made up 10 per cent of CCC workers, close to their overall population share but utterly inadequate to meet their disproportionate relief needs.

As the CCC exemplified, the early New Deal tended to reinforce rather than diminish racial separation. Supposedly an experiment in decentralized 'grass-roots democracy', the Tennessee Valley Authority segregated workplaces in its various projects and settlements. In America's cities, the Federal Housing Administration refused to insure dwellings in areas of Black settlement and encouraged the almost exclusively white recipients of its assistance to preserve neighbourhood property values by adopting restrictive covenants prohibiting sale of their home to Blacks. The sole agency to practise racial fairness was the Public Works Administration (PWA). Under the leadership of Harold Ickes, a former president of NAACP's Chicago chapter, it established racial quotas for private contractors on its projects, set in accordance with the percentage of African Americans in the local workforce as recorded in the 1930 occupational census. Centralized oversight of contract observance resulted in increased hiring of Black workers, who came to see PWA as standing for 'Pop's Working Again'.[17]

Two years into his presidency, many in the African-American elite were vehemently critical of FDR's racial record. Langston Hughes published a damning poem that began with a boy's lament about his family's desperate economic plight and his father's response, 'I'm waitin' on Roosevelt, son.' The verses expressed growing anger with the president in progressing to a finale in which the father bitterly avowed that people like him had stopped believing what they had been told by 'Roosevelt – Roosevelt, Roosevelt'. In May 1935, speakers at the National Conference on the Negro and the Economic Crisis, convened at Howard University, Washington DC's all-Black college, likewise condemned the New Deal for failing African Americans. Reporting on the proceedings, scholar and civil-rights activist Kelly Miller summed up the common opinion: 'Nothing good was found in it.'[18]

Within the broader Black community, by contrast, sentiment ran strongly in favour of FDR. Whereas African-American elites predominantly focused on the racial dimension of the 'Negro problem', the Black masses overwhelmingly prioritized economic concerns. For them, historian Nancy Weiss remarked, 'The struggle to survive took precedence over the struggle for equality. And in the struggle to survive, many New Deal programs made a critical difference.'[19] Though fully aware that they were not receiving a fair share, African Americans were grateful for any federal assistance. State and local distribution of Federal Emergency Relief Administration (FERA) grants for relief of unemployables and temporary work on public projects for the able-bodied patently gave preference to whites, but the lesser benefits for Blacks still raised their living standards. 'It is a curious commentary on industrial conditions in the South', FERA racial adviser Forrester Washington remarked, 'that at the height of prosperity many Negroes never earned as much or ate as well as under relief.'[20] Recalling Black gratitude for the New Deal, NAACP lobbyist Clarence Mitchell explained in the 1970s, 'When you start from a position of zero, even if you only move up a point or two on a scale, it looks like a big improvement.'[21]

The federalization of work relief through the establishment of the Works Progress Administration (WPA) in 1935 boosted New Deal socio-economic assistance for African Americans. It employed 250,000 Blacks in its first year of operation and numbers escalated in FDR's second term to reach 15 to 20 per cent of its workforce. In some Northern cities, their proportion ran at three to five times their share of the local population. In 1939 WPA employed 425,000 African Americans, a seventh of its total workforce, making the agency as important as farm labour and domestic service as a source of Black income. It was not free from racial shortcomings, particularly in the South. African Americans could be disbarred from eligibility for work relief if they turned down private jobs paying a pittance of $2 to $3 a week, which was common for farm labourers. Those who were taken on tended to be allocated unskilled work regardless of their qualifications. Unable to sustain a national minimum wage in the face of regional pressures, WPA established a sliding scale that paid $19 a month in the rural South, compared with the national average rate of $52, but this was still very good money for African Americans. As a Black WPA worker in North Carolina commented, 'The gover'ment is the best boss I ever had.'[22]

WPA helped many more African Americans, men and women, than any other New Deal venture. While most were employed as manual labourers, some received skilled positions, others got professional placements as architects, engineers and medical staff, and others still were hired as writers, musicians, actors and artists in the programme known as Federal Project Number One. In addition to providing jobs, WPA constructed public facilities such as schools and recreation centres that improved the lives of many Black communities, enrolled Blacks of all ages in education and vocational training courses, helped nearly 250,000 achieve literacy and established nursery programmes for Black children. Some thirty years later, an African American recalled to interviewer Studs Terkel that WPA, as well as being a financial godsend, had given many Blacks their first sense of being part of American society: 'It made us feel like there was something we could do in the scheme of things.'[23]

A WPA subsidiary, the National Youth Administration directly aided 300,000 African-American youths over the course of its existence. Its director, liberal Southerner Aubrey Williams, made Black education and training a priority. Mary McLeod Bethune, whose appointment as head of the NYA Division of Negro Affairs made her the top-ranking African American in the New Deal bureaucracy, used her power over agency purse strings to ensure local compliance with anti-discrimination rules. Blacks made up some 10 per cent of all college students assisted over the course of its existence. Their representation was even bigger in high-school programmes, in which at least half of them worked on professional or semi-professional tasks related to their occupational aspirations.[24]

Accordingly, many African Americans came to see FDR as their economic saviour. A popular song, 'Mr Roosevelt, you're my man', encapsulated this image of him. Another, entitled 'Relief Blues', identified the president personally as the source of the public assistance on which many Blacks depended.[25] This was a view that found repeated expression in letters that African Americans sent the president, his wife and Black newspapers. Another indicator of their esteem was the common practice of naming newborn boys 'Franklin', 'Delano', 'Roosevelt' or some combination thereof, while 'Eleanor' was a favourite for girls. Millions of African Americans brought FDR into their home by hanging a photograph of him, usually clipped from a newspaper, alongside images of Jesus Christ and Abraham Lincoln. Many spoke of him in religious terms as 'God Sent', 'saviour' and 'Joshua' to Lincoln's 'Moses'. A Texas woman felt moved to write the president, 'It seem lak we got a unseen eye watchin an studyin our troubles an lookin after em. . . . I feels like he's jes another Moses God has done sent to head His chillun. . . . I'se restin easy cause I know he's got his hand on de throttle an' his eye on de rail.'[26]

African Americans blamed the discrimination they experienced in getting work relief and other New Deal aid on local officialdom's subversion of presidential intent. 'If you complain', a Black WPA worker reported from Detroit, 'they say we are running this job – Roosevelt and [Harry] Hopkins haven't anything to do with it.'[27] Blacks commonly believed that FDR would come to their rescue if he knew of their plight. Though untypical of presidential involvement, the story of Sylvester Harris, widely reported by the Black press and told in a blues song 'Sylvester and His Mule' (recorded by the likes of Lizzie Douglas and Memphis Minnie), encouraged that conviction. Under threat of having his mortgage foreclosed, this Black farmer from Columbus, Mississippi, somehow managed to get through to Roosevelt when he telephoned the

White House on 19 February 1934. As reported by the Associated Press, he told the president, 'A man gettin' ready to take my land and I want to know what to do. De papers say call you [for help], and I does, and here I is.' Promising to investigate, FDR duly arranged through an aide for the Federal Land Bank's New Orleans office to provide a mortgage extension that saved Harris from eviction.[28]

Esteem for Eleanor Roosevelt reinforced African Americans' high opinion of FDR. Ordinary Blacks saw her as the person most likely to help them because he was so busy with other duties. In ER's case, the Black elite was as appreciative as the Black masses for her assistance. NAACP executive secretary Walter F. White remarked in his autobiography that in moments of doubt whether his race would ever gain its due, her support gave him renewed hope and kept him from hating all white people.[29] ER's friendship with Mary McLeod Bethune, who had risen through education from poverty as a South Carolina sharecropper's daughter, also informed her racial liberalism. The desire to sit alongside Bethune inspired the First Lady's challenge to local segregation ordinances at the founding convention of the Southern Conference on Human Welfare in the Birmingham, Alabama, Municipal Auditorium on 28 November 1938. Refusing to sit on the stage section designated for white dignitaries, she attempted to move to the Black side until police warned that doing so was illegal. Accordingly, she had her chair placed in the middle of the stage between the racially separated seating.[30]

The foremost advocate of racial justice within the Roosevelt administration, Eleanor Roosevelt turned up, sometimes unannounced, to Black churches, colleges, schools, WPA projects and CCC camps employing African Americans, and integrated PWA projects.[31] Unlike her predecessors, she invited Black leaders, women's groups and students to discuss racial issues and hosted performances by Black artists in the White House. She enthusiastically supported civil-rights organizations, as when addressing a mass meeting to boost the 1935 membership drive of the NAACP's Washington chapter. The First Lady, the *Afro-American* remarked, 'seemed as much at ease as in her own home. Among the humble people she appeared as one of them.'[32]

Meanwhile ER operated behind the scenes as an unofficial ombudsman for Black interests in the New Deal. She emboldened Harry Hopkins, Aubrey Williams and other sympathetic New Dealers to clean house in their agencies. Through her good offices, Mary McLeod Bethune gained an interview with FDR to discuss the economic needs of Black youth in April 1936. 'We have been eating the feet and head of the chicken long enough', she told him. 'The time has come when we want some white meat.' Impressed with Bethune's combination of passion and realism, FDR told NYA boss Aubrey Williams, 'I believe in her because she has her feet on the ground; not only on the ground, but deep down in the ploughed soil.'[33]

In Rexford Tugwell's judgement, Eleanor Roosevelt was free to be 'more unswervingly moral' than FDR, who was constrained by political realities. In her recall, he never sought to muzzle her support for Blacks. 'Franklin', she wrote after his death, 'had such a deep sense of justice and an over-riding wish to see all Americans treated as equals that he never prevented me from taking any stand.'[34] The truth was somewhat different. There were times when FDR reined in the First Lady for fear of adverse reaction from Southern Democrats. In November 1934, she turned down an invitation to speak at a NAACP anti-lynching rally at Carnegie Hall, New York, after the president counselled that doing so would be 'dynamite'. She also heeded his advice not to address the NAACP national conference in 1935 and again in 1936 to avoid offending the white South.[35]

Eleanor Roosevelt did not object to compromise because she knew that racial justice would take time. She counselled Blacks against 'too much demanding' for equality. In her view, it was better to take any chance they got to prove their ability, and if recognition was slow in coming, 'in the end good performance has to be acknowledged'.[36] Nor would she embarrass FDR by breaking Jim Crow laws. In January 1940, to the disappointment of civil-rights activists, she crossed a Black picket line protesting all-white theatres in downtown Washington DC to attend a charity movie premiere (ironically to see *Abe Lincoln in Illinois*, an adaptation of Robert Sherwood's Pulitzer Prize-winning play). Nevertheless, she deservedly earned the trust of African Americans as a spokesperson for their interests. Despite being unable to fight the most flagrant manifestations of racism, she did enough in smaller ways to make Blacks see her as their friend. In the *Chicago Defender's* assessment, 'Never before in the history of this country has there been in the White House a nobler, a fairer and a more courageous First Lady. . . . She has stood like the Rock of Gibraltar against pernicious encroachments on the rights of minorities'.[37]

The president, the First Lady and the New Deal effectively represented a holy trinity for the Democratic faith that most Blacks embraced with all the enthusiasm of new converts in the 1936 presidential election. In contrast to 1932, FDR made a determined bid for their support in the hope of sweeping the urban-industrial states of the North. The Democratic National Convention seated Black delegates, ten in all, for the first time, invited a Black pastor to deliver the invocation at one session and selected Representative Arthur Michell (D-Illinois) – the solitary Black congressman – to second FDR's nomination. The Democratic National Committee made full use of New Deal patronage to beef up the 'Negro divisions' of Democratic organizations in key Northern states and cities. It also despatched Mary McLeod Bethune and other Black New Dealers to address African-American audiences. Most importantly, FDR himself gave his first real address before a Black gathering when dedicating the new PWA-constructed chemistry building at Howard University on 26 October. As well as being broadcast live on national radio, the speech with its avowal that there should be 'no forgotten men and no forgotten races' made front-page headlines in African-American newspapers just before polling day.[38]

Meanwhile, the National Colored Committee of the Good Neighbor League, a supposedly independent group that received generous Democratic Party funding, was very active in promoting the pro-FDR message. Among other things, it enlisted African-American pastors to spread the word of the president's goodness to their congregations, disseminated campaign literature in Black communities and ceaselessly portrayed FDR as a Black saviour. Most notably, it organized mass meetings in the North to mark the seventy-fourth anniversary of Lincoln's issue of the Emancipation Proclamation. The celebrations culminated on 21 September with a nationally broadcast rally at New York City's Madison Square Gardens, whose 16,000 attendees enthusiastically adopted a formal resolution to 'carry forward the real spirit of Abraham Lincoln by supporting the social and economic programs of our great President, Franklin D. Roosevelt'.[39] The event climaxed with the unveiling of a colossal painting of the Second Emancipation, with FDR standing to a height of 20 feet, arms outstretched in benediction over a kneeling group of Blacks and Lincoln's spirit hovering in the background.

Confirming the partisan realignment first evident in the 1934 midterms, African Americans gave FDR 71 per cent of their votes in 1936. An important bloc in the Roosevelt voter coalition, they now received greater assistance from the New Deal. Improved access to WPA work relief was just one element of this. For some African Americans, rural rehabilitation began to make a real difference to their quality of life. Under the Resettlement Administration initially and then the Farm Security Administration, the economically devastated Gee's Bend community of Black tenant farmers near Selma, Alabama, graduated from being recipients of emergency assistance into participants in a cooperative project that supported some 700 people by the early 1940s. They received federal assistance to purchase modern farm equipment, rent decent homes and buy the land they worked with low-interest loans. In urban America, the New Deal began making a small dent in the appalling housing conditions of Black ghettoes. Cleveland's Democratic mayor Carl Stokes remembered his sense of wonderment when moving with his mother and brother into an apartment in a new public-housing project as an eleven-year-old in 1938. It was the first time the family had a sink with hot and cold running water, a refrigerator, a washing machine and separate sleeping quarters for his mother.[40]

Members of the so-called Black Cabinet of racial advisers and Black office-holders within the New Deal bureaucracy were also active in bringing African-American needs to the attention of their departmental superiors.[41] Commencing regular meetings in August 1936, usually in Mary McLeod Bethune's NYA office or her home, it operated as a clearing house for information on how Blacks fared under the New Deal, identified problems that needed addressing and kept the Black press informed about what was going on. In this way, the Black Cabinet made the New Deal somewhat more sensitive to Black needs, made the federal government somewhat more understandable to African Americans and was instrumental in solidifying Black support for FDR and his party. The substantive changes the group brought about in public policy tended to be specific and small scale, and there is no evidence that it had any clout with the president. Nevertheless, it had considerable symbolic significance for African Americans as their first network within national government.

While the Black Cabinet exemplified FDR's skill in deriving political advantage from limited racial change, he came under growing pressure from African-American leaders to deliver more substantive advances in his second and third terms. For the NAACP's Walter White, the president's massive Black vote in 1936 required payback in support for federal anti-lynching legislation, the greatest civil-rights cause of the 1930s. Lynching became an instrument of racial control and enforcement of white supremacy in the post-Emancipation South. Law enforcement officers at state and local levels left victims unprotected and allowed perpetrators to go unpunished. At their peak from 1891 to 1901, recorded Black lynchings averaged 113 annually. Despite a spike in 1918–19, their incidence declined steadily in the early twentieth century and fell off steeply in the 1920s to a low of seven in 1929. This reflected the distaste of Southern elites for racial violence, the increasing urbanization of the region and improved law enforcement at state level. Amid the economic misery of the early Depression years, however, Black lynchings surged to twenty in 1930 and then to twenty-three in 1933.[42]

FDR spoke out against lynching for the first time in late 1933 to rebuke Governor James Rolph (R-California) for his public endorsement of a mob hanging of two white kidnapper-murderers in San Jose on 26 November. In an address to the Churches of Christ in America, carried nationwide on radio, he avowed, 'Lynch law is murder, a deliberate and definite disobedience of the high command, "Thou shalt not kill." We do not excuse those in high places or low who condone lynch law.' These comments went further than anything uttered by a twentieth-century predecessor on the subject. Grasping at the straw of anticipation that Roosevelt might follow words with deeds, *The Crisis* editorialized that it was 'unusual' for a president to acknowledge lynching as murder. 'These things give us hope', it concluded.[43]

In 1934, the NAACP launched a major campaign with widespread support from church and civic organizations to enact an anti-lynching bill drafted under its auspices. This penalized law enforcement officers who failed to avert lynchings, authorized federal prosecution of lynchers if state officials proved unwilling to do so within thirty days of the offence and levied fines of up to $10,000, payable to the victim's dependents, on counties where the crime took place. The measure, sponsored by Senator Edward Costigan (D-Colorado) and Senator Robert Wagner (D-New York), was reported out of the Senate Judiciary Committee with minimal amendment in March 1934, but faced being filibustered to death by Southern Democrats on the Senate floor. Unwilling to have the chamber's business obstructed, Senate Majority Leader Joseph Robinson (D-Arkansas) refused to bring the measure to debate.

Through Eleanor Roosevelt's good offices, White sought presidential help to get the bill to a floor vote but to no avail. At a White House meeting on 6 May, FDR told the NAACP leader,

> I did not choose the tools with which I must work. . . . I would have chosen quite different ones. But I've got to get legislation passed by Congress to save America. The Southerners by reason of the seniority rule in Congress are chairmen or occupy strategic places on the House and Senate committees. If I come out for the anti-lynch bill now, they will block every bill I ask Congress to pass to keep America from collapsing. I just can't take that risk.

The furthest he would go was to state of the Costigan-Wagner bill in a press conference on 25 May, 'I am absolutely for the objective but am not clear in my own mind as to whether that is absolutely the right way to attain the objective. However, I told them to go ahead and try to get a vote on it.' This tepid endorsement put his Senate lieutenants under no obligation to progress the measure.[44]

A parliamentary manoeuvre finally brought the bill before the full Senate in April 1935 at cost of provoking a Southern filibuster that held up consideration of major New Deal measures, including social security. Responding to presidential exhortations to get on with other business, Northern and Western Democrats voted with their Southern colleagues to adjourn debate without a vote. In protest, White resigned from the Advisory Council for the Government of the Virgin Islands, an official appointment he had received in 1934. Roosevelt henceforth saw him as a nuisance. When the NAACP leader's twenty-fifth anniversary of service came around in 1943, FDR's secretary, Grace Tully, relayed his instruction for aides to draft a restrained testimonial in his name: 'The President doesn't think much of this organization – not to be to [sic] fulsome – tone it down a bit.'[45]

Fearful of its divisive effect on Democrats, Roosevelt was keen to keep the anti-lynching bill off the congressional calendar in 1936. Eleanor Roosevelt's efforts to enlist his support for its inclusion got nowhere. 'The President', she wrote White, 'feels that lynching is a question of education in the states, rallying good citizens, and creating public opinion so that the localities themselves will wipe it out. However, if it were done by a Northerner, it will have an antagonistic effect.'[46] Once re-elected, FDR secretly ordered Attorney General Homer Cummings to work with the NAACP to fashion an anti-lynching bill that would satisfy constitutional protections of states' rights, a qualification that ensured there would be no meeting of minds between the two sides. The measure that the House of Representatives approved by 277 votes to 120 in April 1937 was essentially the NAACP original. Despite almost universal opposition from Southern members, this was the first Democrat-promoted civil-rights bill ever to receive a majority in either chamber of Congress. Focused on achieving Supreme Court reorganization, FDR played no part in this success. As the legislation's chief sponsor, Joseph Gavagan (D-New York), Harlem's white congressman, later commented, 'The President was taking first things first and felt that more demanding questions were more vital to the nation at that particular time than any equal rights legislation.'[47] Nor would FDR lift a finger to help the measure in the Senate where a filibuster could prevent consideration of his judiciary bill.

With opinion polls and newspaper editorials showing strong support for the anti-lynching bill, Roosevelt appeared to come off the fence to support manoeuvres that got it to the Senate floor at the start of the 1938 congressional session. This provoked a six-week filibuster in which Southerner after Southerner expressed determination to preserve white supremacy in Dixie and damned the president for meddling in its race matters. Some also tied the issue to communist influences in the New Deal, a tactic henceforth used with increasing frequency to attack federal agencies seen as sympathetic to African Americans. When FDR inquired through backchannels of Senator James Byrnes (D-South Carolina), an administration loyalist, whether the filibuster could be ended, the response was: 'Tell him not until the year 2038, unless the bill is withdrawn before then.'[48] With no prospect of victory, Northern Democrats agreed to end the debate on 21 February in order to take up Roosevelt's request for an emergency relief appropriation necessitated by the worsening economic situation. The diminution of annual lynchings to two, the lowest number since records began, was instrumental in the NAACP bill disappearing from the congressional calendar in 1939. Supporters got it approved once more by the House of Representatives in 1940 but could not bring it to a Senate vote. Unwilling to risk another filibuster with war raging in Europe, Senate Majority Leader Alben Barkley (D-Kentucky) asserted, 'In the midst of our international situation, . . . [it is] impractical to make a futile effort to obtain a vote on the bill.'[49] This effectively signified that anti-lynch legislation was a cause whose time had passed.

Whether the outcome would have been different had Roosevelt made the issue a presidential priority is unlikely. His failure to do so was a moral stain on his presidency, but even his limited interventions evoked charges of betrayal from Dixie Democrats. If African-American leaders expected legislative returns for Black support of FDR at the ballot box, Southern Democrats considered his assistance in preserving the South's racial system their due for a century of party loyalty. Northern Democrats' willingness to support anti-lynching scandalized their Southern counterparts. Giving vent to regional outrage, Representative Edward Cox (D-Georgia) fulminated, 'For more than 100 years, the people in the South have kept life in the Democratic Party. At time they have been its only friends, and now when the party has grown strong and powerful, it turns upon them and proposes to deal to them this wicked and cowardly blow.'[50] Race was henceforth a major cleavage in the Democratic coalition. Knowing that he could not resolve the issue, FDR sought to contain the threat it posed to party and national unity at a time when America faced growing danger from abroad.

Despite Roosevelt's efforts to manage their expectations of change, African Americans had started the long march to the Civil Rights Revolution of the 1960s during the 1930s. Nothing symbolized this more powerfully than Marian Anderson's concert from the steps of the Lincoln Memorial on Easter Sunday, 9 April 1939.[51] The 42-year-old African American had battled prejudice throughout her career to become recognized throughout the music world as a brilliant contralto. At Eleanor Roosevelt's invitation, she had sung at a private White House function in February 1936, where FDR had been a gracious host (and, more significantly, she would do so again to entertain King George VI and Queen Elizabeth during the British royal visit of June 1939). She also fulfilled an annual engagement for the Howard University School of Music, which needed an ever-larger auditorium to accommodate demand to see her perform. For the 1939 recital, it asked to hire Constitution Hall, the largest private venue in the capital, a request that fell afoul of the racial exclusion policy of the blue-blooded owners, the Daughters of the American Revolution (DAR).

The mainstream media paid little heed to the Anderson ban until Eleanor Roosevelt resigned from the DAR in protest. No First Lady had previously interjected herself into a public controversy in such a direct manner. Encouraged by press and popular support for her stance, Walter White suggested that Anderson deliver a free concert at the Lincoln Memorial on Easter Sunday. Despite initial reservations about participation in a political spectacle, the singer recognized that she had become 'whether I liked it or not, a symbol, representing my people'.[52] White took the proposal to Oscar Chapman, assistant secretary at the Department of the Interior, which had charge of national monuments. Chapman relayed it to his boss, Harold Ickes, who had no hesitation in recommending presidential approval. 'Tell Oscar', Roosevelt remarked, 'he has my permission to have Marian sing from the top of the Washington Monument if he wants it.'[53]

The Roosevelts did not attend the concert lest their presence proved a distraction, but this did not diminish its impact. When Anderson began singing just after five o'clock, standing before her on the National Mall was a vast throng of 75,000 people, in which Blacks rubbed shoulders with whites, common folk with high society, while millions nationwide were tuned to their radios to hear her. Introducing the singer with words cleared by the White House, Harold Ickes declared, 'Genius, like justice, is blind. . . . Genius draws no color line.' Anderson's recital began with an evocative rendition of 'America', moved on to two offerings from her classical repertoire and concluded with three spirituals – with 'Nobody Knows the Trouble I've Seen' for an encore.[54] Lasting just thirty minutes, her performance was an electric and unforgettable experience for those present. Mary McLeod Bethune spoke for many of her race when writing next day, 'Through the Marian Anderson protest concert we made our triumphant entry into the democratic spirit of America.'[55] The first usage of the Great Emancipator's memorial in service of civil rights, the event was linked in spirit, symbol and substance to Martin Luther King's 'I Have a Dream' address at the same venue nearly a quarter century later.

It was the NAACP's progressive allies in the administration who took the lead in getting the concert to go ahead, but the president at least had no hesitation in following them. In contrast to the anti-lynching bill, the issue at stake posed no threat to the South's racial system and states' rights. Nevertheless, FDR was inching forward in other ways to support more substantive protection of Black rights. With his approval, new attorney general Frank Murphy, a former NAACP board member, established a Civil Liberties Unit within the Justice Department's Criminal Division. Later renamed the Civil Rights Section, it legitimized the idea for the first time since Reconstruction that the federal government had the authority and obligation to investigate and prosecute civil-rights violations. Murphy's successor, Nicholas Biddle, ordered the FBI to investigate the killing of Cleo Wright in Sikeston, Missouri, in January 1942, making this the first lynching since the 1880s to attract official Department of Justice involvement. To deter further mob violence, Roosevelt asked Biddle to draft legislation allowing the federal government to investigate mob violence that resulted in death or injury. With no prospect of getting this through the Senate, he ultimately implemented it on the basis of his executive authority.[56]

The president found it more difficult to finesse his next civil-rights challenge pertaining to the desegregation of the armed services and the defence industries. Beginning amid the international crises of 1938, the Black press increasingly agitated against racial discrimination in the military as a denial of African-American citizen rights. Blacks could not enlist in the Marine Corps or the Army Air Corps, could only serve as messmen in the Navy and had very limited opportunities in the Army. As the 1940 presidential election approached, African-American leaders warned that Black discontent over the lack of equal opportunities in the nation's defence effort could lead to mass defections back to the Republicans. The GOP's strong civil-rights platform and the racial liberalism of its presidential candidate, Wendell Willkie, added weight to their admonitions. Though FDR was running on a platform with a 'Negro plank' for the first time, it was much weaker on detail because of need to retain the white South. Some Black newspapers, notably the *Pittsburgh Courier* that had led the charge to Roosevelt in 1932, reverted to endorsing the party of Lincoln.[57]

Using Eleanor Roosevelt as an intermediary, Walter White arranged to see the president in the hope of wringing concessions from him ahead of the election. A delegation consisting of White, Brotherhood of Sleeping Car Porters president A. Philip Randolph and NYA racial adviser T. Arnold Hill met with FDR, Secretary of the Navy Frank Knox and Assistant Secretary of War Robert Patterson at the White House on 27 September 1940. While Roosevelt attempted to assuage the Black trio with expressions of goodwill and vague promises of improvement, the Army and Navy officials drew an unyielding line against desegregation of their services. Accordingly, White handed FDR a memorandum outlining specific requirements for integration of the armed forces, eliciting a promise to study it and get back with proposals about what could be done.[58]

Faced with Knox's threat to resign if he conceded Black demands and Secretary of War Henry Stimson's firm opposition, Roosevelt had limited room for manoeuvre. Dispensing with his promise to consult White's group, he approved for release on 9 October a War Department statement reiterating the necessity for continued racial separation in the armed forces to preserve morale. Adding insult to injury, Press Secretary Stephen Early implied the compliance of White, Randolph and Hill with this policy in remarks to the press. Feeling duped, the trio sent the White House a strongly worded telegram of condemnation: 'Official approval by the Commander-in-Chief . . . of such discrimination and segregation is a stab in the back of Democracy.'[59]

Despite this election-eve donnybrook, Roosevelt's 67 per cent share of the African-American vote on polling day was close to his record tally four years earlier. While there was slippage in support from better-off Blacks, lower-income Blacks remained in his column. With over 319,000 African Americans (6 per cent of their potential labour force), employed on emergency work created by the New Deal, this was a case of economic self-interest. Endorsing FDR for the first time, the *Chicago Defender* urged Black voters to recognize how his programmes had benefited them in socio-economic terms. Nevertheless, emotion was equally at play because most African Americans still saw FDR as their friend and saviour. As Walter White had foreseen, 'The Race is more Roosveltian, "especially MRS Roosveltian," than Democratic.'[60]

For Roosevelt's low-income Black supporters, economic security remained more important than civil-rights advancement, but the two causes soon became one. With the nation's defence industries generating an ever-expanding volume of decently paid jobs, African Americans clamoured for access to this new source of prosperity. The NAACP joined with new organizations like the Committee on the American Negro in Defense Industries and the Committee for Participation of Negroes in National Defense to mobilize local protests. This groundswell of activism found its most significant expression in the formation of the March on Washington Movement (MOWM) under Philip Randolph's leadership.

A trade union leader and a one-time Socialist Party candidate for state office in New York, Randolph believed that collective action, militancy and confrontation were essential to advance Black equality. 'We would rather die on our feet fighting for Negroes' rights', he avowed, 'than to live on our knees as half-men, as semi-citizens, begging for a pittance.'[61] Though his ultimate goal was racial integration in the workplace, Randolph excluded whites from participation in MOWM in the hope of it becoming an instrument for racial liberation. His initial plan envisaged a march in Washington by 10,000 Blacks on 1 July 1941, but it soon became apparent that upwards of 100,000 would participate in a demonstration culminating at the Lincoln Memorial.[62]

Worried that the protest would undermine Democratic unity on war issues, Roosevelt sent a strongly worded memorandum to the National Defense Advisory Commission urging non-discrimination in defence production, but this did not suffice to get the march called off. Agreeing to meet with a presidential delegation led by Eleanor Roosevelt in New York's City Hall on 13 June, Randolph and White were on guard against another betrayal of trust. When the First Lady conveyed her husband's concern that the march would harm the cause of equality by inflaming Southern opposition in Congress, Randolph responded, 'I am certain it will do some good. In fact, it has already done some good, for if you were not concerned about it you wouldn't be here now.' The two Black leaders were adamant that 'jobs not promises' were needed to stop the march.[63]

With time running out, Roosevelt invited Randolph to the White House on the afternoon of 18 June to discuss a way forward. The MOWM leader brought Walter White and two African-American trade unionists, Frank Crosswaith and Layle Lane, to meet the president and top officials involved in defence organization. Cutting off FDR's introductory monologue, Randolph brought the meeting to the business at hand, reiterated what his side wanted and presented a memorandum specifying its terms. These were prohibition of government contracts to firms refusing to hire African Americans, termination of racial discrimination in federal departments, an end to all discrimination and segregation in the armed services and denial of National Labor Relations Act benefits to unions excluding Blacks. To focus minds on his side of the table, the president asked White to confirm Randolph's estimate of 100,000 marchers before asking both groups to repair to another room to thrash out the details of an agreement. None was immediately forthcoming, but FDR appears to have already fixed in his mind what concessions he could make. The next morning, he summoned Joseph L. Rauh, Jr, Lend-Lease chief counsel, to prepare an executive order for Randolph's consideration. It took several drafts to satisfy the MOWM organizer before he agreed on 24 June to call off the demonstration.[64]

Issued the following day, Executive Order (EO) 8802 announced that 'it is the policy of the United States to encourage full participation in the national defense programs by all citizens . . . regardless of race, creed, color, or national origin'. It decreed that government employment and training programmes should comply with non-discriminatory policy, required all future defence contracts to contain non-discrimination provisions and authorized a new Fair Employment Practices Committee (FEPC), located within the Office of Production Management, to investigate discrimination and recommend corrective actions.[65] Largely ignored by the white press, the MOWM was lionized in Black newspapers for wresting the equivalent of a second emancipation proclamation from FDR. For Randolph, the outcome vindicated his belief that collective action by African Americans was the only way to achieve meaningful racial change. 'The Negro', he avowed, 'gets only what he has the power to take . . . we [MOWM] have the masses on the street behind us. And that gives us the power to make conferences produce something.'[66]

More realistically, the real winner in the stand-off, at least in the short term, was FDR. In issuing EO 8802, he secured Black support for his administration's handling of race matters without making major concessions that would offend powerful opponents of racial change in his Cabinet, Congress, the military, business and the labour movement. It made no mention of desegregation of the armed forces, was silent on racial discrimination by trade unions and provided the FEPC with no enforcement powers of its own. In the longer term, however, MOWM had shown the benefits of direct action for the advancement of racial equality. Its linkage of jobs *and* freedom established the agenda of the modern civil-rights movement for the next quarter century and beyond. As Randolph envisaged, this would require the elimination of Jim Crow from all facets of American life, full enforcement of Amendments XIV and XV of the Constitution and the termination of discrimination in public and private employment.[67] If the mass-movement concept that he relied on to pursue these goals did not survive the war years, its eventual revival would be critical to the achievement of the Civil Rights Revolution in the 1960s.

Once America was at war, FDR aimed to subordinate racial issues to the cause of victory. Black leaders, by contrast, considered victory over racism at home to be an equally significant war aim. They were scandalized that the Roosevelt administration slashed FEPC's already small budget when transferring it to the War Manpower Commission in early 1942 and discouraged it from publicizing findings of discrimination against African Americans and Mexican Americans in defence-industry hiring and promotions. The threat of another march on Washington to protest FEPC's limitations induced FDR to issue EO 9346 in May 1943 to grant it independent status within the Executive Office of the President (EOP), more funding for staff and an expanded remit. While FEPC undoubtedly helped to open up employment in industries normally closed to racial minorities in the war years, its achievements fell far short of Black hopes. Wary of offending Southern Democrats, Roosevelt held back from putting the substantive and symbolic power of the presidency behind it. According to FEPC's historian, the White House 'gave it lip service instead of support, used it callously to defuse black protest, and blocked it when political expediency so dictated'.[68]

Despite FEPC's shortcomings, the lure of defence employment encouraged some 700,000 African Americans to leave the South in pursuit of work in the North and the Pacific West. Competition for jobs and housing between whites and Blacks turned a number of cities into powder kegs that eventually exploded in the case of Detroit. Racial rioting on 20–21 June 1943 left twenty-five Blacks and nine whites dead before federal troops were sent to restore order. There were smaller but still significant disturbances that summer in Buffalo, Harlem and Los Angeles. Seeking a presidential statement condemning white violence, Walter White telegraphed Roosevelt, 'No lesser voice than yours can arouse public opinion sufficiently against these deliberately provoked attacks, which are designed to hamper war production, destroy or weaken morale, and to deny minorities, Negroes in particular, the opportunity to participate in the war effort on the same basis as other Americans.' Instead of replying to the NAACP leader, Roosevelt sent a short letter to labour leader Philip Murray, who had called for a government educational campaign to combat racial misconceptions and prejudices. 'I join you and all true Americans', he declared, 'in condemning mob violence, whatever form it takes and whoever its victims.' With Southern Democrats putting the blame for the disturbances on his administration's encouragement of race mixing in the workplace, FDR abstained from further involvement in a matter that would divert his energies from winning the war.[69]

Roosevelt's handling of racial affairs in the Second World War took some of the sheen off his 1930s image as a second emancipator who had improved the socio-economic lot of African Americans. In reality, a common thread linked both phases of his presidency on race, namely willingness to place other priorities ahead of helping Blacks gain equal citizenship. In the 1930s, FDR did little to advance African-American civil rights for fear of provoking Southern Democrats. In wartime, he downplayed them in the interests of national unity required for victory abroad. Significantly he made scant use of the presidential podium to the point of near silence to advocate a better deal for Blacks throughout his tenure. Equally telling, he placed his most substantive wartime contribution to this cause, the FEPC, in his EOP official family, not to support its operations under the wing of his administrative presidency but to constrain its activism and impact. Arguably FDR's most valuable contribution to Black equality in the long term was to nominate in his second and third terms Supreme Court justices dedicated to the protection of personal rights, but the implications of their new jurisprudence for racial issues did not become apparent until after the Second World War.[70]

Roosevelt's trade-offs on racial issues constituted a balancing act that failed to satisfy proponents of either racial change or the status quo. Roy Wilkins of the NAACP later reflected, 'Mr Roosevelt was no friend of the Negro. He wasn't an enemy, but he wasn't a friend.' For Southern Democrats, by contrast, he was altogether too much of a friend to Blacks. In 1936 Senator Carter Glass (D-Virginia) typically adjudged him keener to advance their interests 'than any President except Lincoln . . . [which] has incensed me beyond expression'.[71]

On Roosevelt's death in 1945, bluesman Big Joe Williams recorded a song that encapsulated what ordinary African Americans felt about him. It contained the repeated refrain: 'Oh yes, gonna miss President Roosevelt. Well he's gone, he's gone, but his spirit'll always live on.'[72] Regardless of such plaudits, it is doubtful that FDR could have sustained his balancing act on race had he lived to complete a fourth term. Inadvertently or not, he had encouraged Blacks to look to the presidency for help to uplift them. Though grateful for New Deal assistance because they were accustomed to getting nothing from government, their expectations of support were bound to grow. Roosevelt himself reluctantly recognized racial equality as a legitimate issue for presidential concern in issuing EO 8802, the first executive proclamation of African-American rights since Reconstruction. Black aspirations would also draw sustenance from their growing importance to the Democratic voter coalition in key industrial states as a result of wartime migrations. FDR had promoted racial change within the political limits of his times, thereby establishing precedents for more substantive commitment by his immediate successors. Accordingly, his presidency played its part in helping African Americans on their long march towards equality.

Chief administrator

FDR's institutional presidency

One of the greatest challenges facing Franklin D. Roosevelt in his first two terms as president was to administer the agencies responsible for implementing and giving direction to New Deal initiatives. As public administration expert Luther Gulick observed, once enacted into law, 'the essence of the program is in reality in the gradual unfolding of the plan in actual administration'.[1] FDR initially cobbled together a makeshift oversight system that ultimately fell short in the quest for executive coordination. In March 1936, he established the President's Committee on Administrative Management, better known as the Brownlow Committee (after Chairman Louis Brownlow), to devise a blueprint for more effective executive management. Congressional concern about enhancing presidential power held up enabling legislation for two years until a modified bill was finally enacted as the Executive Reorganization Act of 1939. The consequent establishment of the Executive Office of the President (EOP) resulted in two groundbreaking changes in the character of the modern presidency. First, it marked the rise of the administrative presidency that pursued its policy objectives through programmatic management. The necessary corollary was the institutionalization of the presidency through its development of formal organizational structures to oversee the expansion of administrative operations.[2] Roosevelt took pains to ensure that the new system remained under his control and delivered outcomes he wanted. When war broke out in Europe, he adapted his administrative-institutional presidency to the management of the defence bureaucracy. This laid the foundations for successful execution of commander-in-chief responsibilities when America became a belligerent.

Some of FDR's predecessors had complained about their workload but none carried anything comparable to his. With good cause, Roosevelt told Louis Brownlow that he acted on more matters each day than William McKinley, the last nineteenth-century president, saw in a month. Rudolph Forster, who had served every twentieth-century president hitherto as Executive Clerk, calculated that FDR made at least thirty-five decisions for each one by Calvin Coolidge during his 1920s tenure.[3]

In Roosevelt's first two terms, his White House workday began around eight o'clock in the morning with breakfast in his bedroom during which he ran an eye over half a dozen of the leading newspapers. Early morning conferences with Cabinet members, aides or congressional leaders were a feature of the Hundred Days but rarely happened thereafter, other than in emergencies such as the gold-buying manoeuvres of late 1933.

At nine o'clock, the president usually met with his three staff secretaries and personal secretary to review the day's schedule. Afterwards, he washed, shaved and, with the help of a valet, got dressed, often combining this with a business meeting with one or more government officials. Around half-past ten, he was wheeled down from the second-floor living quarters to the Oval Office in the White House West Wing. FDR usually reserved the rest of the morning for meetings, had a working lunch at his desk (normally poached egg and hash browns) and held more meetings, worked the phones, read official communications and dictated letters in the afternoon. He normally broke off around five o'clock for the 'children's hour' interlude of relaxation and gossip with staff. At half-past five, the end of the official working day, Roosevelt went swimming in the White House pool. After dinner, he often repaired to his private study next to his bedroom for a few hours to hold further meetings if required, peruse a selection of evening newspapers, read official papers and draft his personal correspondence.[4]

This outline barely captures the fullness of FDR's working day. He spent upwards of three hours on the telephone and met with anywhere between ten and fifteen people daily.[5] He usually held two press conferences a week. He was deeply involved in reworking drafts of every major address produced by his team of speechwriters. He also read a vast range of official reports, memoranda and cables. Efforts to impose a one-page limit on the communications flooding through to him in unprecedented volume proved unworkable.[6]

Roosevelt could only sustain this level of engagement by finding time for relaxation. He spent a happy hour many an evening reviewing and adding to a philatelic collection that numbered approximately 25,000 stamps in some forty albums. Another regular diversion was private screenings of movies at the White House with family and invited friends. A great film fan, FDR warmed up for his wartime meeting with Winston Churchill at Casablanca in January 1943 by watching the Warner Bros. classic, *Casablanca*, on New Year's Eve, 1942. Occasional poker evenings with friends and aides offered different entertainment where gossip, cards and drinks mixed by the president were the order of business. Confining himself to two cocktails, usually strong ones because he never measured the ingredients, FDR enjoyed the camaraderie but remained on guard to preserve the dignity of his person and office. While he addressed companions by their first names or nicknames, they had to call him 'Mr President'. As Robert Jackson recalled, 'No person of taste or discernment would take liberties with him, and the few who attempted it were easily put down.'[7]

Of greatest value for recharging presidential batteries were frequent getaways to Hyde Park and Warm Springs and trips that combined official business with recreation further afield. In total FDR spent 92 days away from Washington in 1933, 149 in 1934 and 145 in 1935. Nothing gave him so much enjoyment as going to sea for sailing, fishing or cruising, even though he could not escape being president while on the water. He sent his 'bombshell message' to the London Economic Conference from the USS *Indianapolis* that was ferrying him back to Washington after a yachting vacation along the Maine coast in June 1933. A 14,000-mile vacation cruise aboard the USS *Houston* in July 1934 featured official appearances in Haiti, Puerto Rico, the American Virgin Islands, Colombia, Panama and Hawaii. This trip made FDR only the third president in history after Theodore Roosevelt and Woodrow Wilson to venture abroad when in office. Another sailing holiday along the northeast coast to Nova Scotia ended with him becoming on 31 July 1936 the first president to make a state visit to Canada.

Useful as these distractions were, Roosevelt may have been in less need of them had he employed a different style of administrative leadership. The simplest way to lighten his load would have been to delegate a trusted subordinate to undertake executive coordination. FDR never found the right person in the New Deal years, but even had one been to hand, he would likely have balked at the implicit transfer of any presidential authority. He preferred to share administrative responsibility between subordinates. Exemplifying this approach, he established separate recovery domains by putting Hugh Johnson in charge of the National Recovery Administration (NRA) and Harold Ickes in charge of the Public Works Administration (PWA), and later divided public-works responsibility between Ickes's PWA and Harry Hopkins's Works Progress Administration in 1935. As Arthur Schlesinger, Jr, observed, the essence of Roosevelt's executive method was 'to keep grants of authority incomplete, jurisdictions uncertain, charters overlapping'.[8]

There were several reasons why Roosevelt valued the competitive approach to administrative management. Most importantly, the rivalry between subordinates for the presidential ear provided him with information, advice and understanding of options needed for decision-making. This enabled him to retain power over a rapidly expanding federal bureaucracy populated by ambitious men (and the occasional woman) eager to make policy in their own right. As one official ensnared in FDR's maze of authority remarked, he wanted to 'keep all the reins of government either in his hands or within close reach'.[9] For Roosevelt, administrative competition was also a means of pushing subordinates to greater achievement. 'A little rivalry', he commented, 'keeps everybody going to prove that he is a better fellow than the next man.'[10] It additionally meant that agency chiefs with overlapping responsibilities monitored one another on his behalf, an important factor in keeping disbursement of funds free from major corruption under the New Deal.

On the down side, this mode of management carried huge costs in time spent resolving jurisdictional conflicts between rival lieutenants and smoothing their ruffled feathers. As his Office Secretary Grace Tully commented, 'The maintenance of peace in his official family took up hours and days of Roosevelt's time that could have been used on other matters.'[11] Managing the Hopkins–Ickes feud was especially demanding. Fearing that the president favoured his rival, Ickes made numerous threats of resignation. Hoping that a sea trip would get them to bond, FDR took the pair on his vacation cruise aboard USS *Houston* in October 1935, but their maritime truce did not survive return to land.[12]

Another way of facilitating administrative management would have been to use existing departments to run New Deal operations. Roosevelt preferred to create new ones that devoted their energies wholly to specific tasks and attracted fresh talent with an innovative turn of mind to work in them. When America was at war, he told Secretary of Labor Frances Perkins that he intended to continue this practice. 'We have new and complex problems', he remarked, 'Why not establish a new agency to take over the new duty rather than saddle it on an old institution?'[13] The New Deal agencies had the added advantage of being outside civil service regulations, so he could fill them with liberals not on the civil service list. Despite its benefits for FDR, this system resulted in haphazard administrative growth that increased the problems of coordination. By late 1934, there were nearly 350 interdepartmental committees and subcommittees engaged in this thankless task.[14]

Lacking a formalized management structure, Roosevelt developed a highly personalized mode of addressing his three basic needs as chief administrator: to get information and advice, to make decisions on their basis and to ensure implementation of what he had decided. He constructed what political scientist Matthew Dickinson called 'a jerry-rigged administrative system' based on four components: an expanded Cabinet and staff secretariat, institutional staff agencies, aides borrowed from various federal departments and an assortment of informal advisers, and the White House staff.[15]

FDR's experience underlined the Cabinet's weakness as a collective decision-making body in American government. Many New Deal programmes required interdepartmental collaboration, but department chiefs tended to prioritize their own bureaucratic interests. Weekly Cabinet meetings, held on Friday, rarely discussed significant business. The president asked each member in order of precedence, beginning with Secretary of State Cordell Hull, if they had important matters to report. Their rivalries prevented divulgence of anything more than middling issues for fear of leaks to the press. In his diary, Harold Ickes gave vent to his frustrations at the absence of anything resembling Cabinet government: 'The cold fact is that on important matters we are seldom called upon for advice. . . . The President makes all of his own decisions.'[16] This was par for the handful of previous strong presidents. Like them, FDR preferred to deal with Cabinet secretaries individually on matters of relevance to their departments. The ones he worked with closely were the ones he trusted most – Ickes, Henry Morgenthau (Treasury), Frances Perkins, Henry Wallace (Agriculture) and Homer Cummings (Justice) – but they were far from being a happy band because of mutual jealousies. Significantly, none considered themselves indispensable to FDR. As Morgenthau remarked, 'He never let anybody round him have complete assurance that he would have the job tomorrow.'[17]

Despite creating an administrative system suited to his talent, temperament and taste, Roosevelt was aware of its shortcomings. Seeking a remedy, in July 1933 he created a temporary Executive Council, whose twenty-four members included the ten Cabinet secretaries, the Bureau of the Budget (BoB) director, the heads of nine emergency agencies and the president himself. Intended to be an enlarged Cabinet, this body never functioned effectively because it was too big, lacked sufficient staff to enforce its decisions and suffered from FDR's refusal to base meetings on a formal agenda.[18] In October 1933, Roosevelt created the ten-member National Emergency Council (NEC) to function as the Executive Council secretariat. Its role, he told the first meeting, was to be 'a sort of alter ego . . . going around and acting as my legs and ears and eyes and making certain – what could be called suggestions'.[19] Within this remit, it had three main purposes: to improve coordination of New Deal programmes at state level, to screen legislative proposals emanating from federal departments and agencies, and to gather and disseminate information about New Deal operations. Significantly, the new body had no decision-making capacity, a prerogative the president retained wholly for himself.[20]

Another administrative makeover in October 1934 consolidated the two groups into a 34-member super-committee that retained the National Emergency Council moniker. Roosevelt appointed NRA counsel Donald Richberg as executive director with authority to make any rule necessary to enhance programme coordination. The press's habit of referring to Richberg as Assistant President ensured that his tenure would be brief. When *The New York Times* ran a front-page story about his elevated status, an angry FDR told Press Secretary Steve Early, 'Get hold of [Arthur] Krock and tell him . . . that this kind of thing is not only a lie but that it is a deception and a fraud on the public.'[21] Suspecting Richberg of wanting a government reorganization that brought various New Deal agencies under his personal control, Harold Ickes remarked after the revamped NEC's first meeting, 'He looked like the cat that had swallowed the canary.'[22] Roosevelt's refusal to support him in disputes with department and agency heads caused Richberg to quit in disillusion at the end of 1934. The NEC staggered on under new leadership but never proved an effective instrument for executive coordination owing to Roosevelt's reluctance to delegate it authority. Despite surviving in much slimmed-down form until the EOP's creation, it ceased being a high-level forum in April 1936.[23]

The ultimate answer to FDR's coordination needs, the Bureau of the Budget was incapable of fulfilling this mission until overhauled in 1939. Created by the Budget and Accounting Act of 1921, this provided expert staff resources to develop the president's annual budget plan for submission to Congress, but it was under-resourced even for this task and its location within the Treasury kept it outside the president's institutional family. Like his 1920s predecessors, FDR initially used BoB as a spending watchdog to ensure economy in government. He told journalists that the job of its director, Lewis Douglas, 'is to prevent the Government from spending just as hard as he can. . . . Somewhere between his efforts to spend nothing . . . and the point of view of the people who want to spend ten billion additional on public works, we will get somewhere.'[24] Shortly afterwards, Roosevelt issued Executive Order 6548 requiring BoB approval for obligation of emergency funds, but revoked this three days later when heads of spending departments rebelled at being put under its penny-pinching control.[25] Before long, FDR's own shift from economizer to spender caused the agency's once high-flying boss to quit the administration.

FDR also developed an informal coterie of aides and advisers to help him operate as chief administrator. Some he borrowed from other government bodies for extended sabbaticals, others he enlisted for specific tasks of shorter duration, transfers that disguised the costs of his White House operations as the personnel involved continued to be paid by their host departments. Accordingly, individuals were far more important than titles in his administration. During the first Hundred Days, FDR worked closely with members of the Brain Trust election team whom he had placed in various departments. As one remarked, 'Scattered throughout the service there are numbers of us in important positions to influence policy.'[26] Nominally Assistant Secretary of State, Raymond Moley helped to devise the banking and stock-market initiatives of 1933. Though farm matters engaged much of Rexford Tugwell's energies as Assistant Secretary of Agriculture, a roving brief allowed him to advise FDR on issues pertaining to industrial recovery. Roosevelt later made use of the bill-drafting talents of Tommy

Corcoran and Ben Cohen, who held apparently lowly positions as aides respectively in the Reconstruction Finance Corporation and the Public Works Administration.[27]

Roosevelt's informal assistants hunted information for him, proffered advice on his options, contributed to speechwriting, served as legislative lobbyists and acted as all-purpose troubleshooters. A political dynamo in all these activities, Corcoran became a quintessential New Dealer while in his thirties.[28] He developed a personal network of younger lawyers and economists whom he recruited to serve in the new agencies. As one recalled, 'Tom would see a job that needed to be done and he'd get one of us and say, "How'd you like to try this?"'[29] A five-storey, red-brick residence at 3238 R Street, Georgetown, rented by Corcoran and Cohen, became their headquarters. Once a summer White House for Ulysses S. Grant, it became an adjunct to FDR's White House in the 1930s. The law-drafting, speechwriting, wire-pulling and strategizing undertaken there made it one of the New Deal's engine rooms. In time, it became known as 'the little red house' after Congressman Fred Britten (R-Illinois) identified it on the House of Representatives floor on 20 April 1934 as the venue of 'meetings which promote the communistic legislation we all talk about in the cloakrooms'.[30]

Roosevelt had no compunctions about freezing out members of his informal network once they were no longer useful to his needs. This was Raymond Moley's fate after falling out of sympathy with the president's economic policies in 1933. New Dealers who fell afoul of Congress or the press could not expect his public support. In December 1936 FDR accepted Rexford Tugwell's resignation as Resettlement Administration director because conservative attacks on him as 'Rex the Red' threatened to taint the New Deal as socialistic. Corcoran fell to earth for making so many enemies in Congress through his arm-twisting operations to win votes for FDR's court-packing plan in 1937 and his role in the midterm 'purge' of 1938. Accordingly, he was expendable when Roosevelt's change of priorities to foreign policy put a premium on gaining conservative Democratic support for internationalist initiatives. Passed over for a senior government post, Corcoran resigned in 1941 and reinvented himself as a lawyer-lobbyist, a role in which he made himself very rich.[31]

Long-term confidantes and associates, used by FDR to help in speechwriting, perform research tasks and provide counsel, formed another layer in his informal advisory network. They included Samuel Rosenman, his favourite speechwriter whom he had appointed a New York state judge, businessman Bernard Baruch who advised on the early New Deal and presidential appointments to the agencies it created and Harvard law professor Felix Frankfurter whose factotum role encompassed personnel advice, policy counsel, occasional speechwriting and constitutional interpretation. According to Rosenman, the latter was 'a reliable source of ideas and language' in support of the New Deal.[32] Members of Corcoran's network liked to think of themselves as the 'Happy Hot Dogs' since many of them were Frankfurter's former students. There were times, however, when Frankfurter overstepped in seeking to influence FDR. In 1935 he urged the president to appoint a new assistant to deal with the plethora of business that reached his desk. 'Fat reports are submitted to you without any precis, without any intellectual traffic directions', he declared. 'Equally intolerable is that you should not have at your disposal the kind of preliminary sifting of legislative proposals that you had when you were Governor of New York.'[33] Roosevelt had no interest in creating a post that would limit his decision-making options by determining what reached his desk and how it should be acted upon.

The most visible member of FDR's advisory network was the First Lady. Eleanor Roosevelt had his ear if not always his agreement on issues of concern to her. The president sent her on fact-finding missions about the New Deal's grassroots impact. She was also his bridge to various groups in the New Deal coalition, notably women, African Americans, youth and liberals. FDR additionally entrusted her with trouble-shooting missions within the Democratic Party, notably delegating her to speak to the 1940 national convention that was in turmoil over Henry Wallace's nomination as his running mate. According to columnist Raymond Clapper, Eleanor Roosevelt became 'a Cabinet Minister without portfolio – the most influential woman of our times'.[34] The second part of that statement was certainly true, the first was not.

ER could only exercise leadership within the administration in limited ways. Her partnership with the president was ambiguous, complex and inconsistent in its influence. FDR could not match her idealism because he had to operate in the grey world of political compromise. In the 1932 campaign, Brain Trusters feared that her assertive positions on some issues would overshadow his avoidance of specific commitments. Rexford Tugwell recalled that some of his colleagues saw it as their job 'to get the pants off Eleanor and onto Frank'.[35] As president, FDR valued his wife less as an adviser, owing to his not infrequent doubts about her judgement, than as field reporter. He had utter faith in the observations and information she brought back from her travels about the country. He often reported her commentaries to the Cabinet and the NEC. According to Grace Tully, 'It was not unusual to hear him predicate an entire line of reasoning upon a statement that "my Missus told me so and so."'[36]

Perhaps there was only one person more important to FDR as an intelligence-gatherer – himself. He was a voracious reader of government reports on a wide range of issues. He required regular analyses of mail flooding into the White House from ordinary Americans to gauge the success of New Deal programmes. Many of the meetings and telephone calls that were such an important part of his White House routine had the same purpose. FDR also quizzed departmental and agency subordinates without their boss's knowledge about programmatic progress in their domain. Harold Ickes, for one, complained about his habit of 'calling in members of my staff for consultation on Department matters, without consulting me or advising me'.[37]

The competition Roosevelt fostered between aides was elemental in his intelligence operations. He often put two people to work on the same task without telling them that he had done so. 'He would call you in', one unnamed aide (almost certainly James Rowe) later told political scientist Richard Neustadt,

> he'd ask you to get the story on some complicated business, and you'd come back after a couple of days of hard labor and present the juicy morsel you'd uncovered under a stone somewhere and *then* you'd find out he knew all about it, along with something else you *didn't* know. Where he got his information from, he wouldn't mention, usually, but after he had done this to you once or twice you got damn careful about *your* information.

According to Rowe, 'He delighted in letting you know that he knew something about the problem that you didn't.'[38]

The White House staff who assisted FDR in carrying out his day-to-day business constituted the final part of his administrative set-up. Numbering between forty and fifty, they included stenographers, clerical assistants and the Executive Clerk's staff. At the apex of the staff structure were three senior aides: chief secretary Louis Howe functioned as minister without portfolio and political adviser, Stephen Early ran press relations, and Marvin McIntyre handled appointments. Having been in Roosevelt's orbit for so long – Howe hooked up with him in 1912, the other two in the 1920 vice-presidential campaign – their loyalties were to him personally rather than to the New Deal. Always frail, Howe's health steadily deteriorated from 1934 until his death in April 1936. For Eleanor Roosevelt, his passing removed the only aide fearless enough to tell the president to his face that he was committing a political error.[39] To replace Howe, Roosevelt installed his oldest son James as Secretary to the President in July 1937 over the First Lady's objections that he would become a lightning rod for political attacks. The demands of acting as his father's liaison to various executive agencies combined with critical press scrutiny wore down his health. In November 1938, he resigned after requiring an operation for severe stomach ulcers. FDR promoted his military aide, Colonel Edwin 'Pa' Watson, to fill the third secretary's position and promoted him to brigadier general for good measure.

Two female secretaries who served Roosevelt when New York governor were indispensable to his White House operations. Closer to him than any other aide, Marguerite 'Missy' LeHand, officially designated his personal secretary, performed many of the functions later associated with a White House chief of staff.[40] She acted as a political sounding board, advised on personnel matters and supervised the presidential schedule. Utterly devoted to Roosevelt, LeHand was sensitive to his moods, ensured that he had adequate relaxation and enjoyed his absolute confidence. Despite speculation that they had a long-standing romantic relationship, there is no credible evidence of this. LeHand was something of a surrogate wife to FDR in the emotional rather than sexual sense. The First Lady never resented this because Missy's attentions to her husband enabled her to lead an independent life. Unfortunately LeHand's personal insecurities made her fearful of losing her place in FDR's inner circle, with the consequence that she made increasing demands for his emotional solicitude by the start of the third term. She also lost the ability to entertain and relax him because opioids taken for insomnia left her weary and irritable. When a stroke forced LeHand's retirement in June 1941, many of her duties were taken over by Grace Tully, hitherto FDR's office secretary, who was never as personally close to him.

FDR's personalized system worked well with regard to his information, advice, and decision-making needs, but not for administrative oversight and coordination. Through it, he developed an unrivalled understanding of the executive branch of government. Alben Barkley, a long-standing Washington insider, later commented, 'No President has ever surpassed him in personal knowledge of every department.'[41] Roosevelt welcomed all the advice he could get in order to weigh up his options. He was prepared to tolerate dissenting opinion up to the point that he reached his decision. Thereafter he expected every subordinate to abide by it, even if they had doubts about its wisdom. Not one to worry about a misstep, he once told Frances Perkins, 'We have to do the best we know how to do in the moment. . . . If it does not turn out right, we can modify it as we go along.'[42]

As FDR himself recognized, his mode of executive operation resulted in administrative inefficiency that needed resolution. Worried that his management shortcomings would become an issue in the 1936 election campaign, he was relieved that the Republicans failed to exploit them. As polling day approached, he joked with aides that had he been the Republican presidential candidate, 'I would say "I am for social security, work relief, etc., etc. But the Democrats cannot be entrusted with the administration of these fine ideals." I would cite chapter and verse on WPA inefficiency – and there's plenty of it – as there is bound to be in such a vast, emergency programme.' He added, 'The more I think about it, the more I think I could lick myself.'[43]

By then, Roosevelt had taken steps to remedy matters in readiness for his second term. On 22 March 1936 he announced the establishment of a Committee on Administrative Management to recommend ways of enhancing executive capacity. The panel consisted of three eminent scholars of public administration, Louis Brownlow as chair, Charles Merriam and Luther Gulick, served by a staff of twenty-seven. The trio shared the conviction that a strong presidency was essential for the efficiency of American democracy at a time of growing pessimism in Europe that dictatorships were alone capable of effective leadership. As Brownlow later put it, 'It was our belief that the Presidency of the United States was the institution behind which democrats might rally to repel the enemy. And, to that end, it was not only desirable but absolutely necessary that the President be better equipped for his tremendous task.'[44] The committee did not have a free hand in its work. FDR insisted that it consider a broad executive reorganization rather than focus solely on improving the White House staff system, as the principals had initially envisaged. He met with them on 20 February, a month before their formal appointment, to define their agenda and assure himself of editorial control over the final report. This did not mean that he dictated its recommendations, only that he did not leave them to chance.[45]

After conducting interviews and gathering data over a six-month period, the Brownlow Committee inclined towards the establishment of a two-part division of executive staff based on managerial 'arms' and a coordinating 'brain'. The former would take responsibility for budgetary, personnel and policy planning, the latter for coordinating executive management on the president's behalf. The idea for the 'brain' drew on the model of the British Cabinet secretariat, a corps of permanent government officials headed by a career civil servant that provided administrative support for the prime minister's meetings with his ministers. The limited possibilities for Cabinet government in America prompted a rethink that allocated responsibility for policy planning and coordination to the Bureau of the Budget and staff coordination to a secretariat of five assistants headed by an executive secretary, who would report directly to the president.[46]

Always reluctant to endow executive power in anyone else, FDR scuppered the executive-secretary idea when appraised of it. On 14 November 1936, at his first formal meeting with the Brownlow Committee, he agreed on a compromise whereby one executive assistant would undertake staff coordination without any formal designation of this responsibility.[47] In practice, he would never appoint anyone to manage staff on his behalf, a job he regarded exclusively his own. He wanted his assistants to function as his eyes, ears and voice to gather and transmit information concerning executive-branch operations. In other words, their role was not to formulate policy but to facilitate his decision-making. In limiting presidential assistants to six in total, the Brownlow Committee met FDR's insistence on retaining the prerogative to manage them himself.

Unveiled on 10 January 1937, the final report recommended an institutional framework that established 'a responsible and effective chief executive as the centre of energy, direction and administrative management' within the nation's government. It called for the presidency to be brought abreast of modern advances in administrative management practices to meet the challenges 'of making good the popular will in a people's government'. Where else, it asked, could there be found 'an executive . . . upon whom so much petty work is thrown? Or who is forced to see so many persons on unrelated matters and to make so many decision on what may be, because of the very press of work, incomplete information?' In summing up, it avowed, 'There is but one grand purpose, namely to make democracy work today in our national government. . . . It is for this purpose that the government needs thoroughly modern tools of management.'[48]

The Brownlow Committee Report did more to structure the American presidency as an institution than anything since the political and administrative precedents set by George Washington. It gave modern voice to the ideas espoused by Alexander Hamilton in *Federalist #70* that energy in the executive, 'a leading character in the definition of good government', required its possession of 'firstly, unity; secondly, duration; thirdly, an adequate provision for its support; fourthly, competent powers'.[49] In contrast to the executive-efficiency commissions appointed by Theodore Roosevelt and William Taft, the Brownlow Committee Report placed the president at the heart of the drive for modernization of bureaucratic procedures through enhancing his managerial role. Its most enduring phrase, 'the President needs help', perfectly expressed the need to build a modern presidency capable of meeting the growing needs of the administrative state.[50]

To improve the president's executive capacity, the report made recommendations within five broad categories: expansion of the White House staff; strengthening managerial agencies dealing with budgeting, personnel and planning and placing them under presidential control; expansion and reorganization of the civil service merit system to make a career in public service more attractive to talented individuals; overhaul of the executive branch and the transfer of more than one hundred independent agencies, which threatened to become a 'headless fourth branch of government', into the current Cabinet departments and two new ones, Social Welfare and Public Works; and extensive revision of the fiscal system in light of best public and private practice with regard to financial record-keeping, audit and executive accountability to Congress.[51]

With Brownlow Committee members and senior staff in attendance, FDR gave an extended briefing on the report to seven of the top Democrats in Congress at the White House on the afternoon of Sunday, 10 January. There is no formal transcript of what was said, but the notes taken by Brownlow aide Herbert Emmerich indicated that the exchanges were robust. Afterwards FDR remarked to Brownlow, 'This was quite a little package to give them. . . . Every time they recovered from a blow, I socked them under the jaw with another.'[52] The following morning, with the entire Cabinet present, he shared the Brownlow proposals with journalists in a two-hour press conference. This was another bravura performance that demonstrated FDR's grasp of modern public administration principles. It was soon evident, however, that critics regarded reorganization as a ploy to enhance presidential power under cover of managerial efficiency.

Seeking to assuage this concern, FDR told Congress, 'What I am placing before you is the request not for more power, but for the tools of management and the authority to distribute the work so that the President can effectively discharge those powers which the Constitution now places upon him.'[53] Despite this assertion of administrative need, the unveiling of the court-packing plan a few weeks later strengthened suspicions that he was engaged in a wide-ranging project to expand presidential power beyond anything intended by the Constitution. Unwilling to consider both measures in the same session, Congress shelved consideration of executive reorganization until 1938.

When finally taken up, the proposal aroused even greater opposition than the judiciary bill. The furore showed that FDR was on weak ground when seeking institutional reforms that lacked overt constituencies in the manner of his socio-economic programmes. Funded by Republican media mogul Frank Gannett, the Committee to Uphold Constitutional Government paid for newspaper advertising and mail campaigns against the so-called dictator's bill. For one of its publicity stunts, some 150 horsemen dressed as Paul Revere and carrying banners proclaiming 'NO ONE MAN RULE' cantered down Washington's Pennsylvania Avenue. Meanwhile, the demagogic radio priest, Father Charles Coughlin, prompted supporters to deluge Congress with 300,000 telegrams of protest. This campaign could not prevent the Senate from approving the bill by a small majority but had more effect on the House of Representatives, where a large majority voted to recommit it to committee.[54]

In April 1939, executive reorganization got over the line at the third time of trying, albeit in a much modified form. The legislation required the president to submit reorganization plans for congressional approval rather than enjoy carte blanche to make changes. It also decreed that new Cabinet-level departments could only be created through statute rather than executive order. It further ruled that the president could not unilaterally abolish any of the ten Cabinet departments or any sub-departments in a specified list of twenty-one such bodies. The original provisions giving the president greater authority over the civil service were removed, but he was empowered to appoint six administrative assistants at annual salaries of $10,000. Congress would likely have approved their establishment without the other elements of reorganization two years earlier, something unacceptable to FDR. 'I would hardly know what to do with six Executive Assistants', he told Senator James Byrnes (D-South Carolina), 'if I do not have any authority to put the Government as a whole on a business-like basis. It is a little like giving the President the envelope of the letter without any letter in it!'[55]

On Louis Brownlow's advice, FDR appointed Harold Smith, a professional administrator with a strong record of service in Michigan state government, as Bureau of the Budget director. Though a registered Republican, he was essentially a non-partisan wholly committed to the Brownlow ethos that the presidency was the linchpin of democratic governance in modern America. Like other progressive-minded public administration experts, he regarded the separation of powers as a hindrance to efficient government that only a president supported by administrative experts could bridge. Smith quickly gained FDR's confidence through his neutral competence in overseeing the managerial operations of the executive branch. 'I know of no one whose judgement and integrity and downright common sense the President trusted more completely', Robert Sherwood later remarked.[56]

In consultation with Roosevelt, Smith prepared Reorganization Plans No 1 and 2, respectively sent to Congress on 25 April and 9 May and rapidly approved. Their imaginative use of the seemingly limited powers granted by the enabling legislation confounded the critics who had wanted to contain the president's management authority. The first plan established the Executive Office of the President with the BoB, transferred from the Treasury, as its nerve centre. As a corollary, it created the White House Office (WHO) as the location for the president's personal staff. Finally, it circumvented the need for congressional approval of new Cabinet departments through establishment of the Federal Security Agency, the Federal Works Agency and the Federal Loan Agency, which incorporated a host of hitherto independent agencies under their respective purviews. Thus, for example, the Social Security Board, the National Youth Administration and the Civilian Conservation Corps were placed in the Federal Security Agency, PWA and WPA went into the Federal Works Agency, and the Reconstruction Finance Corporation and the Federal Housing Administration went to the Federal Loan Agency.

Of all the changes, the transfer of BoB into the EOP and the expansion of its resources proved most beneficial for Roosevelt's executive management. The tenfold increase in agency personnel from fifty to five hundred in the next five years enabled Smith to populate it with an army of managerial, financial and legal experts. In addition to scrutinizing every proposal submitted to Congress, analysing every piece of legislation enacted and drafting executive orders, the revamped BoB kept Roosevelt informed of departmental and agency progress with respect to operations they proposed, initiated and managed. As a consequence Smith became the single most important civilian administrator in wartime Washington. As he recognized, the relationship between the president as a political actor and the management arms of his office would be 'worked out in fractions, a kind of adjustment of the harness as the teams pull together'. If FDR did not always follow BoB advice, Smith made sure that he heard it. He was in harmony with the Brownlow ideal that the presidency would benefit in the long term from having a relatively non-partisan, career-based staff of professionals providing neutral managerial competence in an administratively separate capacity from the White House.[57]

Although the White House Office would grow in size and significance under FDR's successors, its importance for FDR was secondary to BoB's expanded role. Under him, it consisted of three sections: the three staff secretaries and their assistants, the Executive Clerk's office and the six presidential assistants mandated by the Executive Reorganization Act. Its budgeted personnel annually averaged just short of fifty from 1940 through 1945 and detailees borrowed from elsewhere in the executive possibly averaged just short of two hundred. Roosevelt had never wanted more than six new assistants, a number small enough for him to oversee. He was scrupulous in ensuring that they engaged solely in staff activities that supported his administrative needs and communicated these to the myriad federal agencies. He left them in no doubt about who was boss. When persisting to argue against a course of action decreed by FDR, James Rowe received a sharp put-down: 'No, Jim, we're going to do it my way and I'll tell you why. The American people may have made a mistake, but they elected me President, not you.' Roosevelt's assistants were presidential 'gofers' occupied in information and liaison operations, whereas their postwar successors increasingly acquired decision-making responsibilities in their own right. 'Now I want you to be a bird dog. I want you to sniff around all over town', Rowe recalled FDR telling him.[58] Accommodated in the State–Navy–War Building (later renamed the Executive Office Building) rather than the White House, FDR's assistants stayed in the background, issued no public statements of their own and generally lived up to the Brownlow Report's requirement that they should display 'a passion for anonymity'. In general, they formed, in Robert Sherwood's words, 'an anonymous and shifting group', most of whose members served two years in post before moving on to other jobs in government.[59]

The outbreak of war in Europe hastened the process of administrative change to meet the emergency. On 8 September 1939 FDR issued EO 8248 reorganizing the EOP into six divisions: the WHO, the BoB, the National Resources Planning Board, the Liaison Office for Personnel Management, the Office of Government Reports and, finally, 'in the event of a national emergency, or threat of a national emergency, such office for emergency management as the President shall determine'.[60] On the same day Roosevelt issued a proclamation of limited national emergency that mandated enforcement of American neutrality and enhancement of national defence. In fulfilment of the second obligation, he set about creating new agencies to oversee the expansion of military production, most of whom reported directly to him. Endowing them with weak or overlapping authority ensured their jurisdictional disputes went to him for resolution. Accordingly, FDR was the one pulling the strings to build the organizational base for putting the American economy on a war footing.

Wary of arousing isolationist ire, Roosevelt proceeded cautiously at first in seeking the voluntary cooperation of business in the conversion of production from civilian to military purposes. The startling success of the German blitzkrieg in spring 1940 prompted the issue of an unpublicized administrative order on 25 May activating the Office for Emergency Management (OEM) as authorized under EO 8248. This became the umbrella organization that enabled FDR to develop what Harold Smith called 'a new government within a government'.[61] Under its ambit he could create, modify and, if need be, discard defence and war agencies without referral to Congress unless new appropriations were needed. In many instances, he could also transfer funds and personnel between agencies under the discretionary power granted him amid the national emergency.

The OEM's creation emerged out of complex presidential manoeuvres over a period of some ten months.[62] On 9 August 1939, Roosevelt established a civilian-based War Resources Board (WRB), composed mainly of business leaders, to advise him on how best to mobilize the nation's economic resources for defence. In line with the M-Day

Plan, drawn up by Army and Navy planners, the Department of War recommended the appointment of a top industrialist as defence 'czar' to oversee conversion to military production. Determined not to empower an executive rival, particularly one from the anti-New Deal corporate class, Roosevelt disbanded the WRB in November and shelved its proposals. Henceforth he looked to manage economic mobilization himself through the EOP. As he told Brownlow, 'If we are really headed for trouble, I will at least be my own boss and will not be compelled to turn over the presidency of the United States to some other man who . . . would never be elected by the people.'[63]

When the European war swung in Germany's favour, Roosevelt established a seven-member National Defense Advisory Commission (NDAC), composed of businessmen and New Dealers, which became part of the new Office of Emergency Management. Asked who was in charge of this body when meeting with it on 30 May 1940, the president responded 'he guessed he was'.[64] Even so, he stopped short of giving NDAC policy-making authority, with the consequence that its efforts to administer economic mobilization ran into bureaucratic resistance from Army and Navy procurement agencies. FDR found himself devoting considerable energy to resolving their jurisdictional disputes that distracted from the primary task of ensuring that the economy's productive capacity kept up with expanding defence needs. The obligation to provide massive resources to Britain under the auspices of Lend-Lease led to another bureaucratic shake-up with the establishment of the Office of Production Management (OPM) within the OEM in early 1941. Though vested with more explicit authority to oversee industrial mobilization than NDAC, the new body had two significant weaknesses. First, it could not determine defence requirements or control the provision of contracts to business, which remained under Army and Navy jurisdiction. Furthermore, Roosevelt's reluctance to create a defence 'czar' induced him to divide executive authority within OPM between General Motors president William Knudsen and labour leader Sidney Hillman. He defended this arrangement as necessary to balance the interests of business and workers in the agency, but the primary purpose was to ensure that he became the ultimate arbiter of their disputes.[65]

OPM's shortcomings became increasingly manifest as production bottlenecks, shortages of civilian goods and inflation grew worse in the summer of 1941. In response, Roosevelt issued an executive order on 28 August creating yet another new agency, the Supply Priorities and Allocations Board (SPAB). This was empowered to determine requirements for defence and civilian production and provide policy directives to guide OPM's operational responsibility for defence mobilization. True to form, Roosevelt stopped short of making it all-powerful by limiting its authority to allocation of supplies necessary for defence production. Issuance of contracts to business and the disbursement of finished products remained the prerogative of the president in consultation with the military services. The new system was an improvement but problems of administrative coordination continued to hamper the mobilization effort.[66] In reality Roosevelt was between a rock and a hard place: isolationists increasingly accused him of speeding up economic mobilization with a view to getting America into the war, while the opposing camp demanded a defence czar to expedite the production process. The surprise Japanese attack on Pearl Harbor rescued him from having to manoeuvre between them. Once America was at war, the economic challenge facing Roosevelt was how to unleash the full potential of the arsenal of democracy.

While America was still neutral, FDR worked on developing a military leadership structure that would best serve his commander-in-chief role. In an early demonstration that he took this responsibility seriously, he had faced down the nation's foremost soldier, Army Chief of Staff Douglas MacArthur, over cuts in the service budget at a White House meeting in May 1933. Accustomed to overawing civilian leaders, MacArthur warned FDR that he would be held responsible for losing America's next war but was told in no uncertain terms, 'You must not talk that way to the President!' The episode showed that Roosevelt did not feel any inferiority in the presence of top brass. As Robert Jackson observed, he was aware that politics and economics had a large part alongside 'seamanship and generalship' in ensuring America's security and often asserted that 'war is too important a matter to be left to the generals'.[67]

As the European crisis intensified in the spring of 1939, FDR decided to appoint new commanders to put America's armed services on a strong defence footing. Passing over more senior officers, he selected Brigadier General George Marshall as Army Chief of Staff and Rear Admiral Harold Stark as Chief of Naval Operations. Both men had a reputation for stating their mind, even to superiors, a quality valued by FDR. Attending a White House military-planning conference in his capacity as Army Deputy Chief of Staff on 14 November 1938, Marshall was the lone voice of scepticism about Roosevelt's proposal to ask Congress for funds to build 10,000 airplanes without also requiring appropriations for air crews to fly them and enhanced infrastructure such as airfields to support them. The other officers present assumed that this dissent meant the end of his career in Washington, but it impressed the president. When interviewed by FDR for the Army's top job, Marshall pointedly insisted on 'the right to say what I think and it would often be unpleasing'.[68] For Roosevelt, this was a price worth paying for his military sagacity, strategic skills and organizational talent.

Stark's qualities of independence and decisiveness had come to FDR's attention when he was Assistant Secretary of the Navy during the First World War. On promoting him to the top job in the service, the president declared, '[Y]ou and I talk the same language.' Stark's value was manifest in his authorship in October 1940 of the strategic plan that outlined the course America would eventually follow on entering the Second World War. To answer its central question, 'Where should we fight the war, and for what objectives?', he outlined four possible options, Plans A, B, C and D, coming down heavily in favour of the last. Plan Dog, as it became known, tied America's fate with Britain's, advocated an Atlantic-first strategy and envisaged a full-scale US land offensive as ultimately necessary to defeat Germany. Roosevelt did not give this blueprint formal approval because he was unwilling to limit his options in a still uncertain situation with regard to Britain's survival. Nevertheless, he indicated tacit acceptance by directing the War, Navy and State Departments to review and refine it. Plan Dog's establishment of a coherent framework for military operations made it the most important statement of American strategy in the Second World War.[69]

FDR's relations with his two main military commanders underwent stresses while America was neutral without ever breaking. Marshall repeatedly expressed concern at the slow defence build-up, urging the president to demand larger appropriations from

Congress to build up the Army that was some 30,000 below its authorized strength of 210,000. He also queried FDR's wisdom in shipping much of America's fighter aircraft production to Britain, thereby denuding the homeland of air power and running the risk that the planes would fall into Germany's hands if the British were defeated. Stark, too, was initially unhappy with the destroyers-for-bases deal that FDR negotiated with Britain in September 1940 despite America's own need for warships.[70]

As with New Deal aides, FDR tolerated dissent from military men during policy debates but expected support for his decisions once taken. While Marshall and Stark had a fine sense of how far they could press their views, some colleagues lacked the same judgement. Meeting with FDR in the White House on 7 October 1940, Admiral James Richardson, commander of the Pacific fleet based at Pearl Harbor, issued a trenchant warning that it should be returned to safe haven on the West Coast while the entire Navy underwent a programme of expansion to ready it for a possible two-ocean war. When informed that election-year realities made this impossible, he effectively voiced lack of confidence in his commander-in-chief. The next day, FDR tersely informed Stark, 'I want Richardson relieved.'[71]

As well as seeking the best service leaders, Roosevelt took steps to improve the civilian leadership of the military departments when the European war reached crisis point in June 1940. Secretary of War Harry Woodring and Secretary of the Navy Charles Edison were the two principal voices of isolationism in the Cabinet. Wary of dismissing them for fear of political backlash, FDR counterbalanced Woodring by appointing Louis Johnson, an advocate of military preparedness, as Assistant Secretary of War in 1937, but their poisonous relationship ill served the Army's cause.[72] Owing to his personal interest in the service, FDR had long acted as de facto Secretary of the Navy, but the de jure one became an irritant in opposing efforts to re-supply Britain with war materials lost in the Dunkirk evacuation. At the Cabinet meeting of 9 June, Edison reported the Navy judge–advocate-general's opinion that the transaction was illegal, only to be told by the president to send the misinformed 'sea lawyer' away on vacation and to dispense the same treatment to any dissenting attorney in his department. When Edison kept repeating his objections, an exasperated Roosevelt told him 'to forget it and do what I told you to do.'[73] Jumping before he was pushed, Edison quit office on 20 June to run for New Jersey governor. Determined to have a supportive Cabinet amid the worsening international situation, Roosevelt gave Woodring his marching orders on the same day, making no pretence that this was anything but an outright sacking.

In a bold stroke, FDR appointed two Republican internationalists in their place. Henry Stimson became Secretary of War, a post he had held in William Taft's administration, and Frank Knox, GOP vice-presidential nominee in 1936, became Secretary of the Navy. Both were vigorous administrators of their departments, consistently supported defence expansion and were strong supporters of aid to Britain but remained subordinate to Roosevelt as commander-in-chief. A secret executive order issued on 5 July 1939 had removed the Secretary of War and the Secretary of the Navy as decision-makers within the military chain of command. It also transferred the Joint Army-Navy Board and a number of other military bodies into the EOP.[74] These monumental administrative changes enabled FDR to transform the Joint

Board, hitherto a consultative body created in the early twentieth century to improve inter-service cooperation, into an instrument of military coordination and execution that reported directly to him. According to historian Eric Larrabee, it became 'the keystone in the structure of authority that made the president the commander-in-chief in fact as well as name'. Further reorganizations that enlarged the strategic role of the service chiefs following America's entry into the war enhanced the president's military leadership prerogatives. To make sure that Stimson knew where he stood in the decision-making hierarchy, FDR wrote him, 'I wish to make it very clear that the Commander-in-Chief exercises his command function in relation to strategy, tactics and operations directly through the Chief of Staff. You, as Secretary of War, apart from your administrative responsibilities, would, of course, advise on military matters.'[75]

As well as embedding his commander-in-chief prerogatives within a formal structure of decision-making, FDR made use of informal channels to grease the wheels of his administrative operations pertaining to defence. No one was more important to him in this regard than Harry Hopkins. Despite lacking any experience in international affairs, this New Deal luminary became an essential factotum whose job encompassed being defence adviser, presidential diplomat and Lend-Lease administrator. According to Harold Smith, 'Hopkins' sole job was to see everything from the President's point of view. He was bound by no preconceived notions, no legal inhibitions and he certainly had absolutely no respect for traditions.'[76]

Ill health had prevented Hopkins achieving much as Commerce Secretary, a position from which he resigned in September 1940. To many Washington observers, this marked the end of his time in the political sun, but he had a remarkable second coming. A successful operation to remove stomach cancer in 1937 had left him permanently debilitated because the procedure had likely refashioned his digestive system in a way that prevented it from absorbing nutrients. While another operation in 1939 saved him from dying in effect of starvation, medical opinion held out little hope for anything but short-term survival. To his doctors' surprise, he lasted another seven years, kept alive by nutrient injections, cigarettes and the determination to play a part in the defeat of Nazi Germany.

Dining at the White House one evening in May 1940, Hopkins looked so ill that FDR urged him to stay the night, a sojourn that lasted until December 1943, when he moved into a Georgetown home on the insistence of his new wife. Accordingly, he was a perennial presence in high-level meetings where Roosevelt discussed strategic options with military and diplomatic officials during the crises of 1940, had informal one-on-one late-evening discussions with the president about what he wanted done and was adept at putting his finger on the nub of any matter in a way that was helpful to Roosevelt's more indirect processes of thought. As a consequence, Hopkins became the person who best understood FDR's intentions as commander-in-chief and how to attain them. [77]

In January 1941, at Hopkins' own suggestion, Roosevelt sent him as his personal representative to discuss issues of common concern with Winston Churchill. What should have been a two-week trip turned into a six-week stay that convinced the American visitor of the British prime minister's greatness as a war leader. 'Churchill', he reported to Roosevelt, 'is the gov't in every sense of the word. . . . He is the one and only person over here with whom you need to have a full meeting of minds'.[78] Returning home with a list of Britain's vital material needs, he became in Churchill's words, 'the most perfect and faithful channel of communication between the President and me'. Using Hopkins as an ad hoc intermediary, the two leaders could bypass official channels to thrash out strategic and operational ideas that their nations could pursue singly or together.[79]

More immediately, Roosevelt recognized that his confidant was perfectly positioned to lead the Lend-Lease programme when enacted into law in March 1941. He designated Hopkins to 'advise and assist me in carrying out the responsibilities placed upon me by the act'.[80] Drawing on his New Deal experience, Hopkins moved expeditiously to turn FDR's vision of Lend-Lease into reality by creating a network of strategically placed Army, Navy and Treasury Department officials to liaise with British military and supply representatives about their armament requirements. Operating out of the Federal Reserve Building, 'the Hopkins Shop', as it was known in government circles, received formal accreditation as the Division of Defense Aid Reports through an executive order that placed it within the Office of Emergency Management in the EOP.[81]

On a second visit to Britain in July 1941 to discuss outstanding issues with Churchill, Hopkins cabled Roosevelt proposing that he fly from there to Moscow to assess how America might help the Soviet Union withstand the recent German invasion. Accepting this offer with alacrity, FDR sent a message via Hopkins to Joseph Stalin that the United States wanted to know how it could 'most effectively and expeditiously' assist Soviet resistance. 'I ask you', the president requested, 'to treat Mr. Hopkins with the identical confidence you would feel if you were talking directly to me'. His Kremlin meetings with Stalin on 30 and 31 July convinced Hopkins that the Red Army would eventually repel Hitler's onslaught if America kept it well supplied with war materials. While FDR unhesitatingly backed his judgement, the Department of War was slow in supplying Russia's needs out of belief that its imminent defeat would result in American weaponry falling into German hands.[82]

On 1 August, Roosevelt left the Cabinet in no doubt that getting military ordnance to Stalin was a priority. Drawing on what Hopkins had communicated, he embarked on a 45-minute lecture explaining why Hitler's Army would not conquer the Soviet Union. This began with a dressing-down of Henry Stimson, whom he held primarily responsible for the delay in delivering the planes and other armaments promised the Russians. 'Whatever we are going to give them', he declared, 'it has to be over there by the first of October, and the only answer I want to hear is that it is under way'.[83] A few days later Stimson recorded for his diary, 'This Russian munitions business has shown the President at his worst. He has no system. He goes haphazard and he scatters responsibility among a lot of uncoordinated men and consequently things never get done'.[84] In reality, many things were getting done to achieve presidential goals that Stimson did not share.

The day after the Cabinet meeting, Roosevelt instructed Wayne Coy, his assistant responsible for defence liaison with the OEM, to expedite transfer of materiel requested by the Soviets. 'Please, with my full authority', he declared, 'use a heavy hand – act as a burr under the saddle and get things moving!' At the end of August, he wrote to Stimson and Knox, 'I deem it of paramount importance for the safety and security of America that all reasonable munitions help be provided for Russia, not only immediately but as long as she continues to fight the Axis powers effectively.' To this end, he ordered them to provide him by 10 September their recommendations for the distribution of war materiel to Britain, Russia and other recipients of American aid by item, quantity and time schedule for the period up to 30 June 1942.[85]

Worn down by his many responsibilities and worried about his health, Hopkins persuaded FDR to endow a trusted ally, Edward Stettinius, formerly chair of United States Steel, with operational charge of the newly created Office of Lend-Lease Administration in September. Such was Roosevelt's confidence in his aide's judgement that the new man got the job without a presidential interview. Nevertheless, he appointed Hopkins to head a new body, the Soviet Protocol Committee, charged with negotiating supply agreements that met Russian war needs. This limited the capacity of anti-Soviet personnel in the State Department and the War Department to interfere with the flow of goods. To administer the Soviet Protocol Committee in Washington, Roosevelt personally chose a military advocate of all-out aid to Russia, Major General James Burns, who in turn selected the like-minded Colonel Philip Faymonville to run the Moscow end of operations.[86]

Despite the very different contexts, FDR's administrative leadership to manage the New Deal and the defence emergency manifested common traits. He sought ultimate control over decision-making by creating structures of information, advice and policy implementation that were responsive to him. The EOP provided a more rational process than the highly personalized pre-1939 system for undertaking his management responsibilities. Having created the administrative-institutional presidency to facilitate his domestic leadership, FDR showed creativity and flair in adapting it to meet the challenges of defence leadership in 1939–41. As his deployment of Harry Hopkins showed, he never lost the penchant for operating outside bureaucratic norms. Just as in the New Deal era, FDR's fluid style of leadership in the build-up to war had its critics. The lawyer and statesman in Henry Stimson inclined him to value order, rules and systematic chains of command in decision-making, which was not Roosevelt's way. 'His mind', the Secretary of War commented, 'does not follow easily a consecutive chain of thought but he is full of stories and incidents and hops about in his discussions from suggestion to suggestion and it is very much like chasing a vagrant beam of sunshine around a vacant room.'[87]

BoB director Harold Smith, another man of tidy mind, also voiced frustration with FDR's opposite tendencies but came to think very differently. Interviewed in 1946, he remarked,

When I worked with Roosevelt – for six years – I thought as did many others that he was a very erratic administrator. But now, when I look back, I can really begin to see the size of his programs. They were by far the largest and most complex programs that any President ever put through. People like me who had the responsibility of watching the pennies could only see the five or six percent of the programs that went wrong through inefficient organization or direction. But now I can see in perspective the ninety-three or -four or -five percent that went right – including the winning of the biggest war in history – because of unbelievably skilful organization and direction. . . . I'd say that Roosevelt was one of the greatest geniuses as an administrator that ever lived. What we couldn't appreciate at the time was the fact that he was a real *artist* in government.[88]

Allowing for some hyperbole in remembrance of the now dead Roosevelt, Smith's observation is very astute. Whatever their shortcomings, FDR's administrative methods met the ultimate test of their value – they worked far more often than not because of his great political skill in getting done what he wanted done. It is not too effusive to describe him as a true artist in the craft of government, a quality with a downside for his legacy. He bequeathed a presidency that had grown in scope, complexity and significance, but few of his successors came close to matching him in the political and administrative skills needed to make it work to best effect.

Constitutional revolutionary

FDR and the Supreme Court

Franklin D. Roosevelt oversaw a constitutional revolution that preserved the New Deal from judicial retrenchment. In 1935–6, the Supreme Court struck down core elements of his programme as improper expansions of federal authority. Roosevelt's court-packing plan to bring the high bench to heel early in his second term resulted in his most abject defeat as president, but success in his broader struggle for constitutional affirmation was at hand. The Supreme Court issued no further rulings against New Deal initiatives pertaining to economic regulation, labour rights and social welfare. From 1937 onwards, its agenda increasingly shifted from defence of private interests to self-restraint in socio-economic affairs and assertion of personal rights. The new personnel that Roosevelt put on the Supreme Court consolidated this transformation. Between August 1937 and June 1941, he nominated seven associate justices and a Chief Justice more than any president other than the obviously exceptional George Washington. Accordingly, it was perfectly valid to designate the Supreme Court as the Roosevelt Court by the time America entered the Second World War, a presidential appellation hitherto unique in third-branch history.

Roosevelt had a healthy respect for the Constitution as a living document capable of being constantly reinterpreted as the times demanded. America's highest law, he declared in 1930, 'has proved itself the most marvellously elastic compilation of rules of government ever written.'[1] In promoting the New Deal, he envisaged a constitutional reordering whereby governing power was largely centralized in Washington, primarily concentrated in the presidency and unambiguously dedicated to socio-economic liberalism. A change in the actual structure of government had no part in his plan. 'Our Constitution', Roosevelt declared in his inaugural address, 'is so simple and practical that it is possible always to meet extraordinary needs by changes in emphasis and arrangement without loss of essential form.'[2] In off-the-record remarks to the Gridiron Club, the social forum of Washington's elite press corps, at its 1934 spring dinner, attended by every sitting member of the Supreme Court, he rebutted critics of the early New Deal's constitutionality: 'They do not know what the Constitution is. They think it means today as applied to present conditions what it meant at the beginning, as applied to conditions of that period. They do not know or realize that the Constitution has changed with the times.'[3]

Roosevelt was similarly dismissive of the common misperception that conflated the nation's highest court with its highest law. This fallacy received validation from no less an authority than Harvard law professor Felix Frankfurter, later to become his third nominee as Associate Justice, who declared in 1930, '[I]n good truth, the Supreme Court *is* the Constitution.'[4] Explaining FDR's contrary mindset, another of his Supreme Court nominees, close confidante Robert Jackson, commented, 'The President had a tendency to think in terms of right and wrong, instead of terms of legal and illegal.'[5] Roosevelt discounted any judicial monopoly of wisdom in interpreting a higher law that was the product of political minds, not legal ones. Celebrating the Constitution's sesquicentennial anniversary in an address delivered at the Washington Monument in September 1937, he emphasized that its principal author, James Madison, was not a trained lawyer and that agreement over its terms at the Philadelphia convention of 1787 was the result of compromise brokered by the non-lawyerly likes of George Washington and Benjamin Franklin. What emerged from the founding deliberations was 'a layman's document, not a lawyer's contract . . . a charter of general principles, completely different from the "whereases" and the "parties of the first part" and the fine print which lawyers put into leases and insurance policies and installment agreements.'[6]

The reading copy of this speech, delivered in the immediate aftermath of his defeat over Supreme Court reorganization, contained a handwritten insertion that Americans saw 'nothing *more* sacred about that branch furthest removed from the people than about either of the others, which are nearest to the people.'[7] These words implicitly voiced his conviction that the political beliefs of Supreme Court justices shaped their interpretation of the Constitution. In an earlier expression of this opinion, he declared at Baltimore on 5 October 1932 that the Republican Party controlled the judicial branch of government, remarks that opponents criticized for disrespecting its independence. An unrepentant Roosevelt told Senator James Byrnes (D-South Carolina), 'What I said last night about the judiciary is true, and whatever is in a man's heart is apt to come to his tongue – I shall not make any explanations or apology for it.'[8]

Accordingly, Roosevelt was not going to take lying down judicial challenges to the constitutionality of the New Deal. As Robert Jackson observed, convinced that 'his motives were always good for the things that he wanted to do, he found difficulty in thinking that there could be legal limitations on them.'[9] To FDR's mind, the Constitution was an instrument to advance the public interest, not an ossified guarantee of limited government. His Fireside Chat of 30 September 1934 quoted the remarks of Chief Justice Edward Douglass White in 1914 (approbation that ignored White's fundamental conservatism):

There is a great danger it seems to me to arise from the constant habit which prevails where anything is opposed or objected to, of referring without rhyme or reason to the Constitution as a means of preventing its accomplishment, thus creating the general impression that the Constitution is but a barrier to progress instead of being the broad highway through which alone true progress may be enjoyed.[10]

In his first term Roosevelt faced a Supreme Court that was a house divided on the issue of whether the Constitution should move with the times. Four of its nine members were consistently hostile to the New Deal, three were broadly supportive and two 'swing' justices held the balance of power. Judicial discord about the proper limits of government had been a recurrent feature of the Supreme Court's history. The disputes of the 1930s were the culmination of wrangling over public regulation of private interests since the turn of the century. Conservative ascendancy in this struggle underwrote judicial activism in support of laissez-faire. Under William Howard Taft, more assertive as Chief Justice from 1921 to 1930 than as president from 1909 to 1913, the Supreme Court struck down more statutes in restraint of public authority than in the previous half-century. Though progressives increasingly demanded legislation to curb judicial power, constitutional crisis was not imminent until FDR became president. Hitherto judicial conservatism had mainly invalidated the social activism of state governments seeking to regulate workplace conditions in an era of economic growth. In the 1930s, it disputed the socio-economic activism of a popular president amid the worst depression in America's history.[11]

The swing duo of Chief Justice Charles Evans Hughes and Associate Justice Owen Roberts held the New Deal's constitutional fate in their hands. The son of Welsh immigrants, Hughes rose from modest circumstances to become a distinguished corporate attorney, Republican governor of New York (1907–10), Associate Justice of the Supreme Court (1910–16), Republican presidential candidate in 1916 and Secretary of State in the Harding–Coolidge administrations (1921–5). With piercing blue eyes, a grey mane and Van Dyke beard, he radiated stern intelligence, moral authority and utter self-assurance on the bench. Progressive in his early judicial career, he had become reliably conservative by 1930, Herbert Hoover's principal criterion for nominating him to replace the dying Taft. Nevertheless, belief in rational, gradual change inclined him to accept incremental expansion of public authority over private enterprise. Of similar outlook, Owen Roberts, another corporate lawyer of Welsh ancestry nominated by Hoover, was initially more beholden to legal precedent. Aligned with anti-New Deal justices in 1935–6, he changed sides in 1937 to validate key elements of Roosevelt's programme, earning himself a place in history for the 'switch in time that saved nine'.[12]

Mocked in the press as the 'Four Horsemen of the Apocalypse', the conservative bloc on the Hughes Court consisted of Willis Van Devanter, a federal appeals court judge nominated by President Taft in 1910; James Clark McReynolds, a Tennessee lawyer who served Woodrow Wilson as Attorney General before being nominated by him as Associate Justice in 1914; George Sutherland, a one-time Utah Republican senator nominated by Warren Harding in 1922; and Pierce Butler, a Minnesota attorney with impeccable conservative credentials nominated by Harding in 1923 at Chief Justice Taft's behest. In their judicial credo, the Constitution demarcated clear boundaries between private freedoms and public authority (particularly in substantive due-process protection of property rights) and between federal and state responsibilities. The quartet had not always ridden together in the 1920s but consistently rejected the constitutionality of New Deal initiatives.[13]

Usually found in opposition to the Four Horsemen were the 'Three Musketeers': Louis Brandeis (nominated by Wilson in 1916), Harlan Fiske Stone (nominated by

Calvin Coolidge in 1925) and Benjamin Cardozo (nominated by Hoover in a like-for-like replacement when Oliver Wendell Holmes retired in 1932). Each had distinguished careers before appointment to the Supreme Court: Brandeis was a vigorous defender of consumer and labour rights in high-profile court cases in the Progressive era; following successful spells in academia and corporate law, Stone cleaned up the scandal-ridden Justice Department as Coolidge's Attorney General; and Cardozo, arguably the most brilliant legal mind of the age, was the intellectual champion of liberal jurisprudence during eighteen years on the New York Court of Appeals. The trio generally observed judicial restraint in deference to the authority of elected legislatures over economic policy and accepted the need to interpret the Constitution in light of changing circumstances.[14]

Consumed by the economic crisis, FDR did not make it his personal priority to build a Justice Department capable of becoming the New Deal's constitutional bulwark. He delegated this responsibility to Senator Thomas Walsh (D-Montana), an experienced Washington insider whom he chose as Attorney General, but the elderly Westerner died from a heart attack two days before Inauguration Day. On Marguerite LeHand's recommendation, Roosevelt appointed Homer Cummings as a temporary stand-in. A former Democratic National Committee (DNC) chairman, Cummings had been a Connecticut state attorney and was a Roosevelt loyalist in 1932. His intuitive understanding that FDR wanted an Attorney General who provided legal justification for New Deal initiatives resulted in his permanent appointment. An appreciative FDR once remarked, 'Homer is a grand fellow. He can always find ways of doing things.'[15]

In reality, the Attorney General's job entailed far more than being the president's legal enabler and required the assistance of competent subordinates. A party loyalist, Cummings acceded to DNC boss Jim Farley's request that he stock the Justice Department with deserving Democrats. The post of Solicitor General, the administration's chief lawyer charged with defending its interests in court, went to the supremely unqualified Crawford Biggs, an undistinguished North Carolina lawyer and judge. 'I wonder if the president realizes how important the efficiency of that office is going to be to his program', Harlan Stone wrote Felix Frankfurter.[16] The hapless Biggs went on to lose ten of the seventeen cases he tried in court in his first fifteen months in office. Louis Brandeis eventually advised FDR that the administration would never win another judgement with Biggs as its advocate. Other hacks got less important but still significant Justice posts. An astute Washington observer commented, 'Mr Cummings' appointments make sad reading. . . . They were wholly inadequate as individuals, and a terrible crew to unload on a Department that was soon to be confronted with some of the most complicated legal cases ever tried in the history of the government.'[17]

At least the cases that Biggs lost were minor ones because the administration eschewed an early test of New Deal constitutionality. It preferred to allow the National Recovery Administration (NRA) and the Agricultural Adjustment Administration (AAA) time to work their hoped-for wonders before undergoing judicial scrutiny. Nearly two years elapsed before government lawyers came before the high bench to argue an important New Deal case. Roosevelt's programme finally began its day in court by getting into hot water over the 'hot oil' provision of the National Industrial Recovery Act of 1933. In Section 9(c), a relatively minor clause, Congress delegated the president authority to prohibit interstate shipments of petroleum produced in violation of oil-state regulations capping output. The abundance of bootleg oil had helped to drag down the price of a barrel of Texas crude to 10 cents, the cost of a can of Campbell's vegetable soup. In December 1934 the Supreme Court heard arguments from a pair of small-scale Texas producers claiming unconstitutional restraints on their operations. Its eight-to-one ruling (Cardozo alone dissented) in *Panama Refining Co. v. Ryan* (1935) held that 9(c) was an improper delegation of congressional authority that afforded the executive branch excessive discretion, a rationale never hitherto used to invalidate a federal statute. Although Congress addressed this objection through the Hot Oil Act of 1935 that specifically authorized executive operations against contraband petroleum, the judgement constituted a portend of things to come.

Of far greater concern to FDR was the imminent ruling on the constitutionality of the abrogation of the gold clause in any contract, private or public, approved by Congress in June 1933. In early January 1935, the Supreme Court heard arguments stretching over three days in the *Gold Clause cases* but did not deliver its rulings until 18 February. The uncertainty during the intervening weeks cast a darker shadow over the White House than anything since the banking crisis of March 1933. If the judgement went against it, the clamour of public bondholders for windfall payment in gold, now over two-thirds higher in dollar-cost than in 1933, would undermine federal solvency and drain the New Deal of fiscal resources. In readiness for a negative ruling, FDR drafted a radio address that announced his intention not to be bound by it. He planned to say:

> It is . . . my duty to protect the people of the United States to the best of my ability. To carry through the decision of the Court to its logical and inescapable end will so endanger the people of this Nation that I am compelled to look beyond the letter of the law to the spirit of the original contracts. I want every individual or corporation, public or private, to pay back substantially what they borrowed.[18]

If delivered, the speech would have provoked constitutional crisis, but the Supreme Court ruled by five-to-four majorities for the government in both *Gold Clause cases*. In *Norman v. Baltimore and Ohio Railroad*, it upheld the right of Congress to regulate the currency without interference from gold-clause contracts. In *Perry v. United States*, it adjudged that Congress had a good-faith obligation not to abrogate gold clauses in Treasury securities, while denying bondholders any right to seek damages for breach of contract. This convoluted ruling implied that the government was in the wrong, but nothing could be done about it.[19] FDR greeted the judgement with a mixture of relief and trepidation. He wrote Securities and Exchange Commission chief Joseph Kennedy, whom he had authorized to shut down stock markets to forestall panic selling if things had gone differently, 'It seems to me that the Supreme Court has at last definitely put human values ahead of the "pound of flesh" called for by a contract.' On more sober reflection, he told a Justice Department official, 'I shudder at the closeness of five to four decisions in these important matters!'[20]

Hoping to avoid further close calls, Homer Cummings moved to improve Justice Department personnel by appointing Stanley Reed as Solicitor General. A loyal New

Dealer who had performed sterling service as Reconstruction Finance Corporation general counsel, the new man had helped write the government brief in the *Gold Clause cases*. He promptly brought in able lawyers from other departments and agencies with first-hand knowledge of laws that were already coming under attack in lower courts.[21] By the time Reed began his defence of the New Deal, however, its ramparts had experienced a serious breach. On 6 May, the Supreme Court by a five-to-four majority struck down *Railroad Retirement Board v. Alton Railway Co.* (1935) on broad grounds that threatened the principles of New Deal social regulation.

An opinion written by Owen Roberts and supported by the Four Horsemen ruled unconstitutional a 1934 federal law creating a mandatory pension programme for railway employees. In the majority judgement, the plan violated the due-process guarantee in Amendment V of the Constitution and was unrelated to interstate commerce, the only area of economic life that Congress could legitimately regulate. Had Roberts confined himself to the due-process argument, a poorly drafted law could have been rewritten, but he placed what Charles Evans Hughes in his minority opinion called 'an unwarranted limitation on the Commerce Clause'. The logic of the ruling implied not only that the NRA was doomed but also that the social security and labour-rights bills currently under congressional consideration faced invalidation if enacted. Harlan Stone, one of the dissenters, declared it the 'worst performance of the Court' since the infamous *Lochner* decision of 1904 that struck down a New York law establishing maximum-hours protection for bakery workers. In an unsigned *New Republic* editorial, Felix Frankfurter repented his earlier conflation of court with Constitution to join fellow Harvard law professor Henry Hart in warning that the ruling reinforced growing concern that neither had 'the capacity . . . to satisfy the needs of our national life'.[22]

For Roosevelt, far worse followed on 27 May, the New Deal's Black Monday, when the Supreme Court handed down three unanimous rulings that seemingly amounted to a judicial declaration of war on his presidency. *Humphrey's Executor v. US* overturned his ouster in 1933 of William Humphrey, a Calvin Coolidge appointee to the Federal Trade Commission. The administration's defence, argued by Stanley Reed in his first case as Solicitor General, rested on the Taft Court ruling over a postmaster's dismissal in *Myers v. United States* (1926) that the president had absolute power of removal over executive-branch personnel. Rejecting this precedent, the Hughes Court adjudged that Humphrey, as a member of an independent regulatory body, could only have been removed with consent of Congress. Adding insult to injury, rather than concede that Roosevelt had acted in good faith based on *Myers*, the ruling made him appear guilty of flagrant disregard of the Constitution. In Robert Jackson's recall, 'that damned little case' made FDR 'madder at the Court' than any other decision because he thought 'they went out of their way to humiliate him personally'.[23] The invalidation of the Farm Bankruptcy Act of 1934 was a pinprick by comparison. The narrow nature of the judgement in *Louisville Bank v. Radford*, which found the law in breach of creditors' property rights, allowed Congress to remove the objectionable features in a redrafted measure enacted as the Farm Mortgage Moratorium Act of 1935.

There was no such salvation for the NRA under the terms of *Schechter Poultry Corp, v. United States* that made the Blue Eagle extinct. From a twenty-first-century vantage, the specific issue in dispute looks trivial, but apparently small-scale cases have often affected broad constitutional interpretation. This one stemmed from the appeal of four Schechter brothers, kosher poultry butchers in Brooklyn, against felony sentences for violating the NRA code regulating their business. The Blue Eagle rules for cleaning up a trade known for price-fixing, short-weighting and sale of diseased birds included a 'straight killing' requirement (the sale of the nearest birds to hand). The Schechters were the first merchants convicted under the new poultry code for selling unhealthy birds and allowing customer selection of fowls (in accordance with kosher rules but not the NRA's). They challenged the agency's jurisdiction in the so-called sick chicken case that came before the Supreme Court on 2 May 1935.

A unanimous opinion, written by the Chief Justice, served a death sentence on the NRA in addressing three issues with broad implications for the entire New Deal. First, extraordinary economic conditions might require extraordinary remedies but did not 'create or enlarge constitutional power'. Second, Congress was not permitted to transfer its legislative functions through sweeping delegation of undefined authority to the president to make public codes that carried the force of law in regulating private economic activity. Finally, the 'commerce power' could not be applied to businesses that were fundamentally engaged in intrastate rather than interstate operations. Even the progressive members of the high bench thought the time had come to draw the line against uncontrolled expansion of federal powers. An exasperated Louis Brandeis warned presidential aide Thomas Corcoran, '[T]ell your President that this Court has told him it is not going to permit the centralization of power which his advisors are imposing on this country'.[24]

FDR's public response to *Schechter* came in his press conference on 31 May. Following an intense tutorial from Frankfurter about its technicalities, he delivered what amounted to a dissenting presidential opinion on what the Chief Justice had argued. He adjudged *Schechter* the most important Supreme Court decision since the Dred Scott judgement that was instrumental in precipitating the Civil War. 'We are facing a very, very great national non-partisan issue', he declared. 'We have got to decide . . . whether in some way we are going to . . . restore to the Federal Government the powers which exist in the national governments of every nation in the world.' For Roosevelt, the real bone of contention was Hughes's stringent interpretation of the commerce clause that was more fitting to the distant past. 'Does this decision', he asked, 'mean that the United States Government has no control over any national economic problem?' To make his point that the court had to move with the times, he asserted, 'We have been relegated to the horse-and-buggy definition of interstate commerce.' As he knew they would, journalists asked to use the words in direct quotation of him, something he rarely allowed but did on this occasion.[25]

Roosevelt told reporters that it might take five to ten years to resolve the impasse. This implied that his solution was a constitutional amendment to curb judicial capacity to overturn legislation enacted by Congress. To test opinion, FDR dictated whole paragraphs for an article that appeared under journalist George Creel's name in *Collier's* in September. This asserted that if the Supreme Court continued to render 'the present generation powerless to meet social and economic problems that were not within the knowledge of the founding fathers', the president would have no alternative 'than to go to the country with a constitutional amendment that will lift the Dead Hand, giving the people of today the right to deal with today's vital issues'.[26] The trial balloon turned out to be a lead one that never got off the ground in the face of popular indifference. Accordingly, FDR decided to await a change in public opinion in response to further judicial attacks on the New Deal.

While the Hughes Court could not recapture the unanimity of Black Monday in its 1936 session, the majority of justices showed themselves not for turning. On 6 January, *US v. Butler* scythed down the AAA in a six-to-three judgement. At the Chief Justice's behest, the majority opinion written by Owen Roberts acknowledged that Congress could spend 'public moneys for public purposes', including the 'general welfare', a significant validation of New Deal expenditure programmes. In the case of AAA, however, it drew a distinction between 'commerce', which Congress could regulate, and 'production', which preceded commerce and fell within the states' regulatory domain under Amendment X of the Constitution. It further adjudged the processing tax that funded AAA production-control payments to farmers an unconstitutional 'expropriation of money from one group for the benefit of another' rather than a true tax to raise revenue. In a scathing dissent, Harlan Stone vented his spleen that judges should be concerned with the constitutionality of legislation rather than its wisdom. Courts, he warned, 'are not the only agency of government that must be assumed to have capacity to govern'.[27]

On 17 February 1936, the Supreme Court made something of an about-turn in *Ashwander et al. v. Tennessee Valley Authority* in upholding a New Deal initiative close to Roosevelt's heart. The Chief Justice manoeuvred adroitly to secure an eight-to-one majority (McReynolds alone dissented) by keeping consideration of the case to the specific issue of TVA's right to dispose of power generated at Wilson Dam. For some legal historians this validation of a quasi-socialist public-power programme demonstrated that the Hughes Court, far from seeking to sabotage FDR's initiatives, invalidated only those it objectively assessed in breach of the Constitution.[28] The Supreme Court's broad assault on the New Deal makes such reasoning unpersuasive. Doubtless, some statutes were poorly drafted in the emergency circumstances, but this did not necessarily make them unconstitutional. Most of the anti-New Deal judgements either revived long-dormant doctrines or employed reasoning never hitherto used to invalidate congressional law.[29]

To make matters worse, most of these decisions were split verdicts by narrow majorities. It was widely rumoured that Hughes had changed his vote in *Butler* to avoid a five-to-four ruling that could damage the court's reputation. The willingness of the bare majority to find ever-narrower rationales for far-reaching pronouncements undermined for good the court's unity of 'Black Monday'. Harlan Stone established himself as the principal voice of judicial restraint in the 1936 cases. Despite his belief that the New Deal was largely misguided, he did not consider this cause to overturn so much of it. The job of the justices, he insisted, was 'to see that the Constitution functions . . . not to approve or disapprove of social policy'. An approach to 'constitutional construction' based on judgement of whether a law was bad or unwise 'tends to increase the dead areas in the Constitution, the lacunae in which no power exists, either state or national, to deal with the problems of government'.[30] Instead of being guided by such thinking, a series of decisions in the spring of 1936 confirmed that *Ashwander* was an aberration not the new norm.

In *Jones v. Securities and Exchange Commission*, a six-to-three majority overturned a Securities and Exchange Commission order imposing sanctions on a registrant who attempted to withdraw his application to sell securities once the agency questioned its truthfulness. The ruling was widely regarded as a warning to every New Deal agency against invading the private rights of property-holders. *Carter v. Carter Coal Company* struck down the Guffey Coal Act of 1935 that aimed to stabilize the bituminous coal industry by revising its now-defunct NRA code. A five-four decision ruled the measure in breach of the commerce power in attempting to resolve labour-management disputes over wages, work conditions and collective bargaining that were local rather than interstate in nature. Yet another five-four ruling, *Morehead v. New York ex rel. Tipaldo*, found a 1933 New York minimum-wage law for women employees an unwarrantable interference with freedom of contract. Despite state rather than federal law being at issue, *Tipaldo* did more to arouse liberal opinion about the dangers of judicial oligarchy than any other case involving New Deal issues.[31]

Far from displeasing Roosevelt, these decisions added grist to his conviction that the judicial branch would eventually be hoist with its anti-New Deal petard. Harold Ickes confided to his diary, 'There isn't any doubt at all that the President is really hoping that the Supreme Court will make a clean sweep of all New Deal legislation. . . . He thinks the country is beginning to sense this issue but that enough people have not yet been affected by adverse decisions so as to make a sufficient feeling.'[32] At Roosevelt's behest, the Democratic platform in the 1936 election contained an opaque commitment to seek a 'clarifying amendment' on judicial-branch power, but he barely mentioned the matter in the campaign. He would be criticized in the court of history for squandering a mandate-creating opportunity, a verdict based on his landslide victory. With opinion polls predicting a close race, FDR did not want to hand the Republicans an issue on which the public mind was not yet clear. His own uncertainty about the best way to effect judicial reform, a conundrum not resolved until after the election, also inclined him to caution.

By late 1936 a constitutional amendment to curb judicial power had lost its appeal for Roosevelt. Despite two years of study, the Justice Department was unable to frame a satisfactory proposal to put before the country. Even with the right form of words, the tortuous amendment process required approval by two-thirds supermajorities in both houses of Congress and ratification by three-quarters of the states, where rural predominance in many assemblies made the outcome uncertain. A statutory strategy looked much simpler by comparison if appropriate legislation could be devised. Even so, the White House discounted proposals currently under consideration by Congress because they focused on constraining the Supreme Court's judicial-review authority over federal and state laws. This derived not from the Article III definition of third-branch powers in the Constitution but from a pair of early Supreme Court rulings, *Marbury v. Madison* (1803) and *Fletcher v. Peck* (1810), making any law that overrode these precedents vulnerable to judicial repudiation.

Expanding the number of justices seemingly offered a better legislative solution. Determined by congressional statute rather than the Constitution, this had changed over time – it was set at six in 1789, five in 1801, seven in 1807, nine in 1837, ten in 1863, eight in 1866 and nine in 1869. Needing an unprecedented expansion to produce a reliable majority, Roosevelt took heart from an analogous British case. In 1911, the Liberal Government's threat to create hundreds of new peers overcame opposition from the Conservative-dominated House of Lords to its 'People's Budget'.[33] Well aware that court-packing on a grand scale violated the separation-of-powers taboo, the president needed the smokescreen of principle to camouflage his power play. Homer Cummings came to his aid with a proposal that emphasized decrepitude rather than doctrine as the rationale for judicial reform.

The current justices had an average age of seventy-one, the oldest being Brandeis at eighty, followed by Van Devanter at seventy-seven, three others pushing seventy-five (Hughes, McReynolds and Sutherland) and the newly septuagenarian Butler. The notion that these ancients were insensitive to contemporary reality was already the subject of a best-selling book, *The Nine Old Men*, by columnists Drew Pearson and Robert Allen.[34] Cummings then discovered that one of their number had railed against elderly jurists in a younger incarnation. In 1913 none other than James McReynolds had unsuccessfully proposed legislation to mandate appointing a new judge to assist any sitting judge who remained on the federal bench below the Supreme Court beyond the age of seventy.[35] Unsolicited corroboration that the high bench needed younger blood also reached Cummings from Princeton professor of jurisprudence and Justice Department consultant Edward Corwin. In his enthusiastic response, the Attorney General observed, 'I realize that there is a good deal of prejudice against "packing the Court." I have been wondering to what extent we have been frightened by a phrase.'[36]

Cummings received Roosevelt's authorization to carry the plan forward at a White House meeting on 26 December. For the president, court-packing had become the only game in town. This was not a decision taken in haste. Roosevelt had been reviewing options about how to deal with the court for nigh on two years. The Supreme Court problem, he told newspaper publisher Joseph Patterson, 'is a mighty difficult one to solve but one way or another I think it must be faced. And it can be faced and solved without getting away from our underlying principles.'[37]

Once FDR decided to move against the Supreme Court, his masterly political touch deserted him. Cloaking his intentions in secrecy to prevent leaks shut off seasoned counsel about the pitfalls of the court-packing proposal. Framing one of the most radical initiatives any president had put to Congress as a common-sense reorganization to improve judicial efficiency was patently deceitful. His worst miscalculation was the hubristic assumption that the voters who had returned him to office in a landslide would follow him unquestioningly on Supreme Court reform. 'The people are with me' became his much-repeated mantra during the battle to enact a bill despite mounting evidence that not enough were. Shrewd, resourceful and finely attuned to political limits on most matters, FDR's leadership was imprudent, devious and overconfident regarding judicial reorganization.

By the time Roosevelt delivered his second inaugural address, the judiciary bill was close to being finalized but he remained silent on what was in store. Sharp-eared listeners would have heard the Chief Justice when administering the oath of office ask the president, with mounting emphasis, whether he would 'preserve, protect and defend the Constitution of the United States' and the equally assertive way that FDR repeated the entire pledge. Roosevelt later told an aide that he longed to cry out, 'Yes, but it is the Constitution as *I* understand it, flexible enough to meet any new problem of democracy – not the kind of Constitution your court has raised up as a barrier to progress.'[38] On 5 February, the president sprang his surprise, stunning Democratic congressional leaders by announcing his intent at an early-morning White House meeting, moving on immediately to break the news to a mid-morning press conference and then sending the proposal over to Congress in the early afternoon.

Roosevelt's message to the legislature claimed that the insufficient number of federal judges had resulted in overcrowded court dockets and unwarranted delays in litigation. Compounding the problem, the advanced age of some judges caused them 'to avoid an examination of complicated and changed conditions'. These older men, 'assuming that the scene is the same as it was in the past, cease to explore or inquire into the present or the future'. It followed that a 'constant and systematic addition of younger blood will vitalize the courts'. To this end, FDR proposed the appointment of new judges, up to a maximum of fifty, for every member of the federal bench who had reached the age of seventy and served for ten years minimum. The bottom line that he would be able to appoint six additional justices to bring Supreme Court membership to the new maximum of fifteen allowed in the bill went unstated. What Samuel Rosenman called 'the cleverness, the too much cleverness' of making age the justification for this sweeping reorganization likely appealed to FDR as delicious revenge on his judicial tormentors. He would have done better to make a clean breast of his desire for judges who embraced a living Constitution.[39]

The White House sought an initial enactment of the judiciary bill in the Senate. A presidential promise to put Senator Joseph Robinson (D-Arkansas) on the Supreme Court at the first opportunity ensured the support of the Majority Leader, who had long sought this elevation. It soon became clear that a tough battle lay ahead when some habitual administration loyalists joined with conservative Democrats in opposition to the measure. These dissenters found their leader in Senator Burton K. Wheeler (Montana), a steadfast progressive and long-standing critic of judicial conservatism. Pique and principle combined to make him the rebel paladin. The first significant Democrat to endorse FDR's presidential candidacy, he had received precious little in return. Wheeler's hopes for the vice-presidential nomination came to nothing, his passion for the coinage of silver as the solution to deflation left the president cold and his baronial expectation of consultation on important matters of state foundered upon FDR's kingly preference to surround himself with courtier aides. Despite his own desire to curb judicial usurpation of Congress's law-making power, he condemned Roosevelt's reorganization plan as an unconstitutional power grab that would make the Supreme Court subservient to the president.[40]

His fighting skills honed in the rough-and-tumble of Montana politics, one of the best parliamentarians in the Senate and a talented orator, Wheeler was a formidable foe, but he was taking on the heavyweight champ of politics. Under the president's close direction, Tommy Corcoran and other aides conducted an aggressive campaign on his behalf. They called in favours owed by some senators, promised pork to others and twisted arms as necessary. While both sides recognized that public opinion was vital to their cause, the opposition had an early advantage on this score. Editorial opinion in the mainly conservative-owned press was uniformly hostile to FDR's court plan. Frank Gannet's National Committee to Uphold Constitutional Government launched a publicity campaign comparing Roosevelt with monarchical tyrants of old and present-day European dictators. The hostile drumbeat that an attack on the Supreme Court was an attack on the Constitution and its separation-of-powers bedrock hit home with the public. In early March, a Gallup survey recorded that 49 per cent of respondents opposed the president's plan, 41 per cent were in favour and the remainder had no opinion.[41]

By then, the president had decided to enter the fray personally to regain the upper hand. At the Democratic Party's Victory Dinner in the Mayflower Hotel in Washington DC on 4 March, the anniversary of his first inauguration, Roosevelt gave one of his greatest addresses, carried by radio link to 1,268 similar dinners across the nation attended by more than half-a-million people. Persuaded by Robert Jackson that he risked losing the battle for public opinion unless he came clean on the real purpose of the bill, the speech marked FDR's abandonment of age as the rationale for judicial reform. He used an agricultural analogy to insist that the three-horse team of American government should pull together to plough the field of national needs. Itemizing the judicial opinions that had already nullified so much of the New Deal, he questioned whether it could be said with any certainty that the same fate would not befall measures promised in the recent campaign. Calling for party unity, he warned that if the Democrats 'do not have the courage to lead the American people where they want to go, someone else will', a veiled warning that the deadlock could bring an authoritarian leader to power.[42]

A Fireside Chat on 9 March, the first of his second term, reinforced the three-horse metaphor for the separate institutions of government. Identifying himself as one of the horses rather than the driver, FDR avowed, 'It is the American people themselves who are in the driver's seat . . . who want the furrow plowed . . . who expect the third horse to pull with the other two.' It was now necessary 'to save the Constitution from the Court, and the Court from itself'. The solution was the appointment not of 'spineless puppets' but of additional justices attuned to the nation's needs as a counterbalance 'to the personal judgement of a few men who, being fearful of the future, would envy us the necessary means of dealing with the present'.[43]

FDR's radio address raised support for his judicial reorganization to 46 per cent, its zenith, in the next Gallup survey, but Charles Evans Hughes spiked his guns. The Chief Justice played his hand to perfection in trumping the most significant assault on judicial authority in American history. Hughes's first move in public was to furnish Burton Wheeler with a letter asserting that the Supreme Court was fully abreast of its work and had no docket congestion, a situation likely to change if there were more justices engaged in conferring upon cases. His ally read this out to great effect when leading off testimony for the opposition before the Senate Judiciary Committee hearings on the judiciary bill on 21 March.

Of even greater significance, the Chief Justice had detached Owen Roberts from the anti-New Deal bloc. Following the *Tipaldo* furore, Hughes and his wife had paid a visit to Roberts and his wife at their Bryncoed farm near Philadelphia in the summer of 1936.

The two men spent much of the time locked together in animated discussion, almost certainly about the danger of continued opposition to the New Deal. Though there is no record of their conversations, Roberts remarked years later, 'Looking back, it is difficult to see how the Court could have resisted the popular urge . . . for what in effect was a unified economy.'[44] The pair doubtless paid close heed to the 1936 presidential election outcome. If the people's vote was not a direct judgement on the Supreme Court, it represented an endorsement of the president and his programme that the judiciary ignored at its peril.

In early 1937, Hughes led the court into a five-four repudiation of *Tipaldo* in the *West Coast v. Parrish* judgement sustaining a Washington state minimum-wage law. Issued on 29 March but actually decided in January, the judgement was a response not to FDR's as yet unlaunched judicial offensive but to the 1936 vote, if never acknowledged as such. The switch by Roberts from the *Tipaldo* majority to the *Parrish* majority represented a constitutional somersault that turned freedom-of-contract sanctity on its head.[45] He then voted alongside Hughes, Brandeis, Cardozo and Stone in decisions that validated core New Deal statutes. On 12 April, four judgements upheld the National Labor Relations Act of 1935, all by five-four majorities. The most significant, *National Labor Relations Board v. Jones & Laughlin Steel Corp.*, ruled that federal authority to regulate interstate commerce permitted Congress also to regulate intrastate commerce that directly impacted interstate enterprise. It found disruption to interstate commerce in a labour dispute that threatened to shut down a large Pennsylvania plant, an opinion that effectively overturned the *Schechter* and *Carter* precedents.

The Chief Justice showed himself a consummate tactician by siding with the Four Horsemen to hear cases pertaining to the Social Security Act. In having the court consider them, his aim was to demonstrate its willingness to validate social legislation, duly rendered in two judgements delivered on 24 May. *Steward Machine Co v. Davis* ruled by five-to-four that the unemployment compensation levy paid by employers and the tax credit received in return was a valid exercise of the taxing and spending powers given to Congress in Article I of the Constitution. *Helvering v. Davis* upheld the old-age retirement levy on employers and workers to fund pension benefits on the same grounds but by seven-to-two, thanks to switches by Van Devanter and Sutherland.[46]

Willis Van Devanter's announcement that he would retire from the court at the end of the current session dealt the final blow to FDR's judicial plan. This gave the president the opportunity to make his first nomination to the high bench, thereby undercutting the rationale for packing it. Public support for his proposal fell to its lowest point of 31 per cent in the next Gallup poll. Washington insiders saw Hughes's hand at work in bringing about his colleague's resignation. Speaking for many Democrats, administration loyalist James Byrnes thought that FDR could now afford to drop the court plan because its purpose was moot. 'Why run for a train', he reportedly queried 'after you've caught it?'[47]

Judicious retreat from the judiciary bill formed no part in FDR's thinking. In his calculation, having promised the next Supreme Court vacancy to the conservative-inclined Joseph Robinson, he needed additional liberal justices to ensure a majority favourable to the New Deal.[48] The Senate Judiciary Committee's adverse report against his original proposal also made it impossible for him to cloak a tactical withdrawal as a strategic victory. According to one historian, 'It was the harshest, most unrestrained indictment of a presidential proposal that had ever reached the Senate floor from a committee in which a ruling party had a commanding numerical majority.'[49] With seven Democrats in the ten-to-eight majority, it almost read like a bill of impeachment against the president in condemning his judicial reorganization as 'a measure which should be so emphatically rejected that its parallel will never again be presented to the free representatives of the free people of America'.[50]

Unwilling to take this indictment lying down, the president sought a substitute bill through a strategy that avoided his errors of early 1937. The Justice Department collaborated with congressional allies to produce a new measure authorizing him to appoint one new justice per calendar year for each sitting member aged seventy-five who declined to retire from the Supreme Court. Under its terms, FDR could have had four additional justices in place by early 1940 if there were no further retirements. At Robinson's suggestion, Roosevelt threw 'a grand Democratic harmony party' at the Jefferson Island Club, formerly a bootlegger's hideout and now a Democratic sanctum in Chesapeake Bay on the weekend of 25–27 June 1937. Every male Democratic member of Congress received an invitation (six women – five from the House, one from the Senate – did not make the guest list), only a handful dared not go, and the attendees arrived in groups of 130 for a day of feasting, boozing and schmoozing. This charm offensive failed in its objective of winning over those opposed in principle to FDR's judicial reorganization.[51]

In desperation, Robinson manipulated Senate rules to call the revised bill for floor debate on 6 July. His hopes rested on putting together a coalition of New Deal stalwarts, undecided Democrats habitually loyal to him and the freshman class elected on FDR's coat-tails in 1936. He carried the main burden of speaking for the measure on the floor and negotiating for votes behind the scenes in the days that followed. The strenuous effort, undertaken in Washington's stifling summer heat, proved too much for the 65-year-old. During the night of 14 July, Robinson suffered a fatal heart attack at his apartment in the Methodist building directly across Maryland Avenue from the Supreme Court building. The prospects of the revised judiciary bill died with him. On reconvening after his funeral in Little Rock, the Senate voted overwhelmingly to recommit the legislation to committee, wherefrom it never re-emerged.[52]

Roosevelt had engaged in two wars – one political, the other constitutional – in seeking to pack the Supreme Court. He had unquestionably lost the political conflict. The New Deal's change of course in 1935 had increased the likelihood of a confrontation with congressional conservatives in his own party, but the court-packing imbroglio precipitated it sooner than expected. If a frontal attack on a popular president's socio-economic agenda so soon after his landslide re-election carried many risks, an assault on his supposedly dictatorial threat to the hallowed Constitution made a safer target. Conservative Democrats comprised the bulk of the troops that Wheeler led into battle to inflict FDR's first legislative defeat on a major domestic issue, thereby shattering his image of invulnerability. Henceforth his intra-party opponents had no qualms about stymying the New Deal and making common cause with conservative Republicans.

By contrast, Roosevelt won the constitutional war, even if his victory was less than total. Reflecting on the battle with the Chief Justice, Robert Jackson told FDR, 'The old man put it over on you.'[53] This was true in the sense that Hughes safeguarded the independence of the Supreme Court from a Roosevelt initiative that would likely have made it the vassal of the executive and created a precedent for further manipulation of its membership in confrontations between later presidents and the judiciary. FDR's defeat ensured that no other president would follow him in launching a comparable effort to pack the third branch. Hughes also preserved the Supreme Court's status as the final interpreter of the Constitution. In 1906, when governor of New York, he had famously remarked, 'We live under a Constitution, but the Constitution is what the judges say it is, and the judiciary is the safeguard of our liberty and our property under the Constitution.'[54] That observation remained true to all intents and purposes after the dust had settled on FDR's court-packing defeat, but victory came at a cost.

Once an advocate of doctrinal stability on the bench, Hughes recognized that the American people would not much longer tolerate having relief, recovery and reform blocked by a set of esoteric legalisms. Retreating in the face of this reality, he sanctioned what one judicial historian adjudged 'a constitutional transformation which, in terms of scope and speed of execution, is unprecedented in the annals of the Supreme Court'.[55] Beginning with the *Jones & Laughlin Steel Corp.* decision, the judicial branch henceforth upheld New Deal statutes in every case pertaining to their constitutionality. With its new sense of self-restraint guiding the reins, the chariot of the living Constitution trampled over precedent previously used to invalidate legislation approved by Congress. According to one estimate, the Supreme Court effectively reversed thirty-two earlier decisions in the ten judicial sessions from 1937 through 1946.[56]

FDR's view of the Constitution prevailed in three key areas. The doctrine of non-delegation of legislative power used to strike down three New Deal statutes in 1935–6 disappeared from judicial review. Delegation without standards to guide executive discretion had a free hand thereafter. One New Deal lawyer drily recalled that he and a colleague had the dubious distinction of being the only federal attorneys in history to produce losing briefs on such delegation (in *Panama*, *Schechter* and *Carter*), becoming more successful on that subject and others from 1937 onwards, 'although not because I had learned to write better briefs'.[57]

Second, the Hughes Court henceforth placed few limits on the scope of the commerce, taxing and general welfare powers of congressional legislation. In a reversal of *Butler*, it upheld the right of Congress to regulate agricultural production, hitherto decreed separate from commerce, in *Mulford v. Smith* (1939). In upholding the Fair Labor Standards Act of 1938 in *US v. Darby Lumber Co.* (1941), it legitimized the authority of Congress to regulate wages, hours and work conditions in enterprises engaged in intrastate activities if these affected interstate commerce. Issued just months before Charles Evans Hughes stepped down from the bench, this judgement put the final seal on the third branch's transformation. As historian Michael Parrish noted, 'The road to *Darby* and federal supremacy over the basic rules of the national marketplace had been a bumpy and twisting one for the Hughes Court prior to 1937, a journey that inspired pungent criticism and helped to provoke the confrontation with the president and Congress.'[58] Ironically, if the 'sick chicken' suit epitomized the jurisprudence of the pre-1937 court, a 'hungry chicken' case embodied that of the post-

1937 court. *Wickard v. Filburn* (1942) ruled that an Ohio farmer growing 23 acres of wheat merely to feed his fowl had sufficient impact on interstate commerce to merit marketing penalties imposed by the Secretary of Agriculture under the terms of the Agricultural Adjustment Act of 1938.[59]

Finally, the doctrine of dual federalism, a construct the Supreme Court had used since the 1890s to keep the federal government out of areas supposedly reserved for the states under the loose terms of the Tenth Amendment, ceased to have validity. Typifying this, *Sunshine Anthracite Coal Company v. Adkins* (1940) sanctioned the Bituminous Coal Act of 1937 despite its resemblance to the Guffey Act struck down in *Carter*. Denying the existence of 'a no man's land' between the state and federal domains, the majority opinion asserted that Congress 'under the commerce clause is not impotent to deal with what it may consider to be dire consequences of *laissez-faire*'.[60] Shortly afterwards, Harlan Stone's opinion in *Darby* drove the final nail into the coffin of dual federalism in asserting the superiority of Congress's inherent powers under Article I of the Constitution over the reserved powers of the states. 'The [Tenth] Amendment', he declared, 'states but a truism that all is retained which has not been surrendered.' It did not deprive the federal government 'of authority to resort to all means for the exercise of a granted power which are appropriate and plainly adapted to the permitted end'.[61]

Another aspect of the constitutional revolution of 1937 was the Supreme Court's shift in emphasis from economic issues to personal rights. In a seemingly minor case, *US v. Carolene Products Co.* (1938), it upheld a federal law prohibiting interstate transportation of 'filled milk', namely skimmed milk mixed with animal fats. In the majority opinion, Harlan Stone wrote what became the most significant footnote in American constitutional history. This fundamentally established separate criteria for judicial review of economic legislation and laws affecting civil liberties and rights. No longer requiring heightened scrutiny, the former would simply be subject to a rational test as to whether Congress possessed appropriate authority to act and reasonable justification for doing so. The latter, in contrast, required 'more exacting judicial scrutiny under the general prohibitions of the 14th Amendment than are most other types of legislation'. In particular, statutes aimed at religious, national and racial minorities as well as 'prejudice against discrete and insular minorities . . . may call for a correspondingly more searching judicial inquiry'. This opinion laid the foundation of the due-process revolution and the civil rights judgements of the Warren Court and Burger Court from the mid-1950s to the mid-1970s.[62]

Roosevelt's nominees to the Supreme Court broadly reinforced this change of approach. One of them, William O. Douglas, commented that FDR liked to make appointments that would 'upset the fat cats' and 'make the established order wince'. As the president himself had remarked in 1936, he wanted judges who 'knew how the other 90 percent live'. Only Stanley Reed of the eight associate justices he put on the Supreme Court had been born to wealth, compared to some two-fifths of all members of the Supreme Court since 1789. Six had held significant positions in his administration or in Congress, another had acted as his informal adviser and none of these had extensive judicial experience. The Roosevelt appointees were New Deal loyalists who shared his impatience with the jurisprudence of the pre-1937 court.[63]

In naming Senator Hugo Black (D-Alabama) to replace Van Devanter in August 1937, FDR was taking revenge on the senators who defeated his court-packing plan in selecting an ardent New Dealer while calculating that the conventions of senatorial courtesy would guarantee his confirmation. Shortly after Black was sworn in, the story broke that he had been a Ku Klux Klan member in the 1920s, a revelation that prompted urban Democrats, Catholic groups and African-American organizations to demand his resignation. Almost certainly aware of Black's past before nominating him, Roosevelt set greater store on his commitment to a living Constitution. The Alabaman had asserted in support of judicial reorganization, 'The time has arrived when those who favour fitting law to modern needs in order to cure social and industrial injustices . . . should have the right to pass laws to accomplish these purposes.' Confounding expectations, the former Klansman became the foremost defender of civil liberties and civil rights on the mid-century court. Black manifested a populist belief in a literal reading of the Constitution, a hitherto conservative philosophy that limited the scope for discretion but to his mind a radical one that unconditionally guaranteed personal rights enshrined in the Bill of Rights and the Fourteenth and Fifteenth Amendments.[64]

In January 1938, FDR nominated Stanley Reed to fill the vacancy created by George Sutherland's retirement. An active New Dealer, he was nevertheless acceptable to Dixie Democrats as a native of Kentucky. He proved a liberal justice in the socio-economic domain but the most conservative Roosevelt appointee regarding civil liberties, civil rights and criminal justice.[65] In January 1939, to fill the vacancy created by Benjamin Cardozo's death, FDR appointed Felix Frankfurter in the expectation that his intellectual firepower would boost liberal jurisprudence. Despite not living up to this hope, the one-time Harvard professor upheld presidential preferences, as well as his own, that judges should defer to congressional will unless there was clear constitutional cause for not doing so. This commitment to judicial restraint induced him to resist Hugo Black's insistence that judges carried a special obligation to protect civil liberties.[66]

On Louis Brandeis's retirement, William Douglas became FDR's fourth appointment in March 1939. Raised in modest circumstances in Yakima, Washington, he rose to become a professor at Yale as an exponent of legal realism, a doctrine that used social science to understand the law and its institutions. In 1934, he was recruited by Joseph Kennedy to join the newly established SEC, becoming its third chairman in 1937. A friend of Felix Frankfurter, Douglas appeared likely to form a jurisprudential alliance with his fellow academician but quickly gravitated towards Black's position on civil liberties. In contrast to the Alabaman's strict positivism, he showed a flair for judicial creativity. His opinion in *Skinner v. Oklahoma* (1942), which struck down a state law requiring involuntary sterilization for felons, established a novel doctrine that individuals had certain 'fundamental interests' such as procreation, which no government could deny without compelling need. Two decades later, he built on *Skinner* to propagate a new right of privacy in the landmark birth-control case, *Griswold v. Connecticut* (1965), which established the precedent for the pro-choice abortion judgement, *Roe v. Wade* (1973).[67]

Appointed in early 1940 to replace the recently deceased Pierce Butler, Frank Murphy was a devout Catholic with a strong social conscience and an avowed liberal. As police court judge in the 1920s, he saw how poverty, ignorance and racism disadvantaged criminal justice defendants; as Detroit mayor in the early 1930s, he did more than any municipal leader in America to commit public resources for relief; and, as Michigan governor, he refused to implement court injunctions obtained by automobile companies against sit-down strikers. After election defeat in 1938, Murphy accepted Roosevelt's invitation to succeed Homer Cummings as Attorney General. Hoping to pursue the presidency one day, he was reluctant to join the Supreme Court until convinced by FDR that this was where he could best serve liberalism. Knowing little about constitutional law, he learned on the job with the help of bright clerks and aligned with the Black-Douglas position that civil liberties held a preferred position in jurisprudence. In *Thornhill v. Alabama* (1940), his first opinion, Murphy overturned a state anti-labour law by ruling that the First Amendment's guarantee of free speech validated peaceful picketing. Dissenting from a majority judgement upholding the conscription of a Jehovah's Witness minister in *Falbo v. United States* (1942), he remarked, 'The law knows no finer hour than when it cuts through formal concepts and transitory emotions to protect unpopular citizens against discrimination and persecution.'[68]

On 12 June 1941, Roosevelt found himself in the remarkable position of making three Supreme Court nominations. He began by naming Harlan Stone to succeed the retiring Charles Evans Hughes. Though no friend of the New Deal, Stone's insistence on judicial restraint reassured liberals, while his opposition to court-packing made him acceptable to conservatives. Usually unforgiving towards critics of his judicial reorganization, FDR relented in Stone's case because appointing a Republican as Chief Justice benefited national unity at a time of controversy over his initiatives to help Britain in its war with Germany. The nomination was met with overwhelming approval from the press and the political establishment. It also held up well in the court of scholarly opinion in recognition of Stone's leading role in bringing constitutional interpretation into the twentieth century.

The last of the Four Horsemen rode off into embittered retirement at the start of 1941. Roosevelt-hating James McReynolds had vowed 'never [to] resign as long as that crippled son-of-a-bitch is in the White House', but the president's election to a third term denied the 79-year-old justice this ambition.[69] In his place, FDR nominated James Byrnes as reward for his loyalty in promoting administration measures in the Senate, demonstrated most recently in his floor management of Lend-Lease legislation. The selection was also a sop to Southern Democrats for providing Roosevelt's foreign policy initiatives with crucial support in a number of tight congressional votes. African-American groups were horrified at the selection of a segregationist, but FDR reasoned that putting Byrnes on the high bench would free him from the electoral constraints of regional racism. The South Carolinian had also put on record his belief that the Constitution's flexibility to address the needs of the times was 'its strength and not its weakness'.[70]

Roosevelt completed his trio of nominees by appointing Robert Jackson to Stone's seat as Associate Justice. Having qualified for the bar through apprenticeship in an attorney's office rather than going through law school, Jackson is the only individual to have been Solicitor General, Attorney General and Supreme Court justice, all positions held before he reached fifty. In January 1941, he published a scathing condemnation of the pre-1937 Hughes Court and its conservative predecessors for making war on legislation that addressed the needs of modern society. As an Associate Justice, he advanced a very broad conception of the commerce power, most notably in his majority opinion for *Wickard v. Filburn*. His preference for judicial deference to majority rule put him closer to Frankfurter than to Black in decisions pertaining to laws curtailing personal rights. Jackson also disliked the Alabaman's efforts to lobby the other justices to support his positions, tactics he considered more suited to the legislature than the bench.[71]

By the time America entered the war, the Supreme Court had become an ally rather than an enemy of New Deal socio-economic regulation. Internal divisions made its record on rights-based jurisprudence less clear-cut, but the momentum still lay in the direction of greater protection for civil liberties.[72] Despite a tarnished record in this field as war president, Roosevelt seemingly signalled sympathy for personal-rights expansion in his final Supreme Court selection. Missing the whiff of political grapeshot, James Byrnes resigned in October 1942 to help FDR manage the problems of the home front. Frankfurter immediately began lobbying for his replacement by Judge Learned Hand of the Second Court of Appeals, a venerable advocate of judicial restraint. Wanting a younger man, Roosevelt opted for 48-year-old Wiley Rutledge, a judge in the Court of Appeals of the District of Columbia who had made his name in academia. His judicial record showed consistent support for New Deal statutes and personal liberties. A Justice Department review appraised him as 'a liberal who would stand up for human rights, particularly during a war when they are apt to be forgotten'. Once on the court, Rutledge joined with Black, Douglas and Murphy in support of rights-based jurisprudence. Since FDR knew what he would get from his final nominee, he was likely signalling his preference for a court that did not defer to state and local officials on matters of civil rights.[73]

Roosevelt's battle with the Supreme Court had two significant consequences for the presidency as an institution. The failure of court-packing reinforced the checks-and-balances ethos of a constitutional system of government in which separate institutions share power. Conversely, the Supreme Court's validation of the New Deal in the 'constitutional revolution' of 1937 showed that the third branch recognized the dangers of resisting a president who could claim to embody the popular will. Charles Evans Hughes would always deny that Roosevelt's attempt to reorganize the judiciary influenced the Supreme Court to change course. This opinion left unspoken the reality that Hughes and Roberts were swayed by his landslide re-election. The duo's switch of votes in 1937 and beyond underlined their understanding that the third branch was as much a political institution as a judicial one. In its political identity, the mid-twentieth-century Supreme Court collaborated with the New Deal coalition of interests from 1937 into the 1970s in working out the judicial implications of the liberal ascendancy. The principal actor in bringing about this change, FDR was vindicated in his conviction that the US Constitution was worthy of reverence 'not because it was old, but because it was ever new'.[74]

Party leader

FDR and the Democrats

Franklin D. Roosevelt achieved greater success as party leader than any president before or since. He had two transformational goals: to elevate the Democratic Party from the minority to the majority party and to make it a liberal party. He was unquestionably successful in achieving his first objective. Having elected just two presidents and only intermittently controlled Congress from 1860 to 1932, the Democrats won all but two presidential elections from 1932 to 1968 and dominated both the House of Representatives and the Senate into the 1980s. FDR also remade the presidential wing of his party into a liberal entity that drew on the support of a new, class-based voter coalition centred in the urban North and West. In Congress, by contrast, conservative Democrats retained considerable influence and eventually established an informal coalition with Republicans to constrain New Deal expansion. Despite this, FDR was instrumental in bringing about one of the greatest political realignments in American history in support of an active national state with the presidency as its driving force.

The Democratic Party inherited by Roosevelt lacked a coherent political identity, had a narrow base and was internally divided. The white, rural small town, Protestant South, its most reliable source of support, had fallen out with the growing but still secondary constituency of urban, predominantly Catholic ethnics over sociocultural issues in the 1920s. The onset of the Great Depression did nothing to unite the Democrats in support of an economic agenda. Conservatives who controlled the Democratic National Committee (DNC) under the chairmanship of corporate executive John J. Raskob, put in charge by Alfred E. Smith in 1928 to boost fundraising, stood for limited government, balanced budgets and a free hand for business amid the crisis. Seeing no hope of change, some intellectuals and trade unionists affiliated with the League for Independent Political Action agitated for a new party representing workers and farmers. University of Chicago economist (and future Democratic senator for Illinois) Paul Douglas commented in 1932 that Woodrow Wilson was 'a far keener thinker and a more determined fighter' than FDR, but the Democratic Party remained 'as cancerous as ever in its composition and as conservative in its policies' under him. If Wilson was unable to change it, 'how can we hope for better things from Franklin Roosevelt?'[1]

The failure of Progressive third-party campaigns in 1912 and 1924 informed FDR's contrary conviction that a new electoral majority could only be built within the existing party system. In his assessment, the Great Depression had made the political environment more conducive to the Democratic transformation project that he first envisaged in the 1920s. In seeking the presidency, Roosevelt intended not only a centralization of power in Washington to correct the economy but also a nationalization of politics to sustain his leadership. Hitherto reformers had conventionally identified as 'progressives' but FDR wanted a new term that encompassed his vision of big government and mass politics while eschewing association with socialism. He found it in 'liberal', a label that lacked a distinctive pedigree in American politics until it became synonymous with the New Deal. Roosevelt launched this designation in the 1932 election campaign to badge the Democrats' change of identity from a party of sectional and local interests into one that was national in character and committed to activist government.[2]

Disdainful of the Raskob-dominated DNC, Roosevelt wrote a Southern ally in 1931 that it was futile to 'make our party . . . a friend of those vested interests which have so completely dominated the Republican organization for so many years. If we win, we must win because we are progressive.'[3] Once his hat was in the ring, Roosevelt moved to establish himself as the only prospective Democratic nominee in favour of broad-based programmatic support for ordinary Americans hard hit by the Great Depression. Speaking on the *Lucky Strike Hour*, a popular radio show, he famously declared, 'These unhappy times call for the building of plans that put their faith once more in the forgotten man at the bottom of the economic pyramid.'[4]

Roosevelt's insistence that in an interdependent national economy restoration of farm prices was essential to industrial recovery had particular appeal to the South and West, helping to reignite Populist-Progressive instincts dormant since Woodrow Wilson's day. Conversely, it did not play well with urban bosses who saw him as a patrician squire with no understanding of metropolitan needs. Voicing their concerns, Jersey City mayor Frank Hague fulminated, 'He cannot carry a single state east of the Mississippi and very few in the Far West.'[5] The Northern chieftains wanted Al Smith, the hero of the cities in the losing race of prosperous 1928, to run again in the more propitious circumstances of depressed 1932. This put them in the same camp as Raskob, who aimed to promote Smith on a Prohibition-repeal platform that would deflect the Democrats from economic activism.

With many Southern and Western state delegations pledged to him, FDR was the clear front runner when the Democratic National Convention met in Chicago in late June 1932 to select a presidential candidate, but was still about a hundred delegates short of the two-thirds supermajority required for nomination. Thanks to the DNC's stop-Roosevelt manoeuvres, delegations pledged to a favourite-son on the early ballots held the balance of power. The longer the balloting continued without a Roosevelt victory, the greater the likelihood that they would switch to another candidate to avoid the marathon roll-calls of 1924 and thereby stampede his supporters into joining them. Accordingly, FDR's lieutenants struck a Faustian bargain with the conservative Speaker of the House of Representatives, John Nance Garner, the favourite-son of the Texas delegation and controller of the California delegation, courtesy of media mogul William Randolph Hearst. His price for switching on the fourth ballot was the vice-presidential nomination, a deal that ensured FDR's presidential candidacy at cost of an all-liberal ticket.[6]

Roosevelt's first priority in his campaign against Herbert Hoover was to unite the various Democratic factions behind his leadership. Of great help to this cause, inclusion of Prohibition repeal in the national platform put an end to 1920s-style cultural cleavage. Without this albatross around his neck, FDR conducted a vigorous cross-country speaking campaign that mixed traditional support for states' rights, balanced budgets and bureaucratic efficiency with innovative commitment to public works, federal assistance for the unemployed and farm relief. Roosevelt was well aware that party unity was not enough for victory as Democrats only constituted a third of registered voters. Accordingly, his nomination-acceptance address invited support from 'those nominal Republicans who find that their conscience cannot be squared with the groping and failure of their party leaders'. This presaged a supra-partisan strategy that eschewed attacks on the opposition party typical of a base-mobilization campaign.[7]

FDR's sometimes anodyne, occasionally contradictory positions on key issues left some commentators confused about his philosophy, but he was following a coherent game plan. As historian Arthur Schlesinger, Jr., observed, '[I]f Roosevelt was evasive about programmes, he had a powerful instinct about directions and a considerable range of commitment to policies.'[8] Throughout the campaign he was steadfast in identifying his candidacy and his agenda with liberalism, broadly defined as federal activism to counteract the Great Depression and establish a more balanced economic system. In its final address, he declared, '[T]here is no glory in a victory only partisan. . . . Unless by victory we can accomplish a greater unity toward liberal effort, we shall have done little indeed.' According to Ernest Lindley, a reporter close to FDR, this strategy reflected his 'consistent ambition for many years . . . to form a new liberal party by attaching the Republican Progressives and miscellaneous liberals to the Democratic Party, thus effecting a new political alignment which had meaning'.[9]

Despite Roosevelt achieving one of the greatest electoral victories in American history, many pundits considered it a qualified triumph owing to his non-partisan approach on the campaign trail. According to *The New Republic*, 'All informed observers agree that the country did not vote for Roosevelt; it voted against Hoover.'[10] In reality the outlines of a new Democratic majority were clearly visible in Roosevelt's huge victory margins in the popular vote and the Electoral College (where he won every state except Maine, Vermont, New Hampshire, Connecticut, Delaware and Pennsylvania). Dominant in every part of the country except New England, he carried a record 2,722 of 3,096 counties nationwide, including 259 that no Democrat had previously won. He re-established the Solid South with 81 per cent of its popular vote, performed strongly in the Northwest and Great Plains where Democrats rarely fared well and swept the big cities. Thanks to his appeal as an Irish-American, Catholic wet, Al Smith had breached the ramparts of Republican urban domination in presidential elections by gaining an aggregate majority of 20,000 in the twelve largest metropolises in 1928. Four years later, FDR carried them by better than 1.5 million votes, running behind Hoover only in Philadelphia. His core support nationwide came from white Southerners, urban ethnics, industrial workers, union members, lower-income voters, the unemployed and farmers. He was also the first Democrat to receive majority support from women since the advent of female suffrage. Meanwhile, his long coat-tails enabled the Democrats to pick up ninety-seven seats in the House of Representatives and eleven seats in the Senate.

Over the course of FDR's first term the political realignment foreshadowed in the elections of 1928 and 1932 reached fruition with the consolidation of a new voter coalition whose constituent elements and associated interest groups were direct beneficiaries of New Deal liberalism. This success came at the cost of sowing discontent among traditional Democratic constituencies and organizations that spilled over into intra-party discord in Roosevelt's second term. Initially this was a conflict over presidential use of patronage to advance the New Deal instead of channelling it exclusively to regular Democrats as a reward for party service. In time, it metamorphosed into a battle for ascendancy over the party's agenda between its liberal and conservative wings.[11]

The early disharmony reflected the tensions between issue-politics and patronage-politics. Roosevelt's liberal priorities put him at odds with regular Democrats, who had anticipated a patronage cornucopia to build up their state and local organizations after twelve years out of power in Washington. FDR showed where his heart really lay in remarks that appeared in his published account of the early New Deal: 'Under a perfect party system a bid for public favour should rest solely on political principles and good administration.'[12] Roosevelt's efforts to operationalize this credo created problems for DNC chair James Farley, his long-standing supporter and campaign manager whom he put in post to run the Democratic Party. Farley's disenchantment with FDR's preference for ideological patronage that promoted the New Deal over organizational patronage that rewarded party regularity would eventually undermine their political alliance.[13]

Bowing to Roosevelt's priorities, Farley restructured the DNC to enhance the role of its special divisions representing women, labour and African Americans, hitherto operated as temporary agencies to mobilize support at election time. This strengthened the influence of reform-oriented groups committed to using the party as a vehicle for their programmatic concerns.

Eleanor Roosevelt was the moving force in the decision to make the Women's Division, established in 1922, a permanent operation in early 1933. She was also instrumental in the appointment as director of her friend and ally, Mary 'Molly' Dewson, whose vigorous leadership made it the most dynamic DNC division.[14] A Wellesley graduate, Dewson was a trained social worker with a long record of activism for better work conditions and wages for women. Debuting as a Democratic organizer in 1928, she took a leading role in mobilizing women in support of FDR's gubernatorial campaign. In common with Eleanor Roosevelt and Frances Perkins, she had a Victorian conception of women as being more deeply concerned than men with humanitarianism, economic security and peace. Dewson's foremost interest was to put like-minded women, ideally with social-work experience, into party positions regardless of any previous Democratic affiliation. Uninterested in appointing party hacks, even female ones, she sought 'women whom the people know on account of their work on unpaid state boards of welfare, education, etc.; in organizations like the Federation of Women's Clubs and the League of Women Voters, etc.; in farm extension work; as leaders in their professions . . .; in short, women who have forged ahead and obtained public standing and confidence'.[15] She had a hand in securing many of the more than 100 important New Deal posts that went to women. Her lobbying for equal representation of women at every level of Democratic organization was also instrumental in all but nine state parties establishing this by 1939.[16]

Dewson shrewdly recognized that her division would gain FDR's strong support if it promoted his goal of liberalizing and strengthening the Democratic Party instead of focusing solely on advancing women within it. To this end, she organized a publicity campaign between elections to educate women about how the New Deal benefited them. The most ambitious initiative, unveiled at Eleanor Roosevelt's press conference in January 1934, was the 'Reporter Plan' that required every Democratic county women's organization to appoint a 'reporter' for each federal agency to learn how it affected their communities and spread the message therein. The best way to win 'independent, stay-at-home, and possible Republican voters', she told FDR, was to make Democratic women 'the mouth to mouth, house to house interpreters and apostles of the New Deal'.[17] By the time ill health forced Dewson to retire at age 64 in 1938, 80,000 women were involved in this enterprise. The Women's Division additionally organized a 73,000-strong army of women workers to get out the vote in the 1936 election and boosted their numbers to 109,000 for the 1940 election. Dewson proudly informed FDR, 'The party organization has been revivified by women who now see it as the instrument to attain their hopes and dreams of a measure of economic stability and security for every-day persons.'[18]

Despite their mutual respect, Dewson's issue-driven politics made for an uneasy relationship with the DNC chair, the epitome of party regularity. She aimed as far as possible to operate independently from him, relying on Eleanor Roosevelt to bend the president's ear to resolve disagreements in her favour, particularly on budget matters. In 1934, Farley turned down her request for $48,000 to keep voter-education operations at high tempo till the election two years hence. With a strong steer from the First Lady FDR resolved the matter by giving Dewson most of what she wanted, a $36,000 budget and the prerogative of controlling it.[19] These ring-fenced outlays enabled the Women's Division to produce and distribute some 80 per cent of all Democratic campaign material in 1936, mainly in the form of colourful 'Rainbow Flyers' that explained and defended New Deal programmes against Republican criticisms.

Organized labour became another key component of the Roosveltian Democratic Party. The craft-based unions in the American Federation of Labor (AFL) had shown only intermittent partisanship before the 1930s. The labour reforms embodied initially in the National Industrial Recovery Act of 1933 and more comprehensively in the National Labor Relations Act of 1935 transformed unions into an integral element of the New Deal coalition. As chair of the DNC Labour Division, Teamsters' president Daniel Tobin brought leadership stability to its organization but the schism that developed between craft and industrial unions hampered coordination of their partisan operations. Fearful that mass unionization threatened its control of the labour movement, the AFL in September 1936 suspended the ten unions that had formed the Committee (later Congress) of Industrial Organizations (CIO) to spearhead the organization of unskilled and semi-skilled workers. In response, the CIO refused to work through the DNC Labour Division because Tobin was an AFL vice-chairman. Two of its chieftains, John L. Lewis of the United Mine Workers and Sidney Hillman of the Amalgamated Clothing Workers, established a separate organization, the Non-Partisan League, to promote New Deal Democrats.[20]

More partisan, more militant and better coordinated than AFL organizations, the industrial unions became the New Deal's predominant interest-group ally. Never at any stage did the CIO give serious consideration to forming an independent labour party akin to that in Britain because the narrow geographic basis of America's working class made this a pipe dream. Recognizing that industrial unions were the creation of the New Deal, Hillman chided left-wingers on his union's executive board in 1936, 'You talk labor party. But can you have a labor party without an economic labor movement?' If FDR failed to win re-election, he warned, the advent of 'a real Fascist administration' would trample over trade union rights.[21] The fledgling CIO became crucial to the electoral success of the Roosveltian Democratic Party by furnishing campaign workers, mobilizing turnout by union families and becoming its foremost financial contributor. Bankers and stockbrokers had funded around 25 per cent of DNC spending in both the 1928 and 1932 elections, making them the party's primary source of finance, but hostility to the New Deal reduced their contributions to insignificant proportions in 1936 and 1940. The CIO's Non-Partisan League contributed some $770,000 to Democrats in 1936, about 13 per cent of the party's total spending. This was less than what five super-rich families (the du Ponts, Mellons, Pews, Rockefellers and Sloans) donated to the GOP presidential candidate, Governor Alfred Landon (R-Kansas). When it came to the basic currency of elections, however, labour votes far outweighed corporate money in the Roosevelt era.[22]

The DNC's Colored Advisory Group, established in 1932, was historically significant as the first Black division that Democrats had organized at any level of politics but was the least effective special division. Starved of funds, it was largely inactive between elections and experienced high turnover of leadership. For fear of offending the white South, FDR and Farley limited its activities to explaining the benefits of New Deal programmes to Northern Blacks.[23] Of greater importance for this cause, all but five of the New Deal agencies had hired African-American advisers by 1937. The highest-ranking ones formed a networking group that the African-American press dubbed the 'Black Cabinet'. According to Robert Weaver, 'Negro affairs adviser' in the Department of the Interior (later to become the first Black member of the actual Cabinet when Lyndon Johnson made him Secretary of Housing and Urban Development in 1965), they constituted 'a new breed of black appointees . . . chosen more for themselves and their ability to define issues relevant to the black community rather than to pay off political debts'. Their overarching goal was 'to maximize the participation of blacks in all phases of the New Deal'.[24]

FDR's willingness to put ideology ahead of regular party interests extended to working with Republican and independent progressives. Impressed with Roosevelt's gubernatorial support for public power, Senator George Norris (R-Nebraska) organized the National Progressive Republican League to mobilize anti-Hoover Republicans in his support in 1932. To strengthen ties with progressive Republicans, Roosevelt offered Senator Bronson Cutting (R-New Mexico) and then Senator Hiram Johnson (R-California) the post of Secretary of the Interior in his new administration, a job neither wanted. It eventually went to Harold Ickes, a reform-oriented Chicago

Republican, who enthusiastically supported FDR's efforts to build a liberal Democratic majority through amalgamation with progressives. Roosevelt also directed New Deal patronage to Governor Floyd Olson's Farmer–Labor administration in Minnesota and Governor Phillip Lafollette's Progressive administration in Wisconsin, bypassing local Democratic organizations in both cases. Further west in Nebraska, when Norris bolted the GOP to seek Senate re-election as an Independent in 1936, FDR endorsed his candidacy over his Democratic opponent. When urged by Farley to show more loyalty to regulars, FDR responded that his motives were 'as clear as the nose on my face'. Cooperation with progressives of any stripe was preferable to dealing with party spoilsmen who were unreliable supporters of his programmes.[25]

Nowhere were the tensions between independent progressives and regular Democrats more evident than in New York City. FDR's animus against Tammany for its leading role in promoting Al Smith's presidential candidacy in 1932 added spice to the vendetta. After his election as mayor on a combined Republican–Fusion Party ticket in 1933, Fiorello La Guardia forged a political alliance with Roosevelt through the good offices of former Brain Truster Adolph Berle. To the disapproval of James Farley and Bronx boss Ed Flynn, who wanted to deploy federal patronage to build a pro-Roosevelt Democratic organization, La Guardia became the local conduit for the massive infusion of federal money that funded public works in the city. At the groundbreaking of the Queens Midtown Tunnel, FDR asserted that New Deal support for the project (through a Reconstruction Finance Corporation loan and a Public Works Administration grant) 'would not have been possible had it not been for an intelligent and aggressive Administration in the City of New York'.[26]

The desire of New York's CIO unions for a city-based political entity free from AFL and DNC influence further complicated local politics. In early 1936, Eleanor Roosevelt, Sidney Hillman, Berle and La Guardia met to agree on the formation of the American Labor Party to organize left-leaning voters' support not only for the president but also for the broader cause of metropolitan progressivism. Holding the balance of power in city politics, this new force ensured La Guardia's re-election in 1937 and 1941. 'It looks as though the great experiment has come off', Berle enthusiastically reported to FDR, 'and that we may have demonstrated that you can run a political situation without patronage or the spoils system provided the administration is first-rate and the ideas are progressive and intelligent.'[27]

Despite his progressive credentials, La Guardia was no slouch when it came to patronage dispensation. As Ed Flynn remarked, appointments to his administration were 'as partisan to him as any appointment a Tammany Hall Mayor ever made was partisan to Tammany'.[28] Far from killing patronage politics, Roosevelt transformed it to serve his ideological purposes, but this did not rule out cooperation with regular Democrats helpful to the liberal cause. Accordingly, New Deal largess formed the basis for an alliance with the metropolitan chieftains who had opposed his nomination in 1932. Only New York's Tammany, with its special connections to Al Smith, remained beyond the pale for Roosevelt.

The city bosses helped to mobilize the urban vote that kept the New Deal in power, constituted a pro-Roosevelt counterweight against rural and small-town conservatives in state Democratic parties and promoted FDR's precedent-breaking third and fourth runs for president. In return, they benefited from federal patronage to sustain their local organizations, New Deal relief that greatly reduced the financial burden of unemployment assistance carried by municipal treasuries and public-works projects that modernized the infrastructure of their cities and boosted local employment. Furthermore, urban machines were not shy about tying themselves to the immensely popular FDR in local elections. Looking back on the good old days, a Chicago Democrat reflected, 'Franklin Roosevelt was the greatest precinct captain we ever had. He elected everybody – governors, senators, sheriffs, aldermen.'[29]

Roosevelt's hostility to New York City's regular Democrats was the exception rather than the rule in his interactions with urban party organizations. He was on good terms with metropolitan bosses like Edward Kelly in Chicago, Frank Hague in Jersey City, Ed Crump in Memphis and Tom Prendergast in Kansas City (until conviction for income-tax evasion put him in a federal penitentiary). New Deal programmes supported the development of new Democratic machines in hitherto Republican cities like Philadelphia and Pittsburgh. In addition to spending $70 million for work relief in Pittsburgh's Allegheny County in its first two years of operation, the Works Progress Administration provided supervisory jobs for most of its Democratic ward chairmen and precinct captains. Once the mediocre boss of a weak local party, David Lawrence became a force in state and national politics and transitioned into the municipal manager who oversaw Pittsburgh's renaissance after the Second World War.[30]

While Roosevelt built a mutually profitable relationship with urban bosses, his efforts to build an administrative state rather than rely on party government to formulate, promote and manage New Deal programmes alienated many regulars. The plethora of new agencies had Democrats in Congress licking their lips in anticipation of fresh pork to reward their supporters and replenish their organizations after long years of famine. They greased the patronage wheels by exempting these institutions from the merit system that had insulated civil service posts from political control for the previous half-century. By 1936, only some 60 per cent of federal public-service jobs featured on the classified list, compared with 80 per cent four years earlier. Despite his reform credentials, FDR winked at a practice that expanded presidential patronage and facilitated rapid staffing of new agencies. Initially, the scale of resources at his disposal enabled him to satisfy regular Democrats in dispensing some patronage their way, but he grew bolder in appointing individuals whose primary loyalty was to the New Deal as his first term progressed.[31]

To build an executive-led administrative state, Roosevelt increasingly staffed the New Deal agencies from the pool of well-educated, young, idealistic lawyers and academics established by his informal aides, Thomas Corcoran and Benjamin Cohen. This mode of recruitment produced what one approving commentator termed 'a psychic "blood transfusion," which invigorated political administration beyond belief'.[32] Voicing the opposite sentiment of regulars, Ed Flynn remarked,

> Under the leadership of Corcoran, these people became more and more pressing in their urging of appointments. . . . As a result many of the appointments in Washington went to men who were supporters of the President and believed in

what he was trying to do, but who were not Democrats in many instances, and in all instances were not organization Democrats.[33]

Roosevelt's popularity dissuaded the regulars from open rebellion in his first term. The 1934 midterm elections offered clear evidence of his significance to the Democratic ticket. Staying true to his supra-partisan strategy, Roosevelt told an old friend, 'Our strongest plea to the country . . . is that the recovery and reconstruction program is being accomplished by men and women of all parties.'[34] This did not deter him from setting the Democratic midterm theme in a Fireside Chat in late June. '[T]he simplest way for each of you to judge recovery', he told listeners, 'lies in the plain facts of your own individual situation. Are you better off than you were last year? Are your debts less burdensome? Is your bank account more secure? Are your working conditions better? Is your faith in your own individual future more firmly grounded?' Almost every Democrat running for office campaigned on their support for FDR. Sensing the national mood, Speaker Henry Rainey (D-Illinois), shortly before his sudden death in August, counselled congressional candidates in marginal districts that their best hope of victory was 'to preach the Roosevelt philosophy and stand behind the President'.[35]

The New Deal passed its first electoral test with flying colours, thanks to the consolidation of the new Democratic voter coalition. This was the only midterm election between 1902 and 2002 in which a first-term president's party did not lose seats in at least one chamber of Congress. The Democrats added to their already swollen majorities in making a net gain of nine seats in House races and, even more remarkably, capturing nine Senate seats from the Republicans. They lost some House seats in rural districts in the Midwest and West but made compensatory urban gains in Connecticut, Illinois, Massachusetts, Missouri and, most notably, Pennsylvania. In the Senate races, urban support gained them wins in Connecticut, Rhode Island, New Jersey, Pennsylvania, Ohio and Indiana. Their other three pick-ups were in the Border states of Maryland, West Virginia and Missouri. In the latter, future president Harry Truman won a landslide victory with the assistance of massive voter registration drives by Democratic organizations in Kansas City and St Louis. Nowhere was the transformation of the Democrats' urban power more evident than in Pennsylvania, which Hoover had carried by 150,000 votes in 1932. In 1934, the Keystone state elected its first Democratic governor since 1890, its first Democratic senator since 1874 (Joseph Guffey, a '100% New Dealer') and twelve Democrats to GOP-held House seats.

The 1934 midterms were also significant for being the first elections in which African Americans turned Lincoln's portrait to the wall. Northern Blacks were now beneficiaries of New Deal relief and their leaders were being courted with patronage dispensed by urban bosses. In the most significant effort to co-opt them, Chicago's Kelly–Nash organization ran African-American Arthur Mitchell, a recent convert from the GOP, to challenge incumbent Oscar de Priest in the Illinois first congressional district, which included the South Side Black ghetto. Campaigning on a 'Forward with Roosevelt' slogan, Mitchell rolled out a victory by 53 to 47 per cent of the vote to become the first Black Democrat in Congress in place of the solitary Republican one.[36]

Roosevelt's authority over the Democratic Party climaxed with his landslide re-election of 1936 following a highly personal campaign that barely mentioned it by name. He also ignored his Republican opponent, Alfred Landon, who claimed to offer a more efficient and less expensive version of the New Deal. 'There's only one issue in this campaign', FDR told Raymond Moley, 'It's myself, and people must be for me or against me.'[37] Presenting himself as the candidate of the people, he ran as the enemy of the special interests of wealth and privilege rather than of the Republicans. 'We have earned the hatred of entrenched greed', the president declared in his 1936 State of the Union Address. 'They seek the restoration of their selfish power. . . . Give them their way and they will take the course of every autocracy of the past – power for themselves, enslavement for the public.'[38]

Six months later Roosevelt accepted the Democratic presidential nomination with a momentous address broadcast nationwide from Philadelphia's Franklin Field. It drew parallels between the patriots who issued the Declaration of Independence against political autocracy in the city in 1776 and his own battle against the 'economic royalists' who had 'concentrated into their own hands an almost complete control over other people's property, other people's money, other people's labor – other people's lives' before New Deal government freed American citizens from such 'economic tyranny'.[39] Hot stuff this may have been, but its tone was made to look moderate by FDR's final campaign address at Madison Square Garden on 31 October. After receiving a thirteen-minute ovation from the wildly enthusiastic audience, he launched into his 'old enemies', the beneficiaries of 'business and financial monopoly, speculation, reckless banking, class antagonism, war profiteering'. These forces of 'organized money' regarded the federal government 'as a mere appendage to their own affairs' until he seized their 'pass-keys' to the White House. Sounding like an avenging angel, he avowed,

> Never before . . . have these forces been so united against one candidate as they stand today. They are unanimous in their hate for me – and I welcome their hatred. I should like to have it said of my first Administration that in it the forces of selfishness and of lust for power met their match. I should like to have it said of my second Administration that in it these forces met their master.[40]

In 1932, Roosevelt had run a big-tent campaign that welcomed business support for activist government, but four years later he declared political war on corporate America. The other side in this conflict was already engaged in an all-out assault on the New Deal. Having greeted FDR as a saviour in 1933, most of the country's top businessmen came to see him as a traitor to his class within two years. The 1935 legislative programme, featuring a bill of rights for organized labour, social insurance provision, the break-up of public-utilities holding companies and a wealth tax, became their casus belli. Organizations like the US Chamber of Commerce, the American Management Association and National Association of Manufacturers made unrestrained attacks on Rooseveltian collectivism as an existential threat to capitalism. At the latter's 1935 convention, its president declared that 'industry was now in politics to rid the United States of the New Deal'.[41]

At the forefront of the business campaign was the American Liberty League (ALL), co-founded in 1934 by former DNC chair John Raskob, supported by a bipartisan coalition of conservatives with strong corporate connections and bankrolled by the

Du Pont family. Among its luminaries were John Davis and Al Smith, respectively the 1924 and 1928 Democratic presidential nominees. Over the next two years the ALL issued 177 anti-New Deal tracts and distributed 5 million copies for free. To launch its election-year operations, the group wheeled out its biggest gun to fire an hour-long salvo against the New Deal at the Mayflower Hotel, Washington DC, before 2,000 well-heeled guests on 26 January 1936. Training his sights on the president, Al Smith avowed, 'There can only be one capital, Washington or Moscow. There can only be the clear, pure, fresh air of free America, or the foul breath of communistic Moscow.'[42]

Joining battle with business made political sense as a re-election strategy: it allowed FDR to continue the supra-partisan approach of 1932; it forced Landon into a defence of business, thereby tying his rival to the corporate donors pouring vast sums of money into Republican coffers; and it shored up his left flank. While the ALL accused FDR of socialism, the trio of Senator Huey Long (D-Louisiana), radio priest Father Charles Coughlin and old-age pension campaigner Francis Townsend damned him for being too close to bankers and business. Long's Share Our Wealth Society quickly grew into a national movement capable of supporting his independent presidential candidacy. A secret DNC poll undertaken in spring 1935 estimated that he could take sufficient votes from Roosevelt to facilitate Republican victory in 1936.[43] The Louisianan's assassination at the State Capitol on 8 September 1935 removed this threat, but Coughlin, Townsend and Gerald L. K. Smith, a one-time field organizer for Share Our Wealth clubs, created the Union Party, which nominated Representative William Lemke (R-North Dakota), a prairie progressive, as its presidential candidate. Initial DNC concerns that Lemke would eat into Roosevelt's working-class support in some key Northern states proved unfounded. The Union Party turned out to be the dampest of squibs – its leaders' increasingly frantic attacks on FDR could not dent his popularity, it failed to get on the ballot in 14 states and it amassed only 892,000 votes in the others.

As the election approached, some polls predicted a tight race, but their methodology was unreliable. James Farley famously made the right forecast that FDR would capture every state except Maine and Vermont. This outcome gave him an Electoral College majority of 523 to 8, the largest in history. His popular-vote share of 60.8 per cent and his eleven million plurality over Landon set new records. Presidential coat-tails helped the Democrats win majorities of unprecedented scope over the GOP in the House (333 seats to 89) and the Senate (76 seats to 16). Roosevelt carried every part of the country to make his victory a nationwide one. About 20 per cent of his support came from voters who usually identified as Republicans. Of the six million increase in turnout over 1932, he captured close to five million, running particularly well among first-time voters. The foundations for his success lay in the cities: his margins were better than 2 to 1 in Baltimore, Chicago, Cleveland, Detroit and Los Angeles, 3 to 1 in San Francisco and New York, 4 to 1 in Milwaukee and bigger still in Southern metropolises like Atlanta, Birmingham and Houston. In becoming the first Democrat since 1856 to carry Pennsylvania, his plurality was based on massive majorities in Philadelphia (where his vote share was 60.5 per cent) and Pittsburgh.

These numbers marked the final stage in the creation of the Democrats' urban power base that had been in the making since 1928. In all, FDR won 102 of the nation's 106 cities with a population of 100,000 or more. A class-based New Deal-forged electoral coalition, drawing support from urban voters in the lower half of the income distribution regardless of their race or ethnicity, was now in being. Among participating voters in 1936, Roosevelt's winning numbers were 74 per cent of semi-skilled workers, 81 per cent of unskilled ones and 80 per cent of labour-union members; 84 per cent of relief recipients; 86 per cent of Jews; 81 per cent of Catholics; and 71 per cent of African Americans.[44]

The scale of victory emboldened FDR's efforts to liberalize his party. In early 1937, former White House insider Stanley High published an article in *The Saturday Evening Post* predicting a second-term battle 'to determine whether the Democratic Party is to be . . . as it has always been or whether it is now to become the liberal party'.[45] The president's controversial efforts to pack the Supreme Court had a direct effect on the outcome of this struggle. His aura of invincibility punctured by defeat over judicial reorganization, FDR's party liberalization project faced growing opposition within Democratic ranks. For some of his adversaries, the bone of contention was still patronage, but for a growing number the central issue had become their philosophical disagreements with the New Deal since the leftward turn of 1935.

In FDR's first term, the main challenge to the New Deal had come from the Supreme Court; in his second, it came from conservative Democrats in Congress, abetted in second-fiddle role by conservative Republicans. Conservative Democrats came from every region, mainly represented rural districts and states, and resented Roosevelt's growing alignment with urban liberalism. The epicentre of anti-New Deal sentiment was the South, home to half of the conservative Democratic bloc in the House and a third of its Senate counterpart.[46] Despite the many benefits the New Deal brought their region, Dixie conservatives disliked its increasingly anti-business tone, resented its growing association with urban interests and worried about its consequences for racial hierarchies. Above all, they fretted over their diminished influence in the party they once dominated. As historian Susan Dunn observed, the illusion that 'they were merely leasing out their party on a short term basis' to Roosevelt was no longer sustainable.[47]

The 1936 Democratic National Convention's abolition of the two-thirds rule requiring a supermajority of delegates to nominate presidential and vice-presidential candidates offered the clearest proof that the South no longer ruled the roost. Adopted in 1832, this rule effectively guaranteed that no one could gain a spot on the national ticket without its support. At FDR's behest, Jim Farley stacked the convention rules committee to ensure a recommendation for its termination, which non-Southern delegations overwhelmingly approved in a floor vote. Its removal, Senator Josiah Bailey (D-North Carolina) lamented, would 'enable the Northern and Western Democrats to control the party, nominate its candidates and write its platform. All this will come out in 1940'.[48] Like many Southerners, Bailey had been a Roosevelt loyalist before disenchantment with his liberal party-building. 'What we have to do', he told fellow conservatives in 1937, 'is to preserve, if we can, the Democratic Party against his efforts to make it the Roosevelt party'.[49]

FDR himself was optimistic that the New Deal would enable a new generation of Southern liberals to wrest regional leadership from conservatives.[50] In early 1938 there were signs that this process was in train. On 4 January, Lister Hill, a liberal-leaning congressman running with Roosevelt's endorsement, won the special Democratic primary to fill Alabama's Senate seat (vacated by Hugo Black on elevation to the Supreme Court) by a margin of 61 to 34 per cent over race-baiting, anti-New Dealer Thomas Heflin. Buoyed by this success, FDR used his Jackson Day dinner address to hammer out the message that the Democratic Party stood for 'the essential unity of our country' and the common welfare of the majority. It could not, he asserted, be home to those who put sectionalism ahead of national interest.[51] Acting through his White House secretary, James Roosevelt, the president's next step was to endorse liberal incumbent Claude Pepper for re-nomination as Florida senator against the primary challenge of anti-New Dealer Neil Wilcox. 'The issue', Pepper wrote in his diary, 'is the New Deal or not – liberalism versus reaction.' With the administration's patronage assistance, he ran out the clear winner with 58 per cent of the vote on 3 May. The outcome, Roosevelt wrote a British friend, 'seemed to prove that the voters' hearts (and heads!) seem still to be in the right place'.[52]

Pepper's success in Florida encouraged what the press called an 'elimination committee', consisting of James Roosevelt, Thomas Corcoran and Harry Hopkins, to seek the ouster of Senator Guy Gillette (D-Iowa), a moderate conservative whose sin was to oppose FDR's judiciary bill. With the state party in the incumbent's corner, their hasty, disorganized and under-resourced efforts to unseat him got nowhere. At this point, Roosevelt himself decided to take charge of the campaign to promote liberals in the Democratic primaries. By now, he was widely perceived in Congress and the press as its moving force, so other setbacks would inevitably be interpreted as signalling his declining hold over the national party. In a Fireside Chat on 24 June, he urged primary voters to consider whether the candidate they supported adhered to the liberal or conservative 'school of thought'. Distinguishing between his role as president and party leader, FDR asserted his responsibility in the latter capacity to carry out 'the definitely liberal declarations of principle set forth in the 1936 Democratic platform'. Signalling his intent to support liberals, he claimed 'every right to speak in those few instances where there may be a clear issue between candidates for the Democratic nomination involving these principles, or involving a clear misuse of my own name'.[53]

Roosevelt proceeded in the months that followed to endorse liberal-leaning Democrats facing conservative primary opponents. On his train trip west in July to take a Pacific cruise vacation, he stopped off in various locations to voice support for Senator Alben Barkley (D-Kentucky), Senator Hattie Caraway (D-Arkansas), Senator Elmer Thomas (D-Oklahoma) and Representative Lyndon B. Johnson (D-Texas), all of whom won their primary races. Roosevelt probably regretted not making a detour to endorse Senator James Pope (D-Idaho), a New Deal loyalist narrowly defeated by a conservative primary challenger. Nevertheless, his approval did not bestow certainty of victory on its recipients as Representative Maury Maverick (D-Texas) and Senator William Gibbs McAdoo (D-California) discovered, but the latter at least went down to a liberal challenger.[54]

Only in five primary contests did presidential involvement entail more than rhetorical endorsement of liberal incumbents. In Kentucky, Alben Barkley benefited from increased Works Progress Administration spending for his state and the votes of relief workers, whom the agency directed to support him. He eventually took 56 per cent of the primary vote to defeat Governor Albert Chandler, who had state government resources at his disposal. More was involved than just the re-election of a New Deal stalwart. Roosevelt had used his influence to secure Barkley's election as Senate Majority Leader by a one-vote margin over Pat Harrison (D-Mississippi) in July 1937. If this administration loyalist had fallen, the Senate leadership would have passed to a conservative Southern Democrat.[55]

Roosevelt also attempted in vain to oust three senatorial incumbents, Walter George (D-Georgia), Ellison 'Cotton Ed' Smith (D-South Carolina) and Millard Tydings (D-Maryland). Prudence deterred him from moving against strongly entrenched conservatives in Connecticut, Colorado, Missouri and Nevada. He mistakenly assumed that the earlier victories of Lister Hill and Claude Pepper signified that the New Deal had made the South and its environs fertile terrain for liberalism. Calling the region 'the Nation's number one economic problem', he commissioned the National Economic Council to produce *The Report on Economic Conditions in the South*, a manifesto for uplift under the New Deal. Released in August, its vision for economic reform was clearly dependent on a new breed of Southern liberals gaining office in place of traditional conservatives. 'It takes a long, long time to bring the past up to the present', a chastened FDR admitted after his efforts to promote their succession ended in failure.[56]

Roosevelt only campaigned vigorously in Maryland but could not transfer his popularity to his hand-picked challenger, David Lewis, an obscure congressman. Tydings benefited from greater name recognition, aroused animus against outside interference and outspent his rival by nearly two-to-one. In Georgia and South Carolina efforts to mobilize relief workers had little effect because most were poor whites and African Americans ineligible for suffrage. George and Smith also whipped up popular outrage against presidential interference as the modern-day equivalent of the Reconstruction carpetbaggers, outsiders who sought to impose racial equality on the South. For good measure, George spoke of a 'second march through Georgia' to remind voters of the Civil War episode that lived in infamy in their memory.[57]

The purge campaign's solitary success was the ouster of Representative John O'Connor (D-New York), who had stymied New Deal legislation as Rules Committee chair. The president's endorsement of his challenger, James Fay, carried more weight in an urban district where low-income voters predominated. Whereas the attempted Senate purges involved half-measures, FDR aides worked systematically to defeat O'Connor. 'This single victory', *The New Republic* exulted, 'is enough to justify the whole [purge] effort.'[58] That assessment underestimated what Roosevelt achieved in the midterm primaries. His principal interventions preserved a loyal Senate leader and removed an obstructive House committee chair, while other intercessions helped a number of liberal incumbents to win their primaries. Nevertheless, the failure to purge George, Smith and Tydings signified that the Democratic Party could not be remade into an entirely liberal one. Many congressional conservatives were too strongly entrenched in their home districts and states. This was particularly the case in the South, whose political traditions, racial hierarchy and relatively backward economy pre-empted the emergence of the kind of electoral coalition that sustained the New Deal in the urban North.

Following the failed purges, the Republican midterm revival made the future of liberalism, seemingly so secure two years previously, appear to *The New Republic* 'full of danger and uncertainty'.[59] The unpopularity of the new farm bill resulted in farmers outside the South becoming the first group to desert the Roosevelt voter coalition. More generally, disenchantment with FDR's court-packing scheme, the CIO sit-down strikes and, in particular, the recession caused middle-class defections. The GOP captured eighty-one seats in the House (including nine from minor parties), among them thirteen in Ohio, twelve in Pennsylvania and eight in Wisconsin, and seven Senate seats.[60] Democrats still retained huge majorities of 262 to 169 in the House and 68 to 23 in the Senate, but the loss of reliable New Dealers made conservatives relatively stronger in both chambers.

In the new House of Representatives, some fifty anti-New Deal Democrats regularly aligned with the enlarged Republican contingent to block Roosevelt's initiatives. Their Senate colleagues, numbering between twenty and thirty depending on the issue, lacked comparable firepower because GOP numbers were proportionately smaller, but were still a force to be reckoned with. Democratic dissidents had a further asset in the disproportionate influence of Southerners in the standing committees of both chambers through which every legislative proposal had to pass. Effectively sent to Congress for life by their one-party region, Dixie conservatives profited from the seniority system that made advancement in these bodies dependent on the longevity of service. At the end of the bitterly disappointing congressional session of 1939 for liberals, Claude Pepper rose in the Senate to express outrage at 'the unrighteous partnership of those who have been willing to scuttle the American government and the American people . . . because they hate Roosevelt and what Roosevelt stands for'.[61]

If FDR's political fortunes were at their lowest ebb in the wake of the midterms, he had not given up on his party-transformation project. Accepting an honorary degree from the University of North Carolina, he avowed that liberalism, far from being on its 'way to the cemetery', would 'come to life again with more strength than . . . before'. With fascism on the move abroad, a liberal America was essential for 'the maintenance of successful democracy at home', which was vital in turn for the survival of democracy elsewhere.[62] Accordingly, Roosevelt was determined that his successor as Democratic leader should be a liberal. He wrote his old Navy Department boss, Josephus Daniels, that he would find it impossible to support a conservative-headed Democratic ticket in 1940. In July 1939, he intimated to James Farley that the next Democratic presidential candidate should be 'someone who is sympathetic to my administration and who will continue my policies'. Making such sentiments public in a communication to the Young Democratic Clubs of America in August, he avowed, 'If we nominate conservative candidates, or lip-service candidates, on a straddle bug platform, I personally . . . will find it impossible to have any active part in such an unfortunate suicide of the old Democratic Party.'[63] These strictures effectively ruled out the candidacy of Vice President John Garner, who had colluded openly with congressional conservatives in FDR's second term. They also constituted a blow to Farley's own presidential ambition because he was essentially a party regular rather than a liberal.[64]

The lack of an electable liberal to continue the New Deal crusade left FDR with no alternative but to run himself in 1940. Despite complaining in private that he was worn down by the presidency, fed up with politics and anxious for retirement to his beloved Hyde Park, he allowed Mayor Edward Kelly of Chicago to line up delegate support without a formal declaration of candidacy.[65] If he chose to run, he wanted the national convention to draft him, ideally by acclamation, to circumvent anti-third term sentiment expressed by the majority of respondents to a Gallup poll in early 1940. Exploiting this popular mood, Republicans accused him of dictatorial ambition, encapsulated in the slogan 'No Crown for Franklin', for wanting to break the two-term tradition set by George Washington. Jumping on this bandwagon, Farley and Garner collaborated to unite dissident Democrats against a third term to boost their own candidacies.

FDR probably made the final decision to run after the Nazi blitzkrieg transformed the war in Europe, but events abroad arguably confirmed rather than kindled his resolve. The need to sustain Democratic liberalism had been driving him inexorably towards a third-term candidacy since the midterms.[66] Victories for pro-FDR slates in a string of presidential primaries affirmed his overwhelming popularity with Democratic voters. Whatever their patronage gripes, many regulars now acknowledged that his popular appeal was essential to elect down-ticket candidates. Despite the nomination being his for the asking, Roosevelt was determined to maintain the charade of being spontaneously drafted. The selection of Chicago to host the national convention made it possible for Mayor Kelly and Cook County Democratic chairman Pat Nash to arrange this outcome. On the evening of 16 July, day two of the convention, Chairman Alben Barkley read out the president's statement denying any desire to be re-nominated and releasing his delegates. A stunned silence was broken by a booming and repeated chant from the sound system, 'We Want Roosevelt'. On cue, Kelly–Nash men flooded the floor followed by delegates from other states to participate in a prolonged demonstration for FDR. The voice that launched it belonged to Chicago superintendent of sewers Thomas Garry, posted in the basement with microphone in hand to whip up the crowd. The next evening, Roosevelt stormed to a first-ballot victory, prompting his rivals to accept his nomination by acclamation.[67]

Determined to have an all-liberal ticket, FDR wanted Henry Wallace, a New Deal stalwart, as his running mate. The Secretary of Agriculture would shore up farm support in the Midwest, was a committed internationalist in foreign affairs and had bipartisan appeal as a one-time Republican. Wanting one of their own in second spot, many regulars came out in support of Speaker William Bankhead (D-Alabama). Facing a mutiny, FDR's convention managers urged him to come to Chicago to put the case for Wallace in person, but he remained in the White House and sent the First Lady instead. When the rebellious mood of the anti-Wallace forces came across via the radio, Roosevelt decided that a personal intervention was necessary. He summarily drafted a statement withdrawing his own candidacy for delivery to the convention if it failed to nominate the running mate of his choice.

In final form, the message asserted:

Until the Democratic Party through this Convention makes clear its overwhelming stand in favor of social progress and liberalism, and shakes off all the shackles of control fastened upon it by the forces of conservatism, reaction and appeasement, it will not continue its march of victory. . . . I wish to give [it] the opportunity to make its historic decision clearly and without equivocation. The party must go wholly one way or wholly the other. It cannot face in both directions at the same time. By declining the honor of its nomination for the Presidency, I can restore that opportunity to the Convention. I so do.

FDR allowed his managers to communicate his threat when working the various state delegations on Wallace's behalf. The First Lady's gracious speech urging the convention to honour the president's preference also went down well. Prodded by big-city leaders, Northern and Western delegations delivered the votes to nominate Wallace by a two-to-one majority over Bankhead, whose support came mainly from the South and Border states. The speechwriter who polished the withdrawal announcement from FDR's original draft adjudged that he was in deadly earnest about refusing the nomination unless the party approved his vice-presidential choice. '[I]f I ever saw him with his mind made up', Samuel Rosenman reflected, 'it was that night.'[68]

Despite the war in Europe having taken a critical turn with the fall of France just weeks earlier, this episode indicated the primary significance of domestic political considerations in FDR's decision to run in 1940. As further confirmation, he told Senator George Norris that he had accepted the nomination to prevent conservative Democrats from regaining control of the party. 'I was frankly amazed', he remarked, 'by the terrific drive which was put on by the old-line conservatives to make so many things adverse to liberalism occur.' To his mind, the nomination of the Roosevelt–Wallace ticket constituted 'a great victory' over the forces that wanted to put the Democratic Party 'back where it was in 1920, 1924 and 1928'.[69] FDR had actually achieved three triumphs at Chicago: his own nomination for a third term, Wallace's nomination and his lieutenants' success in securing a party platform endorsing New Deal liberalism. All told, these successes constituted a veritable purge of conservative influence from the presidential wing of the Democratic Party. To reinforce what this meant for the future, his radio address accepting the presidential nomination emphasized that the social legislation of his first two terms embodied 'the constantly growing sense of human decency . . . throughout the nation', which was leading inexorably to 'a war against poverty and suffering and ill-health and insecurity, a war in which all classes are joining in the interest of a sound and enduring democracy'.[70]

Roosevelt found himself running against the most progressive Republican that he faced in his four presidential races. Though Wendell Willkie had made his name as a utility executive opposed to FDR's interventions in his industry, he now acknowledged the New Deal's broader merits. The darkest of dark horses, he was virtually unknown in the party prior to its 1940 national convention. Desperate to regain national power, a group of mainly Northeastern GOP leaders came to the conclusion that the party's best chance for victory lay in having a candidate as similar as possible in his political positions to FDR.

A former Democrat, who had voted for Roosevelt in 1932, Willkie ran on a platform that effectively legitimized New Deal reforms in recognition of their popular support. In a *Fortune* article that brought him to the attention of GOP leaders, he had declared, 'There has grown up a new concept of public welfare. . . . Government, either state or federal, must be responsible not only for the destitute and the unemployed, but for elementary guarantees of public health, the rehabilitation of farmers, rebuilding of the soil, preservation of the national forests, clearance and elimination of city slums, and so forth.' His candidacy signified that the GOP was not ready to embrace the conservative identity that Roosevelt's vision of political realignment assigned it. In acknowledgement of this, the president told Frances Perkins, 'You know Willkie would have made a good Democrat. Too bad we lost him.' Equally important, his opponent was strongly in favour of the United States supporting Britain in its struggle with Nazi Germany by all means short of war. In FDR's opinion, his nomination had been a 'Godsend to the country' because it ensured that the election would not be fought on interventionist-versus-isolationist lines.[71]

Instead of attacking the New Deal's socio-economic reforms, Willkie condemned it for throttling the capacity of private enterprise to generate full recovery from the Great Depression, but the steady growth of defence-related jobs throughout 1940 undercut this message. In desperation, he turned to accuse Roosevelt of intent to join the war against Germany once re-elected, which improved his poll numbers. This forced FDR to abandon his strategy of standing above the campaign while fulfilling his commander-in-chief obligations to keep the international situation under review and ensure America's defences. In October he delivered major addresses in five cities reasserting his determination to keep the nation at peace but took the opportunity in each to assert the New Deal's achievements and its ongoing agenda. In an election-eve address at Cleveland, he outlined a vision of America's future that encompassed, among other things, an end to poverty, universal educational opportunity, fair taxation and enhanced labour rights 'if we but follow the charts and the guides of our democratic faith'.[72]

Despite polls pointing to a close contest, Roosevelt eventually ran out a convincing winner. He carried the Electoral College by 449 votes to 82, taking all but 10 states (Willkie added Indiana, Michigan, Iowa, both Dakotas, Nebraska, Kansas and Colorado to Landon's Maine and Vermont), and the popular vote by 54.7 per cent to 44.8 per cent. Though Roosevelt was 'Safe on Third', this was his narrowest victory hitherto. Willkie's popular-vote deficit of 4.9 million votes was a huge improvement on Landon's in 1936. He captured some 4.7 million voters who had cast ballots for FDR four years earlier, but won just 3.8 million new voters against FDR's 6.5 million. It is likely that 70 per cent of the 1940 voters stayed with their 1936 party, 14 per cent were switchers and 16 per cent were new voters. To win, Willkie needed about a million more switchers than he gained and something like a half-share of new voters. Roosevelt's top-heavy majorities in the nation's 12 biggest cities with populations over 500,000 accounted for 45 per cent of his popular-vote margin. His huge metropolitan numbers overcame Willkie's superiority in rural and small-town counties in New York, Illinois, Ohio and Wisconsin, and contributed significantly to his carrying Massachusetts, Pennsylvania, Maryland, Missouri and California.[73]

Outside the South, voting was largely a reflection of class: Gallup's post-election survey estimated that FDR won 28 per cent of the upper-income vote, 53 per cent of the middle-income vote and 69 per cent of the lower-income vote. Roosevelt won a third of business and professional voters, nearly half of white collars, two-thirds of labour and four-fifths of Social Security and federal relief recipients. John Lewis's endorsement of Willkie in protest at FDR's neutrality in the sit-down strikes

– and promise to resign as CIO boss if the president was re-elected – did not cause substantial defections by industrial-union workers. Those who switched may have been responsible for Roosevelt's narrow failure to carry Michigan and Indiana. Meanwhile, African Americans gave FDR 67 per cent of their votes, a little down on their 1936 levels because Willkie's stronger stance on civil rights attracted better-off Blacks. Tracking the 1940 vote in thirteen big cities (twelve of them Northern ones stretching from Boston to Seattle, plus Los Angeles), election analyst Samuel Lubell concluded that it followed economic lines. In his assessment, the 'little fellow' re-elected Roosevelt and the 1940 vote confirmed that the New Deal had 'drawn a class line across the face of American politics'.[74]

These statistics underlined the continued significance of the class-based New Deal coalition for the presidential wing of the Democratic Party. This in turn suggested that domestic issues outweighed international matters in deciding the election outcome. That said, a majority of the public changed from opposing to approving a third term for FDR on account of his foreign policy experience in Gallup polls taken after the fall of France. Nevertheless, the clearest conclusion to be drawn from the election was that the New Deal had become embedded in America's political life. Far from conducting an autopsy on a programme that appeared moribund in 1939, the rival presidential candidates were agreed on its permanence and both envisioned how it would develop in the future.[75]

Once America became a belligerent in the global war, FDR had little time for his party liberalization project, but he had made considerable progress in its advancement by then. He had transformed the Democratic Party into the majority party in national politics through endowing it with a liberal identity. Presenting himself as the defender of 'the people' against 'special interests', he had created a class-based voter coalition that would underwrite Democratic ascendancy for close on half-a-century. Despite intra-party strife, he had preserved the fundamental New Deal idea that government had a duty to protect Americans from socio-economic vicissitudes as the core principle of Democratic political philosophy. Finally, he had deployed the patronage accrued from electoral success to build up a liberal administrative state that insured the consolidation of the New Deal.

The Democratic mainstream became to all intents and purposes a Roosevelt party as the New Deal era progressed, but the continued influence of a conservative minority signified that the presidential transformation was far from total. Though no longer able to control the national party, this faction retained sufficient influence in Congress to defeat, diminish or delay reform initiatives. While the head, front legs and one back leg of the Democratic donkey followed Roosevelt, the right hind leg did not march to the same drum, which slowed its liberal progress without ever reversing it.

Communicator-in-chief

FDR's public presidency

If Franklin D. Roosevelt did not invent the public presidency, he was indispensable to its becoming an essential instrument of modern presidential leadership. Early twentieth-century presidents were the first to make campaign-like appeals for popular support, a practice that became routine after FDR. As much teacher as spokesman, Roosevelt was uniquely skilled in pursuing a communications strategy of civic education to help Americans understand his response to economic depression in the 1930s and global war in the 1940s. 'The presidency', he declared in 1932, 'is pre-eminently a place of moral leadership. All our great Presidents were leaders of thought at times when certain historic ideas in the life of the nation had to be clarified. . . . Without leadership alert and sensitive to change, we . . . lose our way.'[1]

Though well established by the 1930s, the public presidency only came into being around the turn of the century. Hitherto, all but a handful of presidents scorned public rhetoric as demagogic violations of the deliberative spirit of republican government. On the infrequent occasions when nineteenth-century presidents engaged in it, they did so primarily in written rather than spoken form, addressed to Congress rather than the people.[2] Communication with the nation eventually acquired democratic legitimacy in response to the growth of education, literacy, newspaper readership and suffrage. This form of presidential politics came into its own with Theodore Roosevelt's public campaigns to check the power of big-business trusts. The concept of a direct relationship between the presidency and the people underwrote his conviction that an activist chief executive should take the lead in determining how the federal government addressed the national interest and should mould popular support for his initiatives. TR's legacy was a presidency that set the political agenda through speeches, interactions with the press and other forms of media and close association with the public will.[3]

Initially associated with Progressivism, the public presidency was deployed for different ends during the Republican ascendancy of the 1920s. Its most successful practitioner, Calvin Coolidge, built up his personal popularity as a shield against censure of his pro-business agenda through regular press conferences, frequent newsreel appearances and occasional radio addresses, a strategy that critics decried as 'government by publicity'.[4] When prosperity gave way to depression, Herbert Hoover could not provide the public leadership that the times demanded. His failure to uplift the nation's spirits made him the perfect foil to put FDR's later accomplishments in best light. His impersonal speaking style did not connect with radio audiences, his press conferences were largely devoid of real news and his public statements highlighting his efforts to get business to boost employment came under attack for being 'relief by publicity'. As the economic crisis deepened, Hoover's sensitivity to press criticism caused him to retreat within the White House. His abandonment of the public presidency showed a fatal misunderstanding of the importance of image to leadership. As columnist Walter Lippmann commented, Hoover lacked 'the capacity . . . to fight fire with fire, passion with passion, and slogans with slogans'.[5]

For reporters, FDR was a breath of fresh air following Hoover's sullen stuffiness. Shortly before his inauguration, press secretary-designate Stephen Early leaked to some prominent newsmen that Roosevelt wanted 'to make the White House assignment an important one and not a watchdog affair, one that would require the very best correspondents to swing'.[6] Washington consequently became the hottest centre of news in America. By 1934, United Press (UP) coverage of affairs in the nation's capital was three times the volume of 1930 and a quarter of all Associated Press (AP) stories featured the same locus. The bulk of this news torrent flowed from the White House and the new executive agencies that were being created with breathtaking rapidity, rather than Congress – and the most important point of origin was the president himself. Attesting to this, the Press Club of faraway San Francisco dedicated its annual publication, *Scoop*, 'to the "best news source" in America, Franklin D. Roosevelt' in 1935. Veteran AP correspondent Jack Bell later remarked of FDR, 'He talked in headline phrases. He acted; he emoted; he was angry; he was smiling. . . . He was exciting. He was human. He was copy'. Adjudging Roosevelt peerless in his handling of journalists, columnist Heywood Broun decreed him 'the best newspaperman who has ever been President of the United States'.[7]

Roosevelt did not think well of the press in return. If he never went as far as Richard Nixon and Donald Trump in attacking the media, he certainly foreshadowed the former in suspecting it of ideological conspiracy against his presidency, and some of his accusations had parallels with the latter's condemnation of 'fake news'. This outlook reflected the Jeffersonian tenets that FDR incorporated into his liberal political philosophy when pondering the Democratic Party's future after the disastrous 1924 elections. The inspiration for this thinking came from reading *Jefferson and Hamilton: The Struggle for Democracy in America*, authored by newspaper editor and popular historian Claude Bowers.[8]

With Theodore Roosevelt to the fore, many progressives had disdained Thomas Jefferson as the champion of states' rights, limited national government and restrained engagement abroad. They correspondingly acclaimed arch-rival Alexander Hamilton's assertive use of federal authority to promote the young republic's prosperity and power. Breaking with this orthodoxy, Bowers eulogized Jefferson as America's first great democrat in his defence of the common people against the special interests of industry, commerce and finance during the political battles of the 1790s with the Hamiltonian Federalists. Reviewing the book for the Bowers-edited *New York Evening World*, FDR sang Jefferson's praises for organizing the working masses and small farmers into a majority coalition that defeated 'the organized compact forces of wealth, of birth, of commerce, of the press' to win the election of 1800. To his mind, 'Jefferson's faith in mankind was vindicated; his appeal to the intelligence of the average voter bore fruit; his conception of a democratic republic came true.' Roosevelt concluded his review by warning that the struggle between democracy and plutocracy was never ending. 'I wonder', he remarked, 'if . . . the same contending forces are not again mobilizing. Hamiltons we have today. Is a Jefferson on the horizon?' Shortly afterwards, he wrote a fellow Democrat, 'Jefferson brought the government back to the hands of the average voter, through insistence on fundamental principles, and the education of the average voter. We need a similar campaign of education today, and perhaps we shall find another Jefferson.' It soon became evident that FDR saw himself as playing this role.[9]

The celebration of the Jeffersonian past as the dawning of American democracy looks hopelessly anachronistic to twenty-first-century eyes. A number of state Democratic parties have renamed their annual Jefferson–Jackson Day fundraising dinners in acknowledgement that commemoration of two slave-owning and Indian-land-grabbing presidents sits uncomfortably alongside their own commitment to inclusivity. FDR, by contrast, was at the forefront of Jefferson's remembrance as the symbol of the nation's founding principles, his dominant image in the mid-twentieth century.[10]

Roosevelt did everything he could when president to promote this understanding of him. In *Looking Forward*, the volume he published to coincide with his inauguration, he lauded Jefferson as the supreme exponent of 'government based on a universality of interest', who gave Americans of his day an understanding of the 'essential principles of self-government'.[11] In 1938, he approved placement of Jefferson's facial image on a new nickel coin and on a new 3-cent postage stamp. Most significantly, FDR was instrumental in commissioning the Jefferson Memorial, constructed near the Tidal Basin in Washington. Speaking at the monument's consecration on 13 April 1943, the 200th anniversary of Jefferson's birth, he dedicated it to the 'Apostle of Freedom' who epitomized present-day America's ideals amid its 'great war for freedom'.[12] The four panels within the memorial were each engraved with quotations from Jefferson, selected through consultation with Roosevelt to show him in the best light as an opponent of oppression.

Prior to making Jefferson the symbol of wartime unity against external tyranny, Roosevelt had used him to justify his own conception of domestic politics as a struggle between the people and the special interests. In April 1930, he portrayed present-day Democrats and Republicans as representing these opposing forces in an address via radio hook-up to thirty Jefferson Day luncheons nationwide. Despite his kinsman's GOP affiliation, he blithely appropriated Theodore Roosevelt's famous slogan to assert the Democratic Party's engagement in 'an age-old conflict for the square deal for the average man and woman'.[13] To his mind, its enemies in this struggle used their disproportionate ownership of the press to mislead the common people. In January 1932, at a Democratic Victory Dinner, Roosevelt reminded his audience that the forces of democracy had faced a significant disadvantage in the young republic because 'the "machinery of publicity" lay almost wholly in the hands of the conservative, privileged group – the political ancestors of the Republican leadership of today'. To overcome them, Jefferson and his supporters had to wage a campaign to educate the people about 'the fundamentals of government'.[14] FDR clearly saw himself as needing to follow the same course when president. 'The American people', he told one newspaper publisher in 1938, 'are sufficiently intelligent, if given the facts, to draw their own conclusion – to form their own opinions'.[15]

Roosevelt's belief in the wisdom of an informed citizenry was one of his strongest convictions. His public presidency served two essential purposes of civic education: to enlighten the common people about the broad objectives and policies of their government, and to act as a conduit for the exchange of ideas between them. Addressing a Jackson Day dinner in 1936, FDR hailed 'the rebirth of the interest and understanding of a great citizenry in the problems of the nation'.[16] Two years later, he avowed confidence that 'in the long run the instincts of the common man . . . work out the best for the common good'.[17] Following Democratic setbacks in the 1938 elections, his next Jackson Day address reassured the party faithful, 'If we deliver in full on our contract to the American people, we need never fear the Republican Party so long as it commands the support of – and in fact down underneath is actually directed by – the same people who have owned it for several generations.' In his 1940 address, FDR voiced pride in having made his presidency 'the most important clearing house for the exchange of information and ideas, of facts and ideals, affecting the general welfare'. In his credo, the circulation of information between the president and the citizenry constituted the lifeblood of American democracy by enabling them to reach mutually agreed decisions. '[I]f the people were free to get and discourse all the facts', Roosevelt asserted, 'their composite judgement would be better than the judgement of a self-perpetuating few'.[18]

The greatest threat to this ideal system of governance in Roosevelt's eyes was the capacity of hostile publishers to use their newspapers for biased coverage of his administration. In corrupting the free flow of information from the president to the people, the owners of what FDR called the 'Tory press' were an impediment to his Jeffersonian responsibility as a civic educator. According to columnists Joseph Alsop and Robert Kintner, newspaper publishers were 'the group more resented by the President than any other in American life'.[19] While he sometimes assailed his most vituperative critics – the likes of *Chicago Tribune* owner Robert McCormick and *New York Daily News* owner Joseph Patterson – for having 'unbalanced mentalities', he generally focused his animus against the entire group. Meeting with journalism professors in December 1935, FDR commented that public confidence in the press had declined 'because of colored news stories and a failure on the part of some papers to print the news. . . . It is not the man at the [editorial] desk in most cases. It is not the reporter. It goes back to the owner of the papers'.[20]

Roosevelt was wont to claim that 85 per cent of the papers – 'the famous eighty-five percent' as he disparagingly termed them – were opposed to him, a charge repeated by others in his circle, but this misrepresented the complexity of press opinion.[21] Newspaper owners overwhelmingly applauded FDR's early display of leadership in tackling the economic crisis. Among the first to experience a change of heart, press-baron William Randolph Hearst established himself as the nation's foremost Roosevelt-hater through his antipathy towards New Deal support for organized labour and tax-the-rich initiatives. His fulminations against 'demo-communism' and 'Stalin Delano

Roosevelt' produced red-baiting editorials throughout a huge media empire. Not content with putting out this message just in his own press, Hearst bought full-page ads in leading newspapers across the country just before the 1936 election. 'Moscow', these proclaimed, 'has told all the Communists in America to vote for Roosevelt, the friend of Russia, the camarade of Communism.'[22] By comparison, Henry Luce's criticisms of New Deal spending extravagance and anti-business impulses, which found expression in his *Time*, *Life* and *Fortune* newsmagazines, were more measured. Moreover, he later supported FDR against isolationist criticism prior to American entry into the Second World War. In inverse fashion, Joseph Patterson's newspapers backed the New Deal until he became a virulent critic of presidential internationalism in 1939.

On the other hand, temporary breaches notwithstanding, Roy Howard, head of the Scripps-Howard chain that owned over forty daily titles and the UP-wire service, was often in the president's corner. The influential and independently owned *New York Times* editorially supported FDR far more often than it opposed him. Roosevelt similarly enjoyed the approval of independent publishers Marshall Field (owner of the *Chicago Sun*, established in 1941), Ralph Ingersoll (publisher of the New York daily *PM*, founded in 1940 with backing from Field), David Stern (publisher of *The Philadelphia Record* and, from 1933 to 1939, the *New York Post*) and Dorothy Schiff (who bought the latter in 1939). For the most part, too, FDR could count on the backing of the Southern press – though regional newspapers were hostile to Supreme Court reform, the attempted purge of 1938 and any New Deal association with racial liberalism. Additionally, Roosevelt found a significant reservoir of support for his policy of helping Britain short of becoming involved in the European war in 1940–1 from the top four newsmagazines – *Life*, *Look*, *Newsweek and Time* – that reached a large national readership in contrast to the local ones of newspapers.[23]

That said, FDR had far greater support from the public than the press, particularly at election times. In 1932, he carried 57 per cent of the popular vote but received the editorial support of only 41 per cent of dailies and 45 per cent of weeklies; four years later, the respective figures were 61 per cent compared with 37 and 40 per cent; and the gap grew to its widest level since Jefferson's day in 1940 when Roosevelt's 55 per cent vote share contrasted with his 25 per cent editorial support among daily newspapers and 33 per cent among weekly ones. According to one analysis, this trend deviated significantly from the historical pattern of editorial support for winning presidential candidates staying within 10 per cent of their popular vote in every election from 1860 to 1928.[24] *The New Republic* adjudged press coverage of the 1936 race 'one of the most slanderous campaigns in the entire history of American journalism'. It found that in the nation's fifteen largest cities, daily newspaper editorials ran two-to-one against FDR, while voters supported him by virtually the same proportion.[25]

A keen student of the press, Roosevelt knew full well that his newspaper support was greater than he admitted. As Eleanor Roosevelt observed, he 'reserved certain periods for his study of the press . . . [and] was always closely informed on all shades of opinion in the country'. In addition to personally scrutinizing New York and Washington newspapers plus *The Baltimore Sun* and *Chicago Tribune* on a daily basis (morning ones while breakfasting in bed, the others in the evening), he received a digest of coverage from Louis Howe (until his death in April 1936), occasional special reports on opinion in some 400 newspapers undertaken by the Division of Press Intelligence (established at Howe's instigation in 1933), regular clippings from administration officials and analysis of news wire despatches from Stephen Early.[26]

FDR's Jeffersonian view of politics as a conflict between the people and the special interests conditioned him to regard the emergence of press animosity following the 1933 honeymoon as inevitable. From his perspective, as historian Graham White put it, 'the hostility of some owners became the hostility of all; the faults of a minority were attributed to the majority'. Newspaper opposition became a badge of honour that confirmed his Jeffersonian destiny as the people's tribune. Accordingly, Roosevelt ignored Roy Howard's plea in August 1935 to temper his hostility towards the press by voicing 'appreciation that all American journalism is not to be judged on the basis of its most partisan units'. A year later aide Raymond Moley cautioned the president against needlessly provoking the press only to receive a Jeffersonian riposte: 'All [newspapers] were, from time to time, guilty of falsifying news.... They were destroying themselves.... Their readers were losing faith in them.' In Roosevelt's estimate, Moley recounted, 'Nothing would help him more than to have it known that the newspapers were all against him.'[27]

Circumventing the hostility of newspaper publishers, real and imagined, to get the truth to the people was essential in Roosevelt's calculation for mobilizing their support. His appointment of Stephen Early as presidential Press Secretary was critical to this task. This was the first formally titled designation of the post, which all-purpose presidential aides had hitherto undertaken since William McKinley's day. The innovation signified that Early's singular duty was news management. He brought diverse media experience to a post that he occupied almost throughout FDR's tenure. A veteran of both UP and AP wire services, Early was an early enthusiast for radio's utility in political communication and employment as Washington editor with the Paramount Newsreel Corporation gave him appreciation for another new medium.[28] He agreed to become Press Secretary on condition of having access to FDR whenever he wanted and having his own comments to reporters attributed to him personally rather than to 'the White House spokesman' – the construct since Coolidge's day. Confident of his standing with Roosevelt, whom he had known since working in the 1920 vice-presidential campaign, Early was, in Samuel Rosenman's words, 'very frank in his criticism' whenever his boss needed putting right on public-relations matters.[29]

While the president valued Early, the same was not true of Eleanor Roosevelt, whose press relations he also oversaw. Their main bone of contention concerned the First Lady's liberal stand on racial issues, which he feared would hurt her husband with Southern opinion. Early's own racial prejudices – born in Virginia, he lived most of his life in Washington DC, very much a Southern city with attendant segregation throughout the first half of the twentieth century – made him resistant to Black attendance at White House press conferences, whether conducted by FDR or ER. His rule that only regular Washington correspondents could be admitted was the formal instrument of exclusion. Originally intended to keep out visiting editors and publishers, it also disbarred journalists from the predominantly weekly African-American press. Early revealed the hypocrisy of this regulation by denying admission to Frederick Weaver of the *Atlanta Daily World*, the first successful African-American daily of the twentieth century.[30]

As well as setting and enforcing the rules for White House news conferences, Early prepped FDR for questions that would likely turn up, used favoured correspondents to plant questions that he wanted asked and sometimes clarified presidential remarks. His original intention not to hold his own press conferences was soon abandoned because too much was happening on the New Deal front. Accordingly, Early held regular briefings after his morning meetings with FDR in the presidential bedroom. He also scrutinized speech drafts, often suggesting revisions to improve their reception, and established rules governing how FDR could be photographed by the press and filmed by newsreels.

Early's public-relations responsibility extended beyond the White House to encompass the entire executive branch. During the interregnum between FDR's election and inauguration, he undertook a personal review of publicity methods and personnel to assess what improvements were needed. Breaking with tradition, he insisted on experienced journalists being appointed information officers for departments and agencies, positions hitherto treated as patronage plums for party hacks. The Great Depression having hit newspapers hard, there was a pool of out-of-work talent readily available. The primary responsibility of the former newsmen who entered government service was to produce informative publicity dramatizing what their department was doing with a view to rallying public approval of presidential policies. As well as writing speeches and ghosting articles for their chiefs, press officers produced a flood of mimeographed handouts that provided essential information for reporters to keep abreast of the momentous changes happening in Washington.[31]

Working journalists were not blind to the danger that government information might indoctrinate them but could not get by without the intelligence it provided.[32] Commentators on the right were generally hostile to this publicity offensive as akin to Nazi propaganda. The *Chicago Tribune* characterized Early as an 'American Goebbels', while *The American Mercury* lashed out at 'Dr Roosevelt's Propaganda Trust'.[33] FDR's supporters conversely regarded New Deal publicity as a necessary corrective to the disinformation of the conservative press. Disdainful of the 'professional poisoners of the public mind', Harvard law professor Felix Frankfurter wrote FDR, '[I]t becomes even more important than it was in the days of T.R. and Woodrow Wilson for the president to do what you are able to do with such extraordinary effectiveness, namely to give guidance to the public in order to rally them to the general national interest.'[34]

If Early was the director of Roosevelt's public presidency, FDR's peerless communication skills made him the star essential for its success. In an apt metaphor, William Allen White, publisher and editor of *The Emporia Gazette*, once told him, 'For box office attraction you leave Clark Gable gasping for breath.'[35] Roosevelt's vivid personality, knowledge of the issues and remarkable quality of speaking voice combined to make him quite simply the greatest show in town, whether in Washington or on his travels and whatever the medium of communication.

Regular news conferences were FDR's most important means of co-opting the press into his public-communications strategy. Uniting the president and the Washington correspondents in what one called 'holy newslock', these made all his predecessors seem 'like Trappists who didn't even talk to themselves'.[36] Roosevelt generally conducted them twice a week, racking up nearly 1,000 in total during his 12-year tenure, a record likely to stand for all time. Open, usually frank and always newsworthy, they made FDR the focal point of national affairs, thereby ensuring in the words of columnist David Lawrence that he 'dominated the best pages in the American newspapers'.[37] Roosevelt immediately dispensed with the written-question-in-advance rule, in place since Warren Harding's day. This had enabled his three Republican predecessors to ignore queries they disliked or deliver propaganda responses to ones they wished to address – including those never actually submitted. Roosevelt's elimination of it meant that he was meeting reporters on terms of parity, subjecting his knowledge of issues to their scrutiny and satisfying their hunger for information about his intentions. As Arthur Krock, *The New York Times* Washington bureau chief remarked, 'Genial, charming, shrewd, and daring, he meets the press on its own ground and wins most of the battles.'[38]

Most news conferences were held in the Oval Office, where FDR conducted them seated behind the large presidential desk. The journalists stood in rows before him. There were usually between 75 and 125 correspondents in attendance, but the number could be as high as 200 if there was a hot news topic. It was a notoriously uncomfortable assignment. Constructed in 1909, the original Oval Office had only 546 square feet of floor space. At Roosevelt's behest, the room was expanded to 800 square feet and relocated from the centre of the West Wing south wall to the southeast corner in 1934. Conditions could still be cramped, and FDR rarely switched on the air conditioning, installed by Hoover for use in the unpleasantly humid summer months, because it played havoc with his sinuses. At one news conference in 1942, Richard Strout of the *Christian Science Monitor*, who had just received anti-toxin shots to go overseas as a war correspondent, fainted away but the room was so crowded that he never hit the ground. Reporters thought the discomfort a small price for the news they got from FDR.[39]

Roosevelt began his first news conference, held on the morning of 8 March 1933, by laying out four ground rules for participating correspondents: all stories based on news announcements were to be without quotation, direct quotations required the press secretary's written permission, background information given to help reporters was not to be attributed to the White House and anything designated off-the-record was to be confidential, released only to those journalists present (the most difficult rule to enforce).[40] The Oval Office press conferences alternated between 10.30 am and 4.00 pm on Wednesdays (later Tuesdays) and Fridays to maximize FDR's chances of front-page coverage in both afternoon and morning newspapers. He used them to break news, comment on the big stories of the week or trial new ideas. His flair for capturing the headlines with dramatic metaphors was often on display, never more so than when discussing Lend-Lease aid to Britain on 17 December 1940, a month before the enabling legislation came before Congress. In depicting this as the equivalent of letting one's neighbour borrow a hosepipe when his home was on fire, Roosevelt cannily camouflaged its giveaway intent.[41]

Roosevelt's popularity with the Washington correspondents was another factor in getting him largely favourable coverage in their news stories, even in editorially hostile papers. *The Washington Post's* Raymond Clapper estimated that some 60 per cent of reporters covering the president held liberal inclinations regarding the New Deal, but fully 90 per cent were for FDR personally. Speechwriter Samuel Rosenman recalled, 'We soon learned to distinguish politically between the newspapermen and the papers they represented. . . . [M]any of the men employed by rabidly anti-Roosevelt papers were on our side and, in confidence, would tell us so.' During the 1936 campaign, the White House often knew in advance of calumnies due to appear in the Hearst press, thanks to leaks from its reporters.[42]

More open and friendly with journalists than any predecessor, Roosevelt cultivated their goodwill.[43] Within his first hundred days, he established what became an annual tradition of hosting a White House party for Washington correspondents and their spouses. As part of the extensive remodelling of the West Wing in 1934, FDR made sure that the press quarters were enlarged and provided with card and chess tables to while away the time. Top journalists, like Raymond Clapper, Anne O'Hare McCormick of *The New York Times* (one of only 15 women on the White House correspondents roster of 363 in 1934) and George Creel of *Collier's*, occasionally received personal briefings. FDR grew more cautious about this practice after an exclusive interview on Supreme Court reorganization for Arthur Krock aroused accusations of favouritism from other correspondents.

Employed to cover capital news in its entirety, most correspondents only attended the White House for the bi-weekly news conferences. For elite reporters from the wire services and high-circulation dailies, in contrast, it was the place where they spent their working day. They also attended the select press conferences given by FDR when at Hyde Park and Warm Springs or on his travels elsewhere in the United States. Roosevelt was particularly solicitous towards these correspondents: he swam with them in the newly installed White House pool, hosted them for occasional Sunday suppers and watched them participate in square-dance sessions organized by Eleanor Roosevelt, all the while feeding them background information of common interest.

FDR's interactions with the Washington correspondents formed part of a concerted strategy for news management. Seeing journalists' goodwill as a counterweight to their employers' enmity, he prepared assiduously for the news conferences that constituted the focal point of his relationship with them. The conference transcripts reveal FDR's virtuoso knowledge in answering questions on a wide range of national, local and international questions. His remarks were broadly successful in shaping the news agenda, but he occasionally miscalculated their effects. In June 1937 correspondents were allowed to quote him that Shakespeare's words, 'A plague on both your houses', best summed up the public mood towards the sit-down strike confrontations between industrial unions and business. When newspaper reports represented this dictum as his own sentiment, union chieftain John Lewis accused FDR of betrayal. 'It ill behooves one who has supped at labor's table and who has been sheltered in labor's house', he fulminated in a nationally broadcast address, 'to curse with equal fervor and fine impartiality both labor and its adversaries when they become locked in deadly embrace.'[44] In general, however, Roosevelt had the skill, confidence and composure to manage the news conferences to his best advantage.

As skilled in non-communication as in communication, Roosevelt used evasive techniques to avoid discussion of subjects he did not wish to consider. He refused to answer 'iffy' questions that called for speculation; he rarely allowed follow-up questions to those that he had not answered fully – 'no cross-examination', he would assert; sometimes he simply refused to answer a question by claiming to have no knowledge of the subject; and on occasions he was untruthful. Though some reporters resented the evasions, few stopped attending Roosevelt's news conferences because he never sent the press away empty-handed.

While journalists kept close tabs on FDR as an unrivalled news source, he spent an inordinate amount of scarce presidential time reviewing what they wrote about him. He held them to higher standards of truth than his own. Woe betide any Washington correspondent falling foul of him on this score as his wrath would descend on the offender at the next news conference. 'Mr Roosevelt', commented one subjected to his anger, 'could be as rough and tough as a Third Avenue blackjack artist.' At times, FDR also felt it necessary to give publishers a dressing-down, usually by letter but sometimes by summoning them to the White House, about what he perceived as inaccuracies in stories and editorials appearing in their newspapers.[45]

Nevertheless, Roosevelt could not turn back a new trend in journalism that he detested. Faced with the momentous changes of his presidency, reporters increasingly sought to explain the 'how' and 'why' of developments instead of just reporting news in unfiltered fashion. For Roosevelt, this threatened his Jeffersonian mission to get the facts put before the people. He was especially wary of syndicated columnists, whose stock-in-trade interpretive opinions reached a wide readership in the 1930s. Though willing to court those he considered sympathetic, like Joseph Alsop, Raymond Clapper and Drew Pearson, he was disdainful of critical ones like Frank Kent, Paul Mallon, H. L. Mencken and Westbrook Pegler. Reporters who posed interpretive questions in his press conferences got short shrift with the refrain that they should stick to the facts. Invoking what he regarded as the eleventh commandment for the press, he told one news conference: 'I am going to have a sign – I am going to place it right behind me: "Don't interpret."'[46] Journalists paid him little heed, not least because they regarded FDR as interpreter-in-chief of the news. Asked to name the best columnist in America, one editor answered, 'That's easy – Franklin Roosevelt. He can hit the front page with a column of his own opinions any day he wants to. And we've got to print it.'[47]

The First Lady's public operations provided another significant avenue for FDR's outreach to the country. Though far fewer in number than her husband's (her highest annual tally was thirty-eight in 1934), Eleanor Roosevelt's news conferences, covered by female correspondents, often dealt with issues of concern to women and were occasionally used by the White House to break news stories. In late 1935, she began writing a daily column, *My Day*, which initially focused on White House life but could be used as a channel of political communication (as when she resigned from the Daughters of the American Revolution in February 1939 over its refusal to allow Marian Anderson to sing in Constitutional Hall). By 1938, it was syndicated in sixty-two newspapers with a total circulation in excess of four million. The following year the august *New York Times* began running the column that Arthur Krock considered 'required political reading for those seeking insight into administration policy'. FDR considered *My Day* a valuable supplement to his presidential communications, even offering to write a column when the First Lady fell ill in September 1936, a suggestion she wisely declined.[48]

Also vital to FDR's public presidency was his mastery of radio, which enabled him to speak to the American people in direct, immediate and unfiltered fashion. To his mind, the relatively new medium counteracted Washington's isolation from the rest of the country by enabling 'direct contact between the masses and their chosen leaders'.[49] While broadcasts provided less frequent opportunities for presidential news management than the bi-weekly press conferences, radio eclipsed the newspapers as the chief means of disseminating news in the 1930s, an ascendancy strengthened during the Second World War. With some 90 per cent of households owning a radio by 1945, one poll found that 67 per cent of respondents adjudged it the medium that had best served the public during the war, while just 17 per cent listed newspapers.[50]

Most of Roosevelt's important addresses, notably the four inaugurals, the annual State of the Union messages, key campaign speeches, significant domestic and foreign policy pronouncements, and the Fireside Chats, were broadcast nationwide.[51] Some of these went through twelve or more drafts until Roosevelt was satisfied that the final version sounded right for radio. Judged purely on rhetoric, they were impressive efforts. A team of speechwriters helped in their production: Samuel Rosenman was involved throughout Roosevelt's presidency, joined by Harry Hopkins and Robert Sherwood during the war; Raymond Moley was a regular first-term contributor until FDR's anti-business re-election campaign provoked their final break; at other times, the likes of Adolf Berle, Benjamin Cohen, Tommy Corcoran, Donald Richberg and Rexford Tugwell came in to help. After contributing general ideas in the early stage of the speechwriting process, Roosevelt always put his personal stamp on the final version through his fine understanding of how to select, manage and deliver words to best effect. 'No matter who worked with him in the preparation', Rosenman declared, 'the finished product was always the same – it was Roosevelt himself.'[52]

If Bing Crosby had the best singing voice for contemporary radio, FDR was the champ of the speaking one. Even critics acknowledged, in the words of one, '[He] possessed a golden voice and a seductive . . . radio technique.'[53] Speech delivery in terms of rate, pitch, volume and voice quality was as important as content for his rhetorical success. An untrained but naturally expert performer on the public stage, he reportedly told Orson Welles, 'There are two great actors in America today. You are the other one.'[54] Roosevelt settled into a speaking rate of 100–120 words per minute for his Fireside Chats, dropping to 88 in the one that followed the Pearl Harbor attack. To ensure clarity, key speeches delivered simultaneously to in-person and radio audiences proceeded at 95–100 words per minute, slow to the point of hesitancy by the standards of his television-era successors. Roosevelt's speaking rate projected the image of a calm, authoritative and wise leader. For this reason, he did not vary the volume of his delivery, managing a well-modulated tenor pitch that contrasted with the shrillness of domestic demagogues and foreign dictators of this era. Though patrician in tone and pronunciation, his voice emanated confidence, conviction and compassion, a winning combination for listeners. As Eleanor Roosevelt observed, it 'unquestionably helped him to make the people of the country feel they were an intelligent and understanding part of every government undertaking during his administration'.[55]

What made Roosevelt's success as a public speaker even more remarkable was that most of his important public addresses – excepting the Fireside Chats – were delivered from a standing position. Leg braces and leaning on a podium kept him upright. The only time he fell was just before delivering his presidential nomination acceptance before an audience of 100,000 at Franklin Field, Philadelphia, on the night of 27 June 1936. Arriving by motorcade, Roosevelt made his way slowly up a curtained-off ramp on son James's arm to the speaker's platform. Near the top, a leg brace gave way when he reached out to greet a well-wisher, causing him to fall face down. Aides quickly lifted the shaken president to his feet, cleaned him up and retrieved his scattered speech pages, all without the crowd knowing what had happened. FDR proceeded to deliver flawlessly an address that went out live to a prime-time national audience on 256 radio stations.[56]

Despite regular broadcasts of his other speeches, the Fireside Chats became the signature feature of FDR's radio presidency, thanks to their innovative, intimate and informal use of the medium. They were employed to explain policy, report on developments and offer reassurance of progress. Above all, Roosevelt used them to take the American people into his confidence in order that they could comprehend his intentions. The day before giving the first, he issued a public statement of its purpose: 'The Constitution has laid upon me the duty of conveying the condition of the country to the Congress assembled at Washington. I believe I have a like duty to convey to the people themselves a clear picture of the situation in Washington itself whenever there is a danger of any confusion as to what the Government is undertaking.'[57]

To whet the public's appetite, the White House usually provided two weeks' notice for a Fireside Chat but delayed divulging details of its subject, thereby making press speculation about this news in its own right. Most were less than thirty minutes in duration but about a quarter were longer (the one explaining the declaration of unlimited national emergency in May 1941 lasted a record forty-four minutes). The average length ran to twenty-six minutes. Their infrequency – four in 1933, sixteen over the course of his first two terms and thirty-one in total – turned the Fireside Chats into special events.[58] Many radio stations re-broadcast them the day after original delivery in recognition of their popularity. As well as being offered airtime for weekly broadcasts by both CBS and NBC, Roosevelt received regular requests from the public to do more Fireside Chats. He resisted the temptation because 'the one thing I dread is that my talks would be so frequent as to lose their effectiveness'.[59]

Despite being a private man who kept his inner self hidden, FDR was remarkably successful in the Fireside Chats in forging a sense of intimacy with the listener. Someone as conditioned to hearing political speeches as Washington correspondent Richard Strout commented, 'You felt he was there talking to you, not to 50 million others, but to you personally'. The talks created a sense of community because most listeners heard them not in isolation but in groups, whether small gatherings of family and friends at home or larger ones in public places like churches, hotel lobbies, movie theatres and restaurants. The experience could even be a shared one for people listening alone. Novelist Saul Bellow reminisced about hearing one Fireside Chat during his student days through the open windows of a line of automobiles parked on Chicago's Midway, their occupants tuned into FDR on the car radio. 'You could follow without missing a single word as you strolled by', he wrote. 'You felt joined to these unknown men and women smoking their cigarettes in silence, not so much considering the President's words as affirming the rightness of his tone and taking assurance from it.'[60]

As their many letters to FDR attested, the Fireside Chats buoyed his listeners, even if there was no change in their material condition as a result of his words. The sense that he was engaging in dialogue with them made them feel better. This was true even of African Americans whose concerns attracted barely any mention in Roosevelt's radio rhetoric. In explaining this, Black poet Ruth Albert Cook thought that the Fireside Chats made listeners of her race feel they were part of America alongside the white audience – even if the next day they '[b]ecame Negroes again'.[61]

The White House was not responsible for designating the talks as 'Fireside Chats', a title that the press employed but FDR considered corny – and unsuited for addresses on hot summer evenings. CBS news executive Harry Butcher coined the term for the second talk on 7 May 1933 after hearing Stephen Early remark that the president liked to think of his listeners 'as being a few people around his fireside'.[62] To maximize audience size nationwide, the talks were usually delivered at ten o'clock in the evening EST, so they could be heard at seven o'clock on the West Coast. Twelve aired on a Sunday, six each on a Monday and Tuesday, thereby enabling FDR to dominate the week's news. There were just two each on the other weekdays and only one on a Saturday (the very last talk on 6 January 1945 when FDR delivered portions of the State of the Union Address submitted earlier that day in written form to Congress). An accomplished radio performer in his gubernatorial days, he told NBC's Carleton Smith before the first talk, 'You'll never have any trouble from me, I'm an old hand at this.' Nevertheless, he put a lot of work into the Fireside Chats, estimating that 'every time I talk over the air it means four or five days of long overtime work in the preparation of what I say'.[63]

In contrast to his other radio addresses, FDR was heavily involved from the outset of the drafting stage because of what happened with the first Fireside Chat on the banking crisis. According to Charles Michelson, the president cast aside the various drafts that he and others had prepared, 'lay on a couch, and dictated his own speech'. His eyes fixed on a blank wall, Roosevelt imagined how to put over what he wanted to say to the ordinary people of his own Duchess County, 'a mason, at work on a new building, a girl behind a counter, and a farmer in his field', all of them needing reassurance that their money was safe in the local bank.[64] To make the talks universally comprehensible, he kept to a basic vocabulary, with 70 per cent of his words being among the 500 most commonly used in the English language and 80 per cent in the 1,000 commonest ones. Labor Secretary Frances Perkins offered a revealing example of the power of Roosevelt's phrase-making through simple language. Asked to draft an address on the Social Security programme, she summed up one section, 'We are trying to create a more inclusive society.' When the talk was broadcast, FDR's 'instinct for simplicity' produced this reformulation: 'We are going to make a country in which no one is left out.'[65]

The approach to the first talk set the routine for the others. Roosevelt would rehearse each chat many times, make changes down to the last minute and improvise some phrases when broadcasting. Shortly before airtime, he would have an aide swab his nostrils to ensure tonal clarity, he would then place a dental bridge in his mouth to prevent the microphone catching a whistle caused by a gap in his teeth and some ten minutes before the broadcast, he would be wheeled into a makeshift studio – normally in the White House Diplomatic Reception Room. A small group of family members, aides and guests would gather to listen but he was oblivious to them once he began speaking. To Frances Perkins, a frequent attendee, Roosevelt was focused on communicating with an American family somewhere far beyond Washington: 'His face would smile and light up as though he were sitting on the front porch or in the parlor with them.'[66]

The first Fireside Chat, delivered from the Oval Office on 12 March 1933, was the most successful in terms of immediate impact in restoring popular confidence in banks that received federal approval to reopen. While listening figures are imprecise, it is likely that between one-third and a half of the total radio audience tuned in. Whatever the actual number, it was evidently a smaller share than heard some wartime addresses – the post-Pearl Harbor talk of 9 December 1941 reached a record 79 per cent of homes.[67] What made the first one an unforgettable experience for those who heard it was the sense that the president had paid them a personal visit. Among the letters that deluged the White House, one from a married couple in Dubuque, Iowa, typically remarked, 'He came into our living room in a kindly, neighborly way.' Another correspondent from Joliet, Illinois, wrote, 'Until last night, to me, the president . . . was merely a legend. A picture to look at. But you are real. I know your voice, what you are trying to do.'[68]

The address opened with the words, 'My friends, I want to talk for a few minutes with the people of the United States about banking.' For the benefit of listeners who primarily used them for modest savings and checking accounts, FDR outlined how banks worked in terms of investing deposits. He then explained the roots of the current financial crisis, the necessity for federal intervention and what he planned to do. He insisted that the government would reopen every bank deemed to be sound, even if continuing checks on their solvency delayed some from resuming business the next day, but he also acknowledged that others would not meet the required standard. In a remarkably candid statement that enhanced the credibility of his broader message about the trustworthiness of reopened banks, he declared, 'I do not promise you that every bank will be reopened or that individual losses will not be suffered, but there will be no losses that possibly could be avoided; and there would have been more and greater losses had we continued to drift.'[69]

Not every Fireside Chat had such positive effect on FDR's listeners. The address of 9 March 1937 in support of reorganizing the Supreme Court did not make the public warm to the proposal. In general, however, the radio talks were a vital instrument of FDR's leadership because they brought America's president and people closer than ever before – or since. Even the addresses that failed to sway opinion contributed to that connectivity by making listeners feel that they were engaged in a dialogue with Roosevelt. The large volume of correspondence from ordinary people to the White House reached peak flow after each Fireside Chat. The sack-loads of letters delighted the president for providing 'the most perfect index to the state of mind of the people.'[70]

Reinforcing their impact, Roosevelt reproduced five-minute highlights of the Fireside Chats for the benefit of newsreel cameras. Filming usually took place a few minutes after each radio address, but occasionally happened several days in advance to enable movie-theatre showings simultaneously with the broadcasts. While some cinemas ran the full address live by radio hook-up to satisfy audience demand, the newsreel versions were even more popular. A New Yorker wrote the president about the showing of his Fireside Chat of 11 September 1941 on the need to maintain freedom of the seas in the face of German attacks on US ships in the North Atlantic: 'I was at a movie last night where there was a packed house, at least 4,000 people. When the reading of your speech was shown on screen, there was loud and vigorous applause.'[71]

The newsreels were more than mere supplements to the Fireside Chats for FDR's public presidency. They made him a vibrant, fully animated, moving and talking personality to movie audiences. Even his disability became a cinematic advantage because he was filmed talking directly to the audience, usually from behind a desk, rather than orating to an auditorium from a lectern. A natural performer for the cameras, his frequent newsreel appearances as Governor of New York had projected him to a national audience. The newsreels emblazoned FDR's inauguration, the first ever recorded by sound-on-film motion pictures, as far more than a customary transition of presidential power. Over the next hundred days, Roosevelt got more newsreel time than Herbert Hoover in his first two years in office. Just as he cultivated reporters, he lavished personal attention on cameramen and film editors, which paid off in the consistently favourable coverage he received throughout his presidency. Even when visibly infirm in the last year of his life, newsreels continued to portray him as exuding vitality. As well as showing him in the White House, they filmed his cross-country travels, vacation trips and ceremonial appearances. This helped to project him as an active, authoritative and assured leader. To guard against oversaturation, Stephen Early used his contacts with the industry to ensure Roosevelt's appearance in what he called 'big news newsreel'. Arranging to have the president filmed when signing the Lend-Lease Act in March 1941 was one such case.[72]

As with radio and the press, FDR and the newsreels had a symbiotic relationship based on mutual need. As the Great Depression intensified, the steep decline in weekly movie ticket sales from 80 million in 1930 to 55 million in 1932 forced the closure of some 6,500 of the nation's 20,000 cinemas. To restore profitability, theatres expanded film programmes to provide greater value for ticket-price by featuring double bills, cartoons and better-quality newsreels. Roosevelt's importance for the latter was reflected in the revival in some big cities of theatres specializing in newsreel exhibition. The new owners of the 550-seat Embassy Newsreel in New York found that Fireside Chats and other presidential appearances substantially increased ticket sales – even if some in the audience came to hiss. 'We quickly discovered', they reported, 'that in Franklin D. Roosevelt we had the greatest single attraction.'[73]

In addition to being captured on the newsreels. FDR's travels were an important instrument of public communication in their own right. As president, he logged over 500,000 miles by rail and racked up additional mileage by automobile, sea and – in the Second World War – international air travel.[74] Many of the domestic excursions brought him to far-flung parts of the United States whose residents would not otherwise have the chance to see him in person. In a dig at congressional and judicial critics, he portrayed his travels as fulfilling the obligation that 'anyone charged with proposing or judging national policies should have first-hand knowledge of the nation as a whole.'[75] Sojourns into the American heartland also reassured Roosevelt of his continuing popularity with the people when the going got tough in Washington. The two-week 'look see' train trip to inspect the New Deal dams (Bonneville, Grand Coulee and Fort Peck) in the Pacific Northwest in late September to early October 1937 following his defeat over Supreme Court reorganization met this need. In a rear-platform address at Boise, Idaho, FDR likened himself to Antaeus, a character in Greek mythology whose strength doubled every time his feet touched the ground. 'I feel that I regain strength by just meeting the American people', he remarked.[76]

Legions of print-media photographers and newsreel crews accompanied FDR wherever he went, raising issues pertaining to control of his pictorial image. Every effort was made to ensure that apparently candid shots of him, whether eating lunch at Grand Coulee, posing in stand-up positions or interacting with other officials, were carefully stage-managed. Though relatively easy to impose rules in the White House, this was not the case in other locations. Stephen Early prohibited truly candid shots unless officially sanctioned, limited the distance from which photographs could be taken to 12 feet in small group situations and 30 feet in large crowds, allowed cameras to be snapped only when the Secret Service announced the president's readiness (after a shot of a pensive FDR made the front pages in 1935) and rigorously policed the greatest taboo – no shots of Roosevelt's disabled condition. Newsreel film-makers were very willing to abide by the rules for fear of risking their recently granted right to cover the White House. Most news photographers also observed them, but when FDR's troubles mounted in 1937 some newspapers and newsmagazines were briefly emboldened to publish shots of him being pushed along in his wheelchair.[77]

Notwithstanding these image-control efforts, FDR was extremely anxious to hear ordinary Americans' candid opinions of him. According to communication expert Hadley Cantril, he was 'the most alert responsible official I have ever known to be concerned about public opinion systematically'. Tracking the popular mind enabled him, in his own words, to 'build up a great mosaic of the state of the union from thousands of bits of information'. Confident of having his finger on the popular pulse, he was not dependent on members of Congress to learn what their constituents were thinking. While newspapermen comprised another barometer of opinion for previous presidents, FDR told a group of editors and publishers in 1938, 'I am more closely in touch with public opinion in the United States than any individual in this room. I have got a closer contact with more people.'[78]

The many millions of letters that ordinary people from a broad spectrum of society sent him during his twelve-year tenure constituted Roosevelt's main pipeline into the public mind. Some fifteen million are held in his presidential library, millions more are in the National Archives. Many were written in response to the Fireside Chats, most were not. Often, they came from people in desperate straits asking for assistance in getting a job, relief, mortgage aid and the basic needs of life – food, clothing and shelter. More significant for Roosevelt were the myriad letters sharing the writer's thoughts about his course of action. As two analysts of this correspondence remarked,

Plate 1 FDR delivering his inaugural address, 4 March 1933.

Plate 2 FDR giving the first of his 998 news conferences, a key element in his public-communications strategy, 8 March 1933.

Plate 3 FDR visiting Civilian Conservation Corps Camp Big Meadow, Virginia, 12 August 1933, with Secretary of Agriculture Henry Wallace and Assistant Secretary of Agriculture Rexford Tugwell (on his left), Secretary of the Interior Harold Ickes (second right) and aide Louis Howe (third right).

Plate 4 FDR signing the Gold Reserve Act of 1934, the culmination of the early New Deal's currency programme, with Treasury Secretary Henry Morgenthau standing to his right.

Plate 5 FDR delivering his seventh Fireside Chat on 28 April 1935 to explain the New Deal's goals for work relief and social insurance.

Plate 6 A billboard announcing a Works Progress Administration work-relief project in Baton Rouge, Louisiana, with FDR's name prominently displayed.

Plate 7 FDR signing the Social Security Act, 14 August 1935, with Senator Robert Wagner (D-New York) and Secretary of Labor Frances Perkins immediately behind him.

Plate 8 Eleanor Roosevelt visiting a Works Progress Administration Negro Nursery School, Des Moines, Iowa, 8 June 1936.

Plate 9 1936 campaign publicity, Women's Division, Democratic National Committee.

Plate 10 New Deal liberalism at high tide: FDR, Governor Herbert Lehman (D-New York) and Senator Robert Wagner greet the crowd at the president's final address in his successful re-election campaign at Madison Square Gardens, New York, 31 October 1936.

Plate 11 FDR with leading New Dealer and wartime aide Harry Hopkins, 11 September 1938.

Plate 12 Eleanor Roosevelt and Mary McLeod Bethune, the highest-ranking African-American New Dealer, Washington DC, May 1943.

Plate 13 FDR and Press Secretary Stephen Early.

Plate 14 FDR being helped to the speaker's podium, a shot that Stephen Early would never allow press cameramen to take – this one was by presidential confidante Daisy Suckley.

Plate 15 The 'Hughes Court': back row, left to right – Owen Roberts, Pierce Butler, Harlan Fiske Stone, Benjamin Cardozo; front row – Louis Brandeis, Willis Van Devanter, Chief Justice Charles Evans Hughes, James McReynolds, George Sutherland.

Plate 16 Cartoon satirizing FDR's court-packing plan by Clifford Berryman of *The Washington Star*.

Plate 17 FDR (on the arm of bodyguard Tommy Qualters) and Eleanor Roosevelt at the Jackson Day Dinner, Mayflower Hotel, Washington DC, 8 January 1938, with Democratic National Committee chair James Farley (left).

Plate 18 FDR being sworn in by Chief Justice Hughes for an unprecedented third term, 20 January 1941.

Plate 19 FDR and Winston Churchill at the Sunday Service aboard HMS *Prince of Wales*, Placentia Bay, Newfoundland, 10 August 1941; their military chiefs, General George Marshall and Field Marshal Alan Brooke, stand behind.

Plate 20 FDR asking Congress to declare war on Japan, 8 December 1941; Vice President Henry Wallace and Speaker Sam Rayburn (D-Texas) seated behind, and son James, his escort, to his left.

Plate 21 FDR signing the US declaration of war against Germany, 11 December 1941, while Senator Tom Connally (D-Texas) holds a watch to fix the precise timing.

Plate 22 FDR refers to a map of the world to explain America's global strategy in the war against Germany, Italy and Japan in his Fireside Chat of 23 February 1942.

Plate 23 War Production Board poster.

Plate 24 FDR reviewing troops at Rabat, Morocco, 21 January 1943.

Plate 25 The FDR-Churchill press conference at Casablanca, where the policy of Axis 'unconditional surrender' was announced, 24 January 1943.

Plate 26 FDR at the Cairo conference with, left to right, Chinese leader Chiang Kai-shek, Churchill and Madam Chiang Kai-shek, 25 November 1943.

Plate 27 FDR, Joseph Stalin and Churchill, the Big Three, at the Tehran conference, 29 November 1943.

Plate 28 Clifford Berryman cartoon following FDR's news conference remarks of 28 December 1943 that winning the war took precedence over expanding the New Deal.

Plate 29 FDR discussing Pacific war strategy at the Waikiki conference with, left to right, General Douglas MacArthur, Admiral William Leahy and Admiral Chester Nimitz, 28 July 1944.

Plate 30 Plenary session at Yalta: FDR, Stalin, Churchill and advisers, 4 February 1945.

Plate 31 The Big Three at Yalta, 9 February 1945.

Plate 32 A seated FDR addressing Congress on the Yalta conference, 1 March 1945.

it revealed the multiple images Americans held of FDR as 'father, brother, neighbor, friend, fellow Christian, leader, protector, crusader, and to a considerably lesser extent . . . power-hungry traducer of America's sacred political traditions, incompetent bureaucrat, relentless enemy of American business, reckless destroyer of sound economics, fomenter of war, dictator, Antichrist'. Supportive or critical, the letter-writers deemed him accessible for the cost of a 3-cent stamp. Many felt a compulsion to get in touch, like the Newark, New Jersey, man who declared, 'I don't know what exactly impels me to write you but I must tell you the following or else I know I'll never feel happy'.[79]

The bulk of the correspondence was opened and read by White House clerks and secretaries. The letters asking for help were despatched to the relevant federal department or agency for reply. Of those engaging in dialogue with the president, some positive messages received answers, usually form ones signed by an aide; many elicited none, particularly if they were critical of Roosevelt. Nevertheless, FDR wanted to keep broadly abreast of popular concerns expressed in this correspondence. White House chief of mails Ira Smith remarked that he saw 'a good many letters, and the summaries and other data that are supplied him make it possible for him to keep a close tab on public opinion and on the problems that are uppermost on the minds of ordinary people'. On important issues, the president also received 'mail briefs', analyses of opinion – both for and against him – from a spread of groups. Lela Styles who chose representative letters for Roosevelt's perusal claimed not to spare his feelings when the bulk of correspondence was hostile. The recipient of a huge volume of mail in her own right, over 300,000 letters in 1933 alone, Eleanor Roosevelt shared the most interesting ones with her husband, often placing them by his bed for night-time reading.[80]

While the letters and mail summaries he read gave FDR an understanding of what Americans thought, he increasingly looked for quantitative evidence in support of this. His use of press conferences, radio, newsreels, travel and popular correspondence analysis built on the public-presidency initiatives of his twentieth-century predecessors, but the employment of opinion polling broke new ground. The development in 1932 of the first modern marketing poll, the 'Psychology Barometer', was a revolutionary breakthrough in the testing of consumer preferences. Adapting its methodology, professional pollsters like George Gallup and Elmo Roper put their expertise at the service of those seeking to gauge the popular mind regarding politics.[81]

Accomplished in the new field, Democratic National Committee (DNC) executive director Emil Hurja came to FDR's attention for his accurate estimates of voting intentions that were used to target key constituencies in the 1932 elections. The 'Wizard of Washington', as he became known, pulled off another coup in correctly predicting Democratic gains in the 1934 congressional elections in defiance of presidential parties habitually losing seats at midterm. Drafted as Roosevelt's own pollster for the 1936 election, he tested reaction to the president's programmes, speeches and tours, which informed his advice to concentrate funds and energy on the large states. This triumph marked the height of Hurja's celebrity as a pollster. His predictions were completely wide of the mark in 1940, by when he was no longer working for FDR. Hurja's disappointment not to be made Ambassador to Finland (his ancestral homeland), feuding with DNC chair James Farley who resented his high profile, and opposition to court-packing led him to resign in 1937.[82]

Seeking another guru, FDR turned to Hadley Cantril, who opened the Office of Opinion Research at Princeton University in 1940. As Nazi armies stormed to victory in Western Europe, the new man's analysis of public opinion showed growing support in the country for some kind of involvement in the war short of actual military intervention. In his assessment, Americans were open to persuasion on this score because 'public opinion does not anticipate emergencies; it only reacts to them.'[83] Roosevelt was an avid reader of his reports tracking popular sentiment on the war but did not want to get too far ahead of it before winning a third term. Shortly after being re-elected, he was sufficiently encouraged by Cantril's polling to trail the Lend-Lease idea in a press conference and give it full-throated endorsement in a Fireside Chat that invoked 'the spirit of patriotism and sacrifice' in the cause of making America 'the great arsenal of democracy'. In Robert Sherwood's recall, 'Roosevelt really enjoyed working on this speech . . . it was the first chance he had had in months and even years to speak his mind with comparative freedom.' He could finally dispense with 'namby-pamby euphemisms in all references to the international situation. Now, for the first time, he could mention the Nazis by name. He could lash out against the apostles of appeasement. . . . He could speak plainly on the subject which was always in his mind – the disastrous folly of any attempt at negotiated peace.'[84]

Some 60 per cent of the listening audience tuned in to hear him, about 80 million people, making it at the time the largest radio audience in history. Over 90 per cent of White House mail responses backed FDR's call to provide aid to Britain, while opinion polls showed some 80 per cent of respondents were of the same mind. Based on this success, Cantril proposed that Roosevelt should make more systematic use of his services. 'I shall be glad to make the facilities available to you at any time', he asserted. 'We can get confidential information on questions you suggest, follow up any hunch you may care to see tested regarding the determinants of opinion, and provide you with answers to any questions asked by the Gallup or Fortune polls.'[85] Roosevelt's enthusiastic acceptance of this offer formalized the modern presidency's dependence on opinion polling that would grow ever greater under his successors.

When America became a belligerent, FDR's public presidency adapted to the emergency conditions of wartime, but the fundamentals established in peacetime broadly stayed in place. In the crisis times of economic depression and global conflict, he gave his country a sense of common purpose to meet its great challenges. In his Fireside Chat in October 1937, FDR asserted,

> Five years of fierce discussion and debate, five years of information through the radio and the moving picture, have taken the whole nation to school in the nation's business. Even those who have most attacked our objectives have, by their very criticism, encouraged the mass of our citizens to think about and understand the issues involved, and understanding, to approve.[86]

FDR had effectively reinvented the public presidency beyond anything imagined by his predecessors, even TR and Woodrow Wilson. His use of it may not have engendered consensus but neither did it produce polarization. The dialogue between president and people kept animosities within proper limits at a time when the nation needed to come together rather than be pulled apart. Accordingly, FDR's public presidency was one of the most significant aspects of his transformational tenure and was elemental to his roles as chief legislator, socio-economic reformer, chief diplomat (at least from the late 1930s onward) and commander-in-chief.

Chief diplomat

FDR as foreign policy leader

Franklin D. Roosevelt wanted the United States to take the lead in establishing a liberal, rules-based international order to promote lasting peace and prosperity. He conceived America's interests as global in scope and necessarily attained through a foreign policy of engagement with allies, support for collective security and advancement of democratic values abroad.[1] As chief diplomat, the greatest challenge he faced in pursuing this agenda was the management of opinion at home. The American public wanted to stay out of any future war in Europe or Asia, a sentiment that found strong support in Congress. Accordingly, Roosevelt played second-fiddle to the legislature in the neutrality debates of the mid-1930s. Following the Munich crisis of 1938, he grew progressively bolder in supporting Anglo-French resistance to Nazi aggression. Nevertheless, he remained cautious about moving too far ahead of domestic opinion when war broke out in Europe. The success of Adolf Hitler's blitzkrieg of 1940, which culminated in the fall of France, convinced most Americans of the need to help Britain, short of their country going to war itself. Building on this, Roosevelt secured enactment in March 1941 of the Lend-Lease programme that supplied the financially straitened UK with weaponry. Thereafter, he engaged in incremental confrontation with Hitler until the Japanese attack on Pearl Harbor pitched the United States into a war of necessity rather than a war of choice. His approach to the international crisis laid the foundations of popular support for his wartime strategy to establish a lasting peace based on US interests and values. Accordingly, FDR's foreign policy leadership initiated a decisive shift in America's role in the world that endured into the twenty-first century.

Roosevelt's Republican predecessors had sought to exercise leadership in world affairs outside the League of Nations through harnessing America's economic muscle to promote peace and stability, but their strategy lay in tatters by the time he became president. Following the reparations crisis of 1923, the US government extended massive loans to ease France and Germany's financial problems, negotiated reductions in war debts and oversaw the transatlantic flow of private capital that helped revive European economies. Under the so-called Washington System, it also negotiated naval-reduction agreements in the Pacific, arranged international guarantees of China's territorial integrity and persuaded Japan that its security and prosperity were best served through cooperation with the United States. Republican internationalism collapsed when the Great Depression undermined America's economic vitality, the prop on which it depended. Without the life support of US credit, Europe fell back into the economic chaos of the immediate postwar years. In Germany, this enhanced the popular appeal of Adolf Hitler's call to repudiate the Versailles settlement and follow the Nazi route to national redemption. Cut off from American credit, shut out of the US market by new protective tariffs and denied raw materials when the European powers closed their colonies to foreign trade, Japan seized Manchuria from China in late 1931 as the first step in creating a self-sufficient empire in East Asia.[2]

FDR brought to office his long-standing Wilsonian conviction that nations were interdependent in their common need for long-term peace and prosperity but tempered this with recognition, drawn from the experience of 1919, that a foreign policy of international cooperation required popular support at home. Seeing Hitler's accession to the German chancellorship as a threat to peace, he told French ambassador Paul Claudel in pre-inauguration talks that the United States, Britain and France should cooperate in deterring Nazi aggression. He also affirmed support for the Stimson Doctrine (promulgated by Secretary of State Henry Stimson) of non-recognition of Japan's acquisition of Chinese territory.[3] However, his internationalist ambitions narrowed in scope when his early initiatives failed to elicit support abroad and aroused opposition at home.

Two months into his presidency, Roosevelt addressed a letter to fifty-four heads of government urging arms reduction, commitment to non-aggression and expansion of world trade.[4] This was meant to benefit the World Disarmament Conference, now convened at Geneva, and the forthcoming World Economic Conference in London. It earned FDR a short-lived reputation abroad as a leader in the cause of international peace. Congressional concerns that selective embargoes might draw the United States into foreign conflict forced him to shelve efforts to secure a resolution prohibiting arms sales to aggressor states, which he considered essential for American participation in collective efforts to promote peace. Without a firm commitment of US support if attacked, France grew increasingly intransigent in resisting Hitler's rearmament demands. The German dictator resolved the impasse by withdrawing his country from the Geneva Conference and the League of Nations on 14 October, an outcome that persuaded Roosevelt to abstain from further efforts to promote disarmament. 'In the present European situation', he wrote Presbyterian pastor Harry Emerson Fosdick, 'I feel very much as if I were groping for a door in a blank wall.' Only an improvement in the transatlantic state of affairs would 'enable us to give some leadership'.[5] In reality, there was no chance of things getting better if the United States was not involved in bringing this about.

Meanwhile, Roosevelt's concerns that Britain and France wanted to broker a pact on currency exchange rates led him to issue the 'bombshell' message of 3 July that blew up the London Economic Conference. The war-debt controversy then pushed America and Britain further apart. In late 1933, the UK offered $460 million in full settlement of Great War loans that heavy interest charges had inflated to $8 billion, double the original value. Rejecting this as derisory, Roosevelt supported a punitive measure proposed by Senator Hiram Johnson (R-California) to prohibit foreign nations in arrears on their war-debt repayments from marketing bond issues to raise funds in the

United States. Unable henceforth to make partial repayments, debtor nations had little incentive to pay what they owed. With no hope of redress from its own war debtors to cover its American obligations, Britain joined the ranks of defaulters, a considerable blow to national pride. Sir Ronald Lindsay, its ambassador in Washington, bitterly commented, 'There is something completely sadistic about the way in which the American Democracy – or rather Demagogy – operates in a case like this. . . to indulge its anger in a frenzy of cruelty.'[6]

Making no headway on the big diplomatic stage, Roosevelt found other means of advancing his internationalist agenda. The United States still withheld recognition from the Bolshevik regime that had come to power in Russia in 1917. Sharing the liberal fascination of the 1930s with the Soviet Union as a progressive force dedicated to creating a more equal society at home and resisting fascism abroad, FDR sensed an opportunity for rapprochement. 'Gosh, if I could only, myself, talk to some one man representing the Russians, I could straighten out this whole question', he confided to Henry Morgenthau.[7] With the State Department unenthusiastic about Soviet recognition, FDR used trusted intermediaries to make informal approaches to Moscow about holding high-level talks. Meanwhile he set about building domestic consensus by emphasizing the trade benefits from formal recognition. This opened the way for Soviet foreign minister Maxim Litvinov to visit Washington in November 1933 to discuss 'outstanding questions'. The resulting agreement, brokered in White House talks with FDR, ended the anomaly of America being the only country of note not to recognize the Soviet Union.[8] The normalization of relations did not bring their governments closer in the 1930s but eventually facilitated Lend-Lease aid to Russia after Hitler's invasion in 1941.

FDR reaped more immediate benefits from a new approach to Latin America, where America's habit of military intervention during the first third of the twentieth century generated resentment of 'Yankee imperialism'. Addressing the Pan-American Union on 12 April 1933, he proclaimed US commitment to equality and cooperation between the nations of the western hemisphere, acknowledged their independence and urged removal of trade barriers.[9] This laid the foundations for the Good Neighbour policy whereby the United States cultivated friendly relations with Latin American governments with the aim of enhancing hemispheric solidarity in a dangerous world and boosting trade. As proof that change was afoot, Roosevelt desisted from sending troops to quell political turmoil in Cuba, effectively America's ward since gaining independence from Spain in 1898. Following recognition of the conservative nationalist government that came to power in early 1934 with the support of military strongman Fulgencio Batista, the United States provided it with a $4 million loan, agreed a new commercial treaty and abrogated the Platt Amendment of 1903 that enshrined its right of intervention in Cuba's affairs. FDR also honoured Herbert Hoover's agreement to terminate the twenty-year presence of US marines in Haiti, thereby leaving Latin America wholly free from American military occupation.[10]

Hemispheric solidarity received another boost when the US delegation at the Pan-American Conference in Montevideo in December 1933 negotiated the settlement of hitherto divisive issues regarding sovereignty, trade and debt repayment. The following summer Roosevelt added a personal touch to rapprochement by stopping off at

Columbia during a vacation cruise, making him the first sitting president to set foot in South America. The huge crowds that turned out to cheer him at stopovers on his 12,000-mile sea voyage to attend the Pan-American Conference in Argentina in late 1936 confirmed the huge improvement in US–Latin American relations. Heartened by the shouts of 'viva la democracia!' that greeted his disembarkations, FDR wrote Ambassador William Dodd in Berlin, 'Those people down there were for me because I have made democracy function and keep abreast of the time and that as a system of government it is, therefore, to be preferred to Fascism or Communism.'[11] As the situation in Europe deteriorated, the Good Neighbour policy enabled US defence planning to become hemispheric in scope. The Pan-American Conferences of 1938, 1939 and 1940 all produced important agreements pertaining to mutual security, neutrality and economic cooperation.

The stabilization of the dollar's value in early 1934 encouraged Roosevelt to request a reciprocal trade bill authorizing him to negotiate bilateral agreements with other nations that allowed mutual adjustments of up to 50 per cent in existing tariffs without need for treaty approval by the Senate. Secretary of State Cordell Hull, a passionate free trader, believed the resultant boost to international commerce would reduce the likelihood of war. Roosevelt was more realistic in hoping only for greater trade between treaty partners. The nineteen bilateral agreements negotiated by the end of 1939 (including eleven with Latin American states) would prove chiefly advantageous to the United States, evidenced by the near doubling of its positive balance of trade since 1934.[12]

The trade agreements negotiated with Canada in 1935 and with Britain and France in 1938 were politically important in demonstrating the solidarity of the Atlantic powers at a time of growing international crisis. The first of these brought to an end an unofficial trade war between the North American neighbours. Following its implementation, FDR wrote Canada's long-serving Liberal prime minister William Mackenzie King, 'In a sense, we both took our political lives in our hands in a good cause and I am very happy to think that the result has proven so successful.'[13] This marked the start of a long-standing partnership whereby the two leaders interacted informally through correspondence, telephone calls and personal meetings to discuss world affairs. More broadly, the reciprocal trade programme provided an important foundation for multilateral trade liberalization that followed the Second World War. In 1947 the tariff negotiation procedure developed under its auspices became the model for the General Agreement on Tariffs and Trade signed by twenty-three countries.

As FDR was well aware, economic internationalism was insufficient to halt fascist aggression that was gaining momentum. In 1935, Hitler revealed the existence of a German air force and plans to build a 550,000-strong army in violation of Versailles disarmament clauses, Italian dictator Benito Mussolini launched a colonial war in East Africa and Japan signalled its Pacific ambitions by demanding parity of naval power with the United States and Britain. Warning that world peace was under threat, FDR declared in his 1936 message to Congress, 'A point has been reached where the people of the Americas must take cognizance of growing ill-will, of marked trends towards aggression, of increasing armaments, of shortening tempers – a situation that has in it many of the elements that lead to the tragedy of general war.' Despite this, the American public overwhelmingly opposed the modest steps he proposed to preserve peace.[14]

In one of history's ironies, the Supreme Court, which voided various New Deal domestic initiatives as unconstitutional in 1935–6 decreed in *United States v. Curtiss-Wright* (1936) that the president was not subject to congressional or judicial constraint as the 'sole organ' in foreign policy. The case arose from a legal challenge to FDR's establishment of an embargo on arms shipments to the Chaco War belligerents, Bolivia and Paraguay. Using the 'sole organ' justification, Cold War presidents would assert their inherent supremacy in foreign affairs to determine the nation's best interests abroad. Wary of claiming such authority, Roosevelt found it expedient in the mid-1930s to accommodate the dominant opinion in Congress and the country that opposed his efforts to counter international aggression beyond the western hemisphere. '[F]or the moment', biographer Robert Dallek observed, 'he was a foreign policy leader without a following.'[15]

In private, Roosevelt denounced 'the very large . . . school of thought which holds that we can and should withdraw wholly within ourselves and cut off all but the most perfunctory relations with other nations'.[16] This diatribe grossly misrepresented the beliefs of those on the other side of the debate on America's world role in the 1930s, which encompassed absolute opposition to America's involvement in another foreign war, unless it came under attack; insistence on total rather than selective embargoes on belligerents to ensure that US neutrality was never compromised; rejection of collective security and membership of international organizations; support for military force levels capable of defending the homeland but insufficient to intervene beyond the Americas; and certainty that America's success in building freedom, democracy and prosperity at home ensured its influence abroad.[17]

Absolute neutrality in foreign conflicts was the primary credo of so-called isolationists, a term that only came into widespread use as a denigratory epithet once America entered the Second World War.[18] Neutralism was strongest in regional terms in the Midwest and Great Plains, weakest in the South; was most prevalent in ethnic terms among German Americans, Italian Americans and Irish Americans; and was marginally stronger among women than men. Though it had more support among voters with less formal education than well-educated ones, a goodly number of intellectuals and scholars were adamant that the United States should not get drawn into another European conflict. Eminent historian Charles Beard, for example, trenchantly insisted that America, acting alone or in coalition, simply lacked the power to restore peace and democracy to a continent 'encrusted in the blood-rust of fifty centuries'.[19] Stronger in the Republican Party than in the Democratic Party, advocates of strict neutrality were to be found among conservatives and liberals in both.

Popular conviction that US involvement in the Great War had been a mistake strengthened determination not to be drawn into another conflict. Walter Millis's best-selling *The Road to War, 1914-1917* asserted that America's insistence on defending its neutral right to trade with the belligerents had effectively made it a silent partner to the Anglo-French alliance. Its arguments fuelled demands for new legislation that would preserve America's impartial neutrality through forbidding commerce with any country at war. Advancing a parallel 'merchants-of-death' argument, a Senate special committee investigating the munitions industry, chaired by arch-neutralist Gerald Nye (R-North Dakota), contended that collusion between the Wilson government, weapon-manufacturers and bankers instigated the call to arms of 1917. Another common belief held a cabal of pro-British advisers to blame for misleading Woodrow Wilson into belligerency.[20] In the public mind, accordingly, strict limitation on presidential discretion in foreign affairs was essential to keep America out of another war. This outlook precipitated the defeat in early 1935 of FDR's request for Senate approval of US membership of the World Court, the judicial arm of the League of Nations created to arbitrate international disputes and uphold the Versailles treaty system.

A complacent president did not undertake a public campaign for what he considered a largely symbolic gesture of support for the international rule of law, but he underestimated the widespread hostility to any suggestion of involvement with the League of Nations. Radio priest Charles Coughlin and William Randolph Hearst's newspapers together raised popular agitation to fever pitch with warnings that the American way of life was at risk. Deluged with 40,000 telegrams of opposition and an even larger volume of hostile mail, the Senate fell seven short of the two-thirds majority required for ratification.[21] Never acknowledging his own misjudgement, an exasperated FDR told Senate Majority Leader Joseph Robinson (D-Arkansas) that those voting nay had damaged the cause of peace. '[I]f they ever get to Heaven', he remarked, 'they will be doing a great deal of apologizing for a very long time – that is if God is against war – and I think He is.' Unwilling to risk further defeats, he told Henry Stimson, 'I fear common sense dictates no new method for the time being.'[22]

Neutrality legislation enacted by Congress constituted further setbacks for presidential foreign policy leadership. As tensions between Italy and Ethiopia grew in the spring of 1935, Roosevelt's manoeuvres to obtain an arms embargo against aggressor nations aroused suspicion that he was seeking implicit authority to support League of Nations sanctions. Determined to exclude America from implied participation in collective security, the Senate insisted on a bill mandating impartial neutrality. To avoid a prolonged legislative battle that would delay consideration of major domestic measures, including Social Security, Roosevelt settled for a six-month ban on trade in weapons and war materials with all belligerents. When Mussolini's invasion went ahead in October, it steamrolled to victory in a matter of months against an ill-equipped adversary. The president hoped in vain that popular sympathy for the outgunned underdog would induce Congress to grant him discretionary power to invoke embargoes against aggressors when the Neutrality Act came up for renewal. Opponents countered that this would only encourage European dependence on America to stiffen collective security. With his eye on re-election, Roosevelt accepted a compromise that extended the existing law with added provisions banning loans and credits to belligerents until April 1937.[23]

Political difficulties at home early in his second term made FDR loathe to court additional troubles on foreign affairs. Although the neutrality legislation did not prohibit arms sales in the case of internal conflict, Cordell Hull enjoyed a rare moment of influence in counselling the president not to take a stand against congressional approval of a joint resolution extending the embargo to the Civil War precipitated in Spain by General Francisco Franco's fascist uprising against the Republican government.

This aligned the United States with the Anglo-French position, but it was a case of three blind mice rather than three wise men. While the democracies abstained from involvement, Germany and Italy acted as co-belligerents fighting alongside Franco's rebels. The Civil War became, in the words of Claude Bowers, America's ambassador to Madrid, 'a foreign war of the Fascist Powers against the government of Spain'.[24] The embargo tied Roosevelt's hands for the duration of the conflict, which ended in victory for Franco in early 1939. In a rare admission of error, he told the Cabinet that America had committed 'a grave mistake' in not selling Loyalist Spain 'what she needed to fight for her life'.[25]

In the meantime, Congress enacted another Neutrality Act in May 1937 reaffirming the mandatory ban on arms sales and financial loans to countries at war and prohibiting Americans from travelling on their passenger vessels. It also imposed a 'cash-and-carry' rule requiring belligerents to pay in cash for non-military commodities like oil and copper and ship these away in their own vessels. The Supreme Court imbroglio made Roosevelt a bystander during congressional deliberations over a bill that denied the United States any leverage over aggressor powers as conflict in Europe and Asia drew ever closer. Barely two months after FDR signed it, skirmishes between Japanese and Chinese troops on the outskirts of Beijing turned into full-scale but undeclared war.

To secure control over Manchuria, now vital to its economy, Japan launched an invasion of China that captured the largest city, Shanghai, in November 1937 and, a month later, the capital, Nanking, where its troops ran wild in massacring civilians and committing mass rape. While the fighting was in its early stages, Cordell Hull urged the president to make a dramatic speech calling for international cooperation in support of peace. FDR agreed to do so in Chicago, a neutralist stronghold, on 5 October on the return leg of his trip to the West. His most important address on foreign policy since taking office, it marked the start of a systematic public campaign to persuade Americans that greater engagement abroad was a national obligation.

Roosevelt substantially reworked the draft provided him by the State Department to make his message more cogent. Without naming any aggressor, he warned, 'The landmarks and traditions which have marked the progress of civilization towards a condition of law, order, and justice are being wiped away. Without a declaration of war and without warning or justification of any kind, civilians, including women and children, are being ruthlessly murdered with bombs from the air.' It was impossible for any nation, even America, 'completely to isolate itself from economic and political upheavals in the rest of the world, especially when such upheavals appear to be spreading and not declining'. The most noteworthy passage of the address, authored by the president himself, called for action against the 'epidemic of world lawlessness' to prevent 'the contagion of war'. To this end, he drew an analogy with the imposition of a 'quarantine' to prevent the spread of an infectious physical disease. 'The will for peace on the part of peace-loving nations', Roosevelt asserted, 'must express itself to the end that nations that may be tempted to violate their agreements and the rights of others will desist from such a course.'[26]

Thanks to popular indignation over Japanese atrocities in China and the bombing of the Spanish village of Guernica by German warplanes, the address received a generally warm response from press and public opinion, but there was little support for follow-up measures. Worried that Roosevelt's 'quarantine the aggressors' remarks had gone too far, Cordell Hull and Democratic leaders in Congress held back from voicing public support. According to Hull, the speech set back 'for at least six months our constant educational campaign intended to create and strengthen public opinion towards international cooperation'.[27] Roosevelt himself retreated from its implications at his press conference the very next day in denying any intent to impose economic sanctions against aggressors. The quarantine speech, he insisted, 'is an attitude, and it does not outline a program but says we are looking for a program'. Nevertheless, its message laid the foundations for his rhetorical campaign over the next four years to educate the public that the United States had a vital interest in preserving a world governed by laws and the moral norms of civilization rather than unrestrained power politics. 'I verily believe', he told the old Wilsonian, Colonel Edward House, 'that as time goes on we can slowly but surely make people realize that war will be a greater danger to us if we close all the doors and windows than if we go out in the street and use our influence to curb the riot'.[28]

Some two months later Japan infringed US neutrality when its warplanes sank the US gunboat *Panay* on the Yangtze River as it helped Americans fleeing the beleaguered city of Nanking. Roosevelt demanded apologies, compensation and guarantees against further attacks and briefly considered punitive measures in response to an incident that underscored his warnings about international lawlessness.[29] For supporters of strict neutrality, by contrast, the *Panay* incident underlined the dangers of America getting drawn into foreign conflict. It sparked their attempt to secure a constitutional amendment that a declaration of war by Congress required majority approval in a national referendum before coming into effect, except in case of attack or threatened attack. The president's role in its defeat signified that his influence in the national debate over neutrality was finally on the rise.

The idea of deciding war or peace through popular vote had a pedigree dating back to the turn of the century but had failed to attract broad approval. Assuming leadership of the cause in 1935, Representative Louis Ludlow (D-Indiana) energetically built support in Congress for a referendum amendment to the Constitution. With the House Judiciary Committee sitting on his proposal, he was 13 short of the 218 congressional signatures needed for a floor vote for its discharge when the *Panay* sinking put these within reach. For Roosevelt and Hull, the amendment's adoption would 'indicate to the world that the nation no longer trusted the Administration to conduct its foreign affairs' and 'would serve notice on the aggressor nations that they could take any action anywhere in the world . . . with little if any likelihood of any concrete reaction from Washington'.[30] The president delegated Democratic National Committee chairman James Farley to use every political and patronage resource at his disposal to line up votes against discharge. He also wrote to Speaker William Bankhead (D-Alabama) warning that the amendment 'would cripple any President in his conduct of our foreign relations'. During the discharge debate on 10 January 1938, the Speaker stepped down from the podium to give a dramatic reading from the floor of the letter from 'our Commander in Chief, a man who loves peace as passionately and devotedly as any man that breathes the air of God in America this day or anywhere else in the world'.[31] Less than half an hour later the House voted 209 to 188 against release.

There was no prospect that the amendment could have won the required two-thirds majorities in both houses of Congress to be put to the states for ratification over the Roosevelt administration's opposition. Nevertheless, the battle over its release encouraged supporters of greater engagement with the world to become more vocal, among them Northeastern economic and political elites, the internationalist wings of both main parties, veterans' organizations and much of the metropolitan press. Accordingly, the Ludlow amendment would be seen by Henry Stimson as 'the high point in the pre-war self-deception of the American people'.[32]

At this juncture FDR himself was still labouring under the delusion that international society remained fundamentally healthy. He was optimistic that the preponderance of peaceful nations would ensure the success of cooperative efforts to constrain the handful of aggressors. As he remarked in the 'quarantine' address, 'The peace, the freedom and the security of ninety percent of the population of the world is being jeopardized by the remaining ten percent who are threatening a breakdown of all international order and law.' To his mind, the 'ninety percent' wanting to live in peace 'can and must find some way to make their will prevail'.[33] Such thinking underlay his proposal, advanced in various forms from 1936 to 1938, for an international conference to establish standards for world peace, which he hoped would gain domestic support for cooperation with states that endorsed principles promoted by the United States.

In January 1938 Roosevelt adapted an idea originally conceived by Undersecretary of State Sumner Welles for a conference in Washington to discuss rules for international behaviour. He made secret overtures seeking British support for a gathering of representatives from small states – Belgium, Hungary, the Netherlands, Sweden, Switzerland, Turkey, Yugoslavia and three (as yet undesignated) Latin American republics – to devise a protocol in cooperation with the United States for promotion to other nations. This marked the hesitant beginning of his 'tacit alliance' with Britain, a phrase coined by arch-neutralist Senator William Borah (R-Idaho) in early 1938, which would grow in substance and significance in opposition to Nazi Germany over the next three years.[34]

To Prime Minister Neville Chamberlain, the idea for the small-nation conference was a 'preposterous effusion' that 'risked cutting across our efforts' at 'a measure of appeasement' of Germany and Italy. His refusal to back Roosevelt's initiative effectively killed it, at cost of the resignation of Foreign Secretary Anthony Eden, who considered Anglo-American cooperation essential to restrain the dictators. A decade later Winston Churchill recalled his 'breathless amazement' that his predecessor had discarded 'the last frail chance to save the world from tyranny otherwise than by war' through waving away 'the proffered hand stretched out across the Atlantic'.[35] In truth, Chamberlain had no reason to believe that the prospective international conference would rein in Hitler or even that it represented a real change in American policy, since its proposal was accompanied by a declaration of continued intent to abstain from involvement in European affairs. William Bullitt, ambassador to France, sent Roosevelt a blunt but accurate assessment of its utility: 'It would be as if in the palmiest days of Al Capone, you had summoned a national conference of psychoanalysts to Washington to discuss the psychological causes of crime.'[36]

The events of 1938 disabused Roosevelt of his optimism about the basic well-being of international society. Unbeknown to him, Hitler had informed his senior military and political officials in a meeting at the Reich Chancellery on 5 November 1937 that Germany's need for territorial and economic expansion could only be attained through force. In a two-hour exposition, he outlined his war plans and assessed the likely responses of other European powers and Japan (he paid no heed to the United States). To his mind, war had to come within the next few years, possibly as early as 1938 and no later than 1945, for Germany to exploit its current superiority in armaments. Despite his generals' doubts about risking conflict with Britain and France, Hitler took the first step to war by annexing Austria through the *Anschluss* of March 1938. His next foray targeted Czechoslovakia's largely German-speaking Sudeten region in the west of the country. War seemingly loomed with Britain and France, but their governments resolved to settle the crisis through appeasement. After two meetings with Hitler in which he met every concession with further demands, Neville Chamberlain and French premier Edouard Daladier agreed on the immediate incorporation of Sudetenland into Germany in a third conference at Munich on 29 September 1938. The settlement bought Britain and France a year to prepare for eventual war, which Hitler had wanted over Czechoslovakia.[37]

FDR was initially appalled to learn that Britain and France aimed to appease Hitler's demand for Czech territory, telling the Cabinet that their leaders would 'wash the blood of Judas Iscariot from their hands'.[38] Nevertheless, he was unwilling to stiffen Anglo-French resolve with promises of American support. A plea to all the parties to preserve peace omitted any offer of help in resolving the dispute and asserted, for good measure, that America had 'no political entanglements'. On hearing that Chamberlain was heading to Munich for a third effort to find a settlement, Roosevelt sent the prime minister a two-word telegram, 'Good man'. [39]

Despite his disengagement from its outcome, Munich constituted a turning point in FDR's foreign policy leadership. At a White House meeting of military advisers and trusted confidantes, he remarked that 'the recrudescence of German power . . . had completely reoriented our own international relations', putting America itself at risk of attack from across the Atlantic.[40] The *Kristallnacht* pogrom of 9–10 November 1938, Nazi-organized attacks on Jews, their homes, property and synagogues, and the German state's confiscation of all Jewish assets reinforced his conviction that Hitler would never respect international norms. In a brief public statement at his 15 November press conference, he remarked, 'I myself could scarcely believe that such things could occur in a twentieth century civilization.' In response, Roosevelt instructed the State Department to summon home the American ambassador to Berlin for 'report and consultation', a recall that proved permanent.[41]

FDR's growing concern about the fascist threat of international lawlessness reinforced his long-standing conviction that State Department bureaucrats, particularly those in the Division of Eastern European Affairs, were sympathetic to Hitler as a bulwark against the Soviet Union. Effectively his own Secretary of State since taking office, he deferred to Cordell Hull on trade and economic diplomacy but largely bypassed him on political matters. Assuming ever greater authority for policymaking from Munich onwards, he collaborated more closely with Undersecretary of State Sumner Welles, a friend of long-standing and fellow Grotonian, who reinforced presidential determination to take a more active role in world affairs following his appointment in 1937. For information on international issues, Roosevelt continued his practice of relying on men he had appointed to ambassadorial posts, whose loyalties were to him rather than the State Department. Among them were Claude Bowers in Madrid, William Bullitt in Paris, Joseph Davies in Moscow (later Brussels), William Dodd in Berlin and Joseph Grew in Tokyo, but not Joseph Kennedy, an arch-appeaser in his new post as Ambassador to Britain.[42]

Despite his growing outrage, Roosevelt still expected other countries to shoulder the burden of resisting Hitler. Meeting with Lord Lothian in February 1939, he 'got mad clear through' when told by this leading appeaser that America should become the principal defender of Anglo-Saxon civilization. 'What the British need today', he wrote a friend, 'is a good stiff grog, inducing not only the desire to save civilization but the continued belief that they can do it.'[43] The 'grog' he had in mind was air power. Immediately after Munich, Roosevelt received reports from William Bullitt that Anglo-French inferiority in this sphere was largely responsible for their abandonment of Czechoslovakia. This persuaded him that the United States should massively stimulate its own aircraft production largely for purchase by Britain and France to develop aerial forces capable of overawing Hitler or, in the event of war, defeating him without America having to become a belligerent. Retreating to Hyde Park for five days in mid-October 1938, the president conferred with Bullitt, Treasury Secretary Henry Morgenthau and work-relief supremo Harry Hopkins about his goals for aircraft production. Also present were Jean Monnet, the Daladier government's emissary charged with seeking FDR's commitment to supply France with warplanes, and Arthur Murray, a long-standing British anti-appeaser. According to Murray's notes of their conversations, Roosevelt authorized him to inform Chamberlain that in the event of war with Germany, he would have 'the industrial resources of the American nation behind him'. To get around neutrality legislation, their supply would come as partly finished materials sufficient to produce an extra 20,000–30,000 warplanes.[44]

This was a pie-in-the-sky figure that failed to account for productive capacity limits, the US armed services' own defence requirements and domestic political realities. The $500 million supplementary defence request that went to Congress in January 1939 asked for $180 million to produce just 3,000 combat planes, with the balance allocated for other military purposes.[45] Having fallen short on quantity, FDR sought compensatory enhancement of the quality of aircraft available for sale. Authorized to procure 1,000 US warplanes, Jean Monnet found that existing models did not meet French standards. Over the War Department's objections, Roosevelt insisted that the French could inspect and purchase three experimental planes not yet in production – the Curtiss P-40 fighter, the Martin 167 bomber and the Douglas DB-7 bomber. Acting as point man to expedite the buying spree, Henry Morgenthau told the president, 'If your theory [is] that England and France are our first line of defence . . . let's either give them the good stuff or tell them to go home, but don't give some stuff which the minute it goes up in the air it will be shot down.'[46]

Hopes of keeping the sales secret fell to earth along with a Douglas bomber that crashed in California on 23 January 1939 with a French official aboard. Summoned to testify before the Senate Military Affairs Committee, Morgenthau justified foreign sales as beneficial to the development costs of the new planes, but Secretary of War Harry Woodring contended that they undermined Army Air Force procurement.[47] To pre-empt a full-scale investigation, Roosevelt invited the entire committee to a confidential briefing at the White House on 31 January. This turned out to be his most forthright statement on foreign policy to legislators during his first two terms in office. Warning that Germany, Italy and Japan were pursuing 'a policy of world domination', he avowed determination 'to prevent it by peaceful means'. America's 'first line of defence' in this endeavour lay well beyond its borders. In the Pacific, a string of islands held the key to ensuring that US naval and air power could deter Japanese expansion. In Europe, the 'continued independent existence' of twenty nations was essential to contain Germany and Italy. It was in America's interests to help Britain and France acquire the air power to ensure this. Had their capability been twice what it was in 1938, 'there would not have been any Munich'. In selling its best planes to Britain and France, America would blunt the threat of aggressor powers without having to go to war itself. '[A]bout the last thing that this country should do', Roosevelt reassured his audience, 'is ever to send an army to Europe again.'[48]

To the president's fury, a committee member anonymously leaked to the press that he had declared America's frontiers to be on the Rhine, words he never used. Roosevelt's characterization of this claim in a press conference as 'a deliberate lie' caused other participants to reveal that his remarks left no doubt that he intended to support Anglo-French rearmament regardless of neutrality law. Standing firm, FDR used his press conference of 17 February to educate reporters and through them the public that this was necessary for America's security.[49] To his great satisfaction, a Gallup survey taken two weeks after his meeting with the committee found that 69 per cent of respondents approved of doing everything short of war to help Britain and France in a conflict with Germany and Italy.

Any hope that Roosevelt's increasingly open support for Anglo-French rearmament would deter fascist aggression disappeared when Germany occupied what remained of Czechoslovakia. Within weeks, the British government announced that it was committed to defending Poland, presumed to be Hitler's next target. This abandonment of appeasement brought a general European war into sight. On 14 April, Roosevelt made a last public appeal for peace in messages sent to Hitler and Mussolini. His seven-page telegram to the German dictator asked for a ten-year guarantee that he would not attack or invade the territory of thirty-one listed nations in Europe and the Middle East. In return, the United States would participate in an international conference to discuss ways of ending 'the crushing burden of armament' and opening up international trade on equal terms to all countries.[50]

Infuriated that Roosevelt published the message before its official receipt in Berlin, Hitler initially deemed it beneath his dignity to reply to 'so contemptible a creature'. The favourable impression it made throughout much of Europe, including Germany, eventually drew a response in the form of a two-and-a-half hour address to the Reichstag that ridiculed the president's proposal. 'A terrible flogging of Roosevelt', Nazi minister of propaganda Joseph Goebbels crowed. 'That really smacks him around the ears. . . . Anybody publicly attacking the Fuhrer certainly gets his comeuppance. . . . What a pigmy a man like Roosevelt is in comparison.' Some domestic critics also took delight that FDR, in Senator Hiram Johnson's words, 'put his chin out, and . . . got a resounding whack on it'.[51]

Despite this, FDR's initiative had significant consequences for Hitler's strategic calculation. As historian Ian Kershaw observed, the Nazi leader could have no illusions that 'whatever the appearances of neutrality, the United States now had to be regarded as essentially a hostile power'. Hitherto he had paid little attention to a distant country seemingly so weakened by economic crisis that it lacked both the will and the military capability to become involved in European affairs. His Nazi eugenics also impelled him to disdain FDR personally as the crippled leader of a mongrel nation. Seeing the United States anew as a potential threat rather than an irrelevance, Hitler sought to ensure its neutrality in his imminent war with Britain and France. Though not yet precisely formulated, a basic assumption took root in his geopolitical thinking that conflict with America should be deferred until Germany dominated Europe and possessed a mighty fleet capable of contesting control of the seas.[52]

Holding no illusions that the fascist dictators would respond positively, FDR had really aimed his message at the American people. As he told Mackenzie King, 'If we are turned down, the issue becomes clearer and public opinion in your country and mine will be helped.'[53] He hoped to generate support for arms-embargo repeal in order to continue supplying the European democracies with weapons when they were at war with Germany. Popular approval for doing so declined from its high point following his meeting with the Senate Armed Services Committee to 57 per cent in April and continued falling to the point that opposition to repeal enjoyed majority support in August. By contrast, public support for enlarging America's own military forces ran between 80 and 90 per cent throughout 1939, with some two-thirds of poll respondents declaring willingness to pay higher taxes if needed.[54]

The survey returns did not deter Roosevelt from seeking to rescind the arms embargo. Largely uninvolved in earlier struggles over neutrality legislation, he lobbied behind the scenes and eventually out in the open in support of allowing weapons sales to belligerents on a cash-and-carry basis, terms obviously advantageous to the democracies because of Britain's naval supremacy. Neither presidential exhortation nor the public-relations success of the British royal visit of King George VI and Queen Elizabeth to the United States in early June swayed congressional hearts and minds. Thanks to Democratic defections, the House of Representatives upheld the current law by a vote of 200 to 188 on 30 June, while the Senate Foreign Relations Committee voted 12 to 11 to defer consideration of the amendment until the next congressional session. Grasping at straws, FDR invited a bipartisan group of senators to the White House on 18 July to ask their support for revision before the chamber recessed. With William Borah to the fore, GOP attendees expressed scepticism that war was imminent and questioned Hitler's readiness to fight. Even if a repeal bill emerged from committee, it was evident that a Republican filibuster would talk it to death on the chamber floor. Accepting that he could do no more for now, Roosevelt laid the foundations for another effort when war broke out in Europe with some strong statements that the Senate had made this eventuality more likely. Most notably, he asserted at his press conference of 21 July that it had 'accepted the responsibility of saying to the Executive Branch of the Government, "There is nothing further you can do to avert war".[55]

Once the Nazi-Soviet non-aggression pact of 23 August 1939 safeguarded Germany's eastern flank, Hitler launched the invasion of Poland on 1 September, precipitating the Anglo-French declarations of war two days later. On the evening of 3 September, FDR delivered a Fireside Chat in which he declared, 'This nation will remain a neutral nation, but I cannot ask that every American remain neutral in thought as well. Even a neutral has a right to take account of facts. Even a neutral cannot be asked to close his mind or his conscience.' This statement was markedly different from Woodrow Wilson's plea for Americans to be 'impartial in thought as well as in action' at the outbreak of the Great War. Over the next two months, opinion polls showed that Americans by margins of four-to-one favoured an Allied victory, while some three-fifths wanted to do everything possible to help bring that about 'short of going to war ourselves'.[56]

The challenge now facing FDR was to help Britain and France without arousing popular concern that he was manoeuvring to make America a belligerent. The renewal of the campaign to repeal the arms embargo offered a perfect illustration of his juggling act. Calling a special session of Congress on 21 September, Roosevelt declared that putting all trade with belligerents on a cash-and-carry basis was the best way of keeping the country neutral. 'Let no group assume the exclusive label of the "peace bloc"', he asserted. 'We all belong to it.' Thereafter he let Democratic leaders in Congress do the work of securing the legislation, recruited Republican sympathizers to lobby for the bill (notably the 1936 presidential running mates, Alfred Landon and Frank Knox) and encouraged the formation of the Non-Partisan Committee for Peace Through the Revision of the Neutrality Act to promote popular support. 'I am almost literally walking on eggs', FDR told Lord Tweedsmuir, Governor-General of Canada, 'I am at the moment saying nothing, seeing nothing and hearing nothing.'[57] He was rewarded with majorities of 55 to 24 in the Senate and 243 to 181 in the House of Representatives for arms-embargo repeal in early November.

Neville Chamberlain hailed the measure for giving the Allies access to 'the greatest storehouse of supplies in the world', but it was more a case of poorhouse fare. In the British Treasury's estimate, the cash-and-carry provision combined with the continued prohibition on loans to belligerents in the amended neutrality legislation made America 'a limited marginal source of war supplies'. To husband the UK's gold and dollar reserves for a long war, it initially focused on buying food and raw materials rather than weaponry. Despite the US government and people being much more sympathetic to Britain and France in 1939–40 than in 1914–17, America's productive power was far less helpful to their cause in the early stages of the Second World War than in the Great War.[58]

With Germany holding back from offensive operations in Western Europe for the eight-month Phoney War, US policymakers and public opinion shared the expectation of eventual Allied victory. Hitler's blitzkrieg, a new kind of warfare integrating tanks, air power, artillery and motorized infantry into a strategy of speedy movement and maximization of battlefield opportunities, ended such complacency. In barely two months, his forces gained control of Norway, Denmark, the Netherlands and Belgium before forcing France to sue for peace on 22 June. This turn of events convinced the majority of Americans that a victorious Germany would attack the United States.[59]

As France was falling, Roosevelt used an address at the University of Virginia to announce a response to Hitler's success: '[W]e will extend to the opponents of force the material resources of this nation; and, at the same time, we will harness and speed up the use of those resources in order that we ourselves . . . may have equipment and training equal to the task of any emergency and every defense.'[60] Operationalizing the second element of the strategy proved straightforward, albeit at some cost to the first. By the end of 1940, Congress boosted the defence budget to fivefold its pre-blitzkrieg size, but the Walsh amendment to the Naval Expansion Act made foreign transfer or sale of any military equipment contingent on certification by the relevant service chief that it was not essential to America's defence. In September, Congress enacted by large majorities the Selective Training and Service Act of 1940, the first peacetime conscription in American history that required men aged twenty-one to thirty-five to register with local draft boards (later extended to all eighteen to forty-five-year-olds when the United States entered the war) but limited their service to the western hemisphere or American possessions elsewhere. Meanwhile, the public consistently supported sale of aircraft and other weaponry to Britain provided this did not delay America's own defence programme.

In these circumstances Roosevelt manoeuvred to aid Britain without getting too far ahead of domestic opinion. Effectively commanding the military chiefs to classify items as 'surplus', the essential requirement for their legal release, he managed to get half-a-million Enfield rifles, 35,000 machine guns, 500 field guns and ammunition shipped to Britain to replace what had been left behind in the Dunkirk evacuation. Entrusting the management of the enterprise to Henry Morgenthau, FDR told him, 'Give it an extra push every morning and every night until it is on the ships.' Aghast at the scale of the weapons transfer, Major Walter Beddell Smith, one of Army chief of staff George Marshall's top aides, remarked, '[I]f we were required to mobilize after having released guns necessary for this mobilization and were found to be short of artillery materiel, everyone who was a party to the deal might hope to be found hanging from a lamp post.' It still required the president to instruct a reluctant Secretary of War Harry Woodring to authorize the shipment.[61] In November, Roosevelt ordered the sale of B-174 Flying Fortresses so that Britain could bomb Germany's cities while its own endured the Luftwaffe's Blitz. Even though the United States currently had fewer than fifty bombers in commission, the transfer went ahead courtesy of legal gymnastics that decreed the planes non-essential for homeland defence because of their impending replacement by B-24 Liberators, an aircraft not yet on the production line.[62]

The most high-profile arms transfer of 1940 featured fifty First World War destroyers, urgently requested by Prime Minister Winston Churchill, who had succeeded Chamberlain on 10 May, to repel a seemingly imminent German invasion. In truth, the primary purpose of the antiquated vessels, which would take months to refit for modern warfare, was to boost Britain's morale and warn Hitler against straining US neutrality. Even so, FDR hesitated to act until he received legal advice that congressional assent was unnecessary provided the transfer strengthened America's defences. Exchanging the destroyers for Britain's gift of two naval bases in Newfoundland and Bermuda, the lease of additional bases in the West Indies for ninety-nine years and a guarantee never to surrender or scuttle its fleet if defeated by Germany met this requirement. In a message to Congress on 3 September, Roosevelt hyperbolically asserted, 'This is the most important action in the reinforcement of our national defense that has been taken since the Louisiana Purchase. . . . The value to the Western Hemisphere of these outposts of security is beyond calculation.'[63] Some two weeks later Hitler postponed his projected invasion because of the Royal Air Force's success in the Battle of Britain. The destroyers, only nine of which were in Britain's possession by the end of 1940, played no part in its salvation but their significance for the increasingly open Anglo-American alliance was immense.

Within a few months, the destroyer deal seemed a drop in the ocean as FDR stepped up efforts to keep a cash-strapped Britain in the war. On 23 November, returning from talks in London, Lord Lothian, the new UK ambassador, told journalists awaiting him at La Guardia Airport, 'Well, boys, Britain's broke; it's your money we want.' This blunt statement concentrated American minds about the plight of a country that still possessed formidable assets in sterling reserves but had barely enough gold and dollar balances to pay for existing military orders. At a Treasury briefing to put military officials in the picture, Secretary of the Navy Frank Knox remarked, 'We are going to pay for the war from now on, are we?' Speaking for everyone present, he answered his own question: 'Got to. No choice about it.'[64] Roosevelt now had to find a way of circumventing the prohibition on loans to belligerents and the cash-and-carry requirements of the most recent neutrality legislation. To think matters through, he departed Washington for a twelve-day Caribbean cruise on USS *Tuscaloosa* in early December.

Six days into this trip, a Navy seaplane delivered a mail package containing a lengthy message from Winston Churchill that Britain faced a 'mortal danger' less sudden but no less deadly than invasion. Owing to the 'bombshell' message that sank the London Economic Conference in 1933, the war-debt imbroglio and the manoeuvring over the small-nations conference in early 1938, Neville Chamberlain had never wholly trusted FDR. His successor, by contrast, recognized that Britain's survival depended on American aid, which he looked to Roosevelt to provide. The leading voice of anti-appeasement, Churchill had been brought back from ten years in the political wilderness to head the Admiralty in Chamberlain's government on the outbreak of war with Germany. Commencing a personal correspondence with FDR in that post, he maintained this channel of communication after becoming prime minister. Increasingly candid about his country's desperate need for military supplies to continue fighting, he told Roosevelt on 27 October, 'The World Cause is in your hands.'[65] The cable that reached the president aboard USS *Tuscaloosa*, the most painstakingly composed message Churchill ever sent him, laid out two dire threats facing Britain.

The loss of over 900,000 tons of merchant shipping mainly to U-boat attacks in the last three months meant that Britain could 'fall by the way'. The decision for 1941 'lies upon the seas' because convoys of American merchant ships protected by US Navy escorts constituted the only hope of preserving the Atlantic lifeline. This would still leave unresolved the financial peril facing Britain. 'The moment approaches', Churchill warned, 'when we shall no longer be able to pay cash for shipping and other supplies.' Having outlined his country's weakness in the starkest terms, the prime minister put himself in the president's hands to find a solution that would not leave Britain 'stripped to the bone' from the forced divestment of its saleable assets to win a war being fought to save civilization. It was his hope that 'ways and means will be found which future generations on both sides of the Atlantic will approve and admire'.[66]

According to Harry Hopkins, who was travelling with FDR, the president sat for hours on the *Tuscaloosa*'s deck contemplating Churchill's message over the next two days. Then, with some assistance from this most trusted aide, 'he came out with it – the whole program'. The basic idea for what became known as 'Lend-Lease', a term coined by the press, had now taken shape. By his return to Washington, FDR had figured out a way of undertaking this programme legally. Meeting with Henry Morgenthau on 17 December, he outlined a plan to 'get away from a dollar sign . . . [and] say to England "we will give you the guns and ships that you need, provided that when the war is over you will return to us in kind the guns and ships we have loaned to you, or you will return to us the ships repaired and pay us, always in kind, to make up the depreciation"'. For the Treasury Secretary, Roosevelt's brilliant sense of 'trading and intuition' met the public's desire to help Britain without the suspicious baggage of loan finance thought to have drawn the nation into the Great War.[67]

That very afternoon, FDR unveiled the Lend-Lease idea in his press conference. The 'best immediate defense of the United States', he told reporters, 'is the success of Great Britain in defending herself'. As military production hit ever greater heights at home, far better for the UK to use America's surplus armaments 'than if they were kept in storage here'. In a masterclass of political salesmanship, Roosevelt captured the essence of Lend-Lease in the irresistible analogy that combined reason with emotion. It was a case of offering friendly assistance to the British akin to lending a neighbour a garden hose to put out a fire in his home and expecting its return or replacement anew once the blaze was put out. As conceived by FDR, historian Warren Kimball observed, the genius of Lend-Lease lay in being 'a give-away program that did not look like one'.[68]

Roosevelt followed this up with a Fireside Chat on 29 December 1940 that was heard by some three-quarters of adult Americans and listeners in parts of Europe and the Far East, the largest radio audience in history hitherto. America's task, he avowed, was to produce vast quantities of weaponry, some of which would be used to boost homeland defence and some sent abroad to supply Britain and other countries fighting aggression, an apportionment the US government would make on the basis of expert military advice on overall necessity. 'We must be the great arsenal of democracy', he asserted. 'For us this is an emergency as serious as war itself. We must apply ourselves to our task with the same resolution, the same sense of urgency, the same spirit of patriotism and sacrifice as we would show were we at war.'[69]

A week later, FDR announced in the State of the Union Address that he would send Congress a Lend-Lease bill. Supporters in the House of Representatives cleverly affixed the measure with the patriotic number and title, 'H.R. 1776: A Bill further to Promote the Defense of the United States.' Despite Roosevelt's brilliant use of the presidential podium to prepare the way, the legislation faced considerable opposition from strict neutralists, peace groups and the America First organization, formed in the wake of the destroyers-for-bases deal to urge build-up of home defences before all else and featuring famed aviator Charles Lindbergh as its principal spokesman.

FDR and his allies increasingly depicted their opponents as appeasers or unwitting dupes of the dictators rather than address valid questions that they raised about America's national interest, the limits of its power, the fiscal costs of Lend-Lease, the likelihood that the programme would eventually make America a belligerent and whether Hitler, even if victorious in Europe, would attack a securely defended United States. Seeing Lindbergh and other opposition luminaries as tantamount to enemies of the republic, the president authorized the Federal Bureau of Investigation to tap their telephones and open their mail.[70] FDR also worked behind the scenes to outmanoeuvre his critics through more orthodox political means. He persuaded Joseph Kennedy, effectively sacked from his London ambassadorship for doubting Britain's survival, to desist from attacking Lend-Lease when testifying at the invitation of its congressional opponents in House hearings on the bill. Through the good offices of Henry Stimson, formerly Wendell Willkie's lawyer, he also got the 1940 Republican standard-bearer to avow his wholehearted support for Lend-Lease as necessary for Britain's survival when testifying before the Senate Foreign Relations Committee.[71]

Approved by huge majorities in both chambers of Congress, the Lend-Lease legislation went for FDR's signature on 11 March. Nevertheless the opposition had secured important amendments, most notably the prohibition on US Navy convoying of war supplies across the Atlantic. To Churchill's consternation, Roosevelt also agreed that the UK should use its remaining dollar reserves to finance the capital costs of the plant expansion required to manufacture Lend-Lease materials. The Reconstruction Finance Corporation eventually arranged loans to cover this but not before Britain was nearly bled dry through liquidation of its US stock securities. On Lend-Lease's enactment, *The New York Times* editorialized approvingly that it marked 'the day when the United States ended the great retreat which began with the Senate rejection of the Treaty of Versailles and the League of Nations. The effort to find security in isolation has failed.' Congress appropriated a staggering $7 billion to finance the first shipments of aid to Britain, to be followed by requisitions totalling $13.7 billion for America's own defence needs in calendar 1941. As a share of gross national product, defence outlays rose from 1.4 per cent in 1939 to 11.2 per cent in 1941, while Army personnel rose from 190,000 to 1,500,000.[72]

To the frustration of Henry Stimson, Frank Knox, Henry Morgenthau and Harold Ickes, the strongest voices of intervention in the administration, Roosevelt remained heedful of popular opposition to America joining the war. 'I am not willing to fire the first shot', he told the Cabinet in May. To the so-called all-outers, the president appeared to be looking for an incident that would justify a retaliatory belligerency rather than educating Americans that their involvement in the war was essential for Germany's defeat. '[T]he President has not aroused the country; has not really sounded the bell . . . does not furnish the motive power that is required', an exasperated Ickes wrote in his diary. When Hitler invaded Russia, Stimson and Knox urged FDR in vain to order the US Navy to protect merchant vessels supplying Britain, an initiative they deemed certain to get America into the war at an opportune moment of Germany's preoccupations in the east. Instead, FDR appeared to think that the new front diminished need for America to become a formal belligerent.[73]

Whatever the geostrategic case for intervention in the summer of 1941, Roosevelt was being politically astute in not rushing into belligerency. The American people may not have rallied round the flag so enthusiastically if the United States had not come under attack. Holding sole authority to declare war, the House of Representatives may not have done so in the absence of clear provocation. In August, it approved extension of the Selective Service draft for a further fifteen months by just one vote. In reality, of course, Lend-Lease had already consigned America's neutrality to the dustbin of history in establishing a common-law alliance with Britain dedicated to the defeat of Nazi Germany. In the months following its launch, the president took a number of initiatives that moved his country closer to a formal state of war.

In early April, FDR extended America's coastal security zone into the mid-Atlantic, ordered US warships to patrol this entire area and authorized them to inform the British on sightings of any German ships and airplanes. At the same time, he announced that American forces would occupy Greenland, a Danish territory liable to German seizure. In justification, he decreed this remote land to be within the western hemisphere and thereby subject to the Monroe Doctrine's prohibition against European intervention. In June he used the same rationale to send 4,000 marines to Iceland.[74] Three months later, FDR exploited a supposed U-boat attack on the US destroyer *Greer* in the North Atlantic zone of security to move to the brink of belligerency. Claiming the warship was the innocent victim of wanton aggression, whereas in reality it had been reporting the submarine's position to a British aircraft, Roosevelt took to the radio to announce what became known as the 'shoot-on-sight' policy. Denouncing the U-boats as 'the rattlesnakes of the Atlantic', he declared that US warships and aircraft would attack any German and Italian ships entering America's zone of security.[75]

It was only a matter of time before the two sides began firing on each other. On 17 October a U-boat torpedoed the US destroyer *Kearny*, killing eleven sailors and forcing its retreat to safe harbour in Iceland. In response, Roosevelt issued an exceptionally belligerent statement that made clear America's determination to see Nazi Germany defeated. 'The forward march of Hitler and of Hitlerism can be stopped – and it will be stopped', he declared. 'Very simply and very bluntly – we are pledged to pull our own oar in the destruction of Hitlerism.' Instead of asking Congress for a declaration of war, however, he requested authority to arm American merchant vessels and allow them to enter combat zones. In granting this, the legislature effectively repealed the 'carry' provisions of the neutrality legislation, casting them into historical oblivion as Lend-Lease had done for the 'cash' requirements.[76]

America finally became belligerent as a result of conflict with Japan. Starting with Plan Dog, military planners had anticipated war against Hitler but assumed a defensive posture in the Pacific to avoid a two-ocean war. A week before the attack on Pearl Harbor, Army and Navy chiefs George Marshall and Harold Stark jointly counselled FDR, 'An unlimited offensive war should not be undertaken against Japan, since such a war would greatly weaken the combined effort in the Atlantic against Germany, the most dangerous enemy.' In their assessment, it was advisable to make political concessions to Tokyo in order to avoid open rupture.[77] Far from ignoring their advice, Roosevelt sought to maintain peace in the face of Japan's provocations in seeking territorial expansion in East Asia but could not allow a rival to become dominant in the Pacific.

In contrast to his rhetorical assaults on Hitler, Roosevelt did not conduct a public campaign to warn Americans of how Japan threatened international civilization. Geopolitics rather than geo-morality shaped his dealings with the Tokyo government. Germany's blitzkrieg success in mid-1940 had encouraged its aspirations for conquest in East Asia. To restrain such ambition, Roosevelt exploited Japan's dependence on US imports for its strategic resources. On 26 July 1940, he declared an embargo on shipments of premium-grade scrap iron and high-octane aviation fuel, but this did not deter Japan from landing troops in Northern Indo-China in late September. Immediately afterwards, it signed the Tripartite Pact with Germany and Italy that pledged the Axis powers to mutual assistance if attacked by a state not presently involved in the European or Sino-Japanese conflicts. This was a naked attempt to intimidate America into remaining neutral in order to avoid a two-ocean war.[78]

For the next twelve months, Tokyo and Washington engaged in a series of escalations intended to secure their respective objectives without provoking outright conflict. In response to the invasion of Southern Indo-China in July 1941, Roosevelt announced an immediate freeze on all Japanese assets in the United States but allowed continued exports of oil if cleared through a special committee authorized to unblock payments for these. In practice, this became a de facto embargo on oil because the new group, with Assistant Secretary of State Dean Acheson in the lead, refused to release any holdings. It is a matter of debate whether FDR was complicit in this tough approach as a means of sowing uncertainty in Japanese minds or whether second-tier bureaucrats were exploiting the opportunity to implement their hawkish preferences. There is no doubt, however, that Roosevelt wanted, as he told the Cabinet, 'to slip the noose around Japan's neck and give it a jerk now and then'.[79]

Even so, FDR remained confident that these initiatives would not push Japan into war. 'It is terribly important for the control of the Atlantic', he told Harold Ickes in July 1941, 'for us to help to keep peace in the Pacific. I simply have not got enough Navy to go round – and every little episode in the Pacific means fewer ships in the Atlantic.'[80] Significantly, he delegated authority for negotiating with the Tokyo government to Cordell Hull while he focused on the more important European theatre of war. In fact, Japanese leaders had concluded by midyear that war with America was inevitable if their country was to enhance its power and prosperity through expansion in East Asia. They looked to precipitate this before the United States could increase its force levels in the Pacific. 'If for the sake of a temporary peace', warned an Army General Staff report, 'we were now to yield one step towards the United States by a partial retreat from state policy, the strengthening of America's military position will lead to its demanding further retreats of ten steps then a hundred. Ultimately, the Empire will wind up having to do whatever the United States wants it to do.'[81]

A new government headed by General Hideki Tojo decided on a final diplomatic initiative in November, which would be followed by commencement of military operations if, as expected, it came to nothing. In essence, Japan demanded a free hand in China and the termination of US economic sanctions in return for not undertaking further military operations in Southeast Asia. There was no chance of America agreeing to this. FDR considered making a counter-offer but reports of a huge Japanese fleet steaming southward extinguished his willingness to negotiate. Furious at what he considered Tokyo's bad faith, he approved a tough peace plan devised by Cordell Hull that demanded withdrawal of Japanese troops from China and Indo-China. Regarding this as an insulting ultimatum, the Imperial Conference of 1 December decided to launch planned military operations against 'the utterly conceited, obstinate and disrespectful' United States.[82]

This was the go-ahead for the surprise attack on Pearl Harbor that took place on 7 December without a prior declaration of war. During what aide Samuel Rosenman described as 'one of the busiest and most turbulent days of his life', filled with meetings and constant news updates from the Pacific, Roosevelt found time to draft the war message that he would deliver to Congress the following day. To ensure maximum support from the legislature, the president rejected Henry Stimson's entreaty to include Germany and Italy in his request for a declaration of war. He also overruled Cordell Hull's preference for a comprehensive review of the circumstances leading to conflict with Japan that might have prompted questions about whether the administration had done enough to avert it.[83] On 2 April 1917 Woodrow Wilson had delivered a long and argumentative message of nearly 3,700 words that secured a declaration of war against Germany from a divided Congress after several days of debate. FDR's message ran to just 503 words and seven minutes in length, making it the shortest major policy address from a president on record. It asked the joint session of Congress to declare that a state of war existed between the United States and Japan. The legislators required only thirty-three minutes to provide a virtually unanimous resolution (one Representative dissented), which Roosevelt signed at the White House a few hours later.[84]

Despite Pearl Harbor, FDR was adamant that Germany remained America's main enemy. Hitler's declaration of war on the United States on 11 December pre-empted the need to find a casus belli, something Roosevelt would not have shrunk from doing. He had regarded Nazi Germany's defeat as essential to America ever since Munich revealed the insatiable scope of its leader's ambitions. For FDR, Hitler's aggression posed an existential threat to the American way of life that was dependent on the preservation of a liberal and civilized international society. His 1939 annual message to Congress had anticipated US war aims in declaring,

> There comes a time in the affairs of men, when they must be prepared to defend, not their homes alone, but the tenets of faith and humanity on which their churches, their governments and their very civilizations are founded. The defense of religion, of democracy and of good faith among nations is all the same fight. To save one we must all make up our minds to save all.[85]

Once the United States was at war, Roosevelt metamorphosed from diplomat-in-chief to commander-in-chief pursuing victory over enemies that threatened American values and national-security president seeking a peace that upheld them.

Commander-in-chief

Structures and strategies

Franklin D. Roosevelt engaged more deeply with his role as commander-in-chief of the armed services than any president in American history. According to Mark Watson, an official Army historian of the Second World War, 'Every president has possessed the Constitutional authority which that title indicates, but few presidents have shared Mr Roosevelt's readiness to exercise it in fact and in detail and with such determination.' Commander-in-chief became his preferred designation in wartime, hence his instruction to Secretary of State Cordell Hull to address him thus rather than as 'Mr President' when proposing a toast at a Cabinet dinner in January 1942.[1] Excepting the Civil War, the Second World War was the greatest crisis hitherto in American history. As in the Great Depression, now relegated to third in the republic's panoply of perils, FDR met the challenges of leadership in war with calm confidence. When the difficult first year of US involvement in the conflict drew to a close, William Hassett, then his confidential secretary, commented that he remained 'unruffled in temper, buoyant of spirit . . . and can sleep anywhere whenever opportunity affords – priceless assets for one bearing his burdens, which he never mentions'.[2]

FDR was an active, innovative and able commander-in-chief who intervened to better effect in military affairs than British prime minister Winston Churchill and Soviet dictator Joseph Stalin.[3] The only Allied leader with a truly global vision, he was intimately involved in holding together the US–UK–USSR Grand Alliance and shaping its strategy to defeat the Axis powers. The institutional arrangements that he developed to coordinate US military and foreign policy during the war laid the foundations for the National Security Act of 1947 that formalized policy-making structures to wage the Cold War. On the home front, FDR rallied the nation amid early military reversals, educated the public about the need for a Germany-first strategy before turning to defeat Japan and oversaw the economic miracle whereby American industry routinely exceeded military production targets once deemed impossible. His war leadership was also instrumental in aggrandizing presidential power, sometimes in excess of constitutional authority. Later historians would see in this the genesis of the 'imperial presidency', but Roosevelt did not claim inherent presidential right to act as he did in the manner of some successors.

The first challenge facing FDR was to create a command structure that abetted his determination to be the sole coordinator of US military strategy and foreign policy in wartime. Moving the Joint Army-Navy Board (JANB) into the Executive Office of the President (EOP) in September 1939 ensured that the service chiefs reported directly to him rather than to the Secretaries of War and the Navy. Once America entered the war, Roosevelt continued the informal process of interactions with military advisers that he had developed in 1940–1. He treated lines of responsibility as something to be followed when they were useful for his purposes and circumvented when not. Accordingly, he built a personalized commander-in-chief system that got what he needed from his most valuable subordinates. Consulting with the service chiefs on all strategic matters, he reserved the right to overrule them, sometimes on military grounds and sometimes on political grounds, especially pertaining to alliance affairs. Never overawed by military rank, Roosevelt countermanded the service chiefs on matters of strategy on at least twenty-two occasions, by the Army chief historian's count, between late 1938 and the end of 1944.[4]

Accustomed to transparent chains of command and hierarchical modes of operation, the service chiefs were never comfortable with Roosevelt's leadership style but adapted to it. Army chief of staff George Marshall insisted on maintaining a formal relationship with the president – he refused invitations to Hyde Park, ignored suggestions to drop by for a late-afternoon martini in the White House and discouraged being addressed by his first name. When asked his opinion, Marshall gave it in unvarnished and succinct format. He urged his fellow service chiefs to keep their written reports to FDR short and crisp. The president, he advised, 'is quickly bored by papers, lengthy discussions, and anything short of a few pungent sentences of description'. FDR's practice of directing regular written questions at his military chiefs to keep them on their toes renders Marshall's judgement questionable on this score.[5]

Roosevelt intervened less in Army than in Navy affairs, on which he claimed greater expertise. Marshall had no difficulty in persuading him to approve plans for the most dramatic organizational changes in the Army since the early twentieth century, which included reducing direct access to the chief of staff to six officers (compared to sixty-one previously), creation of three 'super commands' (Army Ground Forces, Army Air Forces and Services and Supply) and replacement of the old General Headquarters and War Plans Division with a new Operations Division to plan global strategy, act as the Army secretariat and serve as his Washington 'command post'.[6]

FDR rejected a similar centralization of authority for the Navy to preserve his influence over assignments and promotions, deployment of forces and even warship construction. Although the United States was short of P-C submarine chasers, considered essential for convoy protection, Roosevelt insisted on transferring two of these to Brazil to protect its merchant fleet following its declaration of war on Germany in August 1942. '[T]his is a matter of international relations which has to be gone through with regardless of the purely military desirabilities', he told sceptical Navy chiefs.[7] Moreover, his preference for heavy cruisers and light aircraft carriers was not shared by his admirals. The Navy hierarchy was aghast that he approved through backchannels industrial mogul Henry Kaiser's plan for prefabricated construction of light carriers, a scheme it had already rejected.

Meanwhile, FDR manoeuvred adroitly to ensure his influence over the new organizational structures established to coordinate Anglo-American war planning.

The Arcadia conference brought together US and British military leaders in Washington from 22 December 1941 to 14 January 1942 to plan strategy for the European and Pacific theatres in consultation with Roosevelt and Churchill. The talks produced agreement to establish an Anglo-American Combined Chiefs of Staff (CCS) empowered to undertake strategic planning for both nations and report only to the president and prime minister for their final validation. To establish American parity with the UK Chiefs of Staff Committee, whose members served on CCS, Roosevelt transformed the JANB into the US Joint Chiefs of Staff (JCS). He also insisted that the new body should oversee war strategy in its entirety from Washington.

Churchill had wanted separate committees in London and Washington to be responsible respectively for European and Pacific strategy but consented to a single command based in the American capital in recognition that the United States would eventually provide the bulk of manpower and materials.[8] On Marshall's advice, FDR further prevailed on the prime minister to agree to the appointment of supreme commanders to direct air, ground and naval operations in each theatre of the war, a proposal opposed by his own Navy chiefs (who disliked the notion of any Army man in charge of their ships) and the British. To win over Churchill, FDR accepted that the first appointment should be one of his generals, Sir Archibald Wavell, to lead ABDACOM (American-British-Dutch-Australian Command) in the South Pacific, a post soon terminated in the face of Japanese advances.[9] As an additional concession, he agreed that Field Marshal Sir John Dill should serve as the prime minister's personal representative on the CCS and be permanently based in Washington to liaise with the JCS. Churchill also wanted the Munitions Assignment Board, the most significant of the sub-boards established at Arcadia (others included Shipping Adjustment, Raw Materials, Production and Resources), split into two branches to operate independently of the CCS in Washington and London. Seeing this as a ploy to give Britain control over American war production, Roosevelt had no truck with it.[10]

The end result of this high-level manoeuvring was that Roosevelt kept the levers of strategic authority at his elbow. Confident that his supposedly superior knowledge and his greater experience of military affairs would ensure his ascendancy over Anglo-American combined strategy, Churchill accepted the new arrangements as a way of ensuring FDR's commitment to the joint war effort. His physician, Lord Moran, had a clearer sense of what he had conceded, writing in his diary, 'The Americans have got their way and the war will be run from Washington.' The new Army Chief of Staff, Sir Alan Brooke, thought the Arcadia organizational agreement 'wild and half-baked' in giving the Americans central control of the war when their forces were as yet 'totally unprepared to play a major part' but resentfully recognized it was 'a fait accompli.'[11]

FDR treated the new JCS with the same informality as the JANB. Accustomed to the hierarchical British system, Dill commented in exasperation, 'The whole organization belongs to the days of George Washington.'[12] Keen for greater structure, the service chiefs pressed for regular meetings that included formal minutes documenting discussions and decisions. Instead Roosevelt continued to see them as a group or individually whenever he wanted and prohibited written records in their early encounters. 'Put that thing up', he ordered Major General John Deane, the JCS secretary who brought a big notebook to its first White House meeting.[13] By late 1942, however, FDR recognized the benefits of minuting discussions to have a record of where the JCS stood on second-front issues.

Another source of military frustration was the absence of any formal charter defining JCS powers. FDR eventually signed a statement, drafted by the British and American service chiefs, that offered a broad overview of CCS authority, but there is no record that Churchill ever co-approved this. In contrast, the president refused to tie his hands through any formal authorization of JCS powers. 'It would provide no benefits and might in some way impair flexibility of operations', he told the chiefs. Accordingly, the JCS existed at his discretion without any official status based on legislation or executive order. As its chairman later remarked, 'I have heard that in some file there is a chit or memorandum from Roosevelt setting up the Joint Chiefs, but I never saw it.' In this way, FDR ensured that the JCS remained a useful, pliable and dedicated instrument of his will as commander-in-chief.[14]

JCS membership was not carved in stone. When the group began holding regular Tuesday meetings in the Public Health Building on Nineteenth Street, it consisted of George Marshall, Army Air Force chief Lieutenant General Henry 'Hap' Arnold, Chief of Naval Operations (CNO) Admiral Harold Stark and Commander-in-Chief of the US Fleet Admiral Ernest King. Though not a service chief, Arnold was in attendance because Marshall was a keen advocate of strategic air power and wanted two Army votes to counterbalance Navy representation. 'I tried to give Arnold all the power I could', his boss later remarked. 'I tried to make him as nearly as I could Chief of Staff of the Air.'[15] In March 1942 Stark left his desk job in Washington to command US naval forces in Europe, which put him beyond reach of congressional investigations into the Navy's unpreparedness for the Pearl Harbor attack. The president promptly signed an executive order expanding King's responsibilities to encompass CNO.[16] This meant that the Navy now matched the Army in having a single chief responsible for staff and fighting forces. It also created an imbalance on the JCS that Marshall sought to put right by getting FDR to appoint a senior Navy officer as its chairman. The man he had in mind was Admiral William Leahy, a former CNO who was currently Ambassador to Vichy France.[17]

After much prompting from Marshall, the president finally appointed Leahy to chair the JCS in July 1942 following his recall from Vichy. The assignment silenced calls from Republicans (including Wendell Willkie), some Democrats and a goodly number of newspapers for the appointment of General Douglas MacArthur to run the war as head of a unified Army–Navy–Air command. Aware that MacArthur was not the military genius his admirers imagined, Roosevelt never gave this consideration.[18] Marshall hoped that Leahy would improve the flow of information between the White House and the JCS to become the fulcrum of an orderly process of strategic decision-making. FDR's opposite intent found expression in Leahy's title as 'Chief of Staff to the Commander-in-Chief', whose job was to represent his views and interests on the JCS. When asked whether Leahy would be subject to Senate confirmation in his new post, the president asserted that his commander-in-chief prerogative to give any serving officer 'an order of duty' made this unnecessary. A long interview prior to appointment revealed that the admiral shared his understanding of the job. Leahy later commented, 'The Joint Chiefs of Staff was an instrument of the Commander-in-

Chief and was responsible to him. I was his representative on that body.' A seasoned diplomat, he proved an effective chair in managing inter-service disputes within the JCS, keeping the president's concerns to the fore and acting as a conduit to ensure that FDR received the necessary information on which to base his decisions as war leader.[19]

Given an office in the newly reconstructed East Wing of the White House, Leahy met regularly with FDR during his first eighteen months in post. 'Churchill and Roosevelt really ran the war', he later remarked. 'We [the British and American chiefs] were just artisans, building patterns of strategy from the rough blueprints handed us by our respective Commanders-in-Chief.'[20] In reality, FDR's direct involvement in military affairs diminished as the war progressed partly because plans whose inception he had overseen moved into execution and partly because of his physical infirmity in 1944–5. As his confidence in his chiefs grew, he exercised less oversight of their operational activities, without ever giving them carte blanche. Accordingly, US strategy remained remarkably consistent throughout the war in embodying Roosevelt's insistence on support for Britain, Russia and China to keep them in the war, the imperative of crushing Germany before Japan and demanding the unconditional surrender of both and the need for a postwar 'United Nations' organization supported and directed by the Big Four powers. In the words of historian Eric Larrabee, 'It was a package program, in which war and politics were united to a degree rarely seen, and he stuck with it from start to finish.'[21]

FDR's leadership style meant that he never developed a command centre like Churchill's war rooms in Whitehall, but he had a map room installed in the White House after seeing the portable model the prime minister brought to Arcadia. What he wanted was a secure room to house maps that enabled him to follow the progress of the war and to store secret cables, particularly from Allied leaders. In March 1942 the map room was established in a ground-floor cloakroom measuring just 24 feet by 19. FDR used it as his private reference centre but made most of his key decisions in the Oval Office and the Oval Room private study adjoining his bedroom in the White House living quarters. These were the rooms where he consulted the JCS and dealt with Allied communications. Significantly, incoming messages were received and deciphered through Army channels, and outgoing ones were enciphered and despatched through Navy channels, so Roosevelt alone had a full set of both.[22]

America suffered early reverses in the Pacific war for which military planning was relatively underdeveloped. Holding no illusions of outright victory, the Japanese pursued a multi-pronged strategy aimed at gaining control of the Dutch East Indies to replenish petroleum reserves, establishing an unbreakable hold over Southeast Asia and forcing China into submission by closing down its external supply routes. Once achieved, the Imperial Government hoped that the United States would be overawed into suing for peace in recognition that its power in the Pacific could not be dislodged.[23] Success in this enterprise required Japan first to protect the eastern flank of its 'Southern Operation' through a surprise attack to cripple the US Pacific fleet based at Pearl Harbor, then knock out the huge British naval facility at Singapore and finally take control of the Philippines to prevent the United States using it as a forward base to harry naval operations and troop movements.

The Pearl Harbor attack was executed by some 350 aircraft launched from 6 carriers that had sailed to a point 200 miles north of Hawaii. It sank or badly damaged 18 vessels, including 8 battleships, destroyed over 180 aircraft and severely damaged another 120, and killed 2,403 servicemen. The United States had never before suffered naval losses on this scale in a single action. Away at sea on manoeuvres, the three aircraft carriers regularly stationed at Pearl Harbor escaped the devastation, but the strike left the Pacific fleet in dire straits. Thanks to the Magic intelligence breakthrough, American code-breakers had tracked high-level diplomatic despatches from Tokyo to the Japanese Embassy in Washington that provided forewarning of attack but not its location. Pearl Harbor seemed the least likely target because US naval intelligence assumed that Japanese warplanes lacked the fuel capacity to launch an attack from so far out at sea where they would not be detected, but technological improvements had expanded their flight radius. The Japanese achieved complete surprise in carrying out a precise strike on a target 4,000 miles away from their homeland and just 2,000 miles from the US mainland.[24]

This was the opening move in a coordinated offensive that stretched from the north Pacific to the Indian Ocean. Carrier-launched aircraft sank two British battleships, *Prince of Wales* and *Repulse*, off the coast of Malaya on 10 December 1941, Hong Kong, Guam and Wake Island succumbed to attack and lightning invasions launched from Indo-China advanced through Malaya and Thailand into Burma by mid-January 1942. Meanwhile, Japanese forces moved rapidly down the Malay peninsula towards the supposedly impregnable Singapore, the surrender of whose 85,000-strong garrison on 15 February 1942 marked the worst defeat in British military history. The overwhelming defeat of the hastily assembled ABDACOM fleet in the Battle of the Java Sea on 27 February then enabled the capture of the Dutch East Indies on 12 March.

Another Japanese air raid the day after Pearl Harbor annihilated American air power in the Philippines, leaving this US protectorate exposed to invasion on 22 December. In accordance with War Department planning, some 80,000 American and Filipino ground forces under the command of General Douglas MacArthur (accompanied by 25,000 civilian refugees) retreated from Manila to the Bataan peninsula and the nearby island fortress of Corregidor. Starvation and disease steadily undermined their capacity to hold these defensive positions. Trapped with them, President Manuel Quezon asked the American government in early February 1942 to grant the Philippines immediate independence (legally due in 1946) in order that it could declare itself neutral, disband its army and require that all foreign forces leave its territory.[25]

US military planners had long accepted that the Philippines could not be held against Japanese attack. Nevertheless, Roosevelt turned down Quezon's proposal for fear that neutralization would effectively signal America's incapacity to stomach heavy losses. While sanctioning the surrender of native forces, he vowed, 'As long as the flag of the United States flies on Filipino soil as a pledge of our duty to your people, it will be defended to the death.' To MacArthur, who supported neutralization, he asserted, '[W]e cannot display weakness in spirit no matter how physically weak we may now be at the moment in any particular theatre. It is mandatory that there be established once and for all in the minds of all peoples complete evidence that the American determination and indomitable will to win carries on down to the last unit.' Accordingly, US resistance in the Philippines had to be 'as prolonged as humanly possible'.[26]

These messages had the desired effect of stiffening their recipients' resolve. Although FDR arranged to evacuate Quezon and his entourage on 20 February, Filipino forces fought alongside their American counterparts to the bitter end.[27] Recognizing that further sacrifice was futile, Roosevelt withdrew his no-surrender directive on 8 April. The emaciated and diseased Bataan contingent gave up the fight the next day, the forces on Corregidor followed suit on 6 May. Despite ending in capitulation, the Philippines campaign enhanced FDR's moral authority as commander-in-chief. For George Marshall, he had metamorphosed from a glad-handing peacetime politico into a steely war leader prepared for men to die in battle. When FDR rejected Filipino neutralization, he recalled, 'I immediately discarded everything in my mind I had held to his discredit. . . . I decided he was a great man.'[28]

Roosevelt also proved his commander-in-chief mettle in dealing with the most high-profile and self-serving of America's wartime theatre commanders. Recalled from retirement to lead US Army forces in the Far East in mid-1941, MacArthur mishandled his defence of the Philippines. He allowed a fleet of eighteen Flying Fortress bombers and fifty-three fighter planes to be caught on the ground when Japanese aircraft attacked Manila's Clark Field on 8 December. He then neglected to transfer food and medical supplies from amply stocked storage depots to sustain the defence of Bataan and Corregidor. A smaller force of besieging Japanese simply waited for starvation and sickness to compel their enemies' surrender. Never one to admit error, MacArthur assiduously portrayed himself as a military mastermind through daily press releases, many of them self-written, from his underground headquarters in the Malinta Tunnel on Corregidor. Meanwhile, he pleaded with FDR for an offensive naval strategy to attack the maritime supply routes that served the enemy's scattered armies in East Asia. 'The only way to beat him', he declared, 'is to fight him incessantly. . . . From my present point of vantage I can see the whole strategy of the Pacific perhaps clearer than anyone else.'[29]

Roosevelt would have been justified in firing the errant general but desisted – and not just because of his political connections. Knowing that the Japanese would gain a huge propaganda coup from taking MacArthur prisoner, FDR ordered his transfer to assume command of Allied forces in the Southwest Pacific. On the night of 12 March, the general, his wife and four-year-old son, and seventeen of his staff were evacuated from Corregidor on four PT boats that got round the Japanese blockade to reach safe haven on the island of Mindanao, from where they were flown to Australia. Once there, MacArthur told waiting reporters that his job 'was organizing the American offensive against Japan, a primary objective of which is the relief of the Philippines. I came through and I shall return.' This claim of strategic authority did not earn a presidential rebuke. Following discussions with FDR in late January, Harry Hopkins commented in his diary that some high-ranking Army and Navy officers were unwilling to take 'great and bold risks' and would 'have to be liquidated before we really get on with our fighting'.[30] Whatever his shortcomings, MacArthur at least wanted to take the war to the enemy, which made him valuable to Roosevelt as a symbol of America's unshakeable quest for victory. FDR had the self-confidence not to resent the adulation he received from press and public desperate for heroes and the personal authority to keep him getting out of line.

Of course, the principal source of wartime inspiration for most Americans was FDR himself. Sensing that spirits needed lifting amid news of military setbacks, he scheduled a Fireside Chat on 23 February 1942 that relied on listeners referring to their own maps while he explained the importance of 'strange places that many of them have never heard of – places that are now the battlefield for civilization'. At presidential request, many newspapers printed maps of the world on their front pages on the day of the talk. FDR intimated to speechwriter Samuel Rosenman,

> I want to explain to the people something about geography – what our problem is and what the overall strategy of this war has to be. I want to tell it to them in simple terms of ABC so that they will understand what is going on and how each battle fits into the picture. . . . if they understand the problem and what we are driving at, I am sure that they can take any kind of bad news right on the chin.[31]

Speaking the day after Washington's Birthday, Roosevelt reminded an estimated audience of 61.3 million that the Continental Army had shown great 'moral stamina' to win the War of Independence after early setbacks and voiced certainty that America would similarly triumph over its present-day foes. 'This war', he declared, 'is a new kind of war. . . . It is warfare in terms of every continent, every island, every air lane of the world.' Repeatedly urging his listeners, 'Look at your map', he explained the significance of 'the world-encircling battle lines' that required America 'to fight at distances which extend all the way around the globe'. The far-flung theatres of war were all integrated geo-strategically in the drive of the United Nations, mentioned eleven times in the address, to secure a victorious peace based on disarmament of aggressors, self-determination of nations and guarantees of basic human rights. Accordingly, one historian suggested, 'his *global* thinking, on a geographical plane, reemerged as *universal* thinking on an ideological plane.'[32]

In utter contradiction of the Fireside Chat's paean to individual rights, Roosevelt had four days earlier authorized the most flagrant mass violation of American citizens' freedoms ever perpetrated by the federal government. Executive Order 9066 empowered the Secretary of War to 'prescribe military areas . . . from which any or all persons may be excluded' through whatever restrictions were deemed necessary and to arrange for the transportation, food and shelter of enforced evacuees. Framed in a way that could apply to anywhere in the United States, the decree was aimed solely at Japanese–American residents of California, Oregon and Washington. It resulted in the expulsion and eventual incarceration of 120,000 people, 70 per cent of them native-born US citizens. Initially placed in inadequate temporary facilities, Japanese Americans were interned by the end of 1942 in purpose-built installations, in effect concentration camps ringed with towers, fences and barbed wire, stretching from eastern California to south-eastern Arkansas. To run these places, Roosevelt created the War Relocation Authority within the EOP but was careful to distance himself from its ignominious mission. In a rare diminution of his executive domain, he transferred the agency to the Department of the Interior in February 1944.[33]

FDR never explained his motives for authorizing what was the most shameful episode of his presidency. Despite rumours of fifth-column activity to support invasion or sabotage, there was no evidence of Japanese–American disloyalty. This did not stop General John DeWitt, chief of the Army's Western Defense Command, from declaring, 'A Jap's a Jap. . . . It makes no difference whether he is an American citizen or not. . . . I don't want any of them.'[34] Roosevelt said nothing in public or private to suggest that he shared such blatant prejudice. In September 1943, in response to congressional charges that the internees were living too well off Uncle Sam, he declared, 'In vindication of the very ideals for which we are fighting this war it is important to us to maintain a high standard of fair, equal, and considerate treatment for people of this minority as of all other minorities.'[35]

In all probability, political calculation drove FDR's support for internment. He was all too aware that Woodrow Wilson's loss of control of Congress in the 1918 midterm contests had undermined his peace-treaty plans. Retaining the support of Democratic voters in Pacific-coast states through pandering to their anti-Japanese sentiments was a way of avoiding the same fate in the 1942 midterms. When Americans eventually learned of Imperial Army atrocities against prisoners of war, notably the Bataan death march that had followed the Philippines surrender, the antipathy became national in scope. Accordingly, FDR refused to sanction the internees' return to their West Coast homes before he ran for a fourth term, a restoration acceptable to the War Department by mid-1944 because the security threat no longer existed. As biographer Roger Daniels concluded, Roosevelt's wartime treatment of Japanese Americans 'is a permanent deserved stain on his reputation.'[36]

Executive Order 9066 constituted a grave abuse of power in depriving American citizens of their rights on spurious security grounds but was far from being a unilateral presidential initiative. Congress effectively ratified FDR's decree by making refusal to depart a prescribed area when ordered a federal crime. The Supreme Court ruled unanimously in two cases in June 1943 to uphold coerced internment on the basis of military necessity. Only as the war neared its end was this consensus fractured in the *Korematsu* case that produced a split judgement in which one of three dissenting justices, Frank Murphy, condemned Japanese–American internment as 'legalization of racism.'[37]

The internment policy typified FDR's wartime approach to presidential authority. He had built the New Deal largely through legislative means but from early 1941 he increasingly employed commander-in-chief prerogatives to stake out policy faits accomplis that Congress ratified in laws like the War Powers Act of December 1941 and March 1942. The exigencies of war induced him to rely increasingly on his proclamation of 'unlimited national emergency' in May 1941 giving him authority as commander-in-chief to undertake actions necessary to safeguard the nation. The public's support for this expansive presidential use of emergency powers induced Congress and the courts to follow suit.

Roosevelt's broad interpretation of his commander-in-chief mandate enabled him to pack nearly fifty new agencies involved in managing the war effort into the all-purpose Office of Emergency Management. With the exception of the Office of Price Administration, validated by specific statute as the agency with the most effect on people's lives and therefore in greatest need of public consent, Congress simply accepted the others on the post hoc basis that the president decreed their necessity. FDR's assertion of unilateral authority reached its peak with his declaration on 7 September 1942 that he would refuse to sign the Emergency Price Control Act unless Congress removed a farm parity provision that he considered inflationary. 'The President', he avowed, 'has the powers, under the Constitution and under Congressional acts, to take measures necessary to avert a disaster which would interfere with the winning of the war.' Nevertheless, he was careful to emphasize that when peace returned, 'the powers under which I act automatically revert to the people – to whom they belong'. As Arthur Schlesinger observed, Roosevelt 'knew where he wanted to go and where he believed the nation had to go. But he did not want . . . to go there alone.'[38]

For the war to be won, the United States had to become more engaged in fighting it. Six months after Pearl Harbor, it had not taken an inch of enemy territory, had not defeated the enemy in a major battle and had not opened an offensive campaign, but things were about to change. A bold operation of seemingly limited military relevance, undertaken on FDR's insistence, was indirectly instrumental in bringing about Japan's first defeat of the war. In retaliation for Pearl Harbor, Roosevelt wanted an air raid on Tokyo to shake the Japanese sense of invincibility and demonstrate America's resilience. In response, the JCS approved a plan whereby sixteen Army B-25 bombers launched from a Navy carrier, *Hornet*, part of a small task force that advanced into the Pacific to within 600 miles of Tokyo. Lieutenant Colonel James Doolittle recruited and trained a volunteer team of highly talented aviators for the operation that he led. Roosevelt recognized the risk of high-value airmen being killed at a time of pilot shortage but considered it worthwhile to upset enemy confidence.[39]

Undertaken on 18 April 1942, the raid did little physical damage, but all the planes reached Tokyo and made it back as planned to the coastal region of eastern China, where the crews crash-landed or bailed out. Although eight airmen fell into Japanese hands, the others found ready help from the local Chinese to reach safe havens. These civilians paid a terrible price in wholesale massacres, mass rape and widespread destruction perpetrated by Imperial troops sent to occupy the area where the American planes put down. Anticipating retaliation but not its vast scale, Roosevelt had not given the Chinese government advance notice of the operation lest it objected to use of its territory.[40]

If the human consequences of the Doolittle raid were unimaginably terrible, the military ones had momentous significance for the war. It dealt a psychological blow to the self-esteem of Japan's military leaders who had failed in their scared duty to protect the Emperor and the Homeland. None felt this more than the architect of the Pearl Harbor attack, Admiral Isoroku Yamamoto. Thereafter, a subordinate recalled, 'In [his] mind the idea that Tokyo, the seat of the Emperor, must be kept safe from an air attack amounted to an obsession.'[41] Yamamoto induced the Navy General Staff to defer plans for amphibious invasions of a string of Melanesian islands from New Guinea to Samoa to sever Australia's sea links with America. He won support instead for an operation to destroy the US Pacific fleet, thereby eliminating the danger of carrier-launched air raids on Japan. To lure it out of Pearl Harbor for a decisive engagement, he planned to attack Midway Island, an American-held atoll deemed essential for the protection of Hawaii, some 1,100 miles to the south-east.

The turning point in the Pacific war, the Battle of Midway on 4 to 7 June effectively ended Japanese naval ascendancy in the theatre. In an inspired selection, FDR had promoted Admiral Chester Nimitz over a number of senior officers to take command of the Pacific fleet ten days after Pearl Harbor. 'The one big thing about him', declared Admiral Raymond Spruance, battle commander at Midway, 'was that he was always ready to fight. . . . And he wanted officers who would push the fight with the Japanese. If they would not do so they were sent elsewhere.' Nimitz laid great store on choosing the right subordinates because the Pacific theatre was too large for him to be a seagoing commander. Instead of sailing with the fleet, he remained at Pearl Harbor to deal with organization, planning and communication. In appreciation of his qualities, FDR gave him another promotion in February 1942 to supreme commander of Allied forces in the north, central and south-eastern Pacific, a job George Marshall wanted for Douglas MacArthur.[42]

Guided by his own Magic code-breakers, Nimitz gambled that the Japanese fleet would hit Midway rather than other plausible targets. Despite sending a diversionary force north to the Aleutians, Yamamoto commanded a massive armada that included 8 carriers with over 700 aircraft on board to take on an American force with just 3 carriers, 8 cruisers and 15 destroyers. Though close in its early stages, the battle ended in a devastating Trafalgar-scale defeat for the Imperial Navy. Staggering Japanese losses, mainly the result of aerial combat, included 4 carriers sunk to the US loss of 1, 332 planes destroyed to 147 for the United States and some 3,000 dead (including many of their best pilots) to 307 Americans. Nimitz wasted no time in rubbing salt into enemy wounds. In pronouncing victory, he asserted, 'Pearl Harbor has now been partially avenged. Vengeance will not be complete until Japanese sea power is reduced to impotence . . . we are about midway to that objective.'[43]

Two months later the US invasion of Guadalcanal, an island of 2,500 square miles, marked the first stage in recapturing the Solomons. The Japanese had occupied neighbouring Tulagi with its deep-water anchorage in May in their drive to seize Melanesian islands encircling Australia. Conceived by Ernest King as a Navy and Marine operation, the Guadalcanal offensive received Roosevelt's go-ahead because it promised action in the form of the first US amphibious landings since the Spanish–American War of 1898. When it became apparent that greater resources would be needed, the JCS approved commitment of Army forces, both ground and air, a decision given urgency with the discovery that the Japanese were building an airfield on Guadalcanal.

The Marine landings on 7 August were initially successful but the Imperial Navy's crushing victory at Savo Island on the night of 8–9 August forced the temporary retreat of the US Pacific fleet, allowing the enemy to rush in large troop reinforcements. By mid-October Nimitz assessed the American situation as 'not hopeless but . . . certainly critical'. Adamant that defeat was unthinkable, Roosevelt instructed the JCS 'to make certain that every possible weapon gets into that area to hold Guadalcanal, and that having held it in this crisis munitions and planes and crews are on the way to take advantage of our success'. In short order, substantial reinforcements and resupplies were ready for despatch, but transport vessels remained scarce until William Leahy, acting on presidential authority, ordered the War Shipping Administration to 'provide without delay twenty additional ships . . . for use in the South Pacific'.[44]

FDR felt more personally involved in the battle for Guadalcanal than any other engagement in the war. Between August 1942 and November 1943, he mentioned it in six press conferences, more than any wartime encounter. The fighting on land, sea and air to secure a small atoll largely covered by clammy, fetid and malarial jungle was among the most intense of the Pacific war. The longer it went on, the more important the outcome became for both sides, causing them to commit far greater resources to achieve victory than initially intended. Unsustainable losses finally compelled the Japanese to withdraw in February 1943. Although each side had suffered approximately the same tonnage of ships sunk, the Imperial Navy was left much weaker because the United States could replace its losses with greater ease. The destruction of over 800 Japanese planes and their crews was an even bigger blow to the enemy. Finally, the tally of 24,000 troops dead or taken prisoner against US losses of under 1,600 demolished the Imperial Army's self-image as invincible jungle-fighters. A battleground for the rest of the war, the Solomons became the place where the United States could grind down Japan's more limited military resources. FDR commented to William Hassett on news of another naval victory in June 1943, 'Our war of attrition is doing its work.'[45]

As the marines prepared to land on Guadalcanal, FDR was locked in dispute with his top military advisers over where US forces should launch their first land offensive against Hitler. The president had initially supported an Army plan for a second front in Western Europe to draw German resources away from the invasion of Russia. Devised by the Army's chief planner, General Dwight D. Eisenhower, approved after careful study by George Marshall and supported by the other chiefs, this envisaged three operations code-named Bolero, Sledgehammer and Roundup. Bolero entailed the steady build-up of US air, sea and land forces in Britain, Sledgehammer was an emergency small-scale invasion in 1942 to establish a foothold in Cherbourg that would draw German divisions away from the eastern front if the Red Army looked in danger of collapse and Roundup envisaged a full-scale invasion of France in the spring of 1943.

From Roosevelt's perspective, as he wrote Churchill, 'it was essential to draw off pressure on the Russians [who] . . . are today killing off more Germans and destroying more equipment than you and I put together'. While the British regarded Sledgehammer as a suicidal venture and thought a 1943 invasion premature, they hid their reservations lest the Americans opted for a Pacific-first strategy if European operations were delayed. Fortunately for them, FDR soon cooled on the Army plan for not guaranteeing what he desperately wanted, a second front in 1942. An alternative took shape in his mind on receipt of intelligence from Ambassador William Leahy that French forces in Morocco and Algeria were so disillusioned with the Vichy regime that they would not resist Anglo-American invasion of North Africa, an operation that Churchill had previously proposed in vain under the code name Gymnast. On 18 April, FDR authorized Harry Hopkins, currently in London to press the case for Bolero-Sledgehammer-Roundup, to inform Churchill that Gymnast might be back in play. In early May an 'eyes-only' presidential memorandum to his military principals asserted unequivocally that 'there was need for very great speed in developing actual operations' in the Atlantic theatre 'in 1942 – not 1943'.[46]

Once Midway removed the Japanese naval threat to India, Churchill felt empowered to voice his own opposition to Sledgehammer – and to do so face-to-face with the president. Arriving in Washington on 19 June, he went straight to Hyde Park for consultations with Roosevelt and Hopkins. There he presented a memorandum explaining why the operation could not succeed: the Allies presently lacked trained troops and landing craft, the Wehrmacht divisions in France were sufficient to cope with a small invasion without reinforcements from the eastern front and French civilians would suffer massive reprisals for any assistance given the invaders. If an early cross-channel assault was impossible, Churchill recognized that the Allies could not 'stand idle in the Atlantic theatre' throughout 1942. Accordingly, he recommended Gymnast as an undertaking that would fit within 'the general structure of BOLERO' and 'take some of the weight off Russia'.[47]

By now FDR's service chiefs, with the backing of Secretary of War Henry Stimson, had communicated their insistence that the fastest means of victory in Europe was to assemble overwhelming forces in Britain in 1942, invade northern France in 1943 and then drive into Germany. In their assessment, Gymnast would delay this timetable by diverting resources from Bolero, would be vulnerable to German air and armoured counter-attack and would thin out naval resources currently deployed in the North Atlantic to protect supply lines to Britain and Russia.[48] To resolve the issue, Roosevelt and Churchill returned to Washington for further talks on 21 June, which were disrupted by news of the surrender of the 33,000-strong garrison of Tobruk, supposedly the unbreachable British stronghold in Libya, to Erwin Rommel's Afrika Korps. In a gesture of support, FDR agreed to re-route 300 new Sherman tanks intended for US armoured divisions to help the British Eighth Army defend Egypt and the Suez Canal from the advancing Germans, a transfer that Marshall effected by the end of the day with an additional 100 howitzers. In these circumstances, it was expedient to avoid contentious resolution of the second-front issue. What emerged was a fudge – mutual commitment to Bolero, continued assessment of Sledgehammer's feasibility and investigation of alternatives, including Gymnast.[49]

Knowing that FDR was determined to have American troops fighting in the Atlantic theatre in 1942, Churchill cabled on his return to London that Gymnast alone met this need.[50] An infuriated Marshall saw this as a British ploy to delay the invasion of France in 1943 by draining resources into a North African sideshow. At the JCS meeting on 10 July, he gained support for a Pacific-first strategy if Churchill did not back down on Gymnast, a course recommended to FDR in a memorandum jointly signed with King. In a supplementary communication to the president, Marshall emphatically urged that in the absence of Britain's unswerving commitment to Bolero–Roundup, the United States should go all-out to defeat Japan and maintain a defensive posture with token forces in the European theatre.[51]

FDR had no intention of surrendering his commander-in-chief prerogative to decide war strategy. Furthermore, he saw no wisdom in shifting focus to the Pacific and giving Hitler a free hand in Europe for the two years or so it would take to defeat Japan. Having reviewed the Marshall–King memorandum while at Hyde Park on

Sunday, 12 July, he telephoned the War Department to demand by the end of the day a comprehensive plan for a major Pacific offensive, an explanation of how it would help the Soviet Union, and an assessment of its benefits for the global situation. What was produced in a few hours of frantic effort was wholly inadequate by any measure. The presidential response was a curt note that rapped military knuckles hard:

> I have carefully read your estimate of Sunday. My first impression is that it is exactly what Germany hoped the United States would do following Pearl Harbor. Secondly, it does not in fact provide use of American Troops in fighting except in a lot of islands whose occupation will not affect the world situation this year or next. Third: it does not help Russia or the Near East.
>   Therefore it is disapproved as of the present.
>
> - Roosevelt C-in-C

He followed this up by having an aide read a five-page telephone message to Marshall and King to the effect that US troops had to fight in the Atlantic theatre in 1942, either through Sledgehammer or through another operation if that was not feasible. 'Gymnast', it concluded, 'might not be decisive but it would hurt Germany, save the Middle East and make Italy vulnerable to our air power. The war will be lost this year in Europe and Africa not in the Pacific. I think we are doing well in the Pacific.'[52]

Roosevelt exchanged harsh words with Marshall over the second front on his return to the White House. Years later the general ascribed FDR's stand to 'political necessities'. The military, he asserted, had failed to see that 'the leader in a democracy must keep the people entertained. . . . People demand action'.[53] It was certainly the case that Roosevelt wanted military operations to begin in North Africa before the 1942 midterm elections, ideally on 30 October. Refusing to put politics before prudence, however, he would approve Marshall's request for a delay of seven days to ensure that assault troops were adequately trained and well supplied. Had Sledgehammer taken place instead, it would in all probability have been a sacrifice operation with heavy casualties suffered for no tangible gain. As commander-in-chief, Roosevelt opted for a less hazardous operation that stood greater chance of success and could contribute more to Germany's eventual defeat. American forces' lack of battle experience and the fact that the Allies did not yet have control of the North Atlantic (gained in the second half of 1943) made this the correct military decision, but it delayed the cross-channel invasion of France until June 1944.

To get the chiefs on board, FDR sent Marshall and King, accompanied by Hopkins, to London with instructions, signed 'Commander-in-Chief', to secure agreement for a combined operation in 1942. Knowing the British would reject Sledgehammer out of hand, he opened the way for Gymnast by instructing the trio that the 'cardinal principles' to guide selection of where to strike would be 'speed of decision on plans, unity of plans, and attack combined with defense but not defense alone'.[54] The only location that met these criteria was North Africa. Roosevelt gave Marshall and King one week from their arrival in London on 19 July to sort the matter; Sledgehammer was dead within three days, killed by the British War Cabinet's absolute rejection of it; and the US chiefs came round to accepting Gymnast, renamed Torch, the very next day. As a concession, Churchill agreed that an American should command the operation. The man Marshall wanted was Dwight Eisenhower, a trusted subordinate already in Britain as commander of US forces being built up for Roundup.[55]

That should have been the end of the matter but was not. At the JCS meeting of 30 July, the first chaired by William Leahy, Marshall and King insisted that no final decision had been reached on Gymnast/Torch until Churchill and Roosevelt had explicitly abandoned Roundup in its favour. Informed of this, FDR called the military chiefs to the White House that same evening to reiterate that Torch was the 'principal objective' – though he insisted Roundup was still on for 1943, a patent fallacy that did nothing to reconcile Marshall to the North African diversion.[56] Rumblings of continued opposition to Torch found their way into the press, thanks to Stimson's leaks. On 10 August, Marshall decided that things were getting out of hand when the Secretary of War showed him the draft of a letter he intended sending FDR to urge Torch's cancellation. His refusal to support this led to the collapse of an incipient mutiny against the commander-in-chief's military judgement.[57]

Only Joseph Stalin could now throw a spanner into Torch's works. In late May he had despatched Foreign Minister Vyacheslav Molotov to Washington to lobby for an early second front to draw off forty German divisions. By now, the Wehrmacht had inflicted two crushing defeats on the Soviets at Kerch and Kharkov, where combined Red Army casualties exceeded 350,000, as a prelude to the summer offensive, Case Blue. Desperate to keep the Soviets in the war, FDR told Molotov in a White House meeting on 30 May that the United States expected a second front in Europe in 1942, something his military chiefs considered impossible. Over Marshall's strenuous objections, he later accepted the Foreign Minister's proposed language for a public statement that there was 'full understanding' on this score.[58] This was playing with fire because it was evident that Stalin would assume his Anglo-American allies envisaged the invasion of France. On discovery that their destination was North Africa, there was a danger that he would seek a separate peace with Hitler.

To pre-empt this, Winston Churchill, accompanied by FDR's representative, Averell Harriman, flew to Moscow to explain matters to Stalin in three days of talks at the Kremlin from 12 to 14 August. Understandably anxious about the mission, the prime minister told FDR, 'I feel that things would be easier if we all seemed to be together. I have a somewhat raw job.'[59] Thanks to highly placed spies in London and Washington, Stalin possessed full knowledge of the strategic debates between his allies and knew what was coming. This did not stop him flaying Churchill for Britain's military failures while being complimentary about America's fighting capabilities on the first day of talks. Told the next day of the Torch plan to invade North Africa with combined forces of 250,000 troops, he expressed strong approval of its strategic potential to change the tide against Germany in the desert war and threaten the Italian homeland. 'May God prosper this undertaking', he told Churchill and Harriman.[60] Stalin was under no illusions that Torch would spare the Red Army a bloodbath in repelling Case Blue but accepted its utility in getting the Americans and British into ground combat against Hitler's forces.

The most complex operation of the war hitherto, the invasion of North Africa went ahead in the early hours of 8 November. American forces coming across the Atlantic hooked up in secret with British forces to deploy planes, ships and troops in the three-pronged assault on Algiers, Casablanca and Oran. Roosevelt persuaded Churchill to let US troops make the first landings in the expectation that they would encounter less French resistance, optimism that was misplaced.[61] Heavy fighting at Casablanca and Oran left some 500 Americans and many more defenders dead. Neither the British-backed Free French leader General Charles de Gaulle nor the American-backed General Henri Giraud, a war hero who had escaped from a German prison camp, could get their countrymen to lay down their arms. However, Vichy's deputy premier and commander-in-chief of its armed forces, Admiral Jean-Francois Darlan, who was visiting Algiers, was willing to change sides. On 10 November, he agreed to a ceasefire that recognized the Allies' right to be in North Africa and retained the Vichy colonial administration with him as High Commissioner.

For Torch commander Dwight Eisenhower, this was a necessary pact with the devil to get the French to stop fighting and continue governing their colonial possessions without need for large-scale Anglo-American occupation. The arrangement freed him to focus on driving the Germans out of neighbouring Tunisia, but putting a notorious Vichy collaborator and anti-Semite in charge of supposedly liberated territory set off a political firestorm at home. Typifying the anger, CBS London correspondent Ed Murrow roared, 'Are we fighting Nazis or sleeping with them?' Having initially assured Eisenhower of his full support, FDR retreated somewhat in the face of negative press. On 17 November he issued a statement that the Darlan deal was 'a temporary expedient justified solely by the stress of battle'.[62] Darlan's assassination some weeks later drew a veil over the episode before it could cause further embarrassment.

Despite this fallout, FDR had good reason to believe that the tide had started to turn in the war against Germany by the end of 1942. He told an Armistice Day gathering at Arlington, 'The forces of liberation are advancing . . . [to] make certain the survival and the advancement of civilization.'[63] Shortly before Torch ensconced Anglo-American forces in the west of North Africa, the British Eighth Army's victory at El Alamein forced Rommel's Afrika Korps into full retreat from Egypt in the east. Shortly afterwards, the Red Army encircled the German Sixth Army in Stalingrad to halt Case Blue's invasion of southern Russia. These successes prompted Roosevelt to propose a summit meeting in North Africa with Churchill and Stalin in early 1943 to agree war strategy for the coming year and to discuss postwar issues.

Stalin declined an invitation for talks at Khartoum, the safest equidistant point for the three, claiming he could not leave Russia while battle raged at Stalingrad. For a twosome with Churchill, FDR might have repaid the prime minister's transatlantic sojourns by meeting in London. However, the Republicans, resurgent after their strong showing in the 1942 midterms, and their press-baron allies would have had a field day accusing the president of kow-towing to the British. Accordingly, FDR opted for Casablanca in the North African battle zone, thereby enabling him to travel as commander-in-chief rather than as president and to insist on absolute secrecy without reporters present. As various aides pointed out, the trip posed real risks of enemy interception, accidents or even assassination, but Roosevelt paid them no heed. The gruelling journey began on the evening of 9 January with a two-day train ride from Washington to Miami; from there a flying boat carried the president's party to Trinidad for an overnight stop on 11 January, then on to Belem in Brazil for refuelling, followed by a eighteen-hour flight across the Atlantic to reach Bathurst (now Banjul) in British Gambia on 13 January; and after a night aboard a US warship, the final leg was a 1,200-mile hop in an Army C-54 to alight at Casablanca on 14 January. Doubtless, the chance to record a string of presidential firsts appealed to FDR's love of the dramatic – the first president to travel by air, the first to leave the country during wartime and the first since Abraham Lincoln to visit a war zone.[64]

The first question for resolution in the Casablanca talks was where the Allies would go after driving the Germans from North Africa. The Americans themselves were divided on this score. Meeting with Canadian prime minister William Mackenzie King in the White House in early December, Roosevelt remarked that 'he wished for nothing more than let the fighting continue in Africa indefinitely' because it was 'so much easier' to ship military supplies to there than anywhere else. Well-equipped US forces could therefore gain invaluable combat experience against the Germans and wear them down through a process of attrition. The disastrous raid on Dieppe on 19 August 1942, in which two-thirds of a 5,000-strong Canadian contingent were killed, wounded or captured without even getting off the beaches, reinforced his conviction that any attempt at cross-channel invasion of northern France in 1943 was premature.[65]

When the JCS met with the president on 7 January, George Marshall advocated an amphibious invasion of the Brest peninsula on the Brittany coast, a plan that FDR did not openly oppose but in reality considered even more impractical than a Normandy operation. The Army chief underwent a change of heart after speaking in Casablanca to Allied commanders with experience of the Torch operation. The emphatic assessment of Eisenhower's deputy, General Mark Clark, that there was no chance of a cross-channel invasion succeeding in 1943 was a particularly significant reality check. Once sceptical of Torch, Marshall now regarded it as the first of several Mediterranean operations needed to give American forces the fighting experience they needed before an amphibious invasion of France in 1944.[66]

FDR brought with him a small retinue of aides, including Harry Hopkins, and the service chiefs (minus Leahy, left behind in Trinidad suffering after-effects of influenza), plus their top planners. In contrast, Churchill arrived with a huge contingent of staff officers and aides, their numbers so great that many could only be accommodated in a warship that had participated in the Casablanca landings rather than in venues near where the talks were held. General Albert Wedemeyer, Marshall's chief planner, later complained that the British, by sheer force of numbers, overwhelmed their allies into accepting a Mediterranean strategy instead of a cross-channel course that would have brought the war to a swifter end. 'We came, we listened, and we were conquered', he declared.[67] Nothing could have been further from the truth. Once Marshall had spoken with the officers who had participated in Torch, the service chiefs were on the same wavelength as FDR. This was confirmed at their meeting in the president's bedroom in his conference residence, the Villa dar es Saada, on the morning of 15 January. Just as in the Pacific, the United States would pursue a strategy of attrition in the Mediterranean at the outer edge of enemy lines of communication in 1943. Once Tunisia was cleared of German troops, the next target would be Sicily to give Allied forces experience of amphibious invasion in readiness for the assault on German-held France.

That same day FDR took the opportunity, in the company of his son and conference aide-de-camp Elliott, to talk with the man who had commanded Torch. Eisenhower had taken a hair-raising flight from his headquarters in Algiers to appear before the CCS for a grilling on his failure to seize Tunis at the outset of the operation. The British, in particular, had a poor opinion of his military leadership, exacerbated by resentment that a mere lieutenant general had been given command over their more senior officers. Nevertheless, Eisenhower impressed FDR in giving an honest estimate that it would take till mid-May to dislodge the Germans from Tunisia, where they had poured in reinforcements following the Torch landings. The president also appreciated his success in gaining control of Morocco and Algeria so quickly that there was no chance of the Allies being hit on the flank as Marshall and Stimson had feared.[68]

Buoyed by this encounter, Roosevelt wanted to undertake a frontline inspection of American troops close to the Tunisian border, an idea uncompromisingly vetoed by Marshall as excessively risky. Instead he settled for a 'very stirring day' inspecting three divisions of troops stationed near Rabat, some 85 miles northeast of Casablanca on 20 January. He was driven there in the company of George Patton, who had led the Casablanca landings with distinction, and Mark Clark. Seizing the opportunity to be his own intelligence agent, as in New Deal days, FDR never stopped asking questions of the generals, impressing them with his inquisitive mind. Travelling in an Army jeep for the last leg caused him intense pain, but the resultant photo-opportunities fired up patriotic sentiments at home. It was the first time a president had inspected American servicemen on foreign soil. Harry Hopkins's son, Robert, an Army combat photographer present for the shoot, was amused 'to see their jaws drop open' when they realized who was reviewing them. Later he photographed Roosevelt, Clark and Patton eating a lunch of boiled ham and sweet potatoes alongside some soldiers. Although the men were still green in terms of combat experience, seeing them left FDR in no doubt about their spirit and determination. He told Elliott that evening, 'Those troops, they really look as if they're rarin' to go. Tough, brown, and grinning.'[69]

Far less to Roosevelt's liking was his frosty encounter with Charles de Gaulle in the late evening of 22 January. Resentful of being summoned on home soil to see an American president, the Free French leader took further umbrage at FDR's efforts to force him into a shotgun marriage with Giraud to demonstrate their anti-fascist unity under Anglo-American sponsorship. de Gaulle left the meeting with the realization that 'from the moment America entered the war, Roosevelt meant the peace to be an American peace . . . that the states that had been overrun should be subject to his judgement, and that France in particular should recognize him as its savior and arbiter'. Roosevelt, in return, had his suspicions confirmed that de Gaulle wanted to restore French greatness on the back of its empire. The United States, he told Elliott afterwards, was not in the war to resurrect European colonialism. 'When we've won', he avowed, 'I will work with all my might and main to see to it that the United States is not wheedled into the position of accepting any plan that will further France's imperialist ambitions, or that will aid or abet the British empire in *its* imperial ambitions.'[70]

Unwilling to be party to any foreign intervention in French affairs, de Gaulle refused to sign a conference communiqué of rapprochement with Giraud. He agreed only to be photographed in the garden of Villa dar es Saada shaking hands with his rival in the presence of Churchill and Roosevelt in a public display of supposed unity in front of newsmen gathered there for a press conference. In this case the camera lied because the two Frenchmen remained locked in bitter competition for power in which FDR backed the wrong horse. According to future prime minister Harold Macmillan, on secondment to Eisenhower's staff, 'de Gaulle was strong, but uncertain. Giraud was reliable but weak.' Exasperated by Giraud's ineptitude, Churchill proposed formal recognition of de Gaulle's French Committee of National Liberation as the provisional government of France in April 1943, which FDR resisted. Eisenhower's support for the British position and de Gaulle's growing popularity with the French people eventually induced the president to back down in August. Roosevelt's determination to prevent France falling back into its sorry pre-war condition caused him to underestimate de Gaulle's vision of restoring its greatness through his own image of indomitability. As British foreign secretary Anthony Eden observed, FDR 'wanted to hold the strings of France's future in his own hands'.[71]

The de Gaulle–Giraud handshake would have been a memorable way of ending the Casablanca talks but FDR trumped it in the news conference that followed. The fifty correspondents in attendance were amazed to learn that he had been conferring with Churchill for the last ten days without their knowledge. To the consternation of Propaganda Minister Joseph Goebbels, the Nazis only learned of the talks when the main story given the newsmen hit the headlines. This was Roosevelt's announcement that the Anglo-American allies were in agreement that the elimination of Axis war power was the only way to ensure world peace. The unconditional surrender of Germany, Japan and Italy to the United Nations was essential to that end. Its attainment, FDR was careful to emphasize, required the destruction not of their peoples but of 'the philosophies in those countries which are based on conquest and the subjugation of other people'.[72]

The unconditional-surrender announcement drew much criticism after the war for provoking Germany and Japan to fight to the bitter end. Hanson Baldwin, military editor of *The New York Times*, adjudged it a huge mistake for encouraging 'unconditional resistance'. It came to be seen as a spur-of-the-moment initiative that FDR had sprung on his allies and aides without consultation. Churchill later claimed to have had no foreknowledge of it prior to the news conference. Albert Wedemeyer similarly asserted that the service chiefs, had they been asked, would have advised against demanding unconditional surrender lest it lengthened the war by removing the enemy's inducement to negotiate peace.[73]

Far from being an impromptu decision, taken without consultation, FDR had appraised the JCS of his thinking in their White House meeting of 7 January 1943, without any dissent in response. He had also secured Churchill's enthusiastic support for the policy at a private luncheon at his conference villa on 18 January, a decision shared with the CCS later that afternoon. The prime minister promptly cabled his War Cabinet to report his agreement for a 'declaration of firm intention' that the Anglo-American allies would 'continue the war relentlessly until we have brought about the "unconditional surrender" of Germany and Japan'. That body formally approved the policy on 21 January.[74]

FDR was certainly the prime mover in the adoption of 'unconditional surrender' as Anglo-American policy. He was determined that there would be no Great War-style armistice that could be exploited by another Hitler as a stab-in-the back betrayal of Germany. In Robert Sherwood's words, FDR 'wanted to ensure that when the war was won it would stay won'. The president was also looking to reassure Stalin in the absence of a second front in Europe that his Anglo-American allies would never negotiate a separate peace with Hitler.[75] Roosevelt was mindful that it risked prolonging the war, but none of his later critics produced convincing evidence of it doing so. Militaristic, fanatical and fascist, the leaders of Germany and Japan knew that a peace negotiated from a position of increasing weakness from 1943 onwards would have meant their destruction just as surely as unconditional surrender.

Roosevelt's demand for unconditional surrender signalled that the war had moved into a new phase. What had been for the Americans, British and Soviets a defensive war against Nazi Germany for most of 1942 was becoming an offensive war. The Japanese withdrawal from Corregidor shortly after FDR and Churchill left Casablanca confirmed the same turn in the Pacific war. Roosevelt's strategic leadership was crucial to these developments. In facing down his service chiefs and their Cabinet ally, Henry Stimson, against early cross-channel operations, he had preserved the Anglo-American alliance's Europe-first strategy and saved it from a crushing defeat that could have put final victory over Hitler in doubt. Rommel's overwhelming victory over a corps of Eisenhower's tank and infantry forces at Kasserine Pass, Tunisia, in mid-February 1943 demonstrated that American commanders and their troops needed greater combat experience before they were ready for more hazardous challenges. Roosevelt also laid the foundations of primacy in his partnership with Churchill in 1942. Resistance to early cross-channel operations had put him on the same page as the prime minister, thereby making the strategy agreed at Casablanca appear a triumph for British interests. As 1943 progressed, the reality of FDR's preponderance would become evident in disagreements over military priorities beyond the Mediterranean theatre.

Commander-in-chief

Arsenals and alliances

'I want to tell you, from the Russian point of view, what the President and the United States have done to win the war. The most important things in this war are machines. . . . The United States . . . is a country of machines. Without the use of those machines, through Lend-Lease, we would lose this war.' This was Joseph Stalin's toast to Franklin D. Roosevelt at a dinner hosted by Winston Churchill on the occasion of his 69th birthday during the Tehran conference. In response, FDR remarked, '[W]e have proved here . . . that the varying ideals of our nations can come together in a harmonious whole, moving unitedly for the common good of ourselves and of the world.'[1] He might have added that it required more than machines to achieve these ends – equally essential was the disproportionate burden shouldered by the Soviet Union in fighting Hitler's forces at bloody cost to its soldiers and citizenry. Such an exchange would have encapsulated two of the greatest challenges that Roosevelt faced as commander-in-chief – ensuring that the United States fulfilled its mission as the 'arsenal of democracy' and getting it more involved in the land war in Europe in order to shape world peace.

FDR called on America to be the 'great arsenal of democracy' in a Fireside Chat in December 1940 to build support for the Lend-Lease programme that Congress would soon consider. The designation was intended to signify that supplying war materials to nations fighting Germany would save America from having to send its own sons into combat. Once the United States became a belligerent, Roosevelt endowed it with new meaning. 'We cannot outfight our enemies unless, at the same time, we outproduce our enemies', he avowed in his 1942 budget message to Congress. 'We must outproduce them overwhelmingly, so that there can be no question of our ability to provide a crushing superiority of equipment in any theater of the world war.' These words, a perfect encapsulation of FDR's understanding that America was fighting a gross-national-product war, prefaced his request for a war budget of $53 billion in FY1943, more than double the FY1942 level.[2]

Elaborating on these remarks in next day's State of the Union Address, Roosevelt asserted, 'The superiority of the United Nations in munitions and ships must be overwhelming – so overwhelming that the Axis Nations can never hope to catch up with it. . . . We have the ability and capacity to produce arms not only for our own forces, but also for the armies, navies, and air forces fighting on our side.' He then spelled out new war production targets set for 1942 and the increases projected for 1943, among them 60,000 planes rising to 125,000, 45,000 tanks rising to 75,000, 20,000 anti-aircraft guns rising to 35,000 and 6 million deadweight tons of merchant shipping rising to 10 million.[3] Donald Nelson, a top official in defence mobilization, later remarked, '[Roosevelt] staggered us. None of our production people thought that this volume was possible.' Undeterred by their scepticism, FDR breezily told Lend-Lease supremo Harry Hopkins, 'Oh – the production people can do it if they really try.'[4]

One reason that FDR broadcast these targets was to boost public morale at a time when the war was going badly. As speechwriter Robert Sherwood observed, 'It was in Roosevelt's nature to believe that the surest way to capture the imagination of the American people was to give them the greatest possible challenge.' Equally, he was waging psychological warfare to intimidate the Axis powers about the scale of America's productive capacity. There was also a deeper strategic rationale in his thinking. Roosevelt was fully aware of America's unique advantage among the major belligerents in being able to wage a war of machines rather than men. The 'arsenal of democracy' role allowed the United States to take the least-cost route to victory that left most of the actual fighting to its Allies, notably the Soviet Union. This minimized the risk of incurring heavy casualties that might revive popular opposition to America remaining deeply involved in international affairs when peace returned. It also promised to put the United States in a position of unparalleled economic power in the postwar world. As historian David Kennedy observed, 'That vision may not have been fully formed in Roosevelt's mind in early 1942, but it was consistent with his policies in the neutrality period, and its possibilities were latent both in the military strategy he adopted and in the mobilization program he outlined.'[5]

Despite taking longer than any industrial nation to achieve full recovery from the Great Depression, America was an economic giant whose one-fifth share of world income in 1938 was substantially greater than the 16.5 per cent combined share of Germany, Italy and Japan. With nearly nine million unemployed and huge swathes of industrial plant lying unused in 1940, it had immense spare capacity to expand military production in the eighteen months before Pearl Harbor. Self-sufficiency in many raw materials, most notably a three-fifths share of world oil production, and safety from physical attack were further assets. For all these advantages, the United States still experienced problems in converting its economy onto a full war footing.

The difficulties of getting the all-important steel industry, the critical foundation for military output, to maximize production in the neutrality period offered a foretaste of the challenges that lay ahead. Though suspected by liberals of preferring scarcity to boost prices and profits, steel bosses were more concerned not to be left with excess capacity once the defence crisis receded. The president and his officials employed carrots and sticks to 'get [them] off their asses', as one of those involved in the task, economist John Kenneth Galbraith, put it. The administration relaxed anti-trust laws, accelerated tax write-offs for investment and promised to underwrite plant expansion as needed, while also threatening to encourage new entrants into the sector, notably Henry Kaiser, all of which secured industry agreement in 1941 to expand basic capacity by 13 million tons.[6]

Once America was at war, FDR needed to construct an effective machinery for economic mobilization almost from scratch. Agencies spawned in the neutrality period, notably the Office of Production Management, were not fit for purpose. As with the New Deal, Roosevelt created a plethora of new organizations, often with partial or overlapping jurisdictions, that gave him executive prerogative to resolve disputes. Established in February 1942, the War Production Board (WPB) was far from being the mobilization superagency its title implied. Other bodies, at least a dozen in all, received jurisdiction over domains like labour, manpower and prices. Nor did the WPB wrest control of contract allocation from the military procurement bodies that wanted to deal directly with regular suppliers.[7]

As defence jobs boosted consumer spending, many businesses were slow to convert to war production until the WPB placed curbs on non-essential manufacturing in mid-1942. This did not solve the need for plant construction to meet the targets Roosevelt had set. Corporations remained hesitant to invest in new facilities that could become unprofitable once the war ended. Accordingly, as with steel, the federal government underwrote most of the development costs, issued cost-plus-fixed-fee contracts to guarantee profitability and shelved anti-monopoly restrictions. These carrots created new problems of unrestrained business competition for raw materials in short supply, notably copper, steel and aluminium. Eventually, the Controlled Materials Plan, which came into full operation in mid-1943, required all procurement agencies to estimate their commodity needs for WPB determination of allocations. Meanwhile, inadequate housing, transportation and public services in hitherto underdeveloped industrial areas, notably the Pacific West and the South, made high turnover of war workers a threat to production in key industries. Things improved somewhat after Roosevelt created the Committee for Congested Production Areas within the Executive Office of the Presidency in April 1943 to coordinate the myriad agencies dealing with labour-supply problems.[8]

Jurisdictional conflicts among the tangled skein of agencies involved in economic mobilization were inevitable but one stood out for its high-profile wrangling. When the WPB mooted the Controlled Materials Plan in late 1942, what ensued in the words of Budget Director Harold Smith was 'a public "knock-down and drag-out" fight' with the military, which wanted full control over procurement. Angered that press stories of the feuding contravened his rhetoric of a united war effort, FDR considered sacking WPB chief Donald Nelson. Smith persuaded him, however, that the problem lay in 'the lack of unity, vigor, and definite policy' stemming from the agency's structural incapacity to coordinate the production hierarchy.[9] Accordingly, Roosevelt created a new agency, the Office of Economic Stabilization, to fulfil that role under his one-time political fixer, James Byrnes.

Quitting as Associate Justice on the Supreme Court, which he called the 'marble mausoleum', Byrnes was only too happy to return to the political front line as the official charged with sorting out the so-called mess in Washington. 'It just isn't possible for me to devote sufficient time to the domestic problems', the president reportedly told him. 'All these new agencies . . . mean an increasing number of jurisdictional conflicts which come to me for decision. I want you to settle those conflicts for me; I'll issue an executive order giving you the power to settle them, and I'll let it be known that your decision is my decision.' This meant that Byrnes would for 'all practical purposes be Assistant President'.[10] Anyone so designated by the press in New Deal days found himself cast out by a president jealous of his authority, but FDR now recognized that coordination of economic mobilization required just such a lieutenant.

Given an office in the White House, Byrnes was promoted in May 1943 to head the Office of War Mobilization (OWM), a new agency placed atop the administrative hierarchy of the Executive Office of the President. Superseded by a man with no corporate experience, WPB boss and former Sears Roebuck chairman Donald Nelson wryly recalled Roosevelt telling him that businessmen recruited to government 'don't know how to administer the things they must administer as well as the politicians know how'.[11] Fully conversant with the ways of Washington, Byrnes intuitively understood that his job was to be FDR's home-front troubleshooter. As OWM boss, he focused on adjudicating disputes as they emerged from below rather than undertaking operational or long-term planning responsibilities. His success was based not on any significant organizational innovation but on political know-how, closeness to FDR and eschewal of mission creep. Asked by Roosevelt to assess the need for OWM's establishment, another of his political fixers, Samuel Rosenman, concluded, 'Jimmy is the perfect man for the job. The set up will work . . . and leave you free really to spend most of your time on fighting the war and arranging for "post war".[12]

Almost as soon as OWM was created, the president found himself having to settle a public donnybrook between two giants of his administration too big for Byrnes to control. In June 1943 a long-simmering vendetta between Vice President Henry Wallace and Secretary of Commerce Jesse Jones boiled over. As chairman of the Board of Economic Warfare, Wallace accused Jones of failing to amass stockpiles of vital materials in the neutrality period and thereafter obstructing his agency's efforts to obtain them, charges that his opponent dismissed as malicious. Habitually slow to resolve quarrels between New Deal subordinates, FDR did not tolerate wartime brouhahas. He curtly informed the feuding duo that their 'unfortunate controversy and acrimonious public debate' made it necessary to transfer responsibility for the issues at dispute to other hands. There was no time amid a conflict 'so critical to our national security and to the future of civilization' to investigate the truth of their competing claims. The important thing was 'to clear the decks and get on with the war' under 'new men, unencumbered with interagency dissension and bitterness'.[13] Peremptorily terminating Wallace's agency, FDR put Byrnes in charge of its replacement, the Office of Economic Warfare (OEW), which also gained control of parts of Jones's bureaucratic empire. To pre-empt further public disputes, the president warned every department and agency chief that anyone airing quarrels in the press faced immediate dismissal. This thunderbolt terminated public feuding but not behind-the-scenes bickering between rival officials.[14]

Regardless of mobilization hiccups, the United States won hands down in the war of machines. It built 8,812 major naval warships between 1941 and 1945, dwarfing Britain's total of 951 and Japan's 538. Equally important, the 5,000 merchant vessels launched from its shipyards kept open the supply lines on which Britain and Russia relied. Allied amphibious operations depended on the 90,000 landing craft manufactured Stateside. Meanwhile, the United States produced 306,181 aircraft, easily besting the Soviet, British and German totals respectively of 137,271, 108,560 and 99,339. Lend-Lease largess to the Allies included supplying Britain with a quarter of its wartime munitions, over half of all Red Army motorized vehicles and 90 per cent of UK and Soviet aviation fuel at an octane grade far higher than Germany could refine. To get oil to the fronts, America constructed a 1,400-mile pipeline from Texas to Pennsylvania and built a massive fleet of tankers with an aggregate tonnage of 11.4 million by 1945, compared to 2.5 million in 1941.[15]

To see the production miracle for himself, Roosevelt undertook an epic tour of twenty-six defence plants and military bases that entailed an 8,750-mile train journey across America in September 1942. Donald Nelson's briefing for the trip did not prepare him for the magnitude of what he saw. This only hit home on the first stops, at the new Chrysler Tank Factory in Detroit, which was turning out thirty tanks a day, and the new Ford factory at Willow Run, where the world's first mass-production assembly line would eventually produce B-24 Liberator bombers at the rate of one every sixty-three minutes. The odyssey continued westward to reach the Boeing aviation plant at Seattle, whose weekly production of sixty B-17 Flying Fortresses would nearly double by war's end. The highlight of the tour was witnessing the launch of a 10,000-ton freighter constructed in just ten days at the Kaiser shipbuilding yard in Portland. Roosevelt was then driven around the shops producing vessel parts that would be welded into place on the slipway. The brainchild of Henry Kaiser, a corporate enthusiast for all-out production, this prefabrication process enabled the yard to turn out ships at hitherto inconceivable speed. The next plants Roosevelt inspected were the Mare Island Navy Yard, near Oakland, which specialized in submarine construction and repair, and the Douglas aircraft plant at Los Angeles. On the return leg eastward, he saw another B-24 mass-production plant at Fort Worth, Texas, and the Higgins boatyard in New Orleans, which was revolutionizing manufacture of the landing craft that would play a crucial role in amphibious operations in Europe and the Pacific.[16] The tour confirmed that FDR's vision of America's transformation into an industrial colossus with almost unimaginable capacity to produce war materials had become a reality.

The reputation of big business had sunk along with the economy in the depressed 1930s but wartime production feats restored its image. Unemployment declined from 14.6 per cent of the labour force in 1940 to 1.2 per cent in 1944, workers employed in manufacturing enjoyed a 27 per cent real growth of income between 1940 and 1945 (mainly thanks to overtime) and economic output grew by 52 per cent in inflation-adjusted terms from 1939 to 1944. The expansion of military-related output from 2 per cent GNP in 1939 to 40 per cent GNP in 1943 hastened the development of corporate oligopoly. Between 1941 and 1945 more than two-thirds of prime military contracts went to just 100 firms, with the 33 biggest corporations getting fully half of them – General Motors led the way with a 10 per cent share of all war production. This select band had the virtues of reliability, efficiency and familiarity in the eyes of procurement officials.

Profitability and patriotism went hand-in-hand for big business as post-tax corporate profits skyrocketed from $6.4 billion in 1940 to $11 billion in 1944. Once peace returned, the corporate sector got a whopping bonus when just eighty-seven companies bought up some two-thirds of the $17 billion worth of government-financed plants and equipment being sold off at knockdown prices. The war had laid the foundations for what would become known as the 'military-industrial complex', a

cartelistic partnership between the armed services and big business that lay at the heart
of the Cold War state. Secretary of War Henry Stimson had prophetically remarked in
1940, 'If you are going to try to go to war, or to prepare for war, in a capitalist country,
you have got to let business make money out of the process or business won't work.'[17]

If FDR was unconcerned by the growing concentration of military production, he
was readier to fight for a fair tax system to pay for the war. In 1939 filing of personal
income-tax returns was an obligation for just four million Americans, most of whom
were liable to the basic rate of 4 per cent. The rest of the working population did not pay
any federal income tax because their annual earnings fell below the basic exemption
level of $1,500. The Revenue Act of 1942 transformed the income tax from an elite
levy into a mass tax. In order to drain off inflationary purchasing power, it lowered
the personal exemption rate to $624, bringing thirteen million new taxpayers onto the
rolls. Wartime prosperity enlarged the taxpayer base still further so that 42.6 million
Americans (effectively three-quarters of all workers) paid income taxes at basic rates
of 6 per cent and marginal rates stretching all the way up to 94 per cent for top earners
by 1945. For the first time, individuals paid more in aggregate taxes than corporations,
establishing an enduring pattern. As of 1943, they also forked out regular payments
at work through the new withholding system that made employers responsible for
deducting taxes from their workers' pay packets.[18]

Ordinary Americans adjusted with remarkable tolerance to the new tax regime but
business wanted a line drawn against further levies. In response to corporate lobbying,
conservative Democrats and Republicans baulked at FDR's request in late 1943 for a
new tax that would generate $10.5 billion for the war effort. They enacted a substitute
measure that raised only $2 billion and provided special-interest tax-giveaways. FDR
vetoed this with a stinging rebuke: 'The responsibility of the Congress of the United
States is to supply the Government of the United States as a whole with adequate revenue
for wartime needs, to provide fiscal support for the stabilization program, to hold
firm against the tide of special privileges, and to achieve real simplicity for millions of
small income taxpayers.'[19] Long-standing Roosevelt ally Alben Barkley (D-Kentucky)
promptly resigned as Senate Majority Leader in protest at what he considered a slur
on his own integrity and that of Congress but was re-elected unanimously. Turning
the issue into defence of congressional dignity rather than tax fairness, the House and
Senate both voted by wide margins to override FDR. This was the first occasion that
the legislature had enacted a revenue law over presidential veto. Seeing no purpose
in continuing an unwinnable battle, Roosevelt contented himself with a private blast
against the 'very small number of people who would rather nail my hide on to the barn
door than win the war'.[20]

The United States covered 45 per cent of aggregate war costs from taxes, a much
smaller share than its economy could have afforded. The rest came from the sale
of nearly $200 billion of Treasury bonds, about a quarter of which were bought by
individuals and the rest by banks and other financial institutions. Flush with funds,
purchasing bureaus began issuing war contracts in 1942 with no thought to the
economy's capacity to meet them. This provoked the so-called Feasibility Dispute
between the WPB and the military over the speed and scale of procurement. By year's
end, the Joint Chiefs of Staff reluctantly concluded that there was a serious disjunction

between the economy's productive capacity and overexuberant military demand. They agreed to shrink purchase plans by $13 billion, stretch out production schedules and reduce projected ground-force enlistment by 300,000.[21]

The Feasibility Dispute intersected with two other developments to exert a profound influence on American strategic doctrine. On 17 August 1942 the US Army's Eighth Air Force carried out its first bombing raid on continental Europe to destroy rail yards near Rouen in northern France. The sortie encouraged air-power advocates to press its expansive use as essential for Germany's defeat. Within a few months, the imminent defeat of Hitler's forces on the other side of the continent in the Battle of Stalingrad ended doubts about Soviet capacity to continue fighting. US war strategy was originally predicated on the Victory Program's assumption of 1941 vintage that Hitler's invasion would knock Russia out of the war. Military planners had estimated America would need a gigantic army of 213 divisions for a successful invasion of Western Europe when Germany no longer had to worry about the eastern front. Rouen and Stalingrad made such calculations obsolete. Army estimates of future troop needs were revised downwards first to 125 divisions, then 100 and ultimately in July 1943 to 90, a diminution that accorded with the economic limits revealed by the Feasibility Dispute.

The '90-Division Gamble', as the revised Victory Program Troop Basis became known, received FDR's formal approval as commander-in-chief in November 1943. It embodied his 'arsenal of democracy' vision as amended in the 1942 State of the Union Address. Henceforth, military historian Maurice Matloff observed, American strategic doctrine heeded a new gospel that 'the single greatest tangible asset that the United States brought to the coalition in World War II was the productive capacity of its industry'. In the calculations of military planners, a 90-division Army struck a balance between the minimum strength required to win the war and the maximum number of servicemen that could be inducted without overstretching the resources of war industries that held the key to victory. They put their faith in the sufficiency of a smaller ground force, powered by an overwhelming preponderance of weaponry and equipment, to fight a modern war of mobility. By the end of 1943, accordingly, the United States had stockpiled an arsenal that gave Allied forces a three-to-one munitions advantage over their foes in the critical operations of the year to come. Compensating for a smaller army, it also developed a massive aerial force capable of raining down bombs of unprecedented destructive capacity on enemy territory.[22]

The war ultimately ended with the dropping of two atomic bombs on the Japanese cities of Hiroshima and Nagasaki in August 1945. FDR had authorized their development nearly six years earlier when alerted to the dangers of Germany winning the race to produce weapons of mass destruction. A group of scientists, many of them Jewish refugees, got nowhere in their efforts to warn the military bureaucracy about this threat in the pre-war period. Eventually they put their concerns in a letter to FDR, signed by the great émigré physicist Albert Einstein and delivered in person to the president by economist Alexander Sachs on 11 October 1939. His eyes opened to the danger, Roosevelt set up the Advisory Committee on Uranium, which began meeting on 21 October but made little progress in overcoming the immense scientific challenges of actually fabricating a bomb.[23]

In June 1941, the Office of Scientific Research and Development was established within the EOP's Office of Emergency Management to coordinate atomic research under the leadership of the Carnegie Institution's Vannevar Bush, who reported only to FDR. The British discovery that a few kilograms of plutonium, a man-made uranium, could produce an atomic explosion induced Bush to request presidential authority for a full-scale American effort to develop the A-bomb. The costs, he warned in a briefing paper, would be astronomic. Roosevelt gave the go-ahead in uncharacteristically terse fashion on 19 January 1942: 'OK – returned – I think you had best keep this in your own safe.' This set in motion the process whereby the Manhattan Project would expend the vast sum of $2 billion before successfully testing an atomic device at Los Alamos in the New Mexico desert on 16 July 1945.[24]

According to Harvard's James Conant, a top presidential adviser on atomic development, Roosevelt did not comprehend the revolutionary significance of the new weaponry, hence 'the program never got very far past the threshold of his consciousness'. In reality, the president played a key role in keeping the project going when it experienced critical shortages of money and materials in 1943. Faced with more immediate war matters, he paid only intermittent attention to progress on a weapon whose development was far from certain, but he did not ignore the possibility that it would become reality in time. The question of informing the Russians about the atom project became a bone of contention with Winston Churchill. Despite acceding to the prime minister's insistence that the new weapon should remain exclusively in Anglo-American hands, he kept his options open in practice. Nor did FDR commit to the bomb's usage if developed when the war was ongoing. In the expectation that Germany would by then be defeated, the aide-memoire he agreed with Churchill at Hyde Park in September 1944 stated that it 'might perhaps, after mature consideration, be used against the Japanese, who should be warned that this bombardment will be repeated until they surrender'.[25]

While US production was essential to the Grand Alliance's military success, Roosevelt's leadership was also significant as the political fulcrum for its progress towards victory. Securing Churchill's support for an Anglo-American cross-channel invasion of France proved his greatest challenge in keeping the Big Three together. Establishment of this second front was essential to gain Joseph Stalin's agreement to enter the war against Japan once Germany was defeated and support continued Great Power collaboration in peacetime. Although the Roosevelt–Churchill partnership has gone down in history as the foundation stone of the Anglo-American special relationship, FDR was far more concerned to build good relations with the Soviet leader, whose cooperation he considered essential for building a sustainable peace. In his assessment the early wartime disasters that Britain had suffered in Western Europe, North Africa and Southeast Asia had undermined its psychology and sapped its vitality. The 'United States and Russia are young powers, and England is an old, tired power', he once told Vice President Henry Wallace. In his vision, accordingly, the new world order that emerged from global war would have to be built on Soviet-American entente.[26]

Though FDR professed to detest communism as much as fascism, he worked hard to build a good relationship with his Russian counterpart. Part of a collective leadership that took charge of the Soviet Union in 1924, Stalin consolidated his power into dictatorship in the 1930s. In that capacity he had a brutal record of forced collectivization with appalling human costs and indiscriminate purges to liquidate as many as a million suspected enemies. Making it his business to learn as much about Stalin as possible, Roosevelt was under no illusions about his ruthlessness but thought him 'get-atable' (a term Harry Hopkins had used after first meeting him in 1941). He hoped to convince Stalin that a peace cooperatively guaranteed by the Great Powers was the necessary foundation for Russia to achieve economic modernization after the war. 'I bank on his realism', FDR told his personal physician, Vice Admiral Ross McIntire. 'He must be tired of sitting on bayonets.' A week after he died, close companion Daisy Suckley wrote in her diary of Roosevelt's confidence that the Soviet leader would work with him in building the peace: 'F. himself did not have too much faith in Stalin, but he thought that he & Stalin looked at things in the same *practical* way, & that for that reason, there was much hope that Stalin would follow along.'[27]

A communist ideologue, Stalin was deeply suspicious of the capitalist West and its political leaders. Well aware of this, Roosevelt spared no effort to gain his trust. He was determined to meet all Stalin's supply orders for feeding, clothing and arming Russian forces, even at cost to America's own war effort. To this end, the Hopkins-led Soviet Protocol Committee negotiated a series of yearly agreements specifying deliveries to be made by the United States. The shortest supply route, from New York to Archangel, was also the most dangerous because of the U-boat threat in the North Atlantic. Despite significant losses suffered by American convoys, FDR kept a close eye on progress in maintaining protocol-agreed quotas and let the US Maritime Commissioner know of his dissatisfaction if supply rates were falling behind. In March 1942, he put all US agencies involved in Lend-Lease on notice that making good their commitments to the Soviet Union took precedence over all else.[28]

For Stalin, the early establishment of a second front through Anglo-American invasion of France was the primary yardstick of his allies' trustworthiness. The United States and United Kingdom found strategic harmony difficult to achieve on this score. American service chiefs wanted to end the European war as quickly as possible through direct application of preponderant Allied power against Hitler. The British, by contrast, preferred an indirect strategy of bombing, blockade and peripheral military operations on several fronts to effect Germany's political and economic collapse. Memories of the Great War slaughter and the military disasters of 1940–2 reinforced their scepticism about the prospects of direct conquest. Britain also looked to prioritize operations in locations beneficial to its imperial interests – the Mediterranean, the Balkans and the Middle East in the European theatre and Southeast Asia in the Far East.[29]

As his support for Operation Torch demonstrated, FDR occupied a middle position between his service chiefs and the British on how to defeat Germany. He wanted to ensure that American generals and soldiers had experience of fighting Hitler's battle-hardened troops in a secondary theatre before attempting the perilous invasion of northern France. At the Casablanca conference, he accepted the British recommendation that Sicily should be the next target once the Germans were driven out of North Africa. There were good reasons for this: the Allies would enhance their proficiency in amphibious invasion of enemy territory, possession of the island's air bases put southern Italy within range of bomber raids that could undermine Mussolini's now tottering regime and if a new Italian government looked likely to surrender, Hitler would have to withdraw some of his forces from the eastern front to shore up his southern flank.

The Sicilian campaign, launched on 10 July 1943 and completed on 17 August, provided Allied commanders with invaluable lessons in intelligence gathering, deception measures, integrated US–UK command, and air-, naval- and ground-force coordination. On 19 July, an American force of over 500 B-17s and B-24s conducted the largest air raid of the war hitherto against Rome's railway marshalling yards and nearby airfields. Leaving some 700 civilians dead, it precipitated the overthrow of *Il Duce* on 25 July, the prelude to Italy's acceptance of an armistice on 3 September. The first sundering of the Axis pact exposed Anglo-American fault lines in encouraging Churchill's aspirations to pursue the Mediterranean-Balkan rather than cross-channel route to the destruction of Hitler.[30]

The Americans and British had clashed over war strategy at the Trident conference, held in Washington DC in mid-May 1943. Roosevelt unequivocally insisted that Mediterranean operations had to be curtailed once Sicily was captured in order to prepare for a cross-channel invasion in 1944. Churchill, by contrast, wanted to knock Italy out of the war and then move against German-held positions in the Balkans, where a successful campaign in his estimation would induce Turkey to enter the war on the Allied side. Gnawing away at Nazi Germany's soft underbelly would supposedly bring it to the verge of collapse, thereby opening the way for a cross-channel operation to deliver the coup de grace.[31] The British were adamant that the Allies lacked the manpower to contemplate a 1944 invasion of France where twenty-five German divisions stood ready to repel them. At a meeting of the Combined Chiefs of Staff (CCS), General Alan Brooke asserted, 'No operations would be possible until 1945 or 1946, since it must be remembered that in previous wars there had always been some 80 French divisions available on our side.'[32] After days of wrangling, the military chiefs hammered out an agreement whereby, once Sicily was secured, major offensive operations could be conducted to tie down the relatively small number of German divisions in Italy for the remaining summer months before the most experienced US and UK divisions were transferred to Britain to prepare for the invasion of France in May 1944, now code-named Overlord. For George Marshall, this was a necessary compromise to sustain coalition warfare but he worried that Allied operations would become 'extremely difficult and time consuming' if Hitler decided to reinforce his army in Italy.[33]

If the revised invasion schedule was a year or more too soon for British preferences, it was a year too late for the Russians. In March 1943, Stalin wrote FDR that a new summer offensive planned by Hitler made it 'particularly essential for us that the blow from the West be no longer delayed, that it be delivered this spring or in early summer'.[34] Hoping to square matters, Roosevelt despatched Joseph Davies to Moscow in early May with his personal invitation for a one-to-one meeting on either side of the Bering Straits between Russia and Alaska. Davies had developed a good rapport with Stalin when ambassador to Moscow from 1936 to 1938 and was an important source of counsel for FDR on the need for massive aid to keep Russia in the war.

Accordingly, he was the perfect emissary to bring to fruition Roosevelt's intent, as confided to Daisy Suckley, 'to talk, man to man, with Stalin, & try to establish a constructive relationship'.[35]

As speechwriter Samuel Rosenman observed, FDR 'was firmly convinced of his own ability to get along with people and to work out acceptable agreements with them'.[36] Though he had never met Stalin, FDR was sure that he would do better dealing alone with him, unencumbered by the strongly anti-communist Churchill. 'I know you will not mind me being brutally frank', he had written the prime minister in early 1942, 'when I tell you that I think I can personally handle Stalin better than either your Foreign Office or my State Department. Stalin hates the guts of all your top people. He likes me better, and I hope he will continue to do so.'[37] Of course, Churchill minded very much because he feared his two allies reaching agreements on which he had no say. Fortunately for him, Stalin initially viewed his Anglo-American counterparts as speaking with one voice, so held them equally culpable for delaying a cross-channel invasion while Russia bled dry fighting Germany.

Joseph Davies returned from Moscow with the Soviet leader's agreement to meet at Fairbanks, Alaska, on or around 15 July and a clear warning of his expectations. 'Stalin', he reported to FDR on 2 June, 'said to me expressly that he could accept neither the African invasion nor the Air Attack on Germany as a Second Front. . . . He was suspicious, not only of the British, but of us, as well.'[38] On receiving formal notification of the Trident schedule for Overlord, a furious Stalin fired off identical cables to Roosevelt and Churchill accusing them of breaking their promise to open a second front in 1943. Their decision left the Red Army, 'which is fighting not only for its country, but also for its Allies, to do the job alone, almost single-handed, against an enemy that is still very strong and formidable'. The despatch ended on a menacing note that the Soviet Union could not be reconciled to a decision made 'without its participation and without any attempt at a joint discussion of this highly important matter and which may gravely affect the subsequent course of the war'.[39] On any reading, this message signalled that the proposed Roosevelt–Stalin talks were dead in the water. More ominously, it raised questions as to whether the Grand Alliance could hold together long enough to defeat Hitler let alone to build a sustainable peace.

As Robert Sherwood remarked, 'It was fortunate that Hitler did not know how bad relations were between the Allies at that moment, how close they were to the disruption that was his only hope'.[40] The German discovery in April 1943 of mass graves in the Katyn Forest of over 22,000 Polish army officers, police and intellectuals murdered in cold blood by Soviet occupation forces in 1940 had added to the challenges of maintaining Allied unity. Blaming the Nazis for the massacre, Stalin broke off relations with the Polish government-in-exile in London for demanding an International Red Cross inquiry. FDR remonstrated mildly but in vain that 'with several million Poles in the United States', this action 'would not help the present situation'.[41] Despite clear evidence of Soviet culpability, he placed greater importance on preserving Big Three unity than on condemning Stalin's moral reprehensibility. Roosevelt's only means of gaining leverage with his Russian ally was to put Anglo-American boots on the ground in France, but Churchill now insisted that the Mediterranean-Balkan route was the backway into Eastern Europe before the Red Army could overrun it.

The prime minister began backsliding on Overlord once home from Trident. Visiting Britain to review the US build-up for the cross-channel invasion, Secretary of War Henry Stimson was shocked to discover Churchill gung-ho for operations in Italy as the first step in his own victory strategy. 'We cannot now rationally hope', he reported to FDR, 'to be able to cross the Channel and come to grips with our German enemy under a British commander.' In his assessment, the 'shadows of Passchendaele and Dunkerque still hang too heavily' over Churchill and his generals for their hearts to be in Overlord. 'The difference between us', he concluded, 'is a vital difference of faith.'[42] This was the last thing that Roosevelt wanted to hear because he had just received Stalin's proposal for a Big Three meeting in late 1943. This made it imperative for the Anglo-American allies to display united commitment to Overlord. Accordingly, Roosevelt looked to settle second-front matters once and for all at the Quadrant talks in Quebec, initially scheduled for September but brought forward to mid-August because of the rapidly changing situation in Italy.

Meeting at the White House on 10 August, the president and his military chiefs reached agreement that there should be no Balkan campaign, Overlord should go ahead as scheduled and the Americans should provide the bulk of the manpower for the invasion to ensure one of their own having command. FDR was emphatic in wanting '[our] preponderance of force to be sufficient to make it impossible for the British to disagree'.[43] He was willing to throw Churchill the bone of agreeing to joint operations in Italy provided these did not advance beyond Rome. At an earlier parley with FDR, George Marshall expressed concern that a multi-front strategy would distract tightly stretched resources from Overlord. This counsel of caution received the breezy response that military planners were 'always conservative and saw all the difficulties', and that more could usually be done than they were willing to admit'. From Roosevelt's perspective, it was inconceivable that the American people, any more than Stalin, would settle for nine months without significant ground-force engagement against the Germans in the run-up to Overlord.[44]

To lay the ground for Quadrant, FDR summoned Churchill to a pre-conference retreat at Hyde Park, where they settled two important matters of alliance business. The prime minister had long complained of America not honouring its promise to share atomic research with Britain, a commitment that Roosevelt now renewed. The president in turn compelled Churchill to accept an American commander of Overlord on grounds that the United States would make the greatest contribution of manpower and materials to the venture.[45] This amounted to formal recognition that the United States had become the senior partner in the alliance, thereby limiting Britain's scope to delay Overlord. There is no evidence that sharing atomic research was a quid pro quo, but it cannot have escaped Churchill that he risked losing access by not living up to the cross-channel commitment. The Quebec conference consequently ratified the key decisions reached at Hyde Park and sanctioned continuing operations in Italy conditional on non-diversion of resources from Overlord.[46]

This agreement did not extinguish Churchill's hope that his strategic vision would ultimately prevail, but its folly was quickly exposed. Abruptly terminating the Kursk offensive in western Russia on hearing of Anglo-American landings in Sicily, Hitler sent substantial reinforcements to secure his position in Italy. Though it never regained momentum as an offensive force in Russia – or indeed anywhere else – the Wehrmacht remained very capable of waging defensive war on a multi-front basis. Hitler adapted his military strategy to this new reality. In his assessment, German forces could still hold the line on the eastern front, preserve the Atlantic Wall in the west and contain Anglo-American operations in the south. German reinforcements took control of Italy's industrial north and replaced its occupying forces in the Balkans and the Aegean. 'The fundamental principle of our war strategy', Joseph Goebbels noted after talks with Hitler, 'is to keep the war as far as possible from the borders of the homeland.'[47] It was already there in the skies, of course, evidenced by UK and US air force raids that killed some 37,000 people in laying waste to Hamburg in late July. Nevertheless, Hitler remained confident that the longer the ground war went on without resolution, the greater the probability of either the Soviets or the Anglo-Americans seeking a separate peace. The Red Army's success in pushing beyond the Dnieper in the autumn to recapture Ukraine's bountiful granaries and the industrial heartlands of the northern Caucasus did not dent this hope. In Hitler's calculation, Goebbels wrote in his diary, 'There is only one way for our enemies to win total victory in this war, and that is a successful invasion of the West.'[48]

The post-Sicily floundering of the Anglo-American allies posed no threat to the Third Reich. On 9 September, their amphibious invasion of mainland Italy nearly failed to secure its Salerno beachhead. Establishing a pattern for the entire campaign, a combination of inadequate resources, poor command coordination, bad field decisions and fierce German defence confounded overconfident expectations of an easy advance from there to Naples, which was not taken till 1 October – and only then because Hitler's forces retreated to make a stand just north of the city. Meanwhile, Churchill looked to exploit Italy's surrender by taking control of its garrisons in the Dodecanese islands of the southeast Aegean. The Germans beat him to the punch to win one of their last significant victories of the war. Lacking adequate air cover, the British lost 1,500 men killed, 3,000 captured, 8 warships sunk and several more badly damaged, and 113 aircraft destroyed in a disastrous effort to capture Rhodes and neighbouring isles. When the Americans refused to divert resources from Overlord to bail him out, Churchill grudgingly called off the operation. Roosevelt had been in favour of 'obtaining whatever hold we could in the Dodecanese without heavy commitment' but the situation had changed. 'Strategically', he remarked to Churchill, 'if we get the Aegean Islands, I ask myself where do we go from there and *vice versa* where would the Germans go if for some time they retain possession of the Islands?'[49]

Far from strangling Churchill's obsession with the Mediterranean theatre, Roosevelt's response made him all the more determined to scupper its resource-consuming rival. On 23 October he cabled FDR that the manpower and equipment available for Italy and Overlord were insufficient for 'the tasks set them', so it was better to combine resources in the ongoing campaign rather than the prospective one. It was his contention that the invasion timetable agreed at Quebec 'should not be interpreted rigidly and without review in the swiftly changing situations of war'. Exaggerating the significance of Mediterranean-Aegean operations, he claimed that their success would ensure Hitler's ultimate defeat, whereas their failure could give him 'the chance of a startling come back'.[50]

Seeing Overlord as a political sop to Stalin, Churchill told his physician, Lord Moran, 'I will not allow the great and fruitful campaign in Italy to be cast away and end in a frightful disaster, for the sake of crossing the Channel in May.' Unbeknown to the Americans, he shared with the Soviet leader a highly pessimistic British report of Allied prospects in Italy without commitment of additional resources. An accompanying personal message warned that regaining the ascendancy in this theatre would in all likelihood necessitate Overlord's postponement. To Foreign Secretary Anthony Eden, charged with delivering the bad news in Moscow, Churchill confided, 'The battle [in Italy] must be nourished until it is fought out and won. We will do our very best for OVERLORD but it is no use planning for defeat in the field to give temporary political satisfaction.'[51]

Furious to learn of these machinations, Roosevelt and his military advisers decided they would no longer tolerate Churchill's undermining of agreed positions. As historian David Reynolds observed, 'OVERLORD was no longer merely a strategy; it had become a metaphor for who was on top in the Anglo-American alliance.'[52] FDR also received clear warning from America's new ambassador in Moscow, Averell Harriman, about the Soviet mindset on Overlord: 'It is impossible to over-estimate the importance they place strategically on the initiation of the so-called "Second Front" next spring.'[53] Accordingly, he decided on a clear demonstration of his support for Stalin's position when the three leaders met at Tehran in late November 1943.

The Soviet leader would go no further for a Big Three meeting than the Iranian capital, whose direct telegraph and telephone communications with Moscow enabled him to stay in touch with military operations in Russia. In Roosevelt's reckoning, Daisy Suckley recorded in her diary, Stalin's 'inferiority complex, whether for himself or for his country', was the real reason for making him travel so far. The journey involved a relatively pleasant sea voyage aboard a US warship to Cairo, followed by a long flight from there to Tehran that was bound to be physically challenging, but FDR was determined that the conference should go ahead 'regardless of the cost to himself'.[54]

Churchill's hopes of winning Roosevelt's support for his Mediterranean strategy at a pre-Tehran conference at Cairo came to nothing. Unable to get time alone with the president, he got to put his case at their meeting with the CCS on 24 November. Dominating the discussion, he blamed lost opportunities in Italy and the Aegean on diversion of resources to Overlord. While paying lip service to the cross-channel commitment, he was clearly intent on getting it delayed but got nowhere with the Americans. At Roosevelt's instigation, Harry Hopkins went to see Lord Moran later that day to deliver the message, soon to reach the ears of its intended recipient, that the prime minister should not pursue this line in the Big Three talks. 'Sure, we are preparing for a battle at Tehran', Hopkins warned. 'You will find us lining up with the Russians.'[55]

Another Hopkins exchange with Moran made it clear that Roosevelt was not travelling some 8,000 miles just to clarify Grand Alliance military strategy, which could have been settled through exchange of cables. The purpose of the trip was to establish a personal relationship with the Soviet leader. The president, his emissary declared, is 'determined . . . to come to terms with Stalin, and he is not going to allow anything to interfere with that purpose'. This followed the logic of the Soviet Protocol

Committee's review of the USSR's growing power. 'Since Russia is the decisive factor in the war', it concluded, 'she must be given every assistance and every effort must be made to obtain her friendship. Likewise, since without question she will dominate Europe on the defeat of the Axis, it is even more essential to develop and maintain the most friendly relations with Russia.'[56]

In a symbolic demonstration of this intent, FDR agreed to move residence into the Soviet Embassy on the second day of the Tehran conference. The Russian discovery of a German assassination plot made it unwise for the president to make the long journey from the American compound to attend talks at the British and Soviet legations, which were adjacent to each other. In accepting Stalin's offer to host him, Roosevelt made it easier for them to meet on three occasions without Churchill being present. At their first parley, on 28 November, he wooed the Soviet leader by playing up his differences with the prime minister. In their next one-on-one, he broached his ideas for a postwar world peacekeeping body, one backed by the political and military muscle of 'Four Policemen' – the United States, the Soviet Union, Great Britain and China. Despite his reservations about China's capacity to fulfil such a role, Stalin was clearly interested in Roosevelt's vision. Indeed, he wanted a stronger international body than the president had outlined to ensure that a revived Germany did not embark on renewed aggression. From his vantage as FDR's interpreter, Charles Bohlen, a Foreign Service officer at the Moscow Embassy, gained the impression that 'Stalin felt it would be much more dangerous to be outside any world organization than to be in it', providing the USSR could 'block actions it did not like'.[57]

FDR was also in lockstep with Stalin on military strategy in the plenary meetings of the Big Three and their principal officials. In the first, he unveiled the date set for Overlord at Quebec, which the British had resisted sharing with the Soviets, adding that it should not be delayed by 'secondary operations'. Stalin then urged that Overlord should be 'the basis for all 1944 [Anglo-American] operations' as the surest means of compelling Hitler to transfer forces from the eastern front and ultimately of defeating him. Questioning the wisdom of dispersing forces to other fronts, he counselled the Anglo-American allies to make a secondary landing in the south of France to divert German troops away from the English Channel. This would require the redeployment of all but ten divisions currently fighting in Italy and the postponement of Rome's capture. Seizing on this, FDR proposed that the CCS should devise a plan to strike at southern France shortly before, during or just after the northern invasion. Churchill was left isolated in his habitual advocacy of Mediterranean-Aegean operations. Later that evening, Lord Moran asked the dispirited prime minister if anything had gone wrong in the meeting, to which the response was, 'A bloody lot has gone wrong.' For a buoyant FDR, in contrast, much had gone right – not only had he demonstrated to Stalin his commitment to Overlord but also had received assurances that the Soviet Union would join the war against Japan once Germany was defeated.[58]

The following day's plenary was even more excruciating for Churchill. Stalin was shocked to discover that no one had yet been named to command Overlord, a clear sign to his mind that his allies were not serious about it. He insisted that the appointment be made either at Tehran or as soon as possible thereafter. FDR took the opportunity to affirm that this could only be done once Overlord's priority was formally agreed.

Instead of committing to this, Churchill digressed into talking up the prospects for huge gains in Italy, the Balkans and the Aegean, even if the investment of resources to attain them necessitated some delay to Overlord. Resorting to grandiloquence in place of realism, he declaimed that 'now is the time to reap the crop if we will pay the small price for this reaping'. Roosevelt's unambiguous rejoinder that 'any operation which might delay it [Overlord] cannot be considered by us' should have closed off further discussion but did not. On the verge of losing his temper, Stalin finally asked Churchill an 'indiscreet question, namely, do the British really believe in Overlord or are they only saying so to reassure the Russians?' Avoiding a straight answer, the prime minister responded that if 'conditions' were right, namely that operations in Italy and the Aegean limited Germany's capacity to reinforce its divisions in France, 'it was the duty of the British government to hurl every scrap of strength across the channel'.[59]

The meeting ended in agreement only to refer the matter to the Anglo-American CCS to work out an agreed position. Visibly put out, Stalin was mystified why the Big Three could not resolve the matter right away, but the delay gave FDR the chance to despatch Hopkins on another private mission. Following a Soviet-hosted evening banquet that featured copious quantities of food and alcohol, the aide made a post-midnight visit to Churchill's quarters to make it clear that he was fighting a losing battle against US-Russian unity on Overlord. The basic message was, 'Yield with grace.' This was what the prime minister did the next day in formally agreeing to CCS recommendations that the United States and Britain should launch Overlord along with a supporting operation in the south of France 'during May', while aiming to advance by then to the Pisa-Rimini line in the Italian theatre. Stalin, for his part, reiterated commitment to coordinate Red Army offensives with Overlord to prevent any diversion of German forces from the eastern front.[60]

Had the conference ended there, it would have been an unqualified success for FDR in terms of engaging with Stalin, but their differences on Eastern Europe became evident on the final day. In their last private meeting, FDR signalled personal acceptance of a Soviet sphere of influence while seeking in vain to educate Stalin about American domestic opinion. He also agreed that the USSR could retain Polish territory it had seized through invasion in 1939 in return for Poland receiving German territory as compensation, a settlement he insisted on keeping secret for fear of losing the Polish-American vote should he seek a fourth term. Despite appearing to accept this informal guarantee, Stalin resisted Anglo-American entreaties in the final plenary meeting to negotiate a territorial settlement with Poland's government-in-exile in London, which he regarded as anti-Soviet. The Baltic republics of Estonia, Latvia and Lithuania, annexed by the Soviet Union in June 1940, also aroused contention in this forum. While willing to concede Russian control, FDR wanted them to have some degree of self-determination in line with the expectations of the American public, which conflicted with Stalin's insistence on their retention as Soviet Socialist Republics.[61]

Tehran strengthened the Grand Alliance's military unity in pursuit of victory over Germany and Japan while leaving unresolved the political details of the postwar settlement. The conference communiqué was signed at Stalin's insistence 'Roosevelt, Stalin, Churchill', an order that reflected their changed importance on the world stage. This committed the Allies to seek a 'peace that will command the good will of the overwhelming mass of the people of the world and banish the scourge and terror of war for many generations' and to bring together all nations dedicated to eliminating 'tyranny and slavery, oppression and intolerance . . . into a world family of democratic nations'. This was clearly Roosevelt's personal vision of the future, but he was under no illusions that it was achievable anytime soon. For him, the statement embodied a set of aspirations that the victors could begin working towards in peacetime. As he disclosed to columnist Walter Lippmann before departing for Tehran, 'Sometimes I feel that the world will be mighty lucky if it gets 50% of what it seeks out of the war as a permanent success. That might be a high average.'[62]

In the second Anglo-American conference at Cairo, held on the return journey from Tehran, FDR resolved an issue critical to retaining Stalin's trust in Anglo-American commitment to Overlord. Though command of the operation was widely expected to go to George Marshall, who had the support of Churchill, Stalin, Harry Hopkins and Henry Stimson, it went instead to Dwight Eisenhower. John Pershing, the now-retired commander of US forces in France in the Great War, had written FDR in September insisting that Marshall's 'outstanding strategical ability and experience' made him irreplaceable in his present post of Army Chief of Staff. This was the same message the president heard from Marshall's JCS colleagues.[63] Roosevelt well knew that whoever commanded Overlord would be blazoned in history forever more if successful. On the way to Tehran, the president had stopped off in Tunis for talks with Eisenhower, Marshall's putative replacement in the JCS. Ruminating that field commanders, not staff officers, were celebrated in popular memory of war, he illustrated this point with the observation: 'You and I know the name of the Chief of Staff in the Civil War [Henry Halleck], but few Americans outside the professional service do.' Informing Marshall of the decision over a private lunch on 5 December, FDR managed to find the words to salve his disappointment: 'I could not sleep at night with you out of the country.'[64]

There were positive reasons, not just default ones, for giving command to Eisenhower. An outstanding military planner, he was heavily involved in formulating the cross-channel operation; he had already commanded three successful amphibious invasions; a superb organizer, he had experience of setting up a functioning Allied headquarters for the North Africa-Mediterranean theatre, which became the model for the Supreme Headquarters, Allied Expeditionary Force, established in London in January 1944; he was skilled in managing the fractious relations between his British and American subordinates; and he was accustomed to command operations involving coordination of land, sea and air forces. He was also a known quantity to Roosevelt, who had taken the opportunity to size him up in person at Casablanca and Tunis. When asked by his son, James, the reasons for his choice of Overlord commander, FDR responded, 'Eisenhower is the best politician among the military men. He is a natural leader who can convince other men to follow him, and this is what we need in his position more than any other quality'. The appointment, the most momentous of Roosevelt's presidency, turned out to be a great success and put Eisenhower on the road to the White House. As both soldier and president, he displayed highly effective hidden-hand leadership – he never minded if other actors believed they were the initiating agents provided what he wished got done and in the way he wanted.[65]

Roosevelt delayed the public announcement of Eisenhower's appointment until he delivered a Fireside Chat on 24 December. Much of that address focused on what kind of world would emerge from the war. Reporting on the Tehran conference, he expressed optimism that America, Britain and Russia were united in determination to eliminate the evil of Nazism and work together for international peace, security and prosperity once Germany and Japan were defeated. He was particularly complimentary about Stalin, assuring his listeners 'that we are going to get along very well with him and the Russian people – very well indeed'. His message was most cogent in its insistence that America should not return to isolationism after the war lest new aggressors threaten the peace. In a clear reference to the neutrality laws of the 1930s, he declared,

> The well-intentioned but ill-fated experiments of former years did not work. It is my hope that we will not try them again. No – that is putting it too weakly – it is my intention to do all that I humanly can as President and Commander-in-Chief to see to it that these tragic mistakes shall *not* be made again. . . . If we are willing to fight for peace now, is it not good logic, that we should use force if necessary, in the future, to keep the peace?[66]

However much Roosevelt sought to focus on the peace, the need to win the war as quickly as possible kept demanding his attention in 1944. The year began badly with the Allies getting bogged down in late January on the Anzio beachhead, an amphibious operation personally planned by Churchill to bypass German forces in central Italy and take Rome. His hopes of speedy success ran aground on Anglo-American intelligence underestimation of German forces in the area, which bred false confidence that two infantry divisions without armoured support would suffice for the operation. Looking at one point like another Gallipoli, Anzio gave Churchill what he admitted was his worst moment of the war. As casualties on the beach mounted, he confessed to Eisenhower and Alan Brooke in late February, 'We hoped to land a wildcat that would tear out the bowels of the Boche. Instead, we have stranded a vast whale with its tail flopping about in the water.'[67] Hoping to get more forces to bail out the venture, he vainly requested another conference with FDR. Roosevelt put him off by pleading ill health – he had been suffering influenza and bronchitis since late December – while making clear his absolute refusal to keep Overlord's landing craft in the Mediterranean.

When the Allies finally broke out from Anzio in late May, US general Mark Clark marched on Rome instead of entrapping the German 10th Army as instructed. His entry into the city on 4 June did nothing to bring the war's end nearer because German forces had simply retreated northward to a new defensive line. In a Fireside Chat to mark this success, FDR acknowledged the symbolic importance of Rome being the first Axis capital to fall but warned the nation not to inflate its military significance. '[V]ictory', he declared, 'still lies some distance ahead . . . it will be tough and it will be costly, as I have told you many, many times.'[68]

As FDR well knew, the invasion of France was the essential prelude to the collapse of the Third Reich. In late January, Anglo-American military planners had decided to delay D-Day by a month to ensure adequate ships and landing craft for the greatest amphibious invasion in history. Storms in the English Channel then compelled a twenty-four-hour postponement of the due date of 5 June. Eisenhower's decision to exploit an interlude of better weather to give the go-ahead for invasion on 6 June was the most momentous of his command. Nevertheless, he had already displayed confident and cogent leadership that fulfilled FDR's faith in him. He insisted on having subordinate commanders whom he knew and trusted for Overlord, even at cost of denuding the Mediterranean theatre. On threat of resignation, he had prevailed on the Anglo-American air commanders to divert bombers from the aerial war over Germany to the 'transportation plan', the cutting-off of rail and road communications in northern France in the months before the invasion to isolate the area where it would take place. He also insisted that the Anvil invasion of southern France go ahead in support of Overlord despite Churchill's threat of resignation over its diversion of resources from the Italian campaign.[69]

Despite British scepticism about Overlord's prospects, the invasion was truly a joint effort. Utterly committed to the operation, the Americans were willing to undertake the initial assault with only a slender margin of Allied ground-force superiority to take the beaches before pouring in vastly greater numbers of men and machines for a breakout from the coastal perimeter. As General Sir Frederick Morgan, Chief of Staff to the Supreme Allied Commander and the key figure in invasion planning, later commented, 'I fancy it is little exaggeration to say that the sheer size of Overlord was not appreciated by some of the British higher-ups until very late in the day.' Nevertheless, the decision to land in Normandy rather than Pas de Calais that offered the shortest crossing and the most direct route into Germany and the deception plan to focus German attention on the latter were largely British in conception.[70]

By the evening of the invasion's first day, Allied troops had fought their way a few miles inland from the Normandy coast, where five non-contiguous beachheads stretching along a 60-mile line had been established. FDR went on the radio at 8.30 pm EST to ask that the nation join him in prayer for those engaged in this 'mighty endeavour'. Sombre and solemn in tone, his words expressed a fatalistic resignation reminiscent of Abraham Lincoln's Civil War oratory regarding the necessity of battle on this scale to destroy 'the unholy forces of our enemy' and build a 'peace that will let all of men live in freedom, reaping the just rewards of their honest toil'. The endeavour seemingly satisfied Stalin that his Anglo-American allies were now trustworthy partners in the war against Hitler. Mightily impressed by the amphibious operation, he told Averell Harriman that it was 'an unheard of achievement, the magnitude of which had never been undertaken in the history of warfare'.[71]

The Allies finally broke out of the coastal zone in late July and liberated Paris on 24–25 August. Meanwhile, the Soviet Bagration offensive into Byelorussia destroyed twenty divisions of Hitler's Army Group Centre and advanced 450 miles in five weeks from its launch on 22 June. This constituted the greatest defeat that Germany suffered in the war. Notwithstanding temporary setbacks to come, the Grand Alliance was clearly headed for victory over Hitler. FDR left it to his military chiefs in Washington and Eisenhower to deal with the final stages of the war in Europe. The ill health that he had suffered since his return from Tehran was far more serious than revealed to the public. In the final year of life, he usually worked only four hours a day, sometimes less, and needed regular breaks away from the White House. As his energies dwindled,

FDR dealt with fewer matters of commander-in-chief business to focus on building a sustainable peace.

Nevertheless, Roosevelt felt compelled to make a personal intervention in a controversy over the bi-axial strategy pursued against Japan. As Pacific Ocean Areas commander, Admiral Chester Nimitz inflicted another crushing defeat on the Imperial Navy in the Battle of the Philippine Sea on 19–20 June 1944, opening the Marianas to amphibious invasion, whose success would put Japan itself within reach of new B-29 bombers. As Southwest Pacific commander, General Douglas MacArthur focused on gaining control of the northern coast of New Guinea, from where he could strike at the Philippines. Convinced that his particular strategy offered the route to victory in the Pacific, each commander pressed for massive additional resources to pursue it. To arbitrate between them, FDR took off on a cross-country rail trip from Washington DC to San Diego, embarking from there aboard the USS *Baltimore* for a meeting in Hawaii with MacArthur and Nimitz.[72]

Remarkably, the day after his arrival on 26 July, Roosevelt bade his two commanders join him in the back of an open-top limousine to conduct a six-hour inspection of military installations across Oahu. This was the third time in eighteen months – following North Africa and Sicily, en route home from Tehran – that the commander-in-chief had visited his forces in an active theatre of war. The tour made for great press photographs and newsreel pictures of the renaissance of American power in the Pacific. This entailed more activity than FDR had undertaken in a single day since Tehran, but he held up well enough to spring one last surprise. Expecting to make their strategic presentations the following day, Nimitz and MacArthur found themselves called to do so after dinner on the second evening. Admiral William Leahy, the only JCS member accompanying the president on this trip, was full of praise for his chairing of this session. 'Roosevelt was at his best', he wrote, 'as he tactfully steered the discussion from one point to another and narrowed down the area of disagreement between MacArthur and Nimitz. The discussion remained on a very friendly basis the whole time.'[73]

Deferring a final decision till the following day, FDR had no difficulty in getting both commanders to agree to a compromise that gave each some of what he wanted. Although the Honolulu conference effectively continued the bi-axial approach, it let the air out of the Nimitz–MacArthur rivalry, gave the two theatre commanders greater understanding of their respective thinking and got them to work better together.[74] Successful completion of the Marianas campaign in November enabled Nimitz to set about building airfields on the island chain in readiness for the air assault on the Japanese mainland and the invasion of Iwo Jima and Okinawa in 1945. MacArthur, meanwhile, received as much naval support as could be spared to begin retaking the Philippine islands, a campaign that would deny the Imperial Navy a base from which to attack Nimitz's forward strategy.

The Hawaii conference was to all intents and purposes FDR's swansong as commander-in-chief, but he agreed to Churchill's request for a wholly unnecessary Anglo-American conference at Quebec in mid-September 1944. Shocked at his haggard appearance, British participants worried that his hesitant and disengaged demeanour at plenary meetings signified declining mental faculties. Nevertheless, FDR was still capable of slapping down Churchill's efforts to recast Allied strategy. To the embarrassment of his own subordinates, the prime minister proposed that once German forces were run out of Italy, Anglo-American forces should strike across the Adriatic to Trieste and from there head northward with the aim of reaching Vienna before the Red Army. FDR's tactful but effective rebuttal warned against underestimating the capacity of the Germans to continue fighting and their will to do so. The priority, he insisted, was getting across the Rhine, 'a formidable obstacle', before taking on the immense task of defeating the Wehrmacht in its homeland. With Hitler's final offensive effort, the close-run Battle of the Bulge, just three months away, Roosevelt presciently counselled, 'The Germans could not yet be counted out and one more big battle would have to be fought.' Churchill also got nowhere with another proposal for the Allies to focus on recapturing Singapore in the war against Japan, a naked effort to co-opt US power in rebuilding the British empire in Asia. This elicited a flat refusal from FDR to risk heavy casualties with a direct attack on a strongly defended enemy position.[75]

Roosevelt was no longer the leader of old in his last year of life, when ill health forced him to strike a daily balance between rest and work. With victory in the war now a matter of time, he largely left his military subordinates to execute strategies that he had agreed with them and focused on building a sustainable peace. A remarkably effective and engaged commander-in-chief until early 1944, he had met the challenges of economic mobilization, command structure, strategic leadership and alliance-building with great success. He brought America to the brink of victory in two great wars fought simultaneously on opposite sides of the world while incurring just 2 per cent of overall casualties in the conflict. In the estimation of historian A. J. P. Taylor, 'Of the great men at the top [in the Second World War], Roosevelt was the only one who knew what he was doing: he made the United States the greatest power in the world at virtually no cost.'[76] If this barbed comment underestimated FDR's national-security ideals, it contained more than a kernel of truth. The United States emerged from the war with half the world's manufacturing capacity, two-thirds of its gold reserves, three-quarters of its investment capital, its largest navy and air force and its first atomic weaponry.[77] Roosevelt was instrumental in transforming his country into a superpower and in so doing transformed the presidency from an office of national leadership into one of global leadership.

Practical visionary

FDR's national-security presidency

The idea of security had fundamental significance for Franklin D. Roosevelt's presidency. Through New Deal efforts to protect Americans against the ravages of the Great Depression, he had established himself as the first economic-security president. In the late 1930s, in response to the growing bellicosity of Germany, Italy and Japan, he became the first national-security president. Hitherto an insignificant term in American political vocabulary, FDR pioneered the concept of national security to warn his fellow citizens that these aggressive powers threatened not only their nation's territory but also its core values. In advancing beyond the conventional emphasis on safety from attack to place equal significance on defence of America's belief-system, he promulgated a new strategic doctrine that shaped American foreign policy into the twenty-first century. 'Until FDR,' historian Andrew Preston remarked, 'no American statesman had presented security as having two equal parts – physical *and* normative, territorial *and* ideological – forming an integrated, indivisible whole that applied the world over.'[1]

As war president, FDR sought a peace settlement that ensured America's postwar national security. To his mind, the best way of creating an external environment that did not threaten US interests and values was to ensure that as many countries as possible shared them. Accordingly he envisaged a new world order based on the freedoms embodied by self-determination, improved standards of living and peaceful coexistence. Meanwhile, Roosevelt looked to enhance economic security at home through New Deal expansion once peace returned. Both forms of security were inherently interconnected in his conviction that democracy's well-being in America encouraged its development abroad. If, in practice, he tempered his idealistic visions of national security and economic security with compromises that bowed to contradictory realities, they remained the guiding stars for his wartime thinking. Realism and idealism were not mutually exclusive in his credo that good politics could achieve great things. As historian Warren Kimble observed, 'Franklin Roosevelt was no ideologue but he had an ideology.'[2]

FDR's thinking on a national-security peace had reached an advanced stage before America was at war. The 1941 State of the Union Address, one of his greatest speeches, invoked the Four Freedoms to promote enactment of the Lend-Lease programme.[3] This was, he avowed, 'a moment unprecedented in the history of the Union . . . because at no previous time has American security been as seriously threatened from without as it is today'. It was his duty to report that 'the future and the safety of our country and of our democracy are overwhelmingly involved in events far beyond our borders'. Through arming those who were resisting aggressors, FDR asserted, 'we strengthen the ... security of our nation', but far more was at stake than territorial defence.

In Roosevelt's telling, the strength of America's democracy depended on its ability to deliver certain public goods, notably equality of opportunity, jobs for everyone wanting work, social assistance, ending special privilege, preservation of civil liberties and a rising standard of living. As he acknowledged, 'Many subjects connected to our social economy call for immediate improvement.' This implicit exhortation for New Deal expansion would disappear from memory of the address because the concluding passage would be what defined its meaning in history. Up to this point, the discourse was largely the work of presidential speechwriters, but FDR personally authored the peroration. It looked forward to 'a world founded on four essential freedoms': freedom of speech and expression, freedom of religion, freedom from want, and freedom from fear. The words 'everywhere in the world' followed the invocation of each freedom. Sceptical about their inclusion, Harry Hopkins counselled, 'That covers an awful lot of territory, Mr. President. I don't know how interested Americans are going to be in the people of Java.' An undeterred FDR replied, 'I'm afraid they'll have to be some day, Harry. The world is getting so small that even the people in Java are getting to be our neighbors now.'[4]

The phrase stayed in the speech to signify Roosevelt's vision of a moral world order based on 'the cooperation of free countries, working together in a friendly, civilized society' rather than 'the new order of tyranny' sought by the dictators. The invocation of the Four Freedoms as a global ideal complemented the New Deal's redefinition of freedom at home in FDR's mind. Seeing unfettered capitalism as the cause of the Great Depression, he regarded an unregulated international system as responsible for fascist aggression. If the solution to the domestic crisis lay in the state's guarantee of economic security, it followed that restoration of global peace and stability required a rules-based world order underwritten by multilateral institutions.

Roosevelt did not develop his national-security concept in an intellectual vacuum. The idea gained credence in the late 1930s among geopolitics scholars in top universities, among them Edward Mead Earle of Princeton, Nicolas Spykman of Yale and Albert Weinberg of Johns Hopkins. It also gained adherents among leaders of national thought, notably Walter Lippmann. Giving perfect expression to the concept, America's most influential columnist remarked in 1944,

> This persistent evangel of Americanism in the outer world must reflect something more than meddlesome self-righteousness. It does. It reflects the fact that no nation, and certainly not this nation, can endure in a politically alien and morally hostile environment; and the profound and abiding truth that a people which does not advance its faith has already begun to abandon it.[5]

FDR elevated such thinking into international principle at the Atlantic Conference, his first meeting with Winston Churchill, held aboard ship (the US Navy cruiser

Augusta and the Royal Navy battleship *Prince of Wales*) in Placentia Bay, off the coast of Newfoundland, from 9 to 12 August 1941. According to Harry Hopkins, 'They established an easy intimacy, a joking informality and a moratorium on pomposity and cant – and also a degree of frankness which, if not quite complete, was remarkably close to it.'[6] Their encounter provided a symbolic demonstration of shared values in the Sunday service held aboard the *Prince of Wales* on 10 August. The emotional charge of the hymn-singing caused Churchill to weep openly. FDR told son Elliott, 'If nothing else had happened while we were here, that would have cemented us. "Onward, Christian Soldiers." We *are*, and we *will* go on, with God's help.'[7]

Notwithstanding America's neutrality, Roosevelt and Churchill agreed on a joint declaration of war aims, issued as a radio cable for press release. This 376-word statement became known as the Atlantic Charter, a term coined by the *Daily Herald*, the British Labour Party's newspaper. The two leaders exercised final authority over the contents whose detailed drafting was overseen by Undersecretary of State Sumner Welles and Permanent Undersecretary for Foreign Affairs Sir Alexander Cadogan. Though not formally signed, the statement's non-parchment form anticipated modern summitry's reliance on messaging its achievements through the media.

The Atlantic Charter in final form embodied the world view of American liberalism. It set out eight common principles for 'a better future for the world'. First, America and Britain disavowed ambition of aggrandizement; second, both opposed territorial changes against the wishes of peoples affected; third, each respected 'the right of all peoples to choose the form of government under which they will live' and promised restoration of self-government to those forcibly deprived of it by war; fourth, they aspired to ensure equal access for all nations to trade and raw materials required for prosperity; and fifth, they sought the fullest international cooperation to improve labour standards, economic progress and social security. The sixth principle avowed that both countries wanted a peace that afforded all nations 'the means of dwelling within their own boundaries, and . . . assurance that all the men in all the lands may live out their lives in freedom from fear and from want'. The penultimate commitment was to uphold freedom of the seas. Finally, America and Britain recognized that 'abandonment of the use of force' by all nations necessitated disarmament of aggressors 'pending establishment of a wider and permanent system of general security'.[8]

It is not difficult to find huge gaps between the inspirational rhetoric of the Atlantic Charter and wartime reality. America's response to the Holocaust was the starkest example. In August 1942 Roosevelt issued a warning that those guilty of barbaric atrocities 'shall have to stand in courts of law' to answer for their crimes.[9] When the war was over, the United States took the lead in establishing international justice to punish war crimes. By contrast, it did not prioritize trying to save European Jews from extermination during the conflict. Anti-Semitism within the State Department, bureaucratic wrangling over what steps to take and popular opposition to the relaxation of immigration laws that restricted Jewish refugees entering the country all played a part in this. Focused on winning the war, Roosevelt did not champion the cause of saving Jewish lives as opposed to punishing Nazi crimes against humanity. His most important initiative to help European Jewry was arguably the result of political calculation. In early 1944 Treasury Secretary Henry Morgenthau brought him incontrovertible evidence of wilful obstruction by Assistant Secretary of State Breckinridge Long and his officials against even limited efforts to help European Jewry. Worried about the Jewish vote in the upcoming election if this became public, FDR established the War Refugee Board within the Executive Office of the President. This helped to rescue thousands of Jews, settling them in temporary camps in the Middle East, North Africa and Europe, but by then millions had already perished in the death camps.[10]

The Atlantic Charter's high-toned attempt to establish its Anglo-American proponents, and by implication their later Soviet ally, as defending the cause of civilization inevitably served to highlight their own contradictions of it. Despite this, it was a significant proclamation of aspirations, none of them immediately enforceable, about how the world system ought to operate. For Roosevelt, they set the goal for international society, even if progress towards their achievement was tortuous and slow. 'I am everlastingly angry', he declared in 1943,

> at those who assert vociferously that the four freedoms and the Atlantic Charter are nonsense because they are unattainable. If those people had lived a century and a half ago they would have sneered and said that the Declaration of Independence was utter piffle. If they had lived nearly a thousand years ago they would have laughed uproariously at the Magna Charta. And if they had lived several thousand years ago they would have derided Moses when he came down from the Mountain with the Ten Commandments.[11]

Once America became a belligerent, an anti-Axis alliance of twenty-six nations was formally launched at a White House ceremony on 1 January 1942. Its designation as the United Nations, a name embodying shared commitment in war and peace to universal good, was Roosevelt's idea. The founding declaration affirmed dedication 'to a common program of purposes and principles embodied in the Atlantic Charter'.[12] This raised questions about whether colonial possessions would get postwar independence in accordance with charter commitment to self-determination. Churchill was adamant that this applied only to European nations freed from Nazi occupation, a stand at odds with Roosevelt's conviction that it was all-encompassing. FDR insisted that India should sign the Declaration of the United Nations in common with Britain's white dominions, all of them listed alphabetically among member-nations below the Big Four (United States, United Kingdom, USSR and China) rather than grouped together under the 'mother country'. In his next Fireside Chat, he avowed, 'The Atlantic Charter applies not only to the parts of the world that border the Atlantic but to the whole world.'[13]

Statements of this ilk, intended to assure Americans that the war was not being fought to uphold European empires, embodied FDR's own beliefs. Decolonization (a word he never actually used, speaking instead of 'devolution schedules') was elemental to his vision of a moral world order. The imperial powers, he once told Elliott Roosevelt, felt no obligation to improve living standards, education and healthcare for their overseas subjects, which stored up 'the kind of trouble that leads to war'.[14] National interest reinforced his idealism in wanting to put European colonies on the road to independence as a means of opening them to US commerce. As Anthony Eden observed, dislike for empires 'was a principle with him, not the less cherished for its possible advantages'.[15]

Roosevelt's conviction that colonial peoples were mostly unready for immediate independence made him at best a gradualist on decolonization. He was convinced that they could be educated and trained by their rulers to make a go of orderly self-rule under a scheduled process of devolution that could last in some cases for a quarter century.[16] European insistence that their empires had improved indigenous lives cut no ice with him. The first sitting president to visit Africa, FDR wrote Daisy Suckley that Bathurst, the capital of British Gambia where he stopped en route to the Casablanca conference, was an 'awful, pestiferous hole', whose people suffered 'great poverty and emaciation'. Seeing these conditions made him 'glad the U.S. is not a great Colonial power'. He was more impressed with conditions in Liberia, the only independent Black African state, visited on the return journey from Casablanca to take lunch with its president, Edwin Barclay. Roosevelt repeatedly invoked Gambia as an indictment of British colonialism, notably during a press conference with African-American publishers in early 1944. 'It's the most horrible thing I have ever seen in my life', he declared. 'The natives are five thousand years back of us. Disease is rampant. . . . The British have been there two hundred years – for every dollar they have put into Gambia, they have taken out ten. It's just plain exploitation of those people.'[17]

Signalling his anti-colonial sympathies, FDR conferred with local leaders when attending Great Power conferences at Casablanca, Teheran and Cairo. At Casablanca, he beguiled the Sultan of Morocco during a formal dinner with a vision of post-colonial development once free of France. Listening in, a glum Churchill understood that the president's enthusiasm for the end of empire was equally aimed at Britain. Aware that the imperial powers would band together to resist decolonization, FDR told his son, Elliott, 'The English mean to maintain their hold on their colonies. They mean to help the French maintain *their* hold on *their* colonies. Winnie is a great man for the status quo. He even *looks* like the status quo, doesn't he?'[18]

Roosevelt made India, the embodiment of Britain's empire, the initial focus of his anti-colonial campaign. At the Arcadia conference, he urged Churchill that it be granted autonomy to inspire native resistance against Japan. There is no record of their exchange other than the premier's cryptic remarks in his war memoir, 'I reacted so strongly and at such length that he never raised it verbally again.'[19] In fact, Roosevelt repeatedly prodded him to allow India a form of self-government that could be improved over time through trial and error just as the United States had done in developing the Constitution of 1787 from experience with the Articles of Confederation.[20] He instructed Averell Harriman, his special representative in London, to raise the matter directly with the prime minister. Churchill consequently despatched a special representative of his own, Sir Stafford Cripps, to the subcontinent in March 1942 with a proposal for postwar independence. The mission foundered upon nationalist demands for immediate self-government and Hindu–Moslem differences over whether Pakistan should be a separate state, divisions fomented by British colonial authorities. Roosevelt's next ploy was to despatch Harry Hopkins to London with a message that India should be allowed to begin the process of developing institutions of government, which elicited a Churchillian tirade of unyielding resistance.[21]

In July 1942 nationalist leader Mohandas Gandhi urged FDR to support India's demand for immediate self-rule. If granted, he promised that Allied troops could remain there to resist Japanese aggression 'under treaty with the Free India Government that may be formed by the people of India without any outside interference, direct or indirect'.[22] Following the launch of the Quit India movement a month later, British authorities imprisoned All-India Congress Committee leaders, including Gandhi, and ordered mass detention of protesters. Signalling his disapproval, Roosevelt sponsored Wendell Willkie's forty-nine-day tour of Russia, China and the Middle East as his special representative in September–October 1942. A fervent supporter of self-determination, the former Republican presidential candidate took every opportunity on his travels to urge the colonial powers to make immediate commitment to an independence timetable under international regulation. These strictures provoked Churchill's most famous defence of empire, aimed at Roosevelt as much as Willkie. 'We mean to hold our own', he declared at a Lord Mayor's luncheon shortly after the British victory at El Alamein, 'I have not become the King's First Minister in order to preside over the liquidation of the British Empire.'[23]

In spring 1943 Roosevelt changed tack to promote a Declaration of National Independence that reaffirmed the Atlantic Charter and United Nations commitment to future independence for colonial peoples. Drafted by the State Department, this required colonial powers to act as trustees in preparing their overseas possessions for independence through improved standards of living, greater educational opportunity and phased decolonization, all in accordance with published schedules. They were also to report on the annual progress of their stewardship to the United Nations. Utterly resistant to international oversight, the British asserted absolute sovereignty over their colonial affairs and refused to discuss them further with the Roosevelt administration.[24]

Thwarted over Indian independence, Roosevelt turned his attention to Indo-China, which Charles de Gaulle wanted restored to France once the occupying Japanese were defeated. Sharing his determination to prevent this with Joseph Stalin at Tehran, FDR remarked, 'After 100 years of French rule in Indochina, the inhabitants were worse off than they had been before.'[25] For the British, in contrast, France's imperial restoration was essential to preserving their own empire. In 1944, without clearance from Roosevelt, Churchill approved the integration of de Gaulle's Free French forces into the new, British-led Southeast Asian Command to assist their recovery of Indo-China. Refusing to endorse this, FDR told new Secretary of State Edward Stettinius, 'I . . . do not want to get mixed up in any Indochina decision. It is a matter for post war.'[26]

Roosevelt's conviction that Great Power cooperation was the surest guarantee of postwar peace constrained his efforts to press Britain on colonial independence. This also underlay his limited expectations for the United Nations Organization (UNO). The blueprint for this body was the work of State Department committees that Sumner Welles convened at Roosevelt's request to recommend means of postwar international cooperation on political, military, economic and social matters. 'What I expect you to do', FDR instructed, 'is to have prepared for me the necessary number of baskets so that when the time comes all I have to do is reach into a basket and fish out a number of solutions that I am sure are sound and from which I can make my own choice.'[27] By early 1943, in marked contrast to Churchill and Stalin, he was involved in regular meetings about postwar problems with his principal planners. Among other things, these strategy sessions produced an outline plan for a postwar security organization comprising a General Assembly of all member-nations and an executive council (later renamed the Security Council) that would serve as the forum for Great Power consultation.

For all his interest in UNO development, Roosevelt placed far greater importance on cooperation between the Big Four. Meeting with Foreign Secretary Anthony Eden, Welles and the president were adamant that the real decisions within the new organization should be made by the United States, Great Britain, Russia and China, 'who would be the powers for many years to come that would have to police the world'.[28] Significantly, it was FDR, not Stalin, who insisted on Security Council permanent members having full and equal veto power over its decisions. Otherwise, he feared that any challenge to a Great Power could result in its government quitting the UNO just as Germany, Italy and Japan had left the League of Nations. In the Roosveltian schema, too, the General Assembly was to be little more than a talking shop for smaller nations. An important source of support for presidential thinking about the postwar world, Welles's resignation as Undersecretary of State in August 1943, instigated by Cordell Hull's threatened exposure of his homosexuality, deprived Roosevelt of his valuable counsel.

FDR once remarked, 'I am not a Wilsonian idealist. I have problems to resolve.'[29] The postwar settlement that he envisioned relied on 'Four Policemen' to uphold it. Designating the Big Four as 'policemen' legitimized their postwar retention of huge military arsenals to enforce peace, thereby encouraging other nations to disarm in the knowledge that they were safe from aggression.[30] FDR used the term 'policemen' for the first time at the Atlantic Conference in August 1941 but confined its purview to the Anglo-American democracies. He extended an invitation for the Soviet Union to join the sheriffs when outlining his thoughts on peace protection to Foreign Minister Vyacheslav Molotov in Washington in late spring 1942. An enthusiastic Stalin responded, 'Roosevelt's considerations . . . are absolutely sound. . . . Tell Roosevelt . . . his position will be fully supported by the Soviet Government.' FDR later pinned a sheriff's badge on China to have a non-white nation involved in safeguarding Asia's security and to put postwar planning on a worldwide, rather than merely European, basis.[31]

Roosevelt hoped that the Four Policemen would accept responsibility for leadership within the United Nations and cooperate in enforcing Security Council decisions whenever necessary. In his thinking, each would have a regional role in ensuring peace, order and stability, but he was alert to the danger that this could engender hegemonic unilateralism rather than cooperative multilateralism. Wanting regionalism to be inclusive rather than exclusive, FDR never fully clarified how this was to work. The closest he came was in a *Saturday Evening Post* article, 'Roosevelt's World Blueprint', authored by journalist Forrest Davis with presidential approval and input. This spoke of creating 'security commissions' in various regions and making them accountable to a 'master commission', effectively an international executive committee to deal with crises. Around this time, Roosevelt also mused to an aide how shared responsibility for regional oversight might work on a global basis: America and China would police Asia, Great Britain and Brazil (a curious inclusion made on grounds of proximity to the continent) would police Africa, Britain and the Soviet Union would safeguard Europe and the United States would protect the Americas.[32]

The Davis article lauded the Good Neighbor system as the Roosveltian ideal of 'a highly effective organization capable of expressing the hemisphere's united will . . . [that] functions as a continuing peace conference, which mediates before, not after, hostilities'. In practice, FDR was willing to accept grubby means of achieving regional ends. In October 1944, at the Tolstoy conference in Moscow, Stalin and Churchill reached a 'percentages' agreement on the degrees of Soviet and British influence in South-eastern Europe: respectively, Rumania, 90-10; Bulgaria, 75-25; Hungary, 50-50; Yugoslavia, 50-50; and Greece, 10-90. How these divisions were to work was unclear but Roosevelt implicitly accepted them as a form of Great Power regional cooperation.

For the Four Policemen to underwrite a peaceful world order, mutual trust was essential. Although Britain was the sheriff with the closest historical, cultural and political ties to America, even its cooperation could not be taken for granted. Roosevelt was aware that pushing too hard on decolonization might drive Churchill to pursue a spheres-of-interest approach in violation of Big-Four togetherness. Even with Britain's support, a Great Power peace was impossible without Soviet cooperation. FDR sought to win Stalin's trust by developing a personal relationship with him through regular correspondence and conference meetings at Tehran and Yalta. More substantively, he was prepared to accept effective Soviet control of Eastern Europe as the price for sustaining the wartime alliance in peacetime. Roosevelt succeeded in keeping Churchill and Stalin onside but soon despaired of Chinese leader Chiang Kai-shek's commitment to the cause.

Enlisting China as a policeman found no favour with Churchill and Stalin, neither of whom considered it a Great Power, but was fundamental to FDR's global vision. Most immediately, he wanted to sustain its war against Japan that tied down several million Imperial Army troops. In the medium term, he regarded China as a useful partner in promoting regional stability as Japanese imperialism disintegrated, European colonialism receded and the Soviet Union sought greater influence in Asia. Most importantly, his geopolitical gaze was fixed on a more distant future when China was likely to be a much more significant international actor than it was presently capable of being. According to Sumner Welles, FDR was convinced that the United States had to work with China to prevent an East–West global cleavage.[33] On his insistence, Stalin had reluctantly agreed to China signing the Four Power Declaration on 30 October 1943 at the Moscow foreign ministers' conference. This committed the quartet to continue their wartime association in pursuit of postwar peace and security. A jubilant FDR wrote Lord Louis Mountbatten, Britain's chief of combined operations, 'I really feel it is a triumph to have got the four hundred and twenty-five million Chinese in on the Allied side. This will be very useful twenty-five or fifty years hence, even though China cannot contribute much military or naval support at the moment.'[34]

Roosevelt's hopes for China conflicted with the reality that it was incapable of playing an Asian policeman because Chiang Kai-shek's postwar priority was to destroy his communist adversaries. For the Kuomintang leader, this was essential for attainment of his ultimate goal to modernize his country. To the frustration of his American military adviser, General Joseph Stilwell, Chiang husbanded weaponry and financial aid received from the United States in readiness for that campaign instead of deploying his resources to fight the Japanese. FDR remained hopeful of turning the man known as 'the Generalissimo' into a reliable ally until they met at the first Cairo conference, held en route to the Tehran talks in November 1943. There was no spark between them, always important for someone so predisposed to personal diplomacy as Roosevelt. Chiang also made a bad impression in demanding huge amounts of money and equipment to stay in the war.[35]

For a group of Foreign Service officers in China, the only solution to the Chiang problem lay in forming a coalition government between his Kuomintang regime and the Chinese Communist Party (CCP). When Stilwell voiced support for this, FDR compelled the Generalissimo to allow American diplomatic and military observers to make an unsupervised visit to the Communist Party headquarters at Yenan in north-central China. The United States Army Observation Group, known as the Dixie Mission for going into rebel territory, spent nearly three years from July 1944 to March 1947 monitoring the CCP's potential as a US collaborator.[36] Despite this initiative, Chiang showed no urgency to counter a Japanese summer offensive that threatened to knock China out of the war in 1944. On George Marshall's advice, FDR cabled him on 6 July demanding that Stilwell take charge of all American and Chinese forces to repel this attack. Despite being warned that 'our common cause will suffer a disastrous setback' if this was not done, the Generalissimo continued to prevaricate. Roosevelt finally issued an ultimatum on 16 September that all US aid would cease unless Stillwell was immediately given overall command 'to resist the disaster which has been moving closer to China and to you'. Refusal to do so would mean that America's advance across the Pacific 'will be too late for China'.[37]

In a last effort to resolve the Chiang–Stilwell stand-off, FDR sent a personal emissary to mediate between them, an initiative that inadvertently threw the Generalissimo a lifeline. The man chosen for the task was Patrick Hurley, a serving general who had carried out successful missions for Roosevelt in Moscow and Tehran, but he was out of his depth in China, where he fell under Chiang's influence. On 10 October, he informed the president that 'there is no Chinese leader available who offers as good a basis of cooperation with you . . . no other Chinese known to me who possesses so many of the elements of leadership as Chiang Kai-shek'. Three days later, he advised that if Roosevelt supported Stilwell, 'you will lose Chiang . . . and possibly you will lose China with him'.[38]

FDR now had little option but to back Chiang, whom he had promoted to Americans as a great leader qualified to sit at the Big-Four table. The Generalissimo's lobbyists and many supporters in the United States had similarly boosted this image of him. No one was a bigger cheerleader than *Time-Life* publisher Henry Luce, later described as 'the most powerful man in America who was interested in Asia'. Born in China to missionary parents, he had a passion for the country, saw Chiang as the only hope for its future and suppressed reports from his own field correspondents that told a different story.[39] Rather than risk domestic repercussions, FDR recalled Stilwell and let Chiang continue in power in the hope of getting him to ally with the communists against the Japanese, but the China imbroglio went from bad to worse.

The resignation of US ambassador Clarence Gauss in protest at Stilwell's ouster led to Hurley replacing him. Visiting Yenan in November 1944, he negotiated the 'Five Point Agreement' with communist leader Mao Zedong to create a coalition government and army under the equal control of the Kuomintang and CCP. A delighted Mao wrote FDR to thank him for his 'making possible a united, democratic China'.[40] On conferring with Chiang, however, Hurley rewrote the compact to give the CCP only token power. Furious at this betrayal, Mao and his deputy, Zhou Enlai, asked Dixie Mission officials to cable Roosevelt proposing that the pair confer with him in Washington as the representatives of the 'primary Chinese party'. On Hurley's advice, the president made no response and supported his purge of pro-CCP Foreign Service officers, which eventually expelled every diplomat with real knowledge of China.[41]

By early 1945, Roosevelt's hopes for a strong, unified and pro-American China looked doomed. If civil war broke out between Chiang and the communists, there was no prospect of the putative fourth policeman performing a stabilizing role in postwar Asia. Even worse, China's descent into internecine conflict could divide the United States and USSR as respective protectors of the warring parties. The only way Roosevelt could see of avoiding this outcome was to cut a deal with Stalin at Yalta to stabilize East Asia through Soviet and American oversight of China and US occupation of Japan. In his calculation, the two sheriffs might also prevail on the Chinese adversaries to come together to form a coalition government. While FDR had no illusions about a new China emerging anytime soon, he remained confident of this happening in time. Convinced of its potential to become the leading country in the Far East, he told British Colonial Secretary Oliver Stanley, 'The Chinese are a vigorous, able people. They may acquire Western organization and methods as quickly as did the Japanese.'[42]

While Roosevelt grappled with the challenges of bringing his global vision to fruition, domestic issues demanded attention if he was to lay the foundations for peacetime expansion of the New Deal. On 5 December 1942, over dinner in the White House, FDR and Canadian premier William Mackenzie King discussed the recently issued Beveridge Report on welfare-state expansion in postwar Britain. Enthusing about its vision of cradle-to-grave security, FDR remarked, 'That seems to be a line that will appeal. You and I should take that up strongly. It will help us politically as well as being on the right lines in the way of reform.' King interpreted these remarks to mean that Roosevelt 'has in mind a fourth term and that he feels it will come as result of winning the war, and the social programme to be launched'.[43]

Roosevelt now judged the time right to unveil what became known in liberal circles as 'America's Beveridge report', which he had received just before the Pearl Harbor attack. The National Resources Planning Board (NRPB), an agency within the Executive Office of the President, had produced *Security, Work, and Relief Policies* in fulfilment of its mission to undertake socio-economic planning for peacetime. Released by FDR in late 1942 and published in final form in March 1943, this recommended government management of the economy to ensure full employment, enhanced social insurance and more generous welfare provision.[44] While liberals celebrated this vision, bipartisan congressional conservatives took steps to extinguish it by removing NRPB funding from the FY1944 budget. For good measure, they terminated three other New Deal agencies, the Civilian Conservation Corps, the Works Progress Administration and the Farm Security Administration, as redundant amid wartime prosperity.

Apparently bowing to conservative winds, Roosevelt famously remarked in his final news conference of 1943 that 'Dr New Deal' had been needed in the 1930s but 'Dr Win-the-War' was the physician now required. Dismayed liberals, among them Eleanor Roosevelt, interpreted his words as a farewell to reform, but they overlooked what he went on to say about postwar needs: 'It seems pretty clear that we must plan for, and help to bring about, an expanded economy which will result in more security, in more employment, in more recreation, in more education, in more health, in better housing for all of our citizens, so that the conditions of 1932 and the beginning of 1933 won't come back again.'[45]

Confirming that he had not given up on New Deal revival, Roosevelt's 1944 State of the Union Address, delivered as a Fireside Chat on radio, drew on the NRPB legacy to announce a 'second Bill of Rights'. This set forth the socio-economic aspirations of American liberalism for the remainder of the twentieth century and beyond in calling for an expanded standard of living for every American. FDR laid down eight specific rights to ensure that 'a new basis of security and prosperity can be established for all – regardless of station, or race or creed'. These were useful and remunerative employment; sufficient income for food, clothing and recreation; an adequate living for farmers; fair competition in business; a decent home for every family; adequate medical care for all; protection against the economic scourges of old age, sickness, accident and unemployment; and a good education. Linking his domestic and global visions, Roosevelt avowed, 'America's own rightful place in the world depends in large part upon how fully these and similar rights have been carried into practice for all our citizens. For unless there is security here at home there cannot be lasting peace in the world.'[46]

The State of the Union Address went to Congress as a written message for the first time since Woodrow Wilson established the convention of delivering it in person. Having come down with what was thought to be influenza after Christmas, Roosevelt was too ill to address the legislature. Over the next three months, the White House physician, Admiral Ross McIntyre, put out reassuring bulletins that FDR was variously getting over flu, colds and bronchitis, despite his general weakness, weight loss, high temperatures, headaches and stomach cramps getting worse.[47] At the insistence of Anna Roosevelt Boetigger, who moved into the White House to look after her father, he underwent examination at Bethesda Naval Hospital, on 28 March. Lieutenant Commander Howard Bruenn, chief of cardiology, diagnosed the president as suffering from congestive heart failure which could be treated but not cured. Three heart specialists confirmed his findings after examining FDR at the White House on 31 March. None expected him to survive a fourth term in office. The president was put on low doses of digitalis, a low-calorie diet and confined to ten cigarettes and one cocktail a day to get him through his third term.[48]

A constant carer for the president henceforth, Bruenn desisted from advising him against seeking re-election. Admitting to being 'greatly swayed by the circumstances', the cardiologist reflected, 'Here we were in the middle of a great war, which had been conducted fortunately or unfortunately on an almost personal basis between Stalin, Churchill and Roosevelt.'[49] Removing FDR from the triumvirate did not make sense for America or the world. Never told by his doctors how ill he was, Roosevelt in conversations with Daisy Suckley revealed awareness of having heart problems. He appeared to think that cutting down his workload would enable him to live long enough to achieve a durable peace. Nevertheless, there were times when he felt unable to carry on. 'He is, *I think*', Suckley wrote in her diary on 5 July, 'rather uncertain in his mind about himself: whether he is really strong enough to take on another term – whether he ought to try it, when the future is so difficult.'[50] The bugle call of duty overrode his doubts. Two days later, he met with Democratic National Committee chairman Robert Hannegan to plan the announcement that he would seek a fourth term.

Though Roosevelt usually relied on his own judgement in making important decisions, he valued chewing them over with trusted confidantes, but none of his old circle were to hand. Broken in body and mind, Missy LeHand was long gone from the White House; Tommy Corcoran was in political purdah; Robert Jackson was consumed by Supreme Court duties; and Harry Hopkins was in FDR's bad books for quitting the White House to take up residence with his new wife in Georgetown. Increasingly away from Washington in the war years, Eleanor Roosevelt had no idea how ill her husband was; on the rare occasions they were together, she would raise his blood pressure through badgering him to pay more attention to domestic issues. Fortunately for FDR, there was someone with whom he could talk about a fourth-term candidacy.

Lucy Mercer Rutherfurd, his one-time lover and recently widowed, became a growing presence in his life in its last year. Their regular meetings – among other places, in the White House, Hyde Park, Warm Springs or motoring incognito around Washington DC – gave the ailing president a huge lift. Greatly moved by her deep and undimmed affection, Roosevelt wanted to live up to it by doing his duty. She expected no less of him if her one surviving letter (likely an undated draft) to him is any indication. In a postscript, she wrote. 'One is proud and thankful for what you have given to the world and realizes how much more must be given this greedy world – which never asks in vain – You have breathed new life into its spirit – and the fate of all that is good is in your dear blessed & capable hands.' If, as was likely, she communicated similar thoughts when they were together, Lucy Rutherfurd was certainly instrumental in FDR's fateful decision to seek re-election in 1944.[51]

Once FDR's hat was in the ring, speculation mounted as to whether he would keep Henry Wallace on the ticket. The vice president's outspoken wartime support for progressive causes at home and abroad had made him a hero to liberals and a liability insofar as Southern Democrats and urban bosses were concerned. Having foisted Wallace on a reluctant party four years earlier, Roosevelt was unwilling to do so again. 'I am just not going to go through a convention like 1940 again', he told Samuel Rosenman. 'It will split the party wide open, and it is already split enough between North and South; it may kill our chances for election this fall, and if it does, it will prolong the war and knock into a cocked hat all the plans we've been making for the future.'[52]

The Republican presidential candidate, Thomas Dewey, had a proven record of executive leadership as New York governor, accepted the need for social welfare and labour rights, and supported America's membership of the postwar UNO. Facing a tough race, Roosevelt shared the concerns of other Democratic leaders that the vice president's left-wing leanings could drag down the ticket. With a question mark over his capacity to complete a fourth term, Roosevelt also doubted Wallace's presidential timbre if required to take over the top job and thought his internationalism too utopian to cope with the practical necessities of Great Power politics. Moreover, Wallace's public spat with Commerce Secretary Jesse Jones in 1943 raised doubts about his judgement. A final count against him, in four years of presiding over the Senate, the vice president had not built up personal influence in the body responsible for ratifying whatever postwar peace treaties were negotiated.[53]

Of the three men who received FDR's serious consideration as Wallace's replacement, 'Assistant President' James Byrnes was the most experienced in Washington's ways but was unpopular with African Americans and labour leaders as a Southerner and with Catholic leaders as a Protestant convert from their church. Supreme Court justice William Douglas, formerly chair of the Securities and Exchange Commission, was a committed New Dealer but lacked campaign experience and had no base in the party. Almost by default, the vice-presidential pendulum swung to Senator Harry S. Truman (D-Missouri): he was acceptable to every group within the party, he had been loyal to FDR on domestic and international issues, his popularity in the Senate could be useful in a fight for treaty ratification, and he had a national profile from chairing a special committee investigating waste in war industries.[54]

A number of party bosses later claimed credit for influencing a disengaged Roosevelt to back Truman, but he was really the one calling the plays. More involved than anyone else in the manoeuvres that led to the final choice, he kept his true intentions hidden. At various junctures he allowed Wallace, Byrnes and Douglas to believe that he was in their corner, while offering no direct encouragement to the eventual nominee, whom he barely knew. He relied on Democratic National Committee chair Robert Hannegan to convey the decision to a disbelieving Truman on the eve of the Democratic National Convention in Chicago. It required a presidential phone call to Hannegan's suite in the Blackstone Hotel, where the senator had been summoned, to convince him. Told that his nomination was essential for the ticket, Truman agreed to do the commander-in-chief's bidding. Though Wallace supporters did not surrender tamely, the convention nominated the new man on the second ballot. Truman mounted a vigorous campaign in support of FDR's re-election, constantly telling voters that this was no time to put an inexperienced president in his place, remarks that soon acquired great irony.[55]

Owing to failures of image control, FDR's health became an election issue in 1944. While awaiting embarkation on the USS *Baltimore* for his Pacific war conference, he delivered a rousing nomination-acceptance speech to the Democratic National Convention on 20 July by radio hook-up from the presidential train in San Diego and then re-enacted parts of it for the newsreels. Drained of energy from these exertions, FDR was captured looking exhausted, old and slack-mouthed in an Associated Press photograph sent out by wire for use by most newspapers.[56] Worse was to follow on 12 August when FDR broadcast a speech while standing on the forecastle deck of USS *Cummings*, which lay at anchor in Bremerton Naval Shipyard, Washington. The self-composed address on his Hawaii odyssey came across as unfocused, rambling and overlong, the result of being in acute physical distress. His now ill-fitting leg braces, not worn in half-a-year during which he had lost much weight, dug into his flanks just as an attack of angina caused alarming chest pains. It would take Roosevelt more than a month to recover in body and spirit from the ordeal.

Thomas Dewey's relentless attacks on his leadership as old, tired and feeble, delivered in the accusatory manner of the Manhattan district attorney that he once was, finally goaded FDR out of his torpor. He delivered one of his most famous speeches at the Teamsters dinner in Washington DC on 23 September. Part of the address ridiculed the GOP's new-found enthusiasm for the New Deal and the UNO in contradiction of its long-standing conservatism and isolationism. The message was clear – the Old Guard, not the never-mentioned Dewey, remained the heart of the party. The most memorable passage was a comic rebuttal of wrongful charges by 'Republican leaders' (actually only one congressman) that he had sent a US warship to the Aleutian Islands at huge taxpayer expense to pick up his Scottie dog Fala, supposedly left behind there on his Pacific trip. 'I am', he declared, 'accustomed to hearing malicious falsehoods about myself. . . . But I think I have a right to resent, to object to libelous statements about my dog.'[57]

This political thespianism provoked Dewey into a change of tactics in a major speech in Oklahoma City two nights later, which the Republican National Committee paid to have broadcast on twice the number of radio stations originally planned. He now attacked Roosevelt's record in office as 'desperately bad' and damned New Dealers as 'an ill-assorted conglomeration of city bosses, Communists and career bureaucrats'.[58] Pleasing as this may have been to the party faithful, the negative message was out of touch with the wartime spirit of national unity. With the president maintaining a consistent lead in pre-election polls, Republican newspapers resurrected the infirmity issue to no avail. Demonstrating his renewed vitality, FDR made a campaign trip to New York City on 21 October, where he braved heavy wind and rain during a four-hour, 51-mile tour in an open car through four of the five boroughs. That evening his address to the Foreign Policy Association, broadcast nationwide, offered his most cogent expression of national-security ideals.[59]

Of the postwar world, FDR declared, 'We either work with other great nations, or we might one day have to fight them. . . . If we fail to maintain that relationship in the peace – if we fail to expand it and strengthen it – then there will be no lasting peace.' Showing no misty-eyed idealism, he went on to link what needed to be done at home and abroad:

> We are not fighting for, and we shall not attain, a Utopia. Indeed, in our own land the work to be done is never finished. We have yet to realize the full and equal employment of our freedom. So, in embarking on the building of a world fellowship, we have set ourselves a long and arduous task, which will challenge our patience, our intelligence, our imagination, as well as our faith.

Expressing confidence that Americans had become 'a seasoned and mature people', an implicit contrast to the national state of mind in 1919, he avowed in closing, 'We shall bear our full responsibility, exercise our full influence, and bring our full help and encouragement to all who aspire to peace and freedom.'[60]

The following weekend FDR gave major speeches on succeeding days in Philadelphia and Chicago, interspersed with whistle-stops from the back of the presidential train at various stopovers, and a week later spoke at Boston. Addressing a huge crowd at Soldier Field, Chicago, he repeated his economic bill of rights pledge of postwar socio-economic security while linking this to an expansive vision of peacetime abundance that would provide sixty million jobs in industry and a new age of plenty for the farmer based on the war economy's success.[61] This high-octave campaigning represented a triumph, albeit a temporary one, over his mortality, but he delivered his big speeches from a sitting position to avoid another Bremerton episode.

Roosevelt went on to win a fourth term with a comfortable popular-vote victory of 53.4 to 45.9 per cent, which translated into an Electoral College landslide of 432 to 99 votes. Dewey ran well in the Midwest and the Plains states, adding Ohio, Wisconsin and Wyoming to Willkie's 1940 tally, while losing Michigan, to end up carrying twelve states. Roosevelt swept the entire South, the last time a Democratic presidential candidate has done so. Though an abject failure, the attempt by some segregationist delegates at the Chicago national convention to nominate Senator Harry Byrd (D-Virginia) for president signified that the days of the Solid South were numbered.

Pundits interpreted FDR's victory as a vote of popular confidence in his ability to win the war and build a lasting peace, but domestic concerns were also important. The New Deal voter coalition, particularly its urban elements, provided the foundation for victory. Nearly two-thirds of Roosevelt's popular-vote plurality came from the nation's twelve biggest cities, compared to one-third in 1932. His coat-tails helped the Democrats win a net increase of 20 seats in the House of Representatives, where they secured a majority of 242 to 191. Most gains came at the expense of conservative Republicans, the biggest scalp being arch-isolationist Hamilton Fish (R-New York), FDR's local congressman and sworn enemy. Defending 21 Senate seats to the Republicans' 11, the Democrats did well to maintain their 58 to 37 majority. Nevertheless, the conservative coalition remained unbroken and an obstacle to Roosevelt's vision of postwar domestic reform.[62]

Paradoxically, the outgoing 78th Congress, the most conservative of FDR's presidency, had enacted the most significant social-welfare legislation of the Second World War. In linking government largess with the civic obligation of military service, the Servicemen's Readjustment Act of 1944 found favour even among habitually anti-statist legislators. Memories of veterans' protests over the Great War bonus focused minds on how to reincorporate over fifteen million demobilized servicemen into peacetime society and enable them to lead productive lives. Diverting the returnees into education met both ends. Wanting a better deal for veterans than contained in the administration's proposed bill, the American Legion produced a wide-ranging and costly alternative that formed the basis for the so-called GI Bill of Rights, signed by FDR in June 1944. Under its terms, veterans could renew their education or training without tuition charge, receive a monthly living allowance while doing so, obtain federal loan guarantees for the purchase or renovation of homes, farms and businesses – provided a bank agreed to back them – and get modern healthcare in new veterans' hospitals. As with earlier New Deal measures, Southern Democrats on the reporting committees ensured that African Americans got nothing like their fair share from the programme by making state bodies, rather than the Veterans' Administration in Washington, responsible for benefit provision. Black veterans also found themselves segregated in inadequately funded educational institutions and denied mortgage benefits because banks would not lend on ghetto homes. Accordingly, the GI Bill of Rights widened racial inequality in creating a new suburban middle class that was almost exclusively white.[63]

While political battles raged over the New Deal's revival at home, FDR made significant progress in internationalizing it for the benefit of postwar reconstruction. In October 1942 he had scrutinized Australian official Frank Gardner's memorandum calling for the establishment of a multilateral food-aid programme. Impatient with the turf wars of the Agriculture and State Departments for control of this, he seized the initiative to call a conference in Hot Springs, Virginia, in late spring 1943 to convert the Atlantic Charter's freedom-from-want principle into practice. Attended by delegates from forty-four countries, this gathering established an interim commission with the duty to draft a constitution for what became the United Nations Food and Agriculture Organization. Making food-aid the first item on the agenda of postwar internationalism was smart politics on FDR's part: countering global starvation was a low-risk launch for multilateral cooperation, it was a popular cause with the public, and it was beneficial to farm-surplus countries like the United States that would feed the hungry world.[64]

As Roosevelt had anticipated, the Hot Springs conference afforded a rehearsal for international representatives to work together for the common good. It opened the way for further cooperative ventures, notably the United Nations Relief and Rehabilitation Agency (UNRRA), formally established in a White House ceremony on 9 November 1943. The new organization, FDR told delegates from the forty-four member-nations, would 'utilize the production of all the world to balance the want of all the world' and help countries 'learn to work together . . . by actually working together'. The UNRRA delegates reassembled in Atlantic City for three weeks of deliberations that agreed on the appointment of former New York governor Herbert Lehman as director, created an organizational structure and set a provisional budget of $2 billion – three-quarters from the United States – for initial operating costs.[65]

It took much longer to agree on a system of international monetary management to underwrite postwar prosperity. After much preliminary discussion, largely steered by Harry Dexter White for the US Treasury and John Maynard Keynes for the UK Treasury, the United Nations Monetary and Financial Conference met in Bretton Woods, New Hampshire, from 1 to 22 July 1944 to discuss the establishment of an International Monetary Fund (IMF) and an International Bank of Reconstruction and Development (eventually known as the World Bank). The resultant Bretton Woods Accords established mechanisms to stabilize the global monetary-financial order so as to avoid the currency devaluations and import restrictions that had undermined world trade in the 1930s.

The Bretton Woods system pegged the gold value of the dollar ($35 an ounce since 1934) as the rate at which other currencies could be exchanged. Accordingly, the dollar was on a nationally managed standard of its own and the rest of the world was on a dollar standard. This guaranteed America's financial hegemony as the linchpin of the international monetary system. In creating the IMF, with an initial stabilization-loan fund of $8.5 billion, to which the United States contributed $2.75 billion, Bretton Woods established what was effectively an international bank to manage and correct exchange rates. Each member country was obliged to establish a par value for its currency in relation to the dollar and to peg its exchange rate against other currencies within a range of 10 per cent above or below that. Finally, what became the World Bank was established with a working capital of $9.1 billion, with 10 per cent of each member country's subscription paid immediately and 10 per cent on instant call. America pledged $3 billion to help it finance postwar reconstruction and long-term economic development, mainly undertaken through guaranteeing loans from private institutions rather than as direct lender. Financial quotas determined representation on the governing boards of each body, thereby ensuring that the United States, as the largest contributor to both, had the greatest leverage over their policies.

Though far from perfect, the Bretton Woods system exemplified the Roosveltian rationale that international cooperation required nations to learn how to work together. It also embodied belief that multinational support for economically weak countries was essential for the stability of the world economy. In recognition of this, Treasury Secretary Henry Morgenthau told his fellow Bretton Woods delegates, 'We have come to recognize that the wisest and most effective way to protect our national interests is through . . . united effort to attain common goals. . . . Today the only enlightened form of national self-interest lies in international accord.'[66]

Morgenthau headed the administration effort to secure congressional approval of the Bretton Woods Accords over the opposition of the influential American Banking Association, which regarded a restored gold standard, balanced budgets and low inflation as necessary for economic well-being in peacetime. This group had support from the Hearst media empire and newspapers friendly to metropolitan financial interests, notably *The New York Times*. The Treasury put out the contrary message that Bretton Woods was fundamentally intended to deliver on Roosevelt's Bill of Rights promise of postwar full employment and prosperity. It organized a broad-based coalition of industrial unions, small-city banks, the Southern press, the American Economic Association, the Federal Reserve and the League of Women Voters that eventually gained the upper hand in the battle for public opinion and congressional support. On 11 April, the eve of FDR's death, Morgenthau went down to Warm Springs to inform him that New Deal forces were poised to win a great victory over their oldest enemy, the big bankers of New York.[67]

While Morgenthau campaigned for Bretton Woods, FDR was engaged in his final efforts to create a workable Great Power peace. At the Dumbarton Oaks Conference, formally the Washington Conversations on International Security Organization, held from late August to early October 1944, delegations from the United States, United Kingdom, USSR and China laid the UNO's foundations. Drawing from the American blueprint, they agreed to establish a General Assembly for all members; a Security Council, with four permanent members and other rotating ones, responsible for considering questions of peace and security; an International Secretariat; and an International Court of Justice to rule on legal disputes between member-states. The State Department press release hailing this outcome as evidence of deep-seated

Great Power consensus papered over significant disagreements that were left for later resolution.[68]

What Dumbarton Oaks showed above all was that the Big Three – the talks effectively relegated China from the top table – considered their own interests too important to entrust to the UNO. FDR did not risk a campaign to educate politicians, the press and the public of this reality amid a presidential election. Once re-elected, he met with a group of leading senators in an effort to enhance their understanding that Great Power deals were the foundation for sustainable peace. It was evident, he told them bluntly, 'that the Russians had the power in Eastern Europe, that it was obviously impossible to have a break with them and that, therefore, the only practicable course was to use what influence we had to ameliorate the situation'.[69]

These convictions guided FDR's approach to the Yalta conference in early February 1945, which fleshed out what had been agreed at Tehran, the most significant summit of the war. To get there, FDR underwent a horrendously uncomfortable flight aboard the first purpose-built presidential aircraft (nicknamed *The Sacred Cow*) from Malta, where a US warship had deposited him, to Saki airfield in the Crimea, followed by a five-hour drive in freezing conditions to his final destination. Unsurprisingly, British and Russian attendees thought that Roosevelt looked old and worn but all agreed that his mental and psychological capacities remained sharp. The president returned from Yalta sincerely believing he had achieved all he could have expected: he had secured Stalin's commitment to join the war against Japan, brought him into the UNO on his terms and strengthened the foundations for their sustained cooperation.[70]

On Germany, the Big Three agreed on the need for its unconditional surrender, the eradication of Nazism and the establishment of four zones of military occupation that included a French sector. FDR vaguely envisaged a reformed Germany as a force for peace in postwar Europe, which placed him closer to Churchill's hopes for their defeated foe, but he agreed with Stalin that it should not enjoy a higher standard of living than Russia. How to achieve these differing ends was deferred for a later conference, along with the associated issue of German reparations to help rebuild the shattered Soviet economy.

Stalin reiterated his willingness to declare war on Japan shortly after Germany was defeated and named his price for doing so. FDR and Churchill agreed to his expected demands for the southern part of Sakhalin Island, a former Russian territory ceded to Japan in the war of 1905, the Japanese-governed Kurile Islands and Soviet control of Outer Mongolia. They raised no objections to new requirements affecting China, specifically Soviet use of the ports of Darien and Port Arthur and of the Manchurian railroad, which FDR promised to clear with Chiang Kai-shek once Germany surrendered. For Roosevelt, these terms were a small price for Soviet military assistance to hasten the defeat of Japan, which US military planners anticipated could take another two years and cost 200,000 American lives on a worst-case basis. The agreement of Far Eastern terms also constituted a significant step towards postwar cooperation with the Soviet Union. Most importantly in this regard, it fitted Roosevelt's goal of an American-led China in pre-empting a discontented Stalin from supporting the anti-Chiang communists.

Yalta also settled some issues pertaining to the UNO's establishment, which had become more important for Roosevelt's postwar schema than originally anticipated. The American public's growing enthusiasm for membership offered the best hope of binding Congress to postwar internationalism, the new organization seemingly promised a workable conduit for decolonization as a trustee for the independence process and the Security Council was the obvious forum for continuous Great Power consultation. Accordingly, FDR was anxious to settle issues left unresolved at Dumbarton Oaks. Stalin agreed to settle for Ukraine and Byelorussia having representation in the General Assembly, rather than all sixteen Soviet republics as initially required, and withdrew his demand for Security Council permanent members to have veto power over topics under discussion. These were concessions to FDR as compensation for not giving ground over Poland's future, the most contentious issue of the conference.

At a White House meeting with Harry Hopkins and Anthony Eden in March 1943, Roosevelt had ruled out any bargaining with Eastern European countries at a postwar conference. With regard to Poland, he declared, 'the important thing is to set it up in a way that will help maintain the peace of the world.'[71] By late 1944 FDR was even more determined not to quarrel with Stalin over issues beyond his control. Averell Harriman, US ambassador to Russia, recalled the president telling him that 'the European questions were so impossible that he wanted to stay out of them as far as practicable except for the problems involving Germany.'[72] At Yalta, accordingly, he accepted that there was no budging Stalin – and no instrument for doing so – from his insistence on having a 'friendly' government in Warsaw, namely the communist-dominated Lublin regime. Told by Admiral William Leahy, chairman of the Joint Chiefs of Staff, that the Soviets were effectively getting a free hand, Roosevelt admitted, 'I know it. But it's the best I can do for Poland at this time.' As Charles Bohlen later remarked, 'Stalin held all the cards and played them well. Eventually, we had to throw in our hand.'[73]

FDR placed more importance on the Declaration on Liberated Europe agreed at Yalta – and not from an emotional need to have a window-dressing statement to assuage domestic opinion. It avowed the mutual determination of America, Britain and Russia to build 'a world order under law, dedicated to peace, security, freedom, and the general wellbeing of all mankind', decreed the continuation of their wartime unity 'a sacred obligation' and hailed their victory in the war against aggressors for providing 'the greatest opportunity in all history' to build a stable peace.[74] For Roosevelt this was an important expression of mutual commitment to establishing a new international system based on Big Three cooperation. Getting Stalin's signature on the Declaration on Liberated Europe set the standard for measuring his postwar conduct. Far from denying the contradictions in the new order emerging from the Second World War, FDR was confident that these could be managed satisfactorily if the Great Powers were united in wanting peace and stability. This outlook, naïve to later adherents of the 'Yalta betrayal' narrative, was well grounded in the reality of 1945.

The rapid collapse of the Big Three alliance into Cold War confrontation obliterated the West's memory that Stalin's main concern at war's end in Europe was to ensure Russia's future security from a resurgent Germany. His hard line on Poland primarily evinced determination to secure the Soviet Union's most vulnerable border rather than to communize its neighbour. He was equally dedicated to preserving the Big Three alliance as the surest guarantee of safety from attack. In a 1944 speech celebrating the anniversary of the Bolshevik revolution, a high-profile event comparable to a US president's State of the Union Address, he declared, 'The task [facing the United Nations] is not only to win the war but also to make new aggression and new war impossible – if not for ever, then at least for a long time to come.' Essential for this was the continued cooperation of the Great Powers 'not on casual, transitory considerations, but on vital and lasting interests'. While acknowledging their differences on some issues, Stalin insisted that none were insurmountable nor so serious as their now resolved second-front disagreements. Anticipating renewal of Germany's power in a few decades, he endorsed establishment of a world organization that could preserve peace and security if the United States, USSR and Great Britain continued 'to act in a spirit of unanimity and accord'.[75] The Soviet leader's understanding that FDR was on the same wavelength ensured his respect and admiration for the president. Aghast at their togetherness on many matters at Yalta, Churchill groused to his physician, 'Stalin made it plain at once that if this was the President's wish, he would accept it.'[76]

Having gained Stalin's trust in wartime, Roosevelt saw its maintenance in peacetime as the means to make progress in building a world order closer to his national-security ideals than was possible in 1945. He also hoped that the carrot of postwar US economic aid could help to keep Stalin's external conduct in check. There was certainly no let-up in US military shipments in the last months of the war despite Russian forces being more than adequately equipped by then. With his eye on postwar cooperation, FDR informed Edward Stettinius in January 1945, 'It is my desire that every effort be made to continue a full and uninterrupted flow of supplies to the U.S.S.R.'[77]

Roosevelt found comfort in his conviction that convergence between the United States and Soviet systems was afoot. In the White House talks that led to US recognition of the USSR in 1933, Soviet foreign minister Maxim Litvinov had conjectured that differences between their value-systems would diminish over the next twenty years. As Russia modified its state socialism and America moved towards greater social justice, he anticipated that they would grow closer in world affairs. When the two countries became anti-fascist allies, FDR wrote a prominent supporter of Soviet-American friendship, 'Perhaps Litvinov's thoughts of nine years ago are coming true.'[78] Though cosmetic changes in reality, Stalin's wartime dissolution of the Comintern, the organization founded in 1919 to advance world communism, and granting of unprecedented freedom to the Orthodox Church seemingly offered proof that Soviet ideology was becoming less rigid. In April 1943, Roosevelt allowed correspondent Forrest Davis to quote his opinion that 'the revolutionary currents of 1917 may be spent in this war . . . with progress following evolutionary constitutional lines', leading eventually to 'a modified form of state socialism'. According to Averell Harriman, belief in convergence underlay his strategy of accommodating Stalin's demands in the short term with a view to building a stable peace in the long term.[79]

Even with convergence, Roosevelt was all too aware that developing a new world order with just passing resemblance to Atlantic Charter ideals would be a lengthy, frustrating and incremental process. On returning from the Crimea he set about educating the public on this score, beginning with his report on 1 March to Congress and the American people on the Yalta conference. He had launched his public-communication campaign to share his national-security ideas with the American people and win popular support for them with the high-minded and idealistic invocation of the Four Freedoms four years earlier. He had continued it in this vein during the time that America was at war, most notably in the Fireside Chat about the Tehran conference. Now, as victory approached, what proved to be his last major address offered a more circumspect, sober and realistic assessment of the coming peace.

The speech is best remembered for FDR's solitary public reference to his disability in explaining that speaking from a sitting position saved him having 'to carry about ten pounds of steel around on the bottom of my legs'. Ad-libbing parts of it, he pronounced the Yalta conference 'a successful effort by the three leading Nations to find a common ground for peace'. Nevertheless, he was clear that a world based on the Atlantic Charter would only develop gradually because the postwar settlement 'cannot be a . . . structure of complete perfection at first'. He improvised a passage about peacetime issues being 'very special problems' that the United States would take time to understand. Above all, he insisted on the need for 'give-and-take compromise' because none of the Big Three would have their way on all matters. 'We shall not always have ideal answers to complicated international questions', he warned, 'even though we are determined to strive toward that ideal.'[80]

Roosevelt intended to continue the education campaign in two major orations, a Jefferson Day address on 13 April and his speech opening the United Nations conference in San Francisco on 25 April. In the meantime, he had to deal with Churchill's efforts to separate him from Stalin over Soviet insistence on establishing a communist regime in Poland. FDR himself had a testy exchange of cables with Stalin: he berated Soviet credence in false rumours that America and Britain were negotiating a separate peace with German generals in Switzerland; he also voiced strong concern over the exclusion of non-communists in the new government of national unity in Warsaw, without challenging the Lublin group's primacy within this. Still prepared to play the long game, Roosevelt drafted what was his last cable to Churchill to urge conciliation rather than confrontation as the best way of dealing with their Russian ally. 'I would minimize the general Soviet problem as much as possible', he counselled, 'because these problems, in one form or another, seem to arise every day and most of them straighten out. . . . We must be firm, however, and our course thus far is correct.'[81]

Roosevelt's death the following day brought to office a new president inexperienced in foreign affairs. Harry Truman lacked FDR's combination of vision, realism and subtlety in managing relations with the Soviets. Losing patience with what he considered Stalin's betrayal of the Yalta agreements pertaining to Poland, he gave Vyacheslav Molotov a dressing-down when the Soviet foreign minister called at the White House on 23 April en route to the San Francisco UNO conference. At its end, the flabbergasted Russian protested that he had never before been spoken to in this way, eliciting the response, 'Carry out your agreements and you won't get talked to like that.' Acting as interpreter, Charles Bohlen later remarked, 'How I enjoyed translating Truman's sentences! They were probably the first sharp words uttered during the war by an American President to a high Soviet official.'[82]

Truman instinctively shared the mindset of Soviet experts in the State Department and the Moscow Embassy, chief among them Harriman, Bohlen and George Kennan, that appeasement of Stalin in Eastern Europe and in the Far East could end up having the same disastrous consequences as the earlier appeasement of Hitler's insatiable demands for territorial aggrandizement. In the Cabinet, this position had strong support from Secretary of the Navy James Forrestal. Nevertheless, Truman also felt an obligation to continue FDR's policies in order to buttress his legitimacy as an accidental president. Others in his administration, notably Secretary of War Henry Stimson, William Leahy, George Marshall and Secretary of Commerce Henry Wallace, sought to convince their new boss of the benefits of working with the Russians. Truman heard the same advice from Harry Hopkins and Joseph Davies, both of whom saw US–Soviet cooperation, which they had helped forge as FDR's informal emissaries, as the bedrock of a stable peace. These contrary pressures produced a foreign policy that oscillated between confronting and accommodating the Soviet Union for the remainder of 1945.[83] Stalin's suppression of non-communist parties in Soviet-controlled Eastern Europe, clumsy interference in Iran and aggrandizement in Manchuria and Korea swung the pendulum towards resistance and containment in 1946.

'Let's hope nothing happens to [Roosevelt]', Stalin told the Politburo after Yalta. 'We shall never do business again with anyone like him.'[84] Whereas FDR saw the Crimea talks as laying the foundation for sustained Great Power cooperation, the Soviet leader focused on their more immediate benefits for his country. In his eyes, the bargain struck at Yalta legitimized the Soviet Union's retention of territory seized in 1939–40, its ascendancy in Eastern Europe and restoration of its pre-1905 position in East Asia, in return for which he accepted US and British domination elsewhere in the world. Equally important to his understanding of this settlement was the commitment of the Big Three powers to defend it against any threat of renewed aggression by the former Axis nations. The Soviet leader blamed the descent into Cold War, which was not his preferred option, on the change in US leadership from Roosevelt to Truman. He refused to accept that his own provocations had done much to bring about this development.

Roosevelt never took the time to tutor Truman about ends and means in dealing with the Soviets. Whether his successor would have absorbed his teachings has to be doubted. The new president lacked the guile, patience and confidence to deal with Stalin in Roosevelt's way. Like FDR, he believed the United States to be morally superior to the Soviet Union, but unlike FDR he let this conviction guide his foreign policy. If there was to be a transition to peacetime collaboration, dealing with someone as ruthless, suspicious and sensitive to slights as Stalin required a US leader who possessed, in the words of historian Frank Costigliola, 'the emotional intelligence, elasticity, charm, and confidence of a Franklin Roosevelt rather than the personality of a Harry Truman'.[85]

Without Roosevelt to hold it together, the Big Three alliance quickly fell apart. As the Cold War unfolded over its more than four-decade duration, the onset of the struggle took on the aura of inevitability. Whether history would have turned out differently had FDR lived longer is among the greatest of 'what-if' questions. Among those who had no doubts on this score was Churchill's wartime foreign secretary. In August 1946, in a confidential interview with Robert Sherwood, proscribed from inclusion in his memoir of FDR's wartime collaboration with Harry Hopkins, Anthony Eden lamented the shift towards Cold War confrontation. Roosevelt, he declared, 'would never have permitted the present situation to develop' and pronounced his death 'a calamity of immeasurable proportions'.[86] Anticipating a lengthy transition to an international system that approximated to his national-security vision, Roosevelt's grand strategy to lay the foundations for its development was to build a Great Power peace, hold Stalin's trust and not get distracted into confrontation on issues peripheral to his ultimate goal.

Epilogue

FDR's presidential legacy – Truman to Biden

When Franklin D. Roosevelt died the presidency did not move from centre stage as it had after every strong incumbent in the past, a pattern most recently manifested in the transition from Woodrow Wilson to Warren Harding in 1921. Instead, all of FDR's successors wanted to take the lead in shaping America's politics, programmes and place in the world. None came to the presidency thinking about how to scale back its authority. All bore the national expectation of active leadership to keep the United States strong, secure and prosperous that was their Roosveltian legacy. As Harry Truman recognized, '[B]eing president is like riding a tiger. You have to keep on riding or be swallowed.'[1]

Some of Roosevelt's successors considered him their role model in facing the challenges of their office; most did not. Lyndon B. Johnson was the president for whom he had most meaning. FDR had identified the young LBJ as a prime exemplar of the new Southern liberalism that he hoped would flourish under the New Deal. Accordingly, he helped Johnson win election as a congressman in the Texas tenth district in 1937, endowed him with patronage and told aides that he might become one day the first president from the South since the Civil War. As president, LBJ set himself the task of completing the unfinished work of the New Deal through his Great Society programme but wanted to outdo his mentor to prove his own greatness. The reforms that he sped through Congress in 1965 reflected his ambition to enact more major bills in a single session than FDR had achieved in 1933.[2]

Inheriting a presidency tarnished by Vietnam, Watergate and economic setbacks in the 1970s, Ronald Reagan rebuilt it in the image implanted in his youthful Democratic mind a half-century earlier by FDR. As scholar Richard Neustadt observed, this Republican convert restored the office 'to a fair (if perhaps rickety) approximation of its Roosveltian mould: a place of popularity, influence and initiative, a source of programmatic and symbolic leadership, both pacesetter and tonesetter, the nation's voice both to the world and us, and – like or hate the policies – a presence many of us loved to see as Chief of State.'[3]

Other presidents took different models as their guiding light. Richard Nixon held Theodore Roosevelt and Woodrow Wilson in the highest esteem, Gerald Ford and Jimmy Carter identified with fellow underdog Harry Truman and George W. Bush and Barack Obama admired the leadership skills of Ronald Reagan. Whichever predecessor influenced Donald Trump, if any, it was certainly not FDR. Judging from his assertion before the United Nations in 2018 that his administration had accomplished more in two years than 'almost any administration in the history of our country', the forty-fifth president had no idea of the thirty-second president's achievements.[4]

Whatever they thought about Roosevelt, all his successors were his heirs in the sense that they occupied the office whose modern characteristics he had forged. Though some of them expanded it in significant ways, they were essentially adding to the structure inherited from FDR rather than building anew. Roosevelt's transformation of the presidency as a political institution shaped the leadership of all but one incumbent from Harry Truman to Joe Biden (and likely beyond). The obvious outlier was Donald Trump, but his temporary exception proved the general rule regarding the durability of the Roosveltian legacy. As historian William Leuchtenburg observed, FDR 'created the template for how a modern chief executive was expected to perform'.[5]

This was immediately apparent in the continuation of the president's role as chief legislator, established by FDR in the politically unique circumstances of the Hundred Days of 1933. Within a month of America's final victory in the Second World War, Harry Truman signalled that he would follow his predecessor's example by sending a 21-point programme for peacetime reconversion to Congress on 6 September 1945. 'This legislative program', he asserted in his memoirs, 'was a reminder to the Democratic party, to the country, and to the Congress that progress in government lies along the road to sound reform in our private enterprise system and that progressive democracy has to continue to keep pace with changing conditions.'[6] Even if many proposals did not make it onto the statute book, Truman's initiative confirmed the presidency's status as the principal driver of the national legislative agenda. The first Republican president in twenty years, Dwight Eisenhower encountered criticism within his party for not submitting a first-year legislative programme but ensured that one accompanied his 1954 State of the Union Address. For good measure, he established the legislative liaison office in the White House Office to lobby for his proposals.[7]

FDR's New Deal established socio-economic security as the precondition of personal freedom but left much undone to make this a reality for all Americans. His immediate Democratic successors built on the agenda that he set for postwar liberalism in his 1944 State of the Union Address. Harry Truman's Fair Deal broadened New Deal social-welfare provision, John Kennedy's New Frontier continued the work and Lyndon Johnson's Great Society did much to complete it. Seeking to contain rather than roll back the New Deal, Dwight Eisenhower effectively ratified its legacy in creating the Department of Health, Education and Welfare to coordinate social programmes, significantly expanded Social Security coverage and benefits, and promoted the greatest public-works project in US history in launching the Interstate Highway System (whose genesis lay in the report of the FDR-appointed Interregional Highway Committee, sent to Congress in 1944).[8]

Following a period of transition in the 1970s, Ronald Reagan's election in 1980 signified that conservatism had gained national ascendancy for the first time since FDR took office. During the next quarter century Republican presidents prioritized limited government, free markets and traditional values. In so doing, they succeeded in changing the terms of political debate in portraying big government as the root cause of national problems rather than their solution. What they could not do was eradicate the social-welfare entitlements established by FDR and extended by his immediate successors, which were too strongly embedded in the public's expectations to be dislodged. Arguably, their most substantive reversal of the Rooseveltian legacy was to make low taxes a staple of American political culture, albeit at cost of escalating budget deficits amid prosperity. In utter contradiction of FDR's tax increases to help pay for the Second World War, George W. Bush promoted the third-largest tax cut in American history (after Reagan's in 1981 and his own in 2001) just as the United States embarked on the Iraq War in 2003.[9]

In addition to being chief legislators and programme leaders, Roosevelt's successors followed his lead in assuming the role of economic manager. The Employment Act of 1946 institutionalized this responsibility and created the Council of Economic Advisers within the Executive Office of the President to help in discharging it. Building on FDR's belated embrace of fiscal Keynesianism, presidents from Truman to LBJ used the budgetary tools at their disposal to counter recession, control inflation and stimulate economic growth. In 1971, Richard Nixon did away with the Bretton Woods system and its linchpin, the fixed-exchange rate in gold of the 'Roosevelt dollar', in the belief that these were damaging America's international competitiveness against rival trading nations now fully recovered from the Second World War. This break with the past did not enable Nixon and his immediate successors to overcome the unprecedented combination of stagnation and runaway inflation that made the 1970s the most miserable decade for the economy since the 1930s. Their failure opened the way for the Federal Reserve chair to become co-manager of prosperity, responsible for deploying monetary policy to manage inflation, unemployment and the dollar's international value. Late twentieth and early-twenty-first-century presidents, meanwhile, deployed supply-side fiscal incentives to strengthen the foundations of economic growth. For Republicans Reagan, Bush 43 and Trump, this meant cutting taxes to incentivize individual endeavour, wealth-creation and investment. For Democrat Bill Clinton, it meant balancing the federal budget, a feat he was the first president since Calvin Coolidge to achieve four times, in order to enhance the supply of capital available for private investment through reduction of government borrowing.[10]

For the first time since Reconstruction, Roosevelt established the presidency as an ally of African Americans in their need for socio-economic assistance, but his dependence on Southern Democrat support in Congress made him reluctant to champion their civil rights. His immediate predecessors could not make the same trade-offs because Blacks were increasingly unwilling to tolerate them. Growing civil-rights protest drove Truman, Eisenhower and Kennedy to go further than Roosevelt had dared in making progress towards racial equality. One indicator of the change taking place, Kennedy could not emulate FDR's manoeuvring of 1941 to get organizers to call off the March on Washington for Jobs and Freedom in August 1963. Pressure from the freedom movement in combination with his own convictions induced Lyndon Johnson to promote the Civil Rights Act of 1964 and the Voting Rights Act of 1965, thereby earning him historical accolade as the greatest civil-rights president. However, African-American connectedness with the presidency unravelled when conservative Republicans became regular occupants of the White House. Their retrenchment of public-assistance programmes, appointment of judges and justices unsympathetic to affirmative action and support for the War on Drugs that resulted in disproportionate incarceration of young Black males made many African Americans suspect Abraham Lincoln's modern successors of racial bigotry.[11]

Administrative enhancement of the presidency was another area in which Roosevelt was soon outstripped by his successors, but in this case bigger was not necessarily better. In reaction to FDR's personal style of operation, Truman and Eisenhower institutionalized and regularized White House decision-making, particularly in the field of national security. The fine line between political expediency and administrative efficiency was increasingly breached in later presidencies, however. The Bureau of the Budget, the source of neutral managerial competence from FDR to LBJ, was renamed the Office of Management and Budget and given broader functions by Richard Nixon in 1970. The agency henceforth acted more as a member of the president's political family than a supplier of independent analysis for presidential decision-making. In another departure from the Roosveltian model, presidential staff over time became well-known political figures possessing functional specializations in a hierarchical White House Office (WHO). Some gained notoriety for their part in the fateful decision to Americanize the Vietnam War in 1965 and in the scandals of Watergate and Iran-Contra. Originally conceived as an administrative entity, the WHO metamorphosed into a quasi-separate presidential branch of government, in effect becoming an inner layer of White House bureaucracy that competed on the president's behalf for power in the pluralistic and fragmented American system of government. FDR could hardly be held responsible for this development. In his day, WHO budgeted personnel averaged just short of fifty, including six presidential assistants, a coterie small enough for him to manage personally. Within thirty years of his death, the White House staff numbered in excess of 500, with the consequence that presidents needed help just to manage the help.[12]

The constitutional revolution overseen by FDR in the late 1930s extended into the postwar era. The liberal justices appointed by each of his successors from Truman to Nixon made the Supreme Court the institutional champion of rights for the disadvantaged, exemplified by landmark decisions like *Brown v. Topeka* (1954) and *Alexander v. Holmes* (1969), both of which invalidated racially segregated public schools, *Miranda v. Arizona* (1966), which protected the rights of the accused, and *Roe v. Wade* (1973), which established a woman's right of abortion. From the 1980s onwards, the advent of Republican presidents and the broad reaction against judicial liberalism resulted in the appointment of justices who tilted the Supreme Court rightward without making it a conservative body. A series of decisions restricted but did not eradicate affirmative action, abortion rights and criminal justice reform. Donald Trump's opportunity to nominate three new justices finally gave conservative jurisprudence a clear six-to-three majority in the third branch for the first time since FDR's first term. Whether this leads to another judicial confrontation with a liberal president remains to be seen. Whatever happens, the Supreme Court is unlikely to retrench presidential power, whose expansion it has broadly upheld since FDR's day. Even its most famous judgement on this score, *US v. Nixon* (1973), did not challenge the principle of executive privilege to maintain secrecy to protect national security in its specific insistence that Richard Nixon hand over his Watergate tapes for congressional scrutiny.[13]

FDR did not live to see how his project to transform the American party system played out. It was his hope that Democrats and Republicans would acquire cohesive ideological identities respectively as liberal and conservative parties. In mid-1944, he met with Wendell Willkie, the GOP's 1940 presidential candidate, to discuss how they might cooperate to effect a realignment of liberal Democrats with liberal Republicans. The deaths of both shortly afterwards killed off any prospects for doing so.[14] The two parties continued for another quarter century to be ideologically diffuse coalitions that their presidential leaders experienced difficulty in managing. Like FDR, Truman and Kennedy found that conservative Democrats constituted an obstacle to their domestic goals, while Eisenhower's frustration with the Republican right caused him briefly to contemplate party modernization at the start of his second term. LBJ's long coat-tails in his landslide re-election in 1964 hauled sufficient non-Southern Democrats into Congress to enact his Great Society agenda, but his racially progressive reforms irredeemably embittered the white South against national Democratic liberalism.

Seeing the opportunity for realignment, Richard Nixon began a determined effort to convert Dixie Democrats to the party of Lincoln, a project carried forward by Ronald Reagan. Under these presidents and their partisan successors, the GOP became home to conservative whites, many of them discomfited by the social and cultural changes of the 1960s. Freed from their Southern wing, the Democrats became a liberal party that mopped up non-conservative Republican constituencies. The ideological sorting advocated by FDR became a reality, but the outcome in an environment of tight party competition was intensifying partisan polarization. As a consequence, twenty-first-century presidents operated in contradiction of Rooseveltian tradition as base mobilizers rather than as national leaders. Cooperation, compromise and civility between the parties disappeared from American politics. As revealed by the 2020 presidential election and the storming of the Capitol by Donald Trump supporters in its aftermath, the United States had become politically more divided than at any time since the Civil War.[15]

The public presidency changed in conjunction with the president's changing role as party leader. FDR's communications strategy sought not only popular approval for his leadership but also civic education on the issues facing America. His immediate successors broadly followed this model, particularly to maintain public understanding of their Cold War operations. Just as FDR made radio his personal instrument of communication, Eisenhower and Kennedy proved adept performers on the new medium of television, whose presidential usage reached peak effectiveness under former film star Ronald Reagan. Owing to LBJ's experience over the Vietnam War and Nixon's over Watergate, however, presidents increasingly saw the media as obstacles to getting their message to the public. Further reinforcing this outlook for GOP incumbents was their perception of liberal bias in news reporting. As a consequence, presidents from Reagan onwards downplayed the civic-education purpose of political communication to focus on 'going public', in essence engaging in a permanent campaign for popular approval. The needs of base mobilization in a polarized political environment exacerbated this tendency, one reinforced by the ideologically focused media of the digital age. However effective they were as communicators, twenty-first-century presidents found little support from Americans of differing partisan stripe to theirs. Eisenhower and Kennedy had both averaged 49 per cent Gallup poll approval respectively from Democrats and Republicans. The level sank to 31 per cent Democrat approval for Reagan and 27 per cent Republican approval for Clinton, which looked good compared to what followed. Barack Obama averaged just 13 per cent approval from Republicans, and Trump averaged the all-time low of 7 per cent Democratic approval.[16]

Roosevelt's relative lack of success in gaining popular approval for his limited internationalist initiatives in foreign policy is often overlooked in assessments of his effectiveness as a public president in the 1930s, which are largely based on his domestic pronouncements. Nevertheless, his prescience in identifying the threat posed by fascism and the reluctance of many in Congress to recognize this established the presidency as the voice of wisdom in foreign affairs when America eventually entered the war. FDR's success as commander-in-chief in taking the United States to the brink of victory in the 'Good War' also encouraged national expectations that all conflicts would turn out this way for America under strong presidential leadership.

Roosevelt's hopes of building a Great Power peace through Soviet-American cooperation did not long survive his death. Even so, his foreign policy leadership bequeathed two fundamental legacies to his Cold War successors. The first was a presidency with pre-eminent authority at home to determine America's interests abroad, a status enhanced by the need for speed, secrecy and special sources of information that enabled decision-making unity as the atomic age came into being. The other was the binary conception of global affairs as a battleground between freedom, represented by the United States and its allies, and oppression, represented by their adversaries. In 1947, Harry Truman effectively announced the onset of the long global struggle to contain the Soviet Union in his Truman Doctrine message promising support for all peoples under threat from communist expansion.[17] With the exception of the détente era of the 1970s, his successors continued to portray the United States as engaged in a struggle to defend freedom and civilization against forces aligned with Moscow. A decade after the Cold War was finally resolved on American terms, George W. Bush committed the nation to fight another embodiment of oppression in launching the War on Terror and warning of the threat posed by the Axis of Evil (Iran, Iraq and North Korea).[18]

For some scholars, it was a short step from what they regard as Roosevelt's exaggerations and distortions of fact that went hand-in-hand with his efforts to aid Britain and Russia in 1941 to the abuses of presidential power committed in the name of Cold War national security.[19] In this regard, his exploitation of a German U-boat attack on USS *Greer* to issue 'shoot on sight' orders against any enemy vessels operating in America's expanded zone of Atlantic security could be seen as having parallels with LBJ's manipulation of supposed attacks on the USS *Maddox* in the Gulf of Tonkin in 1964 to legitimize US military intervention in Vietnam. It could be contrarily argued, however, that the clarity of hindsight overlooks the complexity of the past in this case.

Fearful of getting too far ahead of public opinion, FDR had not used naval confrontations in the Atlantic in 1941 as the casus belli against Germany, preferring instead to await developments that ensured national unity in support of war. He eventually secured congressional declarations of war against Japan, Germany, and Italy and their allies (Bulgaria, Hungary and Romania). None of his successors sought the same authority when taking the nation into foreign conflict. Truman invoked America's United Nations collective-security obligations to enter the Korean War, LBJ secured a congressional blank cheque, the Gulf of Tonkin Resolution of 1964, authorizing him to take whatever retaliatory measures he deemed necessary against communist aggression in Southeast Asia, George H. W. Bush secured a joint congressional Authorization to Use Military Force to wage the Gulf War under UN auspices in 1991 and George W. Bush used that same instrument to launch the invasions of Afghanistan in 2001 and Iraq in 2003.[20] To many critics, the war-making power, used in this way, enabled an imperial presidency to exceed constitutional restraints on its authority. According to historian Arthur Schlesinger, Jr, too many of Roosevelt's successors came to see their office 'in messianic terms as the appointed savior of a world whose unpredictable dangers call for rapid and incessant deployment of men, arms, and decisions behind a wall of secrecy'.[21]

More than anything else, FDR bequeathed a heroic presidency that met Americans' expectation for strong, effective and wise leadership in times of crisis. Some analysts thought that demeaning revelations of Bill Clinton's affair with a young White House intern had fatally undermined this image of the office in demonstrating the occupant's human shortcomings. Within a short time, the 9/11 terrorist attacks of 2001 caused Americans to turn once more to their president, in this case George W. Bush, for Roosevelt-like reassurance that the nation would transcend the dangers it faced. Nevertheless, it became evident under Bush's successor that the heroic presidency could not rely on the kind of national unity engendered by FDR amid the political polarization of the twenty-first century.

Facing the Great Recession of 2007–9, the worst economic crisis since the early 1930s, Democrat Barack Obama turned to Roosevelt for inspiration by reading historian-journalist Jonathan Alter's book about the Hundred Days of 1933.[22] With FDR-like speed, he promoted enactment within weeks of taking office of the American Recovery and Reinvestment Act of 2009, the largest stimulus hitherto in US history, to kick-start economic revival. Far from being greeted as a saviour, Obama found himself under conservative attack for seeking to introduce budget-busting socialist measures under cover of crisis. In the polarized times, no Republican supported the measure in the House of Representatives and only three did so in the Senate. GOP attacks on Obama's big-government initiatives hit home with voters, who handed the Democrats in 2010 the greatest defeat suffered by a president's party in midterm House elections since Roosevelt's troubled second term in 1938.

Donald Trump's election in 2016 brought the most un-Roosveltian of modern presidents to power. A populist who rose to office on the slogan 'Make America Great Again', he offered a glimpse of what might have happened had Senator Huey Long wrested the White House from FDR in the 1930s. Showing scant respect for constitutional norms, Trump became the first president in history to be impeached twice by the House of Representatives, before being acquitted in Senate trials that required a two-thirds supermajority for a guilty verdict. Focused on mobilizing his base, he used the new technology of Twitter for live-feed messaging that boasted of his greatness, denounced media critics as peddlers of 'fake news' and attacked opponents as unpatriotic socialists. If the encyclopaedia of presidential lies is ever written, there would be entries for all the great and the good, including FDR, but Trump's untruths were so numerous that they could fill a volume of their own. A nationalist in foreign policy, he weakened the rules-based international system built up by FDR and his successors. Having initially disputed the severity of the Covid-19 pandemic in 2020, Trump proved ill-equipped to manage this crisis on belated recognition of the threat it posed. Finally, he became the only modern president to dispute the outcome of a fairly conducted election and question the legitimacy of his victorious opponent.

Ironically, Trump was succeeded by a president who felt closer to FDR than any incumbent since LBJ. Joe Biden saw the opportunity 'to make hope and history rhyme' (a quotation from Irish poet Seamus Heaney) like his hero. In accepting the 2020 Democratic presidential nomination, he asserted, 'Nearly a century ago, Franklin Roosevelt pledged a New Deal in a time of massive unemployment, uncertainty, and fear. Stricken by disease, stricken by a virus, FDR insisted that he would recover and prevail and he believed America could as well. And he did. And so can we.'[23] Regardless of the historical inaccuracy about Roosevelt's recovery from polio, a claim which fitted the pandemic times, this was a clear statement of intent to follow in his footsteps. As president, Biden's Build Back Better agenda at home was an updated if less transformational version of FDR's 'relief, recovery, and reform' promise.[24] In foreign policy, Biden signed a new version of the Roosevelt-Churchill Atlantic Charter with UK prime minister Boris Johnson, another Roosevelt fan. In addition to reaffirming the aspirations of the original, this called for multilateral cooperation to address emerging threats like cyberattacks, global pandemics and climate change.[25] However Biden's withdrawal of US forces from Afghanistan, which precipitated the rapid Taliban takeover of the country, made a mockery of the new charter's promise to defend the principles and institutions of democracy and open society.

Despite this, Biden should not be judged on the basis of whether he is another FDR. The problems he must deal with and the political environment in which he operates are significantly different. Nevertheless, Roosevelt's shadow hangs over him as surely as it did virtually every president since 1945. The only escape seemingly is to eradicate it in the manner of Donald Trump who became the president as destroyer rather than builder, but disruption is not a strategy for governance in the long term. Taking office when democracy was under threat at home and abroad, FDR wondered whether he would be the last president if he failed to get America out of the Great Depression. Nearly a century later, the presidency that Roosevelt bequeathed faces a crisis of a different kind, namely whether it can heal a fractured America and devise effective solutions to pressing problems at home and abroad. Failure to do so could raise questions as to whether the office has become an impossible one.[26]

Accordingly, FDR's presidency merits revisiting to see what it may tell us about the possibilities for presidential leadership in the 2020s and beyond. First, it underlines the necessity of not arousing unrealistic popular expectations about what the presidency can achieve. Neither the legislative blitz of the Hundred Days of 1933 nor succeeding New Deal initiatives restored America's prosperity. Had Roosevelt not run for a third term in 1940, his reputation in history would likely have been less stellar than it became following America's victory in the Second World War and the corollary recovery of its economy. Nevertheless, he would still have been a very significant president. In essence, he fulfilled theologian Reinhold Niebuhr's definition that democracy was 'a method of finding proximate solutions to insoluble problems'.[27]

Second, the presidency needs to recover its teaching functions to enlighten rather than arouse or antagonize Americans, increasingly the consequence of 'going public'. If this appears a very tall order in current times, it is worth remembering that FDR had to build support for his domestic and international initiatives. That said, the presidency would require assistance in fulfilling this role from societal institutions capable of disseminating fact-based civic education to counter twenty-first-century polarization.

Finally, the presidency needs to rediscover its capacity for long-term strategic leadership that links ends and means. Roosevelt is often characterized in history as an improviser and creative opportunist, whereas in reality he had a long-term vision for the kind of America he hoped to build and its place in the world. As Arthur Schlesinger, Jr., observed, an American president stands or falls 'by his instinct for the future' as much as by 'his mastery of the present'. Without the former, his presidency will be 'static and uncreative'. This was a test Roosevelt passed with flying colours, thanks to his 'extraordinary sensitivity to the emergent tendencies of the age', which enabled him to accept the 'inevitability of change, not by necessity, but by conscious choice'.[28] Despite deviations on the way, he knew where he wanted to lead the country. Too often, by contrast, his successors have appeared to be reactive and short term in their leadership.

As Roosevelt was well aware, presidential leadership on its own cannot be the sole answer to what ails the United States. The American people themselves have to be part of the solution. The disbelief of many in the legitimacy of the 2020 presidential election result signified that the continued well-being of American democracy cannot be taken for granted. In these circumstances, it is appropriate to recall FDR's words in his final address of the 1940 election that spelled out the obligations of the people in terms pertinent for the third decade of the twenty-first century and beyond:

We Americans of today – all of us – we are characters in the living book of democracy.

But we are also its author. It falls upon us now to say whether the chapters that are to come will tell a story of retreat or a story of continued advance.[29]

Notes

Abbreviations

AoR-1:   Schlesinger, Jr., Arthur M., *The Age of Roosevelt*, Vol. 1 – *The Crisis of the Old Order, 1919-1933* (Boston: Houghton Mifflin, 1957)

AoR-2:   Schlesinger, Jr., Arthur M., *The Age of Roosevelt*, Vol. 2 – *The Coming of the New Deal* (Boston: Houghton Mifflin, 1958)

AoR-3:   Schlesinger, Jr., Arthur M., *The Age of Roosevelt*, Vol. 3 – *The Politics of Upheaval* (Boston: Houghton Mifflin, 1960)

APP: The American Presidency Project, online by Gerhard Peters and John T. Woolley, http://www,presidency.ucsb.edu/

CC: Ward, Geoffrey, *Closest Companion: The Unknown Story of the Intimate Friendship between Franklin Roosevelt and Margaret Suckley* (New York: Simon & Schuster, 2009) ·

DMK: Diaries of William Lyon Mackenzie King, Library and Archives Canada, https://www.bac-lac.gc.ca/eng/discover/politics-government/prime-ministers/william-lyon-mackenzie-king/Pages/diaries-william-lyon-mackenzie-king.aspx

ERA: Roosevelt, Eleanor, *The Autobiography of Eleanor Roosevelt* (New York: Harper, 1961)

FDRAFP: Dallek, Robert, *Franklin D. Roosevelt and American Foreign Policy, 1932-1945* (New York: Oxford University Press, 1979)

FDR: HPL   Roosevelt, Elliott, ed., *F.D.R.: His Personal Letters*, 4 Volumes (New York: Duell, Sloan, and Pearce, 1950)

FDRL: Franklin D. Roosevelt Library, Hyde Park, NY

FDRW: Woolner, David, Warren Kimball, and David Reynolds, eds., *FDR's World: War, Peace, and Legacies* (New York: Palgrave Macmillan, 2008)

FFF: Kennedy, David, *Freedom from Fear: The American People in Depression and War, 1929-1945* (New York: Oxford University Press, 1999)

FRUS: *Foreign Relations of the United States: Franklin D. Roosevelt Administration (1933-1945)* [Year and relevant vol. no. provided], Office of the Historian, Department of State, https://history.state.gov/historicaldocuments/roosevelt-fd

GCMP: Papers of George Catlett Marshall, George C. Marshall Foundation, https://www.marshallfoundation.org/library/collection/marshall-papers/#!/collection=7

HMD: Diaries of Henry Morgenthau, Jr. (and relevant vol. no), 27 April 1933 to 27 July 1945, FDRL

MNDIS: Loucheim, Katie, ed., *The Making of the New Deal: The Insiders Speak* (Cambridge MA: Harvard University Press, 1983)

MRP: FDR Papers as President, Map Room Papers, 1941-1945 (and relevant box no.)

MSF: FDR Master Speech File, 1898-1945 (and speech file no.)

NYT: *New York Times*

OF: FDR Papers as President, Official File (and relevant box no.)

PCT: Press Conference Transcripts

PPF: FDR Papers as President, President's Personal File (and relevant box no.)

PSF: FDR Papers as President, President's Secretary's File (and relevant box no.)

R&H: Sherwood, Robert, *Roosevelt and Hopkins: An Intimate History* (New York: Harper, 1948)

SD-1:   Ickes, Harold, *The Secret Diary of Harold L. Ickes*: Vol. 1 – *The First Thousand Days, 1933-1936* (New York: Simon & Schuster, 1954)

SD-2:   Ickes, Harold, *The Secret Diary of Harold L. Ickes*: Vol. 2 – *The Inside Struggle, 1936-1939* (New York: Simon & Schuster, 1954)

SD-3:   Ickes, Harold, *The Secret Diary of Harold L. Ickes*: Vol. 3 – *The Lowering Clouds, 1939-1941* (New York: Simon & Schuster, 1954)

TD: Namaroto, Michael Vincent, ed., *The Diary of Rexford Tugwell: The New Deal, 1932-1935* (Westport CT: Praeger, 1992)

TM: Jackson, Robert, *That Man: An Insider's Portrait of Franklin D. Roosevelt*, ed. John Q. Barrett (New York: Oxford University Press, 2004)

TNR: *The New Republic*

TRIK: Perkins, Frances, *The Roosevelt I Knew* (New York: Viking, 1946)

WWR: Rosenman, Samuel, *Working with Roosevelt* (London: Rupert Hart-Davies, 1952)

Prologue

1 For histories of the times, see McElvaine, Robert, *The Great Depression: America, 1929–1941* (New York: Times Books, 1993); and Watkins, T. H., *The Great Depression: America in the 1930s* (Boston: Little, Brown, 1993).

2 *Theodore Joslin Diary*, 3 March 1933, https://www.archives.gov/exhibits/eyewitness/html.php?section=11

3 Quoted in Burns, James MacGregor, *Roosevelt: The Lion and the Fox, 1882–1940* (New York: Harcourt, Brace, 1956), 165.

4 Peel, Roy, and Thomas Donnelly, *The 1932 Campaign: An Analysis* (New York: Farrar & Rinehart, 1935), 213.

5 For excellent introductions to Roosevelt's presidency, see Graubard, Stephen, *The Presidents: The Transformation of the American Presidency from Theodore Roosevelt to George W. Bush* (London: Penguin, 2006), 243–98; and Leuchtenburg, William, *The American President: From Teddy Roosevelt to Bill Clinton* (New York: Oxford University Press, 2015), 143–242.

6 Genovese, Michael, *A Presidential Nation: Causes, Consequences, and Cures* (Boulder CO: Westview, 2013), 11–83; Leuchtenburg, William, *In the Shadow of FDR: From Harry Truman to Barack Obama* (Ithaca, NY: Cornell University Press, 2009).

7 'Foreword to Theodore C. Sorensen's "Decision-Making in the White House"', June 1963, APP, https://www.presidency.ucsb.edu/node/235837.

8 Roper, Jon, *The American Presidents: Heroic Leadership from Kennedy to Clinton* (Edinburgh: Edinburgh University Press, 2000), 3.

9 'Historical rankings of presidents of the United States', https://en.wikipedia.org/wiki/Historical_rankings_of_presidents_of_the_United_States; Morgan, Iwan, 'The Top US Presidents: First Poll of UK Experts', *BBC News: US and Canada*, 17 January 2011, https://www.bbc.co.uk/news/world-us-canada-12195111. See also McCulloch, Tony, 'Simply the Best: FDR as America's Number One President', in Michael Patrick Cullinane and Clare Elliott, eds., *Perspectives on Presidential Leadership: An International View of the White House* (New York: Routledge, 2014), 113–31.

10 *AoR-2*, 15: Burns, *Roosevelt: The Lion and the Fox*, ix–x.

11 Quoted in Kimball, Warren, *The Juggler: Franklin Roosevelt as Wartime Statesman* (Princeton, NJ: Princeton University Press, 1991), 7.

12 Rudalevige, Andrew, *The New Imperial Presidency: Renewing Presidential Power after Watergate* (Ann Arbor: University of Michigan Press, 2005), 48–9.

13 'Remarks in Riga', 7 May 2005, APP, https://www.presidency.ucsb.edu/node/215234

14 Suri, Jeremi, *The Impossible Presidency: The Rise and Fall of America's Highest Office* (New York: Basic Books, 2017), 177.

15 Alter, Jonathan, *The Defining Moment: FDR's Hundred Days and the Triumph of Hope* (New York: Simon & Schuster, 2006), 168–77; 'Escape', *Time*, 27 February 1933.

16 Carlyle, Thomas, 'On Heroes, Hero-Worship, and the Heroic in History' (1841), https://www.gutenberg.org/files/1091/1091-h/1091-h.htm.

17 'Inaugural Addresses: Washington to Biden', *APP*, http://www.presidency.ucsb.edu/inaugurals.php.

18 'Inaugural Address', 4 March 1933, APP, http://www.presidency.ucsb.edu/ws/index.php?pid=14473&st=&st1=#; Houck, Davis, *FDR and Fear Itself: The First Inaugural Address* (College Station: Texas A&M University Press, 2002).

19 Hassett, William, *Off the Record with FDR, 1942–1945* (London: George Allen & Unwin, 1960), 333.

20 *WWR*, 501.

Chapter 1

1 For discussion of FDR's early life, see Ward, Geoffrey, *Before the Trumpet: Young Franklin Roosevelt, 1882–1905* (New York: Harper & Row, 1985); Maney, Patrick, *The Roosevelt Presence: The Life and Legacy of FDR* (Berkeley: University of California Press, 1998), 1–11; and Dallek, Robert, *Franklin D. Roosevelt: A Political Life* (New York: Viking, 2017), 17–39.

2 James Roosevelt to Franklin Roosevelt, 30 January 1898, quoted in Maney, *Roosevelt Presence*, 4.

3 Ward, *Before the Trumpet*, 11–12.

4 'Last Will and Testament of James Roosevelt', http://www.fdrlibrary.marist.edu/psf/box21/A902at01.html.

5 Burns, James MacGregor, *Roosevelt: The Lion and the Fox* (New York: Harcourt Brace, 1956), 472.

6 Roosevelt, Sara, *My Boy Franklin* (New York: Ray Long & Richard R. Smith, 1933), 4.

7 Persico, Joseph, *Franklin and Lucy: President Roosevelt, Mrs Rutherfurd, and the Other Remarkable Women in His Life* (New York: Random House, 2008), 21.

8 Costigliola, Frank, *Roosevelt's Lost Alliances: How Personal Politics Helped Start the Cold War* (Princeton, NJ: Princeton University Press, 2012), 59–63.

9 *R&H*, 9.

10 Cross, Robert, *Sailor in the White House: The Seafaring Life of FDR* (Annapolis, MD: Naval Institute Press, 1999).

11 FDR to Muriel and Warren Delano, 30 May 1891, in *FDR: HPL-I*, 19–20.

12 Roosevelt, Eleanor, *This Is My Story* (New York: Harper, 1937), 149–50.

13 Ward, *Before the Trumpet*, 230–1.

14 Cook, Blanche Wiesen, *Eleanor Roosevelt, Vol I: 1884–1933* (New York: Viking Penguin, 1992), 154.

15 *AoR-1*, 330.

16 Ward, Geoffrey, *A First-Class Temperament: The Emergence of Franklin Roosevelt, 1905–1928* (New York: Harper & Row, 1989), 88–9.

17 Dallek, *Roosevelt*, 35–6.

18 For campaign notes and materials, see *FDR: HPL-2*, 154–8.

19 Winfield, Betty Houchin, *FDR and the News Media* (New York: Columbia University Press, 1994), 12.

20 'Address before the People's Forum, Troy, N.Y.', 3 March 1912, MSF-14, FDRL, http://www.fdrlibrary.marist.edu/_resources/images/msf/msf00015.

21 *TRIK*, 11–12.

22 *AoR-1*, 341.

23 Stiles, Lela, *The Man behind Roosevelt: The Story of Louis McHenry Howe* (Cleveland: World Publishing, 1954).

24 FDR to SDR, 17 March 1913, *FDR: HPL-2*, 199.

25 *TRIK*, 19–21.

26 FDR to ER, 6 August 1914, *FDR: HPL-2*, 243.

27 *FDRAFP*, 9.

28 FDR to ER, probably 21 October 1914, *FDR: HPL-2*, 256–7.

29 'Address to a Joint Session of Congress Requesting a Declaration of War Against Germany', 2 April 1917, APP, https://www.presidency.ucsb.edu/node/207620.

30 'Trip Diary', 4 and 7 August 1918, *FDR: HPL-2*, 412–32.

31 Roosevelt, *This Is My Story*, 149.

32 Ward, *First-Class Temperament*, 16–18.

33 Persico, *Franklin and Lucy*, 122–35; Ward, *First-Class Temperament*, 709–15; *CC*, ix–xvii.

34 Lash, Joseph, *Eleanor and Franklin: The Story of Their Relationship* (New York: Norton, 1971), 220.

35 *AER*, 279.

36 Cooper, John Milton, *Breaking the Heart of the World: Woodrow Wilson and the Fight for the League of Nations* (New York: Cambridge University Press, 2001); *AER*, 101.

37 'Address at Worcester Polytechnic Institute Commencement', 25 June 1919, MSF-95, FDRL, http://www.fdrlibrary.marist.edu/_resources/images/msf/msf00097.pdf.

38 Tobin, James, *The Man He Became: How FDR Defied Polio to Win the Presidency* (New York: Simon & Schuster, 2013), 13–90.

39 *FDR: HPL-2*, 635; Frankfurter to Harlan Fiske Stone, 3 February 1936, quoted in Shesol, Jeff, *Supreme Power: Franklin Roosevelt vs. the Supreme Court* (New York: Norton, 2010), 507.

40 Lash, *Eleanor and Franklin*, 268, 273.

41 Cook, *Eleanor Roosevelt*, I, 338–42; *TRIK*, 30–2.

42 MacKaye, Milton, 'Profiles: The Governor – II', *New Yorker*, 22 August 1931, 28.

43 Smith, Kathryn, *The Gatekeeper: Missy LeHand, FDR, and the Untold Story of the Partnership that Defined a Presidency* (New York: Touchstone, 2016), 62; Costigliola, *Roosevelt's Lost Alliances*, 68–70.

44 Stiles, *The Man behind Roosevelt*, 82; *TRIK*, 29; Gunther, John, *Roosevelt in Retrospect* (New York: Harper & Row, 1950), 243.

45 Gallagher, Hugh Gregory, *FDR's Splendid Deception* (Arlington, VA: Vandamere, 1994), xi.

46 Tobin, *The Man He Became*, 201–52; 'Georgia Warm Springs Foundation, 1940' (report), Disability History Museum, http://www.disabilitymuseum.org/dhm/lib/detail.html?id=2168.

47 Murray, Robert, *The 103d Ballot: Democrats and the Disaster in Madison Square Garden* (New York: Harper & Row, 1976).

48 Golway, Terry, *Frank & Al: FDR, Al Smith, and the Unlikely Alliance That Created the Modern Democratic Party* (New York: St. Martin's Press, 2018), 148–50, 154–7 (quotation, p. 150).

49 Laycock, Joseph, 'A Party in Peril: Franklin Roosevelt, the Democratic Party, and the Circular Letter of 1924', PhD dissertation, Bowling Green State University, 2016, https://etd.ohiolink.edu/!etd.send_file?accession=bgsu1478211951641714&disposition=inline.

50 'The Press on the Ticket', *NYT*, 4 October 1928.

51 *WWR*, 27–37, 52 (quotation).

52 *TRIK*, 52–3.

53 Golway, *Frank & Al*, 265.

54 *WWR*, 48–55; Burns, *Lion and the Fox*, 118–19.

55 'Gov. Roosevelt Gives Hoover Assurance', *NYT*, 25 November 1929.

56 Maney, *Roosevelt Presence*, 32–3.

57 'Text of Governor Roosevelt's Special Message', *NYT*, 29 August 1931.

58 Daniels, Roger, *Franklin D. Roosevelt: Road to the New Deal, 1882–1939* (Urbana: University of Illinois Press, 2015), 97–9.

59 'Acceptance of Nomination for Governor', 16 October 1928, MSF-261, FDRL, http://www.fdrlibrary.marist.edu/_resources/images/msf/msf00265; Maney, *Roosevelt Presence*, 33–5.

60 'Governor Roosevelt's Candidacy', 8 January 1932, in Lippmann, Walter, *Interpretations, 1931–1932* (New York: Macmillan, 1932), 261–2.

61 Gallagher, *FDR's Splendid Deception*, 87.

Chapter 2

1 For specialist studies, see Alter, Jonathan, *The Defining Moment: FDR's Hundred Days and the Triumph of Hope* (New York: Simon & Schuster, 2006); and Badger, Anthony, *FDR: The First Hundred Days* (New York: Hill & Wang, 2008).

2 'Address Accepting the Presidential Nomination at the Democratic National Convention in Chicago', 2 July 1932, APP, https://www.presidency.ucsb.edu/node/275484.

3 *WWR*, 77–8, 84 (quotation); Chase, Stuart, 'A New Deal for America', *TNR*, 29 June and 6, 13 and 27 July 1932. For New Deal histories, see Leuchtenburg, William E., *Franklin D. Roosevelt and the New Deal, 1932–1940* (New York: Harper & Row, 1963); Biles, Roger, *A New Deal for the American People* (De Kalb: Northern Illinois University Press, 1991); and Smith, Jason Scott, *A Concise History of the New Deal* (New York: Cambridge University Press, 2014).

4 For the contrasting perspectives, see Daniels, Roger, *Franklin D. Roosevelt: Road to the New Deal, 1882–1939* (Urbana: University of Illinois Press, 2015), 131–58; and Rauchway, Eric, *Winter War: Hoover, Roosevelt and the Clash over the New Deal* (New York: Basic Books, 2018), 14–18.

5 *FFF*, 365.

6 Berle to Raymond Moley, 19 September 1932, Adolf Berle Papers, Box 15, FDRL; 'Campaign Address on Progressive Government at the Commonwealth Club in San Francisco, California', 23 September 1932, APP, https://www.presidency.ucsb.edu/node/289312; Houck, Davis 'FDR's Commonwealth Club Address: Redefining Individualism, Adjudicating Greatness', *Rhetoric & Public Affairs*, 7 (Fall 2004): 259–82.

7 Churchill, Winston, 'While the World Watches', *Collier's*, 29 December 1934, 24–5, 49 (quotation).

8 Hoover, Herbert, *The Memoirs of Herbert Hoover: The Great Depression, 1929–1941* (New York: Macmillan, 1952), 61–96 (quotation, p. 80).

9 Tugwell, Rexford, *In Search of Roosevelt* (Cambridge, MA: Harvard University Press, 1972), 141–3; Moley, Raymond, *After Seven Years* (New York: Harper, 1939), 67–77 (quotation, p. 70).

10 'Address at Madison Square Garden in New York City', 31 October 1932, APP, https://www.presidency.ucsb.edu/node/208073.

11 Roosevelt, Franklin D., 'The New Deal: An Interpretation', *Liberty*, 10 December 1932, 7–8.

12 Roosevelt, Franklin D., *Looking Forward* (New York: John Day, 1933), 7–14 (quotation, p. 8). Text available at https://gutenberg.ca/ebooks/rooseveltfd-lookingforward/rooseveltfd-lookingforward-00-h-dir/rooseveltfd-lookingforward-00-h.html.

13 Hoover to FDR, 18 February 1933, and to David Reed, 21 February 1933, in Myers, William Starr, and Walter Newton, *The Hoover Administration: A Documented Narrative* (New York: Scribner's, 1936), 338–40.

14 Roosevelt, Franklin D., *On Our Way* (New York: John Day, 1934), 8.

15 Ballantine, Arthur, 'When All the Banks Closed', *Harvard Business Review*, XXVI (March 1948): 129–43.

16 Burns, James MacGregor, *Roosevelt: The Lion and the Fox* (New York: Harcourt, Brace, 1956), 166–7.

17 'Regulations Concerning the Operation of Banks', 10 March 1933, http://www.fdrlibrary.marist.edu/_resources/images/eo/eo0001.pdf.

18 'Fireside Chat on Banking', 12 March 1933, APP, https://www.presidency.ucsb.edu/node/207762.

19 Quoted in Leuchtenburg, *Franklin D. Roosevelt and the New Deal*, 44.

20 Moley, *After Seven Years*, 155.

21 Cutting, Bronson, 'Is Private Banking Doomed?' *Liberty*, 31 March 1934.

22 Lippmann, Walter, *Interpretations, 1933–1935* (New York: Macmillan, 1936), 35.

23 Moley, Raymond, *The First New Deal* (New York: Harcourt, Brace & World, 1966), 201.

24 'Message to Congress on Economies in Government', 10 March 1933, APP, https://www.presidency.ucsb.edu/node/208818.

25 FDR to John Lawrence, 13 March 1933, *FDR: HPL-3*, 338–9.

26 Moley, *After Seven Years*, 189.

27 *AoR-1*, 3.

28 *TD* (6 January 1933), 52–3.

29 *AoR-2*, 35; Culver, John, and John Hyde, *American Dreamer: A Life of Henry A. Wallace* (New York: Norton, 2000), 109–29.

30 Lord, Russell, *The Wallaces of Iowa* (Boston: Houghton Mifflin, 1947), 330.

31 'Message to Congress on the Agricultural Adjustment Act', 16 March 1933, APP, https://www.presidency.ucsb.edu/node/207923.

32 *AoR-2*, 44–5.

33 Wallace, Henry, 'The Farm Situation', *Vital Speeches*, 3 December 1934.

34 Quoted in Browder, Robert Paul, and Thomas Smith, *Independent: A Biography of Lewis W. Douglas* (New York: Knopf, 1986), 93.

35 'Message to Congress on Unemployment Relief', 21 March 1933, APP, https://www.presidency.ucsb.edu/node/207970.

36 Hiltzik, Michael, *The New Deal: A Modern History* (New York: Free Press, 2011), 66–9; Jackson, Donald, 'They Were Poor, Hungry, and They Built to Last', *Smithsonian*, 25 (December 1994), 66–7.

37 *TRIK*, 183–5; McJimsey, George, *Harry Hopkins: Ally of the Poor and Defender of Democracy* (Cambridge, MA: Harvard University Press, 1987), 45–52.

38 Hopkins, Harry, *Spending to Save: The Complete Story of Relief* (New York: Norton, 1936), esp. chapter 4; Hopkins, June, *Harry Hopkins: Sudden Hero, Brash Reformer* (New York: St Martin's, 1999), 149–74.

39 'Message to Congress on Small Home Mortgage Foreclosures', 13 April 1933, APP, https://www.presidency.ucsb.edu/node/208066.

40 Harris, Lowell, *History and Policies of the Home Owners Loan Corporation* (New York: National Bureau of Economic Research, 1951).

41 FDR to Norris, 14 December 1932, *FDR: HPL-3*, 309–10; *AoR-2*, 323–4.

42 'Huge Development Plan for Six States in South Is Drafted by Roosevelt', *NYT*, 3 February 1933.

43 'Message to Congress Suggesting the Tennessee Valley Authority', 10 April 1933, APP. https://www.presidency.ucsb.edu/node/208057.

44 Perino, Michael, *The Hellhound of Wall Street: How Ferdinand Pecora's Investigation of the Great Crash Forever Changed American Finance* (New York: Penguin, 2010), 60–94.

45 'White House Statement on Securities Legislation', 29 March 1933, APP, https://www.presidency.ucsb.edu/node/208180; Moley, *After Seven Years*, 176–9.

46 Landis, James, 'The Legislative History of the Securities Act of 1933', 28 *George Washington Law Review* 29 (1959–60): 29–49; FDR to John Lawrence, 18 May 1933, *FDR:HPL-3*, 346.

47 'Statement on Signing the Securities Bill', 27 May 1933, APP, https://www.presidency.ucsb.edu/node/208180.

48 Douglas, William O., 'Protecting the Investor', *Yale Review* 23 (March 1934): 521–33 (quotation, p. 528).

49 Berle, Adolf, 'New Protection for Buyers of Securities', *NYT*, 4 June 1933.
50 *Public Papers and Addresses of Franklin D. Roosevelt. Volume 2: The Year of Crisis, 1933* (New York: Random House, 1938), 438–9; Friedman, Milton, and Anna Schwartz, *A Monetary History of the United States, 1857–1960* (Princeton, NJ: Princeton University Press, 1963), 454.
51 *TRIK*, 192–6.
52 Johnson, Hugh, *The Blue Eagle from Egg to Earth* (New York: Doubleday, 1935), 96–7; Moley, *After Seven Years*, 187–9; *TD* (30 May 1933), 350–2.
53 'Message to Congress Recommending Enactment of the National Industrial Recovery Act', 17 May 1933, APP, https://www.presidency.ucsb.edu/node/208154.
54 Hawley, Ellis, *The New Deal and the Problem of Monopoly* (Princeton, NJ: Princeton University Press, 1966), 31–4; Lindley, Ernest, *Halfway with Roosevelt* (New York: Viking, 1937), 156.
55 *SD-1* (29 April 1933), 28; Moley, *After Seven Years*, 173, n. 8.
56 *SD-1* (16 June 1933), 53–4; *TRIK*, 201–3.
57 Ickes, Harold, *Back to Work: The Story of the PWA* (New York: MacMillan, 1935), 50–2.
58 Smith, Jason Scott, *Building New Deal Liberalism: The Political Economy of Public Works, 1933–1956* (New York: Cambridge University Press, 2006), 28–53.
59 Johnson, Hugh, 'Pied Pipers', *Vital Speeches*, 11 March 1935; Tugwell, Rexford, 'The Ideas behind the New Deal', *NYT Magazine*, 16 July 1933; Carter, John Franklin, *The New Dealers* (New York: Simon & Schuster, 1934), 21–3.
60 Essary, Fred, 'The New Deal for Nearly Four Months', *Literary Digest*, CXVI (July 1933): 4.
61 *The Fighting President* (Universal, 1933), https://www.youtube.com/watch?v =SyMsdp2ubJc

Chapter 3

1 Tugwell, Rexford, *The Brains Trust* (New York: Viking, 1968), 157–8.
2 'Message to Congress on the Objectives and Accomplishments of the Administration', 8 June 1934, APP, https://www.presidency.ucsb.edu/node/208398.
3 Edman, Irwin, *Fountainheads of Freedom* (New York: Reynal & Hitchcock, 1941), 196; Foner, Eric, *The Story of American Freedom* (New York: Norton, 1998), 195–218.
4 Hoover, Herbert, *The Challenge to Liberty* (New York: Scribner's, 1934).
5 'Fireside Chat', 30 September 1934, APP, https://www.presidency.ucsb.edu/node /208160.
6 'Fireside Chat (Recovery Program)', 24 July 1933, APP, https://www.presidency.ucsb .edu/node/208789.
7 Johnson, Hugh, *The Blue Eagle from Egg to Earth* (New York: Doubleday, Doran, 1935), 265; *AoR-2*, 117–18.
8 'President Signs the Textile Code: First Major Pact', *NYT*, 10 July 1933.
9 Johnson, *Blue Eagle*, esp. chapter 21; *SD-1* (28 July 1933), 72; Tugwell, Rexford, *Roosevelt's Revolution: The First Year – A Personal Perspective* (New York: Macmillan, 1977), 233–7.
10 Leighton, George, 'In Search of the NRA', *Harper's*, January 1934.
11 Bernstein, Irving, *Turbulent Years: A History of the American Worker, 1933–1941* (Boston: Houghton Mifflin, 1969), esp. chapter 6; Kennedy, David, *Freedom from Fear: The American People in Depression and War, 1929–1945* (New York: Oxford University Press, 1999), 291–6.

12 'Statement on the Avoidance of a Strike in the Auto Industry', 25 March 1934, APP, https://www.presidency.ucsb.edu/node/208541.

13 'Garrison Stands on Houde Decision', *NYT*, 15 September 1934.

14 'Message to Congress on the Gains under NRA', 20 February 1935, APP, https://www.presidency.ucsb.edu/node/208349.

15 Hawley, Ellis, *The New Deal and the Problem of Monopoly* (Princeton, NJ: Princeton University Press, 1966), 126–9.

16 Peek, George, 'In and Out: The Experiences of the First AAA Administrator', *Saturday Evening Post*, 16 May 1936, 7.

17 Quoted in Lord, Russell, *The Wallaces of Iowa* (Boston: Houghton Mifflin, 1947), 366.

18 *AoR-2*, 46.

19 Peek, 'In and Out', 8.

20 *TD*, 401–6; *AoR-2*, 56–9.

21 Gerstle, Gary, *Liberty and Coercion: The Paradox of American Government from the Founding to the Present* (Princeton, NJ: Princeton University Press, 2015), 202–16.

22 'Address at Omaha, Nebraska', 10 October 1936, APP, https://www.presidency.ucsb.edu/node/209230.

23 *AoR-2*, 377–9.

24 Hiss, Alger, in *MNDIS*, 238–40; Biles, Roger, *The South and the New Deal* (Lexington: University Press of Kentucky, 1994), 46–7.

25 Saloutos, Theodore, *The American Farmer and the New Deal* (Ames: Iowa State University Press, 1982), 236–53; Badger, Anthony, *The New Deal: The Depression Years, 1933–1940* (London: Macmillan, 1989), 160–3.

26 Saloutos, *The American Farmer and the New Deal*, 270.

27 *SD-1* (6 November 1933), 116.

28 Hopkins, Harry, *Spending to Save: The Complete Story of Relief* (New York: Norton, 1936), 114, 120.

29 National Emergency Council Proceedings, 23 January 1934, in Seligman, Lester, and Elmer Cornwell, eds., *New Deal Mosaic: Roosevelt Confers with His National Emergency Council* (Eugene: Oregon University Books, 1965), 257.

30 FDR to House, 7 May 1934, *FDR: HPL-3*, 401.

31 Eccles, Marriner, *Beckoning Frontiers: Public and Personal Recollections* (New York: Knopf, 1951), 147 (quotation), 158–61; Biles, Roger, *The Fate of Cities: Urban America and the Federal Government, 1945–2000* (Lawrence: University Press of Kansas, 2011), 7–9.

32 'Message to Congress Recommending a Securities Exchange Commission', 9 February 1934, APP, https://www.presidency.ucsb.edu/node/208356.

33 'Letter on Federal Supervision of Securities Sales', 26 March 1934, APP, https://www.presidency.ucsb.edu/node/208551.

34 FDR to Berle, 15 August 1934, in Berle, Adolf, *Navigating the Rapids, 1918–1971*, ed. Beatrice Bishop Berle (New York: Harcourt Brace Jovanovich, 1973), 103–4.

35 Beauchamp, Cari, *Joseph P. Kennedy's Hollywood Years* (New York: Knopf, 2009), 325–9.

36 Flynn, John T., 'The Jackals of Finance', *TNR*, 18 July 1934, and 'Hail and Farewell to Mr. Kennedy', *TNR*, 9 October 1935.

37 'Annual Message to Congress', 4 January 1935, APP, https://www.presidency.ucsb.edu/node/208864.

38 *FDR: HPL-3*, 444.

39 Coblentz, Edmond, *William Randolph Hearst* (New York: Simon & Schuster, 1954), 178; FDR to Baker, 8 November 1934, *FDR: HPL-3*, 429.

40 'Fireside Chat', 28 June 1934, APP, https://www.presidency.ucsb.edu/node/208443; Hopkins, *Spending to Save*, 180–1.

41 FDR to Garner, 13 November 1934, *FDR: HPL-3*, 430.

42 FDR to House, 27 November 1934, *FDR: HPL-3*, 434.

43 'Annual Message to Congress', 4 January 1935, APP, https://www.presidency.ucsb.edu/node/208864.

44 *R&H*, 65.

45 Federal Works Agency, *Final Report on the WPA Program, 1935–1943* (Washington, DC: Government Printing Office, 1947), 28–30. See, too, Taylor, Nick, *American-Made: The Enduring Legacy of the WPA, When FDR Put the Nation to Work* (New York: Bantam Books, 2008).

46 *SD-1* (6 and 9 September 1935), 429–30, 433–4.

47 *TRIK*, 301. See, too, Rosen, Elliot, *Roosevelt, The Great Depression and the Economics of Recovery* (Charlottesville: University of Virginia Press, 2007), 159–69.

48 *SD-1* (3 August 1935), 407. For a biography, see Downey, Kirstin, *The Woman behind the New Deal: The Life of Frances Perkins, FDR's Secretary of Labor and His Moral Conscience* (New York: Doubleday, 2009).

49 Tugwell, Rexford, *The Democratic Roosevelt* (Garden City, NY: Doubleday, 1957), 337; Perkins, *TRIK*, 282–3, 286.

50 Eliot, Thomas, *Recollections of the New Deal* (Boston: Northeastern University Press, 1992), 95–8.

51 Eliot, *Recollections*, 75.

52 Eliot, *Recollections*, 97; Perkins, *TRIK*, 281.

53 Eliot, *Recollections*, 98, 102; Gulick, Luther, 'Memorandum on Conference with FDR Concerning Social Security Taxation, Summer 1941', www.ssa.gov/history/Gulick.html.

54 Perkins, *TRIK*, 294.

55 Eliot, *Recollections*, 102.

56 Eliot, Thomas, 'The Legal Background of the Social Security Act', 3 September 1961, www.ssa.gov/history/eliot2.html.

57 'Message to Congress on Social Security', 17 January 1935, APP, https://www.presidency.ucsb.edu/node/208633. For Witte's critique of Townsend Plan, see Hearings, *Economic Security Act*, House Ways and Means Committee, 74th Congress: Session I, 110.

58 Hearings, *Economic Security Act* (5 February 1935), 897–9.

59 Katznelson, Ira, *Fear Itself: The New Deal and the Origins of Our Time* (New York: Liveright, 2013), 259–60; *Jackson Daily News*, 20 June 1935, quoted in Leuchtenburg, William E., *Franklin D. Roosevelt and the New Deal, 1932–1940* (New York: Harper & Row, 1963), 131.

60 'Statement on Signing the Social Security Act', 14 August 1935, APP, https://www.presidency.ucsb.edu/node/209017.

61 *SD-1* (15 May 1935), 363–4.

62 *MNDIS*, 205–18 (quotations, Green p. 206, Emerson, p. 212).

63 Katznelson, *Fear Itself*, 260; Sloan, Alfred, 'Comments on the Current Situation', *Vital Speeches of the Day*, 1 (20 April 1935), 472.

64 *AoR-3*, 302–24.

65 'Message to Congress on Tax Revision', 19 June 1935, APP, https://www.presidency.ucsb.edu/node/208848.

66 Leff, Mark, *The Limits of Symbolic Reform: The New Deal and Taxation, 1933–1939* (New York: Cambridge University Press, 1984), 91 (quotation), 93–168; *SD-1* (19 June 1935), 384.

67 Eccles, *Beckoning Frontiers*, 166–78.

68 Kettl, Donald, *Leadership at the Fed* (New Haven, CT: Yale University Press, 1986), 45–55.

69 'Letter from Roy W. Howard on Policies Detrimental to Industry', 26 August 1935, APP, https://www.presidency.ucsb.edu/node/209115; 'Reply to Letter from Roy W. Howard', 2 September 1935, APP, https://www.presidency.ucsb.edu/node/209120.

70 'Inaugural Address', 20 January 1937, APP, https://www.presidency.ucsb.edu/node /209135.

71 Baldwin, Sidney, *Poverty and Politics: The Rise and Decline of the Farm Security Administration* (Chapel Hill: University of North Carolina Press, 2011; original ed. 1968), 157–231.

72 National Emergency Council Proceedings, 11 December 1934, in Seligman and Cornwell, *New Deal Mosaic*, 366–8; Biles, *The Fate of Cities*, 8–9.

73 Paulsen, George, *Living Wage for the Forgotten Man: The Quest for Fair Labor Standards 1933–1941* (Selinsgrove, PA: Susquehanna University Press, 1996).

74 'Transmittal to Congress of a Report of the Social Security Board', 16 January 1939, APP, https://www.presidency.ucsb.edu/node/209215; DeWitt, Larry, 'The Development of Social Security in America', *Social Security Bulletin*, 70/3 (2010) (see section 'The Amendment of 1939'), https://www.ssa.gov/policy/docs/ssb/v70n3/v70n3p1.html.

75 Katznelson, *Fear Itself*, 125–6.

76 McElvaine, Robert, *The Great Depression: America, 1929–1941* (New York: Times Books, 1993), esp. 197–225, 337–42.

77 'Annual Message to Congress', 4 January 1939, APP, https://www.presidency.ucsb.edu/node/209128.

Chapter 4

1 *TM*, 124.

2 'Fireside Chat (Recovery Program)', 24 July 1933, APP, https://www.presidency.ucsb.edu/node/208789.

3 Foster, William Trufant, and Waddill Catchings, *The Road to Plenty* (Boston: Houghton Mifflin, 1928), esp. 54–6, 100; *AoR-1*, 137.

4 Rosen, Elliott, *Roosevelt, the Great Depression, and the Economics of Recovery* (Charlottesville: University of Virginia Press, 2005), 1.

5 Powell, Jim, *FDR's Folly: How Roosevelt and His New Deal Prolonged the Great Depression* (New York: Crown Forum, 2003), xiv.

6 'Diagnosing a Depression', *The Economist*, 30 December 2008, https://www.economist.com/finance-and-economics/2008/12/30/diagnosing-depression.

7 Rosen, *Roosevelt, The Great Depression and the Economics of Recovery*, 120–1; Romer, Christina, 'What Ended the Great Depression?' *Journal of Economic History*, 52 (December 1992): 757–84.

8 Collins, Robert, *More: The Politics of Economic Growth in Postwar America* (New York: Oxford University Press, 2000), 1–10.

9 Tugwell, Rexford, *The Democratic Roosevelt: A Biography of Franklin Roosevelt* (New York: Doubleday, 1957), 34–5.

10 Barber, William, *Designs within Disorder: Franklin D. Roosevelt, the Economists, and the Shaping of American Economic Policy, 1933–1945* (New York: Cambridge University Press, 2006), 50–1.

11 'Fireside Chat', 22 October 1933, APP, https://www.presidency.ucsb.edu/node/207739.

12 Friedman, Milton, and Anna Schwartz, *A Monetary History of the United States,
    1867–1960* (Princeton, NJ: Princeton University Press, 1963), 15–88.

13 Rauchway, Eric, *The Money Makers: How Roosevelt and Keynes Ended the
    Depression, Defeated Fascism, and Secured a Prosperous Peace* (New York: Basic
    Books, 2015), 27–30; Keynes, John Maynard, *The Means to Prosperity* (London:
    Macmillan, 1933) [available at https://gutenberg.ca/ebooks/keynes-means/keynes
    -means-00-h.html].

14 Warren, diary entry, 5 March 1933, quoted in Rauchway, *Money Makers*, 37.

15 'Executive Order 6102 – Requiring Gold Coin, Gold Bullion and Gold Certificates to
    Be Delivered to the Government', 5 April 1933, APP, https://www.presidency.ucsb.edu
    /node/208042; *AoR-2*, 19.

16 Acting Secretary of State to the Chairman of the American Delegation (Cordell Hull),
    20 June 1933, *FRUS:1933-1*, https://history.state.gov/historicaldocuments/frus1933v01
    /d473; President Roosevelt to Acting Secretary of State (for relay to Cordell Hull),
    2 July 1933, ibid., https://history.state.gov/historicaldocuments/frus1933v01/d503;
    Moley, Raymond, *After Seven Years* (New York: Harper & Bros., 1939), 259–60.

17 'Keynes Views Roosevelt as World's Great Realist', *New York Herald Tribune*', 27 June
    1933; Skidelsky, Robert, *John Maynard Keynes: Economist, Philosopher, Statesman,
    1882–1946* (London: Penguin, 2003), 499.

18 Rauchway, *Money Makers*, 74–7, 81–5 (quotation, p. 82).

19 FDR to Sara Roosevelt, 28 October 1933, *FDR: HPL-3*, 366; '20-Cent Set Price Asked
    for Cotton', *NYT*, 19 September 1933.

20 Warren, George, and Frank Pearson, *Prices* (New York: John Wiley, 1933); *AoR-2*,
    229–32; Warburg, James, *The Money Muddle* (New York: Knopf, 1934), 147.

21 Acheson, Dean, *Morning and Noon: A Memoir* (Boston: Houghton Mifflin, 1965),
    161–94; *HMD-Farm Credit Diary*, 19 October 1933, http://www.fdrlibrary.marist.edu/
    _resources/images/morg/md00.pdf.

22 *HMD-Farm Credit Diary*, 29 October 1933, http://www.fdrlibrary.marist.edu/
    _resources/images/morg/md00.pdf.

23 Ibid., 23 October 1933, http://www.fdrlibrary.marist.edu/_resources/images/morg/
    md00.pdf.

24 Ibid., 4 November 1933, http://www.fdrlibrary.marist.edu/_resources/images/morg/
    md00.pdf.

25 Warburg, James, *The Long Road Home: The Autobiography of a Maverick* (Garden City
    NY: Doubleday, 1964), 150; Blum, John Morton, ed. *From the Morgenthau Diaries:
    Years of Crisis, 1928–1938* (Boston: Houghton Mifflin, 1959), 74; 'The Economists', in
    MNDIS, 273 (comments of John Pehle).

26 *HMD-3*, 14 January 1935, http://www.fdrlibrary.marist.edu/_resources/images/morg/
    md0004.pdf.

27 'Money Bill Signed; Reserve Bank Gold Goes to Treasury', *NYT*, 31 January 1934.

28 'Proclamation 2072 – Fixing the Weight of the Gold Dollar', 31 January 1934, APP,
    https://www.presidency.ucsb.edu/node/208125.

29 Blum, *Morgenthau Diaries, 1928–1938*, 120–5; Friedman and Schwartz, *Monetary
    History of the United States*, 512–14; Rosen, *Roosevelt, the Great Depression and the
    Economics of Recovery*, 68–9.

30 FDR to Robert Bingham, 13 November 1933, *FDR: HPL-3*, 369; FDR, Memorandum
    for the Historical Record, 15 December 1933, *FDR: HPL-3*, 376.

31 FDR to House, 21 November 1933, *FDR: HPL-3*, 373; FDR to Vice President John
    Garner, 20 November 1934, *FDR: HPL-3*, 433.

32 Keynes, J. M., 'President Roosevelt's Gold Policy', *New Statesman and Nation*, 20 January 1934.

33 Frankfurter to Roosevelt, 16 December 1933, with 'Open Letter to the President', http://www.la.utexas.edu/users/hcleaver/368/368KeynesOpenLetFDRtable.pdf.

34 Keynes, J. M., 'From Keynes to Roosevelt: Our Recovery Plan Assayed', *NYT*, 31 December 1933.

35 Skidelsky, *John Maynard Keynes*, 507; *TRIK*, 225–6; Rauchway, *Money Makers*, 98–9. For commentary and documentation, see '"The Queer Personality and Floating Mind": What Did Keynes Say to and About Roosevelt?' 17 June 2013, https://crookedtimber.org/2013/06/17/the-queer-personality-and-floating-mind-what-did-keynes-say-to-and-about-roosevelt-2/.

36 'Message to Congress on the Budget', 15 May 1934, APP, https://www.presidency.ucsb.edu/node/208749; 'Press Conference #121, 14 May 1934', PCT, FDRL, http://www.fdrlibrary.marist.edu/_resources/images/pc/pc0007.pdf.

37 Krock, Arthur, 'In Washington: Hand of Keynes Is Seen in Revised Recovery Plan', *NYT*, 5 June 1934; *TD*, 288.

38 Douglas, 'Memorandum for the President', 11 April 1934 and Douglas notes, 'White House Conference', 23 April 1934, Lewis Douglas Paper [LDP], Box 236, Special Collections University of Arizona, Tucson; *SD-1* (30 June 1934), 174.

39 Pearson, F. R., W. I. Myers and A. F. Gans, 'Warren as Economic Adviser', *Farm Economics*, 211 (December 1957): 5597–676, esp. 5663–7, https://fraser.stlouisfed.org/title/3598.

40 Keynes, J. M., 'Sees Need for $400,000,000 Monthly to Speed Recovery', *NYT*, 10 June 1934; Douglas, 'Memorandum for the President', 6 June 1934, and 'Notes of White House Meeting', 11 June 1934, *LDP-236*.

41 Keynes, John Maynard, *The General Theory of Employment, Interest and Money* (London: Macmillan, 1936).

42 Hopkins quoted in *AoR-3*, 267.

43 Table 1.2: 'Summary of Receipts, Outlays, and Surpluses/Deficits as Percentage of GDP, 1930–2024', *Budget of the United States Government 2020: Historical Tables*, https://www.whitehouse.gov/wp-content/uploads/2019/03/hist-fy2020.pdf.

44 Douglas notes, 'White House Conference', 23 April 1934, *LDP-236*; 'Veto of the Bonus Bill', 22 May 1935, APP, https://www.presidency.ucsb.edu/node/208686.

45 Morgan, Iwan, *The Age of Deficits: Presidents and Balanced Budgets from Jimmy Carter to George W. Bush* (Lawrence: University Press of Kansas, 2009), 14–26.

46 Keynes, *General Theory*, 127.

47 Blum, *Morgenthau Diaries, 1928–1938*, 249–59; Zelizer, Julian, 'The Forgotten Legacy of the New Deal: Fiscal Conservatism and the Roosevelt Administration, 1933–1938', *Presidential Studies Quarterly*, 30 (June 2000): 331–58 (esp. 343–8).

48 'Annual Message to Congress', 3 January 1936, APP, https://www.presidency.ucsb.edu/node/20891; 'Address at Forbes Field, Pittsburgh, PA', 1 October 1936, APP, https://www.presidency.ucsb.edu/node/209177.

49 'Big July 4 a Good Business Omen', *Business Week*, 10 July 1937, 13.

50 Morgenthau, Henry, 'The Morgenthau Diaries: 1 – The Fight to Balance the Budget', *Collier's*, 27 September 1948, 12–13, 80–2 (quotation, p. 82); Blum, *Morgenthau Diaries, 1928–1938*, 275–83.

51 Eccles, Marriner, *Beckoning Frontiers: Public and Personal Recollections* (New York: Knopf, 1951), 81; Blum, *Morgenthau Diaries, 1928–1938*, 280.

52 'Group Meeting', *HMD-63*, 5 April 1937, 8–9, http://www.fdrlibrary.marist.edu/_resources/images/morg/md0085.pdf.

53 'Message to Congress on Appropriations for Work Relief for 1938', 20 April 1937, APP, https://www.presidency.ucsb.edu/node/209486; 'Diary Entry', *HMD-65*, 21 April 1937, 272, http://www.fdrlibrary.marist.edu/_resources/images/morg/md0085.

54 Velde, François, 'The Recession of 1937 – A Cautionary Tale', *Economic Perspectives*, 33 (2009): 16–37; Irwin, Douglas, 'Gold Sterilization and the Recession of 1937–1938', *Financial History Review*, 19 (December 2012): 249–67.

55 FDR to John Bankhead, 16 October 1937, and to John McCormack, 22 October 1937, in *FDR: HPL-3*, 717–18, 722.

56 *SD-2* (6 November 1937), 241: Brinkley, Alan, *The End of Reform: New Deal Liberalism in Recession and War* (New York: Knopf, 1995), 56–8.

57 Keynes to FDR, 1 February 1938, FDR to Keynes, 3 March 1938, reproduced at https://www.fdrlibrary.org/documents/356632/390886/smFDR-Keynes_1938.pdf/e6a5bbc6-db07-4d65-8576-e4ea058c5641.

58 *SD-2* (6 November 1937), 242.

59 Eccles, *Beckoning Frontiers*, 304; *SD-2* (13 February 1938), 317.

60 Eccles, Memo to FDR (undated), copy in HMD-112, http://www.fdrlibrary.marist.edu/_resources/images/morg/md0145.pdf.

61 Currie, Lauchlin, 'The Causes of the Recession', 1 April 1938, reproduced in *History of Political Economy*, 12, no. 3 (1980): 316–35; Brinkley, *End of Reform*, 95–7.

62 Morgenthau, 'Memorandum for the President', 10 April 1938, 'Group Meeting', 11 April 1938, 'Diary Entries', 11, 12 and 13 April, 1938, HMD-118, http://www.fdrlibrary.marist.edu/_resources/images/morg/md0156.pdf; Blum, *Morgenthau Diaries, 1928–1938*, 417–26.

63 'Message to Congress on Stimulating Recovery', 14 April 1938, APP, https://www.presidency.ucsb.edu/node/209601.

64 'Fireside Chat', 14 April 1938, APP, https://www.presidency.ucsb.edu/node/209619.

65 'Roosevelt's Expansion Program', *TNR*, 20 April 1938; Burns, James MacGregor, *Roosevelt: The Lion and the Fox* (New York: Harcourt, Brace, 1956), 328–36 (quotations, p. 330, 335).

66 Barber, *Designs within Disorder*, 117–20; Eccles, *Beckoning Frontiers*, 333.

67 Stein, Herbert, *The Fiscal Revolution in America: Policy in Pursuit of Reality*, 2nd rev. ed. (Washington, DC: AEI Press, 1996), 120–3; Gallup Survey, 'Government Spending', conducted 25–30 December 1938, http://ibiblio.org/pha/Gallup/Gallup%201939.htm.

68 FDR to O'Mahoney, 16 May 1939, PPF-1200, FDRL.

69 Barber, *Designs within Disorder*, 124. See, too, Hansen, Alvin, *Fiscal Policy and Business Cycles* (New York: Norton, 1941).

70 Keynes, J. M., 'The United States and the Keynes Plan', *TNR*, 29 July 1940, 158.

Chapter 5

1 F. M. Cotton to Franklin D. Rasenvelt [*sic*], 28 December 1934, PPF-30, FDRL.

2 Bethune, Mary McLeod, 'I'll Never Turn Back No More!' *Opportunity*, 16 (November 1938), 324.

3 Reid, Ira, *The Forgotten Tenth: An Analysis of Unemployment among Negroes and Its Social Costs, 1932–33* (New York: National Urban League, 1933).

4 Wilkins, Roy, with Tom Mathews, *Standing Fast: The Autobiography of Roy Wilkins* (New York: Penguin, 1984), 127.

5 Sitkoff, Harvard, *A New Deal for Blacks: The Emergence of Civil Rights as a National Issue: The Depression Decade* (New York: Oxford University Press, 1978), 40–1.

6 Topping, Simon, *Lincoln's Lost Legacy: The Republican Party and the African American Vote, 1928–1952* (Gainesville: University Press of Florida, 2008), 9–28.

7 Weiss, Nancy, *Farewell to the Party of Lincoln: Black Politics in the Age of FDR* (Princeton, NJ: Princeton University Press, 1983), 14–15.

8 Hawkins, John, 'Why the Negro Should Vote for Mr Hoover', *Crisis* (October 1932), 313–14.

9 Daniels, Roger, *Franklin D. Roosevelt: Road to the New Deal, 1882–1939* (Urbana: University of Illinois Press, 2015), 214.

10 For critical assessment of FDR's racial record, see O'Reilly, Kenneth, *Nixon's Piano: Presidents and Racial Politics from Washington to Clinton* (New York: Free Press, 1995), 109–44.

11 Rollins, Jr, Alfred, *Roosevelt and Howe* (New York: Knopf, 1962), 269; Sitkoff, *A New Deal for Blacks*, 44.

12 Salmond, John, '"Aubrey Williams Remembers": A Note on Franklin D. Roosevelt's Attitude toward Negro Rights', *Alabama Review*, XXV (January 1972), 68–9.

13 Davis, John, 'Blue Eagles and Black Workers', *TNR*, 14 November 1934, 9.

14 Quoted in Wolters, Raymond, *Negroes and the Great Depression: The Problem of Economic Recovery* (Westport, CT: Greenwood, 1970), 145.

15 Salmond, John, *The Civilian Conservation Corps, 1933–1942: A New Deal Case Study* (Duke, NC: Duke University Press, 1967), 88–99, 189–90.

16 Weiss, *Farewell to the Party of Lincoln*, 56.

17 Kruman, Marc, 'Quotas for Blacks: The Public Works Administration and the Black Construction Worker', *Labor History*, XVI (Winter 1975): 37–49.

18 Hughes, Langston, 'Ballad of Roosevelt', *TNR*, 14 November 1934, 9; Miller, Kelly, 'Howard Conference Denounces New Deal', *Chicago Defender*, 8 June 1935.

19 Weiss, *Farewell to the Party of Lincoln*, 212.

20 Washington, Forrester, 'The Negro and Relief', *Proceeding of the National Conference for Social Work* (1934), 190.

21 Weiss, *Farewell to the Party of Lincoln*, 211.

22 Wolters, *Negroes and the Great Depression*, 203–9; *FFF*, 254 (quotation).

23 Terkel, Studs, *Hard Times: An Oral History of the Great Depression* (New York: Pantheon, 1970), 115.

24 Sitkoff, *New Deal for Blacks*, 72–3.

25 Oliver, Paul, *Blues Fell This Morning: Meaning in the Blues* (Cambridge: Cambridge University Press, 1990), 38.

26 Gladys Carroll to Roosevelt, 9 December 1935, PPF-3056, FDRL.

27 Weiss, *Farewell to the Party of Lincoln*, 174.

28 Associated Press, 'Sylvester Wins Objective: Puts in Repeated Phone Calls to President Until He Gets Him; Saves Farm' (as appeared on the front page of *Akron Beacon Journal*, 28 February 1934), https://www.newspapers.com/clip/17816920/sylvester_harris_story/.

29 White, Walter, *A Man Called White: The Autobiography of Walter White* (New York: Viking, 1948), 199.

30 Kirby, John, *Black Americans in the Roosevelt Era: Liberalism and Race* (Knoxville: University of Tennessee Press, 1980), 110–23.

31 Beasley, Maureen, *Eleanor Roosevelt: Transformative First Lady* (Lawrence: University Press of Kansas, 2010), 110–11, 121–2, 127–31.

32 *Afro-American*, 27 April 1935.

33 Holt, Rackham, *Mary McLeod Bethune: A Biography* (Garden City, NY: Doubleday, 1964), 193; Bethune, Mary McLeod, 'My Secret Talks With FDR', *Ebony* (April 1949): 42–51.

34 Tugwell, Rexford, *The Democratic Roosevelt: A Biography of Franklin D. Roosevelt* (Garden City, NY: Doubleday, 1957), 303; Roosevelt, Eleanor, 'Some of My Best Friends Are Negroes', Ebony (February 1953): 26.

35 Lash, Joseph, *Eleanor and Franklin: The Story of Their Relationship* (New York: Norton, 1971), 516.

36 Roosevelt, Eleanor, 'Freedom: Promise or Fact', *Negro Digest*, I (October 1943): 9.

37 Editorial, *Chicago Defender*, 4 March 1939.

38 'Address at the Dedication of the New Chemistry Building, Howard University, Washington, DC', 26 October 1936, APP, https://www.presidency.ucsb.edu/node/208355.

39 Resolution reproduced in *NYT*, 22 September 1936. For the event, see High, Stanley, 'Black Omens', *Saturday Evening Post*, 4 June 1938, 14.

40 Stokes, Carl, *Promises of Power: A Political Autobiography* (New York: Simon & Schuster, 1973), 23–5.

41 Robert Weaver and Charlotte Moton Hubbard oral histories in *MNDIS*, 260–6.

42 'Lynchings: By Year and Race', http://law2.umkc.edu/faculty/projects/ftrials/shipp/lynchingyear.html.

43 'Address before the Federal Churches of Christ in America', 6 December 1933, APP, https://www.presidency.ucsb.edu/node/207887; Editorial, *Crisis*, XLI (January 1934), 20.

44 White, *A Man Called White*, 169–70; 'Press Conference #125, 25 May 1934', PCT, FDRL, http://www.fdrlibrary.marist.edu/_resources/images/pc/pc0008.pdf.

45 O'Reilly, *Nixon's Piano*, 117.

46 ER to White, 19 March 1936, Selected Digitalized Correspondence of Eleanor Roosevelt, http://www.fdrlibrary.marist.edu/_resources/images/ersel/ersel098c.pdf.

47 Weiss, *Farewell to the Party of Lincoln*, 241.

48 Sitkoff, *A New Deal for Blacks*, 293.

49 Barkley quoted in *Pittsburgh Courier*, 19 October 1940; Zangrando, Robert, *The NAACP Crusade against Lynching, 1909–1950* (Philadelphia: Temple University Press, 1980), 165.

50 *Congressional Record*, HR, 1st Session, 15 April 1937, 3550; Katznelson, Ira, *Fear Itself: The New Deal and the Origins of Our Time* (New York: Liveright, 2013), 179–82.

51 Arsenault, Raymond, *The Sound of Freedom: Marian Anderson, the Lincoln Memorial, and the Concert That Awakened America* (New York: Bloomsbury, 2009), esp. 145–68.

52 White, *A Man Called White*, 181–2; Anderson, Marian, *My Lord, What a Morning: An Autobiography* (New York: Viking, 1956), 189.

53 Quoted in Sitkoff, *A New Deal for Blacks*, 327.

54 Arsenault, *Sound of Freedom*, 159–61. For video and sound recording, made by the Department of the Interior, see 'Marian Anderson Performs on the National Mall', *National Geographic*, https://www.nationalgeographic.org/media/marian-anderson-concert/.

55 White, *A Man Called White*, 184–5; Bethune quotation in Arsenault, *Sound of Freedom*, 163.

56 O'Reilly, *Nixon's Piano*, 122–3.

57 Editorials, *Pittsburgh Courier*, 24 and 31 August 1940.

58 NAACP press release, 5 October 1940, 'Details of White House Conference on the Army-Navy-Industry Discrimination against Negroes Revealed', OF93-3, FDRL.

59 NAACP Press Release, 11 October 1940, 'White House Charged with Trickery in Announcing Jim Crow Policy of Army', OF93-3, FDRL; 'White House Blesses Jim Crow', *Crisis* (November 1940), 350–1, 357.

60 Editorials, *Chicago Defender*, 12 and 26 October, 2 November 1940; White quoted in Ibid., 1 April 1939.

61 Randolph, Philip, 'Call to Negro America to March on Washington for Jobs and Equal Participation in National Defense', *Black Worker* (May 1941).

62 For MOWM, see Lucander, David, *Winning the War for Democracy: The March on Washington Movement, 1941–1946* (Urbana: University of Illinois Press, 2014).

63 White, *A Man Called White*, 189–92.

64 'Proposals of the March-on-Washington Committee for President Roosevelt's Urgent Consideration', OF-391, FDRL; White, *A Man Called White*, 192–3; Rauh, interview, in Studs Terkel, *The Good War: An Oral History of World War II* (New York: Pantheon, 1984), 337–42.

65 'Executive Order 8802 – Reaffirming Policy of Full Participation in the Defense Program by All Persons, Regardless of Race, Creed, Color, or National Origin, and Directing Certain Action in Furtherance of Said Policy', 25 June 1941, APP, https://www.presidency.ucsb.edu/node/209704.

66 Randolph, Philip, 'The Negro March on Washington', *Black Worker*, July 1941.

67 Randolph, Philip, 'Why Should We March?', *Survey Graphic*, November 1942, 489.

68 'Executive Order 9346 Establishing a Committee on Fair Employment Practice', 27 May 1943, APP, https://www.presidency.ucsb.edu/node/210091; Reed, Merl, *Seedtime for the Modern Civil Rights Movement: The President's Committee on Fair Employment Practice, 1941–1946* (Baton Rouge: Louisiana State University Press, 1991), 345.

69 White to FDR, 21 June 1943, and FDR to Murray, 14 July 1943, OF93-C, FDRL; Wynn, Neil, *The Afro American and the Second World War* (London: Elek, 1976), 112–14; Klein, Maury, *A Call to Arms: Mobilizing America for World War II* (New York: Bloomsbury, 2013), 611–18.

70 For this, see McMahon, Kevin, *Reconsidering Roosevelt on Race: How the Presidency Paved the Road to Brown* (Chicago: University of Chicago Press, 2004).

71 Wilkins quoted in Weiss, *Farewell to the Party of Lincoln*, 222; Glass quoted in Patterson, James T., *Congressional Conservatism and the New Deal: The Growth of the Conservative Coalition in Congress, 1933–1939* (Lexington: University Press of Kentucky, 1967), 98.

72 Oliver, *Blues Fell This Morning*, 261–2.

Chapter 6

1 Gulick, Luther, 'Politics, Administration, and the New Deal', *Annals*, 169 (September 1933): 55–66 (quotation, p. 64).

2 Nathan, Richard, *The Administrative Presidency* (New York: Wiley, 1983); Burke, John, *The Institutional Presidency* (Baltimore: Johns Hopkins University Press, 1992).

3 Brownlow, Louis, *The President and the Presidency* (Chicago: Public Administration Service, 1949), 62; Brownlow, Louis, *A Passion for Anonymity* (Chicago: University of Chicago Press, 1958), 384.

4 *AoR-2*, 511–13.

5   Wann, A. J., *The President as Chief Administrator: A Study of Franklin D. Roosevelt* (Washington, DC: Public Affairs, 1968), 34, 196 n. 7.

6   Brownlow, *President and Presidency*, 61–2.

7   *TM*, 15–16.

8   *AoR-2*, 528.

9   Richberg, Donald, *My Hero: The Indiscreet Memoirs of an Eventful but Unheroic Life* (New York: Putnam, 1954), 166.

10 *AoR-2*, 535.

11 Tully, Grace, *FDR, My Boss* (New York: Scribner, 1949), 170.

12 *SD-1* (27 October 1935), 446–61.

13 *TRIK*, 359.

14 'Proceedings of the National Emergency Council', 11 December 1934, in Seligman, Lester, and Elmer Cornwell, eds., *New Deal Mosaic: Roosevelt Confers with his National Emergency Council* (Eugene: Oregon University Books, 1965), 355–7.

15 Dickinson, Matthew, *Bitter Harvest: FDR, Presidential Power, and the Growth of the Presidential Branch* (New York: Cambridge University Press, 1997), 45–52 (quotation, p. 45).

16 *AoR-2*, 518–20; *SD-1* (3 March 1935), 308.

17 Quoted in *AoR-2*, 539.

18 Dickinson, *Bitter Harvest*, 52–3.

19 'Proceedings of the National Emergency Council', 19 December 1933, in Seligman and Cornwell, *New Deal Mosaic*, 3.

20 'Executive Order 6433-A – Creation of the National Emergency Council', 17 November 1933, APP, https://www.presidency.ucsb.edu/node/207827.

21 'Richberg Put Over Cabinet in New Emergency Council. . . Now No. 1 Man', *NYT*, 1 November 1934; FDR to Early, 3 November 1934, quoted in *AoR-2*, 546–7; 'Assistant President?' *Time*, 12 November 1934.

22 *SD-1* (4 November 1934), 220–1 (11 December 1934), 242–3.

23 For FDR's administrative experimentation, see Dickinson, *Bitter Harvest*, 52–8, 71–9.

24 Dickinson, Matthew, and Andrew Rudalevige, '"Worked Out in Fractions": Neutral Competence, FDR, and the Bureau of the Budget', *Congress and the Presidency*, 34 (Spring 2007): 1–26 (esp. 3–6); 'Press Conference #77, 13 December 1933', http://www.fdrlibrary.marist.edu/_resources/images/pc/pc0201.pdf.

25 *SD-1* (6 January 1934), 134–6.

26 *TD* (21 April 1933), 340.

27 For presidential interactions with the pair, see Marvin McIntyre to Rudolph Foster, 7 September 1934, FDR, Memorandum to Thomas Corcoran, 8 November 1935, and FDR to Benjamin Cohen, 14 May 1936, *FDR: HPC-3*, 420, 518, 590–1.

28 Janeway, Michael, *The Fall of the House of Roosevelt: Brokers of Ideas and Power from FDR to LBJ* (New York: Columbia University Press, 2004), 13–43.

29 Frank Watson oral history, *MNDIS*, 105–10 (quotation, p. 108). See, too, commentaries by other members of the Corcoran-Cohen group, Joseph Rauh, Jr. and Kenneth Crawford, 110–18.

30 *Congressional Record*, 73rd Congress, Session II, 7086–7; Loucheim, Katie, 'The Little Red House', *VQR*, 56 (Winter 1980), https://www.vqronline.org/articles/little-red-house.

31 Janeway, *Fall of the House of Roosevelt*, 21–2.

32 *WWR*, 197.

33 Quoted in Lash, Joseph, *Dealers and Dreamers: A New Look at the New Deal* (New York: Doubleday, 1988), 230.

34 Beasley, Maurine, *Eleanor Roosevelt: Transformative First Lady* (Lawrence: University Press of Kansas, 2010), 124.
35 Lash, Joseph, *Eleanor and Franklin: The Story of Their Relationship* (New York: 1971), 49.
36 Tully, *FDR*, 107.
37 *SD-1* (23 March 1935), 325.
38 Neustadt, Richard, *Presidential Power and the Modern Presidents: The Politics of Leadership from Roosevelt to Reagan* (New York: Free Press, 1990), 132; James Rowe oral history, *MNDIS*, 285.
39 Roosevelt, Eleanor, *This I Remember* (New York: Harper, 1949), 113, 145, 167.
40 Smith, Kathryn, *The Gatekeeper: Missy LeHand, FDR and the Untold Story of the Partnership that Defined a Presidency* (New York: Touchstone, 2016), 127–40.
41 Barkley, Alben, *That Reminds Me* (New York: Doubleday, 1954), 144.
42 *TRIK*, 164.
43 *WWR*, 131.
44 Brownlow, *A Passion for Anonymity*, 335–6.
45 Brownlow, *President and Presidency*, 106.
46 Dickinson, *Bitter Harvest*, 95–104.
47 Brownlow, *President and Presidency*, 105–6, and *Passion for Anonymity*, 381–2.
48 President's Committee on Administrative Management, *Administrative Management in the Government of the United States* (Washington, DC: Government Printing Office, 1937) (quotations, p. 2 and 3).
49 Hamilton, Alexander, 'The Executive Department Further Considered', *The Federalist*, LXX, in *The Constitution of the United States and Selected Writings of the Founding Fathers* (New York: Barnes & Noble, 2012), 568–9.
50 PCAM, *Administrative Management*, 5.
51 'Summary of the Report of the Committee on Administrative Management', 12 January 1937, APP, https://www.presidency.ucsb.edu/node/209074.
52 Brownlow, *Passion for Anonymity*, 390. For meeting notes, see Emmerich, Herbert, *Federal Organization and Administrative Management* (Birmingham: University of Alabama Press, 1971), Appendix I.
53 'Message to Congress Recommending Reorganization of the Executive Branch', 12 January 1937, APP, https://www.presidency.ucsb.edu/node/209079.
54 Polenberg, Richard, *Reorganizing Roosevelt's Government: The Controversy over Executive Reorganization, 1936–1939* (Cambridge, MA: Harvard University Press, 1966), chapter 10.
55 Roosevelt to Byrnes, 26 July 1937, *FDR: HPL-3*, 696.
56 Brownlow, *Passion for Anonymity*, 414–29; Harold Smith, 'Daily Memoranda and Records of Conferences with the President', 28 July 1939, Smith Diary, FDRL; *R&H*, 72–3.
57 Smith Diary, 21 July 1939, *FDRL*; Dickinson and Rudalevige, 'Worked Out in Fractions', 10–22.
58 Rowe in *MNDIS*, 284–5; Dickinson, *Bitter Harvest*, 104–13.
59 *R&H*, 208.
60 'Executive Order 8248 Reorganizing the Executive Office of the President', 8 September 1939, APP, https://www.presidency.ucsb.edu/node/210008.
61 Brownlow, *Passion for Anonymity*, 431.
62 Dickinson, *Bitter Harvest*, 119–32.

63 Polenberg, Richard, *War and Society: The United States, 1941–1945* (Philadelphia: J. B. Lippincott, 1972), 6–7; Brownlow, *Passion for Anonymity*, 424–7 (quotation, p. 425).

64 *SD-3* (2 June 1940), 194. A full transcript of the meeting is erroneously filed among FDR's press conference transcripts as 'PC #647-A', PCT, FDRL. http://www.fdrlibrary .marist.edu/_resources/images/pc/pc0099.pdf.

65 'Special Press Conference #703-A, 20 December 1940', PCT, FDRL. http://www .fdrlibrary.marist.edu/_resources/images/pc/pc0111.pdf.

66 'Executive Order 8875 Establishing the Supply Priorities and Allocations Board', 28 August 1941, APP, https://www.presidency.ucsb.edu/node/209914; Nelson, Donald, *Arsenal of Democracy: The Story of American War Production* (New York: Harcourt, Brace, 1946), 159–70.

67 Larrabee, Eric, *Commander in Chief: Franklin Delano Roosevelt, His Lieutenants, and Their War* (London: Andre Deutsch, 1987), 307–8; *TM*, 81.

68 Stoler, Mark, *George C. Marshall: Soldier-Statesman of the American Century* (Boston: Twayne, 1989), 65–6.

69 FDR to Stark, 22 March 1939, *FDR: HPL-4*, 864; Stark, Harold, *Plan Dog Memo*, 12 November 1940, https://en.wikisource.org/wiki/Plan_dog_memo; Dunn, Susan, *A Blueprint for War: FDR and the Hundred Days That Mobilized America* (New York: Oxford University Press, 2018), 44–9.

70 Pogue, Forrest, *George C. Marshall. Vol. 2: Ordeal and Hope, 1939–1942* (New York: Penguin, 1965), 46–79.

71 Dunn, *Blueprint for War*, 31–3.

72 Pogue, *Ordeal and Hope*, 19–23.

73 *SD-3* (9 June 1940), 202.

74 Cline, Ray, *Washington Command Post: The Operations Division* (Washington, DC: Center for Military History, 2003 – reprint of 1951 original), 45.

75 Larrabee, *Commander in Chief*, 167; FDR to Stimson, 26 February 1942, copy, Harry Hopkins Papers, Organization of Military Forces File, FDRL.

76 *R&H*, 2–3, 159.

77 Roll, David, *The Hopkins Touch: Harry Hopkins and the Forging of the Alliance to Defeat Hitler* (New York: Oxford University Press, 2012), 52–5, 406–9.

78 *R&H*, 243 (full text of letter, 243–6).

79 *R&H*, 269, 948–9.

80 Roosevelt to Hopkins, 27 March 1941, OF-4117, FDRL.

81 'Executive Order 8751 Establishing the Division of Defense Aid Reports', 2 May 1941, APP, https://www.presidency.ucsb.edu/node/209560.

82 FDR to Hopkins, 26 July 1941, *FDR: HPL-4*, 1189; *R&H*, 326–45.

83 *SD-3* (2 August 1941), 592; HMD-427, 4 August 1941 (quotation), http://www .fdrlibrary.marist.edu/_resources/images/morg/mpd11.pdf.

84 Stimson Diary, 4 August 1941, quoted in Jordan, Jonathan, *The Warlords: How Roosevelt's High Command Led America to Victory in World War II* (New York: NAL Caliber, 2015), 82.

85 FDR to Wayne Coy, 2 August 1941, FDR to Stimson, memorandum 30 August 1941, *FDR: HPL-4*, 1195–6, 1201–2.

86 Roll, *The Hopkins Touch*, 152–3; Butler, Susan, ed., *My Dear Mr. Stalin: The Complete Correspondence of Franklin D. Roosevelt and Joseph V. Stalin* (Princeton, NJ: Princeton University Press, 2005), 12.

87 Stimson Diary, 18 December 1940, quoted in Jordan, *Warlords*, 53.

88 *R&H*, 72–3.

Chapter 7

1 Radio Address on Collier's Hour, 'States' Rights', 2 March 1930, MSF-367, FDRL, http://www.fdrlibrary.marist.edu/_resources/images/msf/msf00371.

2 'Inaugural Address', 4 March 1933, APP, https://www.presidency.ucsb.edu/node /208712.

3 'Gridiron Speeches', 14 April 1934, MSF-1581, FDRL http://www.fdrlibrary.marist .edu/_resources/images/msf/msf01467.

4 Frankfurter, Felix, 'The United States Supreme Court Molding the Constitution', *Current History*, 32 (May 1930): 240.

5 *TM*, 59.

6 'Address on Constitution Day, Washington, DC', 17 September 1937, APP, https:// www.presidency.ucsb.edu/node/208747.

7 'Reading Copy: Washington DC – Constitution Day Address', 17 September 1937, 13, MSF-1072, FDRL, http://www.fdrlibrary.marist.edu/_resources/images/msf/msf01104.

8 Byrnes, James, *All in One Lifetime* (New York: Harper, 1958), 65.

9 *TM*, 74.

10 'Fireside Chat', 30 September 1934, APP, https://www.presidency.ucsb.edu/node/208160.

11 Kammen, Michael, *A Machine That Would Go of Itself: The Constitution in American Culture* (New York: St Martin's, 1994), 260–6.

12 Parrish, Michael, *The Hughes Court: Justices, Rulings and Legacy* (Santa Barbara, CA: ABC-CLIO, 2002), 101–6; Leuchtenburg, William, 'Charles Evans Hughes: The Center Holds', *North Carolina Law Review* 83 (2005): 1187, https://scholarship.law.unc.edu/ nclr/vol83/iss5/3/.

13 Parrish, *Hughes Court*, 13–15, 56–67, 73–85.

14 Parrish, *Hughes Court*, 67–73, 85–90, 106–13.

15 McKenna, Marian, *Franklin D. Roosevelt and the Great Constitutional War: The Court-Packing Crisis of 1937* (New York: Fordham University Press, 2002), 1–11; Shesol, Jeff, *Supreme Power: Franklin Roosevelt vs. The Supreme Court* (New York: Norton, 2010), 43 (FDR quotation).

16 Stone to Frankfurter, 17 May 1933, copy in OF10-27, FDRL.

17 Carter, John Franklin, *The New Dealers* (New York: Simon & Schuster, 1934), 261–2.

18 Shesol, *Supreme Power*, 99. For a slightly revised draft, see *FDR: HPL-3*, 456–60.

19 Hart, Henry, 'The Gold Clause in United States Bonds', *Harvard Law Review* 48 (May 1935): 1057–99.

20 FDR to Kennedy, 19 February 1935, *FDR: HPL-3*, 455; FDR to Angus MacLean, 21 February 1935, OF10F-29, FDRL.

21 'The Solicitor General', *MNDIS*, 78–104.

22 Leuchtenburg, William, *The Supreme Court Reborn: The Constitutional Revolution in the Age of Roosevelt* (New York: Oxford University Press, 1995), 26–51 (quotations, p. 45, 48, 50); 'A Dred Scott Decision', *TNR*, 22 May 1935, 34–5.

23 Leuchtenburg, *Supreme Court Reborn*, 52–81 (Jackson quotation, p. 79).

24 *A.L.A. Schechter Poultry Corp. v United States*, 295 U.S. 495 (1935), https://supreme .justia.com/cases/federal/us/295/495/; Brandeis quoted in Hiltzik, Michael, *The New Deal: A Modern History* (New York: Free Press, 2011), 282.

25 'Press Conference #209, 31 May 1935', PCT, FDRL, http://www.fdrlibrary.marist.edu/ _resources/images/pc/pc0022.pdf.

26 Creel, George, 'Looking Ahead with Roosevelt', *Collier's*, 7 September 1935, 7–8.
27 *United States v. Butler*, 297 U.S. 1 (1936), https://supreme.justia.com/cases/federal/us /297/1/; *AoR-3*, 470–4.
28 See, in particular, Cushner, Barry, *Rethinking the New Deal Court: The Structure of a Constitutional Revolution* (New York: Oxford University Press, 1998).
29 Leuchtenburg, *Supreme Court Reborn*, 215.
30 Stone quoted in Mason, Alpheus, *Harlan Fiske Stone: Pillar of the Law* (New York: Viking Press, 1956), 411–12, 417.
31 McKenna, *Great Constitutional War*, 180–217.
32 *SD-1* (29 January 1936), 530.
33 *SD-1* (13 November 1935), 468, (27 December 1935), 494–5.
34 Pearson, Drew, and Robert Allen, *The Nine Old Men* (Garden City, NY: Doubleday, Doran, 1936).
35 Cummings, Homer, and Carl McFarland, *Federal Justice: Chapters in the History of Justice and the Federal Executive* (New York: Macmillan, 1937), 531.
36 Shesol, *Supreme Power*, 251–8 (quotation, p. 257).
37 FDR to Patterson, 9 November 1936, *FDR: HPL-3*, 625.
38 *WWR*, 141.
39 'Message to Congress on the Reorganization of the Judicial Branch of the Government', 5 February 1937, APP, https://www.presidency.ucsb.edu/node/209236; *WWR*, 143–6 (quotation, p. 144).
40 Shesol, *Supreme* Power, 315–24.
41 Caldeira, Gregory, 'Public Opinion and the U.S. Supreme Court: FDR's Court-Packing Plan', *American Political Science Review*, 81 (December 1987): 1139–53.
42 'Address at the Democratic Victory Dinner. Washington, DC', 4 March 1937, APP, https://www.presidency.ucsb.edu/node/209418.
43 'Fireside Chat', 9 March 1937, APP, https://www.presidency.ucsb.edu/node/209434.
44 Roberts, Owen, *The Court and the Constitution: The Oliver Wendell Holmes Lectures* (Cambridge, MA: Harvard University Press, 1951), 61.
45 The scholarship of William Leuchtenburg strongly informs this analysis: 'Charles Evans Hughes: The Center Holds'; and 'When the People Spoke, What Did They Say?: The Election of 1936 and the Ackerman Thesis', *Yale Law Journal*, 108 (1999), https:// digitalcommons.law.yale.edu/ylj/vol108/iss8/8; *Supreme Court Reborn*, 163–79.
46 McKenna, *Great Constitutional War*, 423–37.
47 Alsop, Joseph, and Turner Catledge, *The 168 Days* (Garden City, NY: Doubleday, Doran, 1938), 237.
48 'Robinson Will Not Do', *The Nation*, 29 May 1937, 607–8.
49 McKenna, *Great Constitutional War*, 484.
50 Senate Committee on the Judiciary, *S. 1392, Reorganization of the Federal Judiciary, Senate Report No. 711*, 75th Congress, 1st Session, 23; Leuchtenburg, William, 'FDR's Court Packing Plan: A Second Life, a Second Death', *Duke Law Journal* (1985): 673–89, https://scholarship.law.duke.edu/dlj/vol34/iss3/4.
51 'Outing Promises Gain in Good-Will', *NYT*, 28 June 1937.
52 McKenna, *Great Constitutional War*, 488–521; Shesol, *Supreme Power*, 461–500.
53 Quoted in Gerhart, Eugene, *America's Advocate: Robert H. Jackson* (Indianapolis: Bobbs Merrill, 1958), 117.
54 Hughes, Charles E., *Addresses of Charles Evans Hughes* (New York: Putnam, 1916), 185–6.
55 Mason, Alpheus, *The Supreme Court from Taft to Warren* (Baton Rouge: Louisiana State University Press, 1968), 124–5.

56 Leuchtenburg, *Supreme Court Reborn*, 233.

57 Robert Stern oral history, *MNDIS*, 80.

58 Parrish, *Hughes Court*, 146.

59 Chen, James, 'Filburn's Legacy', *Emory Law Journal*, 52, 1719 (2003), https://papers .ssrn.com/sol3/papers.cfm?abstract_id=901026.

60 *Sunshine Anthracite Coal Company v. Adkins, Collector of Internal Revenue*, 381 (1940) (quotation, p. 396), https://scholar.google.co.uk/scholar_case?case=10237101119 751433897&hl=en&as_sdt=6&as_vis=1&oi=scholarr.

61 *United States v. Darby*, 312 US 100 (1941) (quotation, p. 124), https://scholar.google .com/scholar_case?case=1183543472021488573.

62 Urofsky, Melvin, 'The Roosevelt Court', in William Chafe, ed., *The Achievements of American Liberalism: The New Deal and Its Legacies* (New York: Columbia University Press, 2003), 73–4.

63 Harrison, Robert, 'The Breakup of the Roosevelt Supreme Court: A Contribution of History and Biography', *Law and History Review*, 2 (1984): 165–221 (quotations, p. 198, 193).

64 McMahon, Kevin, *Reconsidering Roosevelt on Race: How the Presidency Paved the Road to Brown* (Chicago: University of Chicago Press, 2004), 110–12 (quotation, p. 111).

65 Breen, Daniel, 'Stanley Forman Reed', in Melvin Urofsky, ed., *The Supreme Court Justices: A Biographical Dictionary* (New York: Garland, 1994), 367–72.

66 Urofsky, Melvin, *Felix Frankfurter, Judicial Restraint and Individual Liberties* (New York: Twayne, 1991).

67 Urofsky, Melvin, 'William O. Douglas as a Common Law Judge', *Duke Law Journal*, 41 (1991): 133, https://scholarship.law.duke.edu/cgi/viewcontent.cgi?article=3163 &context=dlj.

68 Howard, Jr, Woodford, *Mr. Justice Murphy: A Political Biography* (Princeton: Princeton University Press, 1968); Parrish, *Hughes Court*, 122–4.

69 Shesol, *Supreme Power*, 6.

70 McMahon, *Reconsidering Roosevelt on Race*, 133–6.

71 Jackson, Robert, *The Struggle for Judicial Supremacy: A Study of a Crisis in American Power Politics* (New York: Knopf, 1941); Urofsky, Melvin, *Division and Discord: The Supreme Court under Stone and Vinson* (Columbia: University of South Carolina Press, 1997), 25–8.

72 Urofsky, *Division and Discord*, 85–110.

73 Harrison, 'Breakup of the Roosevelt Court', 288–91; McMahon, *Reconsidering Roosevelt on Race*, 138–40 (quotation, p. 138).

74 'Address on Constitution Day, Washington, DC', 17 September 1937, APP, https:// www.presidency.ucsb.edu/node/208747.

Chapter 8

1 Douglas, Paul, *The Coming of a New Party* (New York: McGraw-Hill, 1932), 168–70.

2 Rotunda, Ronald, 'The "Liberal" Label: Roosevelt's Capture of a Symbol', in John Montgomery and Albert Hirschman, eds., *Public Policy* (Cambridge, MA: Harvard University Press, 1968), 377–408.

3 Roosevelt to Herbert Nixon, 27 February 1931, New York Governor Papers, box 60, FDRL.

4 'Radio Address From Albany, New York: "The Forgotten Man Speech"', 7 April 1932, APP, https://www.presidency.ucsb.edu/node/288092.

5 *AoR-1*, 306–7.

6 Farley, Jim, *Jim Farley's Story: The Roosevelt Years* (New York: Whittlesey House, 1947), 19–27.

7 'Address Accepting the Presidential Nomination at the Democratic National Convention in Chicago', 2 July 1932, APP, https://www.presidency.ucsb.edu/node /275484. For the campaign, see Ritchie, Donald, *Electing FDR: The New Deal Campaign of 1932* (Lawrence: University Press of Kansas, 2007).

8 *AoR-1*, 468.

9 'Campaign Address at Madison Square Garden in New York City', 5 November 1932, APP, https://www.presidency.ucsb.edu/node/288089; Lindley, Ernest, *The Roosevelt Revolution: First Phase* (New York: Viking, 1933), 10.

10 'The Week', *TNR*, 16 November 1932, 1.

11 For excellent analysis, see Milkis, Sidney, *The President and the Parties: The Transformation of the Party System since the New Deal* (New York: Oxford University Press, 1993), 52–74.

12 Roosevelt, Franklin D., *On Our Way* (New York: John Day, 1934), 248.

13 Scroop, Daniel, *Mr Democrat: Jim Farley, the New Deal, and the Making of Modern American Politics* (Ann Arbor: University of Michigan Press, 2006), 143–90.

14 Savage, Sean, *Roosevelt the Party Leader 1932–1945* (Lexington: University Press of Kentucky, 1991), 91–4.

15 Farley and Dewson to State Democratic Women Leaders, 19 December 1934, Molly Dewson Papers, box 2, FDRL.

16 For Dewson, see Ware, Susan, *Partner and I: Molly Dewson, Feminism and New Deal Politics* (New Haven, CT: Yale University Press, 1987).

17 Dewson to FDR, 29 May 1935, OF-300, FDRL.

18 Dewson to FDR, 18 April 1936, OF-300, FDRL.

19 Dewson to FDR, 15 December 1934, Molly Dewson Papers, box 4, FDRL.

20 Scroop, *Mr Democrat*, 114–15. See, too, Zieger, Robert, *The Rise of the CIO, 1935–1955* (Chapel Hill: University of North Carolina Press, 1997), esp. chapters 2–5.

21 Leuchtenburg, William, *The FDR Years: On Roosevelt & His Legacy* (New York: Columbia University Press, 1995), 132.

22 Overacker, Louise, 'Campaign Funds in the Presidential Election of 1936', *American Political Science Review* 31 (June 1937): 473–98; Gerstle, Gary, *Liberty and Coercion: The Paradox of American Government from the Founding to the Present* (Princeton, NJ: Princeton University Press, 2015), 244–5.

23 Savage, *Roosevelt the Party Leader*, 94–5.

24 Weaver, Robert, 'The Black Cabinet', in *MNDIS*, 261–4.

25 FDR to Farley, 24 April 1939, quoted in Milkis, The *President and the Parties*, 56–7.

26 'Remarks at the Ground-Breaking Ceremonies of the Queens Midtown Tunnel, New York City', 2 October 1936, APP, http://www.presidency.ucsb.edu/ws/?pid =15152.

27 Berle to FDR, 2 September 1937, Adolf Berle Papers, Box 10, FDRL; Schwarz, Jordan, *Liberal: Adolf A. Berle and the Vision of an American Era* (New York: Free Press, 1987), 91–103.

28 Flynn, Edward, *You're the Boss* (New York: Viking Press, 1947), 141.

29 Leuchtenburg, *The FDR Years*, 150.

30 Savage, *Roosevelt the Party Leader*, 48–79.

31 Van Riper, Paul, *History of the United States Civil Service* (Evanston, IL: Row, Peterson, 1958), 318–29.

32 Carter, John Franklin, *1940* (New York: Viking Press, 1940), 31–2.

33 Flynn, *You're the Boss*, 153.

34 Roosevelt to Colonel Edward House, 10 March 1934, in *FDR: HPL-3*, 394.

35 'Fireside Chat', 28 June 1934, APP, https://www.presidency.ucsb.edu/node/208443; Ritchie, *Electing FDR*, 184–5.

36 Sitkoff, Harvard, *A New Deal for Blacks: The Emergence of Civil Rights as a National Issue: The Depression Decade* (New York: Oxford University Press, 1978), 88–90.

37 Quoted in Maney, Patrick, *The Roosevelt Presence: The Life and Legacy of FDR* (Berkeley: University of California Press, 1998), 83.

38 'Annual Message to Congress', 3 January 1936, APP, https://www.presidency.ucsb.edu/node/208916.

39 'Acceptance Speech for the Renomination of the Presidency, Philadelphia, PA', 27 June 1936, APP, https://www.presidency.ucsb.edu/node/208917.

40 'Address at the Madison Square Garden, New York City', 31 October 1936, APP, https://www.presidency.ucsb.edu/node/208385.

41 Wolfskill, George and John Hudson, *All But the People: Franklin D. Roosevelt and His Critics, 1933–1939* (New York: Macmillan, 1969), 159.

42 Wolfskill and Hudson, *All But the People*, 160–6 (quotation, p. 166).

43 Farley, James, *Behind the Ballots: The Personal History of a Politician* (New York: Harcourt, Brace, 1938), 249–50.

44 Leuchtenburg, *The FDR Years*, 145–6, 154–8.

45 High, Stanley, 'Whose Party Is It?' *Saturday Evening Post*, 6 February 1937, 10–11.

46 Patterson, James, *Congressional Conservatism and the New Deal: The Growth of the Conservative Coalition in Congress, 1933–1939* (Lexington: University Press of Kentucky, 1967), 339–52.

47 Dunn, Susan, *Roosevelt's Purge: How FDR Fought to Change the Democratic Party* (Cambridge, MA: Belknap Press, 2010), 81–92 (quotation, p. 82).

48 Savage, *Roosevelt the Party Leader*, 120–3; Milkis, *The President and the Parties*, 69–71 (quotation, p. 71).

49 Bailey quoted in Patterson, *Congressional Conservatism*, 191.

50 Badger, Anthony, *New Deal/New South* (Lafayette: University of Arkansas Press, 2007), 58–71.

51 'Address at the Jackson Day Dinner, Washington, DC', 8 January 1938, APP, https://www.presidency.ucsb.edu/node/209617; Dunn, *Roosevelt's Purge*, 97–9.

52 Pepper, Claude, *Pepper: Eyewitness to a Century* (New York: Harcourt Brace Jovanovich, 1987), 52–73 (quotation, p. 66); Roosevelt to Arthur Murray, 13 May 1938, *FDR:HPL-4*, 781; Savage, *Roosevelt the Party Leader*, 133–4.

53 'Fireside Chat', 24 June 1938, APP, https://www.presidency.ucsb.edu/node/208978.

54 Dunn, *Roosevelt's Purge*, 120–46.

55 Belair, Felix, 'Not Interfering', *NYT*, 9 July 1938; Savage, *Roosevelt the Party Leader*, 138–43.

56 *FFF*, 346, 348; National Emergency Council, *Report on Economic Conditions in the South* (Washington: Government Printing Office, 1938), https://archive.org/details/reportoneconomic00nati/page/n1/mode/2up.

57 Patterson, *Congressional Conservatism*, 279–85; Dunn, *Roosevelt's Purge*, 152–201.

58 'After the "Purge" at Home', *TNR*, 19 October 1938, 292–3.

59 'What the Election Means', *TNR*, 23 November 1938, 59.

60 Plesur, Milton, 'The Republican Congressional Comeback of 1938', *Review of Politics*, 24 (October 1962): 525–62.

61 Patterson, *Congressional Conservatism*, 288–324; *Congressional Record*, 76th Congress, 1st session, 11165–8.

62 'Address at University of North Carolina, Chapel Hill, North Carolina', 5 December 1938, APP, https://www.presidency.ucsb.edu/node/209376

63 FDR to Daniels, 14 November 1938, *FDR:HPL-4*, 827; Farley, *Jim Farley's Story*, 180–91 (quotation, p. 188); 'Advice to the Convention of Young Democratic Clubs of America', 8 August 1939, APP, https://www.presidency.ucsb.edu/node/209836.

64 Jeffreys, John, *A Third Term for FDR: The Election of 1940* (Lawrence: University Press of Kansas, 2017), 83–6, 104–5.

65 Edward Kelly to Roosevelt, 1 April 1940, PPF-3166, FDRL.

66 See Jeffreys, *A Third Term for FDR*, for a similar assessment, while the primacy of international events is advanced in Dunn, Susan, *1940: FDR, Willkie, Lindbergh, Hitler – The Election amid the Storm* (New Haven, CT: Yale University Press, 2013).

67 Dunn, *1940*, 146–9.

68 Rosenman, *WWR*, 203–7.

69 FDR to Norris, 21 July 1940, *FDR: HPL-4*, 1046–7.

70 'Radio Address to the Democratic National Convention Accepting the Nomination', 19 July 1940, APP, https://www.presidency.ucsb.edu/node/209818.

71 Willkie, Wendell, 'We the People: A Foundation for a Political Platform for Recovery', *Fortune* (April 1940); *TRIK*, 119; *R&H*, 174.

72 'Campaign Address at Cleveland, Ohio', 2 November 1940, APP, https://www.presidency.ucsb.edu/node/209343.

73 Key, V. O., with Milton Cummings, *The Responsible Electorate: Rationality in Presidential Voting, 1936–1960* (Cambridge, MA: Harvard University Press, 1966), 18–21; Eldersveld, Samuel, 'The Influence of Metropolitan Pluralities in Presidential Elections since 1920: A Study of Twelve Key Cities', *American Political Science Review*, 43 (December 1949): 1189–206.

74 Lubell, Samuel, 'Post-Mortem: Who Elected Roosevelt?' *Saturday Evening Post*, 25 January 1941. See, too, Jensen, Richard, 'The Cities Re-elect Roosevelt: Ethnicity, Religion, and Class in 1940', *Ethnicity*, 8 (June 1981): 189–95.

75 Davies, Gareth, 'The New Deal in 1940: Embattled or Entrenched?' in Gareth Davies and Julian Zelizer, eds., *America at the Ballot Box: Elections and Political History* (Philadelphia: University of Pennsylvania Press, 2015), 153–66.

Chapter 9

1 'Roosevelt on the Presidency', *NYT*, 13 November 1932.

2 Tulis, Jeffrey, *The Rhetorical Presidency* (Princeton, NJ: Princeton University Press, 1987), 25–87.

3 Greenberg, David, *Republic of Spin: An Inside History of the American Presidency* (New York: Norton, 2016), 13–23.

4 'Government by Publicity', *TNR*, 22 September 1926, 111; Gould, Lewis, *The Modern American Presidency*, 2nd ed. (Lawrence: University Press of Kansas, 2009), 56–78.

5 'Relief by Publicity', *The Nation*, 12 November 1930; Lippmann, Walter, 'The Peculiar Weakness of Mr. Hoover', *Harper's* (June 1930), 6.

6 Winfield, Betty Houchin, *FDR and the News Media* (New York: Columbia University Press, 1994), 28.

7 White, Graham, *FDR and the Press* (Chicago: University of Chicago Press, 1979), 6; Stein, M. L., *When Presidents Meet the Press* (New York: Messner, 1969), 86; Halberstam, David, *The Powers That Be* (Knopf: New York, 1979), 8–10.

8 White, *FDR and the Press*, 143–8.

9 Bowers, Claude, *Jefferson and Hamilton: The Struggle for Democracy in America* (Boston: Houghton Mifflin, 1925); FDR review in *New York Evening World*, 3 December 1925, reprinted in Rauch, Basil, ed., *The Roosevelt Reader: Selected Speeches, Messages, Press Conferences, and Letters* (New York: Rinehart, 1957), 43–7; FDR to D. C. Martin, 9 December 1925, General Political Correspondence, 1921–1928, Box 4, FDRL.

10 For changing perspectives on Jefferson, see Cogliano, Frank, *Thomas Jefferson: Reputation and Legacy* (Edinburgh: Edinburgh University Press, 2006).

11 Roosevelt, Franklin D., *Looking Forward* (New York: John Day, 1933), 12.

12 'Address at the Dedication of the Thomas Jefferson Memorial at Washington DC', 13 April 1943, APP, https://www.presidency.ucsb.edu/node/209959.

13 'Radio Address to Thirty Luncheons in Honor of Thomas Jefferson, April 12, 1930', MSF-374, FDRL, http://www.fdrlibrary.marist.edu/_resources/images/msf/msf00378.

14 'American System of Party Government', Address at Democratic Victory Dinner, Hotel Astor, New York City, 14 January 1932, MSF-458, FDRL, http://www.fdrlibrary.marist.edu/_resources/images/msf/msf00468.

15 FDR to Joseph Pulitzer, 2 November 1938, PPF-2403, FDRL.

16 'Jackson Day Dinner Address, Washington DC', 8 January 1936, APP, https://www.presidency.ucsb.edu/node/208635.

17 'Address at the Jackson Day Dinner, Washington DC', 8 January 1938, APP, https://www.presidency.ucsb.edu/node/209617.

18 'Address at Jackson Day Dinner', 8 January 1940, APP, https://www.presidency.ucsb.edu/node/209474.

19 Quoted in Pollard, James, *The Presidents and the Press* (New York: Macmillan, 1947), 816–17.

20 FDR to Archibald MacLeish, 13 July 1942, PPF-245, FDRL; 'Excerpts from the Press Conference Held for Journalism School Faculty', 27 December 1935, APP, https://www.presidency.ucsb.edu/node/208373.

21 FDR to Norman Davies, 14 January 1936, in *FDR: HPL*-3, 545; 'Press Conference #661, 16 July 1940', PCT, FDRL, http://www.fdrlibrary.marist.edu/_resources/images/pc/pc0104.pdf.

22 Hearst to Bainbridge Colby and Edward Coblenz, 19 June 1935, in Hearst, William Randolph, *A Portrait in His Own Words*, ed. Edward Coblenz (New York: Simon & Schuster, 1952), 179; Wolfskill, George and John A. Hudson, *All But the People: Franklin D. Roosevelt and His Critics* (London: Macmillan, 1969), 193–4.

23 Carew, Michael, *The Power to Persuade: FDR, the Newsmagazines, and Going to War, 1939–1941* (Lanham, MD: University Press of America, 2005).

24 Mott, Frank Luther, 'Newspapers in Presidential Campaigns', *Public Opinion Quarterly*, 8 (Fall, 1944): 348–67.

25 'The Press and the Public', *TNR*, 17 March 1937.

26 *ERA*, 101–2; Tully, Grace, *FDR: My Boss* (New York: Scribner's, 1949), 76–7; Houchin, *FDR and the News Media*, 63–4.

27 White, *FDR and the Press*, 153; Roy Howard to Stephen Early, 9 August 1935, PPF-68, FDRL; Moley, Raymond, *After Seven Years* (New York: Harper & Bros., 1939), 337–8.

28 Nelson, Dale, *Who Speaks for the President? The White House Press Secretary from Cleveland to Clinton* (Syracuse, NY: Syracuse University Press, 1998), 66–88. See, too, Levin, Linda Lotridge, *The Making of FDR: The Story of Stephen Early: America's First Modern Press Secretary* (Amherst, MA: Prometheus Books, 2007).

29 Rosenman, *WWR*, 414–15.

30 *ERA*, 193–4; Rosten, Leo, *The Washington Correspondents* (New York: Harcourt, Brace, 1937), 86; Early to Frederick Weaver, 15 November 1933, OF-36, FDRL.

31 Herring, Pendleton, 'Official Publicity under the New Deal', *Annals*, 179 (May 1935): 167–75; Rosten, *The Washington Correspondents*, 71.

32 'Official Propaganda and the New Deal', *NYT*, 7 April 1935; 'Publicity and the New Deal', *Washington Post*, 3 May 1936.

33 Manly, Chesly, 'Stephen Early's Propaganda', *Chicago Tribune*, 13 October 1934; Carroll, Gordon, 'Dr Roosevelt's Propaganda Trust', *American Mercury* (September 1937), https://www.unz.com/print/AmMercury-1937sep-00001/.

34 Freedman, Max, ed., *Roosevelt and Frankfurter: Their Correspondence, 1928–1945* (Boston: Little, Brown, 1967), 214.

35 Winfield, *FDR and the News Media*, 83; 'Press Conference #540 – American Society of Newspaper Publishers, 20 April 1939', PCT, FDRL, http://www.fdrlibrary.marist.edu/_resources/images/pc/pc0079.pdf.

36 Davenport, Walter, 'The President and the Press', *Collier's*, 27 January 1945, 11–13, 46.

37 Lawrence, David, 'The Battle for the Headlines', *United States News*, 21 June 1937, 5.

38 'Arthur Krock Sees Threat to Press', *NYT*, 8 October 1940.

39 Brandus, Paul, *Under This Roof: The White House and the Presidency* (Guilford CT: Lyons Press, 2015), 176–8; 'Oral History Interview with Richard L. Strout, 5 February 1971', Harry S. Truman Presidential Library, https://www.trumanlibrary.org/oralhist/strout.htm.

40 'Press Conference #1, 8 March 1933', PCT, FDRL, http://www.fdrlibrary.marist.edu/_resources/images/pc/pc0183.pdf.

41 'Press Conference #702, 17 December 1940', PCT, FDRL, http://www.fdrlibrary.marist.edu/_resources/images/pc/pc0111.pdf.

42 Clapper, Raymond, 'Why Reporters Like Roosevelt', *Review of Reviews and World's Work*, June 1934, 15, 17; Rosenman, *WWR*, 124; Wolfskill and Hudson, *All But the People*, 192.

43 Winfield, *FDR and the News Media*, 53–78.

44 'Press Conference #377, 29 June 1937', PCT, FDRL, http://www.fdrlibrary.marist.edu/_resources/images/pc/pc0049.pdf; 'Text of John L. Lewis Radio Talk', *NYT*, 4 September 1937.

45 Smith, Merriman, *Thank You, Mr. President* (New York: Harper Brothers, 1946), 22 (quotation); White, *FDR and the Press*, 133–5.

46 'Press Conference #783, 14 November 1941', PCT, FDRL, http://www.fdrlibrary.marist.edu/_resources/images/pc/pc0125.pdf.

47 Quoted in Davenport, 'President and Press', 12.

48 Beasley, Maurine, *Eleanor Roosevelt: Transformative First Lady* (Lawrence: University Press of Kansas, 2010), 105–22 (Krock quotation, p. 119). See, too, the 'My Day' Digitalized Collection at George Washington University's Columbian College of Arts and Sciences website https://erpapers.columbian.gwu.edu/my-day.

49 Quoted in *AoR-2*, 559.

50 Field, Harry, and Paul Lazarsfeld, *The People Look at Radio* (Chapel Hill: University of North Carolina Press, 1946), 99.

51 The most comprehensive but not complete collection, numbering over 230 recordings, is *Recorded Speeches and Utterances of Franklin D. Roosevelt, 1920–1945*, FDRL, http://www.fdrlibrary.marist.edu/archives/collections/utterancesfdr.html.

52 Rosenman, *WWR*, 23–6. See, too, *R&H*, 213.

53 Flynn, John T., *The Roosevelt Myth* (New York: Devin-Adair, 1948), 283.

54 Shenkman, Rick, 'How Hollywood Imagines American Presidents', *History New Network*, 21 October 2003, http://hnn.articles/1749.html.

55 Ryan, Halford, *Franklin D. Roosevelt's Rhetorical Presidency* (Westport, CT: Greenwood, 1988), 19–23; *ERA*, 162.

56 Burns, James MacGregor, *Roosevelt: The Lion and the Fox* (New York: Harcourt, Brace, 1956), 273.

57 'Statement by the President on Reopening Banks', 11 March 1933, APP, https://www.presidency.ucsb.edu/node/207723.

58 Since their designation was not an official term, the number of Fireside Chats is variously put at 21, 28, 30 or 31, but the latter is now the most commonly accepted figure. See Levine, Lawrence, and Cornelia Levine, *The People and the President: America's Conversation with FDR* (Boston: Beacon Press, 2002), 571–2 (henceforth *P&P*). For transcripts and available recordings, see 'Famous Presidential Speeches: Franklin D Roosevelt', Miller Center, https://millercenter.org/the-presidency/presidential-speeches?field_president_target_id[31]=31.

59 Roosevelt to Russell Leffingwell, 16 March 1942, in Rauch, *Roosevelt Reader*, 310.

60 Strout, Richard, 'The President and the Press', in *MNDIS*, 283; Greenberg, *Republic of Spin*, 189–98 (Bellow quotation, p. 194).

61 Cook, Ruth Albert, 'Blackout', *Opportunity: Journal of Negro Life* (March 1942), 82.

62 *P&P*, 571; Houchin, *FDR and the News Media*, 104.

63 Storm, Geoffrey, 'FDR and WGY: The Origins of the Fireside Chats', *New York History*, 88 (Spring 2007): 177–97; Brandus, *Under This Roof*, 179; *R&H*, 212.

64 Michelson, Charles, *The Ghost Talks* (New York: Putnam, 1944), 56–7; *P&P*, 31.

65 *TRIK*, 113.

66 *TRIK*, 72.

67 Winfield, *FDR and the News Media*, 121.

68 Mr and Mrs F. B. Graham to Roosevelt, 13 March 1933, and Mildred Goldstein to Roosevelt, 13 March 1933, *P&P*, 36, 26.

69 'Fireside Chat on Banking', 12 March 1933, APP, https://www.presidency.ucsb.edu/node/207762.

70 Howe, Louis, 'The President's Mailbag', *American Magazine* (June 1934), 118.

71 Samuel Traum to FDR, 16 September 1941, *P&P*, 21–2.

72 Doherty, Thomas, *Pre-Code Hollywood: Sex, Immorality, and Insurrection in American Cinema, 1930–1934* (New York: Columbia University Press, 1999), 77–85; Winfield, *FDR and the News Media*, 116.

73 Fielding, Raymond, *American Newsreels, 1911–1967: A Complete History*, 2nd ed. (Jefferson NC: McFarland, 2006), 124.

74 Gunther, John, *Roosevelt in Retrospect* (New York: Harper, 1950), 139.

75 'Fireside Chat', 12 October 1937, APP, https://www.presidency.ucsb.edu/node/208891.

76 'Remarks at Boise, Idaho', 27 September 1937, APP, https://www.presidency.ucsb.edu/node/208784.

77 Gallagher, Hugh, *FDR's Splendid Deception* (Arlington, VA: Vandamere 1994), 93–4; Winfield, *FDR and the News Media*, 111–18.

78 Cantril quoted in Greenberg, *Republic of Spin*, 224; FDR to Joseph Pulitzer,
    2 November 1938, PPF-2403, FDRL; 'Press Conference with Editors and Publishers of
    Trade Papers in Washington DC', 8 April 1938, APP, https://www.presidency.ucsb.edu
    /node/209573.
79 *P&P*, 561–3.
80 Smith, Ira, with Joe Alex Morris, *'Dear Mr President . . .': The Story of Fifty Years in the
    White House Mail Room* (New York: Julian Messner, 1949), 189–91; Sussmann, Leila,
    Dear FDR: A Study of Political Letter-Writing (Totowa, NJ: Bedminster Press, 1963), 66–9.
81 Greenberg, *Republic of Spin*, 223–37.
82 Holli, Melvin, *The Wizard of Washington: Emil Hurja, Franklin Roosevelt and the Birth
    of Public Opinion Polling* (New York: Palgrave, 2002).
83 Cantril, Hadley, 'America Faces the War: A Study in Public Opinion', *Public Opinion
    Quarterly*, 4 (September 1940): 387–407 (quotation, p. 405).
84 'Fireside Chat', 29 December 1940, APP, https://www.presidency.ucsb.edu/node
    /209416; *R&H*, 236.
85 Greenberg, *Republic of Spin*, 235.
86 'Fireside Chat', 12 October 1937, APP, https://www.presidency.ucsb.edu/node/208891.

Chapter 10

1   See, for example, Schmitz, David, *The Triumph of Internationalism: Franklin D.
    Roosevelt and a World in Crisis* (Dulles, VA: Potomac Books, 2007), 91–3; Thompson,
    John, *A Sense of Power: The Roots of America's Global Role* (Ithaca, NY: Cornell
    University Press, 2015), 145–92.
2   Schmitz, *Triumph of Internationalism*, 1–16.
3   Rauchway, Eric, *Winter War: Hoover, Roosevelt, and the First Clash over the New Deal*
    (New York: Basic Books, 2018), 164–95.
4   'Appeal for World Peace by Disarmament and for Relief from Economic Chaos', 16
    May 1933, APP, https://www.presidency.ucsb.edu/node/208142.
5   FDR to Fosdick, 1 February 1934, PPF-21, FDRL; *FDRAFP*, 42–4, 66–70.
6   'Message to Congress on the Payment of War Debts', 1 June 1934, APP, https://www
    .presidency.ucsb.edu/node/208339; Self, Robert, *Britain, America and the War Debt
    Controversy: The Economic Diplomacy of an Unspecial Relationship, 1917–1941*
    (London: Routledge, 2006), 178–95 (quotation, p. 194–5).
7   HMD-Farm Credit Diary, 9 May 1933, 17, http://www.fdrlibrary.marist.edu/
    _resources/images/morg/md00.pdf.
8   HMD-Farm Credit Diary, 27 September, 63–5, http://www.fdrlibrary.marist.edu/
    _resources/images/morg/md00.pdf; 'Communications between the President Franklin
    D. Roosevelt and Maxim Litvinov of the Union of Soviet Socialist Republics', 16
    November 1933, APP, https://www.presidency.ucsb.edu/node/207819.
9   'Address on the Occasion of the Celebration of Pan-American Day, Washington', 12
    April 1933, APP, https://www.presidency.ucsb.edu/node/208062.
10 *FDRAFP*, 60–5, 86–7.
11 FDR to Dodd, 9 January 1937, *FDR: HPL-3*, 648–9.
12 'Message to Congress Requesting Authority Regarding Foreign Trade', 2 March 1934,
    APP, https://www.presidency.ucsb.edu/node/208437; FDR to Raymond Moley, 23
    November 1935, *FDR: HPL-3*, 523–4; *FDRAFP*, 84–5, 92–3.

13 FDR to King, 16 April 1936, *FDR: HPL-3*, 578–9.

14 'Annual Message to Congress', 3 January 1936, APP, https://www.presidency.ucsb.edu/node/208916.

15 Fisher, Louis, '*The Law*: Presidential Inherent Power: The "Sole Organ" Doctrine', *Presidential Studies Quarterly*, 37 (March 2007): 139–52; Dallek, Robert, *Franklin D. Roosevelt: A Political Life* (London: Allen Lane, 2017), 230.

16 Roosevelt to Colonel House, 17 September 1935, *FDR: HPL-3*, 506–7.

17 Cole, Wayne, *Roosevelt & the Isolationists, 1932–45* (Lincoln: University of Nebraska Press, 1983), 6–8.

18 Blower, Brooke, 'From Isolationism to Neutrality: A New Framework for Understanding American Political Culture, 1919–1941', *Diplomatic History*, 38/2 (2014): 345–73.

19 Beard, Charles, 'Collective Security – A Debate', *TNR*, 2 February 1938, 359.

20 Millis, Walter, *The Road to War, 1914–1917* (Boston: Houghton Mifflin, 1935); Cole, *FDR & the Isolationists*, 141–62.

21 *FDRAFP*, 95–7; Cole, *Roosevelt & the Isolationists*, 119–27.

22 FDR to Robinson, 30 January 1935, and to Stimson, 6 February 1935, *FDR: HPL-3*, 449–51.

23 Dallek, *Roosevelt*, 238–9.

24 Bowers to Cordell Hull, 16 March 1937, *FRUS: 1937-1*, https://history.state.gov/historicaldocuments/frus1937v01/d159.

25 *SD-2* (29 January 1939), 569–70.

26 'Address at Chicago', 5 October 1937, APP, https://www.presidency.ucsb.edu/node/208843.

27 Hull, Cordell, *Memoirs of Cordell Hull: I* (New York: Macmillan, 1948), 545.

28 'Press Conference', 6 October 1937, APP, https://www.presidency.ucsb.edu/node/208847; FDR to House, 19 October 1937, *FDR-HPL-3*, 719.

29 Hull, *Memoirs*. I: 559–62; *SD-2* (18 December 1937), 273–5.

30 Hull, *Memoirs*, I: 563–4.

31 Farley, James, *Jim Farley's Story: The Roosevelt Years* (New York: McGraw-Hill, 1948), 117–18; *Congressional Record*, 75th Congress, 3rd Session, 1938, 83: 276–7.

32 Stimson, Henry, and McGeorge Bundy, *On Active Service in Peace and War* (New York: Harper, 1947), 313.

33 Ninkovich, Frank, *The Global Republic: America's Inadvertent Rise to World Power* (Chicago: University of Chicago Press, 2014), 146–7; 'Address at Chicago', 5 October 1937, APP, https://www.presidency.ucsb.edu/node/208843.

34 'Memorandum by the Under Secretary of State (Welles) to President Roosevelt', 10 January 1938, *FRUS: 1938-1*, https://history.state.gov/historicaldocuments/frus1938v01/d75; McCulloch, Tony, *Tacit Alliance: Franklin Roosevelt and the Anglo-American 'Special Relationship' before Churchill, 1937–1940* (Edinburgh: Edinburgh University Press, 2021), esp. *vi*, 107–26.

35 Self, Robert, *Neville Chamberlain: A Biography* (Aldershot: Ashgate, 2006), 280–3; Churchill, Winston, *The Second World War: The Gathering Storm* (Boston: Houghton Mifflin, 1948), 254–5.

36 Bullitt to FDR, 20 January 1938, in Bullitt, Orville, ed., *For the President: Personal and Secret Correspondence between Franklin D. Roosevelt and William C. Bullitt* (Boston: Houghton Mifflin, 1972), 252.

37 Kershaw, Ian, *Hitler 1936–1945: Nemesis* (New York: Norton, 2000), 46–51, 108–25.

38 *SD-2* (18 September 1938), 467–8.

39 President Roosevelt to the German Chancellor (Hitler), 26 September 1938, *FRUS: 1938*-1, https://history.state.gov/historicaldocuments/frus1938v01/d631; *FDRAFP*, 165–6.

40 'Report of Meeting at the White House', 14 November 1938, HMD-150, FDRL, http://www.fdrlibrary.marist.edu/_resources/images/morg/md0200.pdf.

41 Farnham, Barbara, *Roosevelt and the Munich Crisis: A Study of Political Decision-Making* (Princeton, NJ: Princeton University Press, 1997), 152–6; 'Press Conference #500, 15 November 1938', PCT, FDRL, http://www.fdrlibrary.marist.edu/_resources/images/pc/pc0072.pdf.

42 Dallek, *Roosevelt*, 366–7; *R&H*, 134–5; *SD-3* (29 June 1940), 216–18.

43 FDR to Professor Roger Merriman, 15 February 1939, http://masshist.org/database/viewer.php?item_id=1842&img_step=1&mode=transcript.

44 Watson, Mark, *Chief of Staff: Prewar Plans and Preparations* (Washington, DC: Center for Military History, 1991; original 1950), 132–3, https://history.army.mil/html/books/001/1-1/CMH_Pub_1-1.pdf; Elibank, Viscount (Arthur Murray), 'Franklin Roosevelt, Friend of Britain', *Contemporary Review*, 187 (1955): 362–8 (quotation, p. 365–6).

45 Watson, *Chief of Staff*, 142–3.

46 Blum, John Morton, ed., *From the Morgenthau Diaries: Years of Urgency, 1938–1941* (Boston: Houghton Mifflin, 1965), 65.

47 Farnham, *Roosevelt and the Munich Crisis*, 193–6.

48 Transcript, 'Conference with the Senate Military Affairs Committee, Executive Offices of the White House', 31 January 1939, PPF-1P, FDRL.

49 'Press Conference, #523, 3 February 1939', and 'Press Conference #525, 17 February 1939', PCT, FDRL, http://www.fdrlibrary.marist.edu/_resources/images/pc/pc0077.pdf.

50 Roosevelt to Hitler, 14 April 1939, http://www.fdrlibrary.marist.edu/daybyday/resource/april-1939-7/.

51 Kershaw, Ian, *Fateful Choices: Ten Decisions That Changed the World, 1940–1941* (New York: Penguin, 2007), 393; *FFF*, 423–5.

52 Kershaw, *Fateful Choices*, 386–94 (quotation, p. 394).

53 FDR to King, *FDR: HPL-3*, 16 April 1939, 878–9.

54 *Public Opinion Quarterly*, 3 (October 1939): 597, 600 and 4 (March 1940): 103–5.

55 Alsop, Joseph, and Robert Kitner, *American White Paper: The Story of American Diplomacy and the Second World War* (New York: Simon & Schuster, 1940), 41–6; 'Press Conference #564, 21 July 1939', PCT, FDRL, http://www.fdrlibrary.marist.edu/_resources/images/pc/pc0083.pdf.

56 'Fireside Chat', 3 September 1939, APP, https://www.presidency.ucsb.edu/node/209990; *Public Opinion Quarterly*, 4 (March 1940): 106–9.

57 'Message to Congress Urging Repeal of the Embargo Provisions of the Neutrality Law', 21 September 1939, APP, https://www.presidency.ucsb.edu/node/210082; FDR to Tweedsmuir, 5 October 1939, *FDR: HPL-4*, 934.

58 Reynolds, David, *The Creation of the Anglo-American Alliance, 1937–1941* (Chapel Hill: University of North Carolina Press, 1982), 73–5; Thompson, *A Sense of Power*, 166.

59 Cantril, Hadley, 'America Faces the War: A Study in Public Opinion', *Public Opinion Quarterly*, 4 (September 1940): 398.

60 'Address at University of Virginia', 10 June 1940, APP, https://www.presidency.ucsb.edu/node/209705.

61 Blum, *Morgenthau Diaries, 1938–1941*, 155; Watson, *Chief of Staff*, 312.

62 Jordan, Jonathan, *American Warlords: How Roosevelt's High Command Led America to Victory in World War II* (New York: Penguin, 2015), 51–3.

63 'Message to Congress on Exchanging Destroyers for British Naval and Air Bases', 3 September 1940, APP, https://www.presidency.ucsb.edu/node/209947.

64 Langer, William, and Everett Gleason, *The Undeclared War: 1940–1941* (New York: Harper & Bros., 1953), 229.

65 Churchill to Roosevelt, 27 October 1940, MRP-1, FDRL http://www.fdrlibrary.marist .edu/_resources/images/mr/mr0002.pdf. See, too, Gilbert, Martin, *Churchill and America* (New York: Free Press, 2005), 183–211.

66 Churchill to Roosevelt, 7 December 1940, MRP-1, FDRL, http://www.fdrlibrary.marist .edu/_resources/images/mr/mr0002.pdf.

67 *R&H*, 224; Blum, *Morgenthau Diaries, 1938–1941*, 208–9.

68 'Press Conference #702, 17 December 1940', PCT, FDRL, http://www.fdrlibrary.marist .edu/_resources/images/pc/pc0111.pdf; Kimball, Warren, *The Most Unsordid Act: Lend-Lease 1939–1941* (Baltimore: Johns Hopkins University Press, 1969), 124. See, too, Dunn, Susan, *A Blueprint for War: FDR and the Hundred Days That Mobilized America* (New Haven, CT: Yale University Press, 2018), 66–70.

69 'Fireside Chat', 29 December 1940, APP, https://www.presidency.ucsb.edu/node /209416.

70 O'Reilly, Kenneth, 'A New Deal for the FBI: The Roosevelt Administration, Crime Control, and National Security', *Journal of American History*, 69 (December 1982): 638–58.

71 Jordan, *American Warlords*, 66–7; 'Mr Willkie's Testimony', *NYT*, 12 February 1941.

72 *NYT*, 12 March 1941; Thompson, *A Sense of Power*, 190.

73 *SD-3* (25 May 1941), 523 (30 May 1941), 526–7; Kershaw, *Fateful Choices*, 303–4.

74 FDR to Churchill, 11 April 1941, MRP-1, FDRL, http://www.fdrlibrary.marist.edu/ _resources/images/mr/mr0002.pdf; 'Announcement of New Bases in Greenland', 10 April 1941, APP, https://www.presidency.ucsb.edu/node/209515; 'Message to Congress on Landing Troops in Iceland, Trinidad, and British Guiana', 7 July 1941, APP, https://www.presidency.ucsb.edu/node/209725.

75 'Fireside Chat', 11 September 1941, APP, https://www.presidency.ucsb.edu/node /210065.

76 'Address for Navy and Total Defense Day', 27 October 1941, APP, https://www .presidency.ucsb.edu/node/210207.

77 Marshall and Stark to FDR, 5 November 1941, in US Congress, Joint Committee on the Investigation of the Pearl Harbor Attack, *Hearings* (39 Volumes; Government Printing Office, Washington, DC, 1946), 14: 1061–2.

78 Kershaw, *Fateful Choices*, 91–128.

79 *SD-3* (27 July 1941), 588.

80 FDR to Ickes, *FDR: HPL-4*, 1 July 1941, 1173–4.

81 Quoted in Kershaw, *Fateful Choices*, 347.

82 Hull, *Memoirs*, II: 1074–6, 1081–2; Ike, Nobutaka, ed., *Japan's Decision for War. Records of the 1941 Policy Conferences* (Palo Alto CA: Stanford University Press, 1967), 279–82.

83 Rosenman, *WWR*, 284–5; Kershaw, *Fateful Choices*, 427–8; *R&H*, 432.

84 'FDR's "Day of Infamy" Speech: Crafting a Call to Arms', *Prologue*, 33 (Winter 2001), https://www.archives.gov/publications/prologue/2001/winter/crafting-day-of-infamy -speech.html; 'Address to Congress Requesting a Declaration of War with Japan', 8 December 1941, APP, https://www.presidency.ucsb.edu/node/210408.

85 'Annual Message to Congress', 4 January 1939, APP, https://www.presidency.ucsb.edu/ node/209128.

Chapter 11

1 Watson, Mark, *Chief of Staff: Prewar Plans and Preparations* (Washington, DC: Center of Military History, 1991; original 1950), 5–7, https://history.army.mil/html/books /001/1-1/CMH_Pub_1-1.pdf; Hull, Cordell, *The Memoirs of Cordell Hull*, 2 Vols. (New York: Macmillan 1948), II, 1111.

2 Hassett, William, *Off the Record with FDR, 1942–45* (London: George Allen & Unwin, 1960), 145–6.

3 Emerson, William, 'Franklin Roosevelt as Commander-in-Chief in World War II', *Military Affairs*, 22 (Winter 1958–59): 181–207; Larrabee, Eric, *Commander in Chief: Franklin Delano Roosevelt, His Lieutenants, and Their War* (New York: Harper & Row, 1987), 1–39.

4 *TM*, 81; Greenfield, Kent Roberts, *American Strategy in World War II: A Reconsideration* (Baltimore: John Hopkins University Press, 1963), 80–4.

5 Jordan, Jonathan, *American Warlords: How Roosevelt's High Command Led America to Victory in World War 2* (New York: NAL Caliber 2015), 27–8. See, too, Gullan, Harold, 'Expectations of Infamy: Roosevelt and Marshall Prepare for War, 1938–1941', *Presidential Studies Quarterly*, 28 (Summer 1998): 510–22.

6 'Executive Order 9082 Reorganizing the Army and the War Department', 28 February 1942, APP, https://www.presidency.ucsb.edu/node/210375; Larrabee, *Commander in Chief*, 142–3.

7 Buell, Thomas, *Master of Sea Power: A Biography of Admiral Ernest J. King* (Boston: Little, Brown, 1980), 235–9, 292; FDR to King, 22 August 1942, *FDR: HPL-4*, 1342.

8 Harry Hopkins to Admiral Harold Stark, 30 December 1941, in US Joint Chiefs of Staff, Joint History Office, *World War 2 Inter-Allied Conferences* (Washington, DC: US Government, 2003), 80–1; *R&H*, 467–70.

9 FDR, Memorandum to George Marshall, 9 January 1942, *FDR: HPL-4*, 1271–2.

10 Hamilton, Nigel, *The Mantle of Command: FDR at War, 1941–1942* (Boston: Houghton Mifflin Harcourt, 2014), 139–41; FDR to Harry Hopkins, 21 January 1942, *FDR: HPL-4*, 1279; Roll, David, *The Hopkins Touch: Harry Hopkins and the Forging of the Alliance to Defeat Hitler* (New York: Oxford University Press, 2013), 176–7.

11 Moran, Lord, *Churchill, Taken from the Diaries of Lord Moran: The Struggle for Survival 1940–1965* (Boston: Houghton Mifflin, 1966), 23; Danchev, Alex, and Daniel Todman, *War Diaries 1939–1945: Field Marshal Lord Alanbrooke* (Berkeley: University of California Press, 2001), 215.

12 Dill to Brooke, 1 March 1942, quoted in Bryant, Arthur, *Turn of the Tide* (New York: Doubleday, 1957), 234.

13 Bland, Larry, ed., *George C. Marshall Interviews and Reminiscences for Forrest C. Pogue* (Lexington, VA: George C. Marshall Research Foundation, 1991), 623.

14 Buell, *Master of Sea Power*, 186; Leahy, William, *I Was There* (New York: McGraw-Hill, 1950), 126; Stoler, Mark, 'FDR and the Origins of the National Security Establishment', *FDRW*, 71–2.

15 Jordan, *American Warlords*, 130.

16 'Executive Order 9096 Reorganizing the Navy Department and the Naval Service', 12 March 1942, APP, https://www.presidency.ucsb.edu/node/210434.

17 Bland, *Marshall Interviews*, 431–3, 623–4.

18 'Text of Willkie's Lincoln Day Talk before Boston Club', *NYT*, 13 February 1942; Hamilton, *Mantle of Command*, 157–8.

19 Leahy, *I Was There*, 83–4, 102 (quotation); 'Press Conference #836, 21 July 1942,' PCT, FDRL, http://www.fdrlibrary.marist.edu/_resources/images/pc/pc0137.pdf; Jordan, *American Warlords*, 196–7.

20 Leahy, *I Was There*, 103–6.

21 Larrabee, *Commander in Chief*, 638–9.

22 Oral History Interview with George M. Elsey, Harry S. Truman Library, https://www .trumanlibrary.gov/library/oral-histories/elsey1; Hamilton, *Mantle of Command*, 145–53.

23 Kershaw, Ian, *Fateful Choices: Ten Decisions That Changed the World, 1940–1941* (New York: Penguin, 2007), 343–5, 366–7.

24 See, in particular, Wohlstetter, Roberta, *Pearl Harbor: Warning and Decision: A National Failure to Anticipate* (Palo Alto, CA: Stanford University Press, 1962).

25 Quezon to FDR, 8 February 1942, https://www.gov.ph/1942/02/08/telegram-of -president-quezon-to-presidetn-roosevelt-februar-8-1942/.

26 Marshall to MacArthur (response to Quezon), 9 February 1942, *FRUS:1942*-1, https:// history.state.gov/historicaldocuments/frus1942v01/d784; FDR to MacArthur, 9 February 1942, PSF-46, FDRL, http://www.fdrlibrary.marist.edu/_resources/images/ psf/psfa0059.pdf.

27 Quezon, Jr, Manuel, 'Escape from Corregidor', 8 December 2001, https://philippines freepress.wordpress.com/2001/12/08/escape-from-corregidor-december-8-2001/.

28 Pogue, Forrest, *George C. Marshall: Ordeal and Hope, 1939–1942* (New York: Viking, 1966), 247–8.

29 MacArthur to George Marshall, 4 February 1942, PSF-46, FDRL, http://www .fdrlibrary.marist.edu/_resources/images/psf/psfa0059.pdf.

30 *R&H*, 492.

31 *WWR*, 305.

32 'Fireside Chat', 23 February 1942, APP, https://www.presidency.ucsb.edu/node /210361; Henrikson, Alan, 'FDR and the "World-Wide Arena"', *FDRW*, 44–6.

33 'Executive Order 9066 – Authorizing the Secretary of War to Prescribe Military Areas', 19 February 1942, APP, https://www.presidency.ucsb.edu/node/210838; 'Executive Order 9102 Establishing the War Relocation Authority', 18 March 1942, APP, https:// www.presidency.ucsb.edu/node/210476.

34 *FFF*, 751–2.

35 'Message to the Senate on the Segregation Program of the War Relocation Authority', 14 September 1943, APP, https://www.presidency.ucsb.edu/node/210907.

36 Daniels, Roger, *Franklin D. Roosevelt: The War Years, 1939–1945* (Urbana: University of Illinois Press, 2016), 250–5, 453 (quotation).

37 *Korematsu v. United States*, 323 U.S. 214 (1944), https://supreme.justia.com/cases/ federal/us/323/214/.

38 'Message to Congress on Stabilizing the Economy', 7 September 1942, APP, https:// www.presidency.ucsb.edu/node/210858; Schlesinger, Jr, Arthur, *The Imperial Presidency* (London: Andre Deutsch, 1974), 114.

39 Arnold, Henry, *Global Mission* (New York: Harper & Brothers, 1949), 298.

40 Scott, James, 'The Untold Story of the Vengeful Japanese Attack after the Doolittle Raid', *Smithsonian Magazine*, 15 April 2015, https://www.smithsonianmag.com/ history/untold-story-vengeful-japanese-attack-doolittle-raid-180955001/.

41 Fuchida, Mitsuo, and Masatake Okumiya, *Midway: The Battle That Doomed Japan* (Annapolis, MD: Naval Institute Press, 1955), 65.

42 Larrabee, *Commander in Chief*, 354–63 (quotation, p. 358); Potter, E. B., *Nimitz* (Annapolis, MD: Naval Institute Press, 1976), 1–62.

43 Potter, *Nimitz*, 91–107.

44 *R&H*, 624–5; Larrabee, *Commander in Chief*, 292.

45 Hassett, *Off the Record*, 192.

46 *R&H*, 520–23, 538–41; FDR, Memorandum for the Secretary of War, Chief of Staff, General Arnold, Secretary of the Navy, Admiral King, Harry Hopkins, 6 May 1942, PSF-83, FDRL, http://www.fdrlibrary.marist.edu/_resources/images/psf/psf000332 .pdf.

47 Churchill to FDR, 20 June 1942, MRP-2, FDRL, http://www.fdrlibrary.marist.edu/ _resources/images/mr/mr0012a.pdf.

48 Marshall to FDR, 19 June 1942, Stimson to FDR, 19 June 1942, PSF-4, http://www .fdrlibrary.marist.edu/_resources/images/psf/psfa0044.pdf; Marshall, Memorandum for the President, 23 June 1942, GCMP:3–230, https://www.marshallfoundation.org/ library/digital-archive/memorandum-for-the-president-42/.

49 Roll, *The Hopkins Touch*, 204.

50 Churchill to Roosevelt, 8 July 1942, MRP-2, FDRL, http://www.fdrlibrary.marist.edu/ _resources/images/mr/mr0012a.pdf.

51 Marshall and King, Memorandum for the President, 10 July 1942, MRP-165, FDRL, http://www.fdrlibrary.marist.edu/_resources/images/mr/mr0849.pdf; Marshall to Roosevelt, 'Latest British Proposals relative to Bolero and Gymnast', 10 July 1942, GCMP:3–251, https://www.marshallfoundation.org/library/digital-archive/ memorandum-for-the-president-45/.

52 FDR to Marshall, undated draft, John McCrea Papers, FDRL; FDR to Marshall and King, undated handwritten message for telephone communication, MRP-165, FDRL, http://www.fdrlibrary.marist.edu/_resources/images/mr/mr0849.pdf.

53 Quoted in Stoler, Mark, *George C. Marshall: Soldier-Statesman of the American Century* (Boston: Twayne, 1989), 101.

54 Commander-in-Chief to General Marshall, Admiral King and Harry Hopkins, Memorandum: Instructions for London Conference – July 1942, 15 July 1942, PSF-3, FDRL, http://www.fdrlibrary.marist.edu/_resources/images/psf/psfa0039.pdf.

55 *R&H*, 606–12; Jordan, *American Warlords*, 186–8.

56 Matloff, Maurice and Edwin Snell, *Strategic Planning for Coalition Warfare, 1941–1942* (Washington DC: Department of the Army, 1951), 282–3.

57 Hamilton, *Mantle of Command*, 363–70.

58 'Statement on Roosevelt-Molotov Conversations', 11 June 1942, APP, https://www .presidency.ucsb.edu/node/210700.

59 Churchill to Roosevelt, 4 August 1942, MRP-2, FDRL, http://www.fdrlibrary.marist .edu/_resources/images/mr/mr0014.pdf.

60 Harriman, Averell, and Elie Abel, *Special Envoy to Churchill and Stalin, 1941–1946* (New York: Random House, 1975), 146–61 (quotation, p. 161).

61 FDR to Churchill, 2 September 1942, MRP-2, http://www.fdrlibrary.marist.edu/ _resources/images/mr/mr0013.pdf.

62 Jordan, *American Warlords*, 217; 'Statement on Temporary Political Arrangements in Africa', 17 November 1942, APP, https://www.presidency.ucsb.edu/node/210239.

63 'Armistice Day Address', 11 November 1942, APP, https://www.presidency.ucsb.edu/ node/210182.

64 FDR to Margaret Suckley, 10, 11, 12, 13 and 14 January 1943 in *CC*, 196–8; FDR to Eleanor Roosevelt, 13 January 1943, *FDR:HPL-4*, 1393.

65 DMK, 6 December 1942, https://www.bac-lac.gc.ca/eng/discover/politics-government /prime-ministers/william-lyon-mackenzie-king/Pages/item.aspx?IdNumber=24851.

66 'Joint Chiefs of Staff Minutes of a Meeting at the White House', 7 January 1943, *FRUS: The Conferences at Washington, 1941–1942, and Casablanca, 1943* (hereafter *Conferences*), https://history.state.gov/historicaldocuments/frus1941-43/d329; 'Meeting of Roosevelt with the Joint Chiefs of Staff, January 15, 1943, 10.00 a.m., President's Villa', ibid., https://history.state.gov/historicaldocuments/frus1941-43/ch9subsubch5.

67 Wedemeyer, Albert, *Wedemeyer Reports!* (New York: Henry Holt, 1958), 191–2.

68 Roosevelt, Elliott, *As He Saw It* (New York: Duell, Sloan & Pearce, 1946), 83–4.

69 Hopkins, Robert, *Witness to History: Recollections of a World War II Photographer* (Seattle: Castle Pacific, 2002), 49; Roosevelt, *As He Saw It*, 107.

70 Captain John McCrea notes, 'Roosevelt-de Gaulle Conversation, January 22, 1943', *FRUS: Conferences*, https://history.state.gov/historicaldocuments/frus1941-43/d378; de Gaulle, Charles, *The Complete War Memoirs of Charles de Gaulle, Vol. 2: Unity* (New York: Simon & Schuster, 1964), 392–3; Roosevelt, *As He Saw It*, 115–16.

71 Macmillan, Harold, *The Blast of War, 1939–1945* (London: Macmillan, 1967), 190; Eden, Anthony, *The Reckoning* (Boston: Houghton Mifflin, 1965), 372.

72 Hamilton, Nigel, *Commander in Chief: FDR's Battle with Churchill, 1943* (Boston: Houghton Mifflin, 2016), 129–31; 'Press Conference #875, 24 January 1943', PCT, FDRL, http://www.fdrlibrary.marist.edu/_resources/images/pc/pc0144.pdf.

73 Baldwin, Hanson, *Great Mistakes of the War* (New York: Harper, 1950), 13; Reynolds, David, *In Command of History: Churchill Fighting and Writing the Second World War* (New York: Random House, 2005), 323; Wedemeyer, *Wedemeyer Reports*, 186–7.

74 'Joint Chiefs of Staff Minutes of a Meeting at the White House', 7 January 1943; 'Combined Chiefs of Staff Minutes of Meeting with Roosevelt and Churchill, January 18, 1943, 5.00 p.m.', *FRUS: Conferences*, https://history.state.gov/historicaldocuments/ frus1941-43/d355; Gilbert, Martin, *Road to Victory: Winston S. Churchill, 1941–1945* (London: Heinemann, 1986), 299–300.

75 *R&H*, 697.

Chapter 12

1 Charles Bohlen, 'Log of the Trip', *FRUS: Conferences at Cairo and Tehran, 1943* (*CCT-1943*), https://history.state.gov/historicaldocuments/frus1943CairoTehran/ d353; 'Tripartite Dinner Meeting, November 30, 1943, 8.30 p.m., Soviet Embassy', Major John Boettiger minutes, ibid., https://history.state.gov/historicaldocuments/ frus1943CairoTehran/ch8subsubch18.

2 'Annual Budget Message', 5 January 1942, APP, https://www.presidency.ucsb.edu/node /210394.

3 'State of the Union Address', (SUA) 6 January 1942, APP, https://www.presidency.ucsb .edu/node/210559.

4 Nelson, Donald, *Arsenal of Democracy: The Story of the American War Production Board* (New York: Harcourt, Brace, 1946), 185–7; *R&H*, 473–4.

5 *R&H*, 473; *FFF*, 619.

6 Collins, Robert, *More: The Politics of Economic Growth in Postwar America* (New York: Oxford University Press, 2000), 10–12; Galbraith, John Kenneth, *A Life in Our Times: Memoirs* (Boston: Houghton Mifflin, 1981), 148–9.

7   Dickinson, Matthew, *Bitter Harvest: FDR, Presidential Power, and the Growth of the Presidential Branch* (New York: Cambridge University Press, 1996), 141–7.

8   Klein, Maury, *A Call to Arms: Mobilizing America for World War II* (New York: Bloomsbury, 2013), 511–53.

9   Smith, Harold, 'BoB Monthly Report #29', February 1943, 16, FDRL; Smith to FDR, 8 February 1943, PSF-118, FDRL, http://www.fdrlibrary.marist.edu/_resources/images /psf/psf000438.pdf.

10 Byrnes, James, *Speaking Frankly* (New York: Harper, 1947), 18.

11 Nelson, *Arsenal of Democracy*, 390–2.

12 Dickinson, *Bitter Harvest*, 151–3; Rosenman to FDR, 24 May 1943, PSF-163, FDRL, http://www.fdrlibrary.marist.edu/_resources/images/psf/psfc0102.pdf.

13 Hassett, William, *Off the Record with FDR* (London: George Allen & Unwin, 1960), 16 July 1943 diary entry, 190–1; 'Letter to Henry A. Wallace and Jesse H. Jones on Economic Warfare', 15 July 1943, APP, https://www.presidency.ucsb.edu/node/210225.

14 'Executive Order 9361 Establishing the Office of Economic Warfare', 15 July 1943, APP, https://www.presidency.ucsb.edu/node/210258; 'FDR Cracks Down', *NYT*, 18 July 1943, 1.

15 Nelson, *Arsenal of Democracy*, 259–60; Thompson, John, *A Sense of Power: The Roots of America's Global Role* (Ithaca, NY: Cornell University Press, 2015), 195–7.

16 Klein, *Call to Arms*, 399–404. See, too, Daisy Suckley Diary (17–29 September 1942), *CC*, 174–83.

17 Polenberg, Richard, *War and Society: The United States, 1941–1945* (Philadelphia: Lippincott, 1972), 11–13 (quotation, p. 12), 219–20; *FFF*, 621–2.

18 Klein, *Call to Arms*, 440–3.

19 'Veto of a Revenue Bill', 22 February 1944, APP, https://www.presidency.ucsb.edu/node/210639.

20 FDR to Representative Patrick Drewry (D-Virginia), 7 March 1944 in *FDR: HPL-4*, 1499.

21 Brigante, John, *The Feasibility Dispute: Determination of War Production Objectives for 1942 and 1943* (Washington, DC: Committee on Public Administration Cases, 1950), 83–6; Klein, *A Call to Arms*, 377–98.

22 Matloff, Maurice, 'The 90-Division Gamble', in Kent Roberts Greenfield, ed., *Command Decisions* (Washington, DC: Department of the Army, 1960), 365–81 (quotation, p. 373) (available at https://history.army.mil/books/70-7_15.htm).

23 Einstein to Roosevelt, 2 August 1939, Sachs to Roosevelt, 11 October 1939, Leo Szilard, 'Memorandum' (undated), PSF-5, FDRL, http://www.fdrlibrary.marist.edu/ _resources/images/psf/psfa0064.pdf. See, too, Rhodes, Richard, *The Making of the Atomic Bomb* (New York: Simon & Schuster, 1986), 304–15.

24 'Executive Order 8807 Establishing the Office of Scientific Research and Development', 28 June 1941, APP, https://www.presidency.ucsb.edu/node/209713; Rhodes, *Making of the Atomic Bomb*, 388.

25 Kimball, Warren, *Forged in War: Roosevelt, Churchill and the Second World War* (New York: Morrow, 1997), 279–80; Churchill, 'Tube Alloys' (Aide-Memoire of Hyde Park Agreement, 18 September 1944), https://www.atomicheritage.org/key-documents/ hyde-park-aide-m%C3%A9moire.

26 Costigliola, Frank, *Roosevelt's Lost Alliances: How Personal Politics Helped Shape the Cold War* (Princeton University Press, 2017), 419–21; Blum, John, ed., *The Price of Vision: The Diary of Henry A. Wallace, 1942–1946* (Boston: Houghton Mifflin, 1973), 91.

27 McIntire, Ross, with George Creel, *White House Physician* (New York: Putnam, 1946), 170–1; *CC* (19 April 1945), 423.

28 Butler, Susan, ed., *My Dear Mr. Stalin: The Complete Correspondence of Franklin D. Roosevelt and Joseph V. Stalin* (New Haven, CT: Yale University Press, 2005), 10–16.

29 Reynolds, David, *From World War to Cold War: Churchill, Roosevelt and the International History of the 1940s* (New York: Oxford University Press, 2006), 55–8.

30 Hamilton, Nigel, *Commander in Chief: FDR's Battle with Churchill, 1943* (Boston: Houghton Mifflin, 2016), 262–4, 269.

31 'Meeting of the Combined Chiefs of Staff with Roosevelt and Churchill, May 12, 1943 [14.30]', *FRUS: The Conferences at Washington and Quebec (CWQ-1943)*, https://history.state.gov/historicaldocuments/frus1943/ch2subsubch2.

32 'Meeting of the Combined Chiefs of Staff, May 13, 1943 [10.30]', *FRUS: CWQ-1943*, https://history.state.gov/historicaldocuments/frus1943/ch2subsubch4.

33 'Meeting of the Combined Chiefs of Staff, May 19, 1943 [10.30]', *FRUS: CWQ-1943*, https://history.state.gov/historicaldocuments/frus1943/ch2subsubch20; Jordan, *American Warlords*, 261–5.

34 Stalin to Roosevelt, 16 March 1943, in Butler, *My Dear Mr. Stalin*, 121–2.

35 Roosevelt to Stalin, 5 May 1943, *FRUS: Conferences at Cairo and Teheran (CCT)*, https://history.state.gov/historicaldocuments/frus1943CairoTehran/d2; Suckley diary (19 July 1943), *CC*, 227. For Davies's talks with Stalin, see Butler, *My Dear Mr. Stalin*, 130–5.

36 *WWR*, 404.

37 Roosevelt to Churchill, 18 March 1942, MRP-2, FDRL, http://www.fdrlibrary.marist.edu/_resources/images/mr/mr0009.pdf.

38 Hamilton, *Commander in Chief*, 272.

39 Stalin to Roosevelt, 11 June 1943, MRP-8, FDRL, http://www.fdrlibrary.marist.edu/_resources/images/mr/mr0052a.pdf.

40 *R&H*, 733–4.

41 Roosevelt to Stalin, 26 April 1943, *FRUS: 1943-3*, https://history.state.gov/historicaldocuments/frus1943v03/d293.

42 Stimson to FDR, 10 August 1943, *FRUS: 1943-2*, https://history.state.gov/historicaldocuments/frus1943/d227.

43 'Minutes of a Meeting Held at the White House between the President and the Joint Chiefs of Staff on 10 August 1943 at 1415', *FRUS:CWQ-1943*, https://history.state.gov/historicaldocuments/frus1943/d228.

44 Marshall, 'Memorandum for General Handy', 9 August 1943, https://www.marshallfoundation.org/library/digital-archive/memorandum-for-general-handy-9/.

45 Gilbert, Martin, *Churchill and America* (New York: Free Press, 2005), 280–1.

46 'Quadrant: Report to the President and Prime Minister of the Final Agreed Summary of Conclusions Reached by the Combined Chiefs of Staff', 24 August 1943, *FRUS: CWQ-1943*, https://history.state.gov/historicaldocuments/frus1943/d523.

47 Goebbels Diary, 10 August 1943, in Hamilton, *Commander in Chief*, 302–7 (quotation, p. 305).

48 Kershaw, Ian, *Hitler: 1936–45 Nemesis* (New York: Norton, 2000), 600–3, 616–17; Goebbels Diary, 14 November 1943, quoted in Hamilton, Nigel, *War and Peace: FDR's Final Odyssey – D-Day to Yalta, 1943–1945* (Boston: Houghton Mifflin Harcourt, 2019), 40.

49 Roosevelt to Churchill, 8 October 1943, MRP-4, FDRL, http://www.fdrlibrary.marist.edu/_resources/images/mr/mr0025.pdf.

50 Churchill to Roosevelt, 23 October 1943, MRP-4, FDRL, http://www.fdrlibrary.marist.edu/_resources/images/mr/mr0026.pdf.

51 Moran, Lord, *Churchill: Taken from the Diaries of Lord Moran: The Struggle for Survival, 1940–1965* (Boston: Houghton Mifflin, 1966), 122; CHAR 20/122/43, Churchill to Eden, Most Secret and Personal, 26 October 1943, Churchill Papers, Churchill Archives Centre (accessed via Bloomsbury Publishing).

52 Reynolds, David, 'The Diplomacy of the Grand Alliance', in Richard Bosworth and Joseph Maiolo, eds., *The Cambridge History of the Second World War, Vol. 2: Politics and Ideology* (New York: Cambridge University Press, 2015), 312.

53 Harriman to Roosevelt, 4 November 1943, *FRUS: CCT-1943*, https://history.state.gov/historicaldocuments/frus1943CairoTehran/d94.

54 Roosevelt to Stalin, 14 October 1943, Stalin to Roosevelt, 19 October 1943, *FRUS: CCT-1943*, https://history.state.gov/historicaldocuments/frus1943CairoTehran/d43/d47; diary entry, 30 October 1943, *CC*, 250.

55 'Meeting of the Combined Chiefs of Staff with Roosevelt and Churchill, 11 a.m', 24 November 1943, *FRUS: CCT-1943*, https://history.state.gov/historicaldocuments/frus1943CairoTehran/d263; Moran, *Churchill*, 140–2.

56 Moran, *Churchill*, 143; The Executive of the President's Soviet Protocol Committee (Burns) to the President's Special Assistant (Hopkins), 10 August 1943, *FRUS: CWQ-1943*, https://history.state.gov/historicaldocuments/frus1943/d317.

57 Bohlen minutes, 'Roosevelt-Stalin Meeting, 2.45 p.m., 29 November 1943', *FRUS: CCT-1943*, https://history.state.gov/historicaldocuments/frus1943CairoTehran/ch8subsubch10; Bohlen, Charles, *Witness to History, 1929–1969* (New York: Norton, 1973), 145.

58 Bohlen minutes, 'First Plenary Meeting, 4 p.m', 28 November 1943, *FRUS: CCT-1943*, https://history.state.gov/historicaldocuments/frus1943CairoTehran/d360; Moran, *Churchill*, 135.

59 Bohlen minutes, 'Second Plenary Meeting, 4 p.m', 29 November 1943, *FRUS: CCT-1943*, https://history.state.gov/historicaldocuments/frus1943CairoTehran/ch8subsubch11.

60 Bohlen, *Witness to History*, 148; Bohlen minutes, 'Roosevelt-Churchill-Stalin Luncheon Meeting, 1.30 p.m', 30 November 1943, *FRUS: CCT-1943*, https://history.state.gov/historicaldocuments/frus1943CairoTehran/d371.

61 Bohlen minutes, 'Roosevelt-Stalin Meeting, 3.20 p.m', 1 December 1943, *FRUS:CCT-1943*, https://history.state.gov/historicaldocuments/frus1943CairoTehran/ch8subsubch20; Bohlen minutes, 'Tripartite Political Meeting, 6 p.m', 1 December 1943, *FRUS: CCT-1943*, https://history.state.gov/historicaldocuments/frus1943CairoTehran/ch8subsubch21.

62 'The Agreed Text of the Communique', 4 December 1943, *FRUS: CCT-1943*, https://history.state.gov/historicaldocuments/frus1943CairoTehran/d411; Roosevelt to Lippmann, 8 November 1943, PPF-2037, FDRL.

63 Pershing to Roosevelt, 16 September 1943, GCMP: 4–110; https://www.marshallfoundation.org/library/digital-archive/to-franklin-d-roosevelt-from/; Roosevelt to Pershing, *FDR: HPL-4*, 20 September 1943, 1444–5; Hamilton, *War and Peace*, 143–4.

64 Eisenhower, Dwight, *Crusade in Europe* (New York: Doubleday, 1948), 197; Marshall to Robert Sherwood, 25 February 1947, GCMP, 6-028, https://www.marshallfoundation.org/library/digital-archive/6-028-robert-e-sherwood-february-25-1947/; *R&H*, 803.

65 Larrabee, Eric, *Commander in Chief: Franklin Delano Roosevelt, His Lieutenants, and Their War* (London: Andre Deutsch, 1987), 412–28, 447–8; Roosevelt, James, *My Parents: A Different View* (Chicago: Playboy Press, 1976), 176.

66 'Fireside Chat', 24 December 1943, APP, https://www.presidency.ucsb.edu/node/209748.

67 Brooke diary (29 February 1944), in Bryant, Arthur, *Triumph in the West 1943–1946* (London: Collins, 1959), 160.

68 'Fireside Chat', 5 June 1944, APP, https://www.presidency.ucsb.edu/node/210812.

69 Larrabee, *Commander in Chief*, 450–2; Eisenhower, *Crusade in Europe*, 281–3.

70 Larrabee, *Commander in Chief*, 440–3; Harrison, Gordon, *Cross-Channel Attack* (Washington, DC: Office of the Chief of Military History, Department of the Army, 1951), 67–8.

71 'Prayer on D-Day', 6 June 1944, APP, https://www.presidency.ucsb.edu/node/210815; *CC*, 6 June 1944, 310; Harriman to Roosevelt, cable, 28 June 1944, MRP-19, FDRL.

72 Hamilton, *War and Peace*, 306–9.

73 Leahy, *I Was There* (New York: McGraw-Hill, 1950), 251.

74 Hamilton, *War and Peace*, 318–26.

75 McFarland minutes, 'Meeting of the Combined Chiefs of Staff with Roosevelt and Churchill, 11.45 a.m.', 13 September 1944, *FRUS: Conference at Quebec-1944*, https://history.state.gov/historicaldocuments/frus1944Quebec/d177.

76 Taylor, A. J. P., *English History, 1914–1945* (Oxford: Oxford University Press, 1965), 577.

77 Thompson, *Sense of Power*, 230.

Chapter 13

1 Preston, Andrew, 'Monsters Everywhere: A Genealogy of National Security', *Diplomatic History*, 38 (June 2014): 477–500 (quotation, p. 492).

2 Kimball, Warren, *The Juggler: Franklin Roosevelt as Wartime Statesman* (Princeton, NJ: Princeton University Press, 1991), 185.

3 'Annual Message to Congress on the State of the Union', 6 January 1941, APP, https://www.presidency.ucsb.edu/node/209473. See, too, Engel, Jeffrey, ed., *The Four Freedoms: Franklin D. Roosevelt and the Evolution of an American Idea* (New York: Oxford University Press, 2016), 15–36.

4 *WWR*, 246–7.

5 Preston, 'Monsters Everywhere', 494–6; Lippmann, Walter, *U.S. War Aims* (London: Hamish Hamilton, 1944), 22.

6 *R&H*, 363–4. See, too, *CC*, 141.

7 Roosevelt, Elliott, *As He Saw It* (New York: Duell, Sloan & Pearce, 1946), 25.

8 'Atlantic Charter: Joint Statement by the President of the United States and the Prime Minister of the United Kingdom, 14 August 1941', https://www.loc.gov/law/help/us-treaties/bevans/m-ust000003-0686.pdf.

9 'Statement on Axis Crimes in Occupied Countries', 21 August 1942, APP, https://www.presidency.ucsb.edu/node/210814.

10 For critical assessment and defence of FDR's record, see respectively: Wyman, David, *The Abandonment of the Jews: America and the Holocaust, 1941–1945* (New York: Pantheon, 1984), 311–40; and Breitman, Richard, and Alan Lichtman, *FDR and the Jews* (Cambridge, MA: Belknap Press, 2013).

11 'Address at Ottawa, Canada', 25 August 1943, APP, https://www.presidency.ucsb.edu/node/210350.

12 'Declaration by United Nations', 1 January 1942, *FRUS: 1942-1*, https://history.state.gov/historicaldocuments/frus1942v01/d18; Plesch, Dan, *America, Hitler and the UN: How the Allies Won World War II and Forged a Peace* (London: Tauris, 2010), 31–6.

13 *R&H*, 452; 'Fireside Chat', 23 February 1942, APP, https://www.presidency.ucsb.edu/node/210361.

14 Roosevelt, *As He Saw It*, 74.

15 Eden, Anthony, *Memoirs of Anthony Eden, Vol. 2 – The Reckoning. 1938–1945* (London: Cassell, 1965), 593.

16 Minutes, Pacific War Council, 14 August 1942, MRP-168, FDRL, http://www.fdrlibrary.marist.edu/_resources/images/mr/mr0866.pdf.

17 Roosevelt to Suckley, 13, 14 and 26 January 1942, *CC*, 197–8, 200; Daniels, Roger, *Franklin D. Roosevelt: The War Years, 1939–1945* (Urbana: University of Illinois Press, 2016), 311; 'Press and Radio Conference #933, 5 February 1944', PCT, FDRL, http://www.fdrlibrary.marist.edu/_resources/images/pc/pc0156.pdf.

18 Roosevelt, *As He Saw It*, 71 (quotation), 108–16.

19 Churchill, Winston, *The Second World War: IV-The Hinge of Fate* (Boston: Houghton Mifflin, 1950), 209.

20 Roosevelt to Churchill, 10 March and 11 April 1942, MRP-2, FDRL, http://www.fdrlibrary.marist.edu/_resources/images/mr/mr0009.pdf.

21 Kimball, *The Juggler*, 132–40; *R&H*, 511–25.

22 Gandhi to Roosevelt, 1 July 1942, *FRUS: 1942–1*, https://history.state.gov/historicaldocuments/frus1942v01/d575.

23 Willkie, Wendell, *One World* (New York: Simon & Schuster 1943); 'Mr Churchill on Our One Aim', *Manchester Guardian*, 11 November 1942, https://www.theguardian.com/theguardian/2009/nov/11/churchill-blood-sweat-tears. See, too, Zipp, Samuel, *The Idealist: Wendell Willkie's Wartime Quest to Build One World* (Cambridge, MA: Harvard University Press, 2020).

24 'US Draft of a Declaration of the United Nations on National Independence', 9 March 1943, *FRUS: 1943–1*, https://history.state.gov/historicaldocuments/frus1943v01/d683; Plesch, *America, Hitler and the UN*, 90–1.

25 Bohlen minutes, 'Roosevelt-Stalin Meeting, 3 p.m., Roosevelt Quarters, Soviet Embassy', 28 November 1943, *FRUS: The Conferences at Cairo and Tehran, 1943*, https://history.state.gov/historicaldocuments/frus1943CairoTehran/ch8subsubch5.

26 'Memorandum by President Roosevelt for Secretary of State', 1 January 1945, *FRUS: 1945-6*; Kimball, *The Juggler*, 148–9.

27 Welles, Sumner, *Seven Decisions That Shaped History* (New York: Harper, 1951), 182–3.

28 'Memorandum of Conversation, by Mr. Harry L. Hopkins, Special Assistant to President Roosevelt', 27 March 1943, *FRUS: 1943–3*, https://history.state.gov/historicaldocuments/frus1943v03/d23.

29 Quoted in Kimball, Warren, *Forged in War: Roosevelt, Churchill, and the Second World War* (New York: William Morrow, 1997), 201.

30 Welles, *Seven Decisions*, 171–2.

31 Kimball, Warren, 'The Sheriffs: FDR's Postwar World', in *FDRW*, 91–122 (Stalin quotation, p. 95).

32 Davis, Forrest, 'Roosevelt's World Blueprint', *Saturday Evening Post*, 10 April 1943, 20–21, 109–10; Hassett, William, *Off the Record With FDR, 1942–1945* (London: George Allen & Unwin, 1960), 166.

33 Welles, Sumner, 'Roosevelt and the Far East', *Harper's Magazine* (March 1951): 70–80; see, too, Daisy Suckley's diary entry, 28 June 1944, *CC*, 314.

34 Roosevelt to Mountbatten, 8 November 1943, *FDR: HPL-4*, 1468.

35 Schaller, Michael, 'FDR and the "China Question"', in *FDRW*, 145–57; Kimball, *Forged in War*, 234–6.

36 John Service to Stilwell, 'First Informal Impressions of the North Shensi Communist Base', 28 July 1944, PSF-27, FDRL, http://www.fdrlibrary.marist.edu/archives/ collections/franklin/?p=collections/findingaid&id=502.

37 Roosevelt to Chiang, 6 July, 16 September 1944, MRP-10, FDRL, http://www .fdrlibrary.marist.edu/_resources/images/mr/mr0061.pdf.

38 Hurley, additional comments, in Chiang to Roosevelt, 9 October 1944, MRP-10, FDRL, http://www.fdrlibrary.marist.edu/_resources/images/mr/mr0061.pdf; Hurley to Roosevelt, 13 October 1944, MRP-11, FDRL http://www.fdrlibrary.marist.edu/ _resources/images/mr/mr0066.pdf.

39 Halberstam, David, *The Powers That Be* (New York: Knopf, 1979), 69 (quotation), 74–84.

40 Mao to Roosevelt, 10 November 1944, *FRUS: 1944-6*, https://history.state.gov/ historicaldocuments/frus1944v06/d493.

41 Hurley to Roosevelt, 13 and 15 January 1945, MRP-11, FDRL, http://www.fdrlibrary.marist .edu/_resources/images/mr/mr0066.pdf; Schaller, 'FDR and the "China Question"', 160–1.

42 Quoted in *FDRAFP*, 501.

43 DMK, 5 December 1942, https://www.bac-lac.gc.ca/eng/discover/politics -government/prime-ministers/william-lyon-mackenzie-king/Pages/item.aspx ?IdNumber=24837.

44 National Resources Planning Board, *Security Work and Relief Policies* (Washington, DC: Government Printing Office, 1942), https://www.ssa.gov/history/reports/NRPB /NRPBTitlepages.pdf; 'A New Bill of Rights', *Nation*, 20 March 1943, 401; Brinkley, Alan, *The End of Reform: New Deal Liberalism in Recession and War* (New York: Knopf, 1995), 245–53.

45 'Press and Radio Conference #929, 28 December 1943', PCT, FDRL, http://www .fdrlibrary.marist.edu/_resources/images/pc/pc0155.pdf.

46 *WWR*, 390–1; 'State of the Union Radio Address to the Nation', 11 January 1944, APP, https://www.presidency.ucsb.edu/node/268064.

47 Lelyveld, Joseph, *His Final Battle: The Last Months of Franklin Roosevelt* (New York: Knopf, 2016), 89–90. For Daisy Suckley's commentaries on FDR's health, see *CC*, 264–6, 271–2, 278, 280, 284–91.

48 Lelyveld, *Final Battle*, 143–7.

49 Quoted in Hamilton, Nigel, *War and Peace: FDR's Final Odyssey D-Day to Yalta, 1943–1945* (Boston: Houghton Mifflin Harcourt, 2019), 253.

50 Costigliola, Frank, *Roosevelt's Lost Alliances: How Personal Politics Helped Start the Cold War* (Princeton, NJ: Princeton University Press, 2012), 206–9; *CC*, 317.

51 Lelyveld, *Final Battle*, 94–5, 149–50 (Rutherfurd quotation), 207–8, 246–8. See, too, Persico Joseph, *Franklin and Lucy: President Roosevelt, Mrs Rutherfurd, and the Other Remarkable Women in His Life* (New York: Random House, 2008), esp. 294–304.

52 *WWR*, 401–2; *CC* (5 July 1944), 316.

53 Lelyveld, *Final Battle*, 151–61.

54 *WWR*, 405–8; *CC* (14 July 1944), 318–19.

55 Baime, A. J., *The Accidental President: Harry S. Truman, the Bomb, and the Four Months That Changed the World* (Boston: Houghton Mifflin Harcourt, 2017), 112–34.

56 Lelyveld, *Final Battle*, 176–8, 195–8; *WWR*, 413–14.

57 'Address at a Union Dinner, Washington DC', 23 September 1944, APP, https://www .presidency.ucsb.edu/node/209850.

58 'Text of Governor Dewey's Speech in Oklahoma City', *NYT*, 26 September 1944.

59 For the campaign, see Jordan, David, *FDR, Dewey, and the Election of 1944* (Bloomington: Indiana University Press, 2011), 223–92.

60 'Radio Address at a Dinner of the Foreign Policy Association. New York, NY',
    21 October 1944, APP, https://www.presidency.ucsb.edu/node/210407.

61 'Address at Soldiers Field, Chicago, Illinois', 28 October 1944, APP, https://www
    .presidency.ucsb.edu/documents/address-soldiers-field-chicago-illinois.

62 Divine, Robert, *Foreign Policy and U.S. Presidential Elections, 1940–1948* (New York:
    New Viewpoints, 1974), 161–4; Eldersveld, Samuel, 'The Influence of Metropolitan
    Party Pluralities in Presidential Elections since 1920: A Study of Twelve Key Cities',
    American Political Science Review, 43 (December 1949): 1198–206.

63 Mettler, Suzanne, *The GI Bill and the Making of the Greatest Generation* (New York:
    Oxford University Press, 2005), 15–23; Katznelson, Ira, *When Affirmative Action Was
    White: An Untold History of Racial Inequality in Twentieth-Century America* (New
    York: Norton, 2005), 113–41.

64 Borgwardt, Elizabeth, *A New Deal for the World: America's Vision of Human Rights*
    (Cambridge, MA: Belknap Press, 2005), 115–18; Daunton, Martin, 'Nutrition, Food,
    Agriculture and the World Economy', in Naomi Lamoreaux and Ian Shapiro, eds., *The
    Bretton Woods Agreements* (New Haven, CT: Yale University Press, 2019), 146–51, 161–5.

65 'Address on the Signing of the Agreement Establishing the UNRRA', 9 November
    1943, APP, https://www.presidency.ucsb.edu/node/209679; Plesch, *America, Hitler
    and the UN*, 119–39.

66 Borgwardt, *A New Deal for the World*, 121–8 (quotation, p. 128). See, too, Frieden,
    Jeffry, 'The Political Economy of the Bretton Woods Agreement', in Lamoreaux and
    Shapiro, *Bretton Woods Agreements*, 21–37.

67 Rauchway, Eric, *The Money Makers: How Roosevelt and Keynes Ended the Depression,
    Defeated Fascism, and Secured a Prosperous Peace* (New York: Basic Books, 2015),
    203–26.

68 Borgwardt, *A New Deal for the World*, 163–8; 'Text of Statements on Dumbarton Oaks
    and Documents Giving Tentative Security Plans', *NYT*, 10 October 1944.

69 Campbell, Thomas, and George Herring, eds., *The Diaries of Edward R. Stettinius, Jr.,
    1943–1946* (New York: New Viewpoints, 1975), 214.

70 Costigliola, *Roosevelt's Lost Alliances*, 232–5. For the conference, see Preston, Diana,
    Eight Days at Yalta: How Churchill, Roosevelt and Stalin Shaped the Post-War World
    (London: Picador, 2019).

71 'Memorandum by Mr. Hopkins . . .', 15 March 1943, *FRUS: 1943–3*, https://history
    .state.gov/historicaldocuments/frus1943v03/d23.

72 Quoted in Reynolds, David, 'The Diplomacy of the Grand Alliance', in Richard
    Bosworth and Joseph Maiolo, eds., *The Cambridge History of the Second World War*,
    Vol. 2: *Politics and Ideology* (New York: Cambridge University Press, 2015), 314.

73 Leahy, William, *I Was There* (New York: Whittlesey House, 1950), 315–16; Bohlen,
    Charles, *Witness to History, 1929–1969* (New York: Norton, 1973), 192.

74 'Communique Issued at the End of the Conference', *FRUS: Conferences at Malta and
    Yalta 1945*, https://history.state.gov/historicaldocuments/frus1945Malta/d500.

75 'Speech at Celebration Meeting of the Moscow Soviet of Working People's Deputies
    and Moscow Party and Public Organizations', 6 November 1944, https://www.marxists
    .org/reference/archive/stalin/works/1944/11/06.htm.

76 Moran, Lord, *Churchill: The Struggle for Survival, 1940–1965* (Boston: Houghton
    Mifflin, 1966), 279.

77 Quoted in Butler, Susan, ed., *My Dear Mr. Stalin: The Complete Correspondence of
    Franklin D. Roosevelt and Joseph V. Stalin* (New Haven, CT: Yale University Press,
    2005), 12.

78 FDR to Thomas Lamont, 12 November 1942, *FDR: HPL-4*, 1365–6.

79 Davis, 'Roosevelt's World Blueprint', 21; Harriman, Averell, and Elie Abel, *Special Envoy to Churchill and Stalin, 1941–1946* (New York: Random House, 1975), 169–70.

80 'Address to Congress on the Yalta Conference', 1 March 1945, APP, https://www.presidency.ucsb.edu/node/210050.

81 Butler, *My Dear Mr. Stalin*, 309–20; Roosevelt to Churchill, 11 April 1945, MRP-7, FDRL. http://www.fdrlibrary.marist.edu/_resources/images/mr/mr0049.pdf.

82 Truman, Harry S., *Memoirs: Vol 1: 1945 - Year of Decisions* (Garden City, NY: Doubleday 1955), 79–80; Bohlen, *Witness*, 213.

83 White, Mark, *Against the President: Dissent and Decision-Making in the White House: A Historical Perspective* (Chicago: Ivan Dee, 2007), 9–57.

84 Quoted in Preston, *Eight Days in Yalta*, 313.

85 Costigliola, *Roosevelt's Lost Alliances*, 418–28 (quotation, p. 421–2).

86 Quoted in Costigliola, *Roosevelt's Lost Alliances*, 1–2.

Epilogue

1 Gould, Lewis, *The Modern American Presidency*, 2nd ed. (Lawrence: University Press of Kansas, 2009), 287.

2 Leuchtenburg, William, *In the Shadow of FDR: From Harry Truman to Barack Obama* (Ithaca, NY: Cornell University Press, 2009), 121–60.

3 Neustadt, Richard, *Presidential Power and the Modern Presidents: The Politics of Leadership from Roosevelt to Reagan* (New York: Free Press, 1990), 269.

4 'Remarks to the United Nations General Assembly in New York City', 25 September 2018, APP, https://www.presidency.ucsb.edu/node/332698.

5 Leuchtenburg, William, *The American President: From Teddy Roosevelt to Bill Clinton* (New York: Oxford University Press, 2015), 242.

6 Truman, Harry S., *Memoirs: Vol 1: 1945 – Year of Decisions* (Garden City, NY: Doubleday 1955), 485–6.

7 Greenstein, Fred, 'Change and Continuity in the Modern Presidency', in Anthony King, ed., *The New American Political System* (Washington, DC: AEI Press, 1979), 58–61.

8 Hamby, Alonzo, *Liberalism and Its Challengers: From FDR to Bush* (New York: Oxford University Press, 1992), 52–139.

9 Wilentz, Sean, *The Age of Reagan: A History, 1974–2008* (New York: HarperCollins, 2008).

10 Morgan, Iwan, 'Presidents, the Federal Budget, and Economic Good, 1946–2008', in Mark Rose and Roger Biles, eds., *The President and American Capitalism since 1945* (Gainesville: University Press of Florida, 2017), 81–98.

11 Kotlowski, Dean, '"We *Shall* Overcome": Lyndon B. Johnson as the Civil Rights President', and Morgan, Iwan, 'In Black and White: Ronald Reagan's Image on Race', in Iwan Morgan and Mark White, eds., *The Presidential Image: A History from Theodore Roosevelt to Donald Trump* (London: I.B. Tauris, 2020), 117–36, 175–92.

12 Dickinson, Matthew, *Bitter Harvest: FDR, Presidential Power and the Growth of the Presidential Branch* (New York: Cambridge University Press, 1996), 19–42.

13 Burns, James MacGregor, *Packing the Court: The Rise of Judicial Power and the Coming Crisis of the Supreme Court* (New York: Penguin, 2009).

14 Frank, Jeffrey, 'The Willkie What-If: FDR's Hybrid Party Plot', *New Yorker*, 28 July
    2016, https://www.newyorker.com/news/daily-comment/the-willkie-what-if-f-d-r-s
    -hybrid-party-plot.

15 Mason, Robert, *The Republican Party and American Politics from Hoover to Reagan*
    (New York: 2012), 216–81; Abramowitz, Alan, *The Great Alignment: Race, Party, and
    the Rise of Donald Trump* (New Haven, CT: Yale University Press, 2018), esp. 121–74.

16 Kernell, Samuel, *Going Public: New Strategies of Presidential Leadership*, 3rd ed.
    (Washington, DC: CQ Press, 1997); Jones, Jeffrey, 'Last Trump Job Approval 34%,
    Average is 41%', *Gallup*, 18 January 2021, https://news.gallup.com/poll/328637/last
    -trump-job-approval-average-record-low.aspx.

17 'Special Message to the Congress on Greece and Turkey: The Truman Doctrine',
    12 March 1947, APP, https://www.presidency.ucsb.edu/node/232818.

18 'Address Before a Joint Session of the Congress on the State of the Union', 29 January
    2002, APP, https://www.presidency.ucsb.edu/node/211864.

19 See, for example, Maney, Patrick, *The Roosevelt Presence: The Life and Legacy of FDR*
    (Berkeley: University of California Press, 1998), 201.

20 Rudalevige, Andrew, *The New Imperial Presidency: Renewing Presidential Power after
    Watergate* (Ann Arbor: University of Michigan Press, 2005), 57–100, 167–260.

21 Schlesinger, Jr, Arthur, *War and the American Presidency* (New York: Norton, 2005), 66.

22 Alter, Jonathan, *The Defining Moment: FDR's Hundred Days and the Triumph of Hope*
    (New York: Simon & Schuster, 2006); 'First 100 days as Crucial as New Deal, Says
    FDR Author', *The Guardian*, 15 November 2008, https://www.theguardian.com/world
    /2008/nov/15/obama-white-house-barack.

23 'Address Accepting the Democratic Presidential Nomination in Wilmington,
    Delaware', 20 August 2020, APP, https://www.presidency.ucsb.edu/node/342190.

24 Alter, Jonathan, 'The FDR-Biden Connection Runs Deeper Than You Think', *Foreign
    Policy*, 14 September 2020, https://foreignpolicy.com/2020/09/14/the-biden-fdr
    -connection-runs-deeper-than-you-think/; Blumgart, Jake, 'Why Joe Biden Must
    Emulate FDR on More Than Public Spending', *New Statesman*, 9 February 2021,
    https://www.newstatesman.com/world/2021/02/why-joe-biden-must-emulate-fdr
    -more-public-spending.

25 *The New Atlantic Charter*, 10 June 2021, https://www.whitehouse.gov/briefing-room/
    statements-releases/2021/06/10/the-new-atlantic-charter/.

26 For an insightful exposition, see Suri, Jeremi, *The Impossible Presidency: The Rise and
    Fall of America's Highest Office* (New York: Basic Books, 2017), 289–94.

27 Niebuhr, Reinhold, *The Children of Light and the Children of Darkness* (New York:
    Scribner's, 1944), 118.

28 *AoR-2*, 587.

29 'Campaign Address at Cleveland, Ohio', 2 November 1940, APP, https://www
    .presidency.ucsb.edu/node/209343.

Select bibliography

The titles below were the most useful for this FDR study. The footnotes contain a more detailed guide to sources.

Alter, Jonathan, *The Defining Moment: FDR's Hundred Days and the Triumph of Hope* (New York: Simon & Schuster, 2006).

Arsenault, Raymond, *The Sound of Freedom: Marian Anderson, the Lincoln Memorial, and the Concert That Awakened America* (New York: Bloomsbury, 2009).

Badger, Anthony, *The New Deal: The Depression Years, 1933–1940* (London: Macmillan, 1989).

Badger, Anthony, *FDR: The First Hundred Days* (New York: Hill & Wang, 2008).

Barber, William, *Designs within Disorder: Franklin D. Roosevelt, the Economists, and the Shaping of American Economic Policy, 1933–1945* (New York: Cambridge University Press, 1996).

Beasley, Maurine, *Eleanor Roosevelt: Transformative First Lady* (Lawrence: University Press of Kansas, 2010).

Biles, Roger, *A New Deal for the American People* (De Kalb: Northern Illinois University Press, 1991).

Blum, John Morton, ed., *From the Morgenthau Diaries*, 3 Vols. (Boston: Houghton Mifflin, 1959, 1965, 1967).

Borgwardt, Elizabeth, *A New Deal for the World: America's Vision of Human Rights* (Cambridge, MA: Belknap Press, 2005).

Brinkley, Alan, *The End of Reform: New Deal Liberalism in Recession and War* (New York: Knopf, 1995).

Brownlow, Louis, *The President and the Presidency* (Chicago: Public Administration Service, 1949).

Brownlow, Louis, *A Passion for Anonymity* (Chicago: University of Chicago Press, 1958).

Burns, James MacGregor, *Roosevelt: The Lion and the Fox* (New York: Harcourt, Brace, 1956).

Butler, Susan, ed., *My Dear Mr. Stalin: The Complete Correspondence of Franklin D. Roosevelt and Joseph V. Stalin* (New Haven, CT: Yale University Press, 2005).

Churchill, Winston S., *The Second World War*, 6 Vols. (Boston: Houghton Mifflin, 1948–53).

Cole, Wayne, *Roosevelt & the Isolationists, 1932–45* (Lincoln: University of Nebraska Press, 1983).

Costigliola, Frank, *Roosevelt's Lost Alliances: How Personal Politics Helped Start the Cold War* (Princeton, NJ: Princeton University Press, 2012).

Dallek, Robert, *Franklin D. Roosevelt and American Foreign Policy, 1932–1945* (New York: Oxford University Press, 1979).

Dallek, Robert, *Franklin D. Roosevelt: A Political Life* (London: Allen Lane, 2017).

Daniels, Roger, *Franklin D. Roosevelt, 2 Vols: Road to the New Deal, 1882–1939; The War Years, 1939–1945* (Urbana: University of Illinois Press, 2015, 2016).

Davies, Gareth, 'The New Deal in 1940: Embattled or Entrenched?' in Gareth Davies and Julian Zelizer, eds., *America at the Ballot Box: Elections and Political History* (Philadelphia: University of Pennsylvania Press, 2015), 153–66.

Dickinson, Matthew, *Bitter Harvest: FDR, Presidential Power, and the Growth of the Presidential Branch* (New York: Cambridge University Press, 1997).

Dickinson, Matthew, and Andrew Rudalevige, '"Worked Out in Fractions": Neutral Competence, FDR, and the Bureau of the Budget', *Congress and the Presidency*, 34 (Spring 2007): 1–26.

Dunn, Susan, *Roosevelt's Purge: How FDR Fought to Change the Democratic Party* (Cambridge, MA: Belknap Press, 2010).

Dunn, Susan, *1940: FDR, Willkie, Lindbergh, Hitler – The Election amid the Storm* (New Haven, CT: Yale University Press, 2013).

Dunn, Susan, *A Blueprint for War: FDR and the Hundred Days That Mobilized America* (New York: Oxford University Press, 2018).

Eccles, Marriner, *Beckoning Frontiers: Public and Personal Recollections* (New York: Knopf, 1951).

Eliot, Thomas, *Recollections of the New Deal* (Boston: Northeastern University Press, 1992).

Engel, Jeffrey, ed., *The Four Freedoms: Franklin D. Roosevelt and the Evolution of an American Idea* (New York: Oxford University Press, 2016).

Farley, Jim, *Jim Farley's Story: The Roosevelt Years* (New York: Whittlesey House, 1947).

Farnham, Barbara Rearden, *Roosevelt and the Munich Crisis: A Study of Political Decision-Making* (Princeton, NJ: Princeton University Press, 1997).

Flynn, Edward, *You're the Boss* (New York: Viking Press, 1947).

Foner, Eric, *The Story of American Freedom* (New York: Norton, 1998).

Gallagher, Hugh Gregory, *FDR's Splendid Deception* (Arlington, VA: Vandamere 1994).

Gilbert, Martin, *Churchill and America* (New York: Free Press, 2005).

Golway, Terry, *Frank & Al: FDR, Al Smith, and the Unlikely Alliance That Created the Modern Democratic Party* (New York: St Martin's, 2018).

Greenberg, David, *Republic of Spin: An Inside History of the American Presidency* (New York: Norton, 2016).

Hamilton, Nigel, *The Mantle of Command: FDR at War, 1941–1942* (Boston: Houghton Mifflin Harcourt, 2014).

Hamilton, Nigel, *Commander in Chief: FDR's Battle with Churchill, 1943* (Boston: Houghton Mifflin Harcourt, 2016).

Hamilton, Nigel, *War and Peace: FDR's Final Odyssey: D-Day to Yalta, 1943–1945* (Boston: Houghton Mifflin Harcourt, 2019).

Harriman, Averell, and Elie Abel, *Special Envoy to Churchill and Stalin, 1941–1946* (New York: Random House, 1975).

Hassett, William, *Off the Record with FDR, 1942–1945* (London: George Allen & Unwin, 1960).

Hopkins, Harry, *Spending to Save: The Complete Story of Relief* (New York: Norton, 1936).

Hull, Cordell, *The Memoirs of Cordell Hull*, 2 Vols. (New York: Macmillan, 1948).

Ickes, Harold, *The Secret Diary of Harold L. Ickes*, 3 Vols. (New York: Simon & Schuster, 1954).

Jackson, Robert, *That Man: An Insider's Portrait of Franklin D. Roosevelt*, ed. John Q. Barrett (New York: Oxford University Press, 2004).

Janeway, Michael, *The Fall of the House of Roosevelt: Brokers of Ideas and Power from FDR to LBJ* (New York: Columbia University Press, 2004).

Jeffreys, John, *A Third Term for FDR: The Election of 1940* (Lawrence: University Press of Kansas, 2017).

Jordan, Jonathan, *The Warlords: How Roosevelt's High Command Led America to Victory in World War II* (New York: NAL Caliber, 2015).

Katznelson, Ira, *Fear Itself: The New Deal and the Origins of Our Time* (New York: Liveright, 2013).

Kennedy, David M., *Freedom from Fear: The American People in Depression and War, 1929–1945* (New York: Oxford University Press, 1999).

Kershaw, Ian, *Fateful Choices: Ten Decisions That Changed the World, 1940–1941* (New York: Penguin, 2007).

Kimball, Warren, *The Most Unsordid Act: Lend-Lease 1939–1941* (Baltimore: Johns Hopkins University Press, 1969).

Kimball, Warren, *The Juggler: Franklin Roosevelt as Wartime Statesman* (Princeton, NJ: Princeton University Press, 1991).

Kimball, Warren, *Forged in War: Roosevelt, Churchill and the Second World War* (New York: Morrow, 1997).

Klein, Maury, *A Call to Arms: Mobilizing America for World War II* (New York: Bloomsbury, 2013).

Larrabee, Eric, *Commander in Chief: Franklin Delano Roosevelt, His Lieutenants, and Their War* (London: Andre Deutsch, 1987).

Lash, Joseph, *Eleanor and Franklin: The Story of Their Relationship* (New York: Norton, 1971).

Leahy, William, *I Was There* (New York: McGraw Hill, 1950).

Leuchtenburg, William E., *Franklin D. Roosevelt and the New Deal, 1932–1940* (New York: Harper & Row, 1963).

Leuchtenburg, William E., *The FDR Years: On Roosevelt & His Legacy* (New York: Columbia University Press, 1995).

Leuchtenburg, William E., *The Supreme Court Reborn: The Constitutional Revolution in the Age of Roosevelt* (New York: Oxford University Press, 1995).

Leuchtenburg, William E., 'Charles Evans Hughes: The Center Holds', *North Carolina Law Review* 83 (2005): 1187, https://scholarship.law.unc.edu/nclr/vol83/iss5/3/

Leuchtenburg, William E., *In the Shadow of FDR: From Harry Truman to Barack Obama* (Ithaca, NY: Cornell University Press, 2009).

Leuchtenburg, William E., *The American President: From Teddy Roosevelt to Bill Clinton* (New York: Oxford University Press, 2015).

Lelyveld, Joseph, *His Final Battle: The Last Months of Franklin Roosevelt* (New York: Knopf, 2016).

Levine, Lawrence, and Cornelia Levine, *The People and the President: America's Conversation with FDR* (Boston: Beacon Press, 2002).

Lippmann, Walter, *U.S. War Aims* (London: Hamish Hamilton, 1944).

Loucheim, Katie, ed., *The Making of the New Deal: The Insiders Speak* (Cambridge, MA: Harvard University Press, 1983).

McCulloch, Tony, 'Simply the Best: FDR as America's Number One President', in Michael Patrick Cullinane and Clare Elliott, eds., *Perspectives on Presidential Leadership: An International View of the White House* (New York: Routledge, 2014), 113–31.

McCulloch, Tony, *Tacit Alliance: Franklin Roosevelt and the Anglo-American 'Special Relationship' before Churchill, 1937–1940* (Edinburgh: Edinburgh University Press, 2021).

McElvaine, Robert, *The Great Depression: America, 1929–1941* (New York: Times Books, 1993).

McKenna, Marian, *Franklin D. Roosevelt and the Great Constitutional War: The Court-Packing Crisis of 1937* (New York: Fordham University Press, 2002).

McMahon, Kevin, *Reconsidering Roosevelt on Race: How the Presidency Paved the Road to Brown* (Chicago: University of Chicago Press, 2004).

Maney, Patrick J., *The Roosevelt Presence: The Life and Legacy of FDR* (Berkeley: University of California Press, 1998).

Matloff, Maurice, 'The 90-Division Gamble', in Kent Roberts Greenfield, ed., *Command Decisions* (Washington, DC: Department of the Army, 1960), 365–81.

Milkis, Sidney, *The President and the Parties: The Transformation of the American Party System since the New Deal* (New York: Oxford University Press, 1993).

Moley, Raymond, *After Seven Years* (New York: Harper, 1939).

Moran, Lord, *Churchill: Taken from the Diaries of Lord Moran: The Struggle for Survival, 1940–1965* (Boston: Houghton Mifflin, 1966).

Namaroto, Michael Vincent, ed., *The Diary of Rexford Tugwell: The New Deal, 1932–1935* (Westport, CT: Praeger, 1992).

Neustadt, Richard, *Presidential Power and the Modern Presidents: The Politics of Leadership from Roosevelt to Reagan* (New York: Free Press, 1990).

O'Reilly, Kenneth, *Nixon's Piano: Presidents and Racial Politics from Washington to Clinton* (New York: Free Press, 1995).

Parrish, Michael. *The Hughes Court: Justices, Rulings and Legacy* (Santa Barbara, CA: BC-CLIO, 2002).

Patterson, James T., *Congressional Conservatism and the New Deal: The Growth of the Conservative Coalition in Congress, 1933–1939* (Lexington: University Press of Kentucky, 1967).

Perkins, Frances, *The Roosevelt I Knew* (New York: Viking, 1946).

Persico, Joseph, *Franklin and Lucy: President Roosevelt, Mrs Rutherfurd, and the Other Remarkable Women in His Life* (New York: Random House, 2008).

Plesch, Dan, *America, Hitler and the UN: How the Allies Won World War II and Forged a Peace* (London: Tauris, 2010),

Preston, Andrew, 'Monsters Everywhere: A Genealogy of National Security', *Diplomatic History*, 38 (June 2014): 477–500

Rauchway, Eric, *The Money Makers: How Roosevelt and Keynes Ended the Depression, Defeated Fascism, and Secured a Prosperous Peace* (New York: Basic Books, 2015).

Rauchway, Eric, *Winter War: Hoover, Roosevelt and the Clash over the New Deal* (New York: Basic Books, 2018).

Reynolds, David, *The Creation of the Anglo-American Alliance, 1937–1941* (Chapel Hill: University of North Carolina Press, 1982).

Reynolds, David, *From World War to Cold War: Churchill, Roosevelt and the International History of the 1940s* (New York: Oxford University Press, 2006).

Reynolds, David, 'The Diplomacy of the Grand Alliance', in Richard Bosworth and Joseph Maiolo, eds., *The Cambridge History of the Second World War, Vol. 2: Politics and Ideology* (New York: Cambridge University Press, 2015), 301–23.

Ritchie, Donald, *Electing FDR: The New Deal Campaign of 1932* (Lawrence: University Press of Kansas, 2007).

Roll, David, *The Hopkins Touch: Harry Hopkins and the Forging of the Alliance to Defeat Hitler* (New York: Oxford University Press, 2012).

Roosevelt, Eleanor, *The Autobiography of Eleanor Roosevelt* (New York: Harper, 1961).

Roosevelt, Elliott, *As He Saw It* (New York: Duell, Sloan & Pearce, 1946).

Roosevelt, Elliott, ed., *F.D.R.: His Personal Letters*, 4 Vols. (New York: Duell, Sloan, and Pearce, 1950).

Rosen, Elliott A., *Roosevelt, the Great Depression, and the Economics of Recovery* (Charlottesville: University of Virginia Press, 2005).

Rosenman, Samuel, *Working with Roosevelt* (London: Rupert Hart-Davies, 1952).

Saloutos, Theodore, *The American Farmer and the New Deal* (Ames: Iowa State University Press, 1982).

Savage, Sean, *Roosevelt the Party Leader 1932–1945* (Lexington: University Press of Kentucky, 1991).

Schlesinger, Jr, Arthur M., *The Age of Roosevelt*, 3 Vols. (Boston: Houghton Mifflin, 1957, 1958, and 1960).

Schlesinger, Jr, Arthur M., *The Imperial Presidency* (London: Andre Deutsch, 1973).

Scroop, Daniel, *Mr Democrat: Jim Farley, the New Deal, and the Making of Modern American Politics* (Ann Arbor: University of Michigan Press, 2006).

Self, Robert, *Britain, America and the War Debt Controversy: The Economic Diplomacy of an Unspecial Relationship, 1917–1941* (London: Routledge, 2006).

Sherwood, Robert, *Roosevelt and Hopkins: An Intimate History* (New York: Harper, 1948).

Shesol, Jeff, *Supreme Power: Franklin Roosevelt vs. the Supreme Court* (New York: Norton, 2010).

Sitkoff, Harvard, *A New Deal for Blacks: The Emergence of Civil Rights as a National Issue: The Depression Decade* (New York: Oxford University Press, 1978).

Skidelsky, Robert, *John Maynard Keynes: Economist, Philosopher, Statesman, 1882–1946* (London: Penguin, 2003).

Suri, Jeremi, *The Impossible Presidency: The Rise and Fall of America's Highest Office* (New York: Basic Books, 2017).

Thompson, John, *A Sense of Power: The Roots of America's Global Role* (Ithaca, NY: Cornell University Press, 2015).

Tugwell, Rexford, *The Democratic Roosevelt: A Biography of Franklin D. Roosevelt* (Garden City, NY: Doubleday, 1957).

Ward, Geoffrey, *Before the Trumpet: Young Franklin Roosevelt, 1882–1905* (New York: Harper & Row, 1985).

Ward, Geoffrey, *A First-Class Temperament: The Emergence of Franklin Roosevelt, 1905–1928* (Harper & Row, 1989).

Ward, Geoffrey, *Closest Companion: The Unknown Story of the Intimate Friendship between Franklin Roosevelt and Margaret Suckley* (New York: Simon & Schuster, 2009).

Watson, Mark, *Chief of Staff: Prewar Plans and Preparations* (Washington, DC: Center of Military History, 1991; original 1950).

Weiss, Nancy, *Farewell to the Party of Lincoln: Black Politics in the Age of FDR* (Princeton, NJ: Princeton University Press, 1983).

Welles, Sumner, *Seven Decisions That Shaped History* (New York: Harper, 1951).

White, Graham, *FDR and the Press* (Chicago: University of Chicago Press, 1979).

White, Mark, *Against the President: Dissent and Decision-Making in the White House: A Historical Perspective* (Chicago: Ivan Dee, 2007).

White, Walter, *A Man Called White: The Autobiography of Walter White* (New York: Viking, 1948).

Winfield, Betty Houchin, *FDR and the News Media* (New York: Columbia University Press, 1994).

Woolner, David, Warren Kimball, and David Reynolds, eds., *FDR's World: War, Peace, and Legacies* (New York: Palgrave Macmillan, 2008).

Index